D1452435

MISSOURI MARRIAGES BEFORE 1840

MISSOURI MARRIAGES BEFORE 1840

Compiled by

Susan Ormesher

With an Index by Robert & Catherine Barnes

Baltimore
GENEALOGICAL PUBLISHING CO., INC.
1986

NORTH PALM BEACH PUBLIC LIBRARY

929.3778
Mis

Copyright © 1982
Genealogical Publishing Co., Inc.
Baltimore, Maryland
All Rights Reserved
Second Printing 1986
Library of Congress Catalogue Card Number 82-81219
International Standard Book Number 0-8063-0985-7
Made in the United States of America

FOREWORD

The purpose of this book is to assist the researcher in locating early marriage records in Missouri and to provide an additional resource for identifying settlers who were in the state prior to the first and second censuses of 1830 and 1840.

All of the marriage records listed here are available for certification at the appropriate county courthouse. It is recommended that when a marriage is located in this book a copy of the record be obtained from the county recorder's office. This volume is designed as an index to the records, not as a replacement for them.

The marriages herein are arranged in alphabetical sequence by the surname of the groom. Following the groom's name is the name of the bride, then the date and the name of the county in which the record is located. A bride's index appears at the end of the book. Readers should note that the abbreviation *rec.* indicates the date of recording, not necessarily the date of marriage.

The "List of Sources" contains references to the marriage books, or registers, from which the information derives. Some citations are to original registers, while other citations are to previously published compilations. Where more than one record source per county was used, each is separately coded. All Missouri counties with marriage records prior to 1840 are covered in this work, except St. Louis County and City, which have been adequately covered elsewhere.

No book is put together without help. My husband, Ted, and my daughter, Jill, were of immeasurable assistance. Also, the book would not have been possible without the cooperation of the following genealogists who graciously gave permission to use their publications: Elizabeth Prather Ellsberry, Lois Stanley, and Maryhelen Wilson. A very special thanks to one and all.

Susan Ormesher

LIST OF SOURCES

Audr Audrain Co. - <u>Marriage Records of Audrain Co., Mo.</u> 1837-1879
       by Elizabeth Prather Ellsberry

Barr Barry Co. - Marriage Book A,B,C 1837-77
       Recorder's Office, Cassville, Mo.

Bent Benton Co. - Marriage Book A
       Clerk's Office, Warsaw, Mo.

Boon Boone Co. - Marriage Book A.
       Recorder's Office, Columbus, Mo.

Buch Buchanan Co. - <u>Buchanan Co. Marriage Records</u> 1839-1850
       by Elizabeth Prather Ellsberry

Call Callaway Co. - <u>Marriage Records of Callaway Co., Mo.</u> 1820-1840
       by Elizabeth Prather Ellsberry

CG Cape Girardeau Co. - Record A 1826-38   CG-A
       Marriage License Record B   CG-B
       Original Record Book A 1804-1807   CGRA
       Original Record Book 1805-1826   CG-1

Carr Carroll Co. - <u>Carroll Co. Marriage Records</u> 1833-56
       by Elizabeth Prather Ellsberry

Cass Cass Co. - Marriage Book A
       Recorder's Office, Harrisonville, Mo.

Char Chariton Co. - <u>Marriage Records of Chariton Co., Mo.</u> 1821-52
       by Elizabeth Prather Ellsberry

Clar Clark Co. - Marriage Book Dec. 29, 1836- Nov. 29, 1856
       Recorder's Office, Kahoka, Mo.

Clay Clay Co. - Marriage Record A 1822-42
       Recorder's Office, Liberty, Mo.

Clin Clinton - Marriage Book A
       Circuit Clerk's Office, Plattsburg, Mo.

Cole Cole Co. - <u>Marriage Records of Cole Co., Mo.</u> 1821-51
       by Elizabeth Prather Ellsberry

Coop Cooper Co. - <u>Early Marriage Records</u> 1819-1850 & <u>Will Records</u>
       1820-1870 <u>of Cooper Co., Mo.</u>
       by Elizabeth Prather Ellsberry

Craw Crawford Co. - Marriage Records 1 & 2   Cr-1
       Early Pamphlet   Cr-P

Davi Daviess Co. - <u>Marriage Records of Daviess Co., Mo</u> 1836-55
       by Elizabeth Prather Ellsberry

Fran   Franklin Co. - Marriage Book A 1819-1844
                    Recorder's Office, Union, Mo.

Gasc   Gasconade Co. - Marriage Book A-B
                    Recorder's Office, Hermann, Mo.

Gree   Greene Co. - Marriage Book A 1833-54
                    Recorder's Office, Springfield, Mo.

Henr   Henry Co. - Marriage Book A & B
                    Recorder's Office, Clinton, Mo.

Howa   Howard Co. - Marriages 1816-1850 & Wills 1818-1836
                    by Elizabeth Prather Ellsberry

Jack   Jackson Co. - Marriage Records of Jackson Co., Mo. 1827-1860
                    by Elizabeth Prather Ellsberry

Jeff   Jefferson Co. - Marriage Records of Jefferson Co., Mo. 1821-1848
                    by Elizabeth Prather Ellsberry

John   Johnson Co. - Marriage Records of Johnson Co., Mo. 1835-1861
                    by Elizabeth Prather Ellsberry

Lafa   LaFayette Co. - LaFayette Co., Mo. Marriage Records 1825-1844
                    by Elizabeth Prather Ellsberry

Lewi   Lewis Co. - Marriage Record 1 July 1833- Jan. 1848
                    Cir. Clk. & Recorder's Office, Monticello, Mo.

Linc   Lincoln Co. - Lincoln Co., Mo. Marriage Records 1825-1844
                    by Elizabeth Prather Ellsberry

Livi   Livingston Co. - Marriage Records of Livingston Co., Mo. 1837-63
                    by Elizabeth Prather Ellsberry

Maco   Macon Co. - Macon Co., Mo. Will Records 1838-1880 & Marriage
                    Records by Elizabeth Prather Ellsberry

Md   Madison Co. - Marriage Book A 1821-35   Md-A
                    Marriage Record B 1835-47   Md-B
                    Deed Book A   Md-D
                    Recorder's Office, Fredericktown, Mo.

Mari   Marion Co. - Marriage Record A & 2 1827-56
                    Cir. Clk. & Recorder's Office, Palmyra, Mo.

Mill   Miller Co. - Marriage Book A 1837-70
                    Recorder's Office, Tuscumbia, Mo.

Monr   Monroe Co. - Marriage Book A 1831-49
                    Recorder's Office, Paris, Mo.

Morg   Morgan Co. - Marriage Book A 1833-61
                    Recorder's Office, Versailles, Mo.

Perr   Perry Co. - Marriage Book A - pages 29-40 were missing
                    Recorder's Office, Perryville, Mo.

Pett   Pettis Co. - Marriage Book A 1833-47
                    Recorder's Office, Sedalia, Mo.

Pk   Pike Co. - Marriage Record 1 1825-37   Pk-1
                    Marriage Record 2 1837-51   Pk-2
                    Recorder's Office, Bowling Green, Mo.

Plat Platte Co. - Marriage Book A
                Recorder's Office, Platte City, Mo.

Polk Polk Co. - Marriage Book A 1835-65
                Recorder's Office, Bolivar, Mo.

Rall Ralls Co. - Marriage Book A 1821-45
                Cir. Clk. & Recorder's Office, New London, Mo.

Rand Randolph Co. - Early Marriage Records of Randolph Co., Mo.
                1829-59 by Elizabeth Prather Ellsberry

Ray Ray Co. - Marriages 1820-1850 & Wills 1824-1849 of Ray Co., Mo.
          by Elizabeth Prather Ellsberry

Ripl Ripley Co. - Marriage Book A 1833-66
              Circuit Clerk's Office, Doniphan, Mo.

StCh St. Charles Co. - Marriage Records of St. Charles Co., Mo.
                1805-1844; compiled by Lois Stanley, Maryhelen
                Wilson, and Geo. F. Wilson
                St. Louis, Mo. Mar. 1, 1978

StGe Ste. Genevieve Co. - Marriage Book A
                Recorder's Office, Ste. Genevieve, Mo.

StFr St. Francious Co. - Marriage Book A,B,C, 1-A,1,2, & D 1822-98
                Recorder's Office, Farmington, Mo.

Sali Saline Co. - Marriage Records 1820-50
                by Elizabeth Prather Ellsberry

Shel Shelby Co. - Early Marriage Records of Shelby Co., Mo. 1835-1867
                by Elizabeth Prather Ellsberry

Warr Warren Co. - Marriage Book A 1833-46
                Recorder's Office, Warrenton, Mo.

Wash Washington Co. - Marriage Book A
                Recorder's Office, Potosi, Mo.

----, ---- to Sary Cantrel 13 June 1821	Lafa
----, ---- to Nancy Purcell 20 Mar. 1832	Jeff
----, Anthony to Hannah Bainig 25 Sept. 1815	CG-1
----, Landon to Lucy A. Quick 3 Oct. 1829	Jeff
----, Wm. to Catherine ---- 30 May 1835	Jeff
-fee, Wallace to Surana Givens 16 Mar. 1821	Lafa
Abbington, Henry to Marion Smith 31 May 1837	Warr
Abbot, Dudley to Hildah Kerby 8 July 1838	Monr
Abbot, Samuel to Mary Hagood 21 Feb. 1833	Pk-1
Abbott, John to Ann Plummer 4 Apr. 1828	Call
Abbott, Martin to Nancy J. Buchannon 15 Apr. 1838	Monr
Abby, Jean Bte. to Susana Bolin 7 Feb. 1807	StGe
Abbyliss, Nathaniel to Rachel Block 23 Apr. 1837	Pk-A
Abell, Peter T. to Emily Cabbell 19 May 1835	Char
Abell, Wm. to Mahala Pearceall 24 May 1838	Monr
Abernatha, Joab to Nancy Reed 8 Nov. 1829	CG-A
Abernathie, Joab to Mary Smith 1 Sept. 1839	CG-B
Abernathie, Wylie to Sally Hooser 20 May 1830	CG-A
Abernathy, Aaron to Nancy King 21 Sept. 1837	CG-A
Abernathy, Albert G. to Fannie Abernathy 26 Oct. 1837	Perr
Abernathy, Alfonzo to Emily Abernathy 2 Apr. 1835	Perr
Abernathy, Alonzo to Perneely L. Abernathy 21 May 1829	Perr
Abernathy, Battee to Pinerey M. Walker 11 Nov. 1839	Perr
Abernathy, Bellwan E. to Rebeca Pettitt 4 Oct. 1838	Perr
Abernathy, Franklin to Bessie A. Abernathy 1 Aug. 1839	Perr
Abernathy, James R. to Rosannah Davis 11 May 1826	Rall
Abernathy, John H. to Eliza Rutledge 21 Jan. 1830	Perr
Abernathy, Robt. to Rebecca Morton 5 June 1832	CG-A
Abernethy, Joab to Winney Beal 1 Nov. 1831	CG-A
Abington, Lee to Hariet Spurs 25 Apr. 1839	Warr
Abington, Leo B. to Minerva Roy 1 Nov. 1836	StCh
Abington, Taylor to Amanda Penn 14 June 1832	Rall
Abit, Ishmael to Mary Smith 29 Dec. 1835	Rand
Able, Isham to Lewiza Woodson 8 Apr. 1830	Mari
Able, Nelson to Ann Camran 22 Feb. 1818	CG-1
Abrams, Wm. G. to Jane Klein 9 Dec. 1825	StCh
Acock, John to Julian Ross 8 Aug. 1839	Polk
Acors, Wm. to Fanny Jones 23 July 1823	Howa
Acres, Joseph to Elizabeth Hurd 12 Mar. 1825	Lafa
Acton, Cain to Minerva Campbell 10 Jan. 1833	Boon
Adair, Isaac to Mary J. Johnson 3 Sept. 1837	CG-A
Adair, John to Elizabeth Pemberton 28 Mar. 1834	Boon
Adams, Benj. D.W. to Peggy Phillips 11 June 1829	Ray
Adams, Calvin to Katharine Granger 27 Sept. 1838	John
Adams, Charles to Sally Lillard 7 Aug. 1825	Ray
Adams, Edward to Susanah Layton 12 Jan. 1836	Perr
Adams, Eli to Mary J. Robertson 24 Jan. 1833	Coop
Adams, Eli T. to Martha A. Davis 5 Sept. 1839	Coop
Adams, Elijah to Elizabeth Leeper 5 Apr. 1832	Call
Adams, Elijah Jr. to Sarah Michel 14 Nov. 1837	Fran
Adams, Feathergill to Nancy Hasling McMahon 28 Jan. 1836	Clin

1

```
Adams, Geo. to Polly Parmertrek 30 July 1817                        Howa
Adams, Geo. to Polly Childers 23 Mar. 1030                          Fran
Adams, Geo. to Charlotte Carley 9 Mar. 1835                         Ripl
Adams, Geo. to Elizabeth Huste 29 June 1837                         Cr-1
Adams, Geo. to Nancy Gunn 7 June 1838                               Pk-B
Adams, Henry to Sally Huffman 14 July 1834                          Fran
Adams, Henry to Sarah Reed 5 May 1836                               Howa
Adams, Ignatius to Julian Taylor 26 Feb. 1833                      Coop
Adams, Jacob to Conthian McLinn 25 Dec. 1836                        John
Adams, Jacob to Maryan Mark 16 Mar. 1839                            John
Adams, James to Anna Scott 26 Feb. 1824                             Cole
Adams, James to Margaret Miller 20 Nov. 1835                        Rand
Adams, John to Nancy Flannery 12 Mar. 1833                          Jack
Adams, John to Catherine Creeptree 2 May 1834                       StCh
Adams, John to Hannah Baily 13 Nov. 1836                            Fran
Adams, John to Lucinda Philips 11 June 1837                         Perr
Adams, John to Sidney McCrary 18 Jan. 1838                          John
Adams, John D. to May Prewitt 31 Aug. 1834                          Ray
Adams, John Q. to Catherine Brown 6 Jan. 1833                       CG-A
Adams, Joseph to Ellen Moss 11 Apr. 1829                            Jeff
Adams, Joseph to Susan Shobe 18 Nov. 1838                           Warr
Adams, Joshua to Eddy Harwick 2 Nov. 1834                           Jack
Adams, Joshua D. to Amanda M. Tucker 9 Oct. 1838                   Coop
Adams, M. to Elizaberth Parmertree 16 Jan. 1827                     Howa
Adams, Mathew to Lucinda Johnson 23 Oct. 1827                      Coop
Adams, Otho to Mary Johnson 21 Nov. 1827                            Rall
Adams, Ovid to Nancy Yeats 9 July 1835                             Monr
Adams, Peter to Louisa Anderson 17 Dec. 1834                       Lafa
Adams, Thaddeus to Sindrilla Bounds 27 Jan. 1839                   Lafa
Adams, Thomas to Fanny Cornelius 2 Nov. 1826                        Howa
Adams, Thomas to Polly Hudelston 10 Dec. 1829                       CG-A
Adams, Thomas to Sarah Bledsoe 19 Nov. 1835                         Jack
Adams, Turner to Rebecca Eller 26 Jan. 1834                        Coop
Adams, Walter to Matilda Carson 7 Dec. 1820                         Howa
Adams, Wm. to Frances Rice 2 Oct. 1828                              Rall
Adams, Wm. to Mahala Revell 21 Dec. 1830                            CG-A
Adams, Wm. to Martha James 20 Feb. 1831                             Lafa
Adams, Wm. to Nancy Greer 27 Oct. 1832                              CG-A
Adams, Wm. to Elizabeth Hyatt 17 July 1836                          Fran
Adams, Wm. to Mary Short 27 Mar. 1839                               Shel
Adams, Wm. to Frances Grifith 11 Oct. 1839                          Rand
Adams, Wm. G. to Celia Baily 3 Nov. 1836                            Fran
Adams, Winston to Jane Temple 10 Nov. 1836                          Jack
Adamson, Levi to Marry A. Burton 28 Apr. 1836                       Ray
Adderton, Marcus L. to Ann Ruland 3 June 1834                       Linc
Addis, Richard to Sarah A. Davis 4 Mar. 1827                        Pk-1
Adier, Major to Elizabeth Weever 8 July 1827                       Coop
Adkins, Campbell to Rutha Graham 22 Dec. 1826                       Ray
Adkins, Carrol to Elizabeth Welbourn 29 Jan. 1835                  Jack
Adkins, James to Polly Willson 6 Sept. 1822                         Clay
Adkins, James to Mary A. Chapman 9 Mar. 1837                        StFr
Adkins, James to Nancy Simpson 13 Jan. 1839                         Carr
Adkins, James to Susan Kerhn 9 July 1839                            Maco
Adkins, John to Sarah Winifree 22 Oct. 1837                         Carr
Adkins, Lindsey to Polly Winfrey 2 Nov. 1838                        Boon
Adkins, Wm. to Nancy Runnels 10 Jan. 1833                           Howa
Adkins, Wm. P. to Hester Tuggle 3 Nov. 1838                         Shel
Adkins, Willis G. to Polly G. Adkins 10 Jan. 1836                   Carr
Adkins, Wyatt Jr. to Nancy Sollers 5 May 1826                       Clay
Adkins, Wyatt to Mary Bledsoe 5 Nov. 1834                           Jack
Agains, Franklin to Mary A. Waters 8 Apr. 1830                      Boon
Agan, Irvine to Rebecca Jones -- Feb. 1837                          Boon
Agan, James to Elizabeth Harris 12 Nov. 1837                        Boon
Agan, John to Lucy Harris 11 Aug. 1836                              Boon
Agan, Wm. to Jane Godin 1 Apr. 1824                                 Boon
```

2

Agee, Isaac to Cordilly Thornton 25 Nov. 1831	Call
Agee, Ransom to Siam Taylor 23 Mar. 1834	Call
Agee, Tilman to Charlotte Townsend 17 Dec. 1835	Call
Agee, Wm. to Hannah M. Thornton 15 Aug. 1837	Call
Agen, John to Jane Dale 4 Apr. 1832	Boon
Ages, Henry G. to Nancy Wilson 28 Nov. 1839	Clar
Ahmann, Harris to Catharine Subren 16 Sept. 1836	Warr
Ahreys, Frederick to Sophia Ballermeyr 10 Aug. 1839	StCh
Ainslie, Robt. F. to Eliza E. Borron 2 Oct. 1837	Coop
Ainsworth, James to Elizabeth Davis 6 Sept. 1832	Howa
Ainsworth, Levi to Mary Davis -- -- 1827	Char
Aire, Hugh to Elizabeth Duson 12 Nov. 1827	Howa
Aire, Walter G. to Sarah M. Embree 14 Aug. 1838	Howa
Akard, Joseph D. to Kisiah Dunnegan 20 July 1837	Polk
Aker, Martin J. to Ann Rollings 3 May 1838	Clay
Aker, Willis to Nancy Owens 11 June 1833	Clay
Akin, Benj. to Nelly Patterson 5 Oct. 1828	CG-A
Akin, Shannon to Hillnry Durnanq 23 June 1836	Morg
Akins, David to Melve Eads 7 June 1837	StFr
Akins, John to Elizabeth Nunn 16 July 1837	Rall
Akins, Peter to Vancy Keys 12 May 1838	Wash
Akins, Wm. to Elizabeth Blackburn 22 June 1837	Lewi
Alard, David to Polly Weever 30 July 1820	Howa
Albert, Charles C. to Mary McNerwin 21 May 1821	StGe
Alder, John to Frances Rogers 13 July 1833	Fran
Aldridge, Wm. to Jane Carson 15 Mar. 1832	Wash
Aldrige, James to Nancy Paterison 5 Nov. 1829	Wash
Alexander, Ambrose D. to Polly Fuget 23 Oct. 1831	Rall
Alexander, Hiram to Margaret George 12 Oct. 1826	Wash
Alexander, Hugh to Sally Finnell 5 Jan. 1836	Howa
Alexander, James to Emilia Carter 8 Apr. 1838	Boon
Alexander, James to Berebe Cunningham 6 Sept. 1838	John
Alexander, James to Julie A. Dryden 25 Oct. 1838	Linc
Alexander, John to Jane Smith 16 Feb. 1837	Lafa
Alexander, Joseph E. to Mary A. Currin 30 Oct. 1838	Wash
Alexander, Martin to Sarah Thornhill June/July 1821	StCh
Alexander, Nero to Letitia Simmons 7 Jan. 1836	Cole
Alexander, Reuben to Jane Smith 9 Sept. 1830	Md-B
Alexander, Reuben to Edith Embree 12 Sept. 1833	Rand
Alexander, Robt. A. to Dorcas Alexander 13 Sept. 1832	CG-A
Alexander, Thomas H. to Eliza A. Norten 20 Feb. 1834	Gree
Alexander, Walton to Isabella Taylor 6 Feb. 1834	StFr
Alexander, Wm. to Celah Lawless 28 Oct. 1828	Boon
Alexander, Wm. to Jane Kennady 5 Dec. 1831	Pk-1
Alexander, Wm. to Hannah Thomson 10 Jan. 1833	Boon
Alexander, Willis B. to Jane Hopper 8 Mar. 1826	Call
Alfers, Herman to Anna H. Engel 15 Nov. 1839	Warr
Alford, John to Sarah Cook 28 Apr. 1835	Rand
Alford, Johnson H. to Mrs. Adeline Lewis 25 Apr. 1832	Jeff
Alfrey, Joseph W. to Elizabeth R. Robison 19 Nov. 1838	Clin
Alkire, Jesse to Meeky Clay 3 Jan. 1833	StCh
Alkire, Samuel to Mahala Gibson 13 Oct. 1831	Call
Allard, James to Nancy Weaver 7 Nov. 1833	Morg
Allard, James to Elizabeth Parsons 20 June 1838	Cass
Allcorn, Clayton to Eleanor Haff 19 Aug. 1830	Pk-1
Allcorn, James to Elizabeth Rives 1 Aug. 1839	Howa
Allcorn, James M. Jr. to Cinthy F. Wear 14 Feb. 1833	Coop
Allderage, James G. to Luiza M. Shannen 24 Mar. 1836	Perr
Allee, Charity to Kesiah Howard 1 Apr. 1825	Coop
Allen, Aaron to Eliza White 2 Aug. 1838	Barr
Allen, Alfred H. to Verina Velinger 21 Nov. 1839	Cole
Allen, Baranabas to Amelia Lafernait 12 Sept. 1819	CG-1
Allen, Benj. to Margaret McAllister 29 Sept. 1831	Pk-1
Allen, Billings to Milly Graves 19 Apr. 1836	Lewi
Allen, Billings to Ann Woodson 13 June 1837	Lewi

3

```
Allen, Burdett to Lucinda Kemper 19 Jan. 1837                    Md-B
Allen, Cary to Elizabeth Crum 31 Aug. 1837                       Linc
Allen, David to Ann Boone 9 Aug. 1829                            Call
Allen, Edgar to Parthena Harrison 31 Dec. 1833                   Howa
Allen, Edward to Jane Wade 30 May 1826                           Linc
Allen, Eligy to Charlotte Givens 28 Nov. 1839                    Plat
Allen, Geo. to Permelia Palmer 25 Apr. 1832                      Linc
Allen, Henry F. to Sodoiski Haggons 18 July 1839                 CG-B
Allen, Henry W. to Catharine L. Cox 18 Sept. 1839               Char
Allen, Isaac to Rebecca Clevenger 1 Nov. 1826                    Ray
Allen, Jacob to Sarah Cox 16 Oct. 1834                           CG-A
Allen, James to Phoebe Inglish 17 Feb. 1836                      Polk
Allen, Jesse to Nancy Davis 13 Jan. 1831                         Call
Allen, John to Mulah Crowley 20 Dec. 1820                        Howa
Allen, John to Eliza Stone 21 Jan. 1822                          Sali
Allen, John to Mary Eads 3 Apr. 1823                             Cole
Allen, John to Mary Cox 11 Sept. 1834                            CG-A
Allen, John to Martha Sheley 15 Sept. 1836                       Call
Allen, John to Emilene White 17 Oct. 1839                        Barr
Allen, John C. to Polly Fuqua 31 July 1833                       Mari
Allen, John M. to Martha A. Smart 5 Sept. 1833                   Call
Allen, John M. to Mary F. Woods 9 Sept. 1839                     Call
Allen, John W. to Martha Allen 3 Mar. 1831                       CG-A
Allen, Joseph to Matilda English 4 July 1833                     Ray
Allen, Joseph to Sarah McClinny 4 Dec. 1834                      StCh
Allen, Joseph to Lucy Morley 2 Sept. 1835                        Clay
Allen, Moses to Nancy Wright 30 Apr. 1838                        Coop
Allen, Oliver H. to Jane Kenton 8 Feb. 1837                      Lewi
Allen, Preston to Mary A. Bartlett 7 Mar. 1839                   Cole
Allen, Reuben to Rhoda Rowland 13 July 1826                      Ray
Allen, Robt. to Elizabeth B. Whaley 31 Dec. 1833                 Clay
Allen, Robt. B. to Louisa J. Chambers 10 Dec. 1836              StCh
Allen, Robt. L. to Phebe A. Pendleton 9 Oct. 1838               Warr
Allen, Samuel to Sarah Benson 11 Sept. 1827                      Coop
Allen, Shubaul to Dinah Trigg 19 Sept. 1822                      Howa
Allen, Soloman to Nancy Poulson 7 Dec. 1826                      Cole
Allen, Thomas to Sarah Meredith 20 June 1830                     Perr
Allen, Thomas to Ealenor George 30 June 1831                     Coop
Allen, Thomas to Sally Stone 24 Oct. 1831                        Clay
Allen, Thomas to Malinda Batterton 10 Mar. 1836                  Boon
Allen, Thomas to Rebecca Johnson 17 Mar. 1836                    Md-B
Allen, Thomas to Jane Jackson 26 Oct. 1834                       Ray
Allen, Thomas J. to Agnes Basett 16 Oct. 1831                    Howa
Allen, Thomas N. to Isabella Hamilton 4 Apr. 1839               Call
Allen, Whitley to Judy Persinger 19 Dec. 1824                    Clay
Allen, Wm. to Nancy Moad 4 July 1822                             Cole
Allen, Wm. to Mary Shelton 1 Nov. 1833                           StCh
Allen, Wm. to Sally Johnston 22 Feb. 1838                        Clin
Allen, Wm. J. to Suckey Abernathy 26 Mar. 1835                   StFr
Allenberry, John to Lucinda Kirby 1 Mar. 1827                    Char
Allensworth, Wm. to Mary Nelson 8 July 1838                      Lewi
Alley, Thomas to Jerrumah Evans 7 Feb. 1832                      Coop
Allis, Samuel Jr. to Emeline Palmer 23 Apr. 1836                 Clay
Allison, Alexander to Sarah A. Mathes 20 Sept. 1837             Rall
Allison, John to Elizabeth Waddell 21 Sept. 1837               Pk-B
Allison, John to Decy Trapp 21 Aug. 1839                        Buch
Allison, John K. to Mary Richardson -- Jan. 1832               Coop
Allison, Joseph to Maria Jackson 23 Jan. 1838                   Pk-B
Allison, Robt. to Louisa J. Carroll 30 July 1829               Pk-1
Allison, Sylvanus to Jane McCrary 13 Oct. 1831                  Wash
Allison, Thomas to Cynthia Edwards 12 Apr. 1838                 Pk-B
Allison, Umphrey P. to Rebecca Linville 20 Feb. 1834            Lafa
Allison, Warren to Elizabeth Smith 16 June 1836                 Pk-1
Allison, Wm. to Francis C. Davis 11 Aug. 1836                   Mari
Alliston, Wm. R. to Martha E. Cockram 26 Apr. 1838             Polk
```

4

```
Allred, Isaac Jr. to July A. Taylor 11 Oct. 1832            Monr
Allred, Reuben W. to Lucy A. Butler 4 Dec. 1836            Ray
Allred, Wiley to Sally Zebriskin 25 July 1836             Ray
Allright, Benj. to Nancy Hunt 6 Nov. 1827                CG-A
Allton, David to Nancy P. Wilcoxen 14 Mar. 1839          Mari
Allton, John to Sobina Berd 1 Mar. 1837                  CG-A
Ally, John to Mary Baker 17 Aug. 1836                    StFr
Ally, W.E. to Margaret Roland 1 Aug. 1833                Wash
Alsman, Andrew to Elizabeth Manuel 3 July 1836           Mari
Alsop, Elliott to Julia A. Gunn 6 Dec. 1838              Howa
Alsup, John P. to Phebe Weaver 21 Oct. 1836              Polk
Altmier, Wm. to Amanda Eastwood 21 May 1832              Jeff
Alvert, Shadrack to Elizabeth West 20 Apr. 1826          Boon
Ambrose, Allen to Jane Smith 30 Mar. 1837                Boon
Amery, Samuel to Mary Aversoll 17 Mar. 1836              StCh
Amic, Alford to Jane Beaty 24 Oct. 1839                  Sali
Amick, Geo. to Amy Kingsberry 25 Dec. 1817               Howa
Amick, Leander to Eliza Cooper 27 Feb. 1834              Howa
Ammeran, Sanford to Susan Awberry 23 May 1839            Gasc
Ammerman, Joseph to Gemima Auberry 26 Jan. 1834          StCh
Ammerman, Samuel to Martha Smith 13 May 1838             Lewi
Amonett, John to Margaret E. Bruffey 5 June 1836         Wash
Ammons, Henry to Isabel Johnson 8 Nov. 1839              Plat
Amos, Anthony W. to Jane Simpson 12 Mar. 1831            Cole
Amos, John to Polly Stephens 13 Nov. 1823                Cole
Amos, Nicholas to Mary Murray 17 Aug. 1822               Gasc
Amos, Ransom to Catherine Enloe 12 July 1832             Cole
Ancell, John to Jane Clark 1 July 1834                   CG-A
Ancell, Pascal to Martha Whitelow 22 Aug. 1833           CG-A
Ancin, Wm. to Amanda Duckworth 23 Nov. 1837              Gasc
Anders, Isaac to Elizabeth Walker 5 Dec. 1831            Howa
Anders, Squire I. to Martha Parks 20 Oct. 1836           Char
Anders, Walter to Rhoda Beason 24 Oct. 1839              Henr
Anderson, Dr. Albert G. to Louisa J. Muldrow 8 Mar. 1836 Mari
Anderson, Andrew to Elizabeth Johnson 28 Jan. 1836       Mari
Anderson, Andrew to Fenelefy Martin 23 Nov. 1838         Char
Anderson, Anthony to Susan Evans 17 Aug. 1837            Barr
Anderson, Buckley B. to Sally Cutler 5 Jan. 1838         Ray
Anderson, Elias to Elizabeth M. Summers 20 June 1839     Clay
Anderson, Elijah to Mary McHugh 9 Sept. 1838             Linc
Anderson, Geo. to Mary Cornett 27 June 1832              Sali
Anderson, Hedgeman to Curtis W. Stephenson 15 June 1839  Warr
Anderson, Henry to Mary Smith 2 Dec. 1827                Boon
Anderson, James to Ester Wilson 4 Apr. 1813              CG-1
Anderson, James to Margaret Ward 7 June 1827             Fran
Anderson, James to Elender Simpson 6 July 1831           Howa
Anderson, James to Emily Young 13 June 1836              Henr
Anderson, James to Jane Hill 21 June 1838                Linc
Anderson, John to Mary Wilson 21 Jan. 1816               CG-1
Anderson, John to Jane Ward 23 Apr. 1820                 Fran
Anderson, John to Lovee Fenton 28 Apr. 1821              Boon
Anderson, John to Nancy Casey 9 Apr. 1829                Cole
Anderson, John to Juliet Speed 14 Nov. 1833              Jeff
Anderson, Joshua to Laurie Baker 13 Nov. 1825            Call
Anderson, Lewis to Mary S. Elliott 29 Jan. 1839          Rall
Anderson, Mathew to Matilda Maxwell 10 Aug. 1837         Polk
Anderson, Matthew to Sally Hinton 5 Aug. 1828            Pk-1
Anderson, Middleton to Nancy Anderson 5 Sept. 1822       Howa
Anderson, Newton to Ann Olson 20 June 1839               Shel
Anderson, Osborn to Sarah Davis 29 Aug. 1839             Carr
Anderson, Pinkney K. to E.C.F. Twyman 29 Dec. 1831       Perr
Anderson, Robt. to Margaret Anderson 29 June 1818        Howa
Anderson, Robt. to Anna Burbridge 15 Apr. 1830           Pk-1
Anderson, Samson to Patience Spears 27 Mar. 1828         Pk-1
Anderson, Samuel M. to Emily Owen 26 Jan. 1837           Monr
```

5

Anderson, Thomas to Nancy Curtis 19 Jan. 1826   Howa
Anderson, Thomas to Columbia English 4 Oct. 1836   CG-A
Anderson, Thomas to Mira A. Wiseman 12 Nov. 1837   Gasc
Anderson, Thomas to Letha Foeguson 6 Dec. 1838   Fran
Anderson, Thomas L. to Rusella Easton 19 Apr. 1832   StCh
Anderson, Washington to ---- Leeper 14 Feb. 1839   Livi
Anderson, Wm. to Margaret Jeffers 2 Apr. 1818   Howa
Anderson, Wm. to Delila Funk 26 Dec. 1822   Boon
Anderson, Wm. to Malinda Scott 18 Apr. 1830   Coop
Anderson, Wm. to Rebeckey Donnaldson 6 Sept. 1832   Lafa
Anderson, Wm. B. to Elizabeth Williams 2 May 1839   Warr
Anderson, Wm. G. to Anna Frickey 5 Mar. 1839   CG-B
Anderson, Willis to Hetta W. Sadler 15 Sept. 1836   Lewi
Andrews, Aaron to Celia Hargis 19 Oct. 1824   Howa
Andrews, Aaron to Mildred Barnes 24 Dec. 1838   Maco
Andrews, Abraham to Patsey Wooten 29 Apr. 1821   Rall
Andrews, David to Caty Jacks -- Sept. 1823   Howa
Andrews, Eli to Elizabeth Jacks 4 Mar. 1827   Howa
Andrews, Eli M. to Mary Davis 16 Aug. 1838   Sali
Andrews, Green to Jemimah Tinnel 8 Feb. 1827   Howa
Andrews, Jacob to Margaret Duff 15 Apr. 1827   StFr
Andrews, James to Mary Owens 2 Feb. 1837   Howa
Andrews, John to Sally Beatty -- Aug. 1823   Howa
Andrews, John to Peggy Snowden 15 Jan. 1832   Ray
Andrews, Joseph to Lucretia Jameson 9 July 1839   Henr
Andrews, Moses to Polly Fields 4 Sept. 1828   Howa
Andrews, Wesley to Eliza Swinney 5 Feb. 1832   Monr
Andrews, Wm. to Elizabeth Pershall 2 Mar. 1827   StFr
Angel, John to Jemima Hill 21 Jan. 1836   Boon
Angle, Alfred to Evaline Stafford 15 Jan. 1834   Cr-1
Annette, James to Polly Nail 27 Aug. 1826   Howa
Ansell, Washington to Eliza Whitelow 19 Nov. 1829   CG-A
Anson, Franklin to Polly M. Robbins 5 May 1835   Pk-1
Anson, Peter to Lorinda Grooms 1 Sept. 1831   Pk-1
Anson, Thomas to Polly Burbridge 4 Oct. 1832   Pk-1
Anthony, Alfred R. to Permela Coppedge 30 Nov. 1834   Cr-1
Anthony, Jonas M. to Nancy Twittey 3 May 1831   Wash
Anthony, Thomas to Cassey Sutton 20 Oct. 1833   Boon
Anthony, Wm. to Delily Morrow 13 Sept. 1827   Boon
Antony, Wm. to Emey Bennett 4 Jan. 1835   CG-B
Apperson, Gabriel L. to Catherine Fine 13 Feb. 1834   StCh
Apperson, Gilbert to Martha Berkley 16 Mar. 1837   Coop
Apperson, Melton to Elizabeth P. Nowlin 3 Oct. 1839   Gree
Apperson, Peter to Melinda N. Edwards 17 Nov. 1839   Gree
Applebury, John P. to Eliza A. Stevens 30 June 1831   Jeff
Applegate, Charles to Malinda Miller 4 Aug. 1829   Cole
Applegate, Jesse to Cynthia A. Parker 13 Mar. 1831   Cole
Applegate, Joseph to Elizabeth Mackey 1 Oct. 1833   Gree
Applegate, Lindsay to Elizabeth Miller 13 Feb. 1831   Cole
Applegate, Milton to Jane Drewitt 6 Jan. 1827   StCh
Apsley, Wm. to Sarah Conyers 2 Oct. 1838   Rall
Arasmith, Wm. to Mary Humphrey 24 Aug. 1837   Monr
Arbuckle, John to Louisa Jones 22 Dec. 1833   Coop
Arbuckle, Samuel to Frances Evans 29 Dec. 1834   Morg
Arbuckle, Silas P. to Dianna Evans 7 Sept. 1831   Coop
Archer, Creed T. to Anny Tagart 14 Feb. 1837   StCh
Archer, Felds to Frances Wood 22 Mar. 1838   Warr
Archer, Wm. to Abigail Tolliver 27 June 1833   Gree
Archy, John to Winnefred Giles 25 Oct. 1838   Linc
Argent, John to Edney Comegys 1 Dec. 1831   StCh
Argull, Archibald to Eliza J. Miller 9 June 1830   Boon
Armenter, Anthony to Polly Biddy 23 June 1839   Plat
Armon, Willis to Susanna Mosteller 15 Mar. 1835   StFr
Armstrong, Abel W. to Malinda Fergison 4 July 1837   Mill
Armstrong, Abner to Susan Nichols 19 Apr. 1838   Boon

6

```
Armstrong, David to Caroline Cadwallader 15 Oct. 1829          Jeff
Armstrong, Dennis to Mahala Shelton 6 Dec. 1835               Jeff
Armstrong, James to Katharine Reed 31 Aug. 1837              Mill
Armstrong, John to Polly Farar 27 May 1824                  Fran
Armstrong, John to Emilie V. Jollin 27 July 1829           Wash
Armstrong, Joshua D. to Elizabeth Boilston 27 June 1839    Plat
Armstrong, Thomas to ---- Turner 21 Sept. 1837            Boon
Armstrong, Thomas B. to Nancy J. Harris 12 Dec. 1833      Fran
Armstrong, Thomas R. to Eveline Cadwallader 25 Apr. 1839  Jeff
Armstrong, Westley to Patsy Phillips 16 Dec. 1832         Wash
Armstrong, Wm. to Mary Edge 1839                          Call
Arnell, John M. to Nancy Hinds 26 Apr. 1838              Warr
Arnold, ---- to Nancy Morris 26 Nov. 1833               Coop
Arnold, Harvey to Nancy J. Hill 30 Aug. 1837            Monr
Arnold, James to Charity Rathburn 6 Oct. 1839           Clar
Arnold, John to Caty Head 22 Mar. 1816                  Howa
Arnold, Mark to Sarah Winn 17 Sept. 1837                Lewi
Arnold, Price to Ann Barnett 23 Feb. 1817               Howa
Arnold, Wieatt B. to Ann R. Turnham 6 Sept. 1836        Clay
Arpion, Bemigins to Elouisa Mane 1 July 1839            StCh
Arquette, Francois to Mrs. Marguarete Portell 6 Nov. 1827  Wash
Arrent, ---- to Mary J. Hill -- Sept. 1839              Sali
Arter, Abner to Nancy Beesley 2 June 1831               Jack
Arther, Joseph B. to Elizabeth A.W. Sydnor 6 Apr. 1837  Linc
Arthur, David to Eleander Malone 19 Sept. 1839          Cass
Arthur, James to Sary Key 3 Jan. 1830                   Cr-P
Arthur, John to Elizabeth Hire 23 July 1839             Cr-1
Arthur, Levi to Malinda Harris 11 Dec. 1833             Cr-1
Arthur, Mastin to Basheba Butt 23 July 1829             Pk-1
Arthur, Wm. to Amelia White 6 Feb. 1838                 Sali
Artman, John to Nancy Mizee 6 Jan. 1824                 Howa
Artman, Michael to Ann Tarwater 27 Dec. 1835            Ray
Ash, Isaac to Susanna Plunket 16 Nov. 1828              Linc
Ashabranner, Daniel to Catherine Bollinger 22 Oct. 1805 CGRA
Ashabranner, Ezekial to Fanny Bullinger 25 Aug. 1833    CG-A
Ashbaugh, Andrew to Margaret McMillin 30 Aug. 1832      Linc
Ashbraner, Orben to Barborah Bulinger 16 July 1805      CG-1
Ashburn, Gilmore to Armilda Bower 27 Feb. 1834          Linc
Ashby, Benj. L. to Mrs. Martha Cock 2 July 1830         Char
Ashby, Geo. to Clancy Sportsman 2 Mar. 1826             Char
Ashby, John to Anjilinah Cross 10 July 1828             Char
Ashby, Newton to Matilda Warren 8 Dec. 1832             Clay
Ashby, Samuel W. to Mary J. Peery 5 Feb. 1839           Livi
Ashby, Thomas T. to Mary E. Bryan 2 Sept. 1839          Monr
Ashcraft, Jesse to Dicy Hines 17 Apr. 1814             StCh
Ashcraft, Valney to Cynthia Hall 6 June 1833            Howa
Asherbraner, Henry to Catherine Perringer 9 Aug. 1821   Md-A
Ashley, Allen to Elender Huff 1 Jan. 1839               Clay
Ashley, Benj. to Alvira Standley 25 Jan. 1833           Carr
Ashley, Wm. H. to Marry Able 17 Nov. 1806               CG-1
Ashley, Wm. H. to Elizabeth Wilcox 17 Oct. 1832         Boon
Ashlock, Samuel to Sarah D. Hunt 31 May 1838            Call
Ashly, Chesly to Mary Elliott 4 July 1821               StGe
Askern, Wm. to Elizabeth A. Price 6 Sept. 1838          Cole
Aslade, James to Ellin Smith 10 Nov. 1839               Perr
Asterburn, Nevil to Caroline Fair 24 Nov. 1833          Carr
Atchison, Peter to Hetty Blais 25 Sept. 1835            Wash
Athneburry, Samuel to Catherine Rice 20 May 1838        Cole
Atkins, Ephraim to Esenau Cottle 24 July 1806           StCh
Atkins, Hiram to Elizabeth Norwood 26 July 1838         Howa
Atkins, James to Tempy Wilbourn 23 Feb. 1837            Cass
Aton, Isaac to Betsy Bradley 5 Dec. 1818                Howa
Aton, Wm. to Mary Drinkwater 14 Aug. 1836               Coop
Atteberry, Wm. to Charlotte Hungerford 10 Jan. 1839     Clin
Attebury, Greenberry to Elizabeth Butler 4 Mar. 1824    Howa
```

7

```
Atterberry, Michael to Rhoda Gee 18 Aug. 1831                         Rand
Atterberry, Seamon to Nancy Weatherford 12 Oct. 1837                  Mont
Atterberry, Wm. Jr. to Nancy Grogan 25 Jan. 1838                      Monr
Atterbery, Henry to Emily McDaniel 27 Feb. 1838                       Henr
Atterbury, Asberry to Eliza Harris 2 Apr. 1839                       Howa
Atterbury, Ashford to Sarah Myers 4 May 1826                          Howa
Atwell, John to Elizabeth Rhynehart 16 Aug. 1835                      CG-B
Aubason, Zenon to Pelagie Chevallier 30 July 1833                     Md-A
Auberry, Thomas to Ann Grubb 20 Apr. 1828                             Ray
Aubery, Henry to Margaret Pru-- 25 Dec. 1836                          StCh
Aubry, John to Jane Drain 9 Aug. 1829                                 StCh
Aubuchon, Louis to Marie Carron 11 Apr. 1837                          StFr
Audrain, Peter to Mahalah Keitheley 5 Mar. 1835                       StCh
Audrin, James H. to Mary Gatty 1 May 1834                             StCh
Aught, Louvina to Margaret Simmerman 17 Nov. 1839                     Cole
Augull, Hezekial to Elizabeth Davis 24 Dec. 1818                      Howa
Augustine, Theodore to Heculen Hanks 13 Aug. 1834                     Warr
Auld, Michael to Elizabeth Harlerod 1 Feb. 1814                       CG-1
Aull, Robt. to Matilda Donohoe 16 June 1835                          Howa
Aull, Thomas to Clarinda Fugate 14 Oct. 1838                         Clay
Aullerson, Buckley B. to Sally McCulter 31 Dec. 1837                  Ray
Austin, Absalom to Lydia Sitton 7 Jan. 1834                          Call
Austin, Benj. to Elizabeth Austin 26 Jan. 1826                        Boon
Austin, Dabney to Jane Freeman -- Oct. 1836                           Boon
Austin, James to Nancy Nicely 20 Jan. 1831                            Boon
Austin, James to Rosey Maupin 20 Mar. 1836                            Carr
Austin, Joel to Sally Austin 16 Nov. 1827                             Boon
Austin, Joel to Charlotte Harrington 22 Dec. 1839                     Boon
Austin, John to Nancy Buckner 24 Nov. 1836                            Cole
Austin, John to Caroline Waddell 20 Dec. 1838                         Lafa
Austin, John F. to Susannah Wilson 6 Oct. 1835                        Rall
Austin, Robt. to Eliza A. Watkins 15 Dec. 1834                        Jack
Austin, Walker to Euphonia McKinney 16 July 1833                      Rand
Austin, Wm. to Jane Gordan 21 May 1839                                Boon
Avants, Daniel to Elizabeth Ealam 21 Sept. 1815                       CG-1
Avants, Isham to Sarah Campbell 14 Apr. 1814                          CG-1
Averett, Elisiah to Ann Byrd 15 Apr. 1800                             CGRA
Averett, James to Purlina Hopkins 19 Dec. 1837                        Clay
Avery, Willis to Elvina Weeks 24 July 1828                            Linc
Avrett, Weston to Hannah Crockett 8 Mar. 1829                         Clay
Awbrey, Wm. T. to Martha Edwards 9 July 1837                          Davi
Ayers, Lind G. to Susan Hargrove 2 Feb. 1837                         Carr
Ayot, Joseph to Mary DeRoy 2 Mar. 1835                               StCh
Ayres, Anthony to Catherine Bewley 19 Oct. 1837                       Polk
Ayres, Ebenezer D. to Louisianna Overall 12 May 1826                 StCh
Ayres, Jepthah to Margaret Thomas 3 June 1839                        Lewi
Ayres, Richard to Isabella Findley 3 Feb. 1832                        Pk-1
Ayres, Samuel to Martha Crain 27 Dec. 1831                           Boon


B-nie, Benj. to Sally Toomis 13 Nov. 1831                             Cole
Babb, Wm. to Elizabeth Bradley 3 Dec. 1829                            CG-A
Baber, John W. to Juliann Aker 15 Feb. 1838                           Clay
Bacchin, Othneal to Permelia Montgomery 31 May 1839                  Maco
Backster, John to Patsy Mullins 16 July 1820                          Coop
Backus, Thomas to Matilda Kenny 20 Dec. 1838                         Gasc
Bacon, Edward to Eliza Hurt 31 Aug. 1828                              Fran
Bacon, Geo. to Catherine C. Lockwood 6 Sept. 1837                    Mari
Baeine, Joseph to Marcelite Lebeau 26 Feb. 1838                       StCh
Baer, Constantine to Josephine Albrecht 9 June 1839                   StCh
Bagby, Joshua T. to Lucy J. Allen 19 Jan. 1837                        Call
Bagby, Thomas to Mary Cruse 13 Sept. 1832                            CG-A
Bagby, Wm. to Virgane Harrison 24 Sept. 1833                         Rand
Bager, Martin to Kesire Johnston 30 Dec. 1833                         Morg
Bagwell, Cary to Mary Johnson 21 June 1829                            Howa
```

```
Bagwell, Wm. to Mary Johnson 4 Apr. 1832                          Howa
Bail, Wm. to Margaret Wells 17 July 1828                          Linc
Bailey, Calvin to Sydney A. Hurt 1 Mar. 1835                      Howa
Bailey, Charles to Amelia Jameson 12 Feb. 1838                    Call
Bailey, Gulliam to Pernely Myers 21 Aug. 1836                     Jack
Bailey, Harmon to Polly Fisher 16 Jan. 1828                       Coop
Bailey, Henry to Elizabeth Glover 29 Sept. 1834                   Call
Bailey, Jesse to Rachel Ginnings 31 May 1835                      Howa
Bailey, John to Mary Dicken 12 May 1835                           Howa
Bailey, Kindred to Maria Grooms 14 Sept. 1834                     Boon
Bailey, Martin to Nancy Bradley 6 Feb. 1834                       Howa
Bailey, Reuben to Maria Wise 1 Oct. 1829                          Cr-P
Bailey, Rial to Polly Foster 5 Aug. 1821                          Howa
Bailey, Robt. to Lucinda Zumwalt 23 May 1833                      StCh
Bailey, Thompson L. to Martha Sprowl 4 July 1837                  Monr
Bailey, Samuel to Charlotte B. Ward 15 Nov. 1829                  Linc
Bailey, Samuel to Mahala Nickerson 23 Oct. 1836                   Howa
Bailey, Wm. to Rebecca H. Baker 7 Sept. 1836                      Call
Bailey, Wm. to Elizabeth Emberson 2 July 1837                     Rand
Bailey, Wm. to Hetty C. Moore 5 May 1839                          Shel
Bailstron, James to Sarah A. Avery 26 Apr. 1832                   Cr-1
Baily, James to Senia Maupin 8 July 1832                          Fran
Baily, Samuel to Polly Jamison 28 Nov. 1816                       StCh
Baily, Uaril to Jane Mosely 13 Mar. 1835                          Fran
Bain, Abner to Sally McFarland 8 Apr. 1834                        CG-A
Bain, John H. to Polly Gwinn 17 Feb. 1831                         Linc
Baines, Morgan to Elizabeth English 3 Apr. 1836                   Cass
Bair, Wm. to Nancy Baldin 6 Sept. 1837                            Wash
Baird, Miles B. to Mary A. Herrington 12 Sept. 1839              Rall
Baker, Adam to Susanah Aairs 24 Feb. 1822                         Fran
Baker, Anderson J. to Roberta G. Wayne 13 Aug. 1839              Call
Baker, Andrew to Nancy Noble 9 Jan. 1831                          Rand
Baker, Andrew to Elizabeth McCully 23 May 1833                    Howa
Baker, Austin to Martha Houk 23 Aug. 1838                         Wash
Baker, Calvin to Nancy Murrell 2 Oct. 1834                        Jeff
Baker, Carter to Lucinda Crimm 21 May 1835                        Monr
Baker, Charles to Emelia J. Simpson 10 Apr. 1838                  Lafa
Baker, David to Catherine Coplin 24 May 1828                      Wash
Baker, Edmund to Mary Baily 8 Nov. 1836                           Boon
Baker, Felix to Polly Gooding 7 Mar. 1833                         Rand
Baker, Floyd to Rachel Bell 23 Sept. 1830                         Call
Baker, Geo. to Sally McCollum -- -- 1835                          Char
Baker, Geo. to Fanney Crader 17 Jan. 1836                         CG-B
Baker, Henry to Elisibeath Paneck 25 June 1805                    CG-1
Baker, Henry to Mary Handon 27 Oct. 1839                          Gasc
Baker, Henry F. to Elizabeth Hambright 4 Sept. 1834              Jack
Baker, Hiram to Cynthia Rayfield 22 Aug. 1839                     Wash
Baker, Isaac to Jane McCully 19 Aug. 1824                         Char
Baker, Isaac to Ann Baker 18 Jan. 1826                           Call
Baker, Isaac to Rachel McKee 22 Jan. 1835                         StFr
Baker, Isaac to Elizabeth Johnson 8 Oct. 1835                     Monr
Baker, Jacob to Malinda Smith 3 Jan. 1839                         StCh
Baker, Jacob to Mahala Shakleford 17 Dec. 1839                    Plat
Baker, James to Jemima Wideman 2 Mar. 1834                        Jeff
Baker, Jeptha to Nancy Roberts 27 Feb. 1830                       Boon
Baker, John to Susannah Wills 22 Oct. 1829                        CG-A
Baker, John to Mrs. Fanny Adams 17 Nov. 1837                      CG-A
Baker, John G. to Catharine Blevins 9 Oct. 1839                   Polk
Baker, John T. to Nancy DeVore 29 Dec. 1831                       Call
Baker, John W. to Ann Cogdell 21 Sept. 1828                       Clay
Baker, Jonathan to Elizabeth Hurley 31 Dec. 1835                  Gree
Baker, Joseph to Catherine Nyswonger 22 Oct. 1805                CGRA
Baker, Joseph to Eleanor Portis 11 Dec. 1831                      Jack
Baker, Joseph to Ann Young 15 Dec. 1831                           CG-A
Baker, Joshua to Sarah Riggs 13 Sept. 1832                        Boon
```

9

```
Baker, Lawson to Prissilar Kelley 8 June 1826                          Clay
Baker, Lemanion to Mary A. Mobley 19 Jan. 1838                         Rand
Baker, Martin to Ann M. Laurence 21 Apr. 1834                         Lewi
Baker, Mathias to Viney Honsinger 29 Apr. 1830                        Cr-P
Baker, Morris to Hily Haines 27 June 1822                             Call
Baker, Morris to Susannah Hanks 20 Jan. 1838                          Sali
Baker, Moses to Polly W. Walker 3 Nov. 1831                          StFr
Baker, Moses to Lydia R. Kinkead 30 Nov. 1836                        StFr
Baker, Moses to Polly Tate 7 Mar. 1839                               Boon
Baker, Moses J. to Amanda Malugeon 22 July 1838                      Barr
Baker, Peter to Elizabeth Miller 2 June 1824                         CG-1
Baker, Peter to Elizabeth Miller 2 June 1825                         CG-A
Baker, Robt. C. to C. Susannah Devore 30 Apr. 1833                   Call
Baker, Samuel to Mary Lewis 4 Dec. 1825                              CG-A
Baker, Thomas to Ann Adair 10 Jan. 1833                              Call
Baker, Tyre to Louisa McDaniel 3 Jan. 1833                           Rand
Baker, Westly to Emily Nichols 9 Dec. 1836                           Boon
Baker, Wm. to Elisabeth Fisher 30 Dec. 1813                          StGe
Baker, Wm. to Sarah Montgomery 7 Nov. 1822                           Howa
Baker, Wm. to Elizabeth Lagate 26 Oct. 1826                          CG-A
Baker, Wm. to Elizabeth Frazier 20 Mar. 1832                         Coop
Baker, Wm. to Catharine Bagwell 4 Apr. 1837                          Davi
Baker, Wm. to Ruth Standerford 2 Jan. 1839                           Monr
Baker, Wm. B. to Pamela Lewis 16 Dec. 1836                           Call
Balden, Wm. B. to ---- Thornbill 6 Apr. 1834                         Ray
Balders, Ezekiel to Sarah Napear 14 Jan. 1835                        Gasc
Baldridge, Alexander to Jane Collins 12 Oct. 1837                    StCh
Baldridge, Daniel to Christine Huffman 17 June 1805                  StCh
Baldridge, Daniel to Susan Gausney 19 May 1833                       Linc
Baldridge, Daniel to Eliza A. Jamey 30 Mar. 1837                     StCh
Baldridge, Isak to Celia Thornhill 24 Aug. 1837                      StCh
Baldridge, Irving to Mary Thornhill 1 June 1837                      StCh
Baldridge, John to Jane Ringo 15 Oct. 1835                           StCh
Baldridge, Joseph L. to Mary A. Gosney 27 May 1832                   StCh
Baldridge, Wilson to Mahala Taggart 23 Feb. 1837                     StCh
Baldwin, Benj. to Emily Placet 27 Aug. 1830                          Wash
Baldwin, Martin to Claricy Buckston 3 Jan. 1838                      Clay
Baldwin, Thomas to Elizabeth English 18 Dec. 1838                    CG-A
Bales, David to Sally Burns 27 Mar. 1836                             Perr
Bales, Hugh to Susannah Tooney 29 Apr. 1833                          Jack
Bales, Perry to Elizabeth Adamson 26 Mar. 1837                       Ray
Bales, Walter to Sally Johnson 3 June 1832                           Jack
Baley, Edmond M. to Elizabeth Haden 7 May 1834                       Rall
Baley, John to Mrs. Nancy Smith 20 Apr. 1826                         Fran
Baley, Reuben to Celia Sneed 10 Feb. 1832                            Cr-1
Balieu, Leander N. to Sally Liggett 15 Dec. 1833                     Clay
Ball, Austin to Nancy Mayberry 2 Sept. 1832                         Ray
Ball, Isaac to Abigail Howland 3 Jan. 1838                           StCh
Ball, James to Hanna Sinclair 27 Sept. 1826                          Gasc
Ball, John to Juleete Poague 13 Dec. 1838                            Mari
Ball, John W. to Eliza M. Miller 22 June 1834                        Gree
Ball, Singaton to Lucinday Timberlick 10 Sept. 1829                  StCh
Ball, Thomas to Lucinda Roberts 28 Dec. 1833                         Boon
Ball, Thomas B. to Susan Q. Mallery 30 Aug. 1837                     Mari
Ballard, Abner H. to Rebecca Bailes 26 Nov. 1839                     Ripl
Ballard, Alfred to Elizabeth Smith 19 July 1838                      Henr
Ballard, Elijah W. to Lucretia Earls 8 Apr. 1838                     Clay
Ballard, James to Racheal Hitt 18 Nov. 1830                          CG-A
Ballard, Thomas J. to Mary V. Hodges 20 Mar. 1836                    Cole
Ballenger, Elijah to Deborah Warren 21 Apr. 1835                     Boon
Ballenger, James to Amanda Ballenger 10 Mar. 1835                    Boon
Ballenger, Minor to Missouri A. Parks 22 Mar. 1827                   Boon
Ballew, Barnabay to Margaret Burton 26 Sept. 1822                    Howa
Ballew, Wm. to Lottey McClain 7 Apr. 1836                            Howa
Balthrope, Thomas E.A. to Martha F. Kemper 1 Feb. 1838              Mari
```

```
Baly, Thomas to Hilda Gobel 25 Feb. 1838                           Fran
Bancroft, Timothy to Nancy B. Davis 25 Aug. 1825                   Sali
Bane, John to Rachel McFarland 17 Mar. 1833                        CG-A
Bane, Robt. to Mary McFarland 13 May 1828                          CG-A
Bane, Wm. to Ann Brown 11 Dec. 1838                                Clay
Banister, Henry to Margaret Hill 27 June 1832                      StFr
Banks, Henry M. to Nancy Turpin 28 Dec. 1837                       Mari
Banks, Nathaniel to Mary Umphries 6 July 1838                      Carr
Banks, Wm. L. to Jedidah Lewis 29 Dec. 1833                        Howa
Banks, Wm. M. to Eliza J. Cottin 26 June 1834                      Mari
Bankson, Holman F. to Polly Bowles 17 Dec. 1829                    Coop
Bankston, Pleasant to Mariah Smith 21 Nov. 1833                    Coop
Banning, Frazier to Rebecca Watson 11 July 1827                    Char
Banning, James to Margaret Hammett 30 Sept. 1838                   Rand
Banning, Jerry to Isabel M. Campbell 24 Dec. 1829                  Char
Barbar, Geo. to Lydia Ross 9 Mar. 1830                             Perr
Barbee, Owen T. to Ruth Neal 12 Oct. 1837                         Rall
Barber, Jesse to Mary McKown 3 Feb. 1825                           Clay
Barbey, Marshel to Susan Browning 26 June 1835                     Pk-1
Barbrick, David to Elizabeth Westy 14 Dec. 1837                    Gasc
Barger, Gilford P. to Patsy Summers 21 Oct. 1833                   Morg
Barger, Henry to Phoebe Wilfley 26 Feb. 1824                       Call
Baribeau, Francois to Euphrosene Saulier 12 Sept. 1806            StCh
Barker, Elias to Sarah Dennis 20 July 1829                         Coop
Barker, John to Cintha A. Trail 5 Nov. 1829                        Linc
Barker, John to Sary McFarland 26 Aug. 1830                        Lafa
Barker, John to Jane Helton 1 Aug. 1837                            CG-A
Barker, Joseph to Margaret Hopper 11 Mar. 1830                     Lafa
Barker, Lewis to Hester A. Prestley 16 Feb. 1837                   Linc
Barker, Richard to Elizabeth Reeder 24 Dec. 1834                   Lafa
Barker, Starting to Phana Ratten 3 Dec. 1829                       Wash
Barker, Wilson to Ann Lamon 26 Oct. 1828                           Linc
Barkley, Thomas S. to Lucinda Brizandine 31 Jan. 1838            Rall
Barks, Alexander to Fanny Masters 3 Jan. 1833                      CG-A
Barks, Daniel to Malinda Hartle 11 Dec. 1834                       CG-B
Barks, Isaac to Sarah Wise 19 Jan. 1826                            CG-A
Barks, Jacob to Sary Deck 18 Mar. 1830                             CG-A
Barlow, Martin B. to Elizabeth Deering 10 Nov. 1836              Monr
Barltey, Geo. to Elizabeth Moore 8 July 1827                       Call
Barnard, Elijah P. to Anstria Foreman 15 Oct. 1839               StCh
Barnard, John to Mary Baldridge 3 Aug. 1828                        StCh
Barnard, Johnson to Nancy Colliver 23 Jan. 1832                    Pk-1
Barnard, Wm. to Elizabeth Baldridge 25 Sept. 1831                 StCh
Barner, Phillip to Mary A. Roberson 21 Feb. 1839                   Coop
Barnes, Abraham to Gracy Jones 26 Apr. 1816                        Howa
Barnes, Amos to Dorcas Couiard 15 Mar. 1812                        StCh
Barnes, Amos to Mary Tucker 13 Jan. 1834                           Jack
Barnes, Anderson to Scotha Cannon 26 July 1833                     Howa
Barnes, Benj. to Lucrecy Sims 10 Oct. 1819                         Howa
Barnes, Dudley to Rutha E. McMillen 4 Apr. 1835                    Boon
Barnes, Dudley to Lucinda Hulen 7 Aug. 1838                        Boon
Barnes, Francis to Belinda Guess 19 Oct. 1837                      Boon
Barnes, Geo. to Elizabeth Bishop 3 June 1838                       Boon
Barnes, Geo. to Bertha A. Greening 5 Sept. 1839                    Monr
Barnes, Harrison to Eleandor Patten 16 July 1837                   Boon
Barnes, James to Rachel Hewsett 21 Sept. 1837                      Boon
Barnes, James to Amanda Bingham -- Sept. 1838                      Sali
Barnes, John to Sally Hubbard 8 Sept. 1812                         StCh
Barnes, John to Nancy Simons 18 July 1839                          Boon
Barnes, John J. to Elizabeth Burnsidy 3 Nov. 1825                  Fran
Barnes, Joseph to Mary Cox 18 Apr. 1839                            Boon
Barnes, Larkin to Tilpha Lawson 10 Dec. 1834                       Warr
Barnes, Lewis to Elizabeth A. Patton 26 Mar. 1835                  Boon
Barnes, Luster to Margary Shoure 8 Nov. 1835                       Fran
Barnes, Mathew to Jane Sanderson 17 Jan. 1833                      Boon
```

11

Barnes, Miller to Amelia P. Wayne 18 Dec. 1831	Boon
Barnes, Nathan to Lemandia Garrett 24 Sept. 1829	Boon
Barnes, Phillip to Jane Crews 17 Nov. 1823	Boon
Barnes, Robt. to Frances Tucker 11 Oct. 1838	Polk
Barnes, Scott to Mary Matthew 13 June 1833	Boon
Barnes, Silas to Sarah Holman 13 Sept. 1836	Rand
Barnes, Talton T. to Jane R. Patterson 24 Dec. 1839	Coop
Barnes, Thomas to Susanna Field 19 June 1832	Howa
Barnes, Thomas to Elizabeth Henley 4 July 1833	Cole
Barnes, Thomas to Lydia Smallwood -- Dec. 1838	Boon
Barnes, Thomas J. to Sarah L. McCray 28 Apr. 1836	Call
Barnes, Wm. to Margaret Duncan 25 Apr. 1819	Howa
Barnes, Wm. to Polly Roberts 6 Mar. 1829	Cole
Barnes, Wm. to Malrissa Callaway 6 Mar. 1834	Warr
Barnet, James to Lucretia Striklin 21 Dec. 1838	Clin
Barnett, Alfred to Beverly Owens 31 Aug. 1837	Howa
Barnett, Alteriasuis to Jane Areman 5 Sept. 1838	Boon
Barnett, Andrew to Susan Van Daven 4 June 1839	Boon
Barnett, Daniel to Susan Roads 3 Jan. 1839	Boon
Barnett, David to Nancy Conner 18 Feb. 1830	Howa
Barnett, Davis to Lucy McFarland 23 Dec. 1824	Rall
Barnett, Geo. H. to Polly Francis 4 May 1837	John
Barnett, Hutchins to Mary Delaney 29 Mar. 1838	Monr
Barnett, John to Arrella Willingham 1 Jan. 1823	Boon
Barnett, John to Peggy Agen 23 July 1829	Boon
Barnett, John to Elizabeth J. Kerr 8 Apr. 1838	Pk-B
Barnett, Joseph to Becky Cannon 26 June 1827	Linc
Barnett, Joseph to Mary Fry 23 Dec. 1831	Pk-1
Barnett, Morgan to Celey Ernest 15 Nov. 1824	Rall
Barnett, Otheas to Amerlia Overton 1 Nov. 1834	Jack
Barnett, Robt. to Matilda Prichard 16 Oct. 1832	Pk-1
Barnett, Robt. to Mary McMahan 24 Oct. 1839	John
Barnett, Washington to Jane Kincaid 26 Jan. 1837	Mari
Barnett, Wilson C. to Cynthia A. Gunn 17 May 1838	Howa
Barnett, Zacheus to Martha Smith 26 July 1829	Howa
Barnett, Zacheus to Minna Tindal 17 Jan. 1836	Howa
Barngrover, Cornelius to Delia Ravencroft 15 Aug. 1839	CG-B
Barns, Anderson to Elizabeth Gentry 26 Dec. 1839	Carr
Barns, Geo. to Elizabeth Williamson 6 Mar. 1828	Fran
Barnsback, Jacob to Emily McCoy 2 May 1837	StFr
Barr, Wm. T. to Amisititia H. Poor 5 Nov. 1834	Mari
Barradas, Sylvester to Marguerite Beauchemin 22 Jan. 1838	StCh
Barre, Dederick to Christina Tolle 25 Nov. 1837	Warr
Barree, Baptiste to Polly Owen 15 Aug. 1839	Jeff
Barrett, Jackson to Eliza A. Sorrel 3 June 1836	Rand
Barrett, Thomas to Sarah Wright 15 May 1838	Boon
Barrett, Wm. to Patsy Ellington 20 Feb. 1832	Boon
Barringer, Mathias to Elisa Mattingly 24 Nov. 1835	Perr
Barron, Charles to Susan Cockrill 7 Jan. 1836	Rand
Barry, Antion to Salla Webb 1 Nov. 1827	StFr
Barry, James to Nancy Profit 3 Oct. 1824	Boon
Bars, James to Elizabeth Burkheart 13 Aug. 1815	StCh
Bartee, Peyton Y.T. to Elizabeth Longate 9 Sept. 1832	Clay
Barthrett, Henry to Elen Rimon 8 Oct. 1835	Wash
Bartlet, Samuel to Sereny Butcher 13 Jan. 1834	Perr
Bartlett, Geo. W. to Cynthia A. Hatton 25 Aug. 1836	Monr
Bartlett, John to Sally Barclay 19 Dec. 1833	Gasc
Bartlett, Orson to Clarissa Matthews 4 May 1837	CG-A
Bartlett, Reuben to Susanna Hickman 8 Nov. 1835	Perr
Bartlett, Sanders H. to Margaret Hobbs 9 Dec. 1830	Pk-1
Barton, Abraham to Harriett S. Asken 25 Sept. 1834	Cole
Barton, Abraham to Rebecca A. Rice 10 Oct. 1839	Cole
Barton, Andrew to Elizabeth Wigham 19 Dec. 1839	Boon
Barton, John to Frances Burton 17 Apr. 1838	Boon
Barton, Nimber to Margaret Lockhart 7 Nov. 1821	Coop

Barton, Squire to Rachel Dougherty 22 May 1823	Rall
Barton, Wharton to Jane Warren 12 Jan. 1832	Howa
Barum, John to Mariah Minor 14 Nov. 1839	Mari
Basey, John J. to Mary Rogers 6 May 1838	Clin
Basket, Robt. to Mary Potts 16 Dec. 1838	Boon
Baskett, Wilford to Melvina Sulivan 28 Mar. 1839	Polk
Baskin, John C. to Rebecca J. Neale 25 Sept. 1839	Call
Bass, Adam to Eliza Graham 29 Nov. 1836	Rall
Bass, Dabney to Elizabeth Heaslip 23 June 1836	StCh
Bass, David to Martha Davies 9 June 1833	CG-A
Bass, Eli to Margaret Johnston 26 Feb. 1829	Boon
Bass, Tolberd to Martha G. Martin 10 Jan. 1839	Mill
Bass, Wm. to Mary Epperson 17 Apr. 1836	Morg
Bassett, Jonah B. to Katherine Mownuy 30 Aug. 1837	Carr
Bassnett, John R. to Mary J. Claypool 11 June 1839	Boon
Bastin, John to Eliza Perry 15 Jan. 1833	Howa
Basy, John C. to Penina Watson 1 Dec. 1831	Pk-1
Batchelor, Wm. C. to Nancy Samuel 22 Mar. 1838	Coop
Bateman, John to Elizabeth Reece 19 Mar. 1823	Ray
Bater, John to Therisa Gaterneau 14 Sept. 1836	StCh
Bates, Asoph to Sarah Owen 3 June 1830	Lafa
Bates, Edward to Julia D. Coulter 29 May 1823	StCh
Bates, Geo. to Elizabeth Bacon 2 Nov. 1837	Fran
Bates, Henry to Mary R. Martin 17 Dec. 1829	Wash
Bates, Nat to Polly Leek 10 Feb. 1831	Cr-P
Bates, Robt. to Lucy Long 5 July 1838	Clay
Batsel, Edmund to Ellis Bennett 27 May 1832	Mari
Batterton, Enoch to Nancy Snell 28 July 1830	Boon
Batterton, John to Nancy Grant 27 Jan. 1825	Boon
Batterton, Lemual to Mary Lynch 5 Nov. 1824	Boon
Batterton, Samuel to Susan R. Allen 18 June 1836	Boon
Battie, Henry to Dorothy Gradavene 29 Oct. 1835	Call
Battle, John to Finetta J. Ball 30 May 1837	Clin
Baty, John to Perenna Sandridge 10 Dec. 1837	Sali
Baty, Robt. to Lavina Dent 5 Apr. 1826	Fran
Baty, Wm. S. to Mahaly M. Cammon 23 Sept. 1838	Ripl
Batz, Joseph to Mary Prigmore 1 Dec. 1836	Pett
Baugh, Benj. to Maria Boone 30 May 1832	StCh
Baugh, James to Louisa Baldridge 16 June 1831	StCh
Baughman, Jacob to Lenis McClard 10 June 1830	Md-A
Baughman, Wm. to Rachel Slater 26 Feb. 1839	Morg
Bauns, Callaway to Cynthia Means 25 Dec. 1834	Carr
Bauns, James to Polly Rusher 25 Mar. 1838	Carr
Bauthman, Jacob to Mary Parks 13 June 1833	Coop
Bawley, Nelson to Silvia I. Milington 16 Jan. 1834	Warr
Baxter, Alexander to Salley Bozarth 21 Dec. 1825	Rall
Baxter, Bryant to Sarah Ross 8 July 1828	Jack
Baxter, Guilford D. to Sarah Laughlin 4 June 1835	Warr
Baxter, Hugh to Malinda Morris 30 Dec. 1824	Howa
Baxter, James to Hannah Morrison 13 July 1823	Howa
Baxter, James to Magdalene Duncan 8 Nov. 1827	Clay
Baxter, James to Lavina Price 28 Nov. 1835	Pk-1
Baxter, Jesse to Amanda M.G. Gill 25 Jan. 1838	Clin
Baxter, John to Sarah Wallis 6 May 1828	Clay
Baxter, John to Ruth Stayton 10 Feb. 1831	Jack
Baxter, John to Mahala Stadley 1 Nov. 1836	Pk-1
Baxter, Joseph to Frances George 12 Feb. 1829	Clay
Baxter, Wm. to Susanna McCown 1 Sept. 1818	Howa
Baxter, Wm. B. to Catherine Mase 25 Oct. 1835	Pk-1
Bay, James to Rosannah Cole 3 Oct. 1838	Fran
Bay, John to Fedelia King 20 Dec. 1838	Fran
Bay, John to Catherine J. Christwell 19 May 1839	Fran
Bay, Joseph to Emily Parker 24 Nov. 1836	Fran
Bay, Numan to Nancy Johns 20 Feb. 1834	Fran
Bay, Thomas to Nancy Jameson 23 Mar. 1834	Fran

Bayless, Samuel P. to Margaret A. Simpson 28 Mar. 1837 Lafa
Bayliss, Wm. to Mary J. Pierce 22 June 1834 CG-A
Bayne, John H. to Nicy A. Hawkins 25 Oct. 1838 Lewi
Baynham, Grief H. to Martha Barnes 4 Dec. 1839 Call
Baynham, Wm. G. to Tabitha Irvin 10 Oct. 1832 Call
Baynham, Wm. G. to Ann Grant 3 Apr. 1838 Call
Bazark, Jonathan to Isabella Short 7 Feb. 1839 Boon
Beach, Harvey H. to Eleanor I. Henry 8 Sept. 1839 Lewi
Beach, Hiram to Judith A. Price 1 May 1839 Lewi
Beall, Geo. W. to Nancy Harmon 6 Oct. 1838 Jeff
Bealy, Andrew to Juliann Martin 23 Dec. 1825 Lafa
Beaman, James to Mary E. Early 7 Nov. 1839 Pett
Bean, John H. to Malinda Douglas 22 Dec. 1831 Howa
Bear, James to Sinthy Givens 5 Mar. 1839 Wash
Beard, James to Rachel Gwinn 13 June 1833 Linc
Beard, Samuel to Judy Reed 28 June 1832 Linc
Beard, Samuel T. to Elisa Flicher 16 May 1837 Livi
Bearden, Lambert to Redulah Gore 17 Feb. 1839 Barr
Bearding, Wm. to Hannah Cooley 11 June 1828 Char
Bearn, Trotter to Nancy Wilfley 12 Mar. 1837 Call
Beasley, Noah to Catherine Boothe 31 May 1827 Pk-1
Beatie, Ryburn to Amanda Cowan 6 Aug. 1835 Boon
Beatty, David to Namoney Standley 29 July 1819 Howa
Beatty, James to Margaret Davis 26 Jan. 1837 Rand
Beatty, Samuel to Patience Kelly 3 Dec. 1835 Fran
Beatty, Wm. to Nancy Richardson 11 July 1830 Fran
Beaty, Harvey to Elizabeth Campbell 7 Aug. 1838 Carr
Beaty, Orville to Elizabeth Moore 6 Aug. 1832 StCh
Beaty, Wm. T. to Sally Pennall 25 Feb. 1836 Henr
Beauchamp, Asher B. to Lucretia Frazer 1 Feb. 1831 Ray
Beauchamp, Felix to Elizabeth Brown 3 Feb. 1834 Clay
Beauchamp, Joseph D. to Ellen Thompson 26 July 1820 StCh
Beauchamp, Selvenus to Adaline Derbon 8 Dec. 1834 Clay
Beauchemin, Andreas to Louisa Verto 27 Feb. 1838 StCh
Beauchemin, Fr. to Therese Viole 26 Nov. 1833 StCh
Beauchemin, Joseph to Adrienne Tiercero 17 Jan. 1837 StCh
Beauchemin, Louis to Margaretha Bordeaux 19 Feb. 1838 StCh
Beauren, Peter to Sethy Esters 7 Mar. 1830 Lafa
Beauvais, Townsend to Mrs. Rachel Still 8 Apr. 1816 StCh
Beaven, Zadoc to Luretta Miller 23 Oct. 1828 Call
Beavens, Wm. to Lucinda Ferguson 12 Apr. 1832 Call
Bebybee, John to Louisa Parks 30 Aug. 1839 Coop
Beck, Aaron T. to Margaret Cannon 14 Feb. 1839 Linc
Beck, Jeffrey to Susan Hopkins 16 Feb. 1839 Warr
Beck, Joseph C. to Izillar Caun 11 Sept. 1834 StCh
Beckem, Caswell to Sally Prim 20 Dec. 1831 Cr-A
Becker, Johan Geo. to Eva Vetsh 3 Apr. 1839 StCh
Becket, Henry to Polly Clark 24 Oct. 1839 Ray
Becket, Nathan to Rode Patterson 10 Feb. 1828 StFr
Becket, Samuel to Sarah Tennell 17 Jan. 1836 Mari
Beckets, Robt. to Eliza J. Faine 7 Mar. 1837 Boon
Beckett, Geo. to Elizabeth Evans 31 Dec. 1837 Barr
Beckett, John to Rody Morris 22 Sept. 1822 Boon
Beckett, Robt. to Rebecca Shobe 2 Dec. 1832 Mari
Beckett, Wm. D. to Minerva Lampkins -- Feb. 1837 Boon
Beckman, Francis to Mary E. Musid 4 May 1837 Fran
Beckwell, ---- to Elizabeth Fletcher 5 Apr. 1838 Cass
Beckworth, John to Mary Wheeley 14 Jan. 1833 Clay
Becquette, Edmund to Zarah Kunket 17 Oct. 1837 Wash
Becquette, John to Jane L. Fleming 22 Nov. 1832 Wash
Bedford, Augustus to Hannah Shatter 9 Sept. 1838 CG-B
Beecher, Samuel to Margaret J. Smith 29 Mar. 1838 Fran
Beed, Solomon to Susan Brock 14 Aug. 1838 Clay
Beeler, Wm. D. to Catherine A. Hawkes 3 Oct. 1839 Polk
Beeman, James to Elizabeth Smiley 10 July 1834 Pett

14

Beeman, James J. to Sally Crawford 10 Sept. 1836   StCh
Beeman, Ruben to Rebecca Parker -- Oct. 1839   Boon
Beeman, Wm. to Jane Standeford 8 July 1837   Pett
Beggs, Wm. to Hannah Clarke 22 Aug. 1810   CG-1
Belama, James to Zerelda E. Roberts 22 Nov. 1838   Call
Belamy, Wm. to Sarah Keen 25 Oct. 1838   Boon
Belan, Charles to Marguerite Tiercero 24 July 1827   StCh
Belcher, Alexander to Nancy Winn 1 July 1826   Rall
Belcher, Alexander to Sally Brooks 3 Sept. 1827   Boon
Belcher, Isham to Esther Berry 30 Mar. 1837   Gree
Belcher, Jesse to Polly Yates 24 Oct. 1831   Clay
Belcher, John to Elizabeth Mobles 13 Sept. 1821   Howa
Belcher, John N. to Mary Emervine -- Aug. 1836   Boon
Belcher, Moses to Jane Green 16 Oct. 1834   Clin
Belcher, Wm. to Nancy Botts 1 Feb. 1827   Howa
Belcher, Wm. to Frances Amerine 18 Nov. 1839   Boon
Belden, Joseph to Agnes Graves 10 June 1834   Howa
Belieu, Michael to Eliza Hill 6 Feb. 1834   Clay
Belk, James to Emaline Helton 23 Apr. 1838   Gasc
Bell, Andrew to Susan Campbell 19 Aug. 1835   Coop
Bell, Daniel to Dianah Coyle 20 May 1830   Cr-P
Bell, David E. to Nancy Campbell 26 Sept. 1839   Fran
Bell, Geo. L. to Rebecca E. Powell 22 Dec. 1836   Pett
Bell, James to Mary Thomas 29 May 1823   Coop
Bell, James to Elizabeth McNeel 13 Jan. 1826   Coop
Bell, James to Tempy Roy 15 Dec. 1836   Gasc
Bell, James to Susan A. Vest 28 May 1837   Fran
Bell, James to Mary Stephenson 1 June 1837   Perr
Bell, John Jr. to Alemedea Farrar 4 Mar. 1830   Fran
Bell, John to Lucinda Welch 14 Feb. 1838   Warr
Bell, John M. to Rachel Woodson 12 Oct. 1828   Howa
Bell, Mardecii to Mary A. Day 9 Feb. 1832   Call
Bell, Patterson B. to Mary A. Castleman 9 Dec. 1835   Linc
Bell, Robt. C. to Alsada Dearbon 4 July 1836   Clay
Bell, Temple E. to Mary B. Hayes 1 Dec. 1828   Linc
Bell, Thomas B. to Eliza Hockersmith 25 Jan. 1838   Rand
Bell, Valentine to Margaret Houx 2 Dec. 1830   Coop
Bell, Wm. to Polly Armstrong 6 June 1822   Fran
Bell, Wm. to Elizabeth Wimberly 26 Feb. 1835   Linc
Bellama, Wm. to Ann Tharp 9 Mar. 1836   Call
Belland, J.B. to Angelique Barribo 21 Nov. 1829   StCh
Bellew, Cornelius to Elizabeth Conway 8 Mar. 1838   Wash
Bellows, John to Margaret Brown 25 May 1837   Call
Bellups, Robt. to Paulina Davidson 14 Aug. 1839   Fran
Belman, Louis to Polly McDowel 29 July 1838   Md-B
Belood, John to Elizabeth Collet 22 Mar. 1838   Clin
Belsha, Wm. to Catherine Fare 6 Oct. 1831   Perr
Belsha, Wm. P. to Miss Hoskins 6 Jan. 1839   Perr
Belshe, Robt. to Polly Wright 1 June 1834   Rand
Bender, Heinrich to Elizabeth Schwarz 13 June 1836   StCh
Bendorf, Jacob to Polly Parks 22 Nov. 1827   CG-A
Benedick, James to Nancy Downey 23 Nov. 1836   Boon
Benedict, Albert to Constance Palardie 16 May 1839   StCh
Benight, John to Mary Freeman 16 Mar. 1834   Cr-1
Benn, Samuel to Mary A. Mifford 5 Sept. 1830   Pk-1
Bennefon, John to Minerva Billings 18 Oct. 1836   Lewi
Benner, Philip to Katherine Freund 22 Apr. 1839   Warr
Bennet, Anson G. to Mollie A. Moore 14 Apr. 1825   Call
Bennett, Abraham to Martha Hancock 9 Apr. 1837   CG-A
Bennett, Albert to Louiza Adcock 7 May 1837   CG-A
Bennett, Benj. to Rosa Riney 31 Oct. 1839   Clar
Bennett, Caleb to Sally A. Melvin 9 Oct. 1834   Boon
Bennett, Daniel to Louisa A. Haggons 18 July 1839   CG-B
Bennett, Edward H. to Jane Gilliam 2 Apr. 1821   Md-A
Bennett, Henry to Bridget Daly 31 Oct. 1839   Clar

15

Bennett, James to Eliza Rollins 23 Dec. 1830   Boon
Bennett, James M. to Sarah Baker 15 Jan. 1829   CG-A
Bennett, Joel D. to Mary M. McAfee 19 Feb. 1839   Call
Bennett, John to Susanna Holt 31 Aug. 1820   Howa
Bennett, John to Rachel Anderson 13 Jan. 1833   Boon
Bennett, John to Rhoda Evans 11 Apr. 1839   Maco
Bennett, Joseph to Mary Cartwright 17 Nov. 1831   CG-A
Bennett, Larkin to Nancy Freeman 23 Dec. 1834   Boon
Bennett, Lebuz to Margett Henderson 15 Aug. 1837   Md-B
Bennett, Levi to Mary Ware 24 Sept. 1834   Howa
Bennett, Moses to Louisinda McKamey 22 Nov. 1834   Call
Bennett, Reed to Sarah Stoe 14 Nov. 1838   Polk
Bennett, Spencer to Matilda R.A. Compton 7 May 1836   Char
Bennett, Walter to Mary Wood 20 Apr. 1836   Char
Bennett, Wm. to Elizabeth Tudor 7 Mar. 1830   Howa
Bennett, Wm. to Mary B. Hardin 23 Sept. 1838   Rand
Bennett, Wm. H. to Susanna Cartwright 8 Sept. 1831   CG-A
Benoit, Toussaint to Louise Martineau 15 July 1839   StCh
Benson, Adam to Elizabeth Howard 28 Sept. 1834   Warr
Benson, Edward S. to Sarah Tanery 3 Mar. 1839   Livi
Benson, James M. to Ruth Switzer 3 Aug. 1830   Howa
Benson, James S. to Ann Watson 5 Sept. 1837   Lafa
Benson, Jefferson to Sally Hays 15 Mar. 1838   Call
Bentley, Johnson to Abigail Wheeler 16 Feb. 1834   Ray
Benton, Abel to Rodah Goodwin 31 July 1831   Cr-P
Benton, Eliga to Artamus Midlock 27 Sept. 1826   Gasc
Benton, Eliga to Rebecca Davis 17 Mar. 1836   Cr-1
Benton, Henry to Nancy King 17 Apr. 1836   Cr-1
Benton, Isaac to Mrs. Elizabeth Lefler 22 Feb. 1827   Jeff
Benton, James to Elizabeth Evans 8 Jan. 1837   Polk
Benton, Joshua to Mary Davis 1 Feb. 1837   Cr-1
Benton, Mark to Hezziah Mize 30 Apr. 1829   Cr-P
Benton, Matthew T.W. to Nancy Skaggs 23 Mar. 1826   Fran
Benzley, David to Margaret Ligget 10 Sept. 1830   Jack
Bequet, Pierre to Celeste Collmann 27 Jan. 1829   Wash
Bequette, Alexander to Marianne Fleming 7 July 1836   Wash
Bequette, Henry to Mary A. McClenahan 10 Nov. 1824   StGe
Berdsley, Daniel to Lydia Seagraves 5 June 1839   Pett
Berg, Conrad to Eliza K. Fruend 22 May 1838   Warr
Berg, Henry to Louisa Jundrum 23 June 1839   Warr
Bergen, Israel to Elizabeth Null 23 Mar. 1835   Jeff
Bergen, Matthew to Martha A. Stephens 25 May 1837   Mari
Berger, Henry to Polly Titsworth 23 June 1833   Coop
Berger, Joseph to Elizabeth Forshsye 22 Aug. 1832   Coop
Berger, Paul to Terice Moreau 29 May 1824   StCh
Berger, Wm. to Sarah Kimberlin 4 July 1836   Jeff
Bergin, John to Sally A. Holladay 26 May 1839   Plat
Berk, Samuel to Rebecca Bankson 28 July 1822   Coop
Berkly, Benoni to Sarah Williams 10 Oct. 1838   Coop
Bernard, Isidore to Theresa Dubois 12 May 1828   StCh
Bernard, Joseph to Mary Dubois 4 Jan. 1831   StCh
Bernier, Louis to Mary Belmare 6 Mar. 1832   Md-A
Berns, Jeremiah to Jane Sampson 23 July 1820   Howa
Beron, Amos to ---- Micheau 19 Jan. 1826   Wash
Berry, C.H. to Harriett A. Johnson 24 Mar. 1836   Wash
Berry, Charles to Betsey Ewing 16 Dec. 1824   Coop
Berry, Daniel to Matilda Sexton 11 Dec. 1834   CG-B
Berry, Daniel to Alletha Glasscock 17 Nov. 1839   CG-B
Berry, David to Martha Sutton 22 May 1838   Boon
Berry, Dawson to Susanna Sally 21 Aug. 1831   Linc
Berry, Edward G. to Sally A. Galbreath 14 Feb. 1833   Call
Berry, Finis E. to Eleanor Warmick 29 Mar. 1835   Lafa
Berry, Geo. T. to Jane Humphries 12 Dec. 1833   Call
Berry, James S. to Martha Kirkpatrick 1 Jan. 1822   Coop
Berry, John to Nancy Claybrook 15 Sept. 1822   Cole

16

Berry, John to Margaret Galbreath 25 Mar. 1830   Call
Berry, John to Blanche H. Wylie 17 Nov. 1839   Mari
Berry, Joseph to Juleann Paine 5 Nov. 1837   Mari
Berry, Lewis G. to Sarah Weaver 2 July 1837   Jeff
Berry, Lyle A. to Hetty B. Copher 28 June 1821   Boon
Berry, Martin H. to Jane Brown 13 Feb. 1834   Pk-1
Berry, Michael to Sarah Spotts 26 Apr. 1838   Wash
Berry, Nickerson to Polly J. Lemons 20 Dec. 1837   Sali
Berry, Peter to Lucinda May 15 Oct. 1835   Morg
Berry, Richard to Mary E. Watts 15 Aug. 1839   Cass
Berry, Solomon to Lany Linkhorn 6 Dec. 1829   CG-A
Berry, Thomas G. to Juliza Lemon -- Apr. 1827   Boon
Berry, Thomas H. to Mahala Davidson 17 Feb. 1836   Call
Berry, Wm. M. to Malissa E. Lampton 29 Nov. 1836   Coop
Berry, Willis to Sarah Hart 24 Dec. 1839   Jeff
Berry, Willis F. to Aretta Wells 19 Feb. 1839   Pk-B
Berry, Young to Jane Warnick 31 Dec. 1835   John
Berryman, Charles H. to Minerva H. Bivens 29 July 1830   Clay
Berryman, Gerrard to Malinda Brown 10 Apr. 1829   Md-A
Berthelotte, Louis to Margaret Gautier 11 Oct. 1812   StCh
Berthold, John to Agnes Holsheiter 27 Nov. 1838   StCh
Bertling, Daniel to Hannah Probst 9 Dec. 1835   CG-B
Berton, Benj. N. to Sally A. Danilson 14 June 1837   Monr
Beshers, Henry to Mary Stapleton 22 Feb. 1827   Howa
Bess, Christopher to Christina Cline 24 July 1826   CG-A
Bess, Daniel to Haniah Welfong 1 Nov. 1829   CG-A
Bess, James to Sarah Bess 16 Nov. 1834   CG-A
Bess, John to Polly Summers 6 July 1827   CG-A
Bess, Joshua to Mary Whetstone 28 Oct. 1819   CG-1
Best, David to Margaret Harrington 1 July 1834   Clay
Best, Ebenezer to Catherine Wheldon 26 -- 1829   Rand
Best, Ebenezer to Mahulda Munkres 24 Apr. 1833   Clay
Best, Geo. Y. to Leanora Hancock 12 Oct. 1837   Warr
Best, Humphrey to Elizabeth Miller 2 Dec. 1832   Clay
Best, Isaac to Susanna Harrington 15 Nov. 1831   Clay
Best, Joseph to Hannah Parks 7 May 1829   CG-A
Best, Robt. to Jane Taylor 5 June 1823   Cole
Best, Silas to Susan Harrington 20 Jan. 1831   Clay
Best, Stephen to Mary A. Burkleo 1 Mar. 1836   StCh
Best, Thomas to Elizabeth Briscoe 2 May 1819   Howa
Best, Wm. to Salle Best 7 Aug. 1818   CG-1
Beth, Richard to Caroline Foster 29 Oct. 1837   Mari
Bethel, Seaton to ---- Laforce 20 Nov. 1838   Pk-B
Bethrope, Lewis W. to Phianna H. Witman 1 Mar. 1838   Rall
Betticks, Jonathan to Polly Holida 23 Dec. 1819   Howa
Bettis, Ranson to Polle Kelly 13 Feb. 1811   CG-1
Bevans, Tyree T. to Martha A. Baugh 5 July 1833   Jack
Bewford, John to Elizabeth Irwin 2 Jan. 1827   Wash
Bibb, Amos to Mary E. Hansborough 23 Jan. 1838   Mari
Bibb, Henry W. to Judith A. Mundy 30 Nov. 1837   Pk-B
Bibee, John to Mary A. Myers 1 Aug. 1832   Howa
Bice, Luice to Elizabeth Punch 18 Feb. 1834   CG-A
Bidstrop, Christian to Levina Waddle 8 Mar. 1837   Polk
Bidstrup, Herman E. to Sarah Thomas 12 Dec. 1823   Coop
Bidsworth, Wm. to Mary Morgan 5 Oct. 1833   Clay
Bienvenu, Charles to Suzanne Gerardin 15 Feb. 1830   StCh
Bienvenu, Etienne to Brigitte Saucier 22 Sept. 1834   StCh
Bienvenu, John Bte. to Marguerite Lacroix 12 Jan. 1829 StCh
Bienvenu, Joseph to Louise Hebert 3 Nov. 1829   StCh
Bier, Schuyler to Octavo Callaway 18 Feb. 1836   Warr
Bierbaum, John A. to M. Elizabeth Schaberg 6 Sept. 1837 StCh
Bierbaum, John W. to Catherina M. Helwig 5 Apr. 1837   StCh
Bierwirth, Wm. to Anna Eggiman 9 Feb. 1839   CG-B
Bigg, Henry to Elizabeth Banister 2 Nov. 1834   Perr
Biggers, Wm. to Sally Colliver 12 Jan. 1834   Rall

17

Biggerstaff, James M. to Sally Bedford 13 Feb. 1834 — Clin
Biggs, David to Prisila Burns 17 Dec. 1834 — CG-B
Biggs, Geo. to Margaret Jackson 3 Mar. 1835 — Pk-1
Biggs, Jesse to Maria Ramsey 29 Aug. 1830 — Coop
Biggs, John D. to Juliann Vardeman 1 May 1833 — Rall
Biggs, John D. to Harriett Bentley 3 May 1836 — Howa
Biggs, Marlin to Lydia Curnutt 29 June 1837 — Pett
Biggs, Wm. D. to Nancy Reading 3 Sept. 1839 — Pk-B
Bigham, Andrew J. to Louisa Cassaday 29 Apr. 1839 — Clar
Bigham, John to Sarah Evans 14 Feb. 1833 — Lafa
Bigham, Wm. M. to Eliza E. Donham 5 July 1838 — Lafa
Bighum, John to Alminda A. Cathey 16 Oct. 1837 — Coop
Bighum, Wm. to Patience Clark 13 Oct. 1821 — Coop
Bigustaff, Richard to Elizabeth Thornhill 13 Feb. 1817 — StCh
Bilbrew, James to Judy Shaw 22 Nov. 1838 — Pk-B
Billings, Wm. to Eliza Hearn 7 Nov. 1837 — Clar
Billingsley, Jonathan to Mary Powers 18 Feb. 1838 — Barr
Bills, J.M. to Marry Ellis 2 Sept. 1837 — Morg
Biltick, John R. to Syntha Wallace 10 Jan. 1839 — Gasc
Bilyeu, Cornelius to Eliza J. McClain 16 Sept. 1838 — Mill
Bilyeu, Geo. M. to Hester J. Read 24 July 1839 — Mill
Bilyew, John W. to Sarah Harp 24 July 1832 — Cr-1
Bilyew, Solomon to Lydia Bilyew 15 Dec. 1831 — Cr-1
Bingham, Bartlet to Ruthy Cox 19 Aug. 1830 — Lafa
Bingham, Geo. C. to Elizabeth Hutchinson 14 Apr. 1836 — Howa
Bingham, John to Leannah Larison 20 May 1836 — Jack
Bingum, Harmon to Sally Mitchel 30 Apr. 1826 — Lafa
Bingum, James to Nancy Whitsell 30 Apr. 1826 — Lafa
Birch, Joseph to Elizabeth Cheaney 23 July 1835 — Boon
Birch, Wm. to Isabella Pennington 19 Nov. 1818 — StCh
Bird, Abraham to Elizabeth Richmond 11 Apr. 1839 — Mari
Bird, Geo. W. to Emeline Rutter 8 Apr. 1830 — Mari
Bird, Geo. W. to Martha A. Rutter 24 Nov. 1831 — Mari
Bird, Greenup to Eleanor M. Carty 4 Mar. 1830 — Howa
Bird, John to Nancy Cravens 19 Aug. 1830 — Howa
Bird, John S. to Tenny Jones 9 Sept. 1838 — Polk
Bird, Nathaniel J. to Mrs. Ann A. Merrell 26 Oct. 1837 — Mari
Bird, Randolph to Cornelia Brandts 12 Nov. 1835 — StCh
Bird, Wm. H. to Eliza Gash 9 Jan. 1834 — Mari
Birdsong, Geo. to Lilly G. Burnett 4 Jan. 1838 — Mill
Birdsong, James to Mary Parks 1 Aug. 1839 — Coop
Bise, Jonathan to Mahaly Henry 8 Apr. 1839 — CG-B
Bishop, David H. to Mary A. Park 20 Dec. 1834 — Fran
Bishop, David H. to Susan B. Stephens 26 Dec. 1839 — Fran
Bishop, Frederick K. to Nancy A. Homesley 19 Apr. 1838 — Linc
Bishop, John to Jane Robertson 15 Jan. 1839 — Perr
Bishop, Thomas J. to Hany Gray 28 Apr. 1836 — Perr
Bishop, Tyre to Rebecca W. Wilburn 7 June 1838 — Call
Biswell, Jeremiah to Nancy Harvey 14 Aug. 1828 — Char
Biswell, John to Rebecca Wright 14 Jan. 1830 — Rand
Biswell, Richard to Sarah Parker 17 Jan. 1833 — Rand
Biswell, Thomas to Elizabeth Smith 2 June 1819 — Howa
Bittle, Andy to Bethany Tilford 21 Aug. 1828 — Boon
Bittle, Divid to Elizabeth Bittle 26 Sept. 1837 — Boon
Bittle, Emanuel to Arenah Crabtree 30 May 1836 — Jack
Bittle, Frederick to Elizabeth Bullard 14 July 1839 — Boon
Bivans, David M. to Huldy C. Riley 15 Apr. 1830 — Clay
Biven, James to Malcey Williams 20 Mar. 1838 — Howa
Bives, Louis to Julye Caillote 7 Feb. 1832 — Md-A
Bivins, Hudson to Mary A. Wilson 16 Sept. 1838 — Clin
Bivins, Walker W. to Sally P. McGill 25 Aug. 1826 — Clay
Black, Adam to Mary Morgan 6 Sept. 1825 — Ray
Black, Balarmine M. to Mrs. Synthia A. Grounds 9 Apr. 1836 — Perr
Black, Elazor to Lucretia M. Parker 9 May 1839 — Linc
Black, Isaac to Sarah Maupin 14 July 1820 — Boon

18

```
Black, James to Ann Hines 30 Nov. 1828                              Ray
Black, James to Lockky Roland 23 Mar. 1834                          Ray
Black, John Jr. to Susanna Taylor 3 Jan. 1815                       CG-1
Black, John to Elizabeth Sappington 8 Feb. 1830                     Boon
Black, Redmond to Sary Carty 24 Dec. 1832                          Wash
Black, Ruben to Anna Hanna 14 June 1827                             Boon
Black, Thomas to Fanna Price 1 Feb. 1829                           StCh
Black, Wm. to Ann Allen 30 Oct. 1831                               CG-A
Blackaby, John to Elizabeth Sanders 11 Jan. 1838                   Linc
Blackburn, Wm. to Emeline Veach 29 May 1839                        Boon
Blackmon, James to Leah Gallaway 24 Feb. 1839                      Linc
Blackmore, Samuel to Sarah Gallaway 4 Dec. 1834                    Linc
Blackwell, Alexander C. to Eliza A. Earickson 15 Feb. 1838         Howa
Blackwell, Clayton to Malinda Blankenship 25 Aug. 1839             Fran
Blackwell, Jesse to Mary White 10 Sept. 1837                       Fran
Blackwell, John W. to Jane Davis 1 Aug. 1839                       Call
Blackwell, Joseph to Mary Snoddy 11 Jan. 1838                      Howa
Blackwell, Louis to Elizabeth Blackwell 10 Mar. 1832              Wash
Blackwell, Louis to Eliza Flinn 24 Aug. 1839                       Cr-1
Blackwell, Mathew to Margaret Tansy 25 Dec. 1826                   Fran
Blackwell, Robt. to Catherine Reyburn 10 Apr. 1823                StFr
Blackwell, Robt. to Margaret Berry 7 Sept. 1838                   Cr-1
Blackwell, Wm. to Sary Garner 14 Aug. 1834                        Fran
Blackwell, Wm. to Mary Armstead 13 Aug. 1837                      Fran
Blackwell, Wm. to Elizabeth Cummins 14 Mar. 1839                  Wash
Blackwell, Zachariah to Martha Ballard 11 Jan. 1837              Cr-1
Blackwood, Joseph to Catherine W. Jones 19 Nov. 1835             Pk-1
Blackwood, Wm. W. to Jeremia Bohon 14 June 1838                   Mari
Blain, Abraham to Hannah Runnels 31 Jan. 1833                     Ray
Blain, Lawson to Emeline Lesley 11 Mar. 1831                      StCh
Blain, Levi to Susan M. Massey 3 Nov. 1836                        Cr-1
Blain, Permit to Elizabeth Reynolds 2 July 1831                   Ray
Blain, Samuel to Mary A. Waggoner 28 Aug. 1836                    Cr-1
Blair, Geo. W. to Sarah Rook 4 Mar. 1838                          Polk
Blair, Jackson to Elizabeth Downing 4 July 1838                   Linc
Blair, Jesse W. to Emeline Sullivante 11 Aug. 1836               Fran
Blair, Jonathan to Malvina Ross 28 Oct. 1834                      Gree
Blair, Thompson to Sarah M. Downing 21 Mar. 1839                  Linc
Blais, Alexander to Elizabeth Latimore 24 July 1828              Wash
Blakely, Benj. to Marietta Payne 22 Dec. 1835                     Howa
Blakely, Huston to Vireaney Moon 10 Oct. 1839                     Coop
Blakely, Robt. W. to Sarah A. Gridley 18 Mar. 1838               Mari
Blakely, Samuel to Margaret Holiway 8 Aug. 1837                   Cass
Blakely, Samuel to Susan Myrtle 25 Aug. 1839                     Howa
Blakey, Granville to Emeline Smith 29 Oct. 1839                   Mari
Blalock, McHenry to Susan Bollinger 14 Feb. 1839                  CG-B
Blancet, Peter to Margaret Sumpter 19 Jan. 1837                   Monr
Blanchard, Wm. to Emiline Jones 25 May 1839                       Coop
Bland, Isaac to Nancy Floyd 30 Sept. 1832                         Mari
Bland, James W. to Hannah Martin 16 Nov. 1837                     Lewi
Blankenbaker, Joshua to Elizabeth Linyard 23 Oct. 1831           Pk-1
Blankenship, Charles to Mary Lewellen 18 Nov. 1828               Pk-1
Blankenship, James to Eliza Donaghe 21 Dec. 1831                 Coop
Blankenship, Noah to Anna Story 16 Sept. 1827                    Wash
Blankenship, Woodson to Mehala Onstot 3 July 1828               Pk-1
Blann, Zacharrah to Keriak O'Gles 9 Dec. 1837                    Livi
Blanton, Benj. to Mary Robertson 9 Apr. 1835                     Linc
Blanton, Ezekiel to Nancy Yates 3 Apr. 1831                      Jack
Blanton, Geo. H. to Eliza Warren 10 Oct. 1839                    Bent
Blanton, Isaac to Mrs. Elizabeth Gray 12 Feb. 1826             StCh
Blanton, Isaac to Hannah Munkins 12 June 1828                    Clay
Blanton, John to Mary Burger 2 Mar. 1825                         Char
Blanton, John to Mary Morris 23 Dec. 1838                        Clay
Blanton, Joseph to Jane Munkees 4 Aug. 1833                      Jack
Blanton, Lemuel to Maryann Rogers 8 Nov. 1831                    Cr-1
```

19

Blanton, Thomas to Nancy MacCary 27 Dec. 1827	Howa
Blanton, Washington to Elizabeth Head 24 Dec. 1824	Howa
Blanton, Washington to Nancy Williams 4 Apr. 1839	Howa
Blanton, Wm. O. to Polly McCreary 16 Sept. 1827	Howa
Blecher, Moses to Eliza Ricky 7 Aug. 1827	Jack
Bledsoe, Abraham to Betsey Warden 6 Feb. 1834	Jack
Bledsoe, Anthony to Catharine Butler 13 Mar. 1833	Jack
Bledsoe, Harris to Malinda Hamilton 8 Aug. 1839	Fran
Bledsoe, Isaac to Sally Stephens 14 Feb. 1833	Jack
Bledsoe, James to Isabella Bledsoe 14 Mar. 1830	Boon
Bledsoe, Joel to Nancy Luck 5 June 1836	Boon
Bledsoe, John to Mary Adams 20 Sept. 1832	Jack
Bledsoe, Sampson to Sarah Housucker 22 July 1822	Boon
Bledsoe, Valentine to Katherine Bittle 18 Feb. 1836	Jack
Bledsoe, Wm. to Mabel Melton 18 July 1837	Henr
Bledsoe, Willis to Jane Daily 18 July 1824	Lafa
Bleven, Alexander to Emeline Zumwalt 21 Nov. 1833	Call
Blevins, Alexander to Louisa Vanderpool 18 June 1839	Boon
Blevins, Ezekiel to Thurza Young 13 Jan. 1833	Lafa
Blevins, Jesse to Rosa Lower 7 Apr. 1839	Buch
Blevins, Joseph to Elizabeth Whitley 9 Mar. 1826	Boon
Blevins, Stephen to Mahala Young 20 Feb. 1834	Lafa
Blevins, Wm. to Casander Perman 3 Oct. 1839	John
Blew, John to Judith Lingo 9 Aug. 1837	Rand
Blickly, Godfrid to Cecilia Myers 19 June 1834	Perr
Blimmer, Angus to Matilda McLean 20 Dec. 1833	Warr
Blish, Geo. to Irene Young 12 Aug. 1838	Gasc
Blize, John to Evelina Coulter 9 May 1830	Fran
Blize, Martin to Hiley Brown 21 Apr. 1831	Fran
Blize, Wm. to Elizabeth Davis 19 May 1831	Cole
Block, Moses to Sarah Juden 8 Feb. 1827	CG-A
Block, Phenias to Delia Block -- Oct. 1823	CG-1
Block, Zalma to Matilda Renfroe 1 Nov. 1832	CG-A
Blocker, James to Adelia A. Santford 16 Feb. 1837	CG-A
Bloise, James to Munerva Burton 27 Apr. 1836	Howa
Bloise, Levi to Susan M. Massey 3 Nov. 1836	Cr-1
Blood, Joseph Young to Theresa Peters 27 May 1839	StCh
Blore, John M. to Nancy Asherbranner 14 Mar. 1830	Md-A
Blount, John W. to Jane Thomas 2 Jan. 1831	Call
Blue, Daniel to Mary Galbreath 4 Aug. 1825	Rall
Blue, David to Polly Cooper 12 July 1836	Rall
Blue, John to Matilda McClain 19 Apr. 1838	StFr
Blue, Wm. to Priscilla Ramsey 24 Nov. 1836	Rand
Blunkall, John to Mary Hamblin 8 Sept. 1835	Call
Blunt, Peter D. to Sarah Campbill 26 July 1826	Wash
Bly, Wm. to Polly A. Weaver 18 Sept. 1833	Gree
Blythe, John to Sarah Nichols 1 Dec. 1838	Boon
Blythe, Samuel to Sally Russel 15 Dec. 1835	Boon
Blythe, U.R. to Didanna Fletcher 8 July 1830	Ray
Boalwar, John to Elizabeth Nelson 13 May 1834	Monr
Boarding, Wm. to Hannah Cooley 11 June 1828	Char
Boarman, Jesse to Emily Spotswood 8 Dec. 1832	Rall
Boas, Robt. to Sophia Engledon 23 July 1835	Wash
Boaz, David T. to Polly Brown 22 May 1839	Call
Bockhorst, F.W. to M. Bartage 11 Jan. 1837	StCh
Bodine, ---- to Lizy Stone rec. 3 June 1837	Rall
Bodine, Isaac A. to Mary M. Gore 30 Mar. 1837	Monr
Bodine, Wm. to Polly Bigham 24 May 1827	Coop
Boesshearts, Antoon to Elizabeth Twindeman 10 Feb. 1835	StCh
Bogart, Alexander to Mary Keany 22 Dec. 1822	Ray
Boggess, Peter D. to Mary A. Creek 31 Dec. 1835	Clay
Boggs, Andrew to Minerva Owens 3 Feb. 1835	Boon
Boggs, James C. to Barbara Gaw 24 Jan. 1830	Howa
Boggs, Matthew D. to Martha J. Kennett 2 Aug. 1838	Call
Boggs, Robt. to Lucrecy J. Miller 8 Dec. 1832	Call

20

```
Boglido, Mattis to Susan Block 2 Oct. 1837                          CG-A
Bohannan, Charles to Keron H. McFarland 24 June 1828               Rall
Bohannon, Elliot to Jane Moore 1 Jan. 1829                         CG-A
Bohannon, Thomas to Annah Smith 8 Mar. 1838                        Cole
Bohannon, Zeckariah to Patsy Lancaster 14 Dec. 1837               CG-A
Bohart, Jacob to Catherine Cogdell 26 Aug. 1838                    Clin
Bohart, Phillip to Martha Russell 22 Sept. 1838                    Clin
Bohlan, Fredrick A.F. to Mrs. Henrietta Geger 27 Nov. 1839        Perr
Bohon, Jackson F. to Mary Blackwood 13 June 1838                  Mari
Bohon, James to Eliza Mitchell 4 Dec. 1834                         Pett
Bohon, Walter S. to Margaret M. Blackwood 10 Sept. 1835           Mari
Boian, John to Rhoda McPherson 25 Sept. 1834                      Morg
Boice, Aaron to Parthena Galbreath 14 Aug. 1825                   Rall
Boice, Richard to Elisabeth F. Foreman 19 Jan. 1823               Rall
Boiler, Jacob to Ireney Scott 31 Jan. 1838                        Barr
Boiles, James to Polly Miller 28 Dec. 1836                        Coop
Boilston, Nathaniel to Diannah Faubian 21 July 1836               Clay
Boison, James to Martha Prewitt 21 May 1833                       Howa
Boisty, Pierre to Ellen Dihentre 13 Aug. 1839                     Cass
Boland, Phillip to Helena Oyer 30 Jan. 1838                       Perr
Bolcher, John to Hannah Forbush 8 Aug. 1834                       Gree
Bolduc, Louis to Susan Martin 18 Sept. 1827                       Wash
Boler, Geo. H. to Jane E. Hancock 9 Nov. 1837                     Warr
Boles, Dabney A. to Jemima Shobe 15 Apr. 1832                     Mari
Boles, Ed to Lucinda Williams -- Apr. 1838                        Morg
Boli, Davis to Mary Anovey 14 Feb. 1828                           Jeff
Boli, John Jr. to Sary Swaney 21 July 1831                        Jeff
Bollar, James A. to Sarah Button 6 Sept. 1839                     Buch
Bollenger, Nathan to Leyna Randol 27 Apr. 1837                    CG-A
Bolling, Daniel to Sally St. Clair 30 Oct. 1828                   Pk-1
Bollinger, Christian to Sarah Farmer 14 Apr. 1836                 CG-A
Bollinger, Daniel to Mary M. Bollinger 13 Jan. 1822               CG-1
Bollinger, Frederick to Polly C. Bollinger 20 Apr. 1836          CG-A
Bollinger, Henry to Susan Lenard 27 June 1833                     CG-A
Bollinger, Henry to Matilda White 25 Dec. 1834                    Md-A
Bollinger, Jacob to Hanah Polk 12 Oct. 1819                       CG-1
Bollinger, John to Margaret Statler 22 Feb. 1825                  CG-1
Bollinger, Joseph to Mary Spencer 18 Oct. 1836                    Morg
Bollinger, Joseph to Senith Brown 9 Aug. 1838                     CG-A
Bollinger, Joshua to Malinda Seabauch 10 Jan. 1833               CG-A
Bollinger, Levi to Sarah Snider 2 Apr. 1835                       CG-B
Bollinger, Mathias to Fanny Gross 6 Mar. 1836                     Md-B
Bollinger, Matthias to Catherine Seabaugh 18 May 1837            CG-A
Bollinger, Matthias to Belinda Hane 22 June 1837                  CG-A
Bollinger, Matthias to Caroline Hicks 8 Sept. 1839               CG-B
Bollinger, Peter to Elizabeth Wilfong 12 Dec. 1833               CG-A
Bollinger, Phillip to Eliza Seapaugh 6 Dec. 1832                  CG-A
Bollinger, Wm. Jr. to Charlotte Hunt 16 Apr. 1832                 Md-A
Bolton, Waller to Mary Landsdown 14 Mar. 1832                     Cole
Bolton, Wm. to Sarah Lansdown 14 Mar. 1832                        Cole
Bolton, Wm. C. to Nancy A. Canady 19 May 1839                     Plat
Bolware, Alfred to Susan Bryant 10 Apr. 1837                      Monr
Bolware, Barnet to Elizabeth Walker -- Feb. 1831                  Gasc
Bolware, Geo. to Frances Walker 23 May 1831                       Gasc
Boly, Micheal to Jemima Morehead 26 Feb. 1837                     Jeff
Boman, Joshua to Mierria Spencer 29 Aug. 1837                     CG-A
Bomer, Meridith to Polly Calfee 5 Apr. 1833                       Cole
Bomer, Wm. to Elvira Willis 11 Nov. 1833                          Linc
Bond, Edward H. to Eliz. G. Hughes 20 July 1837                   Call
Bond, James to Elizabeth S. Underwood 18 Apr. 1839               Monr
Bond, Jefferson to Delilah Peel 20 May 1827                       StFr
Bond, Kimsey G. to Mary A. Clemmens 2 Aug. 1838                   Clin
Bond, Wm. to Kitta Fugate 11 Feb. 1827                            Rall
Bond, Wm. to Sarah Sullins 7 Nov. 1837                            Mill
Bone, Charles to Elmira Misplay 2 Apr. 1835                       Wash
```

Bone, James to Margaret Harris 7 Aug. 1834   Pett
Bonearant, Rawleigh to Agnes Perkins 26 Oct. 1837   Monr
Bones, Joseph to Anne Patton 24 Jan. 1832   Jack
Bonham, Francis H. to Mary A. Neville 23 Dec. 1830   Pk-1
Bonham, Nehemiah M. to Mahala P. Nevil 11 Jan. 1838   Pk-B
Bonlever, John to Elizabeth Welch 16 July 1823   Howa
Bonner, Wm. to Polly E. Rods 3 Mar. 1833   Perr
Bonney, Prentiss F. to Emily Hayden 7 July 1836   Wash
Bonny, Prentiss F. to Hannah Logan 27 Nov. 1828   Wash
Bonom, Jepson to Chiney Yoakham 22 Aug. 1831   Cr-1
Bookam, Richard to Nancy White 11 Sept. 1836   Boon
Booker, Edward to Mary Lomax 6 Jan. 1836   Call
Booker, James M. to Amanda Gregory 3 Jan. 1839   Fran
Boolin, Benj. to Sopia Dood 30 Jan. 1831   Coop
Boon, Alonzo to Mary J. Jackson 2 Jan. 1834   Call
Boon, Alphonso to Nancy Boon 1 Feb. 1822   Call
Boon, Daniel to Mary Philbert 19 Jan. 1832   Jack
Boon, Daniel to Judah Helton 9 July 1837   Gasc
Boon, Henry to Sarah Wilkison 19 Dec. 1839   Livi
Boon, Lemuel to Nancy Freeman 8 Aug. 1827   Char
Boon, Linsay to Sarah Grooms 14 Jan. 1832   Jack
Boon, Wm. C. to Lucy Daly 10 June 1834   Howa
Boone, Albert G. to Ann R. Hamilton 9 July 1829   Call
Boone, Banton G. to Eliz. C. Boone 26 June 1828   Call
Boone, Daniel to Sarah A. Jones 18 July 1839   Mari
Boone, James to Matilda Wainscott 27 Oct. 1832   Pk-1
Boone, James M. to Mary McMurty 7 Apr. 1831   Call
Boone, Milo to Lucinda Craig 17 Sept. 1839   StCh
Boone, Sydney S. to Sarah J. Jimason 1 Sept. 1836   StCh
Booth, Geo. W. to Sarah Staples 8 Feb. 1827   Jeff
Booth, John to Frances Gallaway 5 Feb. 1833   Linc
Booth, John to Matilda Eastbridge 5 Oct. 1839   Ripl
Booth, Wm. to Delilah Gallaway 29 Mar. 1827   Linc
Boothe, James to Sally A. Tillett 29 Mar. 1835   Pk-1
Boothe, James W. to Sophrona Naylor 20 Dec. 1832   StCh
Boothe, Norman to Sarah J. Lindsey 26 May 1829   Pk-1
Boothe, Peter to Margaret Bishop 20 Dec. 1838   Boon
Boozer, Henry to Lucinda Calloway 29 Jan. 1835   Howa
Bordeaux, Charles to Rosalie Cote 11 Feb. 1839   StCh
Borden, David to Mary Henderson 31 May 1837   Clay
Borden, Henry to Sally Price 26 Oct. 1837   Barr
Borden, Wm. N. to Martha Adamson 15 May 1839   Plat
Boren, Bazel to Elizabeth Roe 13 Nov. 1827   CG-A
Boren, Hiram to Martha Dempsey 5 Aug. 1834   CG-A
Boren, Jacob E. to Dorcas Johnston 19 Jan. 1836   Jeff
Boren, Wm. R. to Sally Wilson 28 Oct. 1830   CG-A
Borgess, Dennis to Nancy Corum 1 Apr. 1830   Clay
Boring, Henry E. to Abigail Scott 11 Sept. 1831   Wash
Boring, Leroy C. to Polly Hulsy 4 Sept. 1827   Fran
Borner, Peter to Ketty A. Mahan 5 Dec. 1827   Coop
Borner, Samuel S. to Sally A. Feland 31 July 1837   Pett
Bornoye, Pierre to Margaretha Obuchon 5 Mar. 1838   StCh
Boroughs, Aphred to Hannah Pritchett 8 Feb. 1838   Pk-B
Bos, Joseph to Lucat Saners 16 Nov. 1837   Perr
Boschert, Joseph to Catherine Lyble 26 Feb. 1838   StCh
Bosjard, John to Regina Byl 26 Apr. 1836   StCh
Bosley, Geo. W. to Martha Morris 18 July 1836   Coop
Boss, Peter to Massey Landers 30 Apr. 1826   CG-A
Boswell, Marshall to Sarah Northcut 24 Dec. 1837   Boon
Botman, Henry to Charity Sutton 24 Sept. 1829   Md-A
Bott, Henry to Catherine Hues 10 Mar. 1836   Wash
Bott, Risdon to Mary Finnell 29 Oct. 1826   Char
Bottom, Jesse H. to Sophia Grimsley 5 Apr. 1838   CG-A
Botts, John to Elizabeth Harvey 11 June 1835   Howa
Botts, Seth to Louisa Harvey 18 June 1835   Howa

22

Boucock, John D. to Elizabeth Gaines 19 July 1838	Rand
Bough, Hiram H. to Nancy Hiatt 2 Aug. 1835	Ripl
Boughman, Jacob to Nancy Carnahan 17 June 1836	Wash
Boughten, Robt. to Betsey Halderman 5 Dec. 1833	Jeff
Boughton, Benj. to Mary Mattingly 18 Apr. 1833	Jeff
Bouldin, Leonard to Catherine Heiromrums 19 Oct. 1837	Howa
Bouldon, James W.M. to Mary A. Loving 16 Nov. 1837	Cole
Boulware, Daniel R. to Martha P. Smith 8 Aug. 1838	Call
Boulware, John N. to Nancy Gash 16 Mar. 1834	Mari
Boulware, Simpson to Elizabeth Stevens 27 Dec. 1836	Monr
Boulware, Stephen to Mary Ratican 29 Apr. 1835	Call
Boulware, Wm. H. to Maria B. Redd 5 July 1835	Mari
Bounds, Isaac to Essabla Morrison 25 Nov. 1827	Md-A
Bourassa, Pierre to Elizabeth Degagnier 12 Oct. 1835	Wash
Bourbonois, Anthony to Josephine Bouche 31 Dec. 1827	StCh
Bourd, John to Jane Callison 1 Oct. 1839	Call
Bourdeaux, J.B. to Ursulle Denoyer 3 Nov. 1830	StCh
Bourland, James to Jane Ashby 9 Jan. 1820	Howa
Bourn, Douglas to Sally Pipes 2 Sept. 1834	Howa
Bourn, John R. to Mary A. McCormick 19 Nov. 1839	Pett
Bourne, Geo. W. to Eliza Butler 13 July 1834	Lewi
Bourne, Hudson to Susan Hayden 7 Feb. 1836	Lewi
Bouyr, Glod to Secil Laplant 14 June 1828	Wash
Bouyse, Paul to Caroline Avna 27 Dec. 1826	Wash
Boveaux, Peter V. to Elizabeth C. Henderson 13 Aug. 1839	Perr
Bowden, Isaac to Polly Woods 18 Apr. 1837	Char
Bowen, Alfred to Elizabeth Boughton 9 July 1838	Jeff
Bowen, Ambrose to Mary A. Jones 29 June 1834	Mari
Bowen, Geo. A. to Ann Powell 3 June 1832	Linc
Bowen, John W. to Mary M. Buckner 25 Feb. 1834	Monr
Bowen, Joshua to Christy A. Hornback 19 Jan. 1832	Rall
Bowen, Morton to Evaline Smith 27 Nov. 1834	Pk-1
Bowen, Thomas to Terry Zumwalt 20 Feb. 1817	StCh
Bowen, Thomas to Lucinda Johnson 14 July 1830	Cr-P
Bowen, Wm. to Sarah Bradford 16 Nov. 1837	Shel
Bower, Charles to Elizabeth Davidson 4 July 1838	Shel
Bower, Jeremiah to Nancy Swindle 12 Nov. 1837	Shel
Bower, Robt. to Anna Morrow 22 Dec. 1831	Gasc
Bowers, Christian to Elvira A. Young 16 Oct. 1834	Jack
Bowin, John to Elizabeth Finney 14 Nov. 1830	Mari
Bowl, Benj. P. to Borelly Tyler 17 Dec. 1829	Mari
Bowlan, Wm. to Selah Williams 6 Oct. 1810	StCh
Bowles, Benj. to Sarah J. Bath 29 June 1834	Coop
Bowles, Dabny to Bertha Tyler 2 Mar. 1834	Mari
Bowles, Thomas to Huldah Stockton 10 Aug. 1832	Cole
Bowlin, Daniel to Eliza Thompson 6 Sept. 1838	Mari
Bowlin, John to Kitty Adkins 18 Oct. 1831	Clay
Bowling, Daniel to Margaret Rivers 30 Oct. 1825	Rall
Bowling, Thomas H. to Jane Winkler 21 Jan. 1836	Rand
Bowling, Thomas J. to Lavina Null 10 Apr. 1834	Jeff
Bowlinger, Wm. to Nancy Lamb 6 June 1836	Morg
Bowls, Jesse to Judith Schofield 17 Feb. 1828	Mari
Bowls, John C. to Mileta A. May 3 Apr. 1833	Pk-1
Bowls, Peter T. to Elizabeth Henderson 26 Sept. 1822	Coop
Bowman, Henry to Elizabeth Russel 20 Sept. 1836	CG-A
Bowman, Ransom P. to Harriet Reavis 4 Aug. 1836	Coop
Bowman, Wm. to Abigail Morgan 1 June 1828	Ray
Bowsfield, Henry to Polly Embree 28 Apr. 1823	Coop
Bowyer, Jesse to Elizabeth Tier 30 Aug. 1827	Howa
Bowyer, Wm. to Patsy Tire 23 Feb. 1827	Howa
Boyce, Aaron F. to Elisabeth J. Ely 1 Aug. 1822	Rall
Boyce, James to Harriet Smith 1 Mar. 1835	Mari
Boyce, Jesse to Harriett Miller 27 Nov. 1832	Ray
Boyce, Robt. C. to Asinah A. Murphy 24 Mar. 1830	Call
Boyce, Wm. to Jane Crain 15 Jan. 1835	Morg

23

Boyce, Willis to Sarah J. Bullock 2 Dec. 1836	Ray
Boyd, Abraham to Polly Harryman 12 Apr. 1827	Cole
Boyd, Abram to Eliza Coatney 26 July 1838	Pett
Boyd, Cary A. to Elizabeth Bayley 23 June 1831	StCh
Boyd, Elemuel to Lydia Johns 18 Jan. 1835	Fran
Boyd, Geo. W. to Mahala Thornhill 23 Aug. 1838	Fran
Boyd, Hiram to Rebecca Dodson -- Apr. 1836	Linc
Boyd, Jackson to Mary A. Shoot 4 Jan. 1838	Monr
Boyd, James to Malinda Adams 4 Dec. 1836	Morg
Boyd, James M. to Martha Sloane 15 Jan. 1835	Clay
Boyd, John to Elizabeth Andrew 19 Sept. 1799	CGRA
Boyd, John to Margaret Harryman 15 Sept. 1814	StCh
Boyd, John to Elizabeth Willingham 13 June 1825	Boon
Boyd, John to Mary A. Scott 15 Apr. 1828	Call
Boyd, John to Vina Goodno 21 Aug. 1833	Coop
Boyd, Joseph to Betsey A. Hasty 6 Feb. 1836	Coop
Boyd, Mathew to Lucy Cary 2 Dec. 1821	Coop
Boyd, Robt. to Lucinda Schrichfield 18 Sept. 1828	Coop
Boyd, Samuel M. to Mary Ely 9 Mar. 1837	Rall
Boyd, Simon to Armanda Wardcastle 24 Sept. 1839	Coop
Boyd, Singleton W. to Nancy Ellis 9 Aug. 1835	Pk-1
Boyd, Thomas to Mary Clifton 20 Nov. 1834	Fran
Boyed, Wm. to Nancy A. Journey 15 Dec. 1836	StCh
Boyer, Amend to Priscilla Jackson 14 Nov. 1839	Maco
Boyer, Anthony to Louisa M. Lambert 25 Sept. 1838	Wash
Boyer, Antoin to Sally Ricar 6 Feb. 1837	Wash
Boyer, Antoine to Marcelite Page' 7 Oct. 1834	Wash
Boyer, Charles to Julie Misplay 9 Aug. 1831	Wash
Boyer, Felix to Aspasie Duclos 2 Mar. 1829	Wash
Boyer, Henry to Adele Portais 12 May 1835	Wash
Boyer, Isidor to Pelagie Robideau 20 Dec. 1826	StCh
Boyer, James J. to Eliza Orear 20 June 1839	Boon
Boyer, Jean B. to Euprosine Collman 19 Jan. 1836	Wash
Boyer, John B. to Adrienne Valois 9 Oct. 1838	StFr
Boyer, Joseph to Marie A. Detchemendy 29 Jan. 1828	Wash
Boyer, Louis to Eulalie Bequet 28 Apr. 1828	Wash
Boyer, Louis to Aslie Perrin 18 June 1832	Wash
Boyer, Pierre to Marie Beauchamp 3 Feb. 1829	Wash
Boyer, Washington to Angeline Willaby 16 June 1836	Wash
Boyes, James to Jemima Freeman 12 Feb. 1833	Call
Boyes, Wm. to Margaret A. Berry 8 Sept. 1831	Call
Boys, James to Lucy Gibson 13 Dec. 1839	Wash
Boys, Wm. to Frances W. Crain 29 Aug. 1833	Morg
Boyse, Alfred to Helen Walker 8 Apr. 1835	Cole
Bozarth, Abner to Nancy Anderson 25 Feb. 1836	Mari
Bozarth, Alfred to Minerva Hanger 24 Mar. 1836	Wash
Bozarth, Andrew to Catharine Loe 15 Jan. 1832	Rand
Bozarth, David to Nancy Smith 16 Feb. 1839	Monr
Bozarth, Elf to Elizabeth Morrison 7 May 1837	Monr
Bozarth, Hiram to Margaret Cleton 14 Oct. 1818	Howa
Bozarth, Ira to Eliza Carnegy 8 June 1834	Lewi
Bozeth, Abner to Millerson Bowles 5 Mar. 1829	Mari
Bozeth, John to Permelia Bowles 5 Mar. 1829	Mari
Bozorth, R. to Susan Bowles 7 May 1831	Mari
Brackee, Wm. to Eliza Vance 6 July 1837	Barr
Bracken, James to Fanny Holley 10 Jan. 1826	CG-A
Bracken, Wm. to Harriett Winters 7 Dec. 1837	Barr
Brackenridge, Asoph to Mary E. Roberts 27 Nov. 1834	Fran
Brackenridge, James to Betsy Bryan 28 Feb. 1833	Wash
Brackenridge, Robt. to Susannah Howard 20 July 1837	CG-A
Bracker, Geo. to Milla Blecher 20 Feb. 1834	Jack
Brackinridge, Palmer to Polly Myres 5 Oct. 1826	Wash
Bracy, John to Rachel Murphy 24 Jan. 1836	StFr
Bradberry, Joseph to Nancy Davis 18 July 1833	Clay
Bradbury, Geo. W. to Lydia Roberts 5 Apr. 1827	Clay

```
Bradbury, Walter to Charity Chisholt 16 Dec. 1813                        StCh
Braden, Felix to Susan J. Yarnold 8 Mar. 1838                            Clay
Bradford, Arthur to Christina Hickam 17 Oct. 1839                        Boon
Bradford, Isaac N. to Martha Duncan 26 June 1828                         Gasc
Bradford, James to Anny Turpen 18 Nov. 1830                              Cr-P
Bradin, Wm. P. to Nancy Gaines 26 Jan. 1837                              Clay
Bradley, Arthur S. to Harriet Alvis 16 June 1836                         Pk-1
Bradley, Austin P. to Caroline Mothershead 30 May 1839                   Monr
Bradley, Calvin to Mary A. Collins 12 June 1836                          Rand
Bradley, Charles to Elizabeth Mock 7 July 1836                           Lafa
Bradley, Elias to Lucy S. Brown 14 Feb. 1839                             Lafa
Bradley, Felix to Lucinda Wilson 29 Oct. 1829                            Howa
Bradley, Geo. W. to Sarah A. Davis 26 Nov. 1835                          Lafa
Bradley, James to Jemima Standford 20 June 1833                          Howa
Bradley, James L. to Sarah A. Smith 26 Apr. 1836                         Pk-1
Bradley, James M. to Lydia Lord 2 Oct. 1834                              Linc
Bradley, John Jr. to Elizabeth Oglesby 20 Mar. 1832                      Howa
Bradley, Joseph to Dinah Stapp 20 Apr. 1820                              Howa
Bradley, Joseph R. to Allis Philbert 18 June 1837                        Howa
Bradley, Levi to Polly James 5 July 1838                                 Rand
Bradley, Levi D. to Sophia Turner 23 Dec. 1832                           Rand
Bradley, Milton to Mary A. Johnson 9 Aug. 1838                           Rand
Bradley, Nathan to Nancy Standiford 6 Sept. 1825                         Howa
Bradley, Nathan to Jemimah Standiford 14 Aug. 1828                       Howa
Bradley, Newton to Elizabeth A. Oliver 28 Sept. 1837                     Rand
Bradley, Samuel B. to Frances Holeman 23 June 1835                       Rand
Bradley, Squire to Rachel Campbell 10 Sept. 1821                         Howa
Bradley, Terry to Ann Owens 26 Mar. 1837                                 Rand
Bradley, Wm. to Elizabeth Ousley 15 Sept. 1831                           Cole
Bradley, Wm. F. to Caroline M. Parker 12 May 1836                        Lafa
Bradley, Wm. M. to Polly Pharis 28 June 1821                             Howa
Bradly, ---- to Patience A. Allen 15 July 1838                           Monr
Bradly, Wm. M. to Mahalah Carter 10 Nov. 1839                           Mill
Bradshaw, Eli to Elizabeth Neice 13 Nov. 1834                           Cole
Bradshaw, John to Sarah A. Turner 5 Apr. 1833                           Cole
Bradshaw, Wm. to Drucilla Harvey 3 Oct. 1831                            Pk-1
Bradshaw, Wm. to Eliza A. Burdoin 20 Apr. 1837                          Wash
Bradshaw, Young E. to Nancy Tripp 8 May 1821                            CG-1
Brady, Benj. to Mary Parker 2 Mar. 1837                                 Md-B
Brady, James to Elizabeth R. Ramsey 15 Oct. 1810                        CG-1
Brady, Jesse to Vicy Parker 2 Apr. 1837                                 Md-B
Brady, John C. to Mildred Baines 7 May 1839                             Howa
Bragg, John to Ruzilla Cannon 16 Apr. 1834                             Howa
Braham, Benj. to Mary A. Tucker 28 Sept. 1832                          Call
Braham, Charles to Margaret Lorien 1 Jan. 1836                         StCh
Braiding, Thomas to Barbary Baker 30 Dec. 1817                         CG-1
Brakenridge, Robberd to Catharina Hahn -- Aug. 1839                    CG-B
Brakin, John to Temperance Hobbs 10 Sept. 1837                         CG-B
Braley, Hugh to Nancy McCreary 25 Mar. 1827                            Howa
Braley, James B. to Manerva Enloe 23 Aug. 1836                         Fran
Braley, John E. to Susannah Moutry 21 Sept. 1830                       Fran
Braly, Frank M. to Elizabeth Madison 19 July 1824                      StFr
Bram, Hezekiah to Eveline Birns 11 Aug. 1833                           Gree
Bramble, Thomas to Amelia Butler 22 Nov. 1827                          Pk-1
Brammell, Washington T. to Martha F. Butts 14 Feb. 1839               Fran
Branen, Andrew to Hannah Lane 3 Dec. 1818                             CG-1
Branen, Mathias to Peggy Hines 14 May 1820                            Howa
Branet, Daniel to Christine White 17 June 1827                        CG-A
Branham, Granville to Eliza Nesbit 1 Mar. 1827                        Boon
Branham, Richard to Emily Johnston 9 Dec. 1834                        Boon
Brannam, John to Pennelipy Moss 5 June 1834                           Clay
Brannum, Richard to Lucy J. Rice 23 Nov. 1837                         Coop
Branson, David to Sally David 14 June 1832                            Gasc
Branson, James to Mary Hains 22 Apr. 1838                             Gasc
Branson, James to Sarah Bumpias 14 Dec. 1839                          Gasc
```

NORTH PALM BEACH PUBLIC LIBRARY

Branson, John to Julian Devenport 7 Jan. 1836   Gasc
Branson, Thomas to Lucinda Hains 10 Jan. 1836   Gasc
Branson, Thomas to Hannah Simpton 11 May 1837   Gasc
Branson, Valentine to Cely Beck 1 Apr. 1832   Gasc
Branson, Valentine to Alpha Shurls 22 Jan. 1835   Gasc
Branson, Washington to Jonah Jott 24 Mar. 1839   Gasc
Branson, Wm. to Matilda Shockley 21 Oct. 1834   Gasc
Branstetter, Findley to Mrs. Lucretia Goodman 7 Dec. 1837   Pk-B
Branstetter, Henderson to Patsy Adams 30 Aug. 1835   Pk-1
Branstetter, Jacob to Ann C. Hodgins 4 July 1839   Ray
Branstetter, James to Elizabeth Branstetter 11 Dec. 1834   Pk-1
Branstetter, John to Jane Woodson 21 Mar. 1837   Pk-A
Branstetter, Simon to Jane P. Branstetter 28 Jan. 1834   Pk-1
Brant, Daniel to Narcissa Longmire 19 Aug. 1830   Mari
Brant, Daniel to Sally Gash 17 Aug. 1837   Mari
Brant, Endicot to Tempy Randol 29 Jan. 1831   CG-A
Brant, Endicut M. to Elizabeth Dowty 15 Mar. 1827   CG-A
Brant, Etienne to Cycile L. Giguere 1 May 1807   StCh
Brant, Mathias to Luija Gillispy 1 Oct. 1829   Mari
Brashear, D.J. to Susan Monroe 22 Mar. 1836   Howa
Brashear, Geo. to Cassel Williams 20 Jan. 1835   Howa
Brashear, Judson to Darcus Wasser 10 Nov. 1836   Howa
Brashear, Mortimore to Sarah Vaughan 9 Nov. 1837   Mill
Brashear, Wm. to Martha Swanzey 2 July 1832   Howa
Brashears, Bazwell to Zephalinda Lewellen 10 Mar. 1836   Rall
Brashears, Cyrus to Julian Rollins 22 July 1832   Clay
Brasill, Samuel to Pheby Tabour 20 May 1832   Gasc
Brassfield, Abner to Cinderalla Gee 17 Apr. 1828   Char
Brassfield, John to Mahala Johnston -- Jan. 1834   Ray
Brassfield, Minter to Jane Splann 24 Feb. 1834   Ray
Brassfield, Thomas W. to Elizabeth Breckenridge 4 Dec. 1837   Clay
Bratten, Wm. to Abigail Davis 7 Sept. 1819   Howa
Bratten, Wm. to Mary Croxel 21 Feb. 1829   Jack
Bratty, Samuel to Polly Denny 11 May 1820   Howa
Brawner, John to Martha Soper 23 Oct. 1839   Clay
Bray, Wm. E. to Elizabeth Phileps 6 Sept. 1838   Fran
Brazee, Elmond D. to Hannah Severe 27 Sept. 1825   Rall
Breanis, James to Matilda Morgan 24 Dec. 1834   Lafa
Breckenridge, Wm. H. to Polly A. Young 15 Oct. 1838   Clay
Breckingridge, Geo. C. to Mary S. Benning 7 Mar. 1839   Wash
Breeding, John to Mrs. Elender Greenstreet 31 May 1836   Fran
Breese, Thomas to Ann Vance 18 Aug. 1836   Cr-1
Breeze, Geo. to Hannah Swiney 17 Nov. 1836   Char
Brenegar, David to Frances Crump 29 Aug. 1835   Boon
Brevard, Adlai to Susan McGuire 8 Nov. 1832   CG-A
Brevard, Albert H. to Juliet Gale 15 Dec. 1831   CG-A
Brevard, R. to Sarah W. Davis 31 Aug. 1837   CG-A
Brewer, Green to Sarah Brown 22 Mar. 1832   Ray
Brewer, Harvy to Sarah Hutson 2 Oct. 1822   Lafa
Brewer, Henry C. to Martha Thereman 1 Oct. 1837   Barr
Brewer, Isaac to Peggy Hines 5 Apr. 1829   Ray
Brewer, Isaac to Polly Brown 25 Oct. 1832   Ray
Brewer, James C. to Lucinda Snowden 23 Nov. 1828   Ray
Brewer, John to Cecilia Layton 28 May 1838   Perr
Brewer, Marc to Mary Layton 13 Feb. 1832   Perr
Brewer, Mark to Fedelia Manning 22 Nov. 1825   Perr
Brewer, Mark to Polly Webb 6 Oct. 1835   Perr
Brewer, Richard to Polly S. McCune 13 Nov. 1825   Pk-1
Brewer, Wiley to Milley Brewer 25 July 1833   Ray
Brewer, Wm. to Rebecca Brown 3 Nov. 1825   Ray
Brewer, Wm. to Anna J. Lemmons 17 Nov. 1839   Md-B
Brewin, David to Elizabeth Morrow 19 Mar. 1837   Md-B
Briant, Absolom to Celia Ferguson 17 Apr. 1828   Wash
Briant, Albert to Polly Winbourn 28 June 1832   Howa
Briant, James to Rosa Davis 2 May 1838   Clin

26

Brice, Benoni to Elizabeth Hammonds 13 July 1837   Pk-A
Brice, Wm. to Thamer Miller 18 Feb. 1834   Pk-1
Bricken, Wm. A. to Susan C. Brock 24 Aug. 1838   Carr
Brickey, Cornelius to Kesiar Hews 31 May 1835   Cr-1
Brickey, Jeremiah to Matilda Simpson 1 July 1832   Wash
Brickey, John to Sally R. Brown 5 Jan. 1825   Wash
Brickey, John S. to Sophia Johnson 1 Feb. 1827   Wash
Brickey, Peter to Mary Wizor 9 Nov. 1834   StFr
Brickey, Preston to Sena Montgomery 2 Oct. 1828   Wash
Brickey, Silas B. to Jemima McAdams 19 Jan. 1826   Wash
Bricky, Jeremiah to Jane Woods 4 Dec. 1835   Cr-1
Bricky, John N. to Polly Webb 15 Sept. 1833   Cr-1
Bridgeford, James to Margaret Campbell 18 Oct. 1838   Monr
Bridgeford, Wm. T. to Sarah M. Noonan 6 Dec. 1837   Monr
Bridges, Elisha to Margaret Costly 22 Mar. 1835   StCh
Bridges, Geo. W. to Agnes Jones 21 Apr. 1836   Clay
Bridges, Hosea H. to Rebecca J. Pyatt 7 Dec. 1837   Gasc
Bridges, John to Susan Johnson 1 June 1826   Clay
Bridges, John to Hannah Owen 8 Apr. 1838   CG-A
Bridges, John Q. to Marthy Rutherford 21 June 1835   Fran
Bridges, John W. to Lucinda Hill 27 Feb. 1838   Henr
Bridgewater, Samuel to Rachel Beaty 6 Dec. 1830   Sali
Bridgewater, Wm. to Martha Dicks 7 Nov. 1839   Coop
Brient, Felix to Maxey Boone 3 May 1832   Call
Briggs, Caleb to Darcus Attleberry 24 Nov. 1830   Howa
Briggs, John C. to Davidella Ely 26 Dec. 1838   Rall
Briggs, Robt. to Nancy Carson 11 Apr. 1819   Howa
Briggs, Robt. C. to Mary Ely 9 Aug. 1838   Rall
Briggs, Robt. M. to Ann E. Jones 22 June 1836   Mari
Briggs, Rufus to Ann Rorer 4 Jan. 1837   Howa
Briggs, Samuel to Nancy Wallace 13 Dec. 1826   Howa
Briggs, Wm. to Rhoda Wright 22 Feb. 1827   Rall
Briggs, Wm. T. to Nancy J. Waters 17 Jan. 1838   Rall
Bright, Aaron to Rachel Robert 1 Apr. 1834   Mari
Bright, Joseph to Betsy Covent 22 Mar. 1832   Jack
Bright, Wm. to Artemetia Johnson 28 Dec. 1838   Lafa
Briles, Milton to Martha A. Thomason 13 June 1839   Linc
Brim, James to Peridance Robertson 31 May 1821   Boon
Brimer, Wm. to Mrs. Polly South 15 Jan. 1829   Pk-1
Brimer, Wm. S. to Lavinia Finley 5 Apr. 1838   Pk-B
Brindley, Michael to Catherine Baldwin 5 July 1838   Jeff
Brinegar, John to Rachel Tate 5 Aug. 1833   Gree
Brink, John H. to Nancy Thornton 29 Dec. 1839   Wash
Brinker, John B. to Sarah Murphy 31 Dec. 1833   StFr
Brisco, Geo. to Ann Fenton 2 Jan. 1834   Linc
Briscoe, Isaac to Nancy Wash 15 Oct. 1835   Lewi
Briscoe, Joel K. to Barnett Miller 30 Oct. 1837   Coop
Briscoe, John to Emily Biggs 29 Sept. 1836   Pk-1
Briscoe, Merett to Alzada Morton 14 Feb. 1839   Mari
Briscoe, Oliver H.P. to Ursula P. Huff 7 Apr. 1836   Morg
Briscoe, Phillip to Amelia Emmerson 1 Apr. 1831   Rall
Briscoe, Wm. to Frances Briscoe 17 July 1823   Coop
Britt, Wm. to Clementine Hopwood 14 Nov. 1837   Pk-B
Brittan, Wm. to Elizabeth Wright 4 Apr. 1827   Wash
Britten, Richard to Sinday Shelton 2 Aug. 1838   Md-B
Britton, Hew to Mary Stover 23 Dec. 1821   Coop
Britton, James to Lucinda Moore 25 Dec. 1838   Cr-1
Britton, Newman to Sarah Cox 28 Dec. 1837   Cr-1
Britton, Richard to Lizzy Couch 21 Feb. 1833   Cr-1
Broaddeus, Benj. F. to Julia Owen 22 Sept. 1839   Howa
Broaddeus, Jeremiah to Polly Herd 28 Nov. 1824   Howa
Broaddues, Andrew to Gracy Askins 8 Apr. 1819   Howa
Broadhurst, Henry to Margaret Faubian 16 Mar. 1837   Clay
Broadhurst, Henry to Katharine Smith 20 July 1839   Clay
Broadhurst, Jacob to Sarah Broadhurst 20 Mar. 1832   Clay

27

```
Broadhusk, Jos. to Zilphy Forbin 2 Apr. 1839          Clay
Brock, Alfred to Henrietta Fall 27 Oct. 1829          Sali
Brock, Blessinggone to Caty McDowell 7 Aug. 1817      Howa
Brock, Elisha to Winna Hinton 23 Jan. 1822            Fran
Brock, James to Elizabeth Holmes 20 Sept. 1819        Howa
Brock, James M. to Elizabeth Slaughter 27 Sept. 1833  Clay
Brock, Joseph to Permelia Collins 11 Nov. 1830        Clay
Brock, Joseph to Mary Crocket 24 Mar. 1839            Clay
Brock, Robt. to Marietta Rice 11 Oct. 1828            Fran
Brock, Sigmund Ch to Mrs. Johanne Ch Elgert 28 Aug. 1839   Perr
Brock, Wm. to Elizabeth Smith 10 Dec. 1827            CG-A
Brockman, Jacob to Elizabeth Embree 20 June 1828      Howa
Brockman, John to Clarisa Thomason 6 Aug. 1837        Perr
Brockman, Sims to Rachel Gartin 26 Feb. 1837          Mill
Brockman, Wm. to Agnes Hill 23 Apr. 1839              Call
Brockman, Wm. W. to Elizabeth Rees 17 Dec. 1835       Ray
Broiles, James to Nancy Berryman 24 Mar. 1838         Coop
Bronhart, Andrew to Elizabeth Spura 19 Aug. 1830      StCh
Broohs, Milton to Betsy Cocheral 11 Feb. 1835         John
Broohs, Philip to Cheldusay Anderson 30 Dec. 1839     John
Brooke, Mathew E. to Julia Barnett 30 Aug. 1838       Rall
Brookes, Charles to Rachel Gragg 18 Feb. 1836         John
Brookes, John L. to Unicia Kelley 18 Oct. 1835        John
Brookes, Newton to Rachel Kelley 29 Nov. 1835         John
Brooking, Robt. to Eliza A. Dehoney 2 Oct. 1839       Jack
Brooks, Gilbert to Sally Moody 21 Aug. 1838           Lewi
Brooks, Green to Mary Hill 24 July 1832               Linc
Brooks, Henry to Polly Roark 11 May 1833              Jeff
Brooks, John to Sarah Bennett 11 Oct. 1831            CG-A
Brooks, John to Harriet Barger 16 Jan. 1834           Boon
Brooks, Matthew to Lucy A. Barnett 30 Aug. 1838       Rall
Brooks, Paschal to Lorenda Roark 22 Mar. 1835         Jeff
Brooks, Robt. to Elizabeth Rhour 28 Sept. 1839        Call
Brooks, Wm. W. to Penelope Terrel 20 July 1837        Howa
Broon, Benj. to Polly Cooper 18 Feb. 1821             Howa
Broshieres, Richard to Amelia Leak 27 Dec. 1832       Rall
Brotherton, John J. to Mary A. Kent 28 Nov. 1839      Warr
Broughton, John to Emeline Stover 14 Feb. 1838        Boon
Browday, Robt. A. to Diana Taylor 21 July 1837        Pk-B
Brown, ---- to Elizabeth Pearce 23 Sept. 1838         Clay
Brown, Alfred to Lucy Thompson 27 Jan. 1834           Gree
Brown, Allen to Emeline Purdom 18 May 1837            Rall
Brown, Allen W. to Frances H. Brown 14 Jan. 1833      Fran
Brown, Anderson to Elvira Matthews 13 July 1830       Mari
Brown, Archibald to Elizabeth E. Huston 27 Nov. 1838  Rall
Brown, Artipus to Elizabeth Crofford 3 Aug. 1836      Clin
Brown, Austin to Sary Herrington 19 Apr. 1835         Jeff
Brown, Bartlet Y. to Decy Degrafton 7 Oct. 1837       Gree
Brown, Benj. F. to Harly A. Kilby 28 July 1836        Pk-1
Brown, Bernard to Marian French 24 May 1828           Perr
Brown, Caleb to Cinthia Hughs 23 June 1833            Pk-1
Brown, Cecero to Elizabeth Jeffries 28 Sept. 1819     Coop
Brown, Chancellor L. to Emily Rhodes 11 July 1833     Mari
Brown, Charles H. to Amanda McKinney 9 Mar. 1837      Call
Brown, Chatham E. to Caroline Morgan 12 Oct. 1838     Morg
Brown, Darius W. to Polly B. Gaddy 30 Mar. 1837       Clay
Brown, Eathen to Sarah Dodson 18 Oct. 1832            Gasc
Brown, Francis to Maria Wilds 31 Mar. 1824            Howa
Brown, Geo. to Irenia Merrit 1 Nov. 1832              Pk-1
Brown, Geo. to Martha A. Todd 17 Apr. 1838            Pk-B
Brown, Haden to Lanna Prewitt 3 Apr. 1836             Boon
Brown, Hanseford to Kessiah S. Penn 10 Jan. 1833      Rall
Brown, Henry to Elizabeth E. Jones 8 Jan. 1835        Fran
Brown, Henry G. to Polly Graham 22 Jan. 1828          Jeff
Brown, Henry T. to Mildred Flint 20 May 1819          Howa
```

```
Brown, Hiram to Catherine Hayden 13 Feb. 1827              CG-A
Brown, Hosea to Ellen Fackler 1 Feb. 1833                  Fran
Brown, Hugh to Celia Taylor 7 Feb. 1836                    Coop
Brown, J. to Winney Moore 5 Dec. 1831                      Ray
Brown, James to Polly Gragg 13 Feb. 1827                   Wash
Brown, James to Jane Campbell 26 Feb. 1829                 Clay
Brown, James to Elizabeth Vapor 19 Apr. 1829              Clay
Brown, James to Malinda Cockran 7 May 1829                Linc
Brown, James to Elmira Merrit 14 Aug. 1832                Pk-1
Brown, James to Rebecca Plummer 5 Nov. 1832              Fran
Brown, James to Hannah A. Alderson 9 July 1835           Call
Brown, James to Abby Lindsey 3 Mar. 1836                  Pk-1
Brown, James to Catharine Sherron 10 May 1836            Rand
Brown, James to Elizabeth Blair 9 Mar. 1837              Fran
Brown, James to Susan Hughes 18 July 1838                Wash
Brown, James to Elizabeth Ripper 27 Aug. 1838            Clar
Brown, James to Emily Staly 24 Dec. 1839                 Bent
Brown, James B. to Eliza R. Durrett 25 Jan. 1838         Sali
Brown, James C. to Stacy Ramsey 13 Sept. 1838           Clin
Brown, James S. to Polly Varner 3 May 1820               StGe
Brown, James S. to Sarah J. Hornbuckle 1 Dec. 1839      Call
Brown, John to Rebecca Adams 20 Mar. 1828               Fran
Brown, John to Catharine Fry 2 Aug. 1829                Jeff
Brown, John to Zurbia Coppedge 17 Dec. 1829             Cr-P
Brown, John to Meaeaney Zumwalt 10 June 1830            Linc
Brown, John to Nancy Richardson 1 Sept. 1831            Fran
Brown, John to Catharine Brison 7 Nov. 1833             Pk-1
Brown, John to Mary Wills 7 Nov. 1833                   CG-A
Brown, John to Margaret S. Lewis 17 Dec. 1833           Mari
Brown, John to Mary A. Davis 15 Jan. 1834               Boon
Brown, John to Nancy Richardson 20 Feb. 1834            Fran
Brown, John to Margaret Petree 3 Apr. 1834              Ray
Brown, John to Mary E. Graham 29 Nov. 1835              Ray
Brown, John to Amelia Donohue 31 Dec. 1835              Perr
Brown, John to Charlotte Williamson 14 Dec. 1837        Fran
Brown, John to Rachel Wilson 9 Feb. 1839                Perr
Brown, John to Mary Cornelius -- Mar. 1839              Howa
Brown, John B. to Martha Adams 7 Feb. 1833              Fran
Brown, John D. to Sarah C. Wake 24 July 1838            Pk-B
Brown, John E. to Mary Darst 10 July 1834               Warr
Brown, John R. to Sarah McClure 25 Feb. 1836            Fran
Brown, John W. to Mrs. Florilda Ashby 11 Dec. 1831      Clay
Brown, Joseph to Nancy King 30 Jan. 1828                Jack
Brown, Joseph to Keziah Raglan 10 July 1828             StFr
Brown, Joseph to Sarah Russell 11 Sept. 1828            CG-A
Brown, Joseph to Sarah Byrd 2 Nov. 1830                 CG-A
Brown, Joseph to Cern Ross 25 Aug. 1835                 Howa
Brown, Joseph to Juliann Pearson 19 Apr. 1836           Call
Brown, Joseph to Lucinda Jackson 28 Feb. 1838           Ray
Brown, Joseph to Patsy Yawbery 25 July 1839             Wash
Brown, Joseph N. to Louisa Collins 25 Sept. 1834        Jack
Brown, Josiah to Amy Alsight 25 Apr. 1839               Polk
Brown, Levin to Lucinda Stone rec. 22 May 1835          Rall
Brown, Maletes to Matilda Linville 4 Aug. 1831          Clay
Brown, Manthane to Catherine Clements 15 Oct. 1837      Ray
Brown, Mason to Lucinda Unsel 14 Nov. 1835              Pk-1
Brown, Michael to Jane Martin 21 Oct. 1830             Coop
Brown, Miller to Margaret A. Faulconer 24 May 1838      Linc
Brown, Moses to Joanna B. Scott 12 Apr. 1835           Pett
Brown, Murphy to Rebecca Jones 30 June 1836            StFr
Brown, Nelson to Rebecca Griffin 7 July 1836           Howa
Brown, Parsons to Orpha Bogges 21 Oct. 1830            Pk-1
Brown, Peter to Mary Layton 19 Aug. 1828               Perr
Brown, Rheuben to Patsy Hines 29 Jan. 1829             Md-A
Brown, Richard to Mrs. Jemima Turner 9 Feb. 1834       Fran
```

```
Brown, Robt. to Catiche Valle' 1 June 1807                          StGe
Brown, Robt. to Amelia Cooper 4 Dec. 1814                           StCh
Brown, Robt. to Patsey McGarey 16 Sept. 1828                        Pk-1
Brown, Robt. to Catharine Weaver 8 Aug. 1837                        John
Brown, Robt. to Emily Hunsicker 10 Sept. 1837                       Lewi
Brown, Robt. to Emely McGuire 11 Oct. 1838                          CG-A
Brown, Robt. to Judith Burton 21 Mar. 1839                          Fran
Brown, Robt. T. to Julia G. Snell 31 Oct. 1829                      Howa
Brown, Robt. T. to Mary Holden 22 Jan. 1838                         Perr
Brown, Samuel to Susanna Woods 16 Mar. 1818                         Howa
Brown, Samuel to Hiley Petree 28 Dec. 1834                         Ray
Brown, Solomon to Ann Edgar 21 Mar. 1821                           Coop
Brown, Thomas to Sarah Knott 23 Nov. 1829                          Perr
Brown, Thomas to Patty Crawley 22 Nov. 1838                        Ray
Brown, Thomas to Mary Battle 3 Mar. 1839                           Clin
Brown, Thomas to Docia A. Cox 27 Aug. 1839                         Ray
Brown, Thomas G. to Patsy Jones 3 June 1818                        Howa
Brown, Timothy to Margery Conway 11 Dec. 1834                      Mari
Brown, Turner to Elizabeth Ausburn 28 Aug. 1835                    Perr
Brown, Vincen to Mary Hamelton 25 May 1837                         StFr
Brown, Walker P. to Susan Jeffries 25 Dec. 1828                    Fran
Brown, Walter to Mary Rochefort 11 Oct. 1836                       Perr
Brown, Washington to Polly Newberry 7 Mar. 1830                    Cr-P
Brown, Wm. to Betsy Brown 26 Mar. 1826                             Fran
Brown, Wm. to Malvina Pearce 18 May 1828                           Pk-1
Brown, Wm. to Mary Love 16 June 1831                               Pk-1
Brown, Wm. to Judith Lovell 5 Apr. 1832                            Ray
Brown, Wm. to Sally Ralph 2 Dec. 1832                              Ray
Brown, Wm. to Lucy A. Guthrie 25 Dec. 1835                         Sali
Brown, Wm. to Mandana Brown 15 Apr. 1837                           Clay
Brown, Wm. to Ruth Markum 21 Sept. 1837                            Gasc
Brown, Wm. to Elizabeth Withington 11 Jan. 1838                    Fran
Brown, Wm. to Sallitha Pullem 30 Jan. 1838                         Clay
Brown, Wm. to Martha Silvey 5 June 1838                            Howa
Brown, Wm. to Jane Menifee 20 Dec. 1838                            Mari
Brown, Wm. to Mary A. Gunn 15 July 1839                            Pk-B
Brown, Wm. A. to Sarah A. Noell 3 Mar. 1839                        Perr
Brown, Wm. B. to Margaret Morrison 30 July 1835                    CG-B
Brown, Wm. P. to Sarah Bowles 17 July 1826                         Rall
Brown, Wm. P. to Melinda Boulware 16 Dec. 1828                     Mari
Brown, Wm. P. to Martha Boulware 22 Jan. 1835                      Mari
Brown, Wm. R. to Ann J. Robinson 26 Oct. 1831                      Coop
Brown, Wm. V. to Elizabeth Keys 19 Oct. 1837                       Rand
Brown, Wilson to Amanda Giboney 13 May 1830                        CG-A
Brown, Zachariah W. to Elizabeth Pritchett 29 Mar. 1838            Pk-B
Brownen, Nicholas W. to Mary E. Hudson 19 Oct. 1837               Barr
Brownfield, John to Susannah Mullins 3 Jan. 1837                   Mari
Brownfield, Jorden to Emely Isbee 7 Feb. 1836                      Howa
Browning, David to Margaret Mozey 10 Mar. 1833                     Linc
Browning, Jasper to Margaret Kirby 31 Dec. 1839                    Lafa
Browning, Wm. to Elizabeth Mifford 14 Nov. 1830                    Pk-1
Browning, Wm. to Nancy Snoddy 24 Dec. 1834                         Howa
Browning, Wm. M. to Elizabeth C. Gep 18 Mar. 1834                  Lafa
Broyles, James to Parthena Robeson 22 Sept. 1839                   Coop
Broyles, Larkin to Melessa Job 5 May 1831                          Clay
Bruce, Alfred to Amanda E. Kinchelee 27 Apr. 1839                  Shel
Bruce, Amos to Rebeca Davidson 4 Jan. 1830                         Wash
Bruce, Amos to Theresa LeClare 12 Dec. 1839                        Wash
Bruce, James to Nancy Bullitt 3 Sept. 1837                         CG-A
Bruce, Richard to Perlina Alexander 23 Dec. 1835                   Cole
Bruchenelle, Doisel to Louise LaPerche 15 May 1830                 StCh
Brue, Daniel to Elizabeth Pigg 31 Dec. 1835                        StFr
Bruer, Wm. to Polly Shock 9 Nov. 1837                              Boon
Bruette, Joseph to Polly Patrick 25 Sept. 1825                     StFr
Bruice, Jacob to Eliza A. Smith 10 Nov. 1836                       Monr
```

Bruion, Evan to Mary Aubury 22 May 1823   StCh
Brumet, Henry to Mariah Brockhaust 5 Oct. 1834   StCh
Brumfield, Richard B. to Sally Boon 5 May 1831   StCh
Brumley, James to Diannah Bilyew 19 Jan. 1832   Cr-1
Brummitt, Wm. to Sally Evans -- July 1827   Char
Brundle, Wm. to Mary Sullivan 15 Dec. 1836   Jeff
Brundrage, David to Susan Williamson 17 Dec. 1826   Wash
Brunes, Jacob to Sarah Colvin 18 Nov. 1834   Boon
Brunk, Wm. to Iyden Coyl 4 Apr. 1835   Linc
Brushwood, John to Sarah Pace 30 Dec. 1834   Boon
Bruster, Daniel to Juliet Corn 28 Dec. 1835   Cr-1
Bryan, Harvey to Mary A. Robnett 23 May 1839   Boon
Bryan, James to Melindy Morgan 16 Apr. 1818   StCh
Bryan, James to Grace Scott 14 Oct. 1830   StCh
Bryan, James H. to Eliza A. Bogart 3 May 1838   Ray
Bryan, Jefferson to Jane Bird 20 May 1837   Livi
Bryan, John to Elizabeth McCutchen 27 Mar. 1832   Boon
Bryan, John to Violina Callaway 14 Feb. 1833   Warr
Bryan, John G. to Avaline McAlvain 6 Nov. 1827   Wash
Bryan, John H. to Eliza A. Gentry 19 Jan. 1836   Boon
Bryan, Joseph to Parthena Bryan 13 Feb. 1812   StCh
Bryan, Joseph to Sarah Winson 29 Sept. 1816   Howa
Bryan, Joseph G. to Patsey Hanley 10 Feb. 1829   CG-A
Bryan, Milton to Zerilda Moss 2 Oct. 1834   Boon
Bryan, Morgan to Elizabeth Callaway 16 Feb. 1815   StCh
Bryan, Wm. to Mary VanBibber 14 Oct. 1838   StCh
Bryan, Wm. B. to Elizabeth J. Hamilton 3 May 1832   Lafa
Bryan, Wm. K. to Elizabeth Hall 6 Dec. 1838   Warr
Bryand, Benj. to Nancy Morris 7 Apr. 1836   Cole
Bryans, Hiram to Missouri Parmer 30 Mar. 1833   Carr
Bryant, Clifton to Elizabeth Jones 15 Aug. 1839   Lafa
Bryant, David to Polly Stroud 29 Mar. 1812   CG-1
Bryant, Edward A. to Sophia J. Baker 20 Dec. 1836   Lewi
Bryant, Geo. W. to Malvina Roden 12 Mar. 1835   Jeff
Bryant, John A. to Nancy Hay 29 Dec. 1836   Clar
Bryant, Joseph to Patsy Bates 11 Feb. 1834   Boon
Bryant, Richard to Elizabeth Johnston 10 Jan. 1837   Monr
Bryant, Thomas to Hannah Jewell 21 Dec. 1837   Mari
Bryant, Toliver to Sarah E. Hackney 26 Jan. 1837   Call
Bryant, Wm. to Betsey Sloan 17 Aug. 1824   Coop
Bryant, Wm. to Vuela Adams 8 Sept. 1833   Jack
Bryon, Rawleigh to Julian Lindsey 26 Feb. 1835   Pk-1
Bryson, Isaac N. to Margaret Love 8 May 1838   Pk-B
Bryson, Wm. to Liza Yates 7 June 1827   Pk-1
Buate, Henry to Julie Ranger 19 Jan. 1828   Wash
Buchanan, Alexander to Ellen Barber 4 Sept. 1838   Linc
Buchanan, Elijah to Elizabeth Stallard 29 Nov. 1838   Linc
Buchanan, James S. to Lucinas Rosson 26 June 1839   Maco
Buchanan, Robt. H. to Polly A. Summer 4 July 1835   Monr
Buchannon, Wm. to Martha Warren 14 Feb. 1831   Call
Buchanon, John to Carline Abbot 6 Dec. 1837   Monr
Buck, Perry G. to Rebecca Thomas 28 June 1823   Sali
Buckhanan, Thomas to Liana Fisher 24 Oct. 1835   Pk-1
Buckhannan, Stephen to Rachel C. Duncan 20 Sept. 1838   Clay
Buckley, Alfred T. to Elizabeth Noland 5 Mar. 1834   Jack
Buckley, John to Eva Berkett 26 Apr. 1837   Call
Buckner, Alexander to Mrs. Rebecca Weems 26 Mar. 1820   CG-1
Buckner, Alexander to Martha A. Lacy 8 Dec. 1839   Md-B
Buckner, Edwin to Hester Wall 10 Nov. 1831   CG-A
Buckner, Wm. to Elizabeth A. Barlow 29 Mar. 1838   Cole
Buckridge, James to Elizabeth Culp 31 Aug. 1836   Clin
Buckridge, Joseph to Nancy Levingston 23 Aug. 1827   Clay
Bud, Robt. to Caroline Young 2 Dec. 1834   Boon
Buey, David to Polly Harvey 29 Mar. 1832   Linc
Buff, Martin to Feely Simpson 20 Sept. 1836   John

Buford, Christopher Y. to Mary Nifong 29 Oct. 1839   Md-B
Buford, Legrand to Eusebia Mallory 17 Jan. 1030   Lafa
Buford, Thomas to Calphurna Carty 26 June 1831   Wash
Bukner, Benj. to Rachel Brooks 5 Oct. 1837   John
Buley, Asberry to Clemmentine Wintine 1 Aug. 1837   Polk
Bulkley, Austarchus to Sarah Landsdale 25 Dec. 1838   Mari
Bullard, Jesse to Fulta Teeters 21 Feb. 1839   Boon
Bullard, Marcus to Susannah Burnet 1 Feb. 1835   Call
Bullard, Nathaniel to Mrs. Sally Langley 21 Oct. 1819   Coop
Bullard, Wm. to Sarah Boyce 2 Sept. 1834   Boon
Bullinger, Daniel to Christina Seabach 11 Feb. 1817   CG-1
Bullinger, Jefferson to Sally Adams 10 Nov. 1831   CG-A
Bullinger, Joseph to Sally Kinder 25 July 1833   CG-A
Bullock, Charles P. to Rowina V. Allen 10 Nov. 1831   Mari
Bullock, John C. to Sally Stewart 6 Jan. 1833   Mari
Bultner, Nicholas to Greitner Kunigunde 22 Dec. 1839   StCh
Bumgardner, Lewis to Hester Halstead 5 Nov. 1833   Howa
Bunch, John to Nancy H. Tally 15 Sept. 1839   Henr
Bunch, Jonathan to Jane Craig 9 Dec. 1821   Char
Bunch, Thomas C. to Ann Rossar 20 Jan. 1824   Howa
Bunch, Thompson to Nancy Hays 26 Aug. 1826   Call
Bunn, Geo. to Sarah Turner 25 Nov. 1830   Pk-1
Bunnard, Isaac to Susanna Mahon 26 Nov. 1820   Howa
Buno, John to Frances Hudson 9 May 1826   Clay
Burbord, Paschel to Mary McVickers 4 Mar. 1838   Lewi
Burbridge, Joseph H. to Sally Jordan 2 July 1829   Pk-1
Burch, Harvey to Sally Smith 9 Mar. 1826   Coop
Burch, John to Margaret Sappington 9 Apr. 1822   Fran
Burch, Lamuel to Eleanor Lock 24 Apr. 1823   Char
Burch, Thomas C. to Celenary Jacobs 23 Jan. 1834   Ray
Burch, Wm. to Malvina James 25 May 1826   Howa
Burcham, Joseph to Mary Reed 16 Mar. 1837   Md-B
Burchard, Andrew to Elizabeth Agee 1 Apr. 1839   Gasc
Burchard, Geo. to Mary Agee 21 Sept. 1837   Gasc
Burchart, Samuel to Barbara Barbark 4 Jan. 1827   Gasc
Burchfield, James to Harriet Sullivant 3 Sept. 1837   Fran
Burchfield, Yong to Lisebeth Jones 31 Jan. 1838   Mari
Burckhart, Christopher F. to Elizabeth Hill 21 Dec. 1837   Rand
Burckhart, Greenberry to Elenor C. Whittenburg 14 June 1833 Monr
Burckloe, Michael to Nancy Moore 12 July 1838   Linc
Burd, Alexander to Matilda Phillips 27 Dec. 1838   Morg
Burden, Eldridge to Patsy Waddell 24 Oct. 1837   Lafa
Burden, John to Nancy Painter 7 Mar. 1837   Gree
Burden, Robt. to Eliza Turnham 16 Feb. 1836   Clay
Burdett, Columbus C. to Jane Campbell 21 Jan. 1827   Md-A
Bures, James to Sary Hughes 21 Oct. 1834   Howa
Burford, Miles W. to Nancy J. Burford 1 June 1839   Monr
Burford, Wm. M. to Nancy F. Nunn 19 June 1839   Clar
Burgan, Wm. to Rhode A. Gibson 9 Sept. 1827   Coop
Burgass, Edward to Eleanor Isgriggs 6 June 1839   Wash
Burge, John to Elizabeth Powell 6 July 1828   Cole
Burger, Conner to Susan ---- 30 Sept. 1830   Cole
Burgess, Thomas to Mary A. Cadwallader 17 May 1832   Jeff
Burgess, Vachel to Catherine Calloway 10 Jan. 1839   Lafa
Burget, John E. to Mary Flynn 16 Sept. 1828   Perr
Burgin, John to Mary Blanton 25 June 1829   Jack
Burgin, John to Sarah A. Green 17 Feb. 1839   Rand
Burgin, Samuel to Betsy Blent 11 Jan. 1834   Jack
Burgoyne, John to Mary Byonids 27 Mar. 1827   Gasc
Burk, Evan H. to Mary W. Overton 5 Jan. 1834   Jack
Burk, James to Anny Mouney 7 June 1830   Perr
Burk, John M. to Keziah Bunnell 22 Jan. 1835   Clay
Burk, Stephen to Elizabeth Howdershell 6 Aug. 1829   Linc
Burk, Thomas T. to Barsheba Summers 11 Feb. 1830   Rand
Burk, Wm. to Lurenna Thornton 5 Sept. 1824   Howa

Burk, Wm. to Levina Reed 5 Nov. 1837	Sali
Burke, Joseph to Mary Rhodes 27 Sept. 1821	Md-A
Burke, Wm. to Milly Shock 20 Mar. 1823	Boon
Burke, Wm. to Polly Foster 21 July 1836	Md-B
Burkett, Thomas W. to Catharine Hyre 10 Aug. 1837	Cr-1
Burklow, Geo. to Engeline Burns 10 May 1838	StCh
Burks, Charles to Elizabeth Murphey 24 Jan. 1836	StFr
Burks, Charles W. to Narcissa Hudson 31 July 1839	Boon
Burks, James to Martha Downey 6 Dec. 1836	Boon
Burks, James P. to Martha Newman 31 Aug. 1831	Call
Burks, Westly to Agness Wright 20 Dec. 1828	Boon
Burksley, Jesse G. to Cornelia Woolsey 9 Nov. 1826	Coop
Burleson, Joseph to Polly Warren 21 Feb. 1821	Sali
Burley, Steven to Polly A. Flecher 4 Jan. 1838	Md-B
Burley, Wm. to Hesteran Graham 1 June 1837	Md-B
Burlison, James to Lucina Hardridge 29 Dec. 1836	Cr-1
Burnam, Diamishus to Nancy Snell 9 Sept. 1830	Howa
Burnam, Elijah to Sarah Reynolds 28 Sept. 1822	Howa
Burnam, Faustor to Mariah Pemberton 28 Nov. 1826	Howa
Burnam, Waston to Cynthia Pemberton 26 Sept. 1827	Howa
Burnard, Wm. to Abigail Harper 4 Aug. 1825	Coop
Burnes, John C. to Jannet F. Kitchen 12 June 1838	Rand
Burnes, Wm. H. to Leviney Wilkerson 10 June 1838	Polk
Burnet, Franklin to Jane Johnston 17 May 1827	Pk-1
Burnett, Aquilla to Judith Chaffin 9 Nov. 1826	Cole
Burnett, Chesley to Elizabeth Burns 13 Dec. 1832	Coop
Burnett, Equilla to Ann E. Finley 4 Oct. 1837	Polk
Burnett, Geo. W. to Sidney S. Younger 10 Nov. 1831	Clay
Burnett, John to Sally Johnson 30 Mar. 1828	Pk-1
Burnett, John to Jane McCombs 18 Jan. 1838	Morg
Burnett, Ruben to Isabella Kelsy 10 Mar. 1839	Morg
Burnett, Thomas to Sarah Howell 18 Aug. 1836	Ray
Burnett, Washington to Eliza Asbury 4 Oct. 1838	Lewi
Burnett, Wilson to Mary Liggett 27 Aug. 1833	Jack
Burnette, Jone to Mariah Burnett 20 Jan. 1839	Henr
Burney, Alexander A. to Elizabeth W. Hall 12 Oct. 1837	Lafa
Burney, Wm. to Sally A. Barnes 26 Mar. 1833	Pett
Burnley, Henry to Laurania Street 25 Nov. 1808	CG-1
Burns, Arthur to Sally Moore 14 Dec. 1825	Pk-1
Burns, Charles to Nancy Sampson 18 June 1834	Clay
Burns, David to Margaret Taylor 28 Apr. 1836	Perr
Burns, Henry to Nancy A. Evans 16 Dec. 1838	Perr
Burns, Ignatius to Elizabeth Bailey 21 June 1832	Pk-1
Burns, Isaac to Phebe Persner 7 Jan. 1821	Howa
Burns, James to Lucinda Brewer 10 Feb. 1834	Perr
Burns, James L. to Joannah Gennings 19 July 1838	Clin
Burns, James M. to Margaret Forsythe 22 May 1834	Coop
Burns, John to Malinda Dixon 23 Dec. 1828	Perr
Burns, John P.W. to Lucinda J. Burke 7 Nov. 1839	Morg
Burns, Michael to Rebecca Long 3 Dec. 1823	Perr
Burns, Michael A. to Mary McLaughlin 7 Mar. 1839	Call
Burns, Reppenson to Polly Garrison 26 Nov. 1833	Perr
Burns, Robt. to Margaret Willis 25 Nov. 1832	CG-A
Burns, Samuel to Elizabeth Ferguson 30 July 1832	CG-A
Burns, Thomas to Elizabeth Green 30 May 1839	Howa
Burns, Wm. to Martha M. Taylor 25 Dec. 1833	Perr
Burns, Wm. to C.H. Throckmorton 24 Dec. 1835	Call
Burns, Wm. to Anna Wood 5 Jan. 1837	Md-B
Burns, Wm. to Malinda Raridon 14 Sept. 1837	Perr
Buros, Thomas to Susan Blith 8 Apr. 1839	Howa
Burress, David to Susannah Monroe 8 Nov. 1812	StCh
Burress, Wm. to Martha Summers 27 Dec. 1831	Rand
Burris, Charles to Emily Bradley 23 Jan. 1837	Boon
Burris, Isaac to Eliza A. Foreman 6 Jan. 1836	Monr
Burris, John to Janaty Bradley 15 May 1835	Lafa

Burris, Thomas to Liddina Barker 4 Apr. 1839   Lafa
Burriss, Maston to Judy Loyd 23 July 1833   Jack
Burriss, Wm. to Lewhetty Burriss 30 June 1833   Jack
Burriss, Wm. to Basheba Masters 30 Jan. 1834   Jack
Burros, Thomas to Ann Byrnside 24 June 1827   Fran
Burrow, Samuel to Catherine Pinkerton 8 Jan. 1834   Perr
Burrus, Benj. to Ann Baxter 10 Jan. 1832   Jack
Burrus, Jeremiah to Sarah Baxter 3 July 1828   Jack
Burshears, Calton to Elizabeth Cook 27 Mar. 1836   Howa
Bursley, Wm. to Sary A. Sawyers 14 June 1838   Cass
Burt, Israel N. to Susan H. January 4 Oct. 1832   Pk-1
Burt, John A. to Basheba Fulkerson 27 Feb. 1827   StCh
Burthall, Wm. to Mary Campbell 6 Nov. 1828   Boon
Burton, Ambrose to Martha Fort 22 Sept. 1836   Rand
Burton, Charles to Lucy S. Nelson 29 Dec. 1833   Monr
Burton, James W. to Phebe Pane 2 May 1836   Char
Burton, Jeremiah to Catharine Swinney 7 May 1837   Monr
Burton, John to Sally Allred 15 Nov. 1832   Monr
Burton, John to Mahala Findley 27 Mar. 1834   Howa
Burton, John to Mary Garnet 22 Nov. 1836   Mari
Burton, John M. to Elizabeth Kelly 11 May 1828   Rall
Burton, John N. to Susan McCord 24 May 1835   Pk-1
Burton, Joseph to Elizabeth Carley 11 Jan. 1829   Howa
Burton, Joseph W. to Orpha J. Brooks 22 Dec. 1838   Rand
Burton, Samuel to Frances L. Dameron 27 May 1834   Rand
Burton, Sharod to Eliza Groomer 10 Dec. 1839   Clay
Burton, Simeon to Nancy Alsbury 22 Nov. 1838   Monr
Burton, Thomas to Elizabeth Hendrickson 14 May 1838   Jeff
Burton, Wm. to Mrs. Mary A. Johnson 29 Feb. 1834   Howa
Burton, Willis to Nancy Standley 14 Aug. 1837   Howa
Burus, George to Durrika Jameson -- June 1836   Linc
Burwell, Walter to Lydia Cox 26 Apr. 1821   Lafa
Busby, John to Rosanna McCall 9 Aug. 1807   StCh
Buscher, H.H. to Christ. M. Kuddlemeyer 20 Jan. 1837 StCh
Bush, Felix E. to Almyra Derbin 19 Apr. 1835   Clay
Bush, George to Ibby James 4 July 1830   Clay
Bush, John to Margaret Gardner 23 June 1825   Rall
Bush, Paleamon to Mary J.S. Devore 30 Dec. 1833   Wash
Bushe, Richard to Katharine Solomon 4 Nov. 1835   Jeff
Busley, John to Sarah Dunnaway 13 Jan. 1829   Jack
Busley, Robert to Rachel Leggett 28 July 1831   Jack
Buster, James to Lucy S. Younger 25 Nov. 1825   Clay
Busurer, A.D. to Elizabeth Gorden 3 Aug. 1837   Ray
Butcher, Bazeles E. to Martha Oliver 29 Nov. 1836   StCh
Butcher, Isam to Margaret Oliver 8 Dec. 1834   StCh
Butcher, Joseph to Rebecca Bruce 30 Sept. 1838   Pk-B
Butcher, Nelsen to Amely Blevins 29 Jan. 1828   Boon
Butcher, Robt. to Elizabeth Wilcoxson 11 June 1822   Howa
Butler, Bledsoe to Ann Royers 8 Dec. 1830   Linc
Butler, David G. to Nancy Welch 20 July 1837   Cass
Butler, Dudley to Matilda Lighter 25 Oct. 1827   Pk-1
Butler, George to Martha Craft 8 Feb. 1839   Clin
Butler, James to Nancy Robison 15 Mar. 1838   Clin
Butler, Jesse to Candais Langston 1 Feb. 1821   Howa
Butler, Joel to Margaret E. Morrison 12 Aug. 1831   Cr-1
Butler, Jonah to Celia Hinshaw 14 Mar. 1837   Cass
Butler, Ransom to Eliza A. Elkins 29 Oct. 1839   Plat
Butler, Thomas to Elizabeth Tackett 29 Aug. 1833   Gasc
Butler, Wm. to Lucinda League 26 Feb. 1837   Jeff
Butler, Wm. R. to Louisa Young 27 June 1837   Pett
Butlers, Thomas to Liza Capehart 8 Mar. 1838   Gasc
Butt, Geo. W. to Martha Wilkinson 17 Dec. 1834   Wash
Butt, John to Matilda Moon 22 Dec. 1835   Jeff
Butter, Joseph to Barbara Tackett 29 Jan. 1829   Gasc
Butter, Wm. to Margaret Warden 1 Apr. 1827   Jack

34

```
Butterfield, David G. to Nancy Grayham 26 Feb. 1827          Jack
Butts, Henry to Elizabeth Drummonds 4 Aug. 1831             Jack
Butts, Jackson to Jane Lovelady 29 Jan. 1835               Jack
Buxton, John to Polly Berman 18 Feb. 1834                  StCh
Buzz, Didymus E. to Sarah Langley 10 Mar. 1839             Call
Buzzard, John to Jane Spergin 19 July 1838                 Barr
Byam, James to Martha A. Knapp 8 Aug. 1837                 Clay
Byars, Preston to Maria Fleming 1 Nov. 1830                Boon
Bybee, James to Elizabeth Kemp 26 Feb. 1839                Morg
Bybee, John to Nancy Adams 10 Dec. 1828                    Howa
Bybee, John S. to Mary Kyle 9 Jan. 1834                    Monr
Bybee, John S. to Jenetta C. Reed 26 April 1837            Monr
Bybee, Levi to Jale Birdsong 20 Feb. 1839                  Morg
Bybee, Nealey to Mildred Wright 21 Aug. 1837               Monr
Bybee, Norman to Cynthia Crigler 31 Oct. 1837              Monr
Byington, Samuel to Emily Breassie 15 Nov. 1832            StFr
Byler, Abraham to Polly Bowman 3 Feb. 1831                 Coop
Byler, David to Nancy Lilly 13 Mar. 1832                   Coop
Byler, Jacob to Louiza Stephens 20 Jan. 1831               Coop
Byler, Joab to Eliza Gilbreath 17 Jan. 1829                Coop
Byler, Joseph to Mary Wilson 10 Aug. 1835                  Coop
Byler, Thomas to Jane Gilbreath 9 Apr. 1829                Coop
Bynum, Gray to Nancy Cooper 20 Dec. 1812                   StCh
Byrd, Amos to Margaret A. Hatcher 11 Apr. 1839             CG-B
Byrd, John to Polly Davenport 17 June 1826                 CG-A
Byrd, Moses to Ellender Hughes 21 Feb. 1805                CG-1
Byrd, Overton to Martha Tesson 25 Feb. 1836                Jeff
Byrd, Richard to Nancy Leegate 7 Dec. 1828                 Howa
Byrd, Wm. to Millyann Rentfro 12 Apr. 1837                 CG-A
Byrd, Wm. G. to Ann Dunn 29 Sept. 1825                     CG-A
Byrem, Benj. to Sarah Ginnings 22 Nov. 1836               Howa
Byrem, Henry to Mahala Roberts 19 Dec. 1838               Howa
Byrne, Morgan to Jane Green 29 Sept. 1811                  CG-1
Byrne, Moses to Rebecca Cox 9 Dec. 1810                    CG-1
Byrnes, Charles to Lucinda J. Cheaney 30 Dec. 1834         Boon
Byrnside, Caldwell to Salina Campbell 22 Sept. 1831        Fran
Byrnsides, John to Betsy Hinton 2 Mar. 1820               Fran
Byrum, Ely to Lydia West 25 Apr. 1832                     Clay
Bysfield, John to Mary J. White 29 Nov. 1838              Boon


Cabishee, Anthony to Nancy Owens 9 Apr. 1837              Polk
Cable, Henry to Rachel Stricklan 24 Jan. 1839             Wash
Cadwallader, Charles to Mariah Bridwell 4 May 1837        Jeff
Cadwallader, Miller to Virginia Shelton 18 Apr. 1838      Jeff
Cady, Thomas to Elizabeth Furgeson 22 Apr. 1833           Perr
Cagill, Wm. to Abagail Vaughn 12 Sept. 1837               Ray
Cahill, Perry to Katharine Triplett 9 Aug. 1835           Fran
Cahill, Perry to Rebecca Rice 10 Feb. 1839                Fran
Cahom, Wm. to Polly Johnson 17 Dec. 1834                  Rand
Cain, Elias to Charlotte Craig 13 Aug. 1837               StCh
Cain, Geo. to Martha Cole 12 Mar. 1835                    Wash
Cain, James to Mahala McCoy 30 June 1831                  StCh
Cain, John to Emily Hill 28 Aug. 1825                     Char
Cain, Jonathan to Narcissa Hinson 4 July 1822             Gasc
Cain, Matthew to Mrs. Frances T. Logan 14 Feb. 1838       StCh
Caisy, Andrew to Therese Heafner 13 Feb. 1838             Wash
Calaway, Wm. P. to Lucinda Sylvey 12 Apr. 1837            StCh
Calbert, Claborn to Anna E. Moss 15 Mar. 1832             Clay
Calbert, John B. to Anna Newel 7 May 1834                 Cole
Caldwell, Alva to Rachel Decker 29 Jan. 1829              Fran
Caldwell, Archable to Priscilla Sumner 31 Oct. 1826       StCh
Caldwell, David to Margaret Able 6 Oct. 1825              CG-A
Caldwell, David to Elizabeth Cowan 12 Mar. 1834           Gasc
Caldwell, David L. to Margaret Manning 17 Apr. 1830       Perr
```

Caldwell, Harmon to Mary Caldwell 30 Oct. 1837	Rall
Caldwell, Harris to Jane Vinyard 22 Oct. 1833	Gasc
Caldwell, James D. to Eliza I. Briggs 1 Jan. 1825	Rall
Caldwell, James P. to Ann Caldwell 6 May 1838	Fran
Caldwell, John to Polly A. Stockton 20 Oct. 1829	Boon
Caldwell, John to Louisa Douglass 26 Nov. 1830	Fran
Caldwell, John G. to Mildred Buckner 8 Oct. 1839	Monr
Caldwell, Kinkead to Mary Clark 25 Mar. 1824	Fran
Caldwell, Kinkead to Polly Cantty 10 Aug. 1828	Fran
Caldwell, McKigy to Lucretia Dauherty 20 Dec. 1824	Fran
Caldwell, Robt. to Indiana Adams 23 Sept. 1830	Rall
Caldwell, Samuel H. to Barbary Briggs 31 Aug. 1830	Rall
Caldwell, Short to Joanna Williams 25 Feb. 1830	Fran
Caldwell, Thomas to Lucinda McBride 2 Sept. 1838	Boon
Caldwell, Wm. to Margaret Mull 15 July 1832	Linc
Calhoon, James to Mary A. Fry 30 July 1835	CG-B
Calhoon, John B. to Jane Pennington 5 Feb. 1833	Gree
Calhoun, John M. to Susan Tracy 12 May 1831	Rall
Call, John to Sarah McCourtney 25 Dec. 1834	Fran
Callaghan, Wm. to Asenath Thompson 17 Jan. 1833	Mari
Callahan, Dennis to Sarah Jewell 3 June 1824	Boon
Callahan, John to Judy Willingham 22 June 1829	Boon
Callas, Rice to Sarah Kelly 1 Dec. 1822	Coop
Callaway, Charles L. to Leannah Wilcox 22 Aug. 1827	Boon
Callaway, James to Caroline Coplin 20 Oct. 1836	Md-B
Callaway, James to Mary J. McKenney 19 July 1838	Warr
Callaway, James V. to Susan Kemp 9 Feb. 1832	Call
Callaway, John B. to Elizabeth Keaton 22 Feb. 1809	StCh
Callaway, Joseph to June E. Craghead 28 Apr. 1839	Call
Callaway, Joseph P. to Nancy Coats 12 Dec. 1822	Call
Callaway, Larkin F. to Susan Howell 21 Dec. 1815	StCh
Callaway, Thomas H. to Patience Keel 24 Dec. 1826	StCh
Callaway, Wm. to Tabitha Coats 9 Apr. 1829	Call
Callihan, Otho S.W. to Henrietta Neuman 26 Apr. 1838	Cole
Callison, Wm. to Nancy Moore 26 Apr. 1832	Call
Callison, Wm. to Polly Cooper 1 June 1837	Morg
Calloway, Ambrose to Susan Jackson -- Oct. 1823	Howa
Calloway, Flanders to Susanna Smith 3 July 1830	Howa
Calloway, James to Ann Waddell 17 Jan. 1839	Lafa
Calloway, Spottswood H. to Polly Tilford 19 Mar. 1828	Boon
Calloway, Stephen to Mary A. Reynolds 2 May 1836	Howa
Callue, Maclain to Louisa Bledsoe 14 Feb. 1835	Cass
Caloway, Andrew to Mrs. Mildred Harrel 14 Feb. 1837	Linc
Caltrum, Calven to Huldah Williams 14 July 1835	Boon
Calvert, Elias to Kesiah Hughes 25 Apr. 1839	Coop
Calvert, John to Enmical Rollin 20 Apr. 1832	Howa
Calvert, Leonard to Rocksey Morley 4 Dec. 1829	Coop
Calvert, Noddy to Jane Bowls 13 Nov. 1823	Coop
Calvert, Peter to Patsy Vaughn 26 Nov. 1835	Coop
Calvert, Wm. Jr. to Martha Mitchell 26 July 1837	Coop
Calvert, Wm. W. to Priscilla Tittsworth 31 Dec. 1839	Coop
Calvin, Elijah to Perlina Lapp 25 Dec. 1828	Linc
Calvin, John to Rosannah Sherwood 6 Jan. 1835	Pk-1
Calwell, Archibald to Susannah Milburn 3 Jan. 1836	StCh
Cambren, Benj. to Adelia Hagen 24 Feb. 1829	Perr
Cambren, James to Elizabeth Grass 1 May 1827	Perr
Cameron, David R. to Susannah Wellborn 15 Mar. 1829	Jack
Cameron, Jonathan to Phebe Conner 27 Sept. 1827	Jack
Camp, Hiram H. to Francis Bishop 21 Feb. 1839	Warr
Campbell, A.B. to Sarah A. Gill 19 Dec. 1837	StCh
Campbell, Alexander to Jane Stuart 21 May 1834	StCh
Campbell, Alexander to Polly Brown 11 Jan. 1835	Ray
Campbell, Benj. to Catherine Short 22 Mar. 1838	Cole
Campbell, Bradley to Meekey Hall 21 July 1829	Coop
Campbell, Caleb W. to Virginia Ashley 11 Nov. 1838	Lafa

Campbell, Colin C. to Lucy A. Eidson 3 Jan. 1838   Md-B
Campbell, Cyrenus to Mary A. Risher 8 May 1828   CG-A
Campbell, David to Amelia Pepper 26 Aug. 1821   Howa
Campbell, Elisha to Rebecca Pence 31 Jan. 1828   Clay
Campbell, Francis to Indianna Boone 22 Oct. 1829   Pk-1
Campbell, Geo. to Mary A. Stones 29 Oct. 1829   Md-A
Campbell, Geo. to Lucinda Vance 12 Sept. 1833   Clay
Campbell, Geo. W. to Louisa G. Pollock 21 Feb. 1839   Coop
Campbell, Harvey to Ann E. Armstrong 23 Nov. 1837   Fran
Campbell, Henry J. to Sophia Palen 2 Apr. 1837   Lewi
Campbell, James to Matilda Allcorn 10 Nov. 1826   Howa
Campbell, James to Eveline Pence 10 Jan. 1828   Clay
Campbell, James to Elizabeth Lee 6 June 1837   Wash
Campbell, James M. to Clarissa Hempstead 15 Aug. 1831   StCh
Campbell, James T. to Mary A. Blackwell 16 May 1832   Cr-1
Campbell, James W. to Sophia A. Henry 1 Aug. 1827   Linc
Campbell, Jefferson to Sarah McCarty 18 Jan. 1838   Lafa
Campbell, Jeremiah to Polly Thompson 23 Jan. 1834   Cr-1
Campbell, Joel to Rosanna Love 8 June 1826   Pk-1
Campbell, John to Armitta Dowty 19 June 1828   CG-A
Campbell, John to Sarah Thomas 17 June 1835   Char
Campbell, John to Elizabeth Lanair 30 Dec. 1838   Morg
Campbell, John to Nancy Boyd 31 Jan. 1839   Call
Campbell, John C. to Mary Herry 8 June 1833   Linc
Campbell, Joseph to Martha Compton 23 Dec. 1830   Wash
Campbell, Joshua to Sidney R. Ewing 6 Feb. 1823   Coop
Campbell, Masters to Sarah Armstrong 21 Feb. 1828   Fran
Campbell, Moses to Nancy B. Hillhouse 5 July 1830   Cr-1
Campbell, Robt. C. to Polly A. McGough 26 Feb. 1834   Carr
Campbell, Samuel to Julian Pence 30 Sept. 1834   Clay
Campbell, Samuel H. to Elizabeth Darby 12 Jan. 1832   Pk-1
Campbell, Squire B. to Emeline Taylor 23 Aug. 1838   Morg
Campbell, Thomas to Frankey Cooper 29 Apr. 1822   Howa
Campbell, Thomas to Pembleton Paul 21 Oct. 1822   Howa
Campbell, Thomas to Elizabeth Paul 11 Mar. 1827   Howa
Campbell, Thomas to Martha West 25 Sept. 1839   Call
Campbell, Wm. to Lufamy Baity 10 May 1821   Coop
Campbell, Wm. to Millindia David 31 Jan. 1828   Md-A
Campbell, Wm. to Hannah Pence 29 Jan. 1829   Clay
Campbell, Wm. to Eliza Hopkins 18 July 1833   Wash
Campbell, Wm. to Matilda Frieze 25 June 1836   Polk
Campbell, Wm. A. to Martha Proctor 24 May 1838   John
Campbell, Winsen to Margaret Morris 5 Dec. 1833   Fran
Campbell, Zachariah to Emily Robinson 22 July 1830   Wash
Campbill, John W. to Serena Byrd 9 Aug. 1836   CG-A
Camplin, Edward to Mary J. Ware 28 Jan. 1836   Boon
Camplin, Elijah to Emily Fisher 8 Apr. 1838   Boon
Camron, Anderson to Elizabeth Baldwin 2 Dec. 1832   Clay
Camron, Calvin to Ann Critesman 22 Dec. 1835   Clay
Camron, Elish to Jane Culp 9 Dec. 1827   Clay
Camron, James to Nancy Roberts 21 Feb. 1830   Clay
Camron, John to Mary Tate 25 Feb. 1830   Mari
Camron, Neal to Mercy Carlile 24 May 1837   Rall
Camster, Geo. to Patsy English 20 Feb. 1823   CG-1
Canada, Ambrose to Mary McDonel 25 Jan. 1827   Coop
Canada, Howard to Eliza J. Wayne 28 Mar. 1839   Boon
Canada, John to Margaret Pew 31 Aug. 1826   CG-A
Cane, David to Mahala Thompson 5 Nov. 1829   Wash
Cannefax, Benj. to Nancy Townsend 18 Dec. 1834   Gree
Cannon, Ephraim to Dorothy Hunter 20 Nov. 1825   Linc
Cannon, Dr. F. to Mary M. Dunklin 15 Mar. 1835   Cole
Cannon, Lewis to Nancy Rods 19 Mar. 1828   StFr
Cannon, Philip to Elizabeth McCoy 15 Mar. 1827   StCh
Canole, Amos to Nancy Daniel 7 Mar. 1836   Howa
Cansler, John to Matilda Renshaw 4 Jan. 1826   Md-A

Canter, Levy to Elizabeth Caton 5 June 1834   Warr
Canterberry, Elijah to Frances Canterberry 25 Dec. 1839   CG-B
Canterberry, Nemrod to Mildred Yancey 10 Apr. 1838   Monr
Canterberry, Reuben M. to Sarah O. Woodson 16 Mar. 1837   Mari
Canterbery, Benj. to Sarah Rete 29 Sept. 1839   John
Canterbury, Geo. to Nancy McPherson 15 Aug. 1837   Mari
Canterbury, Nimrod to Mary Tuckfield 10 Aug. 1837   Mari
Canthron, James to Frances L. Colvin 5 Jan. 1837   Linc
Cantley, John L. to Elizabeth Caldwell 17 Dec. 1837   Fran
Cantrel, Charles to Neoma Cox 26 July 1826   Lafa
Cantrell, Christopher to Narcissa Whaley 24 Nov. 1839   Lafa
Cantrill, Phillip to Polly Richey 1 Apr. 1831   Lafa
Cantrille, Wm. to Margaret Robinson 4 Dec. 1838   John
Cantwell, Wm. to Melvene Calloway 21 Apr. 1835   Md-A
Capehart, James to Juda Crizman 15 Sept. 1831   Gasc
Capehart, John to Louisa Hughes 8 Apr. 1830   Gasc
Capherte, Thomas to Agnes Pryor 19 July 1827   Gasc
Capler, Henry to Polly Jacson 25 May 1834   Wash
Capps, Benj. to Nancy Liggon -- Aug. 1836   Linc
Capps, David to Sarah Goodwin 31 Dec. 1835   Linc
Capps, Silas to Julyann Brumly 1 Apr. 1838   Mill
Caraway, Archibald to Mary J. Serphim 4 May 1834   Wash
Cardinal, Jean M. to Angelique Bruziere 7 Aug. 1820   StCh
Cardwell, John G. to Faith Donmeal 16 Mar. 1837   Gree
Cardwell, Madison to Hannah M. Stipe 13 Oct. 1836   Lewi
Carey, Abijah to Sophiah Woodcock 3 May 1839   Buch
Carey, Creed to Polly Beaty 15 Mar. 1835   Carr
Carey, Daniel to Mrs. Maryann Bivens 1 Feb. 1834   Clay
Carey, James to Elizabeth E. Earheart 7 Feb. 1839   Mari
Carey, Madison to Mary A. Lynch 12 Mar. 1838   Jack
Carico, Benedict to Luvina Hardesty 7 Feb. 1837   Monr
Carle, Edwin to Segia P. Mills 15 Jan. 1835   StCh
Carle, Richmond J. to Frances B.E. Wells 7 June 1837   StCh
Carley, ---- to Elizabeth Laws 11 Oct. 1838   StFr
Carlile, Vincent to Narcissa Black 2 Dec. 1821   Ray
Carlisle, James to Rebecca Crow 7 Mar. 1839   Gree
Carlisle, Ormond to Susan Wright 15 July 1838   Rand
Carlisle, Thomas to Mariah Leach 8 Apr. 1831   Howa
Carlos, Carter M.D. to Frances Hudson 18 Jan. 1838   Boon
Carlton, Baptiste to Mely Gunnville 29 May 1838   Jack
Carman, John B. to Margaret J. Glass 7 Oct. 1838   Lewi
Carmichael, Isaac to Permela Lowery 4 Dec. 1834   Lafa
Carmichael, Martin to Margaret Clendennon 1 Mar. 1838   Cole
Carnal, Jesse to Mahala Blankenship 10 Jan. 1832   Rall
Carnett, Robert to Mary A. Strong 13 Feb. 1838   Cass
Carney, James to Elizabeth Gillcheast 5 Dec. 1839   Howa
Carny, Richard E. to Henrietta Shewmate 17 June 1835   Cr-1
Carothers, Armstrong to Mrs. Margaret Boggs 5 Sept. 1838   Rall
Carpenter, Benj. F. to Matilda Underwood 7 Feb. 1839   Barr
Carpenter, Criston to Elmira Geehon 24 Apr. 1835   Morg
Carpenter, David to Caroline Orsbern 3 June 1838   Monr
Carpenter, Henry to Polly Crouch 21 Sept. 1837   Boon
Carpenter, James to Syntha Johnson 14 Feb. 1833   Lafa
Carpenter, James M. to Mary Milton 17 Mar. 1836   Rand
Carpenter, Joseph to Arrabella Davis 27 Sept. 1831   Boon
Carpenter, Lewis to Lucindy Howell 18 May 1839   Ray
Carpenter, Stephen to Julia Donahoe 26 Sept. 1830   Perr
Carpenter, Thomas to Jannattee Shanklin 8 Aug. 1837   Morg
Carr, John H. to Elizabeth Sumner 12 Jan. 1832   StCh
Carr, Thomas to Susan Kincaid 15 Aug. 1826   Pk-1
Carrall, John to Susannah Hughes 3 Aug. 1837   Coop
Carrel, Casper to Johanah H. Miller 26 Mar. 1838   StFr
Carrell, Samuel to Rebecca Elms 24 Nov. 1839   Buch
Carrico, Ignatius to Louisa Lawrence 2 Apr. 1839   Monr
Carrier, Amos to Charlotty Aynesworth 25 Feb. 1826   Howa

Carrigan, Patrick to Eleanore Lainy 26 July 1828   Wash
Carrington, Henry to Spicy Chldrs 17 Jan. 1830   Fran
Carrington, John to Eliz. T. Randolph 21 Dec. 1837   Call
Carrol, Green to Jemima Shumate 9 July 1837   Cr-1
Carrol, Wm. to Harriet Allison 3 Sept. 1839   Pk-B
Carroll, Birdem H. to Margaret Watson 12 May 1836   Pk-1
Carroll, Jacob to Milly Branson 29 Nov. 1834   Gasc
Carroll, Jesse to Susan Epperson 29 June 1837   Rall
Carroll, Nathaniel to Mahala Mar 23 Feb. 1832   Clay
Carroll, Robt. to Betherna Munkers 11 Aug. 1836   Clay
Carroll, Wm. to Mahaly E. Collins 31 Jan. 1839   Monr
Carrow, Israel to Patsy Carrow 22 Dec. 1835   Jeff
Carrow, John to Martha Lee 3 Sept. 1829   Jeff
Carruck, Isaac to Mary Brown 3 July 1838   Rall
Carruth, Albert G.L. to Parthena Jones 13 Sept. 1838   Call
Carry, Joseph to Mary Cerby 7 Jan. 1838   Barr
Carsner, John to Elizabeth Irons 1 Sept. 1825   Clay
Carson, Andrew to Sarah Amick 22 Dec. 1833   Howa
Carson, Hampton to Arminty Cruse 4 Jan. 1838   Howa
Carson, John W. to Sarah Corlin 21 Jan. 1836   StCh
Carson, Patrick to Polly Kingery 17 Aug. 1837   Cole
Carson, Robert to Harriett Calloway 19 Mar. 1829   Howa
Carson, Wm. to Virginia Sofframaus 8 Dec. 1836   Howa
Carstarphen, Chapel to Margaret P. Briggs 5 May 1825   Rall
Cartee, Joshua to Matilda Finch 16 Sept. 1838   StFr
Cartee, Ransom to Martha Bounds 3 July 1831   StFr
Carter, Asberry to Martha Gibson 26 Nov. 1835   Howa
Carter, Benj. F. to Hannah Huff 1 Aug. 1839   Ripl
Carter, Curtis to Maxamilla Haden 15 Sept. 1836   Rall
Carter, Cyrus to Harriet De-ang 22 June 1837   StCh
Carter, Daniel G. to Nancy Boman 26 June 1832   Lafa
Carter, Duralt to Adeline Thorpe 24 July 1834   Wash
Carter, Eli to Mary Munson 16 Nov. 1837   Warr
Carter, Granville to Sarah M. Pennell 1 Mar. 1836   Cr-1
Carter, James to Mary J. Glenn 23 June 1831   Rand
Carter, James to Mary J. Duncan 4 Apr. 1838   Linc
Carter, John to Jemimah Caton 30 June 1814   StCh
Carter, John to Lucinda Sullivant 12 Nov. 1826   Wash
Carter, John to Judy Wade 12 Jan. 1837   Linc
Carter, John to Rachel Johnson 25 July 1839   Clar
Carter, Liku? to Cintha A. Hodg 4 Dec. 1835   StFr
Carter, Robt. G. to Polly A. Scobie 11 June 1835   Mari
Carter, Tanksley to Eveline Parker 18 Jan. 1838   StFr
Carter, Travis to Martha Fuqua 28 Aug. 1833   Rall
Carter, Wm. to Elizabeth Randol 8 Mar. 1827   CG-A
Carter, Wm. to Agness F. Watts 28 July 1837   Lewi
Carter, Zimri A. to Elizabeth Finney 21 Dec. 1837   Warr
Cartly, Pierson to Martha Sparks 26 May 1832   Cr-1
Cartner, James to Mary Penison 14 Jan. 1830   Coop
Cartwright, Isaac to Sophia Like 16 Jan. 1834   CG-A
Cartwright, Willis to Nancy Pinkston 27 Apr. 1837   Davi
Carty, Greenberry to Juli A. Adams 24 Mar. 1839   StFr
Carty, John to Martha Clatin 27 Oct. 1836   StFr
Carty, Joshua to Catharine C. Mallow 22 Dec. 1829   Wash
Caruthers, Archibald A. to Edith McKay 19 Dec. 1833   StCh
Carver, Geo. to Polly Bedinger 30 Nov. 1838   Barr
Carver, Harrison to Mary A. Rutherford 26 Apr. 1836   Rand
Carver, Joseph to Martha Cunningham 22 Jan. 1835   StFr
Carver, Thomas to Mary Dunn 4 Oct. 1838   Pk-B
Carver, Wm. to Jemima Mathews 16 Jan. 1838   Md-B
Cary, Ambrose to Anna James 27 Nov. 1825   Lafa
Cary, Evins to Sarah Burger 4 Apr. 1822   Coop
Cary, Green to Amelia Fowler 21 Feb. 1839   Boon
Case, Solomon to Mary Morris 19 Aug. 1817   Howa
Case, Wm. to Susa Welker 19 Dec. 1829   CG-A

Casebolt, John L. to Martha Patterson 7 Feb. 1836	Gree
Casebolt, Robt. to Jamima Limes 25 July 1833	Gree
Caseboltz, Jacob B. to Elizabeth Wisdom 7 Oct. 1831	Cr-1
Casey, Francis to Mary Omarrha 22 Jan. 1831	Wash
Casey, James to Elender Sanders 11 Sept. 1836	Clay
Casey, John to Juttitte Detchemendy 14 Feb. 1831	Wash
Casey, Morgan to Margaret Herrington 17 May 1828	Wash
Casey, Morgan to Mary Campbell 6 Aug. 1833	Wash
Casey, Morgan to Ann Johnson 29 Jan. 1837	Wash
Cash, Benj. to Ann Williams 18 Nov. 1826	Char
Cash, James to Mary A. Bastin 17 Dec. 1839	Howa
Cash, Thomas to Martha Parks 24 Dec. 1835	Pk-1
Cash, Thomas Jr. to Permelia Shotwell 20 June 1836	Pk-1
Cashion, Robt. H. to Mary Hagan 27 Dec. 1838	Perr
Cashion, Wm. to Sarrah Hagan 24 July 1837	Perr
Cashon, Robt. to Polly Martin 18 Apr. 1833	Perr
Cashon, Robt. to Cinthy Pinkerton 19 June 1834	Perr
Cask, James to Melinda Davis 23 Feb. 1837	Lewi
Casner, Eben to Mary Woolsey 29 July 1828	Ray
Casner, Harry to Jincy Fields 6 Apr. 1822	Ray
Cason, Benj. to Mary J. Hawkins 12 Dec. 1833	Boon
Cason, D.D. to Julian A. Burck 10 Nov. 1839	Rand
Cason, Larkin to Nancy Sucet 14 June 1832	Call
Cason, Pemberton to Zilphy Stephens 22 July 1825	Coop
Cason, Seth to Sally Moody 26 Sept. 1833	Gasc
Cason, Wm. to Sarah Overton 22 Sept. 1836	Call
Cassell, Robt. T. to Nancy Butler 3 Aug. 1833	Pk-1
Casteel, David to Emily Howland 7 July 1831	Clay
Casteel, Francis to Grace Henderson 10 Feb. 1824	StGe
Casteel, Micah to Martha Abernathy 1 Oct. 1837	Perr
Castlio, John H. to Nancy Callaway 6 Sept. 1818	StCh
Casto, Noah to Martha Cornutt 6 July 1839	Cole
Casy, Andrew to Brigett Flynn 2 Feb. 1836	Wash
Casy, Daniel to Elisa Noel 11 Feb. 1836	Wash
Cates, Charles to Nancy Willis 11 Aug. 1831	Clay
Cates, Frederick to Polly Peacher 11 Apr. 1830	Howa
Cates, Jacob to Elizabeth Covey 12 June 1834	Ray
Cates, John to Sarah Guy 13 Feb. 1834	Ray
Cates, Wm. to Polly Rouch 4 July 1836	Ray
Cathey, Andrew to Jane Ross 22 June 1832	Coop
Cathey, James to Nancy McClenehan 12 Jan. 1822	Coop
Cathey, John to Julietta Moseby 21 Feb. 1835	Pett
Cato, Chapman to Louisa Henson 1 Jan. 1837	CG-A
Cato, Sterling to Jemimah Frizell 10 July 1829	Md-A
Caton, Joshua to Lucinda Caton 23 June 1839	Howa
Caton, Noah to Fanny McDermid 24 Nov. 1814	StCh
Caton, Pitman to Emily Rennick 14 Apr. 1836	Warr
Catron, John to Mary Fletcher 3 Feb. 1833	Lafa
Catron, Menetra to Martha Hill 26 Dec. 1833	Ray
Catron, Richard to Nancy Wilson 26 Dec. 1839	Ray
Catron, Solomon to Elizabeth Gennings 31 Jan. 1822	Lafa
Catron, Stephen to Elizabeth B. Smith 19 Dec. 1833	Lafa
Cavaner, James to Mrs. Odile Isom 18 Dec. 1835	Md-B
Cavashe, Anthony to Mary Pryse 25 Dec. 1830	Wash
Cave, Aadin to Ann Collins 9 Aug. 1832	Boon
Cave, Benj. to Jane Turner 30 June 1825	Howa
Cave, Benj. to Margaret Odin 2 Oct. 1838	Boon
Cave, Ezekiel A. to Catharine Williams 21 June 1838	Boon
Cave, Geo. to Elizabeth Humphreys 25 Dec. 1819	Howa
Cave, Henry to Fanny Graig 8 Sept. 1824	Call
Cave, Hudson to Sophia Gouldan 12 June 1837	Sali
Cave, James to Anna Mason 28 June 1820	Howa
Cave, John to Mary Williams 24 Oct. 1824	Boon
Cave, John to Nancy Hunter 6 Sept. 1836	Jack
Cave, Merit H. to Catherin Rush 21 June 1835	Monr

Cave, Thomas to Polly Jones 8 Oct. 1835	Char
Cave, Wm. to May Cave 29 Sept. 1825	Boon
Cave, Wm. J. to Phebe Moberly 7 Aug. 1835	Monr
Cavet, Hiram F. to Malinda Warmick 24 Oct. 1833	Lafa
Cavit, Isaac to Eliza West 7 July 1825	Md-A
Cawen, Isam to Mary Hensly 12 May 1836	John
Cawfield, James to Ruthy A. Leeper 15 Aug. 1833	Gree
Cawfield, Thomas to Mosila Cunningham 27 Oct. 1833	Gree
Cawlfield, Owen to Mahala Caslier 20 Sept. 1834	Gree
Cawrey, John to Katherine Clingensmith 7 Jan. 1830	CG-A
Cawvey, John to Fanny Miller 20 Mar. 1833	CG-A
Cay, Charles H. to Mary F. Higby 4 Apr. 1839	Clay
Cazy, Edward to Lydia Redmond 25 July 1833	Fran
Cecil, John to Amanda C. Wall 17 Oct. 1839	Henr
Cement, Gustavious to Lucinda Brockman 12 Mar. 1835	Ray
Cerby, Joel to Mary Blevins 3 Feb. 1838	Barr
Cercy, Christopher to Elener Spencer 10 Jan. 1839	Clay
Cerre, Toussaint to Julie Dorlac 10 Aug. 1806	StCh
Cersy, Wm. H. to Cidonay Bourne 14 Oct. 1838	Lewi
Cetre, Joseph to Maurgerite Cothman 2 June 1836	StCh
Chadic, Alexander to Nelly Bass 30 Jan. 1831	Cr-P
Chalmers, James B. to Margaret Evans 14 Feb. 1833	Coop
Chamber, Wm. to Ginne Mcfadden 11 Aug. 1812	CG-1
Chamberlain, Rev. Hiram to Sarah H. Wardlaw 11 Apr. 1836	StCh
Chamberlain, James to Martha Wright 4 Dec. 1834	Pk-1
Chamberlain, Lorenzo to Mrs. Susan Welker 26 May 1833	Jack
Chamberlain, Thomas to Mary Branstetter 10 Sept. 1839	Pk-B
Chamberlin, John B. to Polly Chapman 27 Oct. 1825	Ray
Chambers, Benj. to Jane Woolridge 20 Nov. 1837	Sali
Chambers, Ezekiel to Elizabeth Chambers 12 Apr. 1835	Cole
Chambers, Jack to Polly A. Titus 15 Nov. 1835	Rand
Chambers, James to Margaret Johnson 17 Apr. 1827	Jack
Chambers, Joel to Jane Murry 17 Apr. 1837	Cole
Chambers, John to Elizabeth Allison 10 Nov. 1826	Coop
Chambers, Julius to Sarah Gouge 28 Dec. 1834	Cole
Chambers, Thomas to Elenore Kennedy 19 Sept. 1815	StCh
Chambers, Wm. to Rebecca Gouge 4 Aug. 1831	Cole
Champbell, Samuel to Mary Todd 24 Jan. 1839	Clay
Champion, Jesse W. to Harriett Anderson 15 Dec. 1829	Md-A
Chan, Geo. R. to Paulina McKinney 19 Feb. 1839	Ray
Chance, Dennis to Sarah A. Smith 11 Feb. 1838	Clin
Chancelier, Louis to Magdaline Latreille 25 Nov. 1833	StCh
Chancellier, Alexis to Euphrosine Roy 6 Jan. 1835	StCh
Chandler, Amza to Jael Divine 2 June 1834	Perr
Chandler, Claiborne to Mary J. Grigsby 28 June 1832	Mari
Chandler, James to Mary Gibson 28 Apr. 1838	Clay
Chaney, Henry to Lucinda Allison 29 Nov. 1832	Coop
Chaney, Joel to Anna Dowdan 17 July 1838	Ray
Chaney, Nathan to Elizabeth Milsaps 14 Apr. 1822	Clay
Chaney, Richard Jr. to Catharine McKissick 13 Feb. 1836	Clin
Chaney, Wm. to Eliza Hierommous 9 Aug. 1838	Howa
Chapan, Gad to Nancy Turner 3 Sept. 1829	Pk-1
Chapel, Wm. to Sarah Thomas 1 Mar. 1831	Howa
Chapman, Adeline to Catharine Dooly 7 Sept. 1837	Monr
Chapman, David to Polly Groomes 22 Oct. 1837	Clay
Chapman, Geo. to Eulalie Leaper 25 Sept. 1826	StGe
Chapman, John to Jane Downing 2 Mar. 1820	StCh
Chapman, Joseph to Nancy Gregory 25 Sept. 1837	Mari
Chapman, Samuel to Sarah Langley 7 Feb. 1822	Coop
Chapman, Stephen to Nancy Wood 8 June 1826	Call
Chappell, Elias W. to Patey Thompson 9 July 1837	Sali
Charboneau, Louis to Adelaide H. Delcour 1 Sept. 1835	Wash
Charboneau, Tossant to Marie Laviolett 24 Sept. 1832	Wash
Charlesworth, Walter M. to Mary E. St. Louis 15 July 1839	StCh
Charlott, John B. to Eliza Branmier 29 Sept. 1838	Cass

41

Charlton, Armand to Nancy Farris 24 Feb. 1836   Cole
Charlton, John H. to Nancy Carter 27 Mar. 1833   Call
Chase, Amos to Hannah M. Wells 11 Jan. 1838   Lewi
Chase, Elisha to Anner Donohoe 3 Jan. 1837   Call
Chastam, Benj. to Elizabeth Catron 9 Mar. 1831   Lafa
Chauvin, Jacques to Marie L. Lalande 6 Jan. 1811   StCh
Cheaney, James to Rebecca Kelly 25 Feb. 1835   Boon
Cheatham, David C. to Martha Ratekin 4 July 1838   Call
Cheatham, Turley to Emily Fort 15 Apr. 1839   Call
Cheek, James to Sarah Haghn 30 Oct. 1834   CG-B
Cheiner, Richard to Patsy Fields 25 Oct. 1819   Howa
Cherry, John to Grshuly Henderson 10 Feb. 1837   Perr
Chesney, Pery to Matilda Maggard 5 Mar. 1833   Lafa
Chesunt, Samuel to Jane Renfro 12 Dec. 1839   Livi
Chetwood, Andrew to Amelia Prewitt 7 Aug. 1834   Lafa
Chevallier, Pierre to Archangel Bernier 5 Mar. 1826   Md-A
Chick, Francis to Elenor Hays 16 Dec. 1835   Call
Chilcote, Richard to Sarah Harmon 2 Aug. 1838   Morg
Childers, Daniel to Elizabeth Adams 12 May 1829   Fran
Childers, Henry to Elizabeth Maupin 1 Nov. 1831   Fran
Childers, Johnson to Margaret Blare 20 Jan. 1836   Fran
Childers, Thomas to Polly Hinton 28 Nov. 1831   Fran
Childress, Charles to Ruthie Cox 17 May 1828   Linc
Childress, John M. to Nancy C. Childress 1 Sept. 1839   Clar
Childs, James to Catherine Green 11 Jan. 1835   Boon
Childs, Robt. to Caly Lambert 30 Nov. 1834   Howa
Chiles, Alexander to Litticia Rice 16 Dec. 1835   Jack
Chiles, Wm. C. to Martha Jones 2 Feb. 1837   Fran
Chilton, Francis to Susannah Nifong 25 Sept. 1828   Md-A
Chilton, James to Eliza Kelso 25 June 1839   Pk-B
Chilton, John to Rachel Jackson 17 July 1831   Pk-1
Chinn, Alexander to Mary Kippers 3 Apr. 1838   Monr
Chipley, John to Louisa Amick 9 Dec. 1830   Howa
Chipley, Richard H. to Teressa Matlock 4 Oct. 1837   Shel
Chism, David H. to Teletha Hix 24 May 1837   Morg
Chism, Howard to Mahala Williams 15 Feb. 1831   Howa
Chism, John to Fanny Cooper 8 May 1828   Howa
Chism, Mickel to Diadian Smith 4 Feb. 1830   Coop
Chism, Urbin to America Triplett 16 Mar. 1837   Lewi
Chitwood, Archibald to Caroline Sherron 5 Dec. 1839   Rand
Chitwood, Richard to Sally Sealy 23 Dec. 1827   Rall
Chitwood, Richard Jr. to Rebecca Epperson 16 May 1839   Rall
Chitwood, Seth to Lucinda Caldwell 26 Dec. 1822   Fran
Chrisman, Horatio to Mary Kinchlow 8 Mar. 1818   Howa
Chrisman, Wm. to Margaret Wrattles 1 Jan. 1824   Gasc
Christian, Drury to Nancy Tillett 18 May 1834   Pk-1
Christian, Wm. to Jane Fulkerson 16 Jan. 1831   Cole
Christman, John to Meltina Brashear 15 Dec. 1833   Gasc
Christopher, Geo. to Mary A. Smith 4 Feb. 1834   Mari
Chriswell, James to Jane Allen 15 Oct. 1835   Call
Chrites, Adam to Polly Panack 27 Feb. 1831   CG-A
Chrites, Daniel to Vivan Paneck 21 Jan. 1830   CG-A
Chrites, Daniel to Fanny Leapau 20 Aug. 1835   CG-B
Chronister, Abraham to Nancy Martindill 9 Oct. 1831   CG-A
Chronister, Adam to Hannah Scaggs 7 July 1833   CG-A
Chronister, John to Elizabeth Mills 1 July 1836   Ripl
Chrystial, Wm. to Rhoda Drinkard 8 Apr. 1828   Char
Chuning, Ambrose to Elizabeth Bell 31 Jan. 1839   Fran
Churchwell, Thomas to Susan Tarpley 30 Nov. 1837   Mari
Cilvourn, Benj. D. to Mary Middleton 3 July 1831   Linc
Cisk, Layton to Nancy Byrd 21 May 1829   Howa
Cissel, John to Susan Shufford 23 Apr. 1837   Perr
Cissell, Joseph to Mary Manning 27 Apr. 1835   Perr
Cissell, Joseph to Elizabeth Moore 18 Sept. 1838   Perr
Cissell, Wm. to Elizabeth Tucker 14 Jan. 1834   Perr

Clain, Geo. to Judith Baugh 18 July 1819   StCh
Claipole, Jesse to Clarissa Hasty 8 June 1825   Boon
Clair, Geo. to Manerva Barnes 5 Mar. 1835   Boon
Clairmont, Lewis to Elizabeth Proix 18 Jan. 1830   StCh
Clairmont, Lewis to Helen DuBois 27 May 1839   StCh
Clanton, James to Keziah Tharp 30 May 1830   Call
Clare, John P. to Dorothy Mude 15 Feb. 1821   StCh
Clark, Alexander D. to Sarah Morris 15 Jan. 1835   Fran
Clark, Andrew to Perlina Beaver 3 Jan. 1839   Rall
Clark, Barus to Catharine Thornton 25 Feb. 1836   Sali
Clark, Benj. to Polly Baker 14 Feb. 1829   Char
Clark, Caleb to Polly Davis 10 Jan. 1828   Jeff
Clark, Calvin S. to Nancy A. Carter 14 Sept. 1837   Rand
Clark, Edward to Elizabeth Clark 22 May 1833   Howa
Clark, Elisha to Sinthy Chaney 10 Mar. 1839   Barr
Clark, Galen to Rebecca McCoy 23 Apr. 1839   Clar
Clark, Geo. to Eliza Owen 20 Apr. 1837   Monr
Clark, Green C. to Martha M. Stephens 23 Mar. 1838   Polk
Clark, Henry P. to Frances Whitsett 28 Feb. 1839   Clin
Clark, Isaac to Catherine Turner 5 Nov. 1818   Howa
Clark, Isaac to Hannah Riggs 28 Apr. 1825   Ray
Clark, Isaac to Mrs. Zulica Millsap 29 Dec. 1836   Coop
Clark, Jacob to Phebe Whelman 19 July 1031   Fran
Clark, James to Lucy Smith 17 Aug. 1834   Rall
Clark, James A. to Martha Lewis 19 Mar. 1833   Howa
Clark, James C. to Rebecca J. King 11 Aug. 1829   Clay
Clark, James C. to Mary Baxter 28 May 1836   Clay
Clark, Jeremiah N. to Elizabeth Duncan 4 July 1837   Clay
Clark, John to Emeline Watkin 10 Nov. 1835   Ripl
Clark, John B. to Ellender Turner 19 Oct. 1826   Howa
Clark, John C. to Jane Hyle 3 Oct. 1838   Howa
Clark, John H. to Nancy Kimmberling 27 Oct. 1825   Wash
Clark, John J. to Elizabeth McDaniels 17 Aug. 1825   Cole
Clark, John L. to Keziah Woods 3 June 1832   Linc
Clark, John R. to Mary Collet 8 Oct. 1839   Plat
Clark, Joshua to Elizabeth Davis 31 Jan. 1828   Jeff
Clark, Jotham to Sarah A. Hagan 5 Mar. 1830   Wash
Clark, Mathias to Mary Watkins 18 May 1828   StCh
Clark, Michael D. to Dorcus Fowler 24 Feb. 1829   Cole
Clark, Ostaw to Anny Collins 26 Sept. 1823   Fran
Clark, Potions to Nancy Denny 2 May 1839   Clin
Clark, Ralph to Mary Murphy 2 May 1833   Linc
Clark, Renfrelour to Nancy Tarwater 27 Jan. 1820   Coop
Clark, Robt. N. to Susan Terrill 27 Aug. 1835   Coop
Clark, Thomas to Mary Davis 6 Oct. 1836   Lewi
Clark, Washington to Mrs. Jane Retherford 28 Jan. 1838   Polk
Clark, Wm. to Nancy Nave 16 Apr. 1818   Howa
Clark, Wm. to Sarah Wadley 2 Nov. 1826   Call
Clark, Wm. to Francis Taylor 6 Nov. 1831   Cole
Clark, Wm. to Elizabet Payne 16 Jan. 1832   Mari
Clark, Wm. to Ann Nickles 27 Nov. 1833   Gasc
Clark, Wm. to Prudy Austin 19 Feb. 1834   Wash
Clark, Wm. to Eleanor Irwin 16 Aug. 1838   Linc
Clark, Wm. to Jane Medley 13 Dec. 1838   Rand
Clark, Wm. P. to Narcissa E. Long 16 Oct. 1838   Ray
Clark, Wm. R. to Sarah Baxter 10 Oct. 1839   Jack
Clarke, John S. to Isabella J. Scott 8 Oct. 1838   Pk-B
Clarke, Johnston to Elizabeth Roan 10 May 1827   Wash
Clarkson, Richard to Betsy Brunt 12 Feb. 1824   Howa
Clarkson, Wm. to Susanna D. Lonceford 1 Feb. 1828   Wash
Clarkston, John to Elizabeth Biswell 31 July 1820   Howa
Clarkston, John to Flora Wampucket 7 July 1833   Gree
Clarkston, Wm. to Polly Thompson 30 Nov. 1827   Boon
Clarmont, Francois to Cecille Peyro 8 Nov. 1830   StCh
Clasty, ---- to Sarah Duncan 2 Oct. 1834   Boon

43

Claton, Elbridge to Mary Adams 29 Jan. 1838 — Wash
Claton, John to Susanna Tribue 31 Mar. 1829 — Pk-1
Clatterbuck, John to Martha ---- 29 Apr. 1830 — Call
Clatterbuck, Leroy to Mary Gray 22 Apr. 1831 — Call
Clay, Green to Malva Musick 13 July 1832 — Cole
Clay, Hiram to Mary Carnett 29 June 1836 — Cr-1
Clay, James to Nancy Murdock 11 Feb. 1821 — StCh
Clay, James to Polly A. Spradling 25 June 1831 — StFr
Clay, John G. to Margaret Miller 25 Dec. 1828 — Cole
Clay, Johnson to Rebecky Collet 4 May 1820 — Coop
Clay, Wade H. to Meniea Musick 22 Nov. 1835 — Cole
Clay, Wm. to Sally Colbert 14 June 1822 — Coop
Clay, Wm. S. to Sarah Murphy 29 Sept. 1835 — StFr
Claybrook, Geo. W. to Jemima Hix 1 Sept. 1836 — Cole
Claybrook, James to Lydia Hensley 31 Aug. 1823 — Cole
Claybrook, James to Jane Ray -- Dec. 1825 — Cole
Claybrooks, Joseph to Polly Humphreys 2 Nov. 1824 — Char
Claycomb, John to Rhoda A. Roughton 11 Jan. 1838 — StCh
Claypool, James to Mrs. Elizabeth Lock 18 Nov. 1838 — Wash
Clayton, Beverly W. to Elizabeth Oxford 31 May 1835 — Ripl
Clayton, James to Cynthia Williams 3 Mar. 1829 — Wash
Clayton, James to Anna Daugherty 5 July 1836 — Perr
Clayton, John P. to Louisa Thompson 23 June 1839 — Lewi
Clayton, Perry G. to Teresa Febirghian 3 Nov. 1836 — Jack
Clayton, Thomas F. to Nancy K. Rule 23 Aug. 1829 — Fran
Cleann, John to Elizabeth Strap 23 Sept. 1806 — StGe
Cleaveland, Milton to Susan Beaver 16 Apr. 1830 — Call
Cleaver, Jacob to Eliza Parker 31 Aug. 1824 — Rall
Cleaver, Thomas to Margaret McCune 16 Dec. 1834 — Pk-1
Cleavinger, John to Margaret Wills 3 July 1823 — Clay
Cleeton, Enoch to Kitty Roberts 15 Jan. 1827 — Howa
Cleeton, James to M. Bozarth 7 Aug. 1822 — Howa
Cleeton, Moses to Maria Hargis 21 Feb. 1833 — Howa
Clegel, Benj. M. to Elizabeth H. Ervin 17 Apr. 1834 — Clay
Clemens, James to Lucy Kirby 20 Nov. 1825 — Rall
Clemenson, John to Ly-- Lightnor 5 Jan. 1823 — Lafa
Clement, Wm. to Elizabeth Skaggs 13 Aug. 1829 — Cr-P
Clements, Absalom to Aley C. McGee 19 Mar. 1839 — Ray
Clements, Joshua T. to Mariah Coley 23 Oct. 1834 — Carr
Clements, Peter to Lucy Parrick 27 Aug. 1833 — Md-A
Clements, Wiatt to Cassandra Goode 3 Mar. 1831 — Ray
Clemmons, Anthony to Sarah Job 17 Feb. 1826 — Lafa
Clemons, John to Zerilda Turner -- Jan. 1836 — Boon
Clemson, John to Hannah Rutherford 2 Dec. 1834 — Rand
Clendennen, Daniel to Susannah McDaniel 5 June 1828 — Cole
Clendennen, Matthew B. to Elizabeth Webb 28 Apr. 1829 — Cole
Clendennen, Robt. F. to Mrs. Rebecca Webb 19 Mar. 1829 — Cole
Clendennon, John to Susanna Barton 19 Dec. 1822 — Cole
Cleveland, John T. to Louisianna Hughes 30 Oct. 1823 — Howa
Cleveland, Robt. to Mrs. Frances McGlandin 30 Oct. 1834 — StFr
Clevenger, Archibald to Esther Crop 10 Mar. 1832 — Ray
Clevenger, Ford to Hannah Ramsey 19 Dec. 1822 — Ray
Clevenger, Ford to Elizabeth Allen 10 Jan. 1828 — Ray
Clevenger, Jesse to Jennet Fleming 30 Dec. 1834 — Ray
Clevenger, Pittman to Betsy McCrary 26 Feb. 1835 — Ray
Clevenger, Samuel to Martha Frakes 23 Mar. 1834 — Ray
Clevenger, Thomas to Betsy Odell 30 Aug. 1838 — Ray
Clevenger, Wm. to Dacus Garner 28 Jan. 1829 — Ray
Clevenger, Wm. to Nancy McCorrle 16 Nov. 1838 — Ray
Clevenger, Zachariah to Elizabeth Crop 17 Apr. 1832 — Ray
Clevenger, Zachariah to Eliza Cooper 24 Apr. 1836 — Ray
Clever, Stephen to Mary Hase 7 Mar. 1839 — Rall
Clevinger, James to Tabitha Hatcher 22 Oct. 1835 — Clay
Clevland, Wm. to Rebeca Irvin 1 Oct. 1833 — Wash
Clicker, Martin to Mary Cluck 11 Aug. 1838 — Jack

```
Clifferds, Daniel to Elizabeth Crites 16 July 1818              CG-1
Clifford, Wm. to Joanna Harris 18 Nov. 1834                     Mari
Clifton, Eli to Isabella Cline 6 Feb. 1834                      Perr
Clifton, Franklin to Mrs. Lindy Burns 21 Apr. 1833             Perr
Clifton, Jacob to Katharine Cotner 11 Apr. 1837               CG-A
Clifton, Thomas to Rebecca Lesley 18 Aug. 1837                 Maco
Clifton, Wm. to Polly Hensley -- Mar. 1836                      Rand
Cline, Absolam to Susan Wilson 18 Apr. 1834                    CG-A
Cline, Absolom to Emily Young 7 Apr. 1835                       Pett
Cline, Benj. to Rilla Bess 25 July 1826                        CG-A
Cline, Daniel to Dorcas Sheppard 25 July 1832                 CG-A
Cline, Moses to Nancy Wilson 12 Feb. 1839                      CG-B
Clingensmith, Henry to Barbary Hoofman 1 Aug. 1817            CG-1
Clinton, Jenkins to Basy Clinton 13 Nov. 1830                  Cr-P
Clinton, Wm. to Elizabeth Freeman 2 Mar. 1834                 Cr-1
Clodfelter, Archibald to Mary Hinkle 23 June 1836            CG-A
Clodfelter, Enos to Polly Clodfelter 2 Oct. 1834             CG-A
Clodfelter, John to Lucinda Finison 3 Aug. 1837               Wash
Clodfelter, Wm. to Louisa Matthews 5 Oct. 1837               CG-A
Clopton, Abner to Margaret C. Fristoe 22 Dec. 1836            Pett
Close, Frederick to Mary Gaston 1 July 1824                    Lafa
Clotfelter, Jacob to Elizabeth Smith 26 Apr. 1832            CG-A
Cloyd, Gilbert to Lennia Jones 6 June 1822                     Howa
Cloyd, Gilbert M. to Margaret Roulston 7 May 1839            Howa
Clubb, David to Mily Killion 5 Mar. 1839                      CG-B
Clubb, Samuel H. to Belinda B. Pyatt 7 Dec. 1837             Gasc
Cluck, John to Judy Moody 17 Sept. 1829                       StCh
Clumber, Samuel to Susan Jeffries 25 Mar. 1824               Sali
Coalter, Beverly T. to Elizabeth J. McQueen 24 July 1834     Pk-1
Coatney, Nathan to Catharine Cantrie 27 July 1838            Linc
Coats, Alfred A. to Emaly Akeman 30 Mar. 1834                Lafa
Coats, Henry to Jane Chapman 25 Mar. 1835                    Lafa
Coats, Hiram to Pamelia Walker 20 Sept. 1835                 Call
Coats, John to Sally Smith 16 Aug. 1821                      Call
Coats, Joseph to Martha Roynts 27 Sept. 1838                 Livi
Coats, Wm. to Cena McLaughlin 29 Jan. 1837                   Call
Cobb, Alexander to Catherine Cantaux 10 Oct. 1837            Perr
Cobb, James to Mahala Huddard 14 Feb. 1839                   Boon
Cobb, John to Louisa Handcock 20 Jan. 1838                   Perr
Cobb, Wm. to Temperance Webb 3 Aug. 1833                     Carr
Cobb, Wm. to Eliza Morgan 8 June 1837                        Morg
Cobbs, John A. to Eleanor Cleaver 28 Feb. 1828               Pk-1
Cobelance, Landen to Hannah Thornton 24 Sept. 1837           Ripl
Cobet, Erwin to Margaret Winkler 11 Aug. 1836               Rand
Coche, Lorenzo to Penelope Murry 2 June 1836                 John
Cochran, Geo. to Sarah Anderson 21 Dec. 1837                 Linc
Cochran, James to Emaline Boyd 31 Jan. 1833                  StCh
Cochran, John to Delvina Wilcox 8 Feb. 1827                  Boon
Cochran, Joseph to Jane Miller 22 Apr. 1831                  CG-A
Cochrell, James to Mariah Doke 2 Mar. 1837                   John
Cochrell, Joel to Fanny Brooks 7 Apr. 1836                   John
Cochrell, Westly to Sarah Wilson 25 Feb. 1838               John
Cochron, John to Margaret Clark 10 Sept. 1837               Jeff
Cock, Wm. E. to Rebecca Winsor 15 Jan. 1835                  Lafa
Cockerell, Larky to Hannah Williams 19 Oct. 1831            Jeff
Cockerill, John N. to Loutica Stewart 15 Aug. 1836          Jack
Cockram, Edward to Gabriella Garner 25 Nov. 1829            Mari
Cockran, Geo. C. to Huldah Hunsaken 26 Dec. 1839           Mari
Cockran, James to Susannah Pullam 24 Nov. 1831              Boon
Cockran, LeRoy to Ann Miller 17 Mar. 1831                   CG-A
Cockran, Robt. H. to Mary Allen 16 Jan. 1838               Mari
Cockran, Thomas to Martha Hogard 12 Apr. 1837              Perr
Cockran, Wm. to Mary Ellington 4 May 1834                   Boon
Cockran, Wm. B. to Evaline Allen 20 Oct. 1835              Rall
Cockran, Wm. P. to Mrs. Eliza Scott 2 June 1828            Howa
```

45

```
Cockran, Wm. S. to Manervy Moore 1 Apr. 1830                          Rand
Cockrell, J. Miller to Sucothia M. Ruby 18 May 1834                  Jack
Cockrell, Thomas H. to Emma Donoho 27 Jan. 1831                      Howa
Cockrill, Clinton to Mary E. Crates 29 Sept. 1836                    Rand
Cockrill, F. Grunda to Elizabeth Oxley 11 June 1834                  Rand
Cockrill, Fielding to Martha Chapman 30 Sept. 1834                   Rand
Cockrill, Morgan to Hannah Andrews 3 Feb. 1833                       Lafa
Cocks, Charles to Manerva Shelly 1 Dec. 1835                         Linc
Cocks, Geo. to Mary Wiley 3 Dec. 1832                                CG-B
Cocrille, Peter R. to Sally Steel 25 Dec. 1828                       Coop
Coefelt, Philip to Jane Gobe 13 June 1839                            Cole
Coen, Hardy to Susan Thomason 21 Dec. 1837                          StFr
Cofer, Larkin to Rachel Alexander 17 Mar. 1826                      StGe
Cofer, Thomas B. to Rebecca Turner 7 Jan. 1834                      Linc
Cofer, Thomas L. to Charity A. Whitmire 31 July 1836               Fran
Coffeth, James to Souma E. Winey 9 Mar. 1837                        Livi
Coffett, Pleasant to Clacy Richie 27 Nov. 1837                      Gasc
Coffey, Henry to Isabella J. Guinn 17 Oct. 1838                     Clin
Coffey, Isaac N. to Susan Oakley 25 Oct. 1832                       Linc
Coffin, Joseph to Sary Switzer 2 Nov. 1832                          Howa
Coffman, Andrew to Mary McClanahan 9 July 1826                      Coop
Coffy, Colbert to Catherine Willard 28 Feb. 1830                    Mari
Cogar, Abraham to Polly Corn 29 June 1837                           Jack
Cogdain, Wm. to Susannah Arrington 14 Apr. 1822                     Howa
Coger, James F. to Caroline D. Slaughter 11 Mar. 1830              Mari
Cogsdale, Daniel to Mahala Harrington 8 June 1828                   Clay
Coil, James to Mary J. Brushear 3 Feb. 1834                         Gasc
Coil, Simeon to Elizabeth Russell 27 Sept. 1832                     Jack
Coin, Alexander to Lydia Coffelt 14 Oct. 1833                       Cole
Coker, Wm. to Elizabeth Goforth 26 Oct. 1833                        Gree
Cokes, John to Eliza Trimble 31 Mar. 1833                           Gree
Colans, Wm. to Margaret Scott 7 Sept. 1837                          Pk-A
Colborne, Presley to Louisa Estes 20 Apr. 1837                     Sali
Colburn, John W. to Jane I. Clemins 29 Aug. 1839                    Cass
Colburn, Samuel to Elizabeth A. Cunningham 11 Oct. 1838           StCh
Coldwell, John to Narcissa Land 22 May 1837                         Jack
Cole, Colbery to Rebecca Leach 20 June 1836                         CG-B
Cole, Elijah to Amanda Swearingen 29 Dec. 1833                      Pk-1
Cole, Holbert to Ann Ron 28 Dec. 1819                               Coop
Cole, Jacob to Polly Anderson 8 Oct. 1831                           Cr-1
Cole, James to Elizabeth Ashcraft 15 Oct. 1814                      StCh
Cole, James to Nancy Dickson 25 Jan. 1836                           Coop
Cole, Jesse to Ruth Cox 26 Mar. 1836                                Lafa
Cole, John to Nancy Little 14 Feb. 1833                             Wash
Cole, John to Henrietta Bagley 2 Sept. 1838                         Wash
Cole, Mark to Mary A. Woods 27 Dec. 1834                            Coop
Cole, Micajah to Lavina Turley 22 Jan. 1835                         Wash
Cole, Richard H. to Amanda Eversol 12 Sept. 1837                   Mari
Cole, Samuel to Sarah Briscoe 24 Apr. 1823                          Coop
Cole, Stephen to Nancy Drennan 30 Nov. 1837                        Jeff
Cole, Wm. to Nancy Woods 10 Oct. 1828                               Coop
Cole, Wm. F. to Eliza J. Jamison 15 Sept. 1839                      Wash
Cole, Wm. J. to Elizabeth Jolly 7 June 1838                         Coop
Colelepure, Allen to Sarah Becker 26 June 1829                      Ray
Coleman, Harvey to Elizabeth Williams 30 Aug. 1838                StFr
Coleman, James M. to Martha Turner 2 Nov. 1836                      Pk-A
Coleman, John to Judy Creason 22 July 1822                          Boon
Coleman, Joseph B. to Catherine Murphy 3 July 1839                 Wash
Coleman, Oliver to Mary Brown 4 Jan. 1838                           Rall
Coleman, Pierce to Sarah Coleman 27 Jan. 1834                       StCh
Colens, John to Alsey Hitt 23 May 1839                              CG-B
Coles, Christopher to Martha Burrows 15 Nov. 1823                   Howa
Colgan, Harva H. to Keziah Ferazier 28 Aug. 1831                    Cole
Colivar, Wm. to Polly Grooms 21 Dec. 1830                           Pk-1
Collan, Joseph to Therese Seraphine 25 Nov. 1834                    Wash
```

```
Colle, John to Ann Hardick 18 Aug. 1830                        Boon
Collens, Elisha to Precilla Penrode 12 May 1832                Perr
Collet, Wm. to Lettecia Ball 1 July 1835                       Clin
Collett, Abraham to Elizabeth Gilliam 10 Oct. 1822            Clay
Collett, Wm. to Nancy Moffitt 24 Nov. 1831                     Howa
Colley, Reuben to Maria Hardwick 23 Dec. 1830                  Ray
Colley, Shadrack to Sarah Rimmell 12 Dec. 1839                 Ray
Collier, Geo. to Frances E. Morrison 1 Jan. 1826             StCh
Collier, Hiram to Mildred Sharp 30 Mar. 1825                  Boon
Collier, Ira to Susan Drake 19 Oct. 1837                      Jack
Collier, Isaac N. to Ann Murphey 19 July 1838                 Linc
Collier, Randal to Polly Miles 12 July 1815                   StCh
Collins, Alexander to Rhody Lewis 7 Mar. 1839                 Monr
Collins, Charles to Betsy Proctor 6 Feb. 1827                Wash
Collins, Charles M. to Louisa E. Merry 4 July 1837           Morg
Collins, Christian to Catharine Higbee 15 Sept. 1837         Rand
Collins, Francis K. to Sally McKinney 30 Oct. 1830           Rand
Collins, Henry W. to Rebecca James 16 Dec. 1835              Mari
Collins, James to Rebeckah Chapman 28 Feb. 1820              Coop
Collins, James to Francis More 25 Dec. 1827                  Wash
Collins, James to Mary Tilford 31 Jan. 1831                  Clay
Collins, James to Cordelia Carpenter 25 Sept. 1834           Clay
Collins, James to Sary Moreland 19 Mar. 1838                 Cr-1
Collins, Joseph to Rebeca Wright 21 Feb. 1832               Wash
Collins, Joseph to Nancy Sooney 8 Aug. 1839                  CG-B
Collins, Larkin to Susan McGee 4 Aug. 1836                   Cr-1
Collins, Lemuel to Courtney Robertson 6 June 1833            Rand
Collins, Lewis to Jane Pound 18 Feb. 1833                    Fran
Collins, Martin to Malinda Job 25 Nov. 1834                 Cole
Collins, May B. to Mary F. Hughes 4 Oct. 1837               Howa
Collins, Ruben to Hannah Crisp 11 Mar. 1828                  Jack
Collins, Simeon to Jane A. Tilford 19 Jan. 1833             Clay
Collins, Thomas to Delue Jones 9 Nov. 1821                   Howa
Collins, Thomas to Elizabeth Dyer 29 Oct. 1829              Lafa
Collins, Thomas to Mary A. Morris 29 Aug. 1839              Lewi
Collins, Wm. to Polly Warmouth 1 July 1827                  Char
Collins, Wm. to Elizabeth Alexander 28 June 1832           Cole
Collins, Wm. to Margaret Cylard 30 Sept. 1833              Howa
Collins, Wm. to Mary A. Stewart 12 Sept. 1837             Warr
Collins, Wm. to Rebecca D. Harris 1 Mar. 1838              Mari
Collins, Wm. K. to Mary Lea-- 23 Feb. 1837                StCh
Collman, Joseph to Marie Duclos 4 Feb. 1834               Wash
Collmann, Bernard to Aselie Perrin 24 Oct. 1826            Wash
Colston, Jacob to Elizabeth Goff 15 Sept. 1839            Char
Colter, David to Eliza Stone 13 Apr. 1820                 Coop
Colvan, Stephen to Nancy Pointer 5 Apr. 1835              Gasc
Colvert, Geo. to Willey A. Wood 30 July 1835              Mari
Colvert, Ziba to Mary E. Ferguson 24 Dec. 1834           Mari
Colvin, Benj. to Sophia McBain 25 Apr. 1824              Boon
Colvin, Garlin to Sarah Phillips 20 Feb. 1823            Boon
Colvin, Harris to Susan Steel 28 May 1837                Fran
Colvin, Jacob to Sally Hensley 12 Dec. 1825              Cole
Colvin, James to Sarah Brown 28 Nov. 1833                Pk-1
Colvin, James to Edy Grove 28 Nov. 1839                  Monr
Colvin, Robt. to Elizabeth Cole 10 Apr. 1828             Fran
Colvin, Solomon to Mary A. Gardner 17 Dec. 1835          Fran
Colwell, Wm. to Mrs. Jane Fisher 15 Dec. 1836            Rall
Combs, Levi to Manerva Johnson 17 June 1839              Morg
Combs, Robt. C. to Martha B. Hunt 25 Feb. 1834           Coop
Combs, Robt. M. to Polly White 8 Mar. 1835              Fran
Combs, Stephen to Synthey Wright 27 July 1822            Coop
Combs, Wm. to Eliza Ewing 17 July 1838                   Clar
Combs, Wm. to Mahuldah Roberts 26 July 1838             Clin
Combs, Wm. N. to Matilda Wilson 24 Aug. 1834            Gree
Comegys, Benj. to Lucinda Scott 20 Mar. 1828           StCh
```

47

Comegys, Jacob to Mary Spencer 30 July 1829   StCh
Comegys, Jacob to Engeline P. Mills 19 Apr. 1838   StCh
Comer, John E. to Nancy McCary 8 Oct. 1832   Call
Cometys, Cornelius to Rebecca Ezzell 25 Dec. 1831   Linc
Comiges, Jonathan to Linda A. Scott 23 Feb. 1827   StCh
Compton, Charles to Eliza Doxey 2 June 1839   Char
Compton, Gersham to Jane Davis 27 Feb. 1820   Coop
Compton, James to Mary Winfield 16 Jan. 1826   Perr
Compton, James H. to Mary Wirt 2 July 1839   Clay
Compton, Jonathan to Annis Dollarhide 5 Feb. 1835   Fran
Compton, Joseph to Serena Peirson 14 Jan. 1830   Md-A
Compton, Oliver to Angeline Lincon 18 Apr. 1839   Ripl
Compton, Richard to Nancy Green 28 Feb. 1833   Md-A
Compton, Simon to Ellen Fruman 3 Jan. 1833   Howa
Compton, Thomas to Mary Stepp 28 Sept. 1826   Howa
Compton, Thomas to Mary Liddle 7 Feb. 1830   Md-A
Compton, Yurden to Hannah Anderson -- Feb. 1829   Howa
Coms, Silas to Elizabeth Whitworth 20 July 1836   Md-B
Comstock, James to Susan Mattocks 15 Feb. 1838   Lafa
Comstock, Thomas to Polly Carter 4 Dec. 1836   Ripl
Comstock, Wm. to Delila Carter 10 Mar. 1836   Ripl
Con, Jonathan to Mary Drummond 19 July 1832   Jack
Condry, Elias to Catherine Watson 14 Apr. 1836   CG-B
Conduf, Henderson to Tennessee C. Carter 2 July 1837   Sali
Conger, Stephen to Lucy J. Gordon 8 Mar. 1835   Call
Conger, Thomas D. to Moniza McCampbell 18 Oct. 1827   Call
Conillay, James to Susan M. Spradling 23 Nov. 1829   StFr
Conily, John to Delilah Weldon 23 Aug. 1832   Boon
Conley, Chambers to Eliza Merril 19 July 1838   Mari
Conn, Hugh L. to Hetty A. Boyd rec. 3 June 1837   Rall
Conn, Joel J. to Cleveland Pain 23 June 1835   Coop
Conn, John to Nancy Taylor rec. 8 July 1836   Rall
Conn, Samuel to Melinda Wheeler 14 Jan. 1827   Fran
Conn, Tramuel to Matilda Brasher 2 Dec. 1834   Rall
Connelly, Benj. to Franky Crosthwaite 31 Aug. 1830   Boon
Connelly, Francis to Mariann Turner 18 Sept. 1828   Boon
Connelly, James to Mary A. Dale 13 Dec. 1832   Boon
Connelly, John to Martha Griffith 14 Apr. 1839   Buch
Conner, Allen to Elizabeth Snodgrass 24 July 1827   Coop
Conner, Andrew to Anna M. Bright 17 Oct. 1837   Ray
Conner, Armstrong to Unity Strickland 16 Feb. 1826   Jeff
Conner, James to Jennitta Harl 20 June 1833   Howa
Conner, James F. to Frances E. Chandler 6 June 1838   Coop
Conner, John to Elizabeth Wines 28 Sept. 1824   Cole
Conner, John to Sarah Butcher 1 Dec. 1831   Ray
Conner, John to Sally Howard 23 May 1836   Cole
Conner, John to Harriet S. Hart 30 June 1836   Boon
Conner, John to Sarah Osmon 6 Oct. 1836   Ray
Conner, John to Manerva Apperson 27 Oct. 1839   Mill
Conner, Joseph to Esther Brewer 15 Jan. 1835   Ray
Conner, Lavender W. to Zibba Rice 31 Dec. 1835   Jack
Conner, Lewis to Elizabeth Wilhite 8 Dec. 1836   Boon
Conner, Oliver/Abner? to America Carter 17 May 1832   Cr-1
Conner, Pleasant to Elizabeth Cooper 27 Oct. 1821   Cole
Conner, Shadrack to Letty Brewer 28 Dec. 1837   Ray
Conner, Starling to Mary Cotton 12 Aug. 1829   Coop
Conner, Washington to Celia Cain 28 Feb. 1828   Howa
Conner, Wm. to Patsy Hutson 24 Dec. 1820   CG-1
Conner, Wm. to Delila Wolf 19 July 1830   Coop
Conner, Wm. to Elizabeth Adams 6 May 1832   Mari
Conner, Wm. to Mary Skinner 17 Jan. 1837   Shel
Connots, Geo. W. to Margaret Bell 10 Oct. 1839   Wash
Conoly, Peter to Susan Rue 1 Aug. 1833   StCh
Conorg, Wm. to Mrs. Enice Wells 31 Mar. 1839   Clay
Conrad, David to Mary Bollinger 14 Mar. 1833   CG-A

48

```
Conrader, Louis to Mary A. Stover 4 Mar. 1830                              Sali
Constable, Barton to Martha Francis 4 July 1839                           Cass
Constable, Edward to Brazzlee Arthur 1 Dec. 1836                          Jack
Constable, Thomas to Mahala Malone 18 Aug. 1830                           Jack
Constable, Thomas to Mary Hink 2 Oct. 1838                                Jack
Constable, Wm. to Sarah Dailey 15 Apr. 1832                               Jack
Conway, Clemint to Emma Govreau 19 Nov. 1812                             StGe
Conway, Francis to Nancy Bertin 16 June 1836                             Fran
Conway, Frederick to Mary S. Horine 7 May 1833                           Wash
Conway, Jeremiah to Rachel Morgan 28 July 1811                          CG-1
Conway, Jesse to Nancy Conway 1 June 1837                                Ripl
Conway, John to Sarah Owen 15 Sept. 1839                                 Ripl
Conway, Joseph to Polly L. Hendrick 6 Dec. 1829                         Mari
Conway, Simeon to Polly McRae 2 Oct. 1823                               Rall
Conway, Simeon to Harriet Worthington 12 Nov. 1829                     Mari
Coock, James H. to Permeley Baker 20 May 1828                           Wash
Cook, Allen to Margaret Lovelady 22 Sept. 1835                          Jack
Cook, Charles to Ann Slighton 9 May 1839                                Lewi
Cook, David to Christina Peringen 4 Nov. 1819                           CG-A
Cook, David P. to Sarah Patton 11 June 1834                             Jack
Cook, Geo. to Ann Limbaugh 29 Mar. 1829                                 CG-A
Cook, Geo. W. to Elizabeth Feelan 2 June 1833                           Cole
Cook, Grave to Soffrony Sublet 31 Mar. 1825                             Call
Cook, Henry to Ellaie Millan 17 Nov. 1835                               Mari
Cook, Jackson to Sarah A. Merrett 10 Jan. 1839                          Morg
Cook, James G. to Eliza J. Cook 6 Sept. 1838                            Cass
Cook, James H. to Grizella B. Caldwell 16 May 1839                      Call
Cook, John to Levisey Pennington 31 Aug. 1818                           StCh
Cook, John to Phoebe Strickland 21 Feb. 1828                            Jeff
Cook, John to Elizabeth Robb 7 Sept. 1838                               Howa
Cook, John B. to Mary Wilson 22 Jan. 1835                               Jack
Cook, Joseph to Susan Jones 4 Apr. 1829                                 Jeff
Cook, Nathanial B. to Mary Clark 30 June 1836                           CG-A
Cook, Pascal to Melvina C. Dickey 10 Apr. 1834                          Jack
Cook, Pascal to Nancy Powell 22 Dec. 1839                               Jack
Cook, Phillip St.G. to Rachel W. Hertzog 28 Oct. 1830                   Clay
Cook, Valentine M. to Rachel Holloway 11 Oct. 1838                      Cass
Cook, Wm. to Matilda McCann 10 Apr. 1836                                Warr
Cook, Wm. to Elizabeth Wiggans 9 Dec. 1838                              Maco
Cook, Willson to Patsey Jones 9 Nov. 1826                               Pk-1
Cooke, Henry to Ann W. Sullers 4 Dec. 1836                              Carr
Cooke, Vel-- to Ann Williams 6 June 1839                                Maco
Cool, Wm. to Rodah Smiley 12 May 1822                                    Coop
Coolage, Charles to Marietta Stinson 1 Aug. 1838                        Clar
Cooley, Christopher C. to Nancy Officer 30 Sept. 1834                   Clay
Cooley, Harrison to Nancy Been 12 Jan. 1839                             Clay
Cooley, Isaac to Nancy Massey 9 Oct. 1836                               Rand
Cooley, John to Elizabeth White 2 June 1816                             Howa
Cooley, John to Polly Kitchens 3 Mar. 1821                              Char
Cooley, Joseph to Elizabeth Locke 15 Jan. 1838                          Maco
Cooley, Perrin to Lucy Carter 31 Jan. 1833                              Rand
Cooley, Timothy to Lucinda Mullinick 21 Mar. 1833                       Rand
Cooley, Wm. to Sarah A. Ballinger 10 Jan. 1839                          Rand
Cooly, Elias to Mahalay Lane 2 Oct. 1828                                Howa
Cooly, Isaac to Elizabeth Monroe 15 Jan. 1827                           Howa
Cooly, James to Polly Massey 16 Dec. 1817                               StCh
Cooly, John to Eliza Locke 4 Apr. 1832                                  Howa
Cooly, John to Martha Bierden 23 Nov. 1835                              Monr
Coon, Geo. to Jane Cantrell 29 Oct. 1829                                Linc
Coonce, Jacob to Levina Wamsley 31 Jan. 1839                            Polk
Coons, Felix to Lucinda Gibson 4 May 1837                               Linc
Coons, Geo. to Sallie Bell 29 Dec. 1833                                 Call
Coons, Wm. to Petitia Nichols 26 Nov. 1835                             Boon
Cooper, Albert J. to Eliza J. McDaniel 13 Sept. 1836                    John
Cooper, Benj. to Fanny Hancock 4 July 1816                              Howa
```

49

Cooper, Benj. to Phebe H. Sloan 18 Mar. 1831   Coop
Cooper, Braxton to Jinny Boggs 5 June 1814   StCh
Cooper, Charles D. to Diadana Blankenship 10 June 1839   Maco
Cooper, Charles W. to Josephine Titus 31 Jan. 1833   Rand
Cooper, Daniel C. to Mary Hall 6 Oct. 1836   Mari
Cooper, David to Mary R. Richardson 15 Mar. 1838   Fran
Cooper, Dulaney to Ann Haden 10 Dec. 1835   Howa
Cooper, Garnett to Elizabeth Brown 21 Mar. 1839   Fran
Cooper, Geo. to Sirena Parks 30 July 1834   Fran
Cooper, Hendley to Adaline Carson 23 Oct. 1828   Boon
Cooper, James to Mary Smith 10 Sept. 1839   Rall
Cooper, Jeremiah to Susan Carpenter 2 Aug. 1838   Coop
Cooper, John to Nancy Lakey 13 Oct. 1822   Howa
Cooper, John to Isabella Masters 28 June 1837   Morg
Cooper, John R. to Mrs. Elizabeth Williams 31 July 1831   Cr-P
Cooper, Joseph to Elizabeth Easter 5 Feb. 1818   Howa
Cooper, Joseph to Frances Marshall 13 Sept. 1838   Howa
Cooper, Joseph to Rebecca Davis 10 Feb. 1839   Ray
Cooper, Mathis to Patsy Whitney 11 Dec. 1839   Howa
Cooper, Nathan to Hannah Jones 30 Jan. 1834   Coop
Cooper, Nicholas to Jane E. Long 20 July 1837   Pk-B
Cooper, Patrick to Dotia Hoy 25 Aug. 1832   Howa
Cooper, Robt. to Elizabeth Carson 17 Aug. 1813   StCh
Cooper, Stephen to Malinda Tate 30 Sept. 1824   Howa
Cooper, Thomas to Heziak Stephens 24 Aug. 1826   Cole
Cooper, Walter to Frances Wells 26 Apr. 1832   Linc
Cooper, Wiley B. to Nancy A. Blakely 19 Dec. 1839   Morg
Cooper, Wm. to Susannah Higgins 25 Feb. 1818   Howa
Cooper, Wm. to Mariah Lewis 18 Mar. 1830   StFr
Cooper, Wm. to Mary Williams 18 July 1833   Fran
Cooper, Wm. to Lucetta McClure 28 Apr. 1835   Warr
Coopey, John to Susan Pollard 16 Feb. 1837   Linc
Coots, David to Lydia Linkhorn 12 Feb. 1832   CG-A
Coots, Uriah to Susanna Bryant 25 Dec. 1836   Cr-1
Cope, Geo. to Marthy Creek 14 Nov. 1839   Cass
Cope, John to Suckey Cole 21 Aug. 1826   Wash
Cope, Levi D. to Sarah Prier 23 July 1837   Clin
Copeland, Andrew to Sophia Hiatt 20 Feb. 1821   Howa
Copeland, Ezekiel to Malinda Gwinn 17 July 1822   Sali
Copeland, James to Rebecca Thompson 31 Oct. 1831   Howa
Copeland, John to Mary A. Wiseman 30 Dec. 1838   Gasc
Copeland, Moses to Amyann Ross 13 Mar. 1831   Wash
Copeton, John to Marthey Meals 19 Oct. 1837   Howa
Copher, James to Percilla McQuitty -- May 1837   Boon
Copher, Jessy to Mary A. McQuitty 23 May 1834   Monr
Copher, Samuel to Ann Ferner 29 Aug. 1838   Howa
Copman, Heun to Mana E. Sendker 31 Aug. 1839   StCh
Coppedge, Geo. W. to Sarah Burlison 11 Mar. 1830   Cr-P
Coppedge, Henson to Nancy Kitchens 23 Aug. 1832   Cr-1
Coppenbarger, Peter to Nancy Mathis 12 Dec. 1839   Plat
Corbiere, Joseph to Lisa Clairmont 20 Nov. 1837   StCh
Corbin, Alexander to Phebe Gainer 29 Oct. 1818   Howa
Cordell, Lewis to Ruth Carnegy 18 Aug. 1836   Lewi
Cordell, Lewis C. to Sary E. Hansucker 23 Aug. 1838 Lewi
Corder, Edward to Elizabeth Perman 5 Oct. 1837   John
Cordray, Wm. L. to Mary Wear 29 Mar. 1837   Coop
Cordry, Green R. to Eliza J. Steel 11 Aug. 1839   Coop
Cordry, John B. to Mary E. Wear 4 July 1838   Coop
Corlen, John to Jurughs White 26 July 1836   Boon
Corlew, Robt. to Susan Bridges 3 Mar. 1818   Howa
Corlew, Thomas D. to Margarett Smith 3 Jan. 1839   Mari
Corley, Joseph to Felicity Parue 10 Sept. 1822   Call
Corn, Absolom to Phebe Martin 25 Dec. 1837   Boon
Corn, J. to Saleeta Bridges 19 Dec. 1839   Jack
Corn, John D. to Nancy Brown 3 Nov. 1836   Jack

50

```
Corneile, Louis to Felicite Courcaute 31 July 1805          StCh
Cornelius, Benj. to Elizabeth Means 22 Feb. 1820            Howa
Cornelius, Benj. to Mary Davis 20 Feb. 1821                 Ray
Cornelius, Benj. to Elizabeth Adams 9 Nov. 1826            Howa
Cornelius, Jesse to Sally Skinner 4 Jan. 1838             Boon
Cornelius, John to Jane Means 29 June 1828                Howa
Cornelius, Josiah to Francis Redbetts 28 Apr. 1834        StCh
Cornelius, Levi to Fanny Bozarth 15 Aug. 1822             Howa
Cornelius, Reuben to Betsy Runkle 3 Jan. 1830             Rall
Cornelius, Robt. to Elizabeth Bevel 4 July 1838           Howa
Cornelius, Wm. to Permela Sullons 12 Mar. 1826            Gasc
Cornelius, Wm. to Hannah A. Hays 14 June 1831             Pk-1
Cornet, Edley to Elizabeth Davis 11 June 1828            Jack
Cornet, Literal to Susan Kemper 10 Mar. 1836             Howa
Cornet, Nathan to Elizabeth Wilson 16 Jan. 1831          Boon
Cornett, Wm. to Thursy Cochrean 14 Jan. 1830             Mari
Cornwall, Adamson to Martha Gray 30 Mar. 1833            Pett
Cornwell, Emmerson to Martha Willard 28 Apr. 1836        Jack
Correl, John W. to Elizabeth Penewell 4 Apr. 1839        Mari
Corsey, Henry to Mary Pace 18 Dec. 1839                  John
Corten, Timothy to Helen Casey 8 Oct. 1839               Wash
Corteny, James M. to Charlotte Twitty 19 Feb. 1829       Fran
Corts, Jesse to Patey Vee 13 Aug. 1835                   Sali
Corum, Felix to Mary Robinson 25 Feb. 1836               Coop
Corum, Harden to Agnes Cramer 14 June 1827               Coop
Corum, Harrison to Juliana Tevis 27 Jan. 1835            Coop
Corum, Heli to Eveline Lowrey 23 July 1824               Coop
Corum, Hiram to Mary Marquerer 4 Feb. 1819               Howa
Corum, John to Emeline Estes 17 Dec. 1833                Clay
Corum, Milton to Margarett T. Young 16 May 1837          Clay
Corum, Thompson to Rachel Riggs 7 Oct. 1834              Coop
Corvette, John to Polly Davis 6 Sept. 1822               Boon
Cosby, Josiah B. to Harriet Prince 19 July 1836          StCh
Cosher, David to Cynthia Gray 14 Apr. 1825               Howa
Cosner, Wm. to Sarah Woolsey 27 Feb. 1834                Carr
Cossy, Wm. to Mrs. Sarah McCalester 23 Dec. 1832         Pk-1
Costley, Michael to Mahala Mussett 18 Jan. 1827          Wash
Costner, Emanuel to Katherine Wills 22 Feb. 1838         CG-A
Cote, Joseph to Celeste Tayon 29 June 1807               StCh
Cote, Joseph to Mary M. Bricot 29 Apr. 1834              StCh
Cotes, John A. to Catherine Colvin 3 Feb. 1828           Boon
Cothron, Granville to Maryan Williams 29 Apr. 1827       Pk-1
Cotner, David to Catherine Miller 24 Feb. 1828           CG-A
Cotner, Marten to Elizabeth Moirs 6 Dec. 1838/9          Md-B
Cotner, Phillip to Sarah Miller 7 Oct. 1834              CG-B
Cotrell, John to Elizabeth Tulette 8 Jan. 1835           Lewi
Cotrell, Peter to Cynthian Dunn 28 Jan. 1836             Lewi
Cotte, Baptist to Susan Janis 19 July 1817               StCh
Cottle, Alonzo to Mahala Turner 23 Nov. 1834             Linc
Cottle, Alvora to Harriet Cottle 28 Jan. 1829            StCh
Cottle, John to Julia Hester 1 Nov. 1838                 Linc
Cottle, Stephen to Sally Turner 15 June 1808             StCh
Cotton, Gabriel to Elizabeth Apperson 28 Sept. 1828      Coop
Cotton, Gabriel to Margaret Geyer 14 Oct. 1835           Coop
Couch, Harrison to Julian Fanning 24 July 1836           Rall
Couch, John to Mahala Stroup 30 May 1839                 Jeff
Couch, Thompson to Lussee Hager 9 Oct 1834               CG-B
Coudere, Joseph to Lucille Saucier 22 Feb. 1828          StCh
Coulson, John to Mary Lewis 18 Aug. 1829                 Howa
Coulston, David to Elizabeth Messersmith 6 Feb. 1833     Cole
Coulston, Isaac to Susannah Newton 8 Dec. 1836           Char
Coulston, Jeremiah to Polly Newton 18 Aug. 1838          Char
Coulter, Charles to Agnes Gardner 2 Sept. 1827           Howa
Coulter, Lloyd H. to Emilia Cannon 9 Nov. 1837           Maco
Coumanche, Antoine to Mary L. DuBois 1 Oct. 1834         StCh
```

51

```
Counts, Geo. to Malinda Tongue 3 June 1828                          Md-A
Counts, John to Ellviry Stearman 31 Oct. 1833                      Wash
Counts, Joseph to Edith Griffith 5 Dec. 1833                       Pk-1
Counts, Nicholas to Louisa Shaw 8 Apr. 1833                        Md-A
Counts, Peter to Elender Jonson 28 July 1833                       Wash
Counts, Richard to Julia McClane 11 Sept. 1838                     Wash
Counts, Wm. to Rachel Davidson 2 Apr. 1839                         Warr
Couplin, John to Mary Jarey 14 Nov. 1830                           Rall
Courbe, Francis to Judith LeBeau 19 Jan. 1829                      StCh
Cournoyer, Pierre to Catherine DuBois 29 Oct. 1833                 StCh
Court, Laurence to Patsey Hearty 30 Oct. 1830                      Jeff
Courtley, Isaac to Polly Simpson 22 Sept. 1837                     Fran
Courtnay, Lewis to Cely Love 4 Mar. 1826                           Wash
Courtney, Robt. H. to S.S. McCutcheon 24 Dec. 1826                 StCh
Courtney, Robt. H. to Permelia Allen 27 Oct. 1831                  Mari
Courtois, Antoine to Cecile Oge' 14 Feb. 1831                      Wash
Courtois, Joseph to Scholatique Ronleau 27 Nov. 1830              Wash
Courtois, Stephen to Margaret Sansouci 12 July 1836              Wash
Courts, Jacob to Permelia Ray 1 Aug. 1834                          Howa
Courts, Walter H. to Malinda Northcut 8 Mar. 1838                  Carr
Covall, Wm. to Elizabeth Harriss 1 Apr. 1838                       Md-B
Covey, John H. to Susannah R. Petty 2 Mar. 1834                    Ray
Covington, Henry to Nancy Arnold 14 Nov. 1839                      Call
Covington, James to Narcissa E. Baker 30 Oct. 1838                StFr
Covington, John W.B. to LaPlata T.B. Ellis 19 Sept. 1839          StFr
Cowain, Samuel to Polly Miller 15 July 1838                        Gasc
Cowan, John F. to Elizabeth Hamilton 7 Nov. 1836                   Ray
Cowan, Wm. S. to Sarah Singleton 25 Jan. 1830                      Wash
Cowden, Hezekiah to Elizabeth Inglebart 9 Aug. 1838               Boon
Cowdry, Oliver to Elizabeth Whitner 18 Dec. 1832                   Jack
Cowen, Cornelius to Elizabeth Miller 22 Mar. 1827                  Coop
Cowen, Henry to Honor Howard 8 July 1819                           Coop
Cowen, Horace to Desdamonia Sagers 16 Oct. 1836                    Clay
Cowens, Nicholas to Elizabeth A. Harrington 7 Dec. 1837           Clay
Cowherd, Wm. to Eliza Owens 22 Nov. 1838                           Fran
Cox, Alfred to Sarah Green 18 Sept. 1838                           Rall
Cox, Daniel to Ann Henderson 8 Aug. 1830                           Jeff
Cox, Edward to Hannah Williams 21 Mar. 1833                        Cole
Cox, Ezekial to Nancy Esters 9 Aug. 1835                           Lafa
Cox, Hardin to Martha H. Brown 8 Apr. 1838                         Morg
Cox, Hosea to Nancy Farrer 11 Apr. 1839                            Perr
Cox, Ira to Elizabeth Linville 4 Sept. 1834                        Lafa
Cox, Isaac to Susan Reed 10 Apr. 1832                              Ray
Cox, James to Polly Helms 21 Aug. 1831                             Lafa
Cox, Joal to Malinda Lenor 3 Feb. 1835                             Lafa
Cox, John to Nancy Allen 23 Mar. 1835                              CG-B
Cox, John to Sarah Moberly 21 Apr. 1839                            Livi
Cox, John to Sarah A. Mathews 9 Oct. 1839                          Plat
Cox, John to Milly Keeny 17 Dec. 1839                              John
Cox, John B. to Bathsheba Millson 22 Jan. 1826                     Linc
Cox, Joseph to Dicy Helms 19 Nov. 1825                             Lafa
Cox, Joseph to Jane Odenale 30 July 1839                           Henr
Cox, Joseph M. to Phebe Turpin 17 Nov. 1839                        Lewi
Cox, Joshua to Esthur Kelly 7 Apr. 1823                            Coop
Cox, Joshua to Nancy Mitchel 2 July 1827                           Lafa
Cox, Nathanial to Margaret Cantrell 17 Dec. 1830                   Jack
Cox, Nathaniel to Nancy Maden 20 Aug. 1839                         Linc
Cox, Perry to Margaret Shock 1 Aug. 1838                           Boon
Cox, Pleasant M. to Elizabeth Nash 4 Mar. 1832                     Linc
Cox, Robt. to Louisa McFarland 9 Mar. 1836                         StFr
Cox, Samuel to Mary Stafford 18 June 1823                          Lafa
Cox, Samuel to Nancy Cantril 18 Mar. 1832                          Lafa
Cox, Samuel to Nancy Cantrill 1 Mar. 1833                          Lafa
Cox, Samuel to Eliza Wells 9 Aug. 1834                             Lewi
Cox, Silas to Peggy Helm 1 July 1824                               Lafa
```

52

Cox, Solomon to Polly Lile 8 May 1831   Ray
Cox, Solomon Sr. to Temperance Hendrick 22 Dec. 1831   Ray
Cox, Solomon to Ann Cooper 29 Aug. 1839   Livi
Cox, Stephen to Elizabeth Dowell 29 May 1836   Ray
Cox, Sylvester R. to Susan Harris 15 June 1838   Morg
Cox, Thomas to Elizabeth Hamm 12 Apr. 1838   Sali
Cox, Thomas W. to Martha Murry 15 Aug. 1833   Jack
Cox, Thompson to Nicey J. Whitney 23 Feb. 1837   CG-A
Cox, Wm. to Ruth Dickson 4 Feb. 1822   Lafa
Cox, Wm. to Margaret Barbarick 26 Jan. 1832   Gasc
Cox, Wm. to Elizabeth Cantrell 14 Feb. 1833   Lafa
Cox, Wm. to Lousanna Williams 30 Nov. 1834   Coop
Cox, Wm. to Margaret Farr 6 Sept. 1836   Perr
Cox, Wm. to Precious Campbell 23 Mar. 1837   Gasc
Coxdel, Drury to Margaret Tetherow 10 Aug. 1826   Clay
Coy, Henry to Minny Momouth 23 Jan. 1834   Howa
Coy, Louman to Margaret Leffler 21 Apr. 1821   Boon
Coy, Peter T. to Sarah Alberson 30 May 1839   Lafa
Coyle, Thomas to Louisa Ray 13 Aug. 1835   Jack
Cozens, Geo. W. to Eliza J. White 30 Jan. 1838   StFr
Crabtree, Abraham to Alice Ruraifs 6 Aug. 1829   Cole
Crabtree, John to Matilda Barks 29 -- 1836   Polk
Crabtree, Reese to Rachel Burress 10 Jan. 1839   Jack
Crabtree, Thomas to Eliza McDowell 29 Dec. 1836   Jack
Cracraft, Wm. to Elizabeth Stewart 25 Oct. 1818   CG-1
Craddock, Ransom to Ann Smiley 25 Dec. 1838   Cr-1
Crader, David to Hannah Barks 9 Oct. 1832   CG-A
Crafford, Wm. to Mrs. Nancy Brown 3 May 1829   Clay
Crafford, Wm. to Leah Edmondson 3 Mar. 1830   Jack
Craft, Daniel W. to Elizabeth Prewitt 11 Oct. 1838   Barr
Crafts, Samuel to Margaret Fisher 13 Oct. 1831   Fran
Crage, Alexander to Elizabeth McGee 21 May 1826   Wash
Crage, Samuel B. to Mahaly McGee 8 May 1828   Wash
Craghead, Geo. H. to Sarah Craghead 15 Apr. 1830   Call
Craghead, Robt. to Nancy Hughes 27 Feb. 1831   Call
Craghead, Soloman to Elizabeth Dunlap 13 Nov. 1826   Call
Craghead, Stephen to Nancy Blount 11 Mar. 1834   Call
Cragshead, Jonathan to Amanda Newbill 21 Feb. 1835   Pett
Craig, Carter T. to Mary S. Garner 14 Oct. 1836   Call
Craig, Geo. to Hannah Atwater 15 Mar. 1838   Call
Craig, James to Martha Newton 28 June 1838   Rand
Craig, John to Susan A. Ralph 15 Dec. 1831   Ray
Craig, John S. to Nancy McKey 4 Dec. 1828   Pk-1
Craig, Larkin to Ann Ficklin 7 June 1831   Call
Craig, Peter to Mary Ramsey 19 May 1808   CG-1
Craig, Thomas to Sarah Murrel 8 July 1830   Wash
Craig, Victor to Mrs. Nancy Martin 12 July 1836   Wash
Craig, Wm. Jr. to Mary Rean 8 Oct. 1829   StCh
Craig, Wm. to Sidney Smith 12 Dec. 1838   Call
Crain, Sanders to Isabella McQuitty 3 Mar. 1832   Boon
Crain, Wm. to Harriet Long 19 Apr. 1832   CG-A
Cramer, Henry H. to Ann M. Holzcher 13 Oct. 1839   Cole
Cramer, Wm. to Catherine Houx 1 Feb. 1827   Coop
Crandle, Benjamin to Rebecca Simmons 29 Apr. 1838   Davi
Crandle, Daniel to Perintha Abbot 24 Oct. 1832   Jack
Crane, Joel to Edna Anderson 23 May 1833   Howa
Crane, Joseph to Cassor Sullivan 26 Oct. 1834   Fran
Cranmer, Jonathan to Sarah E. Sexton 21 Jan. 1834   Boon
Cranston, John to Nancy Donneldson 26 Mar. 1835   Coop
Crasento, Thomas to Marandy Ratekin 14 Nov. 1839   Call
Crater, Michael to Eve Teters 19 Feb. 1828   StCh
Craven, David to Catharine Whitton 25 Jan. 1835   Ray
Cravens, Charles to Lucinda Bunch 20 Sept. 1821   Howa
Cravens, Emsley to Sarah Kivett 5 Dec. 1826   Howa
Cravens, James B. to Angelina Gasaway 20 May 1839   Lewi

```
Cravens, Thomas to Matilda Johnson 30 Nov. 1822          Howa
Cravens, Wm. to Perling Estell 9 Feb. 1830               Howa
Crawford, David to Sally Anderson 7 Feb. 1829            Howa
Crawford, Hugh to Mrs. Susan Clark 10 Mar. 1830          Howa
Crawford, James I. to Ann T. McCarty 17 Mar. 1836        Coop
Crawford, Jeptha to Betsey Harris 30 Jan. 1832           Jack
Crawford, John to Jane Bozarth 24 June 1821              Howa
Crawford, John to Sarilda Donohue 22 Apr. 1836           Pett
Crawford, John A. to Elizabeth Scobee 24 Apr. 1838       Monr
Crawford, John M. to Hannah Turnbow 5 Apr. 1838          Monr
Crawford, Robt. to Nancy Forbus 6 June 1837              Monr
Crawford, Thompson to Sarah Fountain 16 June 1831        Md-A
Crawford, Wilkinson to Nancy Sims 2 Aug. 1829            Rall
Crawford, Wm. to Emily Gorden 1 Nov. 1832                Lafa
Crawford, Wm. to Mrs. Lewesia Lane 1 Jan. 1834           Rall
Crawley, Daniel to Sally Howard 14 July 1830             Howa
Crawley, James to Frances Mayes 30 Sept. 1838            Ray
Crawley, Jeremiah to Margaret Anderson 27 Jan. 1831      Howa
Crawley, John to Julia Lee 27 May 1835                   Howa
Crawley, Josiah to Becky Morris 14 Jan. 1820             Howa
Crawley, Littlebury to Nancy Stass 12 Jan. 1826          Howa
Crawley, Thomas to Katherina Linville 3 Aug. 1820        Ray
Crawley, Wm. to Polly Eaton 28 Oct. 1832                 Ray
Creach, Geo. to Parthena Polard 14 Feb. 1839             Linc
Creason, Elijah to Elizabeth Lowell 27 Mar. 1816         Howa
Creason, Hiram to Ann Anderson 28 Aug. 1831              Boon
Creason, Isaac to Elizabeth Burnett 25 Mar. 1838         Ray
Creason, James to Nancy Mullins 16 Apr. 1837             Ray
Creason, James to Mary Bell 26 June 1839                 Sali
Creason, Leroy to Peggy Payne 28 Aug. 1829               Boon
Creason, Nile V. to Sarah Grindstaff 26 Dec. 1836        Char
Creason, Peter to Polly Massingill 15 Mar. 1821          Boon
Creason, Willis to Ruth Moody 2 July 1818                Howa
Creason, Willis to Margaret L. Parker 17 Mar. 1836       Jack
Creasy, John W. to Louisa W. Rains 24 Dec. 1837          Lewi
Creasy, Robt. to Nancy Reading 16 Mar. 1837              Lewi
Creasy, Wm. to Martha Raines 2 Mar. 1837                 Lewi
Creath, Albert to Elizabeth Juden 8 Feb. 1827            CG-A
Creath, John to Harriett Webb 11 Nov. 1829               CG-A
Creech, James to Margaret Rybolt 17 Sept. 1837           Linc
Creed, Geo. W. to Eliza Miller 6 Nov. 1834               Call
Creed, James M. to Martha J. Wilson 26 Feb. 1839         Call
Creeds, Gideon to Eusebell Sims 11 July 1838             Polk
Creeg, Jeromiah to Polly Smeltzer 28 Oct. 1835           John
Creek, Abram M. to Mary A. Beatty 19 Apr. 1838           Clay
Creek, Jacob to Virginia L. Younger 26 Oct. 1826         Clay
Creek, Kellean to Sarah McConnell 2 Oct. 1834            Clay
Creek, Milton to Malinda Riddle 6 Mar. 1836              Cass
Creek, Zacheus C. to Mary Boggoss 4 Mar. 1838            Clay
Crenshaw, Aaron S.H. to Eliza Garner 5 July 1836         Mari
Crenshaw, Joel to Nancy Norton 1831/2                    Linc
Crenshaw, Orvel to Marinday Norton 24 Oct. 1833          Pk-1
Crenshaw, Wm. to Isabella Norton 21 Dec. 1837            Linc
Crews, Caleb to Sally Graham 2 May 1839                  Bent
Crews, Charley to Malinda Lee 12 Dec. 1839               Howa
Crews, Daniel to Malinda Maupon 26 May 1831              Howa
Crews, Enoch to Sally Tolson 27 Jan. 1828                Howa
Crews, Howel to Eleanor Brown 21 Dec. 1834               Cole
Crews, Jesse to Lucca Lamb 11 Feb. 1827                  Char
Crews, Robt. to Mary Callahan 30 May 1823                Boon
Criddle, Edward to Mary Flinn 15 Sept. 1829              CG-A
Crider, Abraham to Mary Owens 5 Nov. 1829                Gasc
Crider, Dayton to Polley Emison 25 Aug. 1831             Pk-1
Crider, Daniel to Elizabeth Reed 24 Aug. 1826            Gasc
Crider, James to Mukey Owens 1 Jan. 1826                 Gasc
```

Crider, Joseph to Priscilla Reed 14 Sept. 1827   Fran
Crigler, Cristopher C. to Malinda Warren 16 July 1837   Carr
Crigler, Geo. L. to Susan J. Fruit 1 Mar. 1838   Monr
Crigler, John to Belinda Utterback 2 July 1835   Rall
Crimm, Gipson to Ann E. Godman 1 Dec. 1836   Monr
Crimshaw, Nicholas to Lerella DeWitt 30 Jan. 1838   Jack
Crisman, Wm. to Parmelia Wommack 18 May 1837   Linc
Crisp, Greenville to Elizabeth Cochell 6 Aug. 1836   John
Crisp, John to Malinda Inglish 28 Apr. 1833   Gree
Criswell, James to Patience A. Sexton 4 Jan. 1838   CG-A
Crites, Coonrad to Mary Wills 26 Dec. 1839   CG-B
Crites, Davault to Margit Johnson 30 July 1835   CG-B
Crites, Jacob to Nancy Shrader 30 Dec. 1819   CG-1
Crites, Joel to Susan Eaker 26 Aug. 1827   CG-A
Crites, Solomon to Sally Skyver 28 May 1829   CG-A
Crites, Solomon to Nancy Cawhorn 2 Aug. 1838   CG-A
Crits, Jacob to Katherine Dellinger 28 Nov. 1825   Md-A
Crits, John to Hethy Clay 11 Feb. 1836   Perr
Critz, Ephriam to Charlotte Critz 9 Feb. 1826   CG-A
Crocker, Hiram to Infinity Brellen 29 Mar. 1835   Cole
Crocker, Wm. to Sarah Manick 18 Feb. 1830   Lafa
Crocket, Wm. W. to Elizabeth Allison 12 Mar. 1839   Pk-B
Crockett, Hugh to Mary A.K. Wright 1 Nov. 1832   Boon
Crockett, Joseph to Nancy Wright 8 Jan. 1835   Boon
Croff, John to Susanna Jones 6 Nov. 1833   Howa
Croley, John to Emerine Stout 26 July 1838   Clay
Croley, Wm. to Lucinda Burnett 22 June 1830   Sali
Cronister, David to Susan Ervins 22 Aug. 1833   CG-A
Crook, Wm. W. to Ann M. Davis 13 Aug. 1839   Morg
Crooks, James to Harriet Bishop 18 Mar. 1838   Lewi
Crop, John to Sally Garman 15 Jan. 1832   Ray
Croplin, Theren to Anna Shipley 8 Mar. 1838   Polk
Cropper, Thomas to Ann Mitchel 29 June 1832   Boon
Cross, Albert to Lovina Howill 14 Nov. 1837   Howa
Cross, Anderson to Mary Hardister 9 Dec. 1830   Rand
Cross, Brown L. to Rachel Hardester 9 Dec. 1830   Rand
Cross, James to Martha Palmer 14 Nov. 1837   Rand
Cross, John to Elizabeth Goodwin 21 Jan. 1812   StGe
Cross, John to Rachel White 4 Jan. 1827   Char
Cross, John to Barbery Horrell 19 July 1836   CG-A
Cross, Noah to Mary Sears 7 Nov. 1839   Rand
Cross, Tolbert to Levice Huffman 27 Sept. 1827   Howa
Cross, Wm. to Elizabeth Smith 29 May 1839   Howa
Crossett, John to Mary Cummins 10 Dec. 1835   Clay
Crosswhite, Jeptha to Nancy Ledford 24 Nov. 1831   Rall
Crosswhite, John to Elizabeth Williams 22 Jan. 1835   Rand
Crosthwaite, John to Fanny Stone 22 Nov. 1832   Boon
Crosthwaite, John to Rozette Mosely 30 Mar. 1834   Boon
Crouch, Pleasant to Nancy Coffett 9 Feb. 1837   Gasc
Crouch, Thomas to Lewisann Fugate rec. 8 July 1836   Rall
Crouch, Wm. to Mahala Martin 11 July 1838   Linc
Crow, Andrew to Christena Zumwalt 30 June 1831   StCh
Crow, Geo. to Mary E. Howdershell 20 Nov. 1838   Linc
Crow, Henry to Susan Ripperton 5 Nov. 1829   Pk-1
Crow, Isaac to Eveline Crow 17 Jan. 1839   Pk-B
Crow, Jacob to Lucinda Worten 5 Dec. 1831   StCh
Crow, Jonathan to Mary Zumwalt 4 Oct. 1831   Fran
Crow, Louis to Nancy Zumwalt 17 Aug. 1828   StCh
Crow, Martin L.G. to Jain Jump 25 July 1839   Fran
Crow, Michael to Nancy Stringer 18 June 1829   Gasc
Crow, Michael to Harriet Foolly 25 Dec. 1834   Gree
Crow, Ross to Nancy Tyre 25 Aug. 1838   Fran
Crow, Ruben to Isabella Miller 17 May 1838   Mari
Crow, Samuel to Polly Jarvis 29 Jan. 1829   Fran
Crow, Samuel to Nancy Simpson 8 Dec. 1836   Jeff

Crow, Sanford to Nancy J. Brown 5 Jan. 1837   Pk-A
Crow, Wm. to Susannah Patton 17 Apr. 1836   Fran
Crowder, Mr. to Mary A. Probison 24 Apr. 1838   Perr
Crowder, John M. to Jane Coleman 19 Nov. 1835   Fran
Crowder, Michael to Rebecca H. Thomas 31 Dec. 1837   Wash
Crowin, Henry to Patsy Williams 17 July 1833   Gasc
Crowley, James to Betsey Thorp 15 Jan. 1829   Clay
Crowley, Samuel to Nancy Loe 15 June 1826   Clay
Crowley, Wm. to Elizabeth Gladdin 24 Dec. 1835   Henr
Crowson, Wm. to Rachel Miller 2 May 1839   Call
Crowther, Henry W. to Eliza Bruffee 19 July 1832   Coop
Croysdale, Abraham to Mary Campbell 13 Sept. 1827   Clay
Crum, Geo. to Polly Moore 12 July 1836   Cole
Crum, Jesse to Luezsa Hutson 18 Sept. 1836   Gree
Crump, Alfred to Lydia Bolin 27 July 1828   CG-A
Crump, Bollinger to Susan May 2 Feb. 1830   Call
Crump, D.W.S. to Mary Love 5 Dec. 1831   Call
Crump, Edmon to Nancy Dowlen 7 Oct. 1838   StFr
Crump, Findoll P. to Martha F. Wingo 15 Oct. 1834   Wash
Crump, Geo. to Betsy Aramen 28 June 1827   StFr
Crump, James to Sally Ratekin 1 Nov. 1832   Call
Crump, James H. to Cela Thompson 22 Oct. 1834   CG-B
Crump, Josiah to Eliza Grindstaff 20 Dec. 1838   Boon
Crump, Samuel to Elizabeth Baker 7 Jan. 1830   Call
Crump, Simpson to Mary J. West 12 Aug. 1830   Call
Crump, Thompson to Louisa Hays 22 Dec. 1825   Call
Crump, Turner to Mrs. Tabitha Saucier 27 Oct. 1833   StCh
Crump, Wm. M. to Mary J. Shull 9 Jan. 1834   Call
Crump, Zachariah to Olly Slinkard 27 Apr. 1837   CG-A
Cruncelton, Wm. to Eliza J. Cole 15 Jan. 1835   StFr
Cruse, Franciscus to Elizabeth Freymuth 17 Jan. 1837   StCh
Cruse, Robt. to America Bohannen 24 May 1827   Rall
Crutcher, Ambrose to Mary Holliday 12 Oct. 1837   Pk-B
Crutcher, Samuel to Eliza A. Holliday 8 Sept. 1836   Pk-1
Crutcher, Thomas to Hester Glenn 12 Apr. 1838   Monr
Crutchfield, Richard to Matilda Nash 15 Aug. 1837   Henr
Cuans, James to Polly Vassar 19 Dec. 1838   Clin
Culbertson, Isaac to Susan Tuggle 3 Oct. 1833   Mari
Culbertson, James to Rebecca Kidder 15 Jan. 1838   Mari
Culbertson, John to Elizabeth Usher 5 Dec. 1835   Char
Culbertson, Joseph to Myra Gash 7 Jan. 1827   Mari
Culbertson, Samuel to Sarah E. Whitelock 12 May 1839   Mari
Cull, Thomas J. to Elizabeth McGinas 19 Dec. 1837   John
Cullen, John P.C. to Beddy L. Tigert 20 Nov. 1828   Gasc
Cullum, R. John to Sarah Vestal 24 July 1834   Rand
Cully, John to Jane Wright 4 Mar. 1821   Howa
Culp, Benj. to Iscey Camron 5 Jan. 1827   Clay
Culp, Jonathan to Melinda Munkres 20 June 1832   Clay
Culp, Nathanial to Elizabeth Camron 31 Dec. 1827   Clay
Culton, Thomas to Mrs. Abigal Boring 13 Nov. 1838   Wash
Cumert, Wm. to Elizabeth Miller 12 May 1836   Cole
Cumming, Hiram to Mary Hall 28 Mar. 1839   Jack
Cummings, Phillip to Patsy Wells 5 May 1836   Wash
Cummings, Thomas to Amy Standage 29 June 1835   Cr-1
Cummins, John to Eliza Wood 10 July 1833   Jack
Cummins, Robt. A. to Catherine C. Long 13 Nov. 1833   StCh
Cummins, Samuel B. to Eleanor C. Crossit 25 Oct. 1832   Clay
Cummins, Wm. to Elizabeth W. Tally 8 Dec. 1836   Pk-1
Cummins, Wm. to Lydia McMurtrie 3 Sept. 1839   Davi
Cummins, Wm. H. to Francis A. Reddish 19 Sept. 1839   Lewi
Cumpton, Isom to Lucy Shoemate 23 July 1834   Cr-1
Cundiff, John to Marilla Phillips 30 Nov. 1837   Clar
Cunduff, James to Elizabeth Wyatt 16 Nov. 1831   Wash
Cunningham, Abner to Betsey A. Woodlan 21 Dec. 1837   Warr
Cunningham, Andrew to Ester Cooper 13 Dec. 1838   Linc

56

```
Cunningham, Andrew W. to Louisa Amick 24 Aug. 1837              Rand
Cunningham, Charles B. to Lucy Wilson 26 Feb. 1829             StFr
Cunningham, Jacob to Sally Thompson 22 Feb. 1826              StFr
Cunningham, Jesey S. to Sary D. Buckner 17 Sept. 1839         Monr
Cunningham, John to Sarah Bain 2 Aug. 1824                    StFr
Cunningham, John to Delina Padgett 20 Dec. 1825              Howa
Cunningham, John to Elizabeth Fountain 9 Nov. 1837           Boon
Cunningham, John to Elizabeth R. Burnen 10 Mar. 1839        Buch
Cunningham, John A. to Amy Cox 8 May 1836                    Carr
Cunningham, Joseph to Caroline Cramer 12 May 1831            Coop
Cunningham, Moses to Huldah Starks 7 Aug. 1825              StFr
Cunningham, Porter to Polly Piles 12 Feb. 1835              Rand
Cunningham, Robt. to Margaret Moris 22 Oct. 1839            Rall
Cunningham, Thomas to Ann E. Christman 18 Sept. 1833        Linc
Cunningham, Thomas to Decilla Simms 4 June 1835             StCh
Cunningham, Wm. to Tempey Cooley 4 Feb. 1819                Howa
Cunningham, Wm. to Abigail Frazier 28 Aug. 1834             StCh
Cunningham, Wm. F. to Sarah Wilson 22 Dec. 1836             Mari
Cunningham, Wm. G. to Elizabeth McCourtney 7 June 1835      Jeff
Cupples, Samuel to Mary Thomas 15 Mar. 1821                 CG-1
Cure, Bartlett to Betsy Hardwick 12 Feb. 1835              Carr
Curnuth, David to Elizabeth Farmer 3 Mar. 1835             Cole
Currell, Edward to Thankful Sears 31 May 1838              Howa
Curren, Waddy T. to Mariah Woods 5 Apr. 1836               Char
Curtis, David to Sarah Walls 3 July 1834                   Howa
Curtis, Enoch to Selah Anderson 15 Feb. 1821               Howa
Curtis, Joel to Elizabeth Smart 14 Apr. 1829               Howa
Curtis, John to Cynthia Mann 15 Nov. 1833                  Ray
Curtis, John to Ann Moore 9 Aug. 1835                      Howa
Curtis, Perry to Eliza J. Mason 17 Dec. 1839               Clin
Curtis, Samuel to Cinthy Elliott 25 July 1836             Char
Curtis, Samuel to Nancy Phillips 8 Feb. 1838              Ray
Curtis, Thomas to Matilda Moore 3 Mar. 1835               Howa
Curtis, Wm. to Hannah David 5 Dec. 1830                   Gasc
Curtis, Williamson A. to Harriet Swearingen 11 July 1819  Howa
Custer, Steven G.R. to Susan Ornbern 15 Mar. 1838         Monr


Dabney, Thomas J. to Cassandra Walker 24 May 1837         Maco
Dace, Herman to Elizabeth Everette 13 June 1825           Jeff
Dace, John to Rachel Quarles 2 Mar. 1837                  Wash
Dace, John to Elender Crump 19 Apr. 1839                  StFr
Daggs, Wm. to Frances Sawyer 12 Apr. 1838                 Clar
Dagien, John L. to Rebecca Williams 20 June 1827          Jeff
Dagley, James to Polly Whitsett 9 June 1839               Clin
Daguette, Peter to Theodosia Rigdon 31 Oct. 1826          StGe
Daile, James to Polly Webb 31 Dec. 1826                   Rall
Dailey, James to Sally Medley 30 Oct. 1830                Rand
Daily, John to Brittannia Arthur 17 Jan. 1833             Jack
Daily, John to Prisey Ross 1 May 1834                     Jack
Daily, Michael to Jane Douglas 30 Dec. 1823               Boon
Dalaney, Joseph to Elizabeth Moore 28 Mar. 1836           Monr
Dalby, Joseph to Margaret LaGatorie 27 May 1809           StCh
Dale, Jacob C. to Margaret Creek 10 Sept. 1829            Clay
Dale, John to Cyntha Woods 12 Feb. 1835                   Rall
Dale, Jonathan to Margaret Almond 15 July 1827            Char
Dallas, Robt. to Peggy A. Feilder 1 Mar. 1838            Cole
Dallas, Wm. to America Conner 30 Aug. 1838                Cr-1
Dalton, James to Nancy Bradley 28 July 1839               Howa
Dalton, Wm. to Sarah Spotts 11 Feb. 1834                  Wash
Daly, James W. to Isabella Morrow 8 Mar. 1827             Boon
Daly, John to Arrenia Morrow 16 July 1829                 Boon
Daly, Wm. to Susanna Burnum 24 Feb. 1836                  Clin
Daly, Wm. to Mary Gilmore 3 Sept. 1836                    Polk
Damron, Nicholas T. to Jane Cannon 25 Feb. 1834          Linc
```

Danel, Alexander to Viney How 21 Sept. 1836   Howa
Danforth, John W. to Precilla Price 19 Dec. 1838   Barr
Danforth, Jonathan E. to Mary Williams 6 Nov. 1838   Barr
Daniel, Ellison A. to Sary A. Turnbeau 31 Oct. 1839   Rall
Daniel, John M. to Amantha Hector 3 Mar. 1828   CG-A
Daniel, John O. to Elizabeth Pennott 8 Apr. 1833   CG-A
Daniels, Alexander to Elizabeth B. Lowell 21 Mar. 1839   Fran
Daniels, David to Huldah Peebly 16 May 1837   Clay
Daniels, Robt. to Nancy Riffle 26 Aug. 1830   Linc
Daniles, David to Metilda Shaws 7 July 1838   Clay
Danilson, David to Julia Burton 29 Aug. 1832   Monr
Danilson, Thomas to Nancy Herryford 25 June 1829   Rall
Danilson, Wm. to Elizabeth Herryford 16 July 1829   Rall
Darby, Aaron to Susannah C. Reser 18 July 1839   Polk
Darby, Andrew to Sally Davis 31 Dec. 1829   Boon
Darby, John F. to Mary Wilkinson 20 Sept. 1836   Perr
Darman, Wm. to Sally Dedrick 7 July 1836   Cr-1
Darney, Geo. W. to Nancy Painter 25 May 1839   Monr
Darr, Wm. to Margaret Parker 10 Mar. 1835   Mari
Darr, Willis to Maria Shobe 8 Apr. 1839   Mari
Darst, Jacob C. to Elizabeth Bryan 25 Mar. 1813   StCh
Dase, Dennis to Catherine Peters 6 Aug. 1835   Wash
Daugherty, Evan to Sarah Green 15 Dec. 1833   CG-A
Daugherty, Franklin to Anny Walker 27 June 1839   Howa
Daugherty, Jabez E. to Harriet Vaughn 8 Aug. 1833   Pk-1
Daugherty, John to Margaret Willson 4 Dec. 1831   Fran
Daugherty, John to Mary Shook 29 May 1836   Wash
Daugherty, John H. to Catherine Summers 28 Feb. 1839   CG-B
Daugherty, Joseph L. to Rosey A. Rich 10 Sept. 1839   Clay
Daugherty, Macajah to Anny Walker 27 June 1839   Howa
Daugherty, Ralph to Sarah Frizell 13 Oct. 1825   CG-A
Daughorty, Geo. to Mary Lucas 9 May 1834   Carr
Daum, Silas to Polly Roe 6 Oct. 1825   CG-A
Davault, Wily to Margaret Rhodes 29 Mar. 1832   CG-A
Davenport, Daniel to Betsey Scot 8 Mar. 1838   John
Davenport, James to Mary Evans 22 July 1830   Clay
Davenport, James to Letitha Turner 26 Sept. 1838   Boon
Davenport, Julius to Sarah Harris 11 Apr. 1839   John
Davenport, Stephen to Elena Holloway 10 Dec. 1839   Boon
Davenport, Zachariah to Lize Whittenburg 17 Mar. 1831   CG-A
David, Lewis to Jane Smith 7 Feb. 1836   Gasc
Davidson, Armstrong T. to Hannah H. Kenady 26 Jan. 1837   Polk
Davidson, Cosby to Ann W. Williams 2 Sept. 1835   Wash
Davidson, Geo. to Sarah Davis 3 Mar. 1836   Mari
Davidson, Geo. to Rebecca Woolard 22 Jan. 1839   Polk
Davidson, Geo. S. to Nancy Montgomery 19 July 1838   Henr
Davidson, John to Mrs. Rebecca Pool 6 Dec. 1836   Gree
Davidson, John K. to Lucy Tillery 7 Nov. 1837   Clay
Davidson, Joseph to Margaret Snider 17 May 1836   Ripl
Davidson, Samuel to America A. Billups 3 Oct. 1839   Fran
Davidson, Thomas to Juleann Pickans 12 Oct. 1836   Morg
Davidson, Thomas to Linda M. Davis 4 July 1839   Mari
Davidson, Wm. Jr. to Harriet Murphy 19 Apr. 1835   Wash
Davidson, Wm. M. to Sarah Snodgrass 15 Oct. 1835   Cr-1
Davis, Abner to Sarah Moon 1 July 1835   Jeff
Davis, Abraham to Sally Burns 1 Sept. 1831   Pk-1
Davis, Abraham to Nancy Waggoner 30 Nov. 1834   CG-B
Davis, Allen to Sally Sheperd 15 Sept. 1830   Jack
Davis, Allen to Betsy Flanery 5 Feb. 1834   Jack
Davis, Allen to Missouri Scott 24 Dec. 1835   Cr-1
Davis, Anderson to Ann Head 18 Aug. 1826   Boon
Davis, Andrew to Caroline McClanahan 29 Aug. 1833   Coop
Davis, Andrew to Louisa Tilford 4 Oct. 1835   Boon
Davis, Andrew J. to Grisellah W. Staley 22 Dec. 1836   Pk-1
Davis, Augustus to Frances Buckner 7 Nov. 1832   Cole

58

```
Davis, Barnabas C. to Julia A. Davis 1 Feb. 1832              Call
Davis, Benj. to Priscilla Butt 3 Apr. 1829                   Wash
Davis, Benj. to Jane Gallet 2 July 1833                      Cole
Davis, Benj. to Matilda Woods 5 Mar. 1835                    Cole
Davis, Benj. to Emily Perten 8 Aug. 1839                     Gree
Davis, Benj. W. to Friediela Barr 19 Apr. 1837               Lewi
Davis, Bowler D. to Lucy Keath 30 Aug. 1838                  Mari
Davis, Buford to Sally Davis 29 Apr. 1827                    Rall
Davis, Burrell to Eliza Lane 2 Dec. 1833                     Mari
Davis, Caswell to Sarah A. White 3 Aug. 1834                 Lafa
Davis, Charles to Jane Cole 14 Apr. 1822                     Coop
Davis, Charles to Lucinda Jackson 23 May 1831                Wash
Davis, Clark to Leviney McBride 12 July 1821                 Howa
Davis, Daniel G. to Harriet E. Medley 1 July 1834            Rand
Davis, Daniel G. to Catherine Rutherford 11 Apr. 1839        Rand
Davis, David to Maryiah Moss 6 Dec. 1827                     CG-A
Davis, David to Matilda Whitelow 3 Nov. 1835                 CG-B
Davis, Edward to Manervy Lawrence 15 Dec. 1835               Howa
Davis, Edward R. to Martha Haynes 2 Feb. 1836               Ray
Davis, Elijah to Lucinda Haynes 15 Jan. 1828                 Call
Davis, Elijah to Lydia Newkern 13 Feb. 1833                  Warr
Davis, Erven to Bothea Duncan 29 Apr. 1836                   Howa
Davis, Evan to Malinda Williams 3 Sept. 1839                 Monr
Davis, Ezra S.E. to Catharine Stetler 23 Mar. 1837          Mari
Davis, Fleming to Martha Logan 28 Mar. 1839                  John
Davis, Frederick to Catherine Gilmore 26 July 1832           StCh
Davis, Gabriel to Cynthia Kinkaid 24 Jan. 1833               Mari
Davis, Garrett to Eve Shookman 25 Aug. 1832                  Fran
Davis, Geo. to Elizabeth Alexander 26 Feb. 1826             Wash
Davis, Geo. to Javel Wilson 15 Apr. 1832                     Jeff
Davis, Geo. to Lucey Clark 9 May 1839                        Polk
Davis, Gillian to Mrs. Rachel Newkirk 12 June 1836           CG-A
Davis, Greer W. to Elizabeth McGuire 20 Sept. 1835           CG-B
Davis, Harper E. to Hulday Hubbard 3 Aug. 1815               StCh
Davis, Henry to Jane Keller 6 Dec. 1839                      Clar
Davis, Henry to Elizabeth Swift 12 Dec. 1839                 Boon
Davis, Henry M. to Catherine Ligon 25 Sept. 1839            Linc
Davis, Hudson to Elizabeth Brewen 6 Mar. 1837               StFr
Davis, Ichabod J. to Elizabeth Haygood 3 Aug. 1837          Pk-A
Davis, Irvine to Margaret Kerr 18 Mar. 1833                  Pk-1
Davis, Isaac to Malinda Gillispy 9 May 1824                  StFr
Davis, Isaac W. to Rebecca M. Baker 13 Oct. 1836            Sali
Davis, James to Elizabeth Fox 9 Nov. 1826                    Rall
Davis, James to Elizabeth Clemments 14 June 1827            Md-A
Davis, James to Susan Hunt 21 Oct. 1827                      Coop
Davis, James to Jennie Francis 28 Jan. 1828                  Jeff
Davis, James to Fanny Carpenter 25 Nov. 1828                 Coop
Davis, James to Margaret Campbell 12 Aug. 1830               Boon
Davis, James to Nancy Johnson 3 Oct. 1832                    Howa
Davis, James to Elizabeth Moody 12 July 1835                 Gasc
Davis, James to Eliza C. Hunter 12 Jan. 1837                 Wash
Davis, James to Ellen Tisdale 14 Mar. 1837                   Pk-A
Davis, James A. to Pernice Lile 10 May 1832                  Ray
Davis, James C. to Frances Mason 4 Apr. 1839                 Rand
Davis, James H. to Letitia R. Staley 26 July 1831            Pk-1
Davis, James M. to Elizabeth Norris 12 Oct. 1837             Clar
Davis, Jared to Nancy Welch 6 Mar. 1834                      Warr
Davis, Jarret to Patsy Harp 1 Aug. 1839                      Mill
Davis, Jeremiah to Dorenda Gilbreath 4 Sept. 1839            Coop
Davis, John to Margaret Clark 28 June 1827                   Jeff
Davis, John to Katherine Rhodes 16 Sept. 1830               Mari
Davis, John to Mary Stephens 11 June 1835                    Coop
Davis, John to Amanda Stevens 20 May 1838                    Monr
Davis, John to Martha Powell 9 Jan. 1839                     Shel
Davis, John A. to Elizabeth Crafts 29 Apr. 1831             Cr-1
```

Davis, John B. to Margaret Young 25 Apr. 1834	Call
Davis, John E. to Clementine Campbell 25 Aug. 1031	Fran
Davis, John S. to Missouri Line Buis 21 Apr. 1831	CG-A
Davis, Joseph to Ann Turley 6 Sept. 1821	Boon
Davis, Joseph to Jane Scribners 1 Apr. 1830	Fran
Davis, Joseph to Margaret Craig 2 June 1831	Boon
Davis, Joseph to Permelia Kirkpatrick 13 Sept. 1832	Rand
Davis, Joseph to Hannah Myers 24 May 1838	Rand
Davis, Joseph to Sarah E. Green 2 Feb. 1839	Howa
Davis, Joseph L. to Susan T. Richardson 14 Jan. 1836	Coop
Davis, Joshua to Eliza Null 2 Oct. 1831	Jeff
Davis, Josiah to Polly Harden 29 Apr. 1824	Howa
Davis, Lenore to Elizabeth Shelton 20 May 1830	Linc
Davis, Leonard to Katharine Gilberts 1 Oct. 1835	Mari
Davis, Lewis to Dicy Morris 8 Aug. 1834	Fran
Davis, Ludwell to Emily Waters 3 Mar. 1820	CG-1
Davis, Luke to Nancy McKee 19 Feb. 1826	StFr
Davis, Madison to Mary Ella 8 Dec. 1836	Call
Davis, Martin to Eveline Vilot 18 May 1837	Carr
Davis, Mathew to Henaretty Lewis 25 Aug. 1836	Mari
Davis, Matthew to Elizabeth Wilfley 7 July 1835	Call
Davis, Mirich to Sary Anderson 14 Feb. 1828	Jack
Davis, Nathanial to Jane Hastings 3 Jan. 1837	Howa
Davis, Nathaniel to Maria A. Allen 19 Oct. 1836	Ray
Davis, Patrick to Eliza J. Dutch 17 -- 1833	CG-A
Davis, Peter E. to Katherine McKinzie 14 Feb. 1832	Cole
Davis, Philip to Rachel Herrod 31 Aug. 1826	StFr
Davis, Pleasant to Catherine O. Edelin 22 Oct. 1839	Linc
Davis, Reese to Catherine Vanmeter 13 May 1837	Sali
Davis, Silas to Minerva Brown 9 Jan. 1834	Jack
Davis, Simon to Susan Elliott 13 Aug. 1837	Rall
Davis, Squire to Paulina Noel 22 July 1838	Monr
Davis, Stephen H. to Martha Lastly 6 Sept. 1838	Gree
Davis, Temple to Francis A. Hendren 16 Feb. 1837	Mari
Davis, Thomas C. to Mary Emmonson 13 May 1830	Howa
Davis, Thomas J. to Ann E. Field 22 Dec. 1825	Rall
Davis, Thomas J. to Lontesia V. Swan 1 Sept. 1829	Call
Davis, Thomas K.H. to Malinda J. McLaughlin 21 Nov. 1839	Mill
Davis, Thomas M. to Catharine Tibbs 6 Dec. 1838	Lafa
Davis, Thomas W. to Emiline Doyle 19 Sept. 1833	Coop
Davis, Timothy to Nancy Wilson 9 Feb. 1823	StGe
Davis, Uriah to Elizabeth Dulany 19 Mar. 1833	Rand
Davis, Warren to Hannah Kenchlee 5 July 1829	Coop
Davis, Wm. to Mahala McFarland 20 Jan. 1823	Coop
Davis, Wm. to Eliza Baker 30 May 1831	Call
Davis, Wm. to Elizabeth Davis 19 Apr. 1832	Coop
Davis, Wm. to Nancy Literal 9 May 1832	Jack
Davis, Wm. to Elizabeth Sumpter 31 Jan. 1833	Wash
Davis, Wm. to Elizabeth Price 24 Dec. 1835	Pk-1
Davis, Wm. to Isabella Shuemaker 17 Mar. 1836	Lafa
Davis, Wm. to Susan Laremore 22 Jan. 1838	Fran
Davis, Wm. H. to Jane E. Crawley 6 July 1837	Howa
Davis, Wm. H. to Editha Davis 20 Mar. 1838	John
Davis, Wm. H.H. to America W. Estes 17 Sept. 1839	Clay
Davis, Wm. M. to Mary Piercy 2 June 1836	Monr
Davis, Wm. R. to Eliza Suttles 22 Dec. 1836	Mari
Davison, Nathaniel to Ann Eastes 29 July 1828	Lafa
Dawson, Alexander to Sarah Haddock 15 Sept. 1835	Boon
Day, Charles to Amanda Hoover 12 Aug. 1838	Gree
Day, Charles A. to Nancy Walker 27 May 1835	Call
Day, Daniel to Permelia May 22 Feb. 1838	Coop
Day, Ezekiel to Sarah Branson 25 Jan. 1838	Call
Day, James to Emila Rochester 5 Apr. 1832	StCh
Day, John to Martha Humphrey 29 Mar. 1823	Gasc
Day, Robt. to Harriet Kelly 24 Jan. 1839	Polk

Day, Valentine to Minerva Oaks 31 Dec. 1837   Wash
Day, Wm. to Eliza Childress 15 Nov. 1832   Call
Dayley, James to Darcus Crawley 29 July 1818   Howa
De--, John to Mary J. Carty 27 Oct. 1836   StFr
Deaderick, John S. to Ellen G. Cotter 19 Dec. 1839   Wash
Deaken, Squire to Susan More 26 Dec. 1832   Cole
Deal, Dennis G. to Mary A. Proctor 18 July 1839   Gree
Dealson, Benj. to Jeanneat L. McClanahan 7 Aug. 1836   Coop
Dean, Abner to Melinda E. Hollans 15 Dec. 1839   Buch
Dean, Geo. to Jane Daly 17 Dec. 1835   Perr
Dean, Geo. W. to Rachel D. Johnston 17 Mar. 1838   Coop
Dean, Greenberry to Jane Nicholson 12 Oct. 1837   Mari
Dean, Henry to Mary A. Tucker 12 June 1827   Perr
Dean, John to Margaret Malone 18 Oct. 1825   Wash
Dean, Laven to Missouri A. Evans 1 June 1834   Rand
Dean, Madison to Nancy McWilliams 16 Nov. 1832   Mari
Dean, Owen R. to Mellisa A. Brashears rec. 3 June 1837   Rall
Dean, Peter to Sarah Tucker 8 May 1832   Perr
Dean, Wm. to Theresa Dunn 27 May 1828   Perr
Deane, Henry to Emily Henderson 17 Mar. 1836   CG-B
Dearing, Albin J. to Mary M. Harris 30 Aug. 1837   Call
Dearing, Joseph W. to Ann Wine 7 Mar. 1835   Rall
Dearmand, Eli to Nancy Vivion 15 Nov. 1832   Cole
Deaver, Jahon M. to Mary B. Hughes 29 Mar. 1838   Fran
Deblois, John B. to Magdalene Calliote 9 Feb. 1832   Md-A
Debo, John to Ann Snell 23 Sept. 1835   Call
Dechouquet, Joseph to Euphemia Valle 26 Jan. 1836   Md-B
Deck, Frederick to Margarett Clubb 2 Aug. 1838   Md-B
Deckard, John to Polly Crawford 6 Sept. 1832   Coop
Decker, Jacob to Betty Withington 13 Aug. 1837   Fran
Decker, John to Mary Nance 13 Jan. 1831   Call
Decker, John to Mrs. Unity Lecount 25 Oct. 1835   Jack
Decker, John Jr. to Luticia Macculla 24 Mar. 1839   Fran
Decker, Wm. to Mary J. Decker 3 Dec. 1835   Fran
Deckins, Wm. to Gane Eavins 9 Jan. 1834   Morg
Decleose, Huett to Mary Lore 14 Apr. 1839   Wash
Declew, Francis to Sally Jackson 14 Feb. 1836   Wash
Declue, Anthony to Emiline Brown 2 May 1833   Wash
Declue, Michael to Tarece Miot 27 Feb. 1827   Wash
Deed, James to Martha A. McGinnis 29 Dec. 1836   Linc
Deeds, Bryant to Sarah Null 25 Jan. 1827   Jeff
Deering, James to Mary J. Duncan 4 Oct. 1839   Ripl
Deering, Sanford to Nancy Hungate 23 Feb. 1837   Monr
Deez, Ezekel to Macolia W. Stephens 21 July 1836   Md-B
Degagnier, John B. to Mary A. Dapron 25 Nov. 1834   Wash
Degagnier, Louis to Marie A. Dagen 25 Nov. 1834   Wash
Degagrie, Nicholas to Maria A. Boyer 6 May 1834   Wash
Degane, A. to Phebey Mier 30 Dec. 1818 (p.15)   Md-D
Degarreth, Josiah to Mahala Boyce 15 Dec. 1822   Boon
Degraffenreed, Monroe to Nancy Johnson 15 Sept. 1839   Polk
DegraftanReed, Vincent to Lucretia Brown 6 Oct. 1837   Gree
Deguer, Francious to Sophia McFarland 20 Dec. 1827   StFr
Deguire, Benj. to Marcellite Isom 19 Feb. 1833   Md-A
Deguire, Frances to Eliza McFarland 28 Nov. 1830   StFr
Deguire, Henry to Mary Bernier 7 Jan. 1835   Md-A
Deguire, John B. to Nancy Brewer 8 Sept. 1818   Md-B
Deguire, Louis Jr. to Judith Lachance 26 Dec. 1828   Md-A
Deguire, Michael to Eliza Kelly 13 Jan. 1829   Md-A
Dehaven, Benj. to Mary White 12 Nov. 1829   Boon
Dejarnett, Jefferson to Malissa Anderson 21 Nov. 1839   Pett
Dek, John to Fanny Baker 24 Feb. 1839   CG-B
Delaney, Dearborn to Matilda Alvis 12 Sept. 1833   Pk-1
Delaney, James to Ruthey Woods 17 Jan. 1828   Howa
Delaney, Wm. to Elizabeth Greening 7 May 1835   Monr
Delanney, John to Tempy Banister 26 Aug. 1832   StFr

Delany, John to Sarah Sparks 20 Mar. 1834   Monr
Delashmuth, John K. to Precilla Thomson 2 Apr. 1834   Perr
Delassus, Leon to Marie L. Elliott 19 Sept. 1837   StFr
Delcomis, David to Nancy Browning 27 Mar. 1834   Linc
Delcour, Nickolas to Mary Missrt 21 July 1835   Wash
Delec, Francis to Unity Frost 29 Aug. 1821   Ray
Delecy, Louis to Nancy Handcock 25 Nov. 1829   Perr
Delitour, Isaac to Mary Moore 16 Jan. 1835   Lafa
Dell, Joshua to Polly Woods 10 May 1821   Coop
Dellinger, Joseph to Elizabeth Sietze 18 Dec. 1825   Md-A
Dellinger, Moses to Hannah Crites 28 Mar. 1831   CG-A
Delmar, John to Cecilia Doran 27 Dec. 1828   Clay
Demare, John L. to Angelique Gotien 11 July 1836   StCh
Demarree, Cornelius Jr. to Delphine Keepers 15 Nov. 1837   Jeff
DeMerrit, Jacob to Glorane E. Ward 21 May 1833   Linc
Demica, Wm. F. to Martha J. Shackleford 11 Dec. 1836   Sali
Dempsey, James to Mary Gibbs 23 Feb. 1837   Pett
Dempsey, James to Mary Gibbs 28 Feb. 1837   Howa
Dempsey, Joseph B. to Mary Walker 19 Mar. 1833   CG-A
Denham, John to Polly Ferguson 6 Dec. 1837   StFr
Denison, Wm. to Sarah A. Cooper 8 Mar. 1832   Cr-A
Dennington, Reuben to Tilitha C. Davidson 19 July 1838   Coop
Dennis, Anthony W. to Emily Houx 3 Dec. 1836   Coop
Dennis, James to Nancy Atterberry 28 July 1834   Howa
Dennis, Lewis to Phebe Sebastian 18 Sept. 1838   StFr
Dennis, Samuel to Elizabeth Arhart 28 Feb. 1831   Coop
Dennis, Samuel to Forlee Green 8 Feb. 1835   Morg
Dennis, Wm. to Sarah Sparks 31 Dec. 1837   Polk
Dennison, Elisha T. to Mary W. Evans 18 May 1830   Howa
Dennison, Joseph to Lucinda Vermillion 18 Oct. 1838   Barr
Denny, Rice to Rebecca Rowland 12 Dec. 1824   Howa
Denoyez, Francois to Angelique Quenelle 29 July 1807   StCh
Densman, Thomas to Nancy Yarnal 7 Sept. 1826   Coop
Densman, Thomas to Sally Robinson 18 Feb. 1827   Coop
Dent, Augustus to Sidney Ravencroft 6 May 1838   CG-B
Dent, Joab to Clerinda Walkins 20 Dec. 1826   StGe
Dent, Josiah to Polly Jameson 12 June 1826   Fran
Dent, Lewis to Eliza A. Simms 8 Jan. 1835   StFr
Denton, Jonathan to Jane Scott 3 Jan. 1833   Gree
Denton, Tipton to Eliza Scott 16 Feb. 1833   Gree
Dentston, John to Didima Bristoe 5 Apr. 1838   Polk
Derbin, Erastus to Sarah A. Riney 18 Aug. 1834   Mari
Derick, Harvey to Carline Feaster 18 Oct. 1832   Cole
Deroi, Michel to Julie Daniel 20 Jan. 1829   StCh
Derosett, Lewis to Melinda Daily 14 Feb. 1839   Polk
DeRoy, ---- to Mary T. Vallie 12 Feb. 1833   StCh
Deroy, Michel to Eulalie Barrada 7 July 1807   StCh
Derrigs, McDaniel to Mary Buckner 4 Jan. 1827   Cole
Derroyer, Francis to Therese Bourdeaux 27 Sept. 1830   StCh
Deruck, Joel L. to Sophia Ridgeway 1 May 1828   Boon
Desange, Geo. to Harriette Moore 1 Mar. 1820   StCh
Desha, Ely to Evy Revel 28 Aug. 1834   Md-A
Deshazer, Robt. to Elizabeth Tovel 27 Sept. 1838   Howa
Deshazo, John T. to Charlotte Walker 22 June 1837   Call
Desloge, Fermin to Cythiann McIlvain 21 June 1832   Wash
Desper, Forest G. to Sarah Jones 24 Aug. 1838   Fran
Detchmendy, Clement to Amelia Wathen 26 Dec. 1837   CG-A
Detchmendy, Edward to Henrietta Wathen 13 May 1839   CG-B
Devault, David to Margaret Holliday 25 Dec. 1833   Md-A
Devault, Samuel to Elvina Folley 9 Feb. 1837   Cr-1
Devel, Wm. H. to Amelia Tice 7 Aug. 1838   Warr
Devenport, Beffee to Mary Beals 5 July 1836   CG-A
Devenport, John Jr. to Nicy Wilkinson 6 Mar. 1838   CG-A
Dever, Wm. to Peraline J.J.P. Hudson 12 Oct. 1838   Warr
Devin, Wm. to Elizabeth Lewellen 6 Nov. 1834   Pk-1

Dewit, Wm. to Sarah Gay 8 Nov. 1838   Mari
Dewitt, Geo. to Minerva Summers 29 Jan. 1832   Rand
Dewitt, Larkin to Hannah Ewing 20 July 1820   Coop
Dewitt, Wm. to Nancy Icenogle 21 June 1839   Jeff
Dewitte, Walter to Hannah Icenogle 1 Oct. 1839   Jeff
Dewren, Mannen to Peggy Gibbs 27 Oct. 1816   Howa
Dial, Hiram to Elizabeth Diggs 13 Sept. 1830   Coop
Dial, Stephen to Deboriah Stone 27 Aug. 1820   Coop
Dick, John to Demaries L. Flint 3 Aug. 1837   Mari
Dickard, James to Christine Crawford 12 Sept. 1819   Coop
Dickerson, Cosby to Mary J. Gaines 22 Aug. 1838   Shel
Dickeson, Layton to Hilray Walton 2 July 1837   Boon
Dickey, David to Barbara McClellan 14 Jan. 1836   Cass
Dickey, John to Sarah Rice 6 Aug. 1829   Rall
Dickey, Lorenzo E. to Mary W. Arnett 8 Oct. 1837   Cass
Dickey, Melvin W. to Emporia Blakely 13 June 1839   Cass
Dickings, Wm. to Pricilla Baley 14 Sept. 1837   Char
Dickle, Archibald W. to Ruth McCray 12 Jan. 1835   Ray
Dickmond, Alford to Sarah Davis 19 Aug. 1838   Ray
Dicks, Carter to Nancy Bridgewater 17 Oct. 1839   Coop
Dickson, Geo. to Nancy Calvert 18 Nov. 1828   Coop
Dickson, Geo. to Prudence Simpson 21 Sept. 1837   Monr
Dickson, J. to Martha Morgan 20 July 1839   Rand
Dickson, Jesse to Barbary Parks 10 June 1834   Perr
Dickson, Jesse to Mary Cox 10 Dec. 1839   Lafa
Dickson, John to Harriet Norris -- Mar. 1822   Lafa
Dickson, Joseph to Sarah B. Curry 31 Aug. 1831   Boon
Dickson, Joseph to Pamale Warren 1 Jan. 1836   Carr
Dickson, Joseph to Charolotte Austin 15 Jan. 1839   Carr
Dickson, Rolly to Tempa McCoy 10 Oct. 1833   Pk-1
Dickson, Soloman to Lydia Wiley 19 June 1831   Lafa
Diel, Antoine to Ann Trammel 14 Aug. 1826   StGe
Diggs, Francis W. to Mary C. Curd 18 Oct. 1838   Call
Diggs, Geo. to Rebecca McCoy 10 Nov. 1839   Linc
Diggs, Thomas to Jane McMillin 20 Jan. 1831   Linc
Dile, Charles to Nancy Wadley 3 July 1825   Call
Dill, Geo. to Ann McCormick 27 Sept. 1823   StFr
Dill, Henry to Margaret Thompson 13 Apr. 1837   Mari
Dill, John T. to Margaret F. Steele 1 Feb. 1838   Call
Dill, Philemon to Elizabeth Collier 19 Nov. 1827   Boon
Dillard, Robt. to Susannah Seely 29 Mar. 1831   Pk-1
Dillard, Robt. D. to Margaret Smith 7 Feb. 1839   Gree
Dillinger, Adam to Mary Fraser 8 June 1837   Fran
Dillinger, Thomas to Polly Killian 2 Mar. 1828   CG-A
Dillon, Levi to Margaret Treese 8 May 1838   CG-A
Dillon, Patrick W. to Ann T. Nash 6 Oct. 1818   StCh
Dimmel, St. Cleare to Celina Keyzer 3 Aug. 1836   Clay
Dinelback, Daniel to Catharine Logan 9 Aug. 1838   Lewi
Dines, James to Elizabeth Bell 29 Dec. 1837   Wash
Dingas, Henry to Elizabeth Ferguson 19 Jan. 1837   Fran
Dingle, Edward to Katharine Woodgate 25 May 1834   Mari
Dingle, Wm. to Ann Cockrell 20 Aug. 1833   Coop
Dingle, Wm. L. to Parmelia Rice 23 July 1837   Mari
Dings, Frederick to Ida Stein 18 June 1835   Fran
Dinning, Colson to Julian Toomey 12 May 1833   Jack
Dinny, Washington to Rebecca Hill 7 Feb. 1828   Boon
Dinwiddie, Franklin to Louisiann Mosby 28 Feb. 1837   Morg
Dinwiddie, John to Elizabeth Kirkpatrick 22 Apr. 1834   Wash
Dittick, James to Eliza Medley 24 Sept. 1835   Jeff
Ditzler, Jacob to Polly Leveridge 19 Mar. 1829   Howa
Divers, Henry to Catharine Divers 9 Apr. 1833   Lafa
Divers, John D. to Caroline D. Allen 21 Aug. 1834   Pett
Divine, Nathanial to Mrs. Ann Griffan 18 July 1836   Perr
Dixon, Christopher to Caroline Johnson 27 Feb. 1834   Jeff
Dixon, David B. to Beveline R. Crawford 2 Aug. 1839   Call

```
Dixon, Henry to Sarah ---- 1 May 1828                                      Fran
Dixon, Robt. R. to Catharine Evean 27 Sept. 1809                          CG-1
Dixon, Samuel to Eliza M. Shannon 18 Nov. 1824                            StGe
Dixon, Wm. P. to Nancy M. Wilks 21 May 1839                               Mill
D'Lashmutt, Lindsey to Margaret Gibony 4 Mar. 1824                        CG-1
Doak, Andrew J. to Rebecca McOnnel 8 Feb. 1838                            Pk-B
Doake, Robt. to Martha C. Beard 24 May 1838                              Rand
Doan, John to Sarah Hinton 9 June 1831                                    Jack
Doane, Harvey to Jane Hunter 20 July 1837                                 Wash
Dobbin, James L. to Mary Simpson 12 Mar. 1833                             Howa
Dobbins, Fleming to Elizabeth Green 4 May 1839                            Boon
Dobbins, John to Elizabeth Richardson 4 June 1837                         Morg
Dobbins, Thomas to Pelina Sullivan 1 Dec. 1839                           Morg
Dobkins, John to Sarah Thompson 29 Mar. 1838                              Cr-1
Dobyns, Wm. to Lucinda Peper 24 Feb. 1833                                 Pk-1
Dockins, Geo. to Mary Rose 17 Nov. 1836                                   Rand
Dodd, Benj. to Evelina Griffith 17 Jan. 1839                             Mari
Dodd, Joseph to Latia Hudson 12 Sept. 1839                               Rall
Dodd, Silas to Rachel Carpenter 18 Apr. 1838                             Monr
Dodds, Hugh L. to Harriett Palmers 5 June 1837                           Clin
Dodds, John B. to Nancy Griffith 6 Nov. 1837                             Pk-B
Dodge, Joseph to Maria A. Coleman 7 June 1838                            Lewi
Dodson, David to Barbary Welty 5 Feb. 1839                               CG-B
Dodson, David to Elizabeth Lester 5 May 1839                            Cr-1
Dodson, Drury to Lucinda B. Pitman 5 Oct. 1837                           StCh
Dodson, Greenup to Verlena P. Pitman 25 Jan. 1835                        StCh
Dodson, James to Elizabeth Young 13 June 1833                            Howa
Dodson, Jeremiah to Margaret Cunningham 17 Dec. 1835                     Linc
Dodson, John to Gerusha Brace 18 Dec. 1834                               Clay
Dodson, John to Margaret Rector 3 May 1839                               Howa
Dodson, John W. to Nancy Pitman 5 May 1831                               StCh
Dodson, Martin to Arminty Quinly 13 Mar. 1834                           Howa
Dodson, Thomas to Kathryn Fletcher 15 Jan. 1839                          Rand
Dodson, Wm. to Sarah Norris 15 Sept. 1821                                Lafa
Dodson, Wm. to Nancy Quinsly 29 June 1837                                Howa
Dodson, Wm. to Heneretta Dawson 14 Feb. 1839                            Clay
Doggett, Wm. to Nancy Armon 28 June 1827                                 StFr
Doherty, Owen to Aurora Sagelle 4 Apr. 1831                              Wash
Dolar, James to Harriet Anderson 8 Dec. 1835                             John
Dollarhide, Wm. to Martha Holt 23 Jan. 1834                              Fran
Doller, Wm. to Gemima Knoston 19 Aug. 1833                               Pett
Dolson, Stephen to Mariah Hutchins 28 July 1836                          Perr
Dolson, Stephen to Lucinda Taylor 23 Apr. 1838                           Perr
Donaldson, James M. to Julia A. Dawson 13 Sept. 1838                     Monr
Donaldson, Philip to Deborah Bowman 31 Mar. 1836                         Cole
Donaldson, Wm. to Elizabeth Thompson 11 Nov. 1834                        Monr
Doncenbock, Francis X. to Mary C. Kenirff 30 Sept. 1838                  Perr
Donelley, James to Polle Logan 28 Apr. 1813                             CG-1
Doniphan, Alexander W. to Elizabeth J. Thornton 21 Dec. 1837            Clay
Donnally, Nathan to Louisa Hagan 9 Feb. 1836                            Rall
Donnell, Thomas L. to Mary McCormack 24 Dec. 1839                        Jeff
Donoho, Joseph to Eleanor Anderson 11 Oct. 1837                          Pett
Donoho, Wm. to Mary Dodson 27 Nov. 1831                                  Boon
Donohue, James to Elizabeth Cissell 24 May 1838                          Perr
Donslap, Joseph to Elizabeth Summers 28 July 1836                        Cass
Dooley, Samuel J. to Darkess Hardwick 7 Apr. 1839                       Rall
Dooley, Underwood to Martha A. Dooley 22 Oct. 1839                       Monr
Doolin, Jordan W. to Eliza Chandler 13 Mar. 1839                         Jeff
Doolin, Thomas to Nancy Lile 25 Jan. 1821                                StCh
Dooly, Esom B. to Ellen Brockman 29 Aug. 1839                            Mill
Dooly, Hyram to Martha J. Johnson 25 Feb. 1836                           Monr
Dooly, Uriah S. to Elizabeth E. Brockman 2 Nov. 1834                     Cole
Dophe, Patrice to Marguerite Noval 24 July 1832                          StCh
Dorilaque, Pierre to Louise Robert 4 Apr. 1836                           Md-B
Dormiers, Peter to Mary Hempstead 5 May 1830                             StCh
```

```
Dorrel, John to Betsy Bradley 16 Dec. 1819                    Howa
Dorrell, James to Agnes Standiford 1 Oct. 1829                Howa
Dorrell, Washington to Agness Osbourne 4 Feb. 1836           Morg
Dorsey, Andrew B. to Mary Wiley 21 June 1835                 Call
Dorsey, Patrick to Lucy West 21 Sept. 1821                    Ray
Dorsey, Patrick to Dica Johnston 23 June 1832                 Ray
Dorsey, Richard to Mary A. Doyle 10 Oct. 1837                CG-A
Dorsey, Sam to Elizabeth Thomson 22 Oct. 1805               CGRA
Dorsey, Sherman to Mary Adams 27 Apr. 1838                   Pk-B
Dorsey, Wm. H. to Jane Nevins 2 July 1829                    Call
Doshile, John to Mrs. Mary Park 27 Mar. 1838                 Shel
Dotsel, John V. to Elizabeth R. Mueller 14 May 1839          Fran
Doty, Azariah to Dicy Alexander 10 Oct. 1836                 Boon
Doty, Azarich to Rebecca Brunts 14 Aug. 1828                Howa
Doty, Enoch to Polly Barnes 17 July 1834                    Boon
Doty, Henry to Polly A. Long 30 Dec. 1834                   Howa
Doty, Joseph to Elizabeth Doty 18 Feb. 1827                 Howa
Dougan, Noah to Nancy Cowie 9 June 1831                     Wash
Dougherty, Henderson to Zerelda Sublett 17 Feb. 1831        Clay
Dougherty, John to Rebecca Hatton 17 Dec. 1835              Call
Dougherty, John F. to Pheba Hawkins 1 May 1831              Clay
Dougherty, Joseph to Elizabeth Grooms 7 Sept. 1831          Clay
Dougherty, Wm. R. to Easter E. Luckey 13 June 1833          Fran
Doughett, John P. to Susannah E. Huff 29 Feb. 1839          Morg
Doughty, Larkin to Maria Howdeshell 21 Nov. 1828           StCh
Doughty, Robt. to Susannah McMillin 24 Feb. 1833           Linc
Douglas, Alexander to Polly Potts 13 May 1823              Boon
Douglas, Geo. N. to Charlotte Stone 20 Dec. 1836          Howa
Douglas, John to Anna Long 12 Nov. 1829                    Boon
Douglas, Samuel to Matilda Golden 15 Dec. 1836            Howa
Douglas, Wm. B. to Martha March 3 Oct. 1839               Boon
Douglass, Jesse to Mary McQuiddy 9 May 1834               Clay
Douglass, Robt. to Ann M. Hall 26 Oct. 1828              CG-A
Douglass, Thomas to Margaret Piles 1 Feb. 1838            Ripl
Douglass, Wm. to Lucy Chick 29 Mar. 1832                  Call
Dow, James to Elizabeth Mahan 13 May 1830                 Coop
Dowell, Martin to Margaret Johnson 20 Dec. 1832          Howa
Dowling, James to Fanny Flauharty 4 Oct. 1812            StCh
Dowling, James to Jane Greenstreet 7 July 1835           StFr
Downey, Michael to Catherine Casey 9 Jan. 1836           Wash
Downing, Absolom R. to Susan A. Kelly 4 Oct. 1835        Mari
Downing, Andrew to Obedience Bell 2 Mar. 1828            Linc
Downing, David R. to Catherine Bird 14 Mar. 1833         Mari
Downing, Ezekiel to Margaret Maricle 29 Oct. 1815        StCh
Downing, Henry to Mary J. Jeffers 13 Dec. 1838           Lewi
Downing, James to Polly Bell 3 Oct. 1837                 Gree
Downing, James V. to Parthenia E. Norris 30 May 1839     Boon
Downing, Randolph to Emily Lyon 30 Oct. 1839             Shel
Downing, Wm. to Catherine A. Allen 13 Oct. 1836          Lewi
Downing, Wm. C. to Margaret A. Reading 26 Mar. 1835      Pk-1
Downs, James M. to Perlina Galliway 14 Nov. 1831         Gasc
Doyel, Edmund to Betsy Fryer 22 Jan. 1829                Fran
Doyle, Alexander J. to Ann E. Suttle 21 Nov. 1837        Howa
Doyle, Farmer to Polly Newberry 6 Oct. 1826              Gasc
Doyle, Owen to Sally Humphrey 29 Nov. 1826               Pk-1
Doyle, Silas M. to Lavicy Keithley 8 Apr. 1832           Pk-1
Dozier, John M. to Lucinda McCoy 7 July 1836             StFr
Drace, Madison I. to Ann R. McDonald 27 Sept. 1838       Clin
Drace, Samuel L. to Menervy Farrar 21 Nov. 1838          Fran
Drace, Silas to Sarah Osborne 21 Jan. 1836               Fran
Drace, Solomon to Comfort Osborn 25 Nov. 1833            Fran
Drace, Thomas to Mrs. Sarah A. McGloflin 25 Oct. 1835    Fran
Drake, James to Jane Mullikin 16 May 1839                Plat
Drake, Jesse to Eliza Stuart 25 Aug. 1836                Howa
Drake, John to Eliza Sharp 28 Aug. 1823                   Ray
```

Drake, Wm. to Sally Glenn 28 Apr. 1836   Jack
Draper, Daniel to Mary Orr 12 June 1834   Pk-1
Draper, Edwin to Urania L. Rouse 14 June 1838   Pk-B
Draper, Henry C. to Mary Jones 11 Nov. 1832   Pk-1
Draper, Philander to Eliza A. Clark 18 Jan. 1835   Pk-1
Draper, Philander to Sarah Fenton 9 Jan. 1839   Linc
Draper, Zachariah to Eleanor M. Briggs 13 Oct. 1823   Rall
Drapper, James to Jane Pierce 21 Apr. 1832   Cr-1
Drennin, John to Emily Stewart 25 Mar. 1826   Wash
Drew, Lewis to Maria Hay 1 Sept. 1836   Lewi
Drew, Peter to Rachel Davis 10 Mar. 1836   Clay
Drewen, Samuel to Jane C. Lizenby 15 Sept. 1836   Mari
Drinkard, Geo. to Martha Hubbard 6 Feb. 1835   Char
Drinkard, Harrison to Jane Hubbard 1 Dec. 1839   Char
Drinkard, James to Anna McHargue 6 Feb. 1831   Char
Drinkard, Stephen to Minerva Johnson 8 Jan. 1834   Howa
Drinkwater, Emanuel to Euphemia Scott 4 Feb. 1821   Coop
Drinkwater, Wm. to Nancy White 24 May 1836   Coop
Drinnon, Wm. to Elizabeth O. Everett 19 Nov. 1826   Jeff
Driren, Addison to Betsy Preston 28 Nov. 1830   Wash
Driskill, Thomas to Mrs. Mary Turner 28 Aug. 1839   Coop
Driskill, Wm. to Susan Williams 27 Jan. 1839   Coop
Droddy, Aron to Elizabeth Dixon 24 Mar. 1825   StCh
Drown, Alfred to Catharine Lester 29 Sept. 1839   Lafa
Druf, Carl to Elizabeth Stiegmier 3 May 1838   StCh
Drum, Joseph to Katherine Peanick 24 Jan. 1832   CG-A
Drummond, Flemmon to Nancy Portis 24 Nov. 1836   Jack
Drummond, Thomas to Susan Prophel 15 June 1826   Lafa
Drummonds, James L. to Sarah Williams 6 Nov. 1839   Plat
Drummons, Wm. to Emaline Rowland 31 Jan. 1830   Pk-1
Drury, Henry to Helen Layton 16 Jan. 1838   Perr
Drury, Wendsor to Mary Bryant 14 Apr. 1831   Jeff
Dry, Wm. to Laura Badley 5 Jan. 1836   Rand
Drybread, Joseph to Mary Windes 25 Dec. 1834   Jeff
Dryden, Constantine F. to Rebecca C. Burford 17 Sept. 1838   Gree
Dryden, Frederick H. to Catherine E. Sharp 11 Jan. 1838   Warr
Dryden, N.J. to Martha Russell 14 Feb. 1837   Char
DuBois, Etienne to Louise Chartran 16 Feb. 1829   StCh
Dubois, Joseph to Helene Danzal 8 Oct. 1805   StCh
DuBois, Louis to Marie L. North 3 June 1839   StCh
DuBois, Stephen to Maria L. Bernard 13 May 1837   StCh
Duckworth, Wiley to Sarah Rowland 29 June 1837   Wash
Duclos, Alexander to Judith Dufour 17 Oct. 1826   Wash
Duclos, Charles to Kiseal Brown 18 Jan. 1835   Wash
Duclos, John B. to Elizabeth Bourassa 12 Nov. 1833   Wash
Duclos, Michael to Agatha Thibeault 31 Aug. 1830   Wash
Dudley, Benj. W. to Eliza J. Dudley 20 May 1834   Mari
Dudley, James to Lucretia Hargrove 25 Oct. 1832   Linc
Dudley, James A. to Permelia Brown 2 May 1839   Rall
Dudley, John to Clarissa Tucker 12 Jan. 1832   Linc
Dudley, Nicholas to Elizabeth Geiger 20 Mar. 1832   Linc
Dudley, Peter to Margaret Tucker 27 Oct. 1830   Linc
Dudley, Wm. to Laurian Coats 12 Jan. 1832   Call
Dudley, Wm. to Alemeda Jameson 10 Dec. 1835   Linc
Dudley, Wm. to Manerva Callaway 15 Feb. 1838   Call
Dudley, Wm. to Mrs. Eliza Tucker 4 Dec. 1839   Linc
Duff, Henry to Ruth C. Braley 6 Dec. 1838   Fran
Duffey, Wm. to Mrs. Elizabeth Jennings -- Oct. 1832   Clay
Duffield, Wm. C. to Ann S. Light 3 Nov. 1835   Rall
Duffner, James to Ann Miles 5 Nov. 1839   Perr
Dufort, Charles to Elizabeth Voizard 27 Dec. 1832   StCh
Dufour, Pierre to Celeste Bauthel 27 Sept. 1825   StGe
Dugal, Haverius to Colastique LaCroix 2 May 1826   StCh
Dugan, Daniel to Nancy L. Lennard 6 Jan. 1839   Cr-1
Dugan, Stephen to Katherine Morris 24 June 1827   Wash

                                   66

Duggins, Lewis to Esther A. Goodridge 15 Aug. 1839	Sali
Duglas, Jesse to Sally A. McQuidy -- Oct. 1838	Clay
Dugles, Robt. M. to Sarah Barnes 13 Feb. 1838	Polk
Duigin, Napoleon B. to Sarah Smiley 29 Mar. 1838	Gree
Duke, Courtney N. to Catharine Jackson 16 Nov. 1838	Pk-B
Duke, Robt. to Ruland Gibson 2 May 1833	Linc
Duke, Thomas to Malissa Pittman 20 Dec. 1839	Buch
Duket, Francis to Rebecca Coil 24 Oct. 1833	Jack
Dull, Geo. to Mahala Upgrove 8 Nov. 1838	Linc
Dumarbant, Warren to Eliza A. Roberts 4 Dec. 1839	Linc
Dumont, Abraham to Felicite Petit 18 Jan. 1830	StCh
Dumont, Thomas to Marie L. Lebeau 9 Feb. 1836	StCh
Dunagin, Mathew to Precilla Acard 13 Oct. 1837	Polk
Dunaway, John to Polly Asher 30 Mar. 1836	Polk
Dunaway, Lewis to Jane English 1 Nov. 1832	Ray
Dunbar, Alexander to Polly Hudson 24 Apr. 1835	Lafa
Dunbar, James G. to Ann Gryam 6 Oct. 1828	Char
Duncan, Alexander B. to Helen M. Bell 17 Aug. 1837	Clay
Duncan, Ashley to Eliza Bowler 28 Feb. 1832	Howa
Duncan, David H. to Eliza A. Morrison 6 Jan. 1836	Call
Duncan, David T. to Sarah C. Turnham 14 Sept. 1837	Clay
Duncan, Frederick to Elizabeth Gibson 24 Jan. 1839	Call
Duncan, Frederick to Martha E. Parks 10 Oct. 1839	Coop
Duncan, Gary K. to Ann M. Dozier 12 Sept. 1827	Linc
Duncan, Henry to Edith Monroe 26 Mar. 1829	Howa
Duncan, Hiram to Nancy Sharp 28 Sept. 1834	Ray
Duncan, Isaac to Delitha Wiley 5 May 1834	Coop
Duncan, James to Jane McLaughlin 15 Feb. 1810	StGe
Duncan, James to Margaret Hulen 14 Apr. 1837	Boon
Duncan, James to Pamelia Duncan 25 Jan. 1838	Clay
Duncan, Jehoida M. to Eliza Crown 24 Jan. 1838	Clin
Duncan, Jeptha to Mary Read 31 Dec. 1834	Coop
Duncan, John to Mary Bernard 6 May 1821	Howa
Duncan, John Jr. to Nancy Bradford 25 Sept. 1828	Gasc
Duncan, John to Sally Kilby 14 July 1830	Pk-1
Duncan, John to Salina Clay 22 Aug. 1832	Cole
Duncan, John to Elizabeth Duncan 18 Oct. 1837	Fran
Duncan, John B. to Polly Bates 8 Oct. 1829	Cr-P
Duncan, Joseph to Rebecca Louallen 15 Nov. 1834	Gree
Duncan, Marshall to Sally King 4 Jan. 1829	Fran
Duncan, Phelemon to Cecelia K. Hutson 23 Oct. 1834	Clay
Duncan, Samuel to Paralee Bass 15 Dec. 1831	Boon
Duncan, Thomas to Polly McClure 21 Jan. 1836	Call
Duncan, Thomas to Nancy Musick 11 Oct. 1838	Fran
Duncan, Wm. to Susan Harris 6 Oct. 1831	Boon
Duncan, Wm. to Sarah Ratliff 5 Aug. 1838	Clin
Duncan, Wm. L. to Emaly Duncan 16 Aug. 1832	Cr-1
Dunegan, James to Elizabeth Logan 16 Feb. 1832	Clay
Dunegan, Joseph to Sarah Jones 9 June 1839	Polk
Dunham, Admiral R. to Martha Brown 20 Nov. 1835	Warr
Dunham, Berry to Margaret Fisher 5 Aug. 1832	Coop
Dunham, John to Saritha Seat 21 June 1832	Coop
Dunham, Joseph P. to Margaret Berry 24 Feb. 1822	StCh
Dunham, Washington to Nancy Griffee 18 Mar. 1827	Pk-1
Dunivin, A.J. to Delilah McDanel 18 Dec. 1836	Polk
Dunkin, Henry to Nancy Woods 26 Dec. 1838	Char
Dunkin, James to Mary Taylor 21 Aug. 1836	Mari
Dunkin, Samuel to Ann Ragsdale 20 May 1832	Md-A
Dunkin, Thomas G. to Emealie Williams 5 Feb. 1829	Pk-1
Dunkin, Wm. to Rhoda Easton 24 Nov. 1831	Mari
Dunlap, Andrew to Martina J. Long 20 Mar. 1838	Cr-1
Dunlap, James to Elizabeth Hainds 9 July 1806	StCh
Dunlap, James to Anna Legate 5 Aug. 1824	Howa
Dunlap, Thomas to Susanna Madison 14 Dec. 1826	StFr
Dunn, Hosea to Matilda Seabaugh 24 Nov. 1833	CG-A

Dunn, James to Mary Hagan 20 Sept. 1827   Perr
Dunn, John to Elizabeth Neal 6 July 1820   CG-A
Dunn, John to Polly Fulbright 9 Jan. 1831   CG-A
Dunn, John F.C. to Elizabeth Duncan 28 June 1831   Clay
Dunn, John W. to Mrs. Lucinda Giboney 23 Apr. 1832   CG-A
Dunn, Leander to Sarah King 2 Mar. 1837   CG-A
Dunn, Miles to Rosa Fulbright 13 Aug. 1837   CG-A
Dunn, Samuel to Margaret Martin 24 Mar. 1808   CG-1
Dunn, Wm. to Nancy OBanion 24 Dec. 1829   CG-A
Dunn, Wm. to Minervy Hays 4 Mar. 1834   CG-A
Dunn, Wm. to Sarah Patton 8 Feb. 1839   Call
Dunnaway, James B. to Sally Howard 28 June 1821   Cole
Dunnegan, Joseph to Mary Davis 3 Apr. 1835   Clay
Dunnica, Fountain to Jane C. Harrison 13 Feb. 1834   Cole
Dunnica, James to Mrs. Nancy Hardaman 5 Mar. 1835   Howa
Dunnica, James P. to Mariah Sites 25 May 1835   Cole
Dunnica, John to Betsey Ferguson 1 Apr. 1822   Call
Durand, Francis to Judith Collmann 17 Sept. 1833   Wash
Durbin, Benedict to Margarite Logsdon 24 Apr. 1838   Lewi
Durbin, Daniel to Theresa Fuget 6 June 1813   StCh
Durbin, Richard to Lucy Logsdon 9 June 1833   Mari
Durfe, Jabez to Elizabeth Brackenbury 3 Mar. 1834   Clay
Durham, Denis to Jane Bigham 11 Jan. 1838   John
DuRicheve, Francis St.C. to Clarisse Reynal 15 Aug. 1827   StCh
Durill, Ira to Mary Smiley 14 July 1836   Pett
Durin, John to Pehuhema Amick 11 Sept. 1827   Howa
Durkee, Chancy to Lucy A. Harris 2 Dec. 1828   Mari
Durkee, Lucian to Elizabeth Bourn 30 July 1829   Mari
Durkee, Roswell to Caroline Hawkins 8 Sept. 1831   Mari
Durkey, James to Jemima Green 13 Mar. 1838   Boon
Durkey, John W. to Mary Green 1 Mar. 1838   Boon
Durocher, Barthelemi to Asphacia Barbeau 23 Jan. 1827   StGe
Dusey, Patrick to Rosa A. Splawn 29 Apr. 1824   Ray
Dutton, John H. to Mary Brown 21 Nov. 1819   StCh
Duval, James C. to Susan Biggs 4 Apr. 1839   Pk-B
Duvall, James to Sarah Howell 2 Mar. 1837   Ray
Duvall, Joseph to Rosa A. Layton 18 Apr. 1837   Perr
Duvall, Louis to Mary Hagan 24 June 1827   Perr
Duvall, Simon to Mary Miles 12 Oct. 1837   Perr
Duvall, Simon to Ann Mattingly -- Nov. 1837   Perr
Duvall, Wm. to Eliza Tully 27 Feb. 1827   Call
Duvatt, Samuel K. to Celina McFarland 25 Dec. 1838   Barr
Duvemer, Jackson to Elizabeth Whitten 11 Dec. 1836   Ray
Duwall, Claiborn to Harriett Miller 25 Mar. 1838   Barr
Dye, Kenneth to Martha A. Burroughs 18 Jan. 1838   Pk-B
Dyer, Wm. to Ester Ritchey 12 May 1831   Lafa
Dysart, James Jr. to Elizabeth James 14 Oct. 1834   Howa
Dysart, John to Matilda Brooks 3 June 1824   Howa
Dysart, John Jr. to Mary Dameron 18 Apr. 1837   Rand
Dysart, Nicholas to Euphamia Givens 22 Nov. 1827   Howa
Dysart, Robt. to Gorham Given 27 Dec. 1827   Char

Eades, Moses to Nancy Walker 9 Jan. 1819   Howa
Eades, Solomon to Susannah Collet 1 Jan. 1823   Cole
Eagen, Louis to Frances A. Ashley 10 Mar. 1835   Lafa
Eaker, Fredric to Betsey Perkins 8 June 1828   CG-A
Eaker, Jonas to Nancy Bailey 24 Apr. 1831   CG-A
Eales, Charles to Lucy Purvis 19 Nov. 1825   Rall
Eames, Ellis to Olive Galebs 5 June 1834   Clay
Earickson, Harrison to Elitha Sharp 30 May 1824   Ray
Earickson, James to Caty Tarwater 7 Feb. 1832   Ray
Earl, James to Polly Sharadine 22 Oct. 1805   CGRA
Early, Charles to Rosanna Welta 22 Feb. 1838   Linc
Early, Dennis to Elizabeth Person 19 Feb. 1837   Clin

```
Early, John to Patsy Person 30 Dec. 1834                        Clin
Early, Peter A. to Sarah McPherson 21 Jan. 1827                 Wash
Earnest, Armstead to Polly Mayberry 13 Aug. 1829               Linc
Earnest, Jacob to Catharine Ashburn 14 Sept. 1837             Mari
Earnest, Thomas to Julia Huss 1 Feb. 1838                      Linc
Earthman, Henry to Rusheba Trammel 23 Feb. 1817               Howa
Earwood, Aaron to Sally Panick 27 Dec. 1829                   CG-A
Ease, John W. to Elizabeth Kelsy 26 June 1836                 Henr
Easely, Edward to Mary A. Faulkner 20 Jan. 1837              Boon
Easly, Green B. to Avaline Johnson 23 Apr. 1837              Boon
Easly, John to Nancy Haddock 23 July 1828                    Boon
Eason, Wm. to Elizabeth Gibson 27 June 1838                  CG-A
East, Urbane to Katharine Kelly 12 May 1823                  Char
Easters, Hyram to Lucy Richardson 15 Apr. 1819               Fran
Eastin, Stephen to Nancy Borbin 22 Jan. 1820                 Howa
Eastin, Stephen G. to Ann Baker 15 Jan. 1824                 StGe
Eastman, Geo. W. to Mary A.D. James 10 Nov. 1836             Mari
Easton, Robt. F. to Mrs. Mary Valle' 8 Jan. 1835            Wash
Easton, Robt. M. to Eleanor McFarland 10 June 1826          Rall
Easton, Wm. to Mary Smith 11 Dec. 1825                      Rall
Easton, Wm. to Phebe Smith 8 Apr. 1821                      Rall
Eastwood, James W. to Jane H. Ustick 7 Mar. 1839            Lafa
Eaton, Eli to Jane Eaton 14 Mar. 1839                       Howa
Eaton, John to Jane Anderson 14 June 1832                   Mari
Eaton, Wm. to Elizabeth Kean 2 Feb. 1826                    Wash
Eckart, Wm. to Fanny Smith 16 Apr. 1818                     StCh
Eddings, Thomas to Elizabeth Harrison 11 Apr. 1833          Howa
Edds, John to Meron Caldwell 19 July 1827                   Gasc
Edelin, Geo. to Ann McElroy 8 Aug. 1837                     Mari
Edgar, Henry R. to Mary Murphy 6 Nov. 1834                  StFr
Edgar, James to Eliza Collins 5 Nov. 1837                   Coop
Edgar, John to Peggy Hannelly 9 Nov. 1815                   CG-1
Edgar, Louis to Margaret Obrien 9 Nov. 1828                 Wash
Edgar, Reuben to Nancy Thompson 27 May 1819 p.20            Md-D
Edgar, W.R. to Jane Long 24 Nov. 1839                       Cr-1
Edgar, Wm. C. to Charlotte Dillin 10 June 1827              Md-A
Edge, Levi C. to Susannah Savage 11 Oct. 1838              Polk
Edinger, Geo. to Matilda McCarty 7 May 1835                CG-B
Edinger, John P. to Mary Burns 3 July 1832                 Perr
Edington, Luke to Mary Stockton 16 Feb. 1836               Polk
Edleman, Joseph F. to Malinda Conrad 10 Dec. 1835          Perr
Edmerson, John H. to Lydia Cockrell 8 Dec. 1836            John
Edmonds, Gilbert to Manerva J. Vandiver 12 Nov. 1835       Shel
Edmonds, Lavender to Elizabeth Hughs 27 Sept. 1832         Wash
Edmonds, Moses to Maria Thomas 11 Feb. 1832               Wash
Edmonns, Lavender to Amanda McCabe 1 Nov. 1837            Ripl
Edmunds, John to Polly Lomax 24 Jan. 1839                Linc
Edmunds, Willis to Abigail Strickland 20 Nov. 1831       Wash
Edson, James to Mary A. Young 16 Jan. 1833               Md-A
Edward, Hiram to Jane Swift 27 Dec. 1837                 Henr
Edward, Wm. to Elizabeth Welton 6 July 1830             Clay
Edwards, Anderson to Elizabeth Larew 24 Jan. 1836       Coop
Edwards, Booker P. to Polly L. McCune 10 June 1833      Pk-1
Edwards, David to Euphema Rule 30 Sept. 1830            Fran
Edwards, Griffin to Harriett McRoberts 22 Mar. 1838     Cole
Edwards, James to Nancy Snodgrass 29 Dec. 1833          Cole
Edwards, John to Lavina Roberts 26 June 1833            Clay
Edwards, Matthew to Margaret Ferguson 24 May 1827       Call
Edwards, Micaah to Matilda Poor 18 Jan. 1835           Morg
Edwards, Morris to Malinda Fox 24 Mar. 1834            Lafa
Edwards, Pleasant C.W. to ---- ---- 14 May 1835        Pk-1
Edwards, Robt. to Elizabeth Loudusky 29 Jan. 1834      Mari
Edwards, Thomas to Mrs. Vaughn 12 July 1826            Linc
Edwards, Thomas to Sally Pinkston 12 Oct. 1828         Ray
Edwards, Thomas to Mary Wall 11 Nov. 1836             Cole
```

Edwards, Wiley to Mary Clark 2 Oct. 1838   Clay
Eggers, Charles to Esther Routbout 22 Feb. 1838   Cole
Eidson, Wm. to Polley Hewitt 6 May 1831   Wash
Eismann, Joseph to Mary Hosekosters 19 June 1836   StCh
Eklunk, Geo. to Risina Shoemaker 25 Nov. 1839   Clay
Elam, Armstead to Eliza A. Rhodes 13 Jan. 1831   Fran
Elam, Wm. to Eliza ---- 9 Oct. 1836   Linc
Elden, Bagley to Elizabeth Goings 24 Dec. 1839   Bent
Elder, Joseph to Harriet Walker 23 Apr. 1839   Perr
Elgan, Alphonso to Martha E. Barkley 23 July 1836   Rall
Elgin, Edward W. to Elizabeth Sinklair 4 Jan. 1838   Pk-B
Elgin, Francis to Dorcas A. Limbrick 13 Oct. 1836   Pk-1
Elgin, Geo. to Dukedella Rust 14 Nov. 1839   Shel
Elgin, Walter W. to Zerrilda Q. Lewis 27 June 1833   Mari
Elington, Pleasant to Armelia Talbot 24 Dec. 1839   Clay
Eliott, Stephen T. to Mary A.L. Hill 7 Aug. 1831   Rall
Elis, Thomas to Mary Mansfield 23 Dec. 1828   Clay
Elkin, Richard to Isabela E. Philips 23 Mar. 1837   CG-A
Elkins, Abel to Frances Williams 9 Dec. 1828   Boon
Elledge, Wm. to Martha Savage 13 Mar. 1834   Jack
Eller, Daniel to Polly Reed 4 Aug. 1836   Cole
Eller, James M.C. to Eleanor Cole 6 Apr. 1832   Coop
Ellice, John to Melinda Brocks 26 Nov. 1829   Sali
Ellifut, Robt. C. to Ann E. Jefferson 20 Dec. 1836   Jack
Ellington, Jacob to Sally Matheny 16 Dec. 1838   Call
Elliott, Amos to Martha A. Sulcher 24 Dec. 1833   Morg
Elliott, Boone to Permelia Anderson 25 May 1834   Pk-1
Elliott, James to Elizabeth Carpenter 15 Jan. 1833   Clay
Elliott, James I. to Jane Griffith 3 Feb. 1829   Pk-1
Elliott, Jesse to Rena Morris 27 July 1837   Ray
Elliott, John to Ann Cooly 17 Sept. 1829   Howa
Elliott, John to Eliza A. Culbertson 26 Dec. 1833   Ray
Elliott, John to Didama Cary 12 Sept. 1837   Clin
Elliott, John to Harriett Penick 4 Sept. 1838   Char
Elliott, Newton P. to Nancy Wilkerson 28 Nov. 1833   Howa
Elliott, Richardson to Jane E. Randol 12 Oct. 1835   CG-B
Elliott, Stephen E. to Ansevilla Manning 2 July 1839   Rall
Elliott, Wiatt to Elizabeth Boucher 4 Sept. 1836   Ray
Elliott, Wm. to Margaret Lewis 13 Feb. 1834   CG-A
Elliott, Wm. to Nancy Sconce 11 Sept. 1838   Ray
Elliott, Wm. to Mary Price 1 July 1834   Char
Ellis, Alfred to Fanny Waters 19 June 1820   CG-1
Ellis, Amos to Mary C. Chitwood 17 July 1834   Rall
Ellis, Asa to Mary Wimberly 26 Feb. 1835   Linc
Ellis, Daniel to Jane Hazelton 20 Oct. 1836   Pk-1
Ellis, Geo. to Mary Bradley 1 Sept. 1836   Pett
Ellis, Isaac to Elizabeth Jeffers 14 May 1829   Rall
Ellis, Jacob to Manerva Anderson 7 Mar. 1839   Pett
Ellis, James to Harriet Elam 2 Sept. 1839   Mari
Ellis, James H. to Mary A. Thomas 13 Feb. 1838   Fran
Ellis, Jeremiah M. to Peggy Jenkins 11 Feb. 1834   Carr
Ellis, John to Catharine Doyle 18 Mar. 1831   Boon
Ellis, Jonathan to Permelia Vaughn 15 July 1831   Clay
Ellis, Josiah to Patsy Poe 25 Oct. 1839   CG-B
Ellis, Lonsford to Kisiah Bull 4 Feb. 1810   CG-1
Ellis, Peter to Amilea Sallee 29 Nov. 1836   Linc
Ellis, Thomas O. to Sarah Gray 22 July 1830   CG-A
Ellis, Wm. to Ellender Hughes 14 Sept. 1829   Coop
Ellis, Wm. to Eliza E. Cox 31 Oct. 1832   Md-A
Ellis, Wm. to Melissa Doyle 29 Jan. 1833   Boon
Ellison, Alexander to Jemima Crawford 15 Sept. 1825   Boon
Ellison, Archibald to Miranda Watson 9 July 1835   Wash
Ellison, James to Polly Ellison 1 June 1837   Polk
Ellison, James to Martha Cowgill 9 Apr. 1839   Clar
Ellison, Robt. to Elizabeth Campbell 30 May 1837   Rall

Ellmore, Joseph to Mrs. Elizabeth Graham 21 Apr. 1829	Howa
Ellson, Wm. to Martha Williams 31 Dec. 1823	Coop
Elmore, Freeman to Martha Orr 20 Dec. 1831	Pk-1
Elsey, John T. to Mary J. Silver 24 Oct. 1839	Mari
Elston, Andrew M. to Jane Anthony 13 Apr. 1828	Boon
Elston, Thomas S. to Mary J. White 13 Nov. 1836	Monr
Ely, Aaron F. to Emily Utterback 26 June 1834	Rall
Ely, Benj. to Martha Gigans 4 May 1837	Mari
Ely, Benj. S. to Nancy Hurley 29 Aug. 1824	Rall
Ely, Boon to Mary A. Percival 11 Nov. 1834	Howa
Ely, David to Rebecca Gooden 14 Mar. 1833	Rall
Ely, Isaac to Mary Goodwin 3 May 1832	Monr
Ely, James to Dulcena Biggers 29 Aug. 1839	Rall
Ely, Joshua to Polly Ralls 8 Nov. 1822	Rall
Ely, Joshua Jr. to Elizabeth Edds 5 Dec. 1833	Rall
Ely, Joshua Jr. to Jane E. Martin rec. 23 Dec. 1837	Rall
Emberson, James to Maria Keach 30 Mar. 1832	Mari
Embree, Cary D. to Lucinda Fowler 30 Dec. 1834	Pett
Embree, David H. to Margaret S. Burress 12 July 1838	Monr
Embree, Joseph to Eliza Harter 25 June 1835	Howa
Embree, Thomas to Phebe Butler 19 Feb. 1838	Pett
Embree, Wm. to Martha Beaman 11 Mar. 1838	Pett
Emerson, Edward to Isabella Shields 23 Nov. 1833	Pk-1
Emerson, Harvey to Katharine McCafety 29 Mar. 1836	Sali
Emerson, John A. to Hester Hill 1 Aug. 1839	CG-B
Emerson, John F. to Keziah Banks 7 Sept. 1837	Mari
Emery, Adam to Mary Hinton 28 Sept. 1837	Lewi
Emison, James to Susan Turley rec. 16 Feb. 1839	Rall
Emmans, Julius to Susannah Hethbran 26 Sept. 1839	Fran
Emmanuel, Joseph D. to Philena Gordon 30 June 1838	CG-A
Emmerson, Hugh to Sevilla Brisco 3 Dec. 1829	Rall
Emmison, Tilly to Lydia Thrash 2 May 1836	Char
Emmons, Elias J. to Mildred Newman 7 Dec. 1830	Call
Emmons, Gibson to Elizabeth Halton 13 June 1828	Boon
Emmons, Jules to Sally Smith 23 Dec. 1817	Howa
Emmons, Julius to Thirza Smith 16 Jan. 1822	Sali
Emmons, Julius to Leuisey Robinett 1 Nov. 1835	Fran
Endicott, Richard B. to Dija Cartwright 13 Aug. 1839	Plat
Endsley, John to Hannah Wells 22 Apr. 1832	Ray
England, James R. to Margaret McCormack 16 Feb. 1835	Jeff
England, Wiley J. to Elvira Blackwell 2 Aug. 1838	Cr-1
English, Albert to Nancy Dunn 16 Jan. 1834	CG-A
English, Benjah to Sarah Taylor 20 Aug. 1836	Linc
English, Benj. F. to Perlina Durben 9 Aug. 1833	Clay
English, Charles to Lydia Whiting 24 May 1835	Clay
English, David to Mary Todd 14 Aug. 1828	Clay
English, Frosty to Mary Brown 25 July 1839	Lewi
English, Howard to Sarah Crockett 3 Nov. 1836	Boon
English, John to Catherine Davis 8 Nov. 1825	Linc
English, John to Polly Morgan 10 Feb. 1831	CG-A
English, John to Jane Morrison 17 Feb. 1831	CG-A
English, Joseph to Columbia McFerron 10 Mar. 1829	CG-A
English, Julius to Temperance Isabell 8 Oct. 1835	CG-B
English, Matthew to Martha Renfroe 5 June 1834	CG-A
English, Robt. Jr. to Agnes M. Lorimier 30 Mar. 1837	CG-A
English, Simeon to Evina McFerron 26 Apr. 1832	CG-A
English, Thomas to Elizabeth Howard 22 Dec. 1808	CG-1
English, Thomas to Louisa Hayden 7 Dec. 1826	CG-A
English, Thomas B. to Sarah Joyce 27 Sept. 1834	CG-A
English, Wm. to Nancy Hunter 19 Nov. 1821	CG-1
Enloe, Anthony to Lucretia Tailor 25 Dec. 1838	Fran
Enloe, Benj. to Isabella Wisdom 29 Sept. 1833	Fran
Enloe, Enoch to Jane Murry 9 Sept. 1837	Cole
Enloe, Felix W. to Jane Burchfield 15 Feb. 1829	Wash
Enloe, John D. to Derses Tailor 9 Feb. 1837	Fran

71

```
Enloe, Wm. to Rebecca Gasperson 15 Dec. 1838          Fran
Ennis, Geo. to Rebecca Cole 29 Apr. 1834              Lafa
Ennis, James to Patsy Hunt 23 Sept. 1831             Lafa
Enochs, David to Nancy Lawson 3 Aug. 1832            Cole
Ensley, Samuel to Anna Pates 6 Oct. 1839             Davi
Enyart, Abram to Nancy Lee 1 Apr. 1832               Howa
Enyart, David to Esther Curtis 2 Mar. 1826           Howa
Enyart, Hezekiah W. to Polly Redwell 16 Nov. 1834    Clin
Enyart, John to Eveline Johnson 18 May 1838          Clin
Enyart, Silas to Charlotte Clavis 3 July 1828        Howa
Eoff, Samuel P. to Jemima Graham 12 Oct. 1831        Jeff
Eoff, Wm. to Sarah Helton 23 June 1815               CG-1
Eoff, Wm. to Patsy Rowland 23 Aug. 1827              Pk-1
Eoff, Wm. to Cordelia Mefford 17 Dec. 1837           Pk-B
Eondson, John to Louisa Rose 16 Feb. 1837            Clay
Epler, Henry to Elsabeth Clark 16 Nov. 1837          Clay
Epperly, Andrew to Mary Burck 15 Nov. 1827           Char
Epperly, Davis to Jane Miller 23 Aug. 1831           Rand
Epperly, Shelton to Elizabeth Lingo 14 Jan. 1836     Rand
Epperly, Solomon to Phebe Gibson 3 May 1829          Howa
Epperly, Wm. to Nancy Lingo 19 Nov. 1835             Rand
Epperson, Anthony to Sarah J. Jeffries 1 Feb. 1838   Rall
Epperson, Samuel to Catharine Robertson 29 Oct. 1829 Pk-1
Epperson, Washington to Nancy Jeffries 8 Feb. 1838   Rall
Eppler, John Jr. to Eliza Booth 19 Jan. 1832         Ray
Epps, Obediah to Delila Taylor 23 June 1836          Ripl
Erhart, Ferdinand to Marie A. Prinster 9 Feb. 1836   StCh
Erickson, John to Lotty Campbell 28 June 1832        Ray
Ervan, Eli to Missenier Brooks 14 Sept. 1826         CG-A
Erven, Wm. to Maryann Harris 8 Dec. 1836             CG-A
Ervin, Ancil to Mary A. Brooks 7 Nov. 1839           CG-B
Ervin, James to Rebecca Willford 28 Mar. 1838        CG-A
Ervin, Wm. L. to Martha A. Lucas 19 Aug. 1833        Jack
Erwin, James to Nancy A. Roy 26 Apr. 1827            CG-A
Erwin, John to Sarah Slagle 20 Jan. 1830             CG-A
Ess, Henry to Catharine Fall 11 June 1839            Sali
Esselman, James C. to Mary A. Kinkead 1 Nov. 1836    StFr
Estes, Anderson to Sally A. Estes 3 Dec. 1833        Lafa
Estes, Anderson to Mary A. Swader 8 Sept. 1836       Clay
Estes, Andrew to Susanna Estes 16 Feb. 1829          Coop
Estes, Archibald to Lovey Stallings 10 Nov. 1828     Clay
Estes, Aron to Elizabeth Wilson 1 Nov. 1838          Morg
Estes, Asa to Polly Cotner 4 June 1839               CG-B
Estes, Beverly to Elizabeth Horne 10 May 1837        John
Estes, Bird to Mary Watson 28 Mar. 1833              Clay
Estes, Burrly to Mary Truitt 24 Apr. 1839            Boon
Estes, Caswel to Dorah Skaggs 16 May 1839            Clay
Estes, Constantine to Malinda Simms 8 Dec. 1839      Morg
Estes, Elisha to Alemeda Soper 10 Dec. 1835          Clay
Estes, Geo. to Matilda Barger 12 Dec. 1833           Morg
Estes, Geo. W. to Elender Clay 31 Jan. 1839          Ripl
Estes, Hiram to Penina Farmer 8 May 1837             Fran
Estes, Hugh to Sarah Huffman 29 May 1834             Gasc
Estes, Jackson to Susan W. Corum 9 June 1836         Clay
Estes, James to Sarah Laughlin 6 Aug. 1825           Gasc
Estes, Joel to Patsy Stollings 12 Nov. 1826          Clay
Estes, Joel to Rebecca Ferrill 25 Sept. 1836         Clay
Estes, John to Caterina Taught 25 Nov. 1814          StGe
Estes, John to Heziah Summers 9 Nov. 1835            Morg
Estes, Littleberry to Nancy Coram 30 Sept. 1830      Clay
Estes, Littleberry to Lucy Holman 8 Feb. 1831        Clay
Estes, Littleberry to Eliza Fristee 30 Jan. 1834     Lafa
Estes, Peyton W. to Polly Davis 17 Mar. 1823         Sali
Estes, Richard to Sarah Martin 26 Feb. 1834          Pk-1
Estes, Robt. to Susannah Nidevar 7 Oct. 1836         Cole
```

```
Estes, Stephen to Susan Holman 27 Jan. 1831                        Clay
Estes, Thomas to Anna Edwards 30 Oct. 1825                         Sali
Estes, Thomas to Martha Estes 19 Jan. 1832                         Clay
Estes, Thomas to Jane Calvin 8 Jan. 1835                           Call
Estes, Thomas to Rody Farmer 27 Oct. 1836                          Fran
Estes, Ward to Gaberela Palmer 24 Aug. 1837                        Clay
Estes, Wm. to Susan Hiete 6 Jan. 1826                              Clay
Estes, Wm. to Elizabeth Sansburry 17 Sept. 1830                    Cole
Estes, Wm. to Margaret Park 1 Dec. 1836                            Linc
Estes, Wm. to Nancy Morgan 28 Nov. 1839                            Polk
Estes, Wm. L. to Malinda H. Doty 29 Mar. 1827                      Clay
Estis, Baxter to Serena Brown 27 July 1832                         Fran
Ethel, Willis A. to Lucy A. Smith 6 May 1820                       Howa
Etting, Daniel to Sylvia Folle 10 Feb. 1837                        StCh
Eubank, John to Susan Ware 5 Jan. 1837                             Howa
Eubanks, Geo. V.W. to Lucinda Davidson 13 Mar. 1839               Monr
Euno, Antoine to Malinda Vaughn 25 May 1825                        Clay
Eustace, Wm. S. to Jane Payne 22 Dec. 1835                         Howa
Evans, Abner A. to Prudence M. McCarty 26 Nov. 1834               Lafa
Evans, Abraham to Linney Thrum 13 Oct. 1825                        Linc
Evans, Augustine H. to Mildred M. James 9 Oct. 1826              Pk-1
Evans, B.P. to Jane Spires 24 May 1831                             Boon
Evans, Cary to Ailsey Lee 6 Aug. 1828                              Ray
Evans, David to Katharine Winder 17 Dec. 1823                      StFr
Evans, David to Rebecca Gibson 27 Sept. 1829                       Howa
Evans, Edward to Cordelia Collier 2 Oct. 1833                      Md-A
Evans, Elija to Polly Watson 8 Apr. 1838                           Clin
Evans, Francis to Jane Keath 20 Apr. 1837                          Shel
Evans, James to Elizabeth S. Allacorn 14 Apr. 1826               Howa
Evans, James to Amanda Jenkins 4 Dec. 1832                         Perr
Evans, James L. to Susan E. Haydon 22 Oct. 1839                    Mari
Evans, John to Katharine Keeny 14 July 1825                        Lafa
Evans, John to Liza Roper 14 Feb. 1827                             Howa
Evans, John to Frances Todd 11 Feb. 1836                           Clin
Evans, Joseph to Rebekah Hicklin 6 Sept. 1821                      Rall
Evans, Lawrence to Elizabeth Goins 23 Dec. 1821                    Howa
Evans, O. to Amelia L. McGee 26 Aug. 1830                          Jack
Evans, Samuel W. to Nancy Riddles 23 Sept. 1836                    Polk
Evans, Thomas to Ann Moore 2 Feb. 1826                             Fran
Evans, Thomas to Mary A. Denny 21 Dec. 1837                        Howa
Evans, Thomas H. to Nancy Donaldson 1 Jan. 1830                    Lafa
Evans, Wm. to Nancy Gregory 12 June 1833                           Lafa
Everett, Jacob to Mary A. Dickinson 24 Dec. 1835                   Perr
Everett, Matthew to Rebecca Church 6 Jan. 1830                     Clay
Everette, John to Mary Brown 2 Oct. 1829                           Jeff
Everette, Louis to Jane Cook 14 Feb. 1832                          Jeff
Everetts, Jacob F. to Sarah Tucker 2 Mar. 1830                     Perr
Everhart, James to Jane Carn 6 Oct. 1839                           Sali
Everly, John to Isaphena Seat 27 Nov. 1839                         Morg
Eversol, Elijah K. to Tabitha A. Godman 15 Oct. 1837             Mari
Eversol, Geo. to Jane Turpin 4 Jan. 1838                           Mari
Evin, Jesse to Patsy Saratt 4 Sept. 1837                           Gasc
Evins, James to Mrs. Sally Whitmire 11 Sept. 1827                  Fran
Evins, Jesse to Martha Surratt 29 Dec. 1835                        Gasc
Evins, John to Meriann Stark 24 July 1831                          Cr-P
Evins, Thomas to Susan Jopling 1 Aug. 1837                         Pett
Ewell, John A. to Eliza Hornshell 21 Mar. 1839                     Plat
Ewell, Joshua to Charlotte Summers 31 June 1838                    Cass
Ewell, Wm. to Polly Blann 30 Nov. 1834                             Carr
Ewing, Chathan A. to Mary B. Young 9 Oct. 1823                     Lafa
Ewing, Geo. N. to Lucinda Rubey 27 May 1824                        Coop
Ewing, James M. to Harriet Witt 19 Sept. 1839                      Monr
Ewing, John to Nancy Gilbert 16 Jan. 1811                          StCh
Ewing, John to Mary A. Wainscott 2 Apr. 1828                       Boon
Ewing, John D. to Ruthy Moore 31 Aug. 1824                         Clay
```

73

Ewing, John R. to Lorina Gehon 27 Oct. 1836	Morg
Ewing, Patrick to Nancy Daurst 25 Dec. 1815	StCh
Ewing, Washington to Alethia J. Ewing 23 Dec. 1834	Lafa
Ewing, Wm. to Elizabeth Creasy 7 Apr. 1835	Lewi
Ewing, Wm. Y.C. to Sally W. McCray 5 Jan. 1836	Lafa
Eyes, Benj. to Polly A. Sullivant 27 Oct. 1829	Wash
Ezeland, Samuel to Christina Keithley 27 Apr. 1828	Linc
Fackler, John to Mary A. Moore 13 Dec. 1838	Clar
Fagan, Thomas T. to Caroline F. Reed 23 Oct. 1834	Clay
Faherty, Peter to Matilda Mattingly 12 May 1835	Perr
Faina, Valerio to Matilda Tucker 9 Nov. 1829	Perr
Fairchild, Oliver H. to Adah W. Brown 16 June 1836	Mari
Falconer, John C. to Martha A. Lamberton 11 Apr. 1837	Lewi
Falkner, David to Mrs. Jane Clark 10 Sept. 1839	Pk-B
Fall, Geo. to Susan Bates 15 Sept. 1836	Sali
Fall, John to Susan Thornton 23 Aug. 1827	Sali
Fallenstein, Berhart to Mrs. Phillipine Blomenberg 19 Nov. 1839	StCh
Famer, Geo. W. to Mary Sikes 25 Apr. 1837	John
Fannin, Thomas to Lida Carter 5 Feb. 1839	Polk
Fanning, Alexander N. to Elizabeth A. Bagby 27 Sept. 1838	StCh
Fanning, Benj. to Mary Nicholas 7 Apr. 1836	Pk-1
Fanning, James to Nancy See 12 May 1836	Rall
Fanning, John to Sarah Shuck 17 Dec. 1836	Rall
Fanning, Michael to Cerdelia B. Kendrick 18 Dec. 1837	Mari
Fare, Elijah to Amanda Randol 1 Nov. 1832	CG-A
Faris, Andrew B. to Martha Baily 8 Dec. 1836	Boon
Faris, Humphrey to Eloiz Lawings 23 Sept. 1832	Howa
Faris, James to Rebecca M. Annett 6 Dec. 1838	Call
Faris, Lewis to Alzady Cornelius 24 July 1817	Howa
Farland, Peter to Espacia Magdeleine 22 Jan. 1838	StCh
Farm, John to Sarah Fanning 25 Oct. 1836	Ray
Farmandes, Samuel to Elizabeth S. Smith 11 July 1837	Monr
Farmer, Axum to Sally Estes 12 Feb. 1835	Pk-1
Farmer, Jesse to Elizabeth E. King 4 Dec. 1833	Call
Farmer, John to Emerald J. Major 12 Nov. 1829	Call
Farmer, John W. to Mary Casey 17 July 1836	Fran
Farmer, Joseph to Martha Samuel 25 Nov. 1835	Call
Farmer, Robt. to Clarinda Brown 1 Sept. 1835	Cole
Farmer, Wilson to Nancy Bivens 19 Nov. 1839	CG-B
Farmes, John to Nancy Hickson 13 Dec. 1821	Ray
Farnish, Elliott to Eliza Burk 7 Jan. 1834	Boon
Farquer, Madison to Maryann J. Martin 21 Mar. 1832	Pk-1
Farr, Anderson to Lusinda Wallice 19 July 1838	Md-B
Farr, John to Susan Burns 20 July 1837	Md-B
Farr, Sandford to Mary Saffarans 31 Sept. 1834	Howa
Farrar, Franklin to Elleanor Pinkerton 25 Jan. 1830	Perr
Farrar, John to Susannah Clifton 8 Apr. 1830	Perr
Farrar, John B. to Mary Hopkins 18 Dec. 1828	Wash
Farrar, Perrin to Adaline Clark 20 Jan. 1831	Fran
Farrer, Franklin to Mary Abernahly 21 Feb. 1839	Perr
Farrer, Moses to Frances McFarland 16 Aug. 1829	StFr
Farrer, Moses to Ann Abernathy 19 July 1838	Perr
Farris, Edward to Louisa Charlton 11 Feb. 1836	Cole
Farris, Eli to Sevina A. Miller 3 Nov. 1837	Coop
Farris, James to Sarah Bankston 15 Jan. 1826	Coop
Farris, James to Rachel C. Burdoin 8 Nov. 1835	Wash
Farris, James to Jane Casady 26 Apr. 1838	Coop
Farris, John to Mary Freeman 29 June 1813	StGe
Farris, John to Mary Westbrook 17 Dec. 1826	Coop
Farris, John to Minerva Morrow 8 Mar. 1832	Cole
Farris, Lewis to Elvira Morrison 5 Feb. 1826	Wash
Farris, Melzar to Jane Murray 11 Oct. 1835	Cole
Farris, Richard to Sarah Shumate 8 May 1837	Cr-1

74

Farris, Robt. P. to Catherine A. Cross 20 Jan. 1826   Wash
Farrough, Joseph L. to Lucinda Cummins 23 Dec. 1830   Jack
Fasen, Charles to Emily Green 31 Dec. 1835   Sali
Fate, Henry C.C. to Mary L. Noell 15 Dec. 1836   Perr
Fatheree, Helund J. to Mary Matthews 21 Dec. 1834   CG-B
Faubian, Isaak to Louisa Smith 14 Nov. 1839   Clay
Faubion, John to Mary Atkins 14 Dec. 1838   Clay
Faublin, Wm. to Elizabeth Bryant 2 Mar. 1837   Boon
Faughender, Samuel to Eliza Emery 12 Feb. 1828   CG-A
Faulk, Jacob to Polly Simon 1 Jan. 1824   Gasc
Faulks, Samuel to Malvina Jones 14 Feb. 1839   Gree
Fauns, Augustus to Martha A. Furguson 8 Dec. 1833   Warr
Fauster, Thomas to Julianna Gwinn 1 Oct. 1837   Sali
Favior, Thomas to Jane Phillips 2 Aug. 1821   Call
Fawbush, Dennis to Eliza A. Bates 14 May 1838   Monr
Fawcett, Wm. to Ann Matthews 30 Aug. 1838   Boon
Fawney, Fredredic to Ann Edelman 28 June 1838   Ray
Fayne, John to Catharine Davis 28 Dec. 1834   Howa
Feagan, Henry Y. to Charlotte White 16 Dec. 1830   Mari
Feagan, Silas M. to Mary A. White 22 Dec. 1831   Mari
Feagan, Wm. to Elvira Kendrick 12 Jan. 1836   Mari
Feakes, Joseph to Perlena Harris 29 Aug. 1830   Boon
Feaster, Robt. to Esther Phillips 17 Dec. 1835   Cole
Feazle, Joshua to Elizabeth Boice 8 June 1822   Rall
Feelds, Nathan to Mary E. Graham 25 Apr. 1839   John
Feland, Wm. to Elizabeth Smith 9 May 1826   Howa
Felps, Wm. to Sarah Early 7 Feb. 1839   Linc
Fenel, Jesse to Selia Bradley 27 Sept. 1832   Howa
Fenley, Joseph to Emily Thomas 26 Feb. 1831   Mari
Fenten, Richard to Clarissa Palmer 27 Mar. 1834   Linc
Fentesche, John A. to S. McClelland Baker 12 Sept. 1839   Call
Fenton, Caleb to Jane Boyce 13 Nov. 1825   Boon
Fenton, Caleb to Letita Foster 8 Jan. 1832   Boon
Fenton, James E. to Susan Hicks 18 Oct. 1820   Boon
Fenton, Joel to Lucy March 23 Nov. 1830   Boon
Fenton, Joseph C. to Hannah Stinson 12 Sept. 1839   Clar
Fenwick, Geo. to Julia A. Hernden 31 Aug. 1837   Coop
Fenwick, James to Rebecca Granberry 10 Feb. 1831   CG-A
Fenwick, Leo to Julia Wheeler 17 Nov. 1831   CG-A
Ferel, Benj. to Susan Black 12 Mar. 1839   CG-B
Fergerson, Wm. B. to Laura Lewis 21 Aug. 1839   StCh
Ferguins, Caleb H. to Nancy P. James 9 Apr. 1829   Mari
Ferguson, Daniel to Susannah Sinclair 4 Jan. 1826   Pk-1
Ferguson, Douglas to Jane Lewis 22 Nov. 1828   Jeff
Ferguson, Henry M. to Eliza H. Bryant 20 Feb. 1837   Lewi
Ferguson, James to Catherine Price 20 Oct. 1834   Call
Ferguson, John to Mary Cooley 29 Dec. 1828   Clay
Ferguson, John to Elizabeth Bullinger 27 Feb. 1830   CG-A
Ferguson, Levan to Jane Holloway 22 Feb. 1822   Call
Ferguson, Thomas to Malinda Carter 5 Oct. 1830   Cole
Ferguson, Thomas J. to Nancy L. Moore 14 Feb. 1833   Call
Ferguson, Wm. to Mary Davis 25 Dec. 1838   Rand
Ferguson, Wm. to Zerilda Landown 11 Dec. 1839   Cole
Ferguson, Willoughby P. to Elizabeth Gee 18 Jan. 1838   Call
Ferill, Robt. to Katharine Lightner 21 Mar. 1839   Pk-B
Ferrel, Benj. A. to Lucy C. Standley 13 Feb. 1829   Coop
Ferrel, Ezekial to Ann Burch 7 Oct. 1828   Pk-1
Ferrel, Hiram to Jane Buckridge 25 July 1828   Clay
Ferrel, Jacob to Jane Ashcraft 12 May 1836   Howa
Ferrel, John to Mary Doyle 1 Oct. 1837   Pk-B
Ferrel, Tandy to Sally A. Haines 26 June 1838   Monr
Ferrell, James to Mary C. Billups 2 Nov. 1837   Fran
Ferrell, Thomas to Lucitha Story 26 Nov. 1829   CG-A
Ferrell, Wm. to Elizabeth Clemmens 5 July 1821   Sali
Ferril, Daniel to Hannah Love 9 June 1833   Clay

Ferril, Eber to Mrs. Lucy Richy 7 June 1833	Fran
Ferril, Wm. E. to Louiza M. Banks 13 Sept. 1838	Lafa
Ferrill, Jessee to Pernina E. Myers 7 Nov. 1839	Jack
Ferrill, Jonathan to Elizabeth Fall 27 Oct. 1825	Sali
Ferrill, Joseph to Anne Rowe 21 June 1835	Clay
Ferrill, Martillus to Mrs. Mary J. Waller 7 Mar. 1837	Coop
Ferrill, Peter H. to Susan J. Meredith 9 Mar. 1836	Coop
Ferrill, Wm. to Tabitha Porter 16 Aug. 1839	Cass
Ferris, Marmaduke E. to Adaline W. Shade 6 July 1834	Perr
Ferry, Charles to Arzella Watts 9 Jan. 1834	Linc
Ferry, John to Anna Young 12 July 1821	Boon
Fetsh, Johann to Marie A. Prinston 11 Feb. 1839	StCh
Fible, Joseph to Mary Wills 7 Feb. 1839	Lewi
Fickle, Abner to Susan Conley 17 Aug. 1828	Lafa
Fickle, Absolom F. to Julian Hopkins 14 Oct. 1838	Clay
Fickle, Henry H. to Fanny White 5 Oct. 1836	Lafa
Fickle, Matthis to Arrena Noland 25 Dec. 1832	Lafa
Ficus, Adam to Susan McDonald 7 Oct. 1819	Howa
Field, Benj. F. to Mary A. Walker 28 Mar. 1839	Mari
Fielder, Geo. W. to Mariah M. Ford 28 Dec. 1837	Pk-B
Fielder, Wm. to Jane Thurman 4 Oct. 1838	Pk-B
Fielding, John to Mary A. Digernt 25 Aug. 1834	Howa
Fields, Benj. to Polly Taylor 4 Sept. 1827	Ray
Fields, Beverly to Louisa E. West 11 Aug. 1836	Call
Fields, Ebenezer to Betsey Taylor 8 Oct. 1834	Ray
Fields, Isaac to Betsy Lovell 8 Apr. 1835	Ray
Fields, James to Lucy Ross 22 Dec. 1831	Coop
Fields, James to Sally McDonald 4 July 1833	Ray
Fields, Jesse to Martha A. Oglesby 14 Nov. 1833	Coop
Fields, John to Sarah Reed 24 Oct. 1816	Howa
Fields, John to Catharine McDonald 13 Apr. 1826	Ray
Fields, John D. to Eunice Hostetter 6 July 1837	Pk-A
Fields, John W. to Harriett S. McCutchen 11 July 1837	Coop
Fields, Joseph to Hannah Lee 6 Aug. 1829	Clay
Fields, Joshua to Delinda Bellamy 18 Mar. 1830	Perr
Fields, Levi to Caty Wallace 26 Feb. 1817	Howa
Fields, Levi to Sarah Fields 30 Nov. 1839	Buch
Fields, Philip F. to Lucy Barnett 18 Dec. 1837	Rall
Fields, Stephen to Elizabeth Jones 20 May 1823	Howa
Fields, Stephen to Mariam McDaniel 5 Apr. 1836	Ray
Fields, Thomas to Rebecca Riggs 22 Jan. 1829	Ray
Fields, Thomas to Sinthy Sisk 12 Sept. 1833	Char
Fields, Wilfred B. to Sarah A. Brashear 24 Jan. 1839	Howa
Fields, Wm. C. to Sally Cook 28 Dec. 1837	Howa
Fien, Wm. to Nancy Garner 21 Feb. 1828	Ray
Fife, Henry H. to Clarissa Woods 4 July 1839	CG-B
Fiffer, Jacob to Mary Miller 7 Mar. 1833	Gree
Figgins, Wm. to Sarah Alvis 2 Feb. 1837	Pk-1
Fight, Andrew to Mary Weaver 8 Nov. 1827	Jeff
Fightmaster, Alvin to Sarah Colvin 27 Sept. 1839	Monr
Fike, Hasten to Polly Simpson 1 Nov. 1827	Rall
Fike, Nelson to Mary J. Hase 15 Aug. 1838	Rall
Filteau, John B. to Bridget Vallee 17 Sept. 1812	StCh
Finch, John P. to Mary A. Walsh 3 Sept. 1835	Perr
Finch, Richard to Sarah Smith 5 Apr. 1837	CG-A
Finch, Thomas to Susan Harold 8 May 1836	StCh
Finch, Thomas J. to Elizabeth Burns 3 Oct. 1837	Perr
Findley, Alexander to Jane Carroll 19 June 1836	Morg
Findley, Brutes to Nancy Crockett 6 Feb. 1839	Boon
Findley, Colby to Sarah Hensley 16 Sept. 1839	Plat
Findley, James to Juliet V. Ryland 12 Dec. 1839	Lafa
Findley, Wm. W. to Margaret J. Campbell 25 Oct. 1838	Call
Fine, Cornelius to Harriotte Hill 30 Jan. 1834	Lafa
Fine, John to Agnes Mitchell 30 Sept. 1826	Coop
Fine, Jonathan to Rachel Houx 22 Nov. 1835	John

```
Fine, Ludgard Jr. to Patsa Cox 6 Aug. 1833                        Lafa
Fine, Morgan to Luisy Porter 30 Jan. 1834                         Lafa
Fine, Quin M. to Louisa B. Hord 24 Oct. 1839                      Jack
Fine, Wm. B. to Elizabeth Cooper 24 Oct. 1839                     Warr
Finger, Peter to Rosy Roades 22 June 1834                         Md-A
Fink, Valentine P. to Louisa P. Wescott 29 Sept. 1835            Wash
Finks, James F. to Caroline M. Hughes 4 Oct. 1837                Howa
Finks, Joel A. to Elizabeth Settle 27 June 1839                  Rall
Finley, Charles to Rachel Ballew 13 Sept. 1832                    Cr-1
Finley, Gilman to Martha Gladney 20 Dec. 1838                    Linc
Finley, James to Polly Dodds 26 July 1836                        Pk-1
Finley, John to Nancy Woodland 7 Jan. 1838                       Call
Finley, Milton to Sally Grant 4 Jan. 1827                        Pk-1
Finley, Milton to Mary Wear 15 Aug. 1833                          Coop
Finley, Morgan to Margaret Cross 8 Sept. 1826                    Howa
Finley, Samuel W. to Cynthia A. Carrell 18 Feb. 1830            Pk-1
Finnell, Hiram to Mary Davis 10 Oct. 1834                        Char
Finnell, Martin to Amy Richardson 14 Apr. 1831                  Howa
Finnell, Wm. to Jane Goodman 15 Sept. 1827                       Char
Finnell, Wm. to Emily J. Craig 24 Feb. 1829                     Howa
Finney, ---- to Polly Willingham 23 Feb. 1830                    Boon
Finney, Harvey A. to Missouri Williams 21 Apr. 1839             Ray
Finney, Hiram to Polly Davis 6 Feb. 1833                         Ray
Finney, Wm. to Elizabeth Wilson 12 Oct. 1832                     Ray
Finney, Wm. H. to Sarah Camp 13 Nov. 1838                        Warr
Firguin, John to Polly Hornback 28 June 1829                    Mari
Firman, Benj. F. to Sarah Rookwood 20 Oct. 1836                 Shel
Fish, Wm. to Lotty Edwards 9 July 1835                           Jack
Fisher, Abram to Mary Fullerton 25 Jan. 1838                    Pk-B
Fisher, Andrew J. to Nancy Daughtey 17 Sept. 1837              Ripl
Fisher, Benj. to Luizea Jones 31 Aug. 1828                      StCh
Fisher, Benj. to Elizabeth Isele 23 Aug. 1835                   StCh
Fisher, Elijah to Viola English 16 Oct. 1838                    Lewi
Fisher, Henry to Nelly Gabainal 13 Dec. 1827                    Coop
Fisher, James T. to Rebecca Smeltezer 22 Dec. 1831             Sali
Fisher, John to Elizabeth Stinson 28 Dec. 1825                  Coop
Fisher, John to Jane Faris 6 Oct. 1831                          Coop
Fisher, John to Sarah J. Haycroft 16 Oct. 1838                  Lewi
Fisher, John P. to America Gilaspie 18 May 1837                 Pk-A
Fisher, Joseph to Mary Craighead 6 Nov. 1827                    Call
Fisher, Joshua to Martha Donovan 11 Nov. 1811                   StCh
Fisher, Joshua to Elizabeth Durham 14 Aug. 1821                 Cole
Fisher, Joshua to Mariah A. Lard 19 Apr. 1835                   Pk-1
Fisher, Manuel to Sally Scott 24 Dec. 1836                      Sali
Fisher, Nicholas to Mrs. Nancy Courtney 9 Feb. 1832            StCh
Fisher, Peter to Cary Carter 23 Dec. 1821                       Coop
Fisher, Peter Sr. to Elizabeth Scott 6 Apr. 1839               Pett
Fisher, Peyton L. to Frances Jordon 8 July 1830                Howa
Fisher, Reuben to Elizabeth Bass 18 June 1832                  Coop
Fisher, Richard to Schursay Wooten 27 June 1833                Morg
Fisher, Richard to Betsy Summers 24 Oct. 1835                  Morg
Fisher, Russell B. to Polly Hays 2 July 1835                   Morg
Fisher, Sidney S. to Jane Jamison 2 Sept. 1830                 Rall
Fisher, Solomon to Susannah Thompson 5 Sept. 1826             Pk-1
Fisher, Solomon to Elizabeth Welthy 26 June 1831              Pk-1
Fisher, Solomon to Elizabeth Welty 18 Apr. 1833               Pk-1
Fisher, Solomon to Matilda Payne 14 Feb. 1839                 Pk-B
Fisher, Trustman to Margaret Gess 19 Mar. 1829                 Coop
Fisher, Wm. to Eliza Smith 25 Dec. 1827                         Coop
Fisher, Wm. to Sarah Woolford 3 July 1831                       Wash
Fisher, Wm. to Eliza Hostetter 16 Feb. 1832                     Pk-1
Fisher, Wm. to America Edwards 29 Mar. 1836                     Sali
Fisher, Wm. to Electa Watson 8 Nov. 1837                        Pk-B
Fisher, Witsoul to Amanda Edwards 17 Dec. 1835                 Pett
Fite, Willis to Ruth Turley 10 Apr. 1828                        Wash
```

```
Fitter, John to Mrs. Regina Saintus 12 Nov. 1833          StCh
Fitts, John to Nancy Burgess 9 Dec. 1839                  StCh
Fitz, Wendelin to Catherine Sherer 3 June 1834           Perr
Fitzgerald, H. Lee to Ailcy Stufflebean 8 June 1834      Jack
Fitzhugh, Soloman to Polly Dickey 19 Oct. 1826           Lafa
Fitzhugh, Wm. to Mary Upton 7 Feb. 1833                  Morg
Fitzwater, John to Elizabeth Isgrig 2 Apr. 1834          Wash
Fitzwater, John to Nancy McCourtney 23 Aug. 1839         Fran
Fitzwaters, Uriah to Frances Fitzwaters 19 Mar. 1837     Wash
Flack, Gursham to Lucinda Sloan 1 July 1839              Boon
Flack, James to Silvey Fisher 9 June 1822                Coop
Flanery, John to Nancy Spiva 15 Oct. 1827                Md-A
Flanery, John to Wineford Perkins 2 Aug. 1832            Monr
Flanery, John J. to Prudence Burriss 24 Dec. 1839        Jack
Flannery, John to Rebecca Crabtree 22 Mar. 1835          Jack
Flannery, Zion to Lucinda Sheperd 11 Dec. 1834           Jack
Flanry, Elijah to Tabitha Brock 3 Oct. 1839              Plat
Flanry, Wm. to Ann Hase 25 Feb. 1838                     Cass
Flatt, John to Polly Pointer 24 May 1835                 Gasc
Fleetwood, Wm. to Patsy Ashby 13 May 1821                Char
Fleming, James to Dicy Lawless 24 Dec. 1826              Boon
Fleming, Nicholas L. to Patsy E. Harris 25 Nov. 1835     StFr
Flemming, Hiram to Jain Stevenson 11 Jan. 1837           Perr
Flemming, John B. to Mary McClain 31 July 1828           Wash
Flemming, Jonathan to Mahaly Lizenby 7 Aug. 1834         Mari
Flemmings, Jackson to Elizabeth Kuton 7 Nov. 1839        Howa
Flemmings, Peter to Ann Dillard 20 Feb. 1832             Howa
Flemmons, Baley to Mary Foster 9 Mar. 1826               Perr
Flenner, Manuel to Martha J. McCafferty 23 Dec. 1838     Sali
Fletcher, Allen to City Ann Hatfield 17 Aug. 1837        Maco
Fletcher, Charles to Cintha Tarwater 4 Sept. 1831        Ray
Fletcher, Drewry to Eliza E. Gates 5 Sept. 1839          Plat
Fletcher, Elije L. to Juliann Cochran 17 May 1838        Maco
Fletcher, Goldsmith to Mary Naave 29 June 1826           Ray
Fletcher, Henry to Jane Estes 18 Apr. 1822               Call
Fletcher, James to Nancy White 12 June 1825              Lafa
Fletcher, John to Catharine Skidmore 6 June 1831         Ray
Fletcher, John F. to Judith Simco 29 Aug. 1839           Call
Fletcher, Joseph O. to Lucy W. Parker 18 May 1837        Call
Fletcher, Moses to Jane McKipic 21 May 1829              Clay
Fletcher, Soloman to Elender Broadhurst 9 Jan. 1834      Ray
Fletcher, Thomas to Rosanna Ordway 24 Feb. 1814          CG-1
Fletcher, Thomas to Eliza Mudd 2 Aug. 1836               Linc
Fletcher, Thomas to Jane Skidmore 4 Aug. 1836            Ray
Fletcher, Wm. to Rachel Burrows 13 Oct. 1831             Pk-1
Fletcher, Wm. to Emaline McGee 9 Apr. 1834               Boon
Fletcher, Wm. to Louisana Murphy 2 Feb. 1837             Rand
Flin, Andrew W. to Mary Flod 13 Jan. 1839                CG-B
Flinn, Lisander to Maria Stephenson 1 May 1827           Wash
Flint, Wm. to Ann Porter 7 Nov. 1833                     Coop
Flippin, Thomas J. to Druscilla Murray 2 Mar. 1826       Cole
Flood, Amos to Nancy Atwell 29 Apr. 1818                 CG-1
Flook, Frederick to Catherine Halter 31 Dec. 1838        CG-B
Floweree, Wm. K. to Matilda A. Caldwell 20 Mar. 1833     Rall
Floyd, A.B. to Delilah Goode -- Oct. 1837                Boon
Floyd, Henry to Mary Phillips 13 Jan. 1837               Clar
Floyd, Jesse to Fanney Colovan 13 Dec. 1809              CG-1
Flud, David to Susannah Roade 2 Feb. 1831                StFr
Fluer, Joseph to Therese Gutter 12 Jan. 1836             StCh
Fly, John to Sarah Todd 18 Mar. 1828                     Howa
Flynn, Royal to Luvica Hall 25 Feb. 1837                 Pk-A
Focke, Ferdinand to Gertrude Deister 31 July 1836        StCh
Foley, Elijah to Nancy Brown 1 Dec. 1825                 Boon
Foley, Thomas to Mary Hawkins 17 July 1834               Linc
Folly, Joseph to Rachel Breese 21 Jan. 1836              Cr-1
```

```
Footman, Reuben to Elizabeth Wilson 30 Nov. 1838                    Clay
Forbes, Andrew H. to Nancy M. Steel 23 Feb. 1831                    Coop
Forbes, John W. to Mary D. Owens 13 June 1838                       Clay
Forbes, Wesley to Ann Smiley 16 Jan. 1834                           Pett
Forbus, John to Eliza Bennett 24 Apr. 1831                          CG-A
Forbus, Robt. A. to Agnes Porter 15 June 1836                      Gree
Force, Charles to Betsey Conner 7 Sept. 1819                        Coop
Ford, Alexander to Lydia A. Hunt 3 Sept. 1835                       Ray
Ford, Ambrose to Ceda ---- 30 Oct. 1835                            StCh
Ford, Andrew J. to Susannah Hay 22 Dec. 1835                       Lewi
Ford, Benj. to Mrs. Rachel Clark 28 Mar. 1837                      Linc
Ford, Harvey to Elizabeth Shannon 3 Nov. 1836                     StCh
Ford, James to Mary A. Duncan 15 Aug. 1839                          Clay
Ford, James N. to Permelia Cockram 25 July 1833                    Mari
Ford, John to Catherine Kirkpatrick 24 Oct. 1833                   Wash
Ford, Joseph to Nancy Benus 30 July 1835                           Pk-1
Ford, Lloyd to Mary A. Orear 6 Oct. 1836                           Rall
Ford, Nathaniel to Lucinda Embree 11 July 1822                     Howa
Ford, Pleasant to Polley Williams 29 Mar. 1832                     Monr
Ford, Samuel to Margaret W. Higgins 18 Dec. 1825                   Howa
Ford, Thomas to Agness A. Scott 12 Dec. 1837                       Clar
Fore, Augustus to Elizabeth Montgomery 9 Sept. 1838                Cr-1
Fore, Charles to Polly Lain 18 Sept. 1839                          Char
Foree, Dr. S.J.M. to Judith P. Mitchell 25 Sept. 1838             Clar
Forehand, Jonathan to Amey Inman 14 June 1832                      Wash
Foreman, James to Polly See 27 Sept. 1822                          Rall
Foreman, Wm. to Susan Parker 26 Jan. 1826                          Rall
Foren, Moses to Mahala Farmer 13 Feb. 1835                        Gree
Forguson, Robt. to Hanah Ohaver 14 Apr. 1831                       Wash
Forman, Inskeep to Elizabeth Taylor 6 Aug. 1829                    Mari
Forman, Vincent to Rose A. Naul 28 May 1833                        Lewi
Forman, Wm. to Sarah Yarnal 24 Dec. 1828                          StCh
Forrest, Geo. to Mary A. Hardy 24 Sept. 1839                       Rall
Forrest, James to Patsy Hill 26 Nov. 1818                          Howa
Forrest, James to Luvecy Littral 6 Oct. 1825                       Howa
Forrest, Preston to Lucinda Lee 31 July 1827                       Howa
Forrest, Thomas J. to Juna Hudt 16 Dec. 1835                       Howa
Forrester, Allen to Catherine B. McAustin 16 Aug. 1836            Jeff
Forrester, Andrew to Electa Everette 1 Jan. 1830                   Jeff
Forrier, Samuel to Alice Shannon 22 Nov. 1827                      Call
Forrister, Geo. to Susannah Riane 1 Feb. 1831                      CG-A
Forsythe, Benj. U. to Nancy Collet 20 Sept. 1838                   Clin
Fort, Elias R. to Harriet Robertson 1 Sept. 1836                   Cr-1
Fort, John to Derinda Bell 19 Oct. 1828                            Coop
Fortener, John to Sally Jentry 21 Sept. 1838                       Clay
Fortune, James to Margery A. Brashears 30 June 1833                Ray
Foster, Alexander F. to Margaret Pollard 20 Aug. 1835             Jeff
Foster, Asy to Clementine Johnston 11 Oct. 1838                    CG-A
Foster, Beverly B. to Adaline Beherst 31 Oct. 1836               Pk-1
Foster, Charles to Belinda Biggs 8 Aug. 1833                      StCh
Foster, Elijah to Elizabeth Powell 12 July 1827                    Call
Foster, Frederick to Martha Minton 16 Sept. 1830                   CG-A
Foster, Garner to Manerva Pinkston 17 Mar. 1836                    Call
Foster, Geo. to Katharine Thomas 18 Dec. 1823                      Howa
Foster, Geo. H. to Zelihe Turner 11 Feb. 1830                     Boon
Foster, Henry to Rebecca Parish 18 July 1838                       Monr
Foster, Henry to Manerva Montgomery -- -- 1839                     Maco
Foster, Henry L. to Margaret Wolfskill 17 Aug. 1828               Howa
Foster, James to Minerva Barnes 1 Dec. 1836                        Boon
Foster, James to Elizabeth Ford 10 Jan. 1839                       Linc
Foster, James to Hannah J. Thompson 12 Dec. 1839                   Clay
Foster, James T. to Isabella Ellis 22 Sept. 1836                   Call
Foster, John to Ann Miler 27 July 1823                            StCh
Foster, John to Sarah Longley 24 Apr. 1828                         Call
Foster, John to Matty Johnson 15 May 1831                          Jeff
```

79

Foster, John to Sarah Gill 19 Apr. 1832   CG-A
Foster, Joniah to Nancy Adams 10 July 1817   Howa
Foster, Pethnel to Margaret Bones 28 Feb. 1822   Sali
Foster, Robt. to Hannah Cercy 2 July 1826   StGe
Foster, Robt. to Sarah Doason 12 May 1834   Gree
Foster, Robt. C.S. to Mary W. Green 12 June 1836   Boon
Foster, Simpson to Eleanor Job 1 Oct. 1835   Cole
Foster, Thomas to Elsie Lacey 5 Sept. 1833   Jeff
Foster, Thomas to Mary Lay 22 Nov. 1833   Jack
Foster, Thomas to Elizabeth ---- 4 Nov. 1835   Coop
Foster, Whitley to Catherine Hannah 10 Dec. 1835   Rand
Foster, Wm. to Rebecca Poe 19 Oct. 1831   CG-A
Foster, Wm. A. to Matilda D. Harris 31 Aug. 1837   Call
Foster, Wm. F. to Manervy Farris 1 Jan. 1834   Pett
Fountain, Absalom to Lucy A. Angell 13 Mar. 1838   Boon
Fountain, Matthew to Sarah Hicks 5 July 1836   Boon
Foushee, Edwin to Amanda Pitzer 31 Aug. 1837   StCh
Fowler, Charles to Eliza A. Frazier 22 Jan. 1839   Rall
Fowler, John to ---- McCullom 6 June 1821   Char
Fowler, Joseph L. to Mahala Huffman 12 Aug. 1832   Fran
Fowler, Leroy P. to Jane Cowsert 21 Sept. 1837   Ray
Fowler, Lienden to Sarah Osten 19 Jan. 1832   Call
Fowler, Robt. to Elizabeth Butler 1 Mar. 1838   Pett
Fox, James C. to Ann Smith 23 June 1822   Rall
Fox, Levi to Mary Nelson 31 Oct. 1833   Lafa
Fox, Madison to Hannah Lynch 5 July 1838   Lafa
Fox, Peter to Sarah A. Trent 22 Sept. 1838   Char
Fox, Silas to Martha A. Akard 12 Sept. 1839   Polk
Fox, Wm. to Caty Herd 11 Aug. 1818   Howa
Fox, Wm. to Elizabeth Thomas 7 May 1829   Char
Fox, Wm. to Polly Pitzer 27 June 1838   Warr
Foy, Nicholas to Susan Roy 23 June 1839   Call
Fraisier, Wm. P. to Mary K. Saddler 11 Nov. 1833   Lewi
Fraizier, James M. to Mary K. Snell 27 Sept. 1836   Mari
Frame, John to Nancy Vaughan 26 Oct. 1836   Lewi
Frams, Wm. to Nancy Shelton 13 Dec. 1832   StCh
Frances, Gideon to Sarah Burcham 25 May 1832   Md-B
Francisco, John G. to Sarah Woods 13 Oct. 1836   Mari
Frank, Wm. to Ruby Brace 25 Jan. 1838   Clay
Frankenberg, Adolph to Maria E. Huevelmeycos 15 Sept. 1837 Fran
Franklin, Edward to Mary Conner 1 Sept. 1833   Lafa
Franklin, Francis to Mary E. Tingle 31 Jan. 1838   Shel
Franklin, James to Christena Ivans 25 Oct. 1838   Polk
Franklin, John to Ann Conner 1 Mar. 1837   Fran
Franklin, John to Sarah Anderson 24 Nov. 1839   Lewi
Franklin, John R. to Lucy A. Walker 4 Aug. 1836   Jack
Frans, James M. to Mary A. Lilly 3 May 1839   StCh
Frasier, Lewis to Susannah Skinner 10 Jan. 1833   Fran
Frasure, James to Mary A. Liles 8 Dec. 1836   Gree
Fray, James to Eliza Dennis 10 June 1830   Howa
Fray, John to Martha Barnes 3 Oct. 1837   Rand
Fray, Wm. to Barbary Dale 11 Mar. 1834   Rand
Frayser, Robt. B. to Mary V. Spoors 1 Jan. 1836   StCh
Frazer, James M. to Mary K. Snell 27 Sept. 1836   Mari
Frazer, Martin to Nancy Evins 10 May 1838   StCh
Frazier, John S. to Tabitha Rains 31 Jan. 1833   Mar
Frazier, Pitman H. to Susan Sherwood 13 Aug. 1835   Ray
Frazier, Wm. to Lucretia Eddington 31 Jan. 1833   Linc
Fredericks, Frederic K. to Delancy Foster 28 Sept. 1835   Jack
Freeman, Abraham to Nancy Deen 16 Nov. 1826   Fran
Freeman, Jonathan to Mary Webb 3 Jan. 1839   Boon
Freeman, Joshua to Elizabeth Lamb 14 June 1838   Rand
Freeman, Michael to Louisa Wilson 17 Nov. 1836   Call
Freeman, Nelson to Elizabeth Johnson 12 May 1836   Howa
Freeman, Orran to Sarah A. Penick 14 July 1839   Ray

```
Freeman, Silas to Epsey Marlow 27 Dec. 1829/30                  StFr
French, Isaac C. to Nancy C. Monroe 23 June 1836               Morg
French, John to Isabella Dillard 11 May 1837                    Call
French, Lewis to Louisa Simpson 1 Aug. 1822                     Call
French, Silas to Maria Mattingly 18 June 1837                   Perr
French, Wm. H. to Comfort E. Parks 29 Mar. 1836                 Morg
Freshans, Andrew to Jane Marcum 5 Mar. 1837                     John
Freshour, John J. to Permealy C. Allen 15 Aug. 1837            Cole
Freshour, Wm. to Elizabeth Wells 23 Dec. 1837                  Cole
Freutly, John to Josephine Mescade 4 May 1835                  StCh
Frey, John to Sophronia Hall 7 Nov. 1822                       Call
Frey, Thomas to Elizabeth McCullock 12 Apr. 1838              Clin
Frickey, Elijah to George Ann K.G. Alexander 6 Feb. 1838      CG-A
Frickey, Wm. to Katherine Garner 22 Aug. 1833                 CG-A
Fricky, Thompson to Mary Garner 23 Feb. 1832                  CG-A
Friend, John to Sarah Friend 18 Nov. 1833                     Gree
Frier, James Sr. to Mrs. Mary P. Luck Sr. 8 Dec. 1833         Pk-1
Frier, James M. to Mary P. Luck Jr. 26 Dec. 1833              Pk-1
Frier, Wm. to Winneford Griffith 21 Apr. 1839                 Fran
Frieze, Alford M. to Amanda A. Campbell 25 June 1835          Polk
Frissell, Willard to Ann M. Austin 20 Jan. 1831               Jeff
Fristoe, John J. to Eliza Hancock 18 Oct. 1836                Howa
Frizel, Joseph to Sarah Bollinger 25 Jan. 1819                CG-1
Frizell, Porter to Lilly Porter 22 Oct. 1834                  Gree
Frizzel, Jason to Odeel Smith 17 Mar. 1836                    Md-B
Frizzel, Medum to Cicilla Lashance 7 Apr. 1836                Md-B
Frizzell, Thomas to Mary A. Parker 25 Apr. 1839               Md-B
Froman, Lorenzo to Cecelcernam Gist 14 July 1831              Clay
Frost, Elijah to Elizabeth Brown 9 Dec. 1821                  Char
Frost, Gilbert to Elizabeth Cogdale 22 Nov. 1829              Clay
Frost, Josiah to Nancy Bradbury 18 Oct. 1834                  Jack
Fruit, Enoch to Margaret Hannah 22 Oct. 1835                  Monr
Frukie, Geo. to Ann Smuing 12 Feb. 1826                       CG-A
Fry, Abraham K. to Betsy Lear 10 Jan. 1822                    Rall
Fry, Abraham K. to Sally McFawl 23 Nov. 1826                  Rall
Fry, Benj. to Margarett Stevenson 14 Nov. 1833               Clay
Fry, Benj. I. to Luceda J. Elmore 15 May 1831                Sali
Fry, Elijah to Polly A. Brassfield 24 Sept. 1835             Clin
Fry, Jacob to Emily Fry 28 Nov. 1837                          Pk-B
Fry, James to Mary J. Downing 27 Apr. 1834                    StCh
Fry, Jefferson to Mary A. Hall 3 Aug. 1830                    Clay
Fry, Peter to Sally Gemerson 13 June 1839                     Bent
Fry, Thomas to Elizabeth A. Hall 17 July 1823                Clay
Frye, James to Elizabeth Becket 3 Feb. 1828                  Mari
Fryer, Richard to Eliza A. Oldham 5 July 1829                Fran
Fryor, Jesse to Susannah Wilson 30 Oct. 1831                 Cr-1
Fudge, Jonathan to Mary A. Spence 12 Dec. 1839               Boon
Fugate, Geo. W. to Mrs. Esther Johnson 27 Apr. 1838          StCh
Fugate, Hiram to Eleanor Crouch 4 Dec. 1828                  Rall
Fugate, Washington to Susanah Hensley 23 May 1833            Cole
Fuget, Joseph to Mariah Kerkindol 24 May 1837                Clay
Fugett, Braxton to Mariah Swope 1 May 1824                   Howa
Fugett, Hiram to Nancy Brown 28 Feb. 1819                    Howa
Fugett, Jonathan to Nancy Burnes 5 July 1821                 Howa
Fugit, Geo. W. to Nancy Hackney 13 Aug. 1839                 Cole
Fulbright, Aaron to Catherine Baker 30 Dec. 1832             CG-A
Fulbright, John L. to Elizabeth Roper 22 Feb. 1835           Gree
Fulcher, Richard to Catharine Floyd 22 Feb. 1837            Maco
Fulkerson, Frederick to Sally Ridgeway 30 June 1831          Howa
Fulkerson, Isaac to Mary Wheeler 6 Sept. 1837                CG-A
Fulkerson, James to Elizabeth Hutchens 28 Sept. 1834         Boon
Fulkerson, James to Elizabeth Houx 5 Jan. 1836               John
Fulkerson, James P. to Louisa Steinbeck 7 Jan. 1830          CG-A
Fulkerson, Reuben to Polly Cochrell 20 Mar. 1838             John
Fulkerson, Robt. C. to Lavina Dickason 6 Dec. 1828           Rall
```

Fulkerson, Wm. N. to Ellen Christie 30 Nov. 1826   StCh
Fulkinson, Richard to Polly Grant 28 Dec. 1828   Boon
Fulkinson, Richard to Polly Laughlin 20 Nov. 1831   Boon
Fullan, Thomas to Mary Eddman 5 Mar. 1839   Ray
Fullbright, John to Elizabeth Yount 2 Oct. 1828   Call
Fullbright, Phillip to Mary Durning 5 Nov. 1838   CG-A
Fullenwider, Caleb P. to Margaret Atwell 10 June 1830   CG-A
Fuller, Andrew to Polly Stanton 13 Feb. 1832   Clay
Fuller, James to Nancy Stotts 14 Dec. 1837   Pett
Fulton, James to Nancy Tenney 5 Jan. 1837   Carr
Fulton, Neal to Lucy Harris 26 Jan. 1821   Sali
Funderburk, Washington 29 Dec. 1836   CG-A
Funk, John to Margaret Henderson 24 June 1836   Boon
Funk, Thompson P. to Sarah Small 24 Aug. 1837   Clar
Fuqua, Alford to Polly Wilson 5 Sept. 1834   Rall
Fuqua, David W. to Jane S. Mifford 1 May 1835   Pk-1
Fuqua, Isham to Eliza A. Smith 14 Jan. 1836   Mari
Fuqua, Moses to Harriet Irvine 5 Feb. 1835   Pk-1
Fuqua, Wm. to Milly Parrish 6 May 1834   Mari
Fuqua, Wm. to Eliza Figgins 24 Dec. 1837   Rall
Fuquay, Nathaniel to Ann Hill 27 May 1836   Lewi
Furgeson, Wm. to Nancy Dike 7 Oct. 1839   Buch
Furguson, James H. to Julian S. Holland 19 Dec. 1839   Warr
Furguson, Wm. to Polly Heard 28 Mar. 1821   Lafa
Furmage, Joseph to Elizabeth Dagley 20 Dec. 1838   Clay
Furnham, David to Sarah J. Ford 27 Apr. 1837   Linc
Furnish, Larkin G. to Alphrama Wilson 9 Feb. 1832   Howa
Furse, Geo. H. to Martha Fall 17 Mar. 1836   Sali

Gabriel, James to Polly A. Goodman 1 Nov. 1838   Coop
Gabriel, John Jr. to Mary Vaught 14 Feb. 1827   Coop
Gage, John G. to Lydia Clement 15 Mar. 1832   Cr-1
Gage, Joseph to Fanny Livingston 21 Sept. 1819   Howa
Gage, Reuben to Martha Mezings 27 Mar. 1839   Buch
Gage, Richmon to Hannah Thurkindoll 18 Sept. 1822   Howa
Gaige, Wm. H. to Lorada House 1 Sept. 1839   Mari
Gain, Jefferson to Emily Barnes 14 Nov. 1833   Boon
Gaines, John to Mary A. Wallace 21 Dec. 1837   Howa
Gaines, Preston to Sarah Warden 23 Apr. 1833   Howa
Gaines, Robt. to Amelia Sears 11 July 1838   Monr
Gaines, Willis to Louisa Crowley 29 Dec. 1831   Clay
Gainor, Robt. to Levina Perkins 11 Mar. 1838   Ray
Gains, Wm. to Sarah A. Haze 31 Oct. 1837   Mari
Gairty, Geo. to Edna Burkleo 30 Oct. 1825   StCh
Galaspie, Samuel to Mahala Dickerson 22 May 1834   Pk-1
Galaspy, Robt. to Catharine Brown 12 Apr. 1836   Mari
Galbraith, Alfred to Margaret Boggs 4 Feb. 1836   Monr
Galbreath, Daniel to Flora Blue 4 Aug. 1835   Monr
Galbreath, James to Elizabeth Galbreath 10 Oct. 1821   Call
Galbreath, James R. to Sarah Petty 17 Nov. 1836   Call
Galbreath, Thomas W. to Manervy Dulaney 11 Apr. 1839   Rand
Galens, Calvin to Casandra A. Parish 11 Oct. 1838   Polk
Galey, David to Mary A.E. Fritzlen 17 Apr. 1828   Clay
Galiher, Henry to Betsey Phillips 6 Nov. 1831   Wash
Gall, David to Mary McDonald 23 Dec. 1827   Fran
Gall, Jacob to Roxana Hurt 7 Sept. 1826   Fran
Gall, John to Elizabeth McWilliams 15 Apr. 1830   Fran
Gallaher, Geo. to Sarena Miner 21 Oct. 1830   Wash
Gallatin, Fishel to Harriette Geiger 4 Dec. 1839   Jeff
Gallaway, Elijah to Rebecca Leard 7 Dec. 1828   Linc
Gallaway, Peter to Matilda Wilson 25 Nov. 1830   Linc
Galliway, David R. to Sarah A. Walker 3 Dec. 1839   Clay
Gallop, Simeon to Emily Eastin 21 Apr. 1832   Boon
Galloway, Jesse to Sally Skaggs 11 May 1834   Gasc

```
Galloway, Jesse to Nancy Spence 15 May 1836                        Cr-1
Gamacho, Louis to Elizabeth Diamond 7 Nov. 1831                    Jeff
Gambell, John to Phenize Pallon 7 Sept. 1837                       Barr
Gamble, Geo. to Hardwitch Isbel 17 Mar. 1827                       Wash
Ganaray, John B. to Sarah James 24 Jan. 1839                       Howa
Gann, Jackson to Rebecca Barker 2 Sept. 1834                       Lafa
Gann, Oliver to Susannah Green 7 Jan. 1836                         Lafa
Gann, Thomas to Rosanna Gann 28 Nov. 1839                          Lafa
Gantt, Edward to Sarah Smith 2 Jan. 1822                           CG-1
Gapen, Governer B. to Minerva Gray 5 Apr. 1835                     Rand
Gardiner, Henry to Sarah Miller 26 Dec. 1835                       StCh
Gardner, James A. to Cynthia J. Shirley 19 Nov. 1835              Coop
Gardner, John to Matilda Bennett 22 Mar. 1838                      Carr
Gardner, Thomas to Martha Leford 1 Mar. 1829                       Clay
Gardner, Wm. G. to Martha H. Jones 14 May 1833                     Mari
Garman, Alfred to Polly Irons 24 Feb. 1831                         Ray
Garman, James to Eliza Turner 3 Oct. 1835                          Carr
Garner, James to Lucinda Adams 6 Mar. 1828                         Clay
Garner, James to Belinda King 23 May 1837                          CG-A
Garner, John to Shelotta Ashbranner 11 Mar. 1832                   CG-A
Garner, John to Katherine Tennill 30 Mar. 1836                     Mari
Garner, John to Nancy Walker 7 May 1839                            CG-B
Garner, Stephen T. to Nancy Snoddy 28 Mar. 1839                    Howa
Garner, Walter S. to Mary A. Wilson 23 Dec. 1834                   Howa
Garner, Wm. to Ann Green 22 Sept. 1829                             CG-A
Garner, Wm. to Virginia A. Moss 15 Nov. 1832                       Mari
Garner, Wm. Jr. to Hannah Spalding 16 Feb. 1833                    Mari
Garnett, Eden to Ann Quisenburg 23 Dec. 1838                       Sali
Garnett, Franklin to Martha A. Garnett 20 Mar. 1831               Mari
Garnett, James R. to Eliza Cleaver 28 June 1830                    Rall
Garnett, Lewis to Patsey Sims 12 Oct. 1837                         Rall
Garret, Mr. to Lucy Scott 13 Aug. 1835                            Call
Garret, Luis to Lavina Pilips 17 Oct. 1835                         Perr
Garrett, Benj. F. to Henrietta Huner 20 Sept. 1838               Lewi
Garrett, James to Marietta Durrett 29 Aug. 1829                    Sali
Garrett, Laban to Rachel Baxter 3 May 1821                         Sali
Garrett, Peter R. to Mary A. Whitelow 26 July 1827               CG-A
Garrison, Abner to Charity Fitzwaters 10 Dec. 1834               Wash
Garrison, Geo. to Elizabeth Tailor 30 Jan. 1834                   Clin
Garrison, John to Elizabeth Thompson 2 Feb. 1826                 Wash
Garrison, John A. to Indiana Speer 11 Mar. 1836                   Wash
Garten, Nathaniel to Clementina Steel 15 Feb. 1831              Coop
Garvin, John B. to Rebecca Reed 2 Mar. 1837                       StCh
Gash, Ebener t Maria McReynolds 26 Oct. 1833                      Lewi
Gash, Joseph t: Uley Culbertson 28 Oct. 1824                      Rall
Gash, Samuel to Nancy Oliver 28 Mar. 1826                         Howa
Gassaway, Wm. to Emily Daugherty 23 Nov. 1838                     CG-A
Gasway, Upton to Melinda White 23 Mar. 1834                       Lewi
Gatch, Henry R. to Caroline Garrison 10 Nov. 1834               Cr-1
Gatch, Phillip P. to Susan Arney 1 Oct. 1835                      Cr-1
Gates, Chesley to Margaret A. Moor 2 Dec. 1839                    Henr
Gates, Michael to ---- Marechall 6 Nov. 1839                     StCh
Gatty, Geo. to Mary Van Burklee 6 Dec. 1804                       StCh
Gatty, John to Gerucy Van Burkelow 11 Oct. 1810                  StCh
Gauge, Wm. to Nancy Hudspeth 5 Oct. 1832                          Cr-1
Gaugh, Gabriel W. to Lucinda A. White 20 Jan. 1839              Coop
Gaunt, John M. to Mary E. Berry 5 Feb. 1839                       Polk
Gausney, Wm. to Susannah Corn 28 Sept. 1834                       Jack
Gaw, Philip to Mary Barnett 5 June 1834                           Boon
Gaw, Wm. to Susan Adams 3 Nov. 1835                               Howa
Gay, Green to Elizabeth Stout 15 Sept. 1836                       Polk
Gay, Zebolin to Sarah Titus 5 Jan. 1839                           Carr
Gearhart, Isaac to Sarah Welch 5 Mar. 1818                        Howa
Geber, Peter to Theresia Dul 29 Apr. 1834                         Perr
Gebhardt, Franz J. to Katherine Pfarr 17 Sept. 1837             StCh
```

Gee, Aaron to Rebeccah Gash 2 Feb. 1828   Char
Gee, Aaron to Margaret Moore 22 July 1837   Maco
Gee, John to Priscilla Gee 25 June 1827   Howa
Gee, Moses to Synthy Sherrin 16 Dec. 1826   Char
Gee, Samuel to Martha Linner 3 Sept. 1835   Carr
Geerler, Eli to Charlotte Scaggs 28 Mar. 1839   Gasc
Geery, John to Elizabeth Causton 11 Oct. 1831   StCh
Geery, Robt. to Sarah Parks 29 Sept. 1831   Rall
Gehon, Geo. to Mary Laurence 31 Dec. 1839   Polk
Gentry, David to Elvira Fry 28 Jan. 1830   Mari
Gentry, Geo. W. to Nancy A. Parsons 14 Mar. 1835   Jack
Gentry, James to Cynthia A. Brook 6 June 1838   Boon
Gentry, Jessy to Elizabeth Smith 12 June 1828   Mari
Gentry, John to Nancy McCollum 15 Dec. 1825   Char
Gentry, John to Dorcas Anderson 15 Oct. 1837   Carr
Gentry, John to Mary Odell 8 Mar. 1838   Ray
Gentry, Joshua to Adaline Henry 20 Apr. 1826   Rall
Gentry, Moses to Nancy Vanlandingham 1 Mar. 1831   Mari
Gentry, Nicholas to Lydia Shelton 28 Oct. 1833   Ray
Gentry, Rhodes to Nancy Culbertson 4 Nov. 1837   Mari
Gentry, Sampson to Sarah Gentry 19 Nov. 1835   Carr
Gentry, Westly to Polly Segnor 22 Mar. 1827   Boon
Geoffre, J.B. to Louisa Marechal 6 Dec. 1831   StCh
George, Alvin to Jane Scott 11 Apr. 1839   Coop
George, Elberton to Elizabeth Goff 31 Oct. 1839   Henr
George, Garnie to Sarah McFarlin 10 Nov. 1822   StFr
George, Huston to Ann Burris 7 Sept. 1835   Coop
George, James to Betsy Eidson 1 July 1828   Wash
George, James to Lusindy Pruett 8 Apr. 1839   Md-B
George, Rubin to Sally McFarland 1 Apr. 1821   Coop
George, Thomas to Mary Farris 3 Nov. 1839   Wash
George, Wm. M. to Serene Moss 1 Nov. 1835   Clay
Gerry, John to Elizabeth Hicklin 21 Mar. 1822   Rall
Gerry, Wm. to Malissa Phillips 24 July 1834   Howa
Gerue, John B. to Sarah Jones 11 Jan. 1826   Howa
Gesler, Casper to Hanner Wilkey 17 Apr. 1836   StCh
Gettis, James to Elizabeth Liebly 27 June 1833   Howa
Geyer, Jacob to Sarah Hoy 17 Apr. 1831   Clay
Ghent, Henry to Mary Boyd 15 Jan. 1839   Clay
Gholson, Felix to Harriet McNeille 19 Jan. 1826   Wash
Gibbin, Daniel to Sarah A. Winn 2 Aug. 1838   Howa
Gibbons, John G. to Elizabeth McSpadden 10 Aug. 1837   John
Gibbons, Morris to Nancy Carman 8 Mar. 1838   Mari
Gibbs, Bennett G. to Sarah Randles 16 June 1839   CG-B
Gibbs, Frederick to Elvina Fields 4 Sept. 1828   Howa
Gibbs, Hiram to Eliza Rutter 2 Feb. 1832   Mari
Gibbs, Hiram to Adaline Parmer 16 Nov. 1834   Mari
Gibbs, Jonas G. to Devicy Aikman 18 Mar. 1834   Jack
Gibbs, Mathew to Susan Williams 30 Mar. 1837   Livi
Gibbs, Valentine to Elizabeth Poor 18 Aug. 1836   Md-B
Gibney, Alexander to Sally A. Hackney 12 Dec. 1831   Boon
Giboney, James to Mary Williams 24 Dec. 1829   CG-A
Gibony, Alexander to Lucinda Hays 26 Aug. 1830   CG-A
Gibs, Thomas to Elizabeth Gibson 11 Nov. 1831   Coop
Gibson, Absolam to Alice Wiggin 22 Nov. 1838   Wash
Gibson, George to Nancy Willson 9 July 1829   Linc
Gibson, Geo. G. to Mary Porter 3 Nov. 1835   Linc
Gibson, Geo. W. to Charlotte Robertson 23 Oct. 1830   StCh
Gibson, Hawkins to Sally Bradley 27 Nov. 1828   Char
Gibson, Hezekiah to Terrissa Bishop 13 Oct. 1831   Pk-1
Gibson, James to Peggy Morrow 11 Oct. 1827   Gasc
Gibson, James to Mary A. Ransdell 11 Aug. 1836   Pett
Gibson, John to Betsy Morgan 26 Mar. 1820   Howa
Gibson, John to Sarah Noland 20 Mar. 1828   Jack
Gibson, Stephen to Lucinda Summers 19 Feb. 1836   Rand

84

Gibson, Thomas to Margaret Burgen 2 Oct. 1834	Jack
Gibson, Wm. to Eloise Duquet 3 Nov. 1825	StGe
Gibson, Wm. to Posy Swift 7 Nov. 1830	Pk-1
Gibson, Wm. to Nancy Tansy 26 Apr. 1831	Fran
Gibson, Wm. L. to Dixy Malone 1 Sept. 1839	Lewi
Giddings, Wm. B. to Mary H. Buckner 27 Mar. 1834	Monr
Gideons, Joshua A. to Mahaly J. Johnson 23 Jan. 1839	Gree
Gieber, Nichalos to Mary Mattingly 8 Sept. 1835	Perr
Gierge, Clement to Clara Miller 12 Feb. 1838	Perr
Gieslar, Noah to Sarah Harrison 14 Oct. 1839	Cr-1
Gilbert, Benj. to Mary Neal 19 Dec. 1838	Coop
Gilbert, David to Betsy McIntire 18 Apr. 1827	StCh
Gilbert, James to Manervy Polly 12 June 1836	Polk
Gilbert, John to Nancy Mobly 1 Dec. 1836	Sali
Gilbert, John to Mary Fagan 2 Jan. 1839	Rall
Gilbert, John J. to Jane M. Anderson 15 Oct. 1832	Monr
Gilbert, Nathanial to Elizabeth Stafford 14 Dec. 1825	StFr
Gilbert, Wardner to Catherine Jones 7 Mar. 1805	StCh
Gilbert, Wm. to Levina Roland 26 May 1833	Rall
Gilbreath, Hugh to Geruna Smiley 30 Apr. 1833	Coop
Giles, Auston to Francis Minton 30 Aug. 1838	CG-A
Giles, Francis H. to Elizabeth Hines 5 May 1836	Warr
Giles, Gordan to Gavrilla Watts 25 June 1839	Linc
Giles, Wm. to Mary A. Weir 3 Feb. 1830	Md-A
Giley, John to Sarah A. Kennady 27 Apr. 1826	Pk-1
Gilham, John P. to Jane F. Holmes 18 Oct. 1831	Jeff
Gill, Ferdinand to Lydia Handsbrough 22 July 1831	Mari
Gill, Ferdinand to Kitty Williams 13 Mar. 1838	Mari
Gill, James to Polly Story 6 June 1832	CG-A
Gill, Wm. to Sarah Musick 28 Apr. 1834	Mari
Gill, Wilson to Catharine Pollard 22 Aug. 1839	Mari
Gillam, Benj. to Nancy Turner 11 Oct. 1835	Wash
Gillam, Edward to Hariatt Hudspeth 22 Feb. 1833	Cr-1
Gillam, Geo. to Polly A. Turner 2 May 1839	Wash
Gillam, Solamon to Elizabeth Huitt 2 May 1839	Wash
Gillaspie, Washington to Susan Snedigar 19 Mar. 1839	Pk-B
Gilleland, Geo. to Malessa Rice 14 Mar. 1832	Lafa
Gillespie, Robt. to Sophie Barnes 20 Dec. 1827	Boon
Gillet, John S. to Mary A. Fristoe 29 Jan. 1826	Char
Gillett, Philo to Mary A. Debs 22 June 1837	Warr
Gilliam, Andrew J. to Sarah F. Clay 12 Dec. 1839	Plat
Gilliam, Fayett H. to Ann E. Ayres 4 July 1837	Sali
Gilliam, John to Eliza J. Clark 10 May 1836	Clay
Gilliam, Mitchel to Henrietta Tailor 15 Nov. 1832	Clay
Gilliham, Wm. T. to Nancy Asbell 25 Sept. 1838	Polk
Gilliland, Elam to Nancy Cooper 19 Nov. 1829	CG-A
Gilliland, Jesse R. to Ann Shaw 1 May 1839	Linc
Gilliland, Lucas to Lucy Jennings 29 Mar. 1839	Henr
Gillim, John W. to Wilmina Suddith 6 Sept. 1832	Pk-1
Gillin, John W. to Mary A. Poor 31 Nov. 1833	Linc
Gillis, Daniel to Frances Caton 28 Mar. 1833	Warr
Gillis, Peter to Nancy E. Webb 22 Aug. 1830	Linc
Gillispy, James O. to Ruth Wisdom 23 Oct. 1832	Cr-1
Gillmore, James J. to Ann L. Miller 14 Apr. 1839	Clin
Gillmore, Millford to Sarah A. Gibson 8 Nov. 1838	Clin
Gillmore, Wm. to Sarah Quinn 22 Dec. 1831	Call
Gillock, Robt. to Sarah Harper 30 Aug. 1838	Barr
Gillum, James L. to Janetta Buford 22 Mar. 1838	Pk-B
Gillum, Nathan to Patience Bryant 21 Feb. 1839	Pk-B
Gillum, Nathan S. to Ann Smith 11 Apr. 1837	Howa
Gillum, Robt. to Myre Jones 27 Jan. 1824	Clay
Gilman, Archibald to Majoicery Ferguson 28 Dec. 1837	Call
Gilman, Wm. to Charlotte Williams 25 Feb. 1830	Call
Gilman, Wm. J. to Vicy A. Callaway 10 Oct. 1838	Call
Gilmore, David to Elizabeth Phillips 16 Aug. 1838	Gasc

```
Gilmore, James S. to Nancy Burch 28 Apr. 1826                      Coop
Gilmore, John to Frances Burch 22 July 1828                       Coop
Gilmore, John to Margaret Savage 3 Mar. 1831                      Jeff
Gilmore, John R. to Rebecca Frier 26 July 1834                    Pk-1
Gilmore, Joseph to Martha W. Ronnols 21 Mar. 1830                 Clay
Gilmore, Samuel to Matilda Shirley 16 May 1830                    Coop
Gilmore, Samuel M. to Martha A. Stevenson 5 Feb. 1837            Clay
Gilmore, Wm. to Keziah McKinny 25 Dec. 1828                       Cole
Gilreash, Thomas P. to Elender Edwards 11 Feb. 1836              Ray
Gilstrap, Bright to Nancy Bradley 8 Sept. 1839                   Rand
Gilstrap, Isaac to Elizabeth King 18 June 1839                   Maco
Gilstrap, Peter to Anny Mullinix 19 Apr. 1835                    Rand
Giltar, Alexander to Fanny Edwards 5 Feb. 1835                   StFr
Ginkins, Aaron to Mrs. Millard A. Willis 3 Mar. 1836            Pk-1
Ginnings, John to Susan Shelton 9 Aug. 1836                      Md-B
Gipson, Elias to Ester Hears 7 Aug. 1823                         Fran
Gipson, John to Tabithy Coots 8 Nov. 1832                        CG-B
Gipson, Smith to Catherine Banning 5 Apr. 1838                   Maco
Girdner, Michel to Rachel Weleron 18 July 1839                   Livi
Gist, Howard to Elizabeth White 10 Oct. 1839                     Coop
Gist, Price to Lavina Fitzhugh 3 May 1835                        Jack
Gist, Samuel to Susan Fisher 11 Sept. 1837                       Clin
Gist, Thomas to Peggy Robison 4 Apr. 1830                        Coop
Givans, Elisha to Margaret Conway 25 Apr. 1839                   Mari
Givens, Alfred to Margaret Price 5 Dec. 1837                     Henr
Givens, Asriel to Polly Winscot 25 Dec. 1823                     Boon
Givens, Geo. W. to Margaret Prewitt 12 Feb. 1834                Howa
Givens, James to Polly Logston 20 Sept. 1828                     Howa
Givens, James to Elenor Chapman 26 Apr. 1830                     Lafa
Givens, John G. to Mary A. Stewart 8 Jan. 1835                   Pk-1
Givens, Merrit to Nancy Allen 10 Jan. 1839                       Davi
Givens, Samuel to Ann M. Sutton 18 Dec. 1832                     Linc
Givens, Thomas J. to Sarah McCoy 16 Sept. 1833                   Jack
Givens, Wm. to Sally Coots 21 Oct. 1831                          Clay
Givins, John to Amy S. Abbet 15 Sept. 1839                       Mill
Givins, Johnson to Ellen Trible 5 Jan. 1837                      Pk-A
Givney, R. to Mary Stocknill 4 Jan. 1831                         Coop
Gladdin, James to Mahala Sollers 24 Aug. 1826                    Clay
Gladney, Wm. S. to Nancy Cannon 16 Feb. 1837                     Linc
Glasby, Albon H. to Nancy L. Adams 13 Feb. 1838                  Pk-B
Glasby, Ezekiel R. to Judy A. Robeson 16 Sept. 1839            Pk-B
Glascock, Asa to Eliza Glascock 13 June 1835                     Rall
Glascock, Charles to Eliza Glascock 29 Jan. 1828                 Rall
Glascock, Charnal to Catherine Morris 13 June 1833             CG-A
Glascock, Fielding to Mrs. Mary Hall 11 Jan. 1827               CG-A
Glascock, Geo. to Lucy A.M. Allen 23 June 1835                   Mari
Glascock, Geo. F. to Maria S. Haskall 15 Jan. 1839             Rall
Glascock, Harrison to Rebecca Cleaver 27 Oct. 1836             Rall
Glascock, Hiram to Sarah A. Settle 21 Nov. 1838                 Rall
Glascock, Robt. to Elizabeth Sullinger 8 Mar. 1829             CG-A
Glascock, Thomas to Ury D. Dodd 10 Aug. 1837                     Rall
Glascock, Thomas O. to Mahala A. Lewellen 3 Jan. 1839          Rall
Glasgow, James to Elizabeth Groff 12 June 1825                   Fran
Glasgow, James H. to Harriet A. Cramer 12 Oct. 1836            Coop
Glaskow, Nathan to Ann B. Allcorn 17 Feb. 1834                   Howa
Glass, James to Hepsabie Morris 28 Oct. 1829                     Jack
Glass, Samuel to Lucinda McFarland 28 Nov. 1827                 Coop
Glass, Samuel to Martha Sincere 24 Apr. 1836                     StCh
Glass, Samuel B. to Sarah Smith 28 Apr. 1839                     Linc
Glass, Wm. to Susan M. Gresham 14 July 1830                     Mari
Glasscock, Hiram to Elizabeth Glasscock 12 Dec. 1833          Rall
Glasscock, Isaac to Henrietta J. Brock 28 Feb. 1836            Jack
Glasscock, Scarlet to Jane Day 22 Sept. 1822                    CG-1
Glavelle, Thomas to Mary Donnell 25 Dec. 1834                   Gree
Glaze, Lawrence to Minerva J. Dale 2 Apr. 1835                   Ray
```

```
Glazebrook, John L. to Mary J. Holand 23 Oct. 1828              Coop
Glazier, John to Linda Forsythe 9 Apr. 1839                     Coop
Gleason, Wm. to Larry Allsop 16 July 1824                       Howa
Gleavis, Thomas H. to Elenor W. Ewing 22 Dec. 1825             Lafa
Glen, Anderson to Catey Triplet 18 Mar. 1835                   Wash
Glendi, Thomas M. to Ellen Shields 15 Jan. 1833               Call
Glenn, Hamilton to Sarah Drinkard 24 Nov. 1838                Maco
Glenn, Hugh to Nelly Drake 28 Dec. 1820                       Howa
Glenn, James to Susan Martin 1 June 1826                      Wash
Glenn, James B. to Elizabeth Elliott 7 Feb. 1837             Clin
Glenn, James E. to Susan Foster 25 May 1826                  Pk-1
Glenn, James E. to Sarah Love 2 July 1835                    Pk-1
Glenn, John M. to America Crag 4 Nov. 1838                   Monr
Glenn, Joseph to Sally Graham 5 Apr. 1821                    Boon
Glenn, Joseph to Nancy Tuggle 3 Oct. 1833                    Mari
Glenn, Joseph to Eliza McMillen 31 Oct. 1833                Jeff
Glenn, Joseph F. to Rosanna Kincade 23 Aug. 1838            Cr-1
Glenn, Silas S. to Marnen Burnem 13 June 1836              Clin
Glenn, Thomas to Eliza Tucker 3 Sept. 1832                 Wash
Glinday, Thomas to Mary Cayce 17 Mar. 1836                 StCh
Glinn, Pleasant P. to Francis Rush 8 Feb. 1827            Mari
Glover, Allen to Elizabeth Harris 15 Sept. 1838           Boon
Glover, Charles to Mahala Davis 3 Oct. 1839               Call
Glover, Milton to Elizabeth Osburn 15 Oct. 1839          Bent
Glover, Philip to Sally Kuntz 13 Nov. 1819               StCh
Goddard, John to Tabitha Phipps 18 Sept. 1831            Rand
Goddard, Wm. A. to Eleanor Selvy 3 Dec. 1837            Rand
Godfroi, James to Louise Tisson 16 Feb. 1836           StCh
Godman, Granville M. to Evalina Sudduth 23 July 1833   Mari
Godsey, Burrell to Nancy Millsap 24 Sept. 1835         Carr
Goe, Noble to Jinny Smith 5 Nov. 1817                  StCh
Goff, Daniel to Elizabeth Stewart 25 Sept. 1828        Howa
Goff, James to America Stewart 9 Apr. 1826            Howa
Goff, John to Airene A. Bowen 4 Oct. 1838            Warr
Goff, Wm. to Mrs. Mary Oglisby 28 Oct. 1834          Wash
Goforth, Benj. to Julia A. Taylor 19 July 1838      Cr-1
Goforth, Gilloughby to Martha Marquiss 13 Jan. 1831  Wash
Goforth, James to Polly Lee 17 Dec. 1810             StCh
Goforth, Zachariah to Mary Hill 30 Oct. 1836        Wash
Gohlston, John M. to Mary Ellis 26 July 1837        CG-A
Gold, Joseph L. to Elizabeth Lock 17 Mar. 1835      Gree
Golden, Daniel to Mathilde Duclos 17 Oct. 1826      Wash
Goll, Lloyd B. to Eleanor Mathews 22 Dec. 1836      Pk-A
Gollecher, Wm. to Elizabeth Waller 15 Feb. 1829     CG-A
Golliher, Medad to Eliza Masterson 1 May 1836       CG-B
Golloway, Samuel to Polly Howard 25 July 1824       Cole
Gooch, Drury to Nancy Verews 23 Dec. 1836           Jeff
Gooch, Gillead to Elizabeth Mammith 24 July 1834    Howa
Gooch, James to Malinda King 27 Dec. 1832           Cole
Gooch, Jesse to Malinda McGuire 21 Mar. 1837        CG-A
Gooch, Phillip to Rosannah Payor 6 Jan. 1839        Gasc
Gooch, Roland to Celila Milsap 18 Dec. 1834         Char
Gooch, Tanly to Susan Duncan 12 Nov. 1835           Shel
Gooch, Wm. A. to Mary States 17 Oct. 1839           Wash
Goodall, Jobe to Sary Enloes 18 Apr. 1827           Cole
Goodall, Terry to Nancy Shiveres 27 Dec. 1838       Gasc
Goode, Allen to Susannah Lee 9 Oct. 1828            Ray
Goode, Mack H. to Paulina A. Brown 1 Aug. 1833      Fran
Gooden, Joseph to Jane Allen 14 Mar. 1820           Coop
Goodin, Joseph to Nancy Cockran 3 Mar. 1825         Char
Gooding, Alexander to Elizabeth Goggin 26 July 1831 Rand
Gooding, John to Elizabeth Purdon 26 Sept. 1836     Lewi
Gooding, Nicholas to Nancy Dodson 1 Mar. 1838       Rand
Gooding, Samuel to Jane Cockran 5 Aug. 1827         Char
Goodlet, Wm. to Susan E. Murphy 21 July 1839        Linc
```

Goodman, Felix G. to Lucinda Wise 14 Mar. 1839   CG-B
Goodman, Peter to Polly Matthens 20 Feb. 1838   John
Goodman, Wm. to Dolly Robertson 19 Feb. 1826   Coop
Goodman, Wm. to Sarah Conner 21 Mar. 1830   Coop
Goodmon, Wm. S. to Delila Boggus 11 Oct. 1838   Pk-B
Goodrich, Asaph to Sarah Stone 11 Dec. 1834   Linc
Goodrich, Benj. to Harriet H. Thomas 8 Oct. 1822   Call
Goodrich, Elijah R. to Sarah Tygart 7 Dec. 1835   StCh
Goodrich, James to Matilda Patten 18 Dec. 1825   StCh
Goodrich, James to Charity Phillips 13 Oct. 1836   Morg
Goodrich, John to Elizabeth Thornhill 3 Feb. 1828   StCh
Goodrich, John to Ardella Wodbridge 19 Apr. 1835   Linc
Goodrich, Martin P. to Cynthia A. McGee 18 Mar. 1836   Monr
Goodright, Edward to Polly Dye 7 June 1833   Rall
Goodson, Wm. to Martha Molder 15 Feb. 1838   Polk
Goodwin, Nicholas to Elender Holmes 4 Apr. 1839   Linc
Goodwin, Robt. to Susannah Henderson 10 Feb. 1837   Perr
Googe, Wm. to Naomi Bogges 21 Oct. 1830   Pk-1
Goolsey, Blackburn to Martha Short 20 Jan. 1836   Char
Gorden, Archibald to Mililda Bruster 24 June 1836   Ripl
Gorden, J.P. to Elizabeth Crump -- Aug. 1827   Boon
Gorden, Patterson to Lucretia Fornbush 31 Jan. 1832   Boon
Gordon, Alexander to Nancy Askens 3 Mar. 1836   Cole
Gordon, Alexander to Elizabeth Christopher 12 Oct. 1837   Clay
Gordon, Andrew to Lucinda Prine 5 Feb. 1829   Jack
Gordon, Geo. W. to Elizabeth Sone 26 Mar. 1835   Cole
Gordon, Jackson to Sally Gordon 12 Mar. 1837   Pk-A
Gordon, John to Emily Davis 10 Jan. 1839   Ray
Gordon, John B. to Nancy Thomas 2 Jan. 1834   Cole
Gordon, Joseph to Matilda Henderson 22 Aug. 1822   Call
Gordon, Reuben W. to Mary A. Brawley 22 Dec. 1833   Ripl
Gordon, Stephen B. to Lydia L. Quick 3 Apr. 1836   Pk-1
Gordon, Thomas to Ne-- C. Reed 3 Nov. 1839   Henr
Gordon, Wm. to Dulanie Bundrum 18 June 1829   Boon
Gordon, Wm. to Elizabeth Craig 3 Nov. 1833   Linc
Gordon, Wm. to Livisa Meur 8 Feb. 1838   Call
Gordon, Wm. P. to Jane F. Williams 17 Nov. 1838   Warr
Gore, Isaac B. to Ann Lynch 17 Apr. 1839   Rall
Gorham, T.R.B. to Martha A.F. Vivion 2 Oct. 1833   Lafa
Gorham, Thomas J. to Burrila Burton 20 June 1828   Char
Gorman, John to Elizabeth Bridges 20 Nov. 1836   Cr-1
Gormann, Ezekial to Elizabeth Mathews 7 Dec. 1828   CG-A
Gosejakob, Frederick to Margaret Cappelman 29 Aug. 1839   StCh
Goslin, Ruben to Mary Davenport 15 Sept. 1836   Boon
Goslin, Sylvester to Abigail Turner 25 Jan. 1831   Boon
Gosney, Henry to Mary Paulard 14 Apr. 1834   Linc
Gosney, James to Malvina Obanion 22 Aug. 1837   Md-B
Goss, David to Elizabeth Carter 25 Mar. 1838   Monr
Goss, Joseph to Mary Patterson 17 Sept. 1837   Monr
Gotcher, Hugh to Sinea Havens 2 Aug. 1832   Clay
Gouge, Allen to Hannah Miller 1 Jan. 1829   Cole
Gouge, Gideon to Nancy Foster 31 Dec. 1833   Rand
Gouge, John to Nancy McKinney 27 Sept. 1827   Cole
Gouge, Joshua to Sarah Chambers 30 Mar. 1837   Cole
Gouge, Martin to Polly Robinson 9 Aug. 1832   Cole
Gourley, Adam to Maranda Norten 27 Dec. 1835   Pk-1
Gouty, Wm. to Elizabeth McKey 26 Feb. 1826   Wash
Gover, Wm. to Julia A. Allen 4 June 1837   Lewi
Gowan, Stephen to Genetta Brooks 13 Jan. 1830   Rand
Grabs, Augustus F. to Helen M. Grabs 22 May 1837   Warr
Grace, Peter to Anne M. Williams 27 July 1834   StCh
Grafford, John W. to Martha Richardson 2 May 1839   Pk-B
Grafton, Joseph to Mrs. Mary Elliott 9 Mar. 1826   Wash
Gragg, Abner to Nancy Johnson 23 Dec. 1830   Clay
Gragg, Jefferson to Polly White 25 Feb. 1836   Clin

```
Gragg, Jefferson to Polly White 25 Feb. 1836                           Clin
Gragg, John to Sairna Cook 22 May 1836                                 Pett
Gragg, John to Elizabeth Ford 16 Jan. 1838                             Clay
Gragg, Robt. to Nancy Brewer 16 Aug. 1827                              Ray
Gragg, Wm. to Catharine Jones 7 Mar. 1830                              Clay
Gragg, Wm. to Mary Jones 24 Dec. 1834                                  Howa
Gragg, Wm. Jr. to Salena M. Gragg 14 June 1838                         John
Graham, Alexander to Jemima Jones 19 Apr. 1827                         Jeff
Graham, Alexander to Elizabeth Miller 17 Apr. 1834                     Char
Graham, Franklin to Parthena Crabtree 7 May 1835                      Jack
Graham, Geo. to Mary Kelly 19 July 1831                                Md-A
Graham, Geo. W. to Margaret West 23 Mar. 1830                          Jeff
Graham, Geo. W. to Jane Braden 30 July 1839                            Carr
Graham, Hiram to Louisa Edmundson 8 May 1834                          Jack
Graham, Jaemes to Polly Whitner 29 Mar. 1838                           Md-B
Graham, James R. to Mahala B. Davis 23 Mar. 1834                       Rall
Graham, Jefferson to Jeannette Guilmaure 1 July 1833                   Wash
Graham, John to Elizabeth Freeman 26 Apr. 1821                         Boon
Graham, John to Margaret Miller 25 Nov. 1832                           Boon
Graham, John to Unice Fabor 11 May 1839                                Bent
Graham, John G. to Nancy Hobson 21 Dec. 1837                           John
Graham, Louis to Mary Penson 4 Feb. 1835                               Wash
Graham, Michial to Lamah Husk 26 Mar. 1829                             Char
Graham, Noah to Sally Meredith 11 Mar. 1830                            Coop
Graham, Robt. to Ann English 7 Feb. 1830                               Ray
Graham, Robt. to Mary A. Gains 7 Jan. 1836                             Boon
Graham, Thompson to Susan Senter 21 Apr. 1836                          Jeff
Graham, Van S. to Ann James 25 Apr. 1833                               Cole
Graham, Wm. to Susan Ruder 22 Dec. 1838                                Henr
Graham, Wm. to Leathy A. Linch 27 Dec. 1838                            Rall
Grahard, Baptiste to Cecil Vincent 27 May 1830                         Gasc
Grahard, Joseph to Mary Denos 27 May 1830                              Gasc
Grandstaff, Isaac to Nelly Noland 25 Mar. 1832                         Boon
Grant, David to America Gilliam 12 Mar. 1839                           Buch
Grant, Geo. to Susan Todd -- Feb. 1838                                 Howa
Grant, Geo. A. to Nancy Williams 7 Oct. 1829                           Howa
Grant, Israel B. to Mary Warren 14 Feb. 1831                           Call
Grant, John to Polly Rice 14 Feb. 1828                                 Lafa
Grant, Peter to Martha Hollad 10 Nov. 1831                             Pk-1
Grant, Samuel M. to Tabitha V. Inskeep 2 Sept. 1834                    Mari
Grant, Vincent O. to Sarah A. Berk 9 Sept. 1839                        Howa
Grant, Wm. to Sally West 26 June 1828                                  Boon
Grant, Wm. to Lavina McFarland 30 Aug. 1838                            Lafa
Grant, Wm. D. to Loucintha Moore 29 Dec. 1833                          Pk-1
Grass, Joseph to Margaret Cannon 17 Mar. 1835                          Perr
Gravely, Samuel to Laro Bass 16 Nov. 1836                              StCh
Graves, Albert G. to Frances J.E. Harrison 22 Oct. 1839               Lafa
Graves, Edward to Lydia Wisdom 2 June 1835                             Boon
Graves, Edward to Elizabeth Merrin 12 Feb. 1837                        CG-A
Graves, James to Elizabeth Waugh 7 Mar. 1839                           Pk-B
Graves, James S. to Susannah Blakely 2 Sept. 1834                      Howa
Graves, John to Matilda Copeland 4 Mar. 1819                           Howa
Graves, John to Beany Rees 4 Feb. 1834                                 Coop
Graves, Wm. L. to Elizabeth J. Dunlap 16 Apr. 1835                     Lewi
Gravier, Joseph to Celeste Petit 9 Nov. 1833                           StCh
Gray, Fincelius R. to Margaret Ferguson 12 Aug. 1835                  Howa
Gray, Geo. to Eliz. C. Holt 16 Nov. 1837                               Call
Gray, Henry H. to Duba Tomlin 20 July 1834                             Lafa
Gray, Jacob C. to Sarah Parkerson 26 Jan. 1837                         John
Gray, James D. to Levicey Fowler 25 Nov. 1837                          Cole
Gray, John to Nancy Ross 23 Mar. 1821                                  Boon
Gray, John to Eliza Bellemy 2 Feb. 1827                                Perr
Gray, Joseph to Nancy Slocum 27 Mar. 1834                             Boon
Gray, Joseph M. to Nancy Isaac 14 Feb. 1837                            Howa
Gray, Joseph M. to Polly Webb 13 Sept. 1839                            Boon
```

89

Gray, Leven to Ann Bellamy 8 Mar. 1827   Perr
Gray, Martin to Ann Even 24 May 1827   Boon
Gray, Nicholas to Lucinda Miller 12 Apr. 1835   Cole
Gray, Robt. W. to Elizabeth Inglish 10 Mar. 1831   Cole
Gray, Sidney to Cynthia Barnett 19 Sept. 1839   Howa
Gray, Thompson to Emmaline Isaac 4 Sept. 1836   Howa
Grayham, Carter to Agnes Henderson 11 Oct. 1827   Md-A
Grayham, John to Malinda Stephens 5 Feb. 1817   Howa
Grayham, Pinkney to Catherine Whitener 13 Nov. 1834   Md-A
Grayham, Thomas to Ann Lewis 17 Aug. 1837   Barr
Grazier, John to Debby Quick 21 Aug. 1839   Gasc
Grear, W.H. to Rebecca Thatcher 22 July 1831   Call
Greeg, Jacob to Nancy Lewis 4 Mar. 1828   Jack
Greegg, John to Margaret Campbell 3 Mar. 1831   Wash
Greemel, Robt. to Eulila Fenwick 25 Oct. 1836   Perr
Green, Benj. to Susan Endicut 21 Nov. 1837   Clay
Green, Benj. to Semira Winn 29 May 1839   Howa
Green, Charles to Madam Julie Bradshaw 7 Mar. 1838   StCh
Green, David to Sophia Miller 25 Dec. 1808   CG-1
Green, David to Elizabeth Smith 11 Nov. 1832   CG-A
Green, Elijah to Rebecca Runis 18 Mar. 1831   Cole
Green, Elijah to Nancy Barnes 23 Sept. 1836   Polk
Green, Esquire to Lucy A. Wainscott 25 Jan. 1832   Boon
Green, Flanders to Nelley Yeager 1 June 1828   Linc
Green, Franklin to Elizabeth L. Fray 2 Jan. 1838   Howa
Green, Geo. to Sary Spoonamore 9 Dec. 1817   Howa
Green, Geo. W. to Mary A. Alfred 26 July 1836   CG-A
Green, Isaac to Martha Green 27 Nov. 1836   Boon
Green, James Jr. to Rachel Yarnel 17 Apr. 1823   StCh
Green, James R. to Nancy Carrington 12 Sept. 1837   Clin
Green, Jesse to Mary Gromer 29 Apr. 1824   Clay
Green, Jesse to Machela Boyd 11 Aug. 1833   Boon
Green, John to Nancy Boyd 6 May 1819   Coop
Green, John to Liddy Hitchcock 30 Aug. 1835   Jack
Green, John to Martha A. Everis 18 Jan. 1838   StCh
Green, John to Remey Brinegar 17 June 1838   Boon
Green, Joseph to Margaret W. Welden 17 Feb. 1839   Lewi
Green, Levin B. to Elizabeth Wright 2 Aug. 1838   Clar
Green, Lewis to Nancy Gross 24 Mar. 1830   Rand
Green, Lewis to Emeline Little 20 July 1837   Boon
Green, Madison to Frances Coy 23 Mar. 1837   Howa
Green, Obediah to Mary Roussin 2 Sept. 1834   Wash
Green, Robt. to Mrs. Elizabeth Maricle 6 Mar. 1810   StCh
Green, Robt. to Rebecca Vestal 12 Mar. 1836   Rand
Green, Squire to Emily Evans 11 Apr. 1836   Howa
Green, Squire to Mary Downing 4 May 1837   Linc
Green, Thomas to Assentha McKnight 27 Oct. 1829   CG-A
Green, Weller to Lucy A. Falconer 12 Sept. 1827   Char
Green, Wm. to Eleanor Cooley 3 Oct. 1816   Howa
Green, Wm. to Susannah Fennell -- Apr. 1821   Howa
Green, Wm. to Lorceney Smith 8 Mar. 1830   Call
Green, Wm. to Hannah Wadkins 2 Jan. 1837   CG-A
Green, Wm. to Melinda Lisenby 12 Jan. 1837   Char
Green, Wm. M. to Cincinnatti A. Montgomery 22 Feb. 1831   Mari
Green, Willie E. to Ann Woods 29 Mar. 1826   Howa
Green, Willis to Polly Kerby 17 Dec. 1836   Howa
Greene, Durant to Jane Maxwell 21 Nov. 1833   Wash
Greenlee, Asha to Nancy Litton 29 Apr. 1831   Wash
Greenlee, James to Jacenthy Hinch 1 Sept. 1829   Wash
Greenly, Elijah to Nancy Little 4 Nov. 1832   Wash
Greenstreet, Allen to Elizabeth Laremore 25 May 1827   Fran
Greenstreet, James Jr. to Sarah Kely 14 Mar. 1821   Fran
Greenstreet, James to Margaret Smith 15 Nov. 1827   Fran
Greenstreet, John to Zippy Laremore 15 Nov. 1827   Fran
Greenstreet, Lewis to Nancy Davis 31 Dec. 1835   Fran

Greenstreet, Wm. to Elizabeth Anderson 27 Aug. 1837	Fran
Greenup, Samuel to Mary Curhat 13 Aug. 1835	Cole
Greenwalt, Joseph to Charlotte Hatten 8 Aug. 1828	Perr
Greenway, Geo. to Abigail Brooshire 21 Aug. 1834	Cole
Greenway, Geo. to Fanny Russell 18 June 1837	Cole
Greenway, Geo. to Mary Walker 7 Sept. 1839	Cole
Greenwood, Wm. to Sophia L. Pugett 5 Feb. 1835	Lewi
Greer, E. Woodledge to Potisha A. Burns 17 Oct. 1839	Perr
Greer, Ephriam to Margaret Willard 13 May 1827	CG-A
Greer, Henry to Rachel Wood -- Apr. 1839	Morg
Greer, James to Elizabeth Cox 23 July 1813	CG-1
Greer, James to Martha Mullikin 2 Oct. 1834	Pk-1
Greer, James to Rachel Eavens 31 Oct. 1839	Mari
Greer, Jesse to Nancy Burch 5 July 1832	Coop
Greer, John G. to Eliza Dale 25 Mar. 1832	Wash
Greer, Martin to Martha Grainger 28 Feb. 1839	John
Greer, Samuel to Sarah Van 24 Dec, 1829	Fran
Greer, Solomon to Ann Lindsey 30 Dec. 1827	CG-A
Greer, Thomas to Nancy Shields 23 Jan. 1834	Coop
Greer, Thomas to Eliza Devault 6 Feb. 1834	CG-A
Greer, Willis to Clarissa Lowe 22 Nov. 1838	StFr
Gregg, Archibald to Lina Eubanks 1 Aug. 1839	Audr
Gregg, David to Nancy Adams 13 Aug. 1818	Howa
Gregg, James to Nancy White 7 Mar. 1833	Clay
Gregg, Matthew to Anna Lewis 20 Oct. 1836	Clay
Gregoire, Francis to Mary Brown 28 Dec. 1831	Perr
Gregoire, Louis H. to Mary Pratte 13 Oct. 1835	Perr
Gregory, Andrew B. to Millinda McKorkle 21 Dec. 1828	Clay
Gregory, Asiriah to Matilda Henson 16 Oct. 1828	Wash
Gregory, Chappel to Polley Underwood 18 Oct. 1832	Pk-1
Gregory, Chappell to Penelope Moore 1 Feb. 1829	Pk-1
Gregory, David to Nancy B. Wade 27 July 1833	Lafa
Gregory, Felix to Juliet Craddock 11 Feb. 1833	Md-A
Gregory, Inglefield to Margaret Davis 7 July 1836	Lewi
Gregory, John to Miss Rush 22 Feb. 1838	Mari
Gregory, Malachi to Catharine Reeves 25 Sept. 1837	Wash
Gregory, Umbleton to Amanda Crooks 27 Oct. 1833	Lewi
Gregory, Uriah S. to Susan Seaman 29 June 1837	Clar
Gregory, Wm. S. to Sarah J. Williams 6 June 1839	Lewi
Greir, Berry to Nancy Bouldin 13 Apr. 1837	Pett
Gremor, Alexander to Nancy Russel 28 Mar. 1839	Linc
Grewe, Christian to Ibby Lincicum 15 Dec. 1839	CG-B
Grewing, ---- to Mary A. Williams 10 Dec. 1835	Boon
Grey, Elijah to Polly Hungate 9 Apr. 1838	Monr
Grey, James to Polly Allen 11 Nov. 1830	Clay
Grey, Moses to Sarah Blocker 1 Jan. 1833	CG-A
Greyer, John J. to Miranda Grant 28 Jan. 1836	Rall
Gribble, Harrison to Martha Mathens 1 Mar. 1838	John
Grice, Jesse to Mary Marshall 24 Mar. 1832	Sali
Grice, John to Sindy Revell 13 Nov. 1836	Md-B
Grice, John A.L. to Rebecca McClanahan 12 Mar. 1837	Coop
Gridley, Amos to Sally Thornhill 16 Jan. 1826	Rall
Griffen, Isaac to Polly Hickam 24 Apr. 1835	Boon
Griffeth, Rolla M. to Margaret Wilson 13 Oct. 1836	Howa
Griffin, James to Tabitha Murley 2 Oct. 1838	Maco
Griffin, James N. to Sarah M. Vardeman 12 Aug. 1837	Mari
Griffin, John to Margaret A. Murley 1 Apr. 1838	Maco
Griffin, Joel W. to Francis Smith 12 Apr. 1832	StCh
Griffin, Soloman to Clarysa Hays 18 July 1823	StFr
Griffin, Wm. to Ann Griffin rec. 16 Feb. 1839	Rall
Griffis, Thomas to Rachel Whitenburg 23 Dec. 1837	Gree
Griffith, Abel G. to May Stadley 13 June 1839	Pk-B
Griffith, Albert G. to Sarah S. Pickett 18 Oct. 1838	Pk-B
Griffith, Amos to Susan Doak 3 May 1838	Pk-B
Griffith, Daniel to Mary F. Snell 2 Feb. 1837	Lewi

```
Griffith, Joel Jr. to Nancy Moore 1 Apr. 1830                              Pk-1
Griffith, Joel S. to Roannah B. Dodds 5 Nov. 1837                          Pk-B
Griffith, John to Eliza M. Williams 25 Nov. 1830                           Call
Griffith, John to Katharine Amos 19 Oct. 1837                             Pk-B
Griffith, Lewis to Nancy Lambkins 15 Apr. 1827                             Call
Griffith, Thomas to Mary James 24 Feb. 1820                               StCh
Griggs, Ambers to Polly Frazuer 1 Aug. 1831                               StCh
Griggs, Ambrose to Isabella Evans 2 Mar. 1837                            Call
Griggs, Joseph to Margery Robinson 6 Feb. 1823                            Md-A
Grigory, Benj. to Rebecca Reed 27 Apr. 1828                              Md-A
Grigory, Daniel F. to Nancy Garret 8 Oct. 1834                           Wash
Grigsby, John to Mrs. Dicey Lewis 17 May 1832                            Mari
Grigsby, John to Dicy Lewis -- -- 1832 rec. 5 Apr. 1834                   Lewi
Grigsby, John T. to Sarah L. White 8 Aug. 1833                           Monr
Grim, John to Margaret A. Standford 5 Sept. 1838                          Pk-B
Grime, Wm. to Sherlotte Right 4 Nov. 1833                                Rall
Grimes, James to Rebecca Mulherin 6 Aug. 1826                            Pk-1
Grimes, Thomas H.S. to Sarah Gibson 11 Dec. 1828                          Linc
Grimsley, Wm. C. to Henrietta E. Bottom 5 Apr. 1838                       CG-A
Grimstaff, David to Mary Masters 22 Dec. 1836/7                          CG-A
Grindstaff, David to Elizabeth Hamond 15 Feb. 1838                        Boon
Grindstaff, Henry to Abby Beckett 15 Feb. 1838                           Barr
Grindstaff, Wm. to Polly Blevins 17 Mar. 1836                            Boon
Griner, Vincent to Rebeck Laferty 30 July 1830                           Perr
Grisham, Jacob to Margaret Rush 24 Jan. 1837                             Mari
Grism, James to Minerva Thomas 19 Sept. 1838                             Char
Grissom, Wm. to Sarah Mosely 25 Sept. 1827                               StFr
Griswold, Frederick to Rebecca Shobe 18 Dec. 1823                         StCh
Griswould, Harvey to Mahala Shobe 9 Aug. 1827                            StCh
Grobe, John G. to Anna C. Kappelmann 10 Apr. 1837                        StCh
Groff, Balsar to Sally Backus 1 Jan. 1835                                Gasc
Groff, Henry to Harriett Pinkleton 15 Feb. 1833                          Fran
Groff, Thomas to Elizabeth Harrison 20 July 1826                         Fran
Grogan, Nelson to Anastatia Ferrel 14 July 1837                          Monr
Grogin, Spencer to Susannah Smith 26 Sept. 1824                          Howa
Grogins, Bartholomew to Mary Fraker 22 Sept. 1825                        Pk-1
Grojan, Elijah to Winifred B. Hicks 19 Jan. 1837                         Rand
Groom, Abraham to Sarah Adams 1 Feb. 1827                                Clay
Groom, Isaac to Sarah Groom 6 Mar. 1828                                  Clay
Groom, James to Rebecca Adams 7 Apr. 1836                                Clin
Groom, Solomon to Margaret McMahan 4 Aug. 1835                           Clin
Groom, Wm. to Polly Nagill 16 Dec. 1819                                  Howa
Grooms, Amos to Sarah Chaney 5 Aug. 1834                                 Clay
Grooms, Amos to Martha A. Drummond 6 Oct. 1836                           Lafa
Grooms, James to Louisa Payne 23 July 1837                               Boon
Grooms, John to Ann Coatney 12 Nov. 1829                                 Rand
Grooms, John to Polly Ambrose 18 Jan. 1838                               Boon
Grooms, Lorenzo to Patsey Story 16 Oct. 1831                             CG-A
Grooms, Samuel to Ann Sidwell 10 Dec. 1829                               Pk-1
Grooms, Samuel to Betsy A. Posey 3 Sept. 1837                            Fran
Grooms, Wm. to Maria Cass 1 Mar. 1837                                    Clay
Grosbong, Jacob to Eliza J. Nichols 14 Aug. 1834                         Linc
Groshong, Jefferson to Martha A. Bainbridge 3 Mar. 1836                  Linc
Gross, Camel to Mahala Reed 25 May 1836                                  Rand
Gross, Christopher to Sophia Yount 21 Mar. 1830                          CG-A
Gross, Geo. to Lookey Perry 17 Nov. 1836                                 Wash
Gross, Isaac to Margaret Tuckenay 30 Sept. 1831                          Rand
Gross, Isaac to Dorcus Pancost 1 Apr. 1833                               Rand
Gross, Samuel to Jelina Martin 21 Mar. 1824                              Howa
Gross, Steven to Margaret Broose 14 Feb. 1838                            Howa
Gross, Wm. to Elizabeth Slinkard 20 May 1827                             CG-A
Grote, Francis to Mary Dorlac 26 Nov. 1839                               StCh
Grou, John to Thisey Smith 7 June 1838                                   Clay
Grounds, Benj. to Louisa Bricky 6 Nov. 1836                              Cr-1
Grounds, John to Mrs. Elizabeth Smith 5 Nov. 1837                        Md-B
```

Grounds, Joseph to Mary Yount 29 Apr. 1832   CG-A
Grounds, Peter to Ann Johnson 3 Mar. 1839   CG-B
Grounds, Sollomon to Mary Moiers 13 June 1839   Md-B
Grove, Samuel to Paulina Camplin 10 Aug. 1839   Boon
Groves, Belimus H. to Elizabeth M. Hayden 12 Mar. 1829   CG-A
Groves, Harrison to Sary A. McLain 3 Sept. 1839   Plat
Groves, Nimrod to Hannah R. Fretwell 11 Oct. 1836   Lewi
Grubb, Benj. I. to Eliza A. Ligget 15 Mar. 1838   Davi
Grubb, Francis to Ann Etherton 7 May 1832   Ray
Grubb, Washington to Amanda Kees 13 Mar. 1835   Carr
Grubbs, Nathan to Martha Monroe 11 June 1835   Char
Grubbs, Wm. to Lucinda Smith 11 Aug. 1839   Char
Grudy, Wm. to Charlotte Hall 10 Mar. 1833   Howa
Grugan, Thomas to Susan Lewis 18 Sept. 1838   Rand
Grundy, P.J.P. to Clarissa Lusky 30 Nov. 1835   Wash
Gudgell, John to Sarey Gregory 6 Oct. 1836   Carr
Guerrant, Stephen to Emily Quinn 27 Dec. 1829   Cole
Guerrant, Stephen to Lucy A. Hardin 2 Mar. 1837   Call
Guess, Henry to Abbigail Conner 29 May 1828   Clay
Guess, Thomas to Mary Glasscock 16 Nov. 1830   CG-A
Guibor, Augustus to Edith P. Herrington 20 Jan. 1835   Jeff
Guibourd, Eugene to Marie T. St. Gemme 15 Nov. 1825   StGe
Guignon, Simon A. to Mary C. Bossier 13 Nov. 1832   Md-A
Guin, John to Talitha Young 19 Apr. 1827   Linc
Guines, John to Catharine Smyth 25 Oct. 1829   Fran
Guinn, Andrew to Frances Dryden 30 Apr. 1837   Gree
Guinn, Benj. to Thesiah Bledsoe 3 Dec. 1836   Clin
Guinn, David to Chiney Cannon 25 Nov. 1827   Clay
Gujnard, Alexis to Mary Prieur 8 Jan. 1838   StCh
Gullett, John to Nancy A. Gaines 7 Apr. 1839   Shel
Gully, Thomas to Lucinda Montgomery 27 Apr. 1834   Rand
Gulyen, John W. to Polin Stowe 12 Jan. 1838   Maco
Gunn, John to Anna Todd 17 Feb. 1822   Howa
Gunn, Wm. to Barbara A. Swanson 17 Jan. 1833   Howa
Gunnell, Nathaniel to Nancy Brown 18 Jan. 1839   Ray
Gunnells, John to Christiana Like 6 Dec. 1832   CG-A
Gunter, James to Peggy Banister 21 June 1835   StFr
Gunteriman, Peter to Nancy Smith 22 Sept. 1829   Lafa
Gunther, John C.A. to Mary Miller 5 Oct. 1837   Barr
Gupton, Arrington M. to Melvina Eament 13 Mar. 1834   Mari
Gupton, Stephen to Elisabeth Simmons 15 Apr. 1824   Rall
Gurrey, John to Mrs. Elizabeth Bridges 23 Oct. 1835   Clay
Guthridge, Wm. to Ruth A. Dunkin 15 Oct. 1835   Char
Guthrie, Allen W. to Eliz. A. Young 16 Sept. 1838   Call
Guthrie, Wm. to Clarissa Griffith 21 Oct. 1838   Monr
Guthrie, Wm. to Elizabeth Humphrey 20 Dec. 1838   Monr
Guthry, James S. to Helen T. Brown 3 Aug. 1837   Sali
Guy, Irvine to Nancy L. Vaughan 2 May 1833   Pk-1
Guy, John to Lucy A. Dawson 18 Feb. 1836   Pk-1
Guyer, Thomas to Mary A. Dobbins 28 May 1837   Morg
Gwin, Thornton to Deborah Camron 2 Mar. 1829   Clay
Gwinn, Elijah to Rebecca McKissie 18 Jan. 1821   Sali
Gylmore, Thomas to Chalotte Coons 20 Oct. 1831   Call

Haasse, Sebastian to Catharine Souter 1 Feb. 1836   Perr
Hackleman, Pleasant to Elizabeth Morris 14 Apr. 1839   Mill
Hackley, James to Nancy Kerby 5 Sept. 1833   Howa
Hackley, Wm. E. to Lucy McCreary 14 Jan. 1833   Howa
Hackney, Hightower to Susan Gallop 11 Jan. 1833   Boon
Hackney, Joseph to Elizabeth Johnson 7 Mar. 1833   Cole
Hackney, Thomas to Nancy Johnson 1 July 1824   Cole
Hackney, Wm. M. to Isabella Rice 24 July 1834   Cole
Hadbrink, John H. to Ann M. Ameling 30 June 1838   Fran
Haddock, Charles to Sarah Collins 12 Oct. 1830   Boon

```
Haddock, Taylor to Catherine Dawson 26 Dec. 1834          Boon
Haddock, Wm. to Polly Collins 27 Oct. 1834               Lafa
Haden, Allen to Sarah McQuitty 19 Mar. 1829              Boon
Haden, Anthony to Agnes Ballew 24 Sept. 1805            CG-1
Haden, Daniel to Mary A. Musick 24 June 1833            Pk-1
Haden, Hendley to Harriet Bailey 8 Mar. 1832           Rall
Haden, James to Christina Seabaugh 6 May 1833          Perr
Haden, Jeremiah to Emily Hulen 6 July 1837             Boon
Haden, Joel to Sarah Talbert 9 Aug. 1832               Boon
Haden, Joel to Zerilda Kirtly 4 July 1838              Boon
Haden, John S. to Mary A. Perry 9 May 1839             Howa
Haden, Lewis to Mary E. Bellum 18 Nov. 1832            Pk-1
Haden, Samuel to Elizabeth Boothe 24 Dec. 1833         Boon
Haden, Sylvester to Sussy Welker 5 Apr. 1832           Perr
Haden, Turner to Louisa Cave 4 Sept. 1826              Boon
Haden, Wm. to Polly Galloway 14 Sept. 1834             Boon
Haden, Wm. to Urissey McHenry 17 Jan. 1838             StFr
Hadin, John to Hester Grimes 13 Jan. 1836              StCh
Hadlock, James to Dillus Pirce 29 July 1813            CG-1
Haeard, John to Lucy Buckner 28 Jan. 1836              Mari
Haff, Abram to Harriet Buford 1 Mar. 1838              Pk-B
Hagan, Benniahs to Penelope Branham 29 Jan. 1839       Clay
Hagan, David to Mary Malott 20 Feb. 1835               Clay
Hagan, David to Mahala Bursby 9 May 1839               Cass
Hagan, Geo. W. to Nancy Tucker 4 Feb. 1833             Perr
Hagan, Henry to Eliza Elliott 2 Feb. 1836              Rall
Hagan, John to Sarah A. Layton 24 July 1827            Perr
Hagan, John to Elizabeth Tucker 5 July 1836            Perr
Hagan, Louis to Rosamund Renner 7 Oct. 1838            Wash
Hagan, Michael to Cecily Layton 5 Feb. 1833            Perr
Hagan, Pius to Mary Tucker 29 July 1834                Perr
Hagar, John to Sinthy Saddler 14 Nov. 1837             Perr
Hagar, Rogert to Judith Briggs 6 Oct. 1825             Rall
Hager, James to Jeanne Lynch 20 Nov. 1832              Rall
Hager, John to Melissa Keatly 26 Sept. 1838            Rall
Hager, John to Elizabeth Saddler 31 Oct. 1839          Perr
Haggans, Wm. to Elizabeth Speery 28 Sept. 1839         Coop
Haggard, James to Sarah Fletcher 5 Mar. 1837           Lafa
Haghn, Davault to Ann Spencer 28 July 1836             CG-A
Haghn, Mathias to Katy Shell 13 June 1833              CG-A
Hagins, Hillery to Sarah Broadhurst 2 Sept. 1838       Ray
Hagler, Eli to Elizabeth Hinkle 31 Aug. 1830           StCh
Hagler, Wm. to Elizabeth Zimmerman 28 Oct. 1833        CG-A
Hagood, James A. to Louisa Estes 27 Feb. 1834          Linc
Hahn, David to Laney Hahn 14 Nov. 1839                 CG-B
Hahn, Jesse to Sophia Settlemire 18 June 1829          CG-A
Haig, Silas to Nancy Smith 6 Jan. 1839                 Howa
Haigh, John B. to May Engledow 7 Mar. 1839             Wash
Hail, David to Nersisse Peen 17 July 1833              Fran
Hail, Jacob to Phebe Vaughn 5 Jan. 1832                Cole
Hail, Reuben to Martha Taylor 27 Jan. 1839             Mill
Hail, Thomas to Jane Wolf 11 Nov. 1830                 CG-A
Haines, Dewit to Elizabeth Taylor 14 Apr. 1839         StCh
Haines, Joseph to Jincy Vincent 17 Apr. 1810           StCh
Hains, Luster to Susannah Branson 1 June 1837          Gasc
Hais, Joseph to Rebecca Barcus 10 Mar. 1839            Sali
Haisless, Robt. to Kesiah Mulkey 1 Apr. 1839           Lafa
Hakmann, John F.W. to Maria E. Winter 14 Oct. 1837     StCh
Hakmann, John F.W. to Maria E. Winter 14 Oct. 1837     Warr
Hale, Edward Jr. to Matilda Story 19 Feb. 1818         CG-1
Hale, Fountain to Severn Bratten 7 July 1830           Cole
Hale, Jesse to Catherine Sweeting 23 Jan. 1820         CG-1
Hale, John to Margaret Shetley 19 Nov. 1835            Md-A
Hale, Wm. to Sarah Wilkinson 30 Nov. 1837              CG-A
Halen, Osborne to Eliza Jones 13 Apr. 1837             Fran
```

Haley, James T. to Cintha Goggin 6 Apr. 1830   Rand
Haley, John to Malinda Goggins 14 Sept. 1834   Rand
Haley, Presley W. to Mrs. Ann Patrick 18 Nov. 1827   Howa
Halford, Wm. C. to Martha N. Martin 31 Mar. 1839   Coop
Hall, B.B. to Mary H. Reed 31 May 1835   Call
Hall, Charles to Caroline Thornhill 15 Jan. 1839   Linc
Hall, Clark to Minervy Moon 15 Oct. 1839   Cole
Hall, David to Amanda Vanlandingham 12 Nov. 1834   Ray
Hall, Drury to Anny Greenstreet 8 Mar. 1827   Fran
Hall, Edward to Mary J. Shannon 6 Oct. 1836   StCh
Hall, Geo. C. to Elizabeth C. Hale 21 Nov. 1839   Clay
Hall, Green W. to Minerva Douglass 8 Jan. 1835   CG-B
Hall, Henry to Nancy Self 30 Sept. 1830   Fran
Hall, Hezekiah to Mary Hill 3 Mar. 1831   CG-A
Hall, Hiram to Fannie Stephens 12 Oct. 1831   Linc
Hall, James to Scinthia Groom 27 July 1824   Clay
Hall, James to Kisire M. Cartright 20 July 1834   Gasc
Hall, James to Nancy Prigmore 24 Dec. 1835   Pett
Hall, Jeremiah to Eleanor Duncan 23 Apr. 1835   Clay
Hall, John to Elizabeth Smith 2 Sept. 1830   Cole
Hall, John to Mary A. Hall 21 Sept. 1837   Mari
Hall, John to Sarah Weaver 4 Apr. 1838   Clar
Hall, John D. to Nancy Duncan 28 Dec. 1826   Clay
Hall, John D. to Adeline Rogers 1 Jan. 1834   Cole
Hall, Jonathan to Matilda Roberts 13 Feb. 1838   Davi
Hall, Joseph to Drusilla Moore 19 May 1835   Ripl
Hall, Levi to Grazilla Hall 14 Jan. 1835   Rall
Hall, Levi F. to Mrs. Susan E. Jameson 7 Nov. 1839   Monr
Hall, Robt. to Mira Tennille 20 July 1806   CG-1
Hall, Samuel to Agness Estes 17 May 1825   Clay
Hall, Samuel to Rachel Gray 29 Oct. 1835   Call
Hall, Samuel to Jane Matherly 3 June 1836   Linc
Hall, Stewart N. to Zerilda McCutchan 10 Oct. 1839   StCh
Hall, Thomas to Sarah Belcher 11 Feb. 1832   Monr
Hall, Wm. to Sally Estes 9 Dec. 1819   Coop
Hall, Wm. to Dolly Dunham 7 June 1835   John
Hallaway, Thomas to Nancy Baul 19 Dec. 1839   Gasc
Halliburton, Westley to Sophia Holman 9 Mar. 1834   Mari
Halloman, Abner to Permelia Dale 27 Dec. 1838   Barr
Halloman, Allen W. to Rachel Counts 15 Jan. 1826   StGe
Hallow, Humphrey to Milda McCoy 14 Nov. 1833   Linc
Halsey, John to Manerva Johnson 27 June 1839   Char
Halsey, Wm. to Harriet Bowling 2 July 1835   Mari
Halstead, John D. to Sarah Powell 18 Mar. 1834   Howa
Halsy, Elijah to Polly Moore 22 Feb. 1824   Fran
Halten, Benj. to Dorcas Hazzard 14 Oct. 1828   Boon
Halton, Wm. B. to Ann Westlake 21 Apr. 1825   Boon
Ham, David to Eunicy Sullivan 29 Nov. 1836   Sali
Ham, J.W. to Mary J. Edrington 18 Apr. 1839   Linc
Ham, John A. to Sarah F. Ruden 14 May 1838   Henr
Ham, Joseph W. to Rebecca B. McDaniel 31 May 1832   Linc
Ham, Mathew to Elizabeth Gray 18 Oct. 1836   Call
Ham, Schuyler to Pamelia A. Jones 21 Feb. 1833   Call
Hamac, Wm. to Dammous Richardson 21 Mar. 1819   Fran
Hamblin, John to Elizabeth Heasick 18 Aug. 1836   Call
Hambright, John to Missouri Hudspeth 22 Aug. 1833   Jack
Hamesby, Geo. M. to Eleanor C. Brown 19 Jan. 1837   Warr
Hamilton, Andrew to Elizabeth Callison 17 Sept. 1835   Call
Hamilton, Benj. to Lucinda Weimer 8 Aug. 1839   Mill
Hamilton, David N. to Lucinda Rash 27 Oct. 1839   Polk
Hamilton, Dudley to Mary Sapp 12 Nov. 1835   Boon
Hamilton, Fenwick to Rebecca A. Granbery 28 Mar. 1837   Perr
Hamilton, James to Elizabeth Pallett 3 Apr. 1832   Jack
Hamilton, James to Ann Callison 31 Oct. 1839   Call
Hamilton, James T. to Margaret Caldwell 11 June 1839   Perr

Hamilton, Jeremiah to Martha Mitchell 5 Jan. 1810   Fran
Hamilton, Jeremiah to Elizabeth Fisher 13 Mar. 1821   Fran
Hamilton, Leroy to Elizabeth Johnson 18 May 1834   Boon
Hamilton, Niman to Eleanor Williams 5 Sept. 1839   Fran
Hamilton, Preston to Levina Florea 23 Nov. 1837   Clay
Hamilton, Richard to Nancy Watsen 2 Apr. 1833   Wash
Hamilton, Robt. K. to Sophia Holeman 14 Nov. 1830   Mari
Hamilton, Samuel to Nancy Reed 29 Dec. 1834   Pk-1
Hamilton, Thomas J. to May Ramsey 24 Nov. 1836   Ray
Hamilton, Wm. to May McChristion 13 Oct. 1836   Ray
Hamilton, Wm. B. to Margaret H. Allen 7 Sept. 1837   Call
Hamlet, Archer to Martha A. Shipley 20 June 1839   Cole
Hamm, Strother S. to Margaret G. Miller 1 Jan. 1839   Sali
Hammett, Joseph to Polly Millsap 28 Feb. 1830   Rand
Hammill, Jacob to Margaret Thompson 23 Sept. 1839   CG-B
Hammock, Jackson to Polly Brown 5 Nov. 1835   Fran
Hammond, John to Frances Maupin 14 July 1836   Jeff
Hammond, John to Rebecca Earney 24 Nov. 1836   Cr-1
Hammond, Samuel to Catharine Story 19 Mar. 1822   Coop
Hammond, Wm. to Emma Lucas 12 Feb. 1828   Jeff
Hammond, Wm. to Ann Kells 20 Nov. 1835   Linc
Hammond, Wm. to Elizabeth Neal 20 Aug. 1837   Pk-A
Hammonds, John to Elizabeth B. Kimler 2 May 1839   Linc
Hammons, Bryant to Sarah Moore 26 Nov. 1837   Ray
Hammons, Harland to Elizabeth Plemons 11 Nov. 1829   Coop
Hammons, John to Sally Shockley 5 July 1829   Coop
Hammuston, Daniel to Frederica Depenn 18 Nov. 1837   Fran
Hampton, Abel G. to Sarah Rennison 27 Jan. 1832   Coop
Hampton, David to Susan Hains 5 Feb. 1835   Howa
Hampton, Henry to Mary Frey 19 July 1827   StFr
Hampton, Henry to Jane Magruder 4 Jan. 1837   Monr
Hampton, James to Mary Strain 17 Aug. 1828   Coop
Hampton, John to Eleanor Burford 10 Sept. 1839   Clar
Hampton, Joseph J. to Elizabeth Cox 24 Aug. 1839   Lafa
Hampton, Lite to Telitha Morris 27 May 1830   Mari
Hampton, Martin to Jacintha Fowler 15 June 1838   Clin
Hampton, Matthew A. to Margaret Brooks 22 Jan. 1835   Cole
Hampton, Thomas to Sarah Hatfield 4 Mar. 1827   Linc
Hampton, Wm. to Obitha Morris 29 Apr. 1830   Mari
Hampton, Wm. D. to Frances Mullins 9 Nov. 1823   Coop
Hamson, Jesse Jr. to Margaret J. Barnett 30 Oct. 1838   John
Hamton, Jourdon to Mary A. Parrish 22 Mar. 1838   Rall
Hancock, Abbot to Sinthy Cavenaugh 30 July 1818   Howa
Hancock, Benj. to Elizabeth Rule 6 Nov. 1834   Gree
Hancock, Henry to Rachel Gragg 16 Apr. 1839   Clay
Hancock, James to Martha O. James 21 Mar. 1839   Maco
Hancock, John to Levina Barton 15 Apr. 1838   Boon
Hancock, Louis C. to Jane Shaw 12 Dec. 1839   Perr
Hancock, Richard to Polly Horn 21 Nov. 1824   Lafa
Hancock, Stephen to Rosetta Darst 22 Nov. 1838   Warr
Hancock, Stephen K. to Joy Roberts 3 Feb. 1830   Coop
Hancock, Thomas to Pusena Bemes 4 Mar. 1839   Maco
Hancock, Wm. to Elizabeth McClain 4 Jan. 1816   StCh
Hancock, Wm. to Elizabeth Gilmore 6 Dec. 1838   Polk
Handcock, Jefferson to Parthena Agen 19 May 1836   Boon
Hane, Soloman to Polly Bollinger 16 Aug. 1836   CG-A
Hanes, Collett to Mrs. Polly Green 25 Dec. 1832   Clay
Hanes, Samuel to Susannah Stephens 14 Apr. 1822   Boon
Haney, John to Elizabeth Ward 12 Sept. 1839   Polk
Haney, Joseph to Nancy Hendrick 4 June 1828   Jeff
Haney, Wm. to Polly Bailey 22 May 1834   Carr
Hankins, David to Belinda Shelly 27 July 1831   StCh
Hankins, Edward to Nancy Rector 21 Dec. 1834   Linc
Hankins, James K. to Margaret Barkley 1 Feb. 1838   Rall
Hanks, David to Sarah Ikherd 11 Feb. 1827   CG-A

96

Hanks, Jesse to Malinda Rea 29 May 1839   Sali
Hanks, Wm. to Nancy Spencer 16 July 1826   Md-A
Hanley, James to Sarah A. Reed 17 Sept. 1839   Mari
Hanley, John to Maria Atchison 21 Mar. 1835   CG-B
Hanly, James to Cassandra Cooley 22 Jan. 1835   Clay
Hanna, Alexander F. to Sarah A. Hall 21 Feb. 1839   Howa
Hanna, Robert to Mary Owen 26 Mar. 1829   Howa
Hannah, Andrew to Martha Houston 4 Oct. 1838   Ray
Hannah, Geo. to Matilda Turner 13 Nov. 1835   Rand
Hannah, Isiah to Mary Rector 22 Nov. 1827   Coop
Hannah, James to Elizabeth Gray 26 Nov. 1835   Monr
Hannah, Patton to Jane Smith 3 Dec. 1835   Rand
Hannah, Samuel to Susan Lowden 18 Nov. 1839   Call
Hannahs, James to Margaret Herrington 1 July 1826   Jeff
Hansberry, ---- to Susannah Boulware 9 June 1835   Call
Hansbrough, Richard to Ambrosha Mays 14 Mar. 1834   Mari
Hansbury, Enoch to Emily McCoy 27 Oct. 1836   Mari
Hanshaw, John to Elizabeth J. Salter 17 Jan. 1829   Clay
Hanson, Benj. to Francis Wollard 5 May 1839   Polk
Harbison, Branton D. to Lucy J. Venible 25 Sept. 1839   Howa
Harbour, Elisha to Elizabeth Reeves 12 Dec. 1833   Fran
Hardack, Henry to Catherine M. Windhorst 17 Dec. 1839   StCh
Harden, Henry C. to Dovey E. Black 19 July 1838   Perr
Harden, Horace H. to Sarah Presley 20 Sept. 1827   Linc
Harden, James to Nancy Estes 13 Mar. 1828   Clay
Harden, John to Rachel Hyatt 25 Dec. 1836   Fran
Harder, Joseph R. to Mary A. Murphy 9 Mar. 1837   Fran
Hardestey, Hilary to Catharine M. Miles 3 Sept. 1839   Monr
Hardgrave, Jesse to Elizabeth Henderson 14 June 1835   Wash
Hardin, Benj. to Margaret Reddick 7 Jan. 1827   Howa
Hardin, Benj. to Susan Hubbard 30 May 1837   Rand
Hardin, Colden to Margaret Jones 25 Oct. 1835   Rand
Hardin, Joseph to Jane Davis 8 Jan. 1833   Howa
Hardin, Samuel to Massey Smith 21 Dec. 1824   Howa
Hardin, Thomas to Ann Cherry 12 Apr. 1838   Wash
Hardin, Wm. C. to Louisa M. Pettibone 13 Mar. 1834   Pk-1
Hardister, Henry to Mahaly Harris 18 July 1833   Rand
Hardister, Henry to Mary A. Harris 24 Nov. 1836   Rand
Hardister, Samuel to Elizabeth Helms 5 June 1826   Gasc
Hardwick, David to Sarah Cooley 12 Sept. 1839   Carr
Hardwick, Lewis to Jane Aikman 20 May 1826   Lafa
Hardwick, Louis to Elizabeth Smith 30 Sept. 1827   Clay
Hardwick, Phillip to Peggy Gray -- Oct. 1821   Howa
Hardwick, Thomas J. to Nancy D. Fair 31 July 1834   Carr
Hardwick, Thomas J. to Louisa Bricken 18 Oct. 1838   Carr
Hardwicke, Alexander to Margaret Officer 18 Oct. 1825   Clay
Hardy, Baptist to Martha Davidson 17 Nov. 1836   Shel
Hardy, Geo. L. to Theresa Leake 17 Jan. 1833   Rall
Hardy, Joseph to Julie A. Gardner 31 June 1831   Rall
Hardy, Richard to Ann Ransdell 1 Aug. 1837   Rall
Harges, Silas H. to Mary J. Lutdington 19 Oct. 1833   Wash
Hargis, Caleb to Elizabeth Cleeton 31 Jan. 1833   Howa
Hargis, Hardin to Katharine Chambers 13 Apr. 1834   Rand
Hargis, Isaac to Elizabeth Reed 3 Feb. 1828   Howa
Hargis, Joshua L. to Samantha Parton 4 Feb. 1839   Howa
Hargis, Whitenidor to Levina Adams 22 Oct. 1826   Jeff
Hargis, Wm. to Patsy Bundridge 7 Aug. 1838   Howa
Hargrave, James to Martha Anderson 7 Mar. 1839   Livi
Hargrave, John to Catherine Fowler 12 June 1836   Henr
Hargrave, Wm. to Margaret Anderson 7 Aug. 1836   Henr
Haris, Tirey to Faney Mellone 2 Aug. 1827   Wash
Harison, Geo. P. to Adaline H. Wash 4 June 1839   Lewi
Harison, John to Margaret Bigham 21 July 1835   John
Harl, Lewis to Eliza Wilhite 6 May 1838   Boon
Harlan, John to Manerva Beard 19 July 1838   Rand

97

Harlan, Wm. to Levon Holman 8 Feb. 1837   Rand
Harley, Andrew B. to Peggy Galbreath 25 June 1820   Coop
Harley, Joseph to Rhoda Lewis 30 May 1839   Plat
Harlington, Elisha to Louisianna Martin 4 Aug. 1825   Ray
Harlow, Kingsolver to Mary L. Price 14 June 1838   Char
Harlow, Mahlon H. to Frances Tandy 23 July 1835   Lafa
Harlow, Martin to Eunice Lyles 2 Oct. 1834   Pk-1
Harlow, Micajah Jr. to Nancy Cordil 10 Mar. 1834   Lafa
Harlow, Nathan to Jane Hollway 20 Oct. 1836   Sali
Harman, Lindsey to Nancy G. Powels 3 Oct. 1839   Cole
Harman, Valentine to Sarah Jones 29 Mar. 1839   Morg
Harmon, Elburton to Parthenia Crump 28 June 1838   Boon
Harmon, Esom to Frances Clarkson 12 Dec. 1837   Howa
Harmon, Jacob to Julia Foster 12 Jan. 1834   Coop
Harmon, Peter to Maria Smith 7 Apr. 1828   Coop
Harmon, Samuel to Polly Bennett 21 Aug. 1838   Coop
Harney, Henry L. to Elizabeth Morris 23 May 1820   StCh
Harold, Geo. to Christina Rybolt 9 July 1806   StCh
Harper, Alexander to Luvina Hayden 31 Aug. 1830   Mari
Harper, Elijah to Sally Roberts 19 Feb. 1833   Pk-1
Harper, Elijah to Mary A. Gassway 18 Aug. 1836   Lewi
Harper, Harvey to Priscilla Peters 8 Mar. 1827   Coop
Harper, Jacob to Mahala Amos 12 Oct. 1837   Linc
Harper, James to Mary Clark 1 Mar. 1836   Polk
Harper, Polemon W. to Nancy Renfro 27 May 1838   Polk
Harper, Wm. to Jain Walker 14 Sept. 1826   Pk-1
Harper, Wm. to Martha Morgan 17 Oct. 1839   Warr
Harrel, Calvin to Frankie Gwinn 20 Dec. 1827   Linc
Harrel, Geo. to Betsy McDaniel 1 Mar. 1829   Linc
Harriford, James to Elizabeth Farrowbank 14 Nov. 1839   Lewi
Harriman, Christopher to Martha Linville 5 Jan. 1839   Cole
Harrington, Abel to Rebecca E. Gilmore 7 Mar. 1839   Buch
Harrington, Bartley to Louisa Ervin -- May 1810   CG-1
Harrington, Miles to Louisa Fowler 25 Aug. 1836   Clay
Harrington, Potter to Mary Brown 30 Oct. 1836   Clin
Harrington, Thomas to Hetty Pitcher 8 Jan. 1826   Clay
Harris, Benj. to Lucinda McKinny 2 Aug. 1827   Fran
Harris, Caleb to Minerva Irvine 1 Apr. 1835   Boon
Harris, Caleb to Fanny Cox 15 July 1838   Cr-1
Harris, Charles to Rebecca Deatherage 19 Mar. 1836   Howa
Harris, David to Sarah Teeter 2 Sept. 1819   Howa
Harris, David to Frances Burden 23 Oct. 1825   Char
Harris, Eli G. to Sarah Thompson Givens 21 Feb. 1839   Cass
Harris, Erastis to Rebecca Davis 7 Aug. 1837   Perr
Harris, Gideon C. to Sarah E. Higganson 16 Jan. 1834   Perr
Harris, Gravest W. to Mary Austin 10 May 1835   Perr
Harris, Henry to Mary A. Hefner 18 July 1837   Wash
Harris, Isaac N. to Elizabeth Laseter 26 June 1836   StFr
Harris, James to Elizabeth Ellis 8 Feb. 1835   Boon
Harris, James to Elvinia Kelly 14 Dec. 1837   Boon
Harris, James to Martha Hoozer 4 Sept. 1839   Coop
Harris, James B. to Eighty P. Gilliam 24 Dec. 1823   Clay
Harris, James C. to Nancy Stewart 26 Sept. 1828   Wash
Harris, Jesse to Susan Medlock 23 Jan. 1835   Fran
Harris, Jesse to Elizabeth David 29 July 1837   Gasc
Harris, John to Sarah Hyranymous 17 Aug. 1826   Howa
Harris, John to Elizabeth Lay 29 May 1829   Howa
Harris, John to Rhody Townson 23 July 1835   Call
Harris, John to Polly Dodson 5 Jan. 1837   Polk
Harris, John W. to Lucinda P. Hornshell 15 Mar. 1838   Clin
Harris, Joseph to Mary Gipson 25 Feb. 1837   Clay
Harris, Joshua to Matilda J. Decker 14 Apr. 1835   Cr-1
Harris, Littleton W. to Sarah E. Hicks 17 Feb. 1835   Wash
Harris, Mastin to Rachel J. Akens 9 June 1835   Call
Harris, Miles to Mrs. Martha A. Warren 4 July 1839   Rand

98

```
Harris, Moses to Mary Roberts 9 Apr. 1828                       CG-A
Harris, Nathan to Matilda Baird 22 Jan. 1835                    Md-A
Harris, Oliver to Mary A.C. Dudley 12 May 1836                  Pk-1
Harris, Overton to Nancy Ellington 9 Apr. 1831                  Boon
Harris, Peter to Betsey Acles 5 May 1833                        Call
Harris, Peter B. to Ann Hook 4 Mar. 1822                        Howa
Harris, Reuben to Laura Fritstoe 13 June 1833                   Jack
Harris, Reuben B. to Ann Brown 22 June 1820                     Coop
Harris, Robt. to Nancy Berger 19 Sept. 1838                     Coop
Harris, Sampson to Midist Westbrook 24 Dec. 1829               Coop
Harris, Samuel to Ann A. Thomas 27 Mar. 1838                    Fran
Harris, Samuel to Sophia Jacks 17 Sept. 1839                    Howa
Harris, Samuel to Nancy Cole 22 Sept. 1839                      Coop
Harris, Sherwood to Elvina Akinson 27 Nov. 1838               Boon
Harris, Thomas to Eliza Forman 19 Mar. 1829                     Mari
Harris, Thomas to Ellender Smith 29 Mar. 1829                  Boon
Harris, Tyre to Margaret Whitenburge 9 Jan. 1823               Rall
Harris, Tyre to Sophia Jacks 17 Sept. 1839                      Howa
Harris, Washington to Elizabeth Feril 25 Dec. 1839            Ripl
Harris, Western to Elizabeth Kavanaugh 17 Sept. 1816          Howa
Harris, Wm. to Christian Jackson 7 Dec. 1823                   Sali
Harris, Wm. to Nancy Davis 31 Dec. 1834                        Coop
Harris, Wm. to Milly Ellington 2 Sept. 1838                    Boon
Harris, Wm. to Emily McEntire 1 Nov. 1838                      Fran
Harris, Wm. to Cecelia Little 3 Sept. 1839                      Rall
Harrison, Abner to Dulcenda Dozier 2 Apr. 1830                 Linc
Harrison, Abner to Nancy Harrison 11 Nov. 1834                 Call
Harrison, Aristedes to Catharine Litton 12 Feb. 1831          Wash
Harrison, Batteal to Ellen Twitty 1 Sept. 1833                Cr-1
Harrison, Benj. to Polly Stevenson 23 Feb. 1808               StGe
Harrison, Benj. to Elizabeth Adkins 4 Dec. 1839               Carr
Harrison, Calvin to Elizabeth Talley 30 Oct. 1838             Monr
Harrison, Elijah to Millender Rowland 28 July 1831            Call
Harrison, Henry to Matilda Davis 29 Oct. 1835                 Rand
Harrison, Hugh to Delia A. Bush 15 Mar. 1831                   Wash
Harrison, J.B. to Maria Griffen 8 Nov. 1836                    Gasc
Harrison, James to Rebecca Crockett 4 Nov. 1821               Boon
Harrison, James to Maria L. Prewitt 23 Dec. 1830              Howa
Harrison, Jason to Sally M. Dunnicak 3 Dec. 1825              Cole
Harrison, Jesse to Mary Simpson 1 Aug. 1830                   StCh
Harrison, John to Cynthia Coppedge 6 May 1828                 Gasc
Harrison, John to Elizabeth Wels 10 Dec. 1837                 Wash
Harrison, John M. to Nancy C. Covington 29 July 1838          Wash
Harrison, Lewis to Easter Hutchason 1 Feb. 1837              Cr-1
Harrison, M. to A. Craig 28 June 1831                          Call
Harrison, Mathew to Elizabeth Quales 30 June 1839            Ripl
Harrison, Michael to Sarah Wells 31 May 1837                  Wash
Harrison, Reuben to Elizabeth Boring 26 Feb. 1829            Fran
Harrison, Robt. to Mary S. North 1 Jan. 1834                 Fran
Harrison, Samuel to Polly Atkins 14 Sept. 1820               Howa
Harrison, Samuel to Charity Irvin 21 Sept. 1826              Wash
Harrison, Samuel to Jane Staples 28 Nov. 1839                Jeff
Harrison, Simeon D. to Sarah Cartwright 18 Aug. 1836         StCh
Harrison, Thomas to Sarah Potts 28 Oct. 1824                  Boon
Harrison, Thomas to Nancy Harler 14 Dec. 1837                Ripl
Harrison, Wm. to Nancy Shepherd 25 Nov. 1834                  Gree
Harrison, Wm. N. to Nancy Lamasters 18 Dec. 1834             StCh
Harrison, Wm. N. to Melissa Green 27 Sept. 1838              Mill
Harrison, Wm. R. to Catherine E. Webb 1 Aug. 1833            Lewi
Harriss, John to Bary Best 22 May 1836                        Jack
Harryman, Hugh to Christenny Zumwalt 10 May 1827             Call
Harryman, James to Jane McCay 20 Mar. 1838                    Cole
Harsel  Anthony to Pelina Huggard 26 May 1835                Clay
Hart, Franklin to Mary Robinson -- Aug. 1836                  Boon
Hart, James to Nancy Ferguson 20 Apr. 1837                    Call
```

Hart, John to Matilda Dean 24 Mar. 1824	Clay
Hart, Madison to Sally A. Monroe 12 Oct. 1836	Boon
Hart, Michael to Elizabeth Madison 10 Feb. 1820	StGe
Hart, Ranson L. to Polly Steele 19 Nov. 1829	CG-A
Hart, Samuel A. to Elizabeth LeBelle 7 Feb. 1828	StCh
Harte, Thomas to Elizabeth Layton 19 Jan. 1829	Perr
Hartel, David to Barbary Lewis 11 Nov. 1827	CG-A
Hartle, David to Fanny Cotner 6 June 1839	CG-B
Hartle, Geo. to Polly Neswonger 30 Dec. 1830	CG-A
Hartle, Jefferson to Christener Sebaugh 23 July 1839	CG-B
Hartle, Jesse to Sarah Sapaugh 5 Mar. 1835	CG-B
Hartle, Logan to Ana Bollinger 6 Jan. 1833	CG-A
Hartle, Peter to Barbary Seabaugh 22 Dec. 1836	CG-A
Hartle, Solomon to Jane Davis 1 Dec. 1836	CG-A
Hartley, Jacob to Mrs. Matilda Patterson 12 Dec. 1837	Gree
Harton, Geo. to Drewcilla Hains 17 Sept. 1835	StFr
Harton, Hezekiah W. to Elizabeth Bradshaw 19 July 1831	StFr
Harver, James O. to Betsey Philips 22 Sept. 1830	Call
Harvey, Augustine to Mildred Palmer 29 Mar. 1838	Linc
Harvey, Elijah to Jane Foster 23 Dec. 1827	Howa
Harvey, Geo. W. to Henrietta McMillen 3 Oct. 1833	Howa
Harvey, Henry to Salinda Turley 4 Dec. 1832	Coop
Harvey, James to Peggy Brunt 11 Apr. 1833	Boon
Harvey, James to Mary Allison 11 Jan. 1835	Coop
Harvey, James to Rebecca Sidenbender 10 Mar. 1838	Mari
Harvey, Reuben V. to Mrs. Barbary A. Allen 7 May 1836	Coop
Harvey, Thomas to Lydia Dickson 31 Aug. 1835	Ray
Harvey, Valentine to Charlotte Bain 2 Feb. 1837	Linc
Harvey, Wm. to Jane Morin 2 Mar. 1826	Howa
Harwell, Thomas to Mrs. Agnes Spann 3 Mar. 1839	Polk
Harwood, Nathaniel to Sally A. McGaugh 8 Dec. 1836	Ray
Hase, Augustine Z. to Elizabeth Simms 17 Sept. 1833	Perr
Hash, John to Millia Elkins 10 Jan. 1839	Barr
Haskell, Friend P. to Elizabeth Fairyer 3 July 1839	Rall
Haskins, Thomas C. to Mary G. Anderson 18 Feb. 1835	Call
Hasler, Alexander C. to Espy Pruett 11 Feb. 1836	Md-B
Haslip, John to Matilda Lynch 11 Nov. 1833	Jack
Hasse, Augustus to Matilda Wurdemann 23 Jan. 1837	StCh
Hassinger, Wm. to Williamen Abel 16 Apr. 1837	Mari
Hastey, John to Elizabeth Westbrook 18 Dec. 1838	Coop
Hastin, Wm. C. to Nancy Dodd 13 Apr. 1836	Cr-1
Hasy, Garritson P. to Catherine Smith 14 Apr. 1833	Cr-1
Hatch, Benj. to Lovey Turner 26 Mar. 1837	Boon
Hatcher, Harrison to Catherine Higens 5 Feb. 1830	CG-A
Hatcher, Joshua to Malinda Becket 10 May 1838	Clin
Hatcher, Lemuel G. to Sarah Chambers 11 May 1834	Mari
Hatfield, Alexander to Elizabeth Smith 20 Aug. 1826	Coop
Hatfield, Alfred to Gustin Cath. Nixon 24 Dec. 1835	Morg
Hatfield, C.P. to Elizabeth Onsley 15 Aug. 1839	Cass
Hatfield, Edward to Sarah Thompson 20 July 1839	CG-B
Hatfield, Geo. to Indianna Morrisson 16 Nov. 1834	Morg
Hatfield, Isham to Martha R. Clay 25 July 1833	Morg
Hatfield, Joseph to Polly Heather 29 Oct. 1836	Morg
Hatfield, Wm. to Polly Bass 14 Oct. 1832	Coop
Hatfield, Wm. to Mrs. Elizabeth Hall 30 July 1839	Lafa
Hathorne, Johnson to Frances Duncan -- -- 1833	Boon
Haton, James to Nancy Cadon 29 Dec. 1836	Ray
Hatton, Fleming to Melinda Barton 23 Dec. 1838	Boon
Hatton, Jacob to Mrs. Narcissa Venandal 13 Mar. 1834	Mari
Hatton, John B. to Catherine Abbott 5 Oct. 1823	Boon
Hatton, John J. to Mary Hunt 14 Nov. 1839	Davi
Hatton, Milton B. to Jane F. Davidson 4 Oct. 1838	Monr
Hatton, Westly to Margaret Leonard 23 June 1836	Boon
Hattrmon, Wilbourn to Safiah Pipes 18 Sept. 1835	Howa
Haugh, Peter to Sarah Slater 22 July 1824	Char

Haughan, David to Emelia Craddock 3 Dec. 1830   Md-A
Haun, Jacob to Polly Moody 1 Aug. 1816   StCh
Haun, Nathan to Bersheba Allen 22 Oct. 1829   StCh
Haun, Peter to Jinny Moody 27 Aug. 1818   StCh
Haunsinger, Jacob to Tabethy Bledsoe 11 Mar. 1819   StCh
Haven, Wilson to Mary A. Crosthwaite 9 Jan. 1838   Boon
Havens, John to Artemicia Gotcher 2 Aug. 1832   Clay
Havens, Joseph to Ada Broyles 5 Dec. 1833   Clay
Haverstick, Geo. to Anna Shoultz 2 Dec. 1827   Jeff
Haverstick, Henry to Catura Huffman 11 Sept. 1810   StCh
Hawk, Geo. to Anna Clark 11 Apr. 1826   Wash
Hawk, Geo. to Clarinda Boyd 9 Aug. 1839   Mill
Hawk, Wm. to Julia A. Rambo 7 Nov. 1839   Wash
Hawker, Parkerson to Hannah M. Miller 28 June 1838   Howa
Hawkins, Abraham B. to Margaret Ross 28 Feb. 1837   Mari
Hawkins, Alan to Margaret Oster 26 July 1839   Wash
Hawkins, Alfred to Elizabeth Rush 26 June 1831   Mari
Hawkins, Andrew B. to Eliza Reno 20 Dec. 1832   Mari
Hawkins, Augustin to Sarah Hutton 7 Aug. 1834   Gasc
Hawkins, Benj. to Ailsey Lowry 6 June 1833   ·   Pk-1
Hawkins, Berry to Elizabeth Crage 5 Sept. 1839   Cr-1
Hawkins, Bin to Susannah Holladay 30 Dec. 1838   Pett
Hawkins, Bird to Sary Holliday 11 May 1826   Howa
Hawkins, Harvey to Elizabeth Campbell 18 Aug. 1836   Gasc
Hawkins, Isaac to Susan M. Wasson -- Aug. 1838   Mari
Hawkins, James to Rachel A. Cole 23 Sept. 1838   Wash
Hawkins, James C. to Mary E. Copitt 25 Apr. 1830   Mari
Hawkins, James L. to Orpha Packwood 6 Mar. 1838   Monr
Hawkins, John to Susan R. Massy 17 Aug. 1836   Wash
Hawkins, John Jr. to Rachel Stevenson 31 May 1838   Pk-B
Hawkins, John C. to Mary Turnham 30 Sept. 1829   Clay
Hawkins, R.L. to Mary M. Hopkins 11 Apr. 1839   Linc
Hawkins, Samuel to Cynthia Reno 8 June 1834   Mari
Hawkins, Strother to Lucinda Reno 4 Nov. 1832   Mari
Hawkins, Warren R. to Marinda Strawhorn 5 Sept. 1833   Cr-1
Hawkins, Washington to Mary Packwood 9 Sept. 1838   Monr
Hawkins, Wm. to Jane Dickey 18 June 1835   Wash
Hawkins, Wm. to Martha Bondurant 19 July 1836   Pk-1
Hawkins, Wm. to Rachel Bates 13 Oct. 1836   Monr
Hawkinsmith, Wm. H. to Susannah Slusher 25 May 1837   Lafa
Hawks, Daniel to Polly Reeves 29 Jan. 1839   Gree
Hawks, David to Maryan Cosner 31 May 1829   CG-A
Haws, Jacob to Catherine Barks 14 Jan. 1821   CG-1
Hay, Isaac to Nancy Langdon 8 Feb. 1832   CG-A
Hay, Joseph to Nancy Coil -- July 1834?   Cole
Hayden, Burges to Neoma Harrison 2 Jan. 1838   Howa
Hayden, Charles to Sarah Walker 7 Oct. 1838   Perr
Hayden, James to Lucretia Riney 25 July 1826   Perr
Hayden, James R. to Purlina Williams 20 Aug. 1829   Pk-1
Hayden, John to Julia Dowty 16 Nov. 1826   CG-A
Hayden, Joseph to Nancy Williams 20 Jan. 1830   Pk-1
Hayden, Nathan to Lucy Barnard 1 Mar. 1838   Rall
Hayden, Peyton R. to Maria Adams 19 Dec. 1819   Howa
Hayden, Samuel to Mery McClure 16 Oct. 1834   Call
Hayden, Solomon to Mary J. Lafo 11 Apr. 1832   CG-A
Hayden, Turner to Sallena Fisher 4 Sept. 1831   Pk-1
Hayden, Webb to Ruth Dunn 26 Jan. 1826   CG-A
Hayden, Wm. to Parthenia Fisher 9 Sept. 1827   Pk-1
Hayden, Wm. B. to Melvina E. Scott 15 Mar. 1837   Howa
Hayden, Wm. C. to Ann C. Cordell 1 Jan. 1839   CG-B
Haydon, Benj. F. to Mary E. Hicks 18 May 1837   Mari
Haydon, Elijah to Amanda J. Haydon 2 Apr. 1839   Mari
Haydon, Enoch to Louisa Neal 17 June 1830   Mari
Haydon, James W. to Emmarina H. Butler 6 July 1837   Mari
Haydon, John G. to Mary W. Price 6 Feb. 1831   Mari

Haydon, John G. to Eliza Bradshaw 20 Aug. 1835   Clay
Haydon, Wm. to Alvira Gentry 24 May 1838   Mari
Hayes, Harvey H. to Maria Tucker 16 Apr. 1839   Mari
Hayes, Howard to Isabel Morris 29 Oct. 1829   Coop
Hayes, Isaac to Susan Anderson 23 Sept. 1834   Boon
Hayes, Jefferson to Jane Mosley 4 Dec. 1834   Rall
Hayes, Wm. to Elizabeth Cowan 4 May 1837   Boon
Hayes, Wm. to Mary Dennis 30 Aug. 1838   Sali
Haynes, Joseph to Eliza J. Vanlandingham 23 Dec. 1838   Shel
Haynes, Samuel to Nancy Scobee 6 Dec. 1837   Rall
Haynes, Wm. to Polly Louder 25 Feb. 1830   Call
Hays, Amos to Paulina Russell 31 Jan. 1833   CG-A
Hays, Andrew to Elizabeth Davidson 1 Mar. 1836   Polk
Hays, Benj. to Penelope Boon 19 Dec. 1834   Howa
Hays, Daniel to Polly Bryan 28 Apr. 1813   StCh
Hays, David to Mrs. Lurinda Noe 16 Feb. 1834   Wash
Hays, David A. to Elizabeth Walton 20 June 1839   Wash
Hays, France to Mary Looney 12 Nov. 1837   CG-A
Hays, Geo. to Sally Byrd 22 Oct. 1805   CGRA
Hays, Greenlee to Eliza J. Keath 8 Dec. 1829   Pk-1
Hays, Harmon to Minervia Scholl 29 Mar. 1832   Call
Hays, Hugh to Polly Blakely 9 June 1831   Jack
Hays, James to Elenor Christopher 16 Sept. 1834   Wash
Hays, John to Nelly Green 6 Apr. 1826   CG-A
Hays, John to Polly Harris 25 Dec. 1839   Char
Hays, Joseph to Nancy Hays 18 Mar. 1825   Call
Hays, Lee to Elizabeth A. Johnson 2 Apr. 1839   Boon
Hays, McKinly to Mrs. Sarah L. Findley 5 June 1839   Linc
Hays, Putnam to Nancy P. Montgomery 1 Aug. 1839   Sali
Hays, Thomas to Sally Owens 31 Jan. 1836   Sali
Hays, Samuel M. to Polly P. Baits 18 Jan. 1838   Clay
Hayse, Robt. Jr. to Margaret Starks 29 Jan. 1826   StFr
Hayter, Wm. to Louisa Means 3 Mar. 1836   Clay
Hayth, Benj. L. to Elvira W. Forsythe 22 Nov. 1837   Lewi
Hayton, Jephta to Elizabeth Fulks 10 Mar. 1833   Call
Haywood, Robt. J. to Amanda M.F. Jackson 21 Feb. 1837   Pk-A
Haywood, Samuel F. to Nancy Johnson 27 Nov. 1838   Clar
Hazel, Edward to Sarah Yarnal 30 Jan. 1831   Coop
Hazlet, Joseph to Lucy Etherenton 27 Aug. 1839   Pk-B
Hazleton, Royal H. to Martha A. Reynolds 21 Dec. 1839   Gree
Hazzard, Henry to Winfred Warer 7 Nov. 1834   Boon
Hazzard, Ivel M. to Lynda A. McClain 15 June 1836   Boon
Head, Alfred to Margaret Hed 9 Apr. 1820   Howa
Head, Alfred to Elizabeth Anderson 17 Nov. 1836   Pett
Head, James to Mary Akers 11 Apr. 1833   Ray
Head, Norville to Sarah More 11 Dec. 1836   Clay
Head, Wm. to Lucinda Rollands 27 July 1826   Howa
Head, Wm. H. to Orpha Hedrick 14 Apr. 1825   Howa
Headlee, Gideon to Nancy Adams 28 Nov. 1839   Gree
Headlee, James S. to Mary Dyzard 7 Nov. 1837   Gree
Headruk, Wm. to Elizabeth Beordin 18 Apr. 1834   Char
Heart, Alfred E. to Nicy Pulham 17 Jan. 1833   Call
Heart, Ferdinand H. to Catharine Paulum 13 Feb. 1833   StCh
Heart, Henry J. to Lucretia Hunt 2 Nov. 1837   Clay
Heath, John G. to Hetty McDowell 5 July 1814   StCh
Heath, Moses to Delila Moon 8 Jan. 1826   Coop
Heath, Richard F. to Rachel Stockdale 21 June 1838   Mari
Heathcock, Wm. to Nancy C. Springer 11 May 1834   Wash
Heatherly, Benj. to Rhoda Kelly 14 Oct. 1838   Fran
Heatherly, James to Sarah Maupin 27 Apr. 1829   Fran
Heatherly, Leonard to Sally Brown 20 Aug. 1829   Fran
Heathman, James F. to Louisa Williams 20 Oct. 1839   Monr
Heber, Frederick to Elizabeth Wat 10 Dec. 1837   Clay
Heberling, James C. to Christian Amick 16 Aug. 1838   Howa
Hebert, Bazil to Therese Morin 6 Sept. 1806   StCh

```
Heckart, Michael to Rachel Baker 28 Mar. 1839                        Shel
Hedrick, Jonathan to Elizabeth Travilion 23 Dec. 1824                Coop
Hedrick, Samuel to Nancy Hutcheon 12 Jan. 1837                       StCh
Hedricks, May B. to Wineford Jinings 21 Feb. 1830                    StCh
Hefferfinger, James to Mildred Dooly 13 Feb. 1832                    Coop
Hefflin, Augusta to Elizabeth Lee 3 Nov. 1834                        Pett
Hegwood, John to Elizabeth Young 5 Apr. 1838                         Pk-B
Heir, Alexander to Isabella Brown 17 Dec. 1829                       Linc
Heisen, Ferdinand L.C. to Susan Ruland 16 May 1839                   Linc
Heison, Frederick A.A. to Ann Paxton 22 Oct. 1837                    Pk-B
Heizard, Robt. to Susan Hunter 17 Dec. 1839                          Rall
Heldeman, John to Fanny Hanly 20 Jan. 1829                           CG-A
Helderman, Augustus to Elizabeth Shatter 8 Feb. 1838                 CG-A
Helfenstine, Wm. to Elizabeth Massey 12 May 1834                     StCh
Helfrey, Charles to Jemina Smith 7 Feb. 1836                         Warr
Hellard, Thomas to Anna Swan 14 Nov. 1833                            Perr
Helm, Hiram to Sarah Nevins 27 Sept. 1837                            Lafa
Helm, Joseph W. to Nancy Mallory 30 July 1835                        Monr
Helm, Tillman to Patsy Tincher 17 Nov. 1836                          Lafa
Helm, Wm. to Susan Butler 14 May 1825                                Clay
Helm, Wm. M. to Martha Brown 19 Dec. 1839                            Fran
Helms, Allen to Elizabeth McClure 27 Dec. 1828                       Lafa
Helms, Anthony to Anna Gilliam 27 May 1830                           Lafa
Heltebrand, Benj. to Mary Moyers 31 Mar. 1831                        Md-A
Heltebrand, Geo. to Joanah Maury 21 June 1832                        Md-A
Heltebrand, Geo. to Marget Higdon 2 May 1839                         Md-B
Heltebrand, Henry D. to Sarah White 22 Oct. 1839                     Md-B
Helterbran, Benj. to ---- Grunt 29 Jan. 1805                         CG-1
Helton, Isaac to Elizabeth Hughes 2 Mar. 1828                        Gasc
Helton, James to Mary Hill 21 June 1831                              Gasc
Helton, James to Bursella Vaughan 10 Oct. 1833                       Gasc
Helton, Peter to Emeline Anderson 30 Sept. 1834                      Gasc
Helwig, John G. to Mrs. Rachel Ritcher 21 Nov. 1839                  Perr
Hemphill, David H. to Elizabeth Turner 23 June 1835                  Pk-1
Hempstead, ---- to Francis Carter 23 Oct. 1834                       StCh
Hempstead, Edward to Permelia McNight 11 Oct. 1836                   CG-A
Hempstedt, John to Margaret Thompson 13 June 1839                    CG-B
Henderson, Alexander H. to Hadissah Finley 15 Mar. 1837             Linc
Henderson, Alexander S. to Adeline R. Giboney 12 Nov. 1835          CG-A
Henderson, Carens E. to Jane Hope 6 Nov. 1828                        CG-A
Henderson, Charles to Elizabeth Wilkinson 3 Jan. 1836              CG-B
Henderson, Daniel to Zerilda Carrington 2 Mar. 1837                 Clin
Henderson, David to Margarett Miller 19 Mar. 1833                    Clay
Henderson, David to Mary Blattenburgh 11 Dec. 1834                  Call
Henderson, Ellison to Elizabeth McClard 25 Nov. 1830                Md-A
Henderson, Fermand D. to Sarah Trap 25 Dec. 1821                     Lafa
Henderson, Geo. to Jane Blair 22 Oct. 1811                           CG-1
Henderson, Geo. to Lucy McCarty 25 Feb. 1817                         CG-1
Henderson, Giles to Nancy Travis 2 Oct. 1834                         Jack
Henderson, Isaac to Mary Woolery 6 July 1839                         Coop
Henderson, Isaac L. to Harriet Benson 18 Nov. 1838                   Livi
Henderson, James to Anna Harris 9 July 1826                          Wash
Henderson, James H.D. to Sarah Vaughn 26 Dec. 1837                   Mari
Henderson, James H.D. to Mary E. Fisher 8 Aug. 1839                  Rall
Henderson, James S. to Emily Boone 6 June 1831                       Call
Henderson, Jesse C. to Nancy Hughart 5 Apr. 1827                     Call
Henderson, John to Mary Steel 21 Feb. 1839                           CG-B
Henderson, John to Mary A. Henderson 7 July 1839                     StFr
Henderson, John T.A. to Malinda Rubey 25 Mar. 1830                   Coop
Henderson, John V. to Elizabeth O'haver 21 Oct. 1829                StFr
Henderson, Jonas to Catherine Rayburn 28 Sept. 1837                 Wash
Henderson, Joseph to Mary Butler 16 Mar. 1837                        Cass
Henderson, Leven H. to Rebecca Wilkinson 26 June 1838               Polk
Henderson, Nathaniel to Rachel Smith 17 Nov. 1836                    Md-B
Henderson, Noah to Caroline Arnold 17 Jan. 1839                      Buch
```

Henderson, Robt. to Lucy Holman 13 Feb. 1834   Clin
Henderson, Samuel to Elizabeth Harris 1 Mar. 1827   Wash
Henderson, Samuel to Hannah Harris 10 Feb. 1833   Wash
Henderson, Sirus to Margaret McNight 9 Oct. 1838   CG-A
Henderson, Thomas to Polly Gunn 12 Oct. 1836   Rand
Henderson, Westley to Sally Green 15 June 1837   Clay
Henderson, Wm. to Charlotte Malone 28 Jan. 1836   Gasc
Henderson, Wm. A. to Amandy Tinnison 7 July 1837   Wash
Hendrick, Benj. D. to Elizabeth Thomas 10 Oct. 1838   Carr
Hendrick, Henry to Christiana Fite 18 Mar. 1807   CG-1
Hendrick, Johnson to Levicy Standford 10 June 1830   Pk-1
Hendrick, Madison to Nancy Brown 3 Oct. 1839   Fran
Hendrick, Moses to Amanda Daniel 15 Sept. 1829   Pk-1
Hendrick, Noah Jr. to Nancy Kilby 9 Apr. 1835   Pk-1
Hendrick, Richard to Mary Mourman 2 Apr. 1818   Howa
Hendrick, Wesley to Huldah G. Clempston 16 Aug. 1836   Pk-1
Hendrick, Wm. to Mildred Dodson 30 Mar. 1825   Fran
Hendrick, Wm. to Mary Strickland 26 Mar. 1834   Jeff
Hendricks, Daniel to Polly Conway 5 Mar. 1837   Mari
Hendricks, David to Katherine Miller 21 Jan. 1830   CG-A
Hendricks, John to Polly Finney 8 Apr. 1830   Ray
Hendricks, John to Francis Dougherty 28 Feb. 1837   Mari
Hendricks, John W. to Matilda Terry 21 Mar. 1839   Polk
Hendricks, Wm. to Elizabeth Shell 10 Feb. 1833   CG-A
Hendricks, Wm. D. to Elizabeth Wilson 2 Jan. 1835   CG-A
Hendrickson, John to Baliza Lucas 25 Dec. 1829   Jeff
Hendrix, Abraham to Mrs. Cassa A. McFarland 9 Oct. 1837   Cass
Hendrix, Cornelius to Lisey Tisdell 29 Sept. 1839   Ripl
Hendrix, Elisha to Sarah Rider 27 Mar. 1838   Cass
Hendrix, Thomas to Polly Conn rec. 22 May 1835   Rall
Hendrix, Wm. to Jemima E. Boyd 5 June 1838   Rall
Hendron, John to Surilda Goss 20 Apr. 1833   Howa
Henley, John to Mary Avants 10 July 1814   CG-1
Henley, Joseph to Mary Bell 2 Jan. 1834   Lafa
Henley, Rolen to Margaret Bollinger 10 Aug. 1834   CG-B
Henly, Alonzo F. to Elizabeth Belt 22 May 1833   Lafa
Hennick, James to Leah Maupin 1 Apr. 1838   Fran
Henning, James S. to Susan J. Peake 11 Sept. 1837   Clar
Henning, John C.J. to Mrs. Johanne R. Hoffman 25 Aug. 1839 Perr
Henninger, John to Eliza Oglenice 21 Jan. 1835   Linc
Henry, Alexander to Susannah Allen 29 Dec. 1839   CG-B
Henry, Isaac to Nancy Grooms 2 Aug. 1838   Clay
Henry, John to Nancy Walker 29 Aug. 1839   Pk-B
Henry, Leonard to Patsy Shaw 24 Aug. 1837   Linc
Henry, Malcolm M. to Miranda Suiter 10 Oct. 1839   Lewi
Henry, Robt. C. to Catherine M. Switzler 18 May 1836   Howa
Henry, Wm. to Nancy Jamerson 15 July 1834   Gree
Henseley, Wm. to Sally Head 5 May 1812   StCh
Hensley, Absalom to Matildah Bradford 16 Jan. 1837   Cr-1
Hensley, Henry to Sally Harrington 7 Dec. 1828   Clay
Hensley, Ichabod C. to Sarah Fulkerson 24 Dec. 1818   Howa
Hensley, James to Elvira Scott 19 Mar. 1835   Cr-1
Hensley, John to Aramenta Hensley 2 Sept. 1827   Clay
Hensley, John Jr. to Marian Sanderson 31 Mar. 1836   Cole
Hensley, John A. to Elizabeth E. Herrington 24 Mar. 1839   Jeff
Hensley, Morgan to Sarah Evans 12 June 1836   Rand
Hensley, Thomas to Junetty Smith 4 Sept. 1834   Ray
Hensley, Wm. to Polly Harrington 17 June 1822   Howa
Hensley, Wm. to Nancy Hensley 22 Nov. 1830   Cole
Hensley, Wm. to Lucinda Cantly 22 Feb. 1838   Fran
Hensly, Clifton B. to Adaline Clemmens 11 Feb. 1837   Boon
Hensly, John D. to Mary Sullins 5 Sept. 1833   Fran
Hensly, Lemuel to Elizabeth Morgan 27 July 1833   Fran
Henson, Damaris to Betsy A. Walker 1 Apr. 1827   Howa
Henson, Zachariah to Armada Williams 27 Oct. 1836   Gree

Hereford, James to Rosy Vincent 24 May 1832   Call
Heriford, Elisha to Lucinda Buster 18 Aug. 1837   Howa
Herin, Allen to Sally Brunts 16 Feb. 1826   Howa
Herman, Joshua J. to Marth A. Woolfolk 14 Oct. 1834   Linc
Hern, Branham to Emeline Barnes 19 Jan. 1837   Boon
Hern, Ferdinand to Camantha Bledsoe 30 Mar. 1833   Pett
Hern, James to July Williams 3 Jan. 1830   Boon
Hern, Oliver to Nancy Burton 17 Apr. 1838   Boon
Herndon, Charles to Rebecca Cramer 12 Nov. 1835   Coop
Herndon, James W. to Ann M. McGruder 6 Dec. 1832   Monr
Herndon, Lewis A. to Mary Williams 3 July 1839   Howa
Herndon, Wm. H. to Nancy Jackson 15 July 1833   Cole
Herod, Samuel B. to Elizabeth Cundiff 16 Oct. 1836   StFr
Herod, Samuel B. to Nancy Haile 10 Dec. 1839   StFr
Herral, Reuben to Phebe Brages 10 May 1835   Pett
Herrell, Henry to Ann Manning 16 Aug. 1829   Perr
Herren, James to Rebecca W. Truitt 12 Aug. 1830   Rall
Herrick, Ezekiel B. to Ann W. Sprigg 6 Sept. 1825   Md-A
Herriford, Hanly to Eliza Selby 5 Apr. 1835   Boon
Herriford, Lekana to Lucille Helm 15 Mar. 1838   Boon
Herriman, Mattis to Roanah Herrel 15 Aug. 1828   Howa
Herrin, Collins to Elizabeth Heeny 11 Dec. 1825   StCh
Herrin, Edmund B. to Levina P. Wilson 1 Oct. 1838   Rall
Herrin, James to Mary Hays 25 Nov. 1838   Sali
Herrin, Robt. to Mariah Bowen 19 May 1838   Lewi
Herring, Edmund to Polly Boyers 30 Dec. 1838   Clin
Herring, Robt. to Triphany Jordan 19 Feb. 1837   Pk-1
Herrington, Bartlett to Eliza Hilterbran 28 June 1829   Jeff
Herrington, Elisha to Jemima Graham 23 May 1830   Jeff
Herrington, Jacob to Elizabeth Beatty 1 Aug. 1822   Howa
Herrington, John to Susan Hones 25 Dec. 1831   Jeff
Herrington, John to Susan Jones 25 Feb. 1832   Jeff
Herrington, Thomas to Rachel Herrington 27 Feb. 1823   Howa
Herrod, Samuel B. to Harriet Smith 11 Dec. 1831   StFr
Heskett, John to Emaley Coward 13 July 1837   Monr
Hester, Avil to Harriet Marlow 18 July 1838   Henr
Hester, Hugh to Isabella McBride 20 Sept. 1831   Gasc
Heston, Wm. L. to Martha A. Martin 27 Dec. 1838   Coop
Hether, Michael B. to Rebeca Bush 13 Nov. 1829   Mari
Hetherly, Leonard to Elizabeth Ogden 6 Sept. 1838   Fran
Hetton, Laton to Rebeca Triplet 2 Nov. 1834   Wash
Hevok, Wm. to Miranda E. Brown 4 Dec. 1835   Sali
Hewell, John to Rosanah Hereford 15 May 1818   Howa
Hewitt, Charles C. to Mary A. Twisdell 21 Mar. 1837   Linc
Hewitt, Green to Polly Sullivant 21 May 1829   Wash
Hewitt, John to Susan Gathy 3 Apr. 1837   StCh
Hews, Abraham to Mary Baker 29 Jan. 1828   Gasc
Heyer, Philip J. to Emilie Kratzenstein 5 June 1837   StCh
Hibbard, John to Nancy Barnes 2 June 1835   Boon
Hibler, James to Ruthy Gragg 25 Oct. 1835   Char
Hiccocks, Charles to Mariah Hill 15 Nov. 1828   StFr
Hick, James to Tabitha Brunk -- Feb. 1830   Boon
Hick, Young E. to Margaret M. Swain 17 Jan. 1822   Boon
Hickam, Ezekial to Nancy Sims 29 Jan. 1829   Boon
Hickam, Geo. to Neoma Smith 23 Mar. 1830   Boon
Hickam, Geo. to Sally Sims 13 Feb. 1834   Boon
Hickam, Jacob to Elizabeth Early 6 June 1833   Boon
Hickam, John to Lucinda Collier 6 Aug. 1834   Boon
Hickam, John to Rebecca Carrot 23 Sept. 1835   Boon
Hickam, Joseph to Elizabeth Turdy 22 Jan. 1822   Boon
Hickam, Joseph to Susan Teeter 30 Aug. 1838   Boon
Hickam, Richard to Catharine Smith 15 Apr. 1835   Boon
Hicker, James to Mary Todd 18 Aug. 1825   Howa
Hickerson, Armstead to Rhoda Bentley 12 Apr. 1832   Call
Hickerson, James to Elizabeth Ashbrooks 7 June 1827   Wash

```
Hickerson, Samuel H. to Margaret Hinton 21 Nov. 1838          Pk-B
Hickerson, Thomas to Susannah VanBibber 21 June 1816           StCh
Hickery, Wm. to Sally Wahhube 20 June 1838                     Fran
Hickill, James to Matilda West 10 Feb. 1833                    Fran
Hicklin, John to Mary F. Gleavis 27 June 1825                  Lafa
Hicklin, Wm. to Nancy Kenney 29 Apr. 1828                      Rall
Hickman, David M. to Ann Bryan 12 Feb. 1829                    Boon
Hickman, Geo. to Ann Bartlett 7 Jan. 1838                      Perr
Hickman, Hardin to Elizabeth Teeter 25 Sept. 1827             Howa
Hickman, Jesse to Martha A. Foresun 5 Oct. 1837               Gree
Hickman, Joseph to Matilda Morman 13 Jan. 1820                Howa
Hickman, Micajes to Catherine Cobb 24 Apr. 1834               CG-A
Hickman, Moses to Katharine Hurt 10 Apr. 1834                 Boon
Hickman, Noah to Ruthe Campbell 7 Jan. 1836                   Clay
Hickman, Robt. Y. to Mary Shewmate 25 Feb. 1830               CG-A
Hickman, Wm. to Virginia McGinniss 28 Aug. 1834               Clay
Hickman, Wm. A. to Brunet A. Burckhart 12 Apr. 1832           Rand
Hicks, Absalom to Theodosia Winn 20 Dec. 1821                 Boon
Hicks, Ammon to Winniford Kelly 11 June 1826                  Howa
Hicks, Ammon to Catharine Shaver 2 Dec. 1833                  Monr
Hicks, Charles to Ann Vinyard 10 Aug. 1837                    Wash
Hicks, James to Polly Bailey 1 Mar. 1827                      Howa
Hicks, Phillip to Polly Simpson 26 Aug. 1824                  Howa
Hicks, Robt. D. to Margaret E. Byrd 21 Dec. 1837             Jeff
Hicks, Wm. to Mary Ownby 18 May 1839                          Buch
Hicks, Willis to Elizabeth Foster 17 May 1827                Boon
Hicks, Willis to Maria Marney 19 Mar. 1835                   Boon
Hickscocks, James to Malinda Gosa 1 Dec. 1828                StFr
Hickson, Andrew H. to Elizabeth Brasfield 2 July 1829        Clay
Hickson, Thomas to Elizabeth Hill 20 Jan. 1824               Clay
Hiett, Samuel to Matilda Estes 14 June 1827                  Clay
Higamight, Daniel to Eliza Stone 27 Nov. 1834                Howa
Higgenbotham, Geo. to Helen Turley 28 July 1831              Wash
Higgins, James to Nancy Eades 17 Dec. 1823                   Cole
Higgins, John to Malinda Witt 27 Feb. 1835                   Howa
Higgins, Philaman to Lucinda Witt 2 Apr. 1836                Howa
Higgins, Robt. to Camila A. Donilson 23 Jan. 1838            Howa
Higgions, Jacob to Elveary Gragg 24 Jan. 1838                Clay
Higgs, Calvin to Dicey Head 19 May 1839                      Perr
Highite, John to Levica Pinkston 2 July 1832                 Ray
Highly, Nathaniel to Melinda Headspeth 15 Apr. 1827          Wash
Highsmith, David to Jane Miller 13 Mar. 1828                 Linc
Highsmith, Samuel to Teressa Turner 4 Sept. 1826             Linc
Hight, Alfred D. to Angeline Springer 12 Jan. 1837           Wash
Hight, Henry to Eliza Ayres 19 Apr. 1807                     StCh
Hightower, Merriman to Margaret Buckhanan 17 Sept. 1837      Monr
Hildebrandt, Joseph to Barbara House 1 Feb. 1838             CG-A
Hilderbran, John to Polly Herrington 23 Mar. 1829            Jeff
Hilderbran, Samuel to Maria Everette 3 Jan. 1828             Jeff
Hilderbrand, David to Polly Parker 11 Nov. 1831              Fran
Hilderbrand, Henry to Elizabeth Herrington 10 Apr. 1836      Jeff
Hilderbrand, John to Susy Parker 10 Dec. 1833                Fran
Hiles, Isaac to Elizabeth Swain 12 Feb. 1829                 Pk-1
Hiley, Wm. B. to Loudicey McKee 28 Sept. 1837                StFr
Hill, Alexander to Loucinda Edminton 21 July 1839            Gasc
Hill, Armstead to Nancy Fenton 25 Dec. 1825                  Boon
Hill, Charles C.P. to Eliza A. McCoy 7 June 1838             StFr
Hill, Claiborn to Patsy Morris 9 July 1819                   Howa
Hill, Daniel to Denicy Roy 13 Aug. 1835                      CG-B
Hill, David to Sally Dandy 15 Oct. 1827                      StCh
Hill, Dawson to Labina Smith 14 July 1835                    CG-B
Hill, Eligah to Polly Teague 10 Mar. 1835                    Jack
Hill, Elisha to Susan Summers 20 Dec. 1832                   CG-A
Hill, Emry to Maria Sullinger 29 Apr. 1830                   CG-A
Hill, Felix G. to Mary A. Steene 1 Mar. 1838                 Jeff
```

```
Hill, Green to Saphronia A. Ford 11 Sept. 1838                    Clay
Hill, Isaac to Elizabeth Tucker 22 July 1833                      Perr
Hill, James to Polly McFarland 1 Oct. 1821                        Coop
Hill, James to Charlotte McGaugh 16 Aug. 1827                     Ray
Hill, James to Mary Ion 9 Dec. 1829                              Md-A
Hill, James to Amanda Moore 16 June 1836                         Md-B
Hill, James to Polly Sexton 16 Feb. 1837                         CG-A
Hill, John to Luckey Jones 15 Oct. 1820                          Coop
Hill, John to Permelia Camplin 27 Oct. 1831                      Boon
Hill, John W. to Lucretia Tyler 28 Dec. 1836                     StFr
Hill, Joseph to Nancy Gentry 18 June 1838                        Carr
Hill, Joseph to Jane Martin 22 Feb. 1839                         Coop
Hill, Joseph to Elizabeth Roberts 25 Nov. 1839                  Buch
Hill, Robt. J. to Catherine Haile 12 Jan. 1837                   StFr
Hill, Samuel to Lucretia Parmer 13 Mar. 1834                     Carr
Hill, Samuel to Susan Potter 27 Oct. 1836                        Clay
Hill, Thomas to Elizabeth Henry 19 Mar. 1829                     Linc
Hill, Thomas to Hetta League 28 Mar. 1839                        StFr
Hill, Wm. to Elizabeth McCroskey 2 Jan. 1823                     Ray
Hill, Wm. to Polly Gragg 25 Dec. 1827                            Wash
Hill, Wm. to Jane Ferril 27 Dec. 1838                            Sali
Hill, Wm. B.D. to Sarah J. Chinn 23 May 1839                     Shel
Hill, Wm. C.A. to Sarah A. Summers 9 Oct. 1836                   Rand
Hillerkamp, Francis to Margaret Blauff 15 Nov. 1835             StCh
Hillhouse, James D. to Nancy Gibson 14 Sept. 1837              Barr
Hillman, Geo. W. to Martha A.F. Gorham 20 June 1839            Lafa
Hilterbran, Jonathan to Sarah Jones 27 Mar. 1829               Jeff
Hilton, John to Margaret Fannin 9 Jan. 1838                      Rall
Hinch, Michael to Polly Grant 4 June 1817                        Howa
Hinch, Samuel to Parthina Gibb 12 May 1808                       StGe
Hinch, Samuel to Nancy L.A. Angle 10 May 1832                   Wash
Hinch, Samuel to Martha A. Richardson 3 Nov. 1838               Polk
Hinch, Uriah to Elizabeth Stephenson 23 Oct. 1810               CG-1
Hinchy, Bilbery to Belinda Warden 4 Aug. 1827                   Gasc
Hinchy, Ezekial to Sarah Shibers 20 Aug. 1827                   Gasc
Hinchy, John to Charlotte Cutbirth 9 May 1833                   Gasc
Hinchy, Uriah to Elizabeth Cutbirth 9 May 1833                  Gasc
Hinckle, Edmund to Mary Mayjors 22 Aug. 1839                    John
Hindes, Wm. to Mary Marlow 23 Feb. 1837                         StFr
Hines, Abram to Susan Shiflett 6 Apr. 1837                      Howa
Hines, Bolser to Lucinda Bellow 6 June 1832                     Ray
Hines, Charles to Sally Tranuih 29 Sept. 1822                   Howa
Hines, Henry to Elizabeth Blackstone 25 Mar. 1823              Char
Hines, Henry N. to Mary Blockley 20 Apr. 1838                   Davi
Hines, James to Elvira C. Patton 7 Aug. 1835                    Ray
Hines, John to Polly Dall 10 Sept. 1826                         Ray
Hines, Levi to Matilda Morgan 25 Dec. 1834                      Warr
Hines, Matthias to Lavina Croff 10 Nov. 1830                    Howa
Hines, Walter to Matilda Johnson 14 June 1829                   Cole
Hines, Wm. to Elender Hackley 12 Feb. 1829                      Howa
Hines, Wm. to Sarah Ramsey 24 Oct. 1831                         Ray
Hines, Wm. G. to Elizabeth G. Fulkerson 25 Apr. 1824           Cole
Hink, Samuel to Charity Bosley 21 June 1821                     Lafa
Hinkle, Alexander to Fanny Hinkle 3 Dec. 1825                   CG-A
Hinkle, Daniel to Sarah Dunn 2 Dec. 1832                        CG-A
Hinkle, Geo. W. to Alsey A. Weltsy 11 Mar. 1834               StCh
Hinkle, Isaac to Catherine Welker 18 July 1825                 CG-A
Hinkle, Levi to Matilda Dempsey 22 June 1834                   CG-A
Hinkle, Lewis to Margaret Fulbright 21 Apr. 1839               CG-B
Hinkle, Nathaniel to Eleanor N. Butts 28 Aug. 1838            Fran
Hinkle, Robt. to Polly Evans 16 Sept. 1830                     CG-A
Hinkle, Wm. to Mary Bess 22 Apr. 1827                          CG-A
Hinkle, Willy to Mary Rhyne 17 Oct. 1837                        Perr
Hinkson, Andrew H. to Matilda Summers 22 Dec. 1833            Wash
Hinkson, Cecero to Eveline E. Bush 11 Mar. 1830                Wash
```

Hinkson, Samuel H. to Polly Greath 2 Feb. 1817   Howa
Hinkston, Harlow to Nancy Hill 28 June 1827   Clay
Hinshaw, Jesper to Nancy Miller 26 Dec. 1836   Cass
Hinson, Phillip to Abigail A. Cooper 8 Mar. 1832   Cr-1
Hinton, David to Rebecca Sullens 13 Mar. 1834   Fran
Hinton, Jacob to Helen McFarland 4 Mar. 1833   Cr-1
Hinton, Job to Nancy Terry 22 Mar. 1836   Fran
Hinton, Rolin to Elizabeth Brammell 29 Aug. 1833   Fran
Hinton, Thomas to Margaret Spotts 13 Feb. 1839   Sali
Hiot, Siprois to Etionetta Janis 21 Feb. 1838   StCh
Hitchcock, Absalom to Lidia Cox 18 July 1830   Lafa
Hitchcock, Jesse to Polly Hopper 4 July 1821   Lafa
Hitchcock, Sampson to Cinthy Lewis 30 Dec. 1824   Lafa
Hitchock, Isaac Jr. to Elizabeth Rop 15 Feb. 1835   Jack
Hitchock, Silas to Margaret Patterson 15 Feb. 1827   Jack
Hiter, Jephtha D. to Margaret Hiter 10 Jan. 1839   Clar
Hitt, Benj. to Sarah Stall 12 Mar. 1839   CG-B
Hitt, Henry B. to Martha E. Barlow 12 Apr. 1838   CG-A
Hitt, James to Mary A. Elliott 24 Apr. 1834   CG-A
Hitt, John G. to Fidella Milton 27 Dec. 1838   CG-B
Hitt, Wm. Y. to Elizabeth Orear 12 Apr. 1836   Boon
Hix, Harden to Altezorah Spencer 24 May 1835   Morg
Hix, John A. to Amanda J. Smith 21 Nov. 1837   Sali
Hix, Samuel to Salina Gehon 13 June 1836   Morg
Hixon, Allen to Leanna Hyatt 5 Feb. 1833   Clay
Hixon, Andrew Jr. to Nancy Rollings 30 May 1833   Clay
Hixon, Solomon to Betsy Watson 22 July 1835   Clay
Hoback, John to Dice Hobeck 26 Dec. 1825   Gasc
Hoback, Wm. K. to Martha E. Herrick 29 Sept. 1839   Lewi
Hobbs, Berry to Sarah Penn 29 Mar. 1835   CG-B
Hobbs, Ezekial to Mariah Ball 4 June 1827   Boon
Hobbs, Ezekiel to Malissa Gibbs 13 Nov. 1834   CG-B
Hobbs, James to Sally Davis 12 Jan. 1826   Pk-1
Hobbs, John to Polly Lemasters 10 Aug. 1834   Pk-1
Hobbs, John to Martha Penn 26 Oct. 1836   CG-A
Hobbs, Joshua W. to Nancy Burton 6 Nov. 1828   Rall
Hobbs, Vincent to Caroline Morgan 3 Sept. 1839   CG-B
Hobs, Geo. W. to Rachel Mooras 7 May 1839   Ripl
Hobs, John to Emely Moore 16 Dec. 1838   Ripl
Hobs, Vinson to Elizabeth Minten 6 Oct. 1836   CG-A
Hockensmith, David to Julian Richardson 25 Feb. 1834   Ray
Hockersmith, Jefferson to Rokyannah Noble 10 Sept. 1835   Rand
Hockins, Lewis to Claudia Thomas 31 Jan. 1828   Call
Hodge, Alfred to Elen Waddle 2 Dec. 1838   Warr
Hodge, Archibald R.M. to Elizabeth Bell 8 Mar. 1832   Monr
Hodge, John to Louisa Meelor 30 Oct. 1832   Call
Hodge, Samuel D. to Sarah Manney 25 Dec. 1831   Monr
Hodges, Andrew to Hanah Price 22 Sept. 1836   Gree
Hodges, Edmond to Jane Durham 8 Dec. 1825   Fran
Hodges, Geo. to Elizabeth Clark 30 July 1827   Wash
Hodges, John to Martha Jamison 9 Aug. 1838   Fran
Hodges, Martin B. to Jane McCreery 25 Feb. 1836   Wash
Hodges, Peter B. to Mary Burt 7 Nov. 1830   Wash
Hodges, Peter B. to Mary Caleasie 7 Apr. 1836   Wash
Hodges, Samuel to Susan Tincher 2 Sept. 1823   Boon
Hodges, Wm. to Melissa Dale 4 Apr. 1837   Rand
Hodges, Wm. V. to Louisanna Lingenfelter 20 Sept. 1827   Clay
Hoeke, B.H. to R. Alaria Rameyer 6 Mar. 1835   StCh
Hoff, Wm. to Emily Stark 20 July 1837   Clin
Hoffman, James to Jane Stephenson 25 Feb. 1838   Barr
Hoffman, John to Elizabeth McConnell 14 Sept. 1828   StCh
Hofft, Wm. to Elizabeth Parsons 4 Aug. 1836   Cass
Hofman, Soloman to Mary Presnell 2 June 1839   CG-B
Hogan, David to Elizabeth Balch 2 May 1832   Cole
Hogan, Henry to Nancy Joiner 28 July 1839   CG-B

```
Hogan, Martin M. to Sophia Myers 10 Nov. 1826                          CG-A
Hogan, Zachariah to Polly McClane 24 Dec. 1826                         Pk-1
Hogard, Austin to Mary Kinnison 19 Mar. 1835                           Perr
Hogue, Hezekiah to Malissa Howard 25 Sept. 1832                        Coop
Hohnsley, Jefferson to Lucy J. Bishop 6 Nov. 1834                      Warr
Holbart, Nathan to Eunice Kinworthy 10 May 1835                        StFr
Holbert, Eli to Frances Sherrel 11 Dec. 1828                           StFr
Holbert, Ewing to Julia Scott 26 Nov. 1839                             Wash
Holbert, Jo-- to Mahala Batony 12 Feb. 1826                            Gasc
Holbert, John to Lithe Robinson 6 Jan. 1829                            Md-A
Holbert, Josiah to Amy Kensworthy 7 July 1833                          StFr
Holbough, Jonas to Lucici L. Poe 19 June 1831                          Gasc
Holcomb, John to Jenisha B. Johnson 15 Nov. 1835                       Howa
Holcomb, Kezzy to Daphia Thompson 19 Apr. 1836                         Lewi
Holcombe, Thomas to Johannah McLary 27 Mar. 1834                       CG-A
Holder, Henry to Honor Reed 10 Apr. 1828                               Gasc
Holder, Jonathan to Elizabeth Williams 29 July 1834                    Gree
Holder, Joseph to Nancy Gordwin 14 Feb. 1837                           CG-A
Holeman, Francis to Mary Croly 25 Aug. 1839                            Buch
Holeman, James R. to Marian Estes 10 Nov. 1833                         Clay
Holeman, Thomas to Sarah Musgrove 11 Apr. 1834                         Monr
Holeman, Wm. to Rebecca Barnes 17 Nov. 1836                            Boon
Holeter, Luke to Elizabeth Bryan 13 Jan. 1814                          StCh
Holiday, Cornelius T. to Elizabeth M. McFearson 1 Feb. 1838            Lewi
Holiday, Elias L. to Elizabeth A. Vandiver 1 Feb. 1838                 Shel
Holiday, Samuel to Elizabeth South 27 Dec. 1838                        Pk-B
Holiway, Barnes to Mrs. Adeline McClellon 28 Feb. 1837                 Cass
Holiway, Flemming to Mrs. Elizabeth Blakely 11 Apr. 1837               Cass
Holl, Ambrose to Mary Shetley 18 Mar. 1838                             Md-B
Holladay, Wm. to Jane Tong 3 Mar. 1833                                 Md-A
Holland, James to Anny Thompson 27 Nov. 1818                           Howa
Holland, James to Sarah Hutchinson 23 Oct. 1832                        Howa
Holland, Samuel W. to Sarah S. Colman 21 Nov. 1826                     Fran
Holland, Samuel W. to Martha Jeffres 26 Apr. 1830                      Fran
Holland, Thomas to Mary Potter 12 Apr. 1838                            Clay
Holland, Wm. to Margaret Dix 21 June 1832                              Mari
Holland, Wm. to Elizabeth Estes 24 Dec. 1837                           Char
Holland, Wm. to Patsy Crane 28 Mar. 1839                               Boon
Hollansworth, Wm. to Martha Donoho 24 Dec. 1837                        Boon
Hollenburge, Alexander to Abigail Cargale 15 May 1839                  Plat
Hollida, John to Mary J. Austin 2 Jan. 1839                            Pett
Holliday, Dandridge to Ann M. Carson 27 Aug. 1834                      Howa
Holliday, Joseph to Elizabeth East 31 Oct. 1837                        Monr
Holliday, Wm. H. to Jennetta Harper 3 Oct. 1839                        Monr
Hollingsworth, Geo. to Elizabeth A. Meason 5 June 1836                 Monr
Hollingsworth, James A. to Margaret Heont 8 Dec. 1836                  Cole
Hollis, Samuel B. to Jemima Drake 23 Oct. 1838                         Howa
Holliway, Jacob to Abigail E. Isbell 7 July 1831                       Gasc
Holliway, Jonathan to Elisabeth Freeman 2 May 1822                     Gasc
Holliway, Samuel to Katharine Johnson 22 Feb. 1821                     Howa
Holloman, John B. to Nancy Bruffie 26 Sept. 1839                       Wash
Holloway, Crowder to Mary Irvine 10 Oct. 1833                          Call
Holloway, Flemming to Ann Hagood 20 Dec. 1832                          Pk-1
Holloway, Henry to Adeline Ward 30 Apr. 1835                           Linc
Hollowman, Thomas to Rebecca Harley 9 Feb. 1831                        Cole
Holly, Wm. to Polly Harriford 8 Feb. 1826                              Char
Holly, Wm. to Elizabeth Landon 20 July 1839                            Boon
Holman, Daniel to Jane Crowley 12 Dec. 1833                            Clay
Holman, Harry to Nancy Wilson 25 Dec. 1836                             Ray
Holman, James to Sarah Williams 10 Mar. 1829                           Howa
Holman, James to Mary Rowland 20 Oct. 1831                             Rand
Holman, John to Eliza A. Williams 15 May 1823                          Char
Holman, John to J. Rusha Titus 13 Nov. 1834                            Rand
Holman, Joseph to Rhoda Miller 4 Aug. 1836                             Ray
Holman, Joseph to Mary Adams 11 Feb. 1838                              Shel
```

Holman, Squire to Arathrisa Barnes 10 Jan. 1839   Rand
Holmes, Samuel to Jane Keeling 19 Oct. 1837   Linc
Holmes, Stephen to Lydia W. Massey 3 Apr. 1828   StCh
Holmes, Sylvester to Nancy Hull 6 Mar. 1836   Pk-1
Holmes, Wm. B. to Mahalia Campbell 2 June 1831   Wash
Holoman, Samuel to Jane Trail 11 Apr. 1831   Wash
Holscher, John H. to Maria E. Drunkrelmaner 24 June 1839   Fran
Holson, Joseph to Rosannah Waters 23 June 1836   Perr
Holster, Felix to Luvicia Flynn 11 Sept. 1838   Perr
Holt, Abner to Elizabeth Berry 28 Feb. 1839   Bent
Holt, Geo. to Lucinda Stevens 24 Nov. 1833   Coop
Holt, Geo. to Elizabeth Hatley 17 Aug. 1834   Cole
Holt, Gideon to Lucindy J. Cockstill 10 Oct. 1839   Cole
Holt, James M. to Elizabeth Luckett 31 Oct. 1839   Mari
Holt, John to Eleanor Munns 8 May 1823   Howa
Holt, John to Sarah Brandon 4 Nov. 1835   Call
Holt, John to Elizabeth Lake 28 July 1836   Mari
Holt, John to Elizabeth Paten 17 Sept. 1837   Gree
Holt, Joseph to Mary Cunningham 2 Nov. 1834   StFr
Holt, Levy to Manerva Williams 10 Jan. 1839   Coop
Holt, Littleton E. to Mary A. Snider 6 Feb. 1839   Barr
Holt, Stephen to Casindy Deny 11 Jan. 1838   Gree
Holt, Timothy to Nancy J. Gordon 14 Jan. 1829   Call
Holt, Wm. P. to Polly Bly 24 Oct. 1839   Call
Holton, Nathan to Margaret Palmetory 15 July 1831   Howa
Holton, Stuart to Alethe Barnes 16 Apr. 1835   Boon
Holtsclan, James to Lucinda Fielding 25 June 1826   Howa
Holtzclaw, Peter to Betsey Duncan 2 Aug. 1827   Clay
Homan, Jesse to Elizabeth Edgar 19 Oct. 1825   Wash
Homes, Samuel to Martha E. Ritchie 9 Jan. 1834   Clay
Hon, John to Elizabeth Hinkle 6 Feb. 1806   CG-1
Honore, Isidore to Margretha Marie 26 Feb. 1838   StCh
Honsinger, John to Matilda Gillespy 9 Oct. 1827   Gasc
Hood, John to Sarah Walker 31 May 1836   Howa
Hoodenpy, J.M. to Sarah Briges 4 Apr. 1830   Gasc
Hook, Elijah to Hannah Shoemaker 20 Aug. 1839   Coop
Hook, James to Mary Proctor 12 Dec. 1833   Coop
Hook, John to Leah Bellemay 6 Aug. 1829   Perr
Hook, John to Elizabeth C. Graves 4 Nov. 1833   Morg
Hoops, David to Louisianna Walton 22 Aug. 1833   Gasc
Hoops, Geo. to Amanda Walton 23 June 1836   Gasc
Hoover, Jacob to Sarah Cave 18 June 1831   Boon
Hope, David C. to Narcissa S. Harris 8 Nov. 1831   CG-A
Hope, Robt. Y. to Margaret Torrence 26 July 1838   CG-A
Hope, Thomas to Margery Lytle 13 Sept. 1831   CG-A
Hope, Wm. to Lucinda Sheppard 3 Apr. 1827   Perr
Hope, Wm. to Elizabeth Jones 30 June 1836   CG-A
Hopkins, B. to Sarah A. Hobbs 3 Mar. 1836   Linc
Hopkins, Elliott to Amaranthe LeFevre 27 July 1837   StCh
Hopkins, Geo. W. to Nancy Sampson 3 Sept. 1835   Clay
Hopkins, Stephen to Sarah Cunningham 13 Oct. 1831   Linc
Hopkins, Thomas to Lydia Beck 22 Oct. 1826   Linc
Hopkins, Thomas W. to Nancy A. Campbell 12 Jan. 1832   Wash
Hopkins, Walker to Nancy Beck -- Aug. 1831   Linc
Hopkins, Walter to Agnes Brickey 13 Sept. 1839   Cr-1
Hopper, Charles to Nancy McClure 4 Jan. 1829   Lafa
Hopper, John to Jane Lee 9 Nov. 1837   Lafa
Hopper, John to Nancy McMurtrie 18 Aug. 1839   Davi
Hopper, Martin to Nancy Stafford 21 Jan. 1836   Howa
Hopson, Alexander to Catherine Coleman 22 Apr. 1837   StFr
Hopson, Hiram L. to Elizabeth M. Tutor 18 Jan. 1833   Mari
Hopton, Abner to Margaret Flack 14 Dec. 1837   Gasc
Hor, Allen to Lucinda March 20 June 1836   Clay
Horine, Alton to Sary Shuffield 20 Nov. 1834   Fran
Horine, Benj. to Louizanna Jones 27 Dec. 1838   Fran

Horine, Elias to Mary Roberson 4 Feb. 1836	Wash
Horine, Mathias to Mary Drury 14 Oct. 1835	Jeff
Horine, Thomas to Susan Quick 27 June 1839	Wash
Horn, Amos to Vina Norris 28 June 1822	Lafa
Horn, Andrew O. to Margaret Steel 29 Mar. 1838	Gree
Horn, Frederick to Nancy Cockran 23 Oct. 1839	Ripl
Horn, James to Jane Bennett 17 Nov. 1835	Clay
Horn, John to Eliza Bink 27 Dec. 1832	Jeff
Horn, Martin to Sarah Richardson 12 Nov. 1835	StFr
Horn, Samuel W. to Catherin Branson 30 Mar. 1838	Gasc
Horn, Wm. to Elizabeth M. Stone 21 July 1829	Clay
Hornback, Andrew to Sally Wood 12 Jan. 1837	Coop
Hornback, James to Mahala A. Field 3 Dec. 1835	Rall
Hornback, Samuel to Eleanor Bass 21 Nov. 1833	Coop
Hornbeck, James to Nancy Cunningham 18 Oct. 1826	Ray
Hornbeck, James to Emaline Scritchfield 27 July 1831	Coop
Hornbuckle, Richard S. to Elvira Smart 1 Oct. 1838	Call
Hornbuckle, Rufus to Amanda Davis 2 Apr. 1839	Call
Hornbuckle, Thomas to Providence Baker 28 May 1826	Call
Horncash, Michael to Martha Sherrin 11 Feb. 1836	Rand
Horner, Gustavus B. to Elizabeth Kelly 4 Mar. 1839	Fran
Hornsby, Crawford to Pheby Longacre 8 Aug. 1839	John
Horrell, Bernard to Sarah Manning 9 Jan. 1837	Perr
Horsley, James R. to Lucy A. Gillman 2 Nov. 1837	Rand
Horton, John to July A. Hickland 28 Dec. 1837	Lafa
Horton, Walker to Sarah Mason 19 Aug. 1838	Char
Hoskins, Daniel to Elizabeth Colbert 9 July 1831	Boon
Hoskins, James to Lucy Fountain 20 Oct. 1831	Boon
Hospes, Lewis to Elizabeth Wurdemann 24 June 1837	StCh
Hoss, Christopher to Catherine Probst 12 June 1828	CG-A
Hostetter, Abram to Polly Mifford 5 Feb. 1829	Pk-1
Hostetter, Ammon to Matilda Jackson 15 Dec. 1833	Pk-1
Hostetter, Enoch to Sarah Floyd 20 Apr. 1834	Pk-1
Houck, Soloman to Rachel C. Francisco 9 Jan. 1838	Howa
Hough, Jackson A. to Laura Davis 16 July 1839	Mari
Hough, Wm. to Martha Jacoby 8 June 1837	Pk-B
Houghton, Wm. to Sarah J. Jackson 28 Jan. 1836	Monr
Hoult, Punphery D. to Nancy Gorden 24 Aug. 1829	StCh
Houn, Geo. to Jane Tooley 18 Mar. 1819	Howa
House, Adam to Nancy England 13 Sept. 1838	Ripl
House, Eli to Irine West 14 Jan. 1836	Jack
House, Fielden to Mrs. Nancy Lane 2 Feb. 1836	Pk-1
House, Fleming to Sally Humphry 6 June 1833	Pk-1
House, Hollandsworth to Milly Thomas 15 May 1836	Ripl
House, John to Maryann House 7 Nov. 1839	Ripl
House, Joseph to Mary Malone 25 Jan. 1825	Call
House, Joseph to Matilda ---- 10 May 1829	Linc
Housen, John to Polly Etter 29 Apr. 1832	StCh
Houser, Thomas to Susanah Hindman 14 Feb. 1839	Clay
Houston, John to Permelia Branum 3 Sept. 1829	Call
Houston, Jonathan M. to Tatimy Estes 14 Apr. 1836	Morg
Houston, Robt. to Nancy Wiseman 16 Oct. 1834	Boon
Housucker, Wm. to Ritta Bledsoe 1 Nov. 1821	Boon
Houtchins, James to Nancy Neele 5 Dec. 1833	Boon
Houts, Christby to Mary Falls 3 Jan. 1823	Sali
Houx, Frederick E. to Elender Crawford 26 Mar. 1835	Coop
Houx, Geo. to Eliza Sloss 16 Jan. 1834	Coop
Houx, Jacob to Peggy Massy 27 May 1827	Coop
Houx, Phillip to Margaret Morrow 14 Sept. 1824	Coop
How, Wm. to Nancy Sorrell 7 Dec. 1834	Monr
How, Wm. to Nancy Thompson 24 Apr. 1838	Mari
How, Wm. S. to Eliza A. Brickey 8 Dec. 1829	Wash
Howard, Abraham to Sally Alexander 1 Mar. 1826	Call
Howard, Abraham to Mary Spalding 7 Jan. 1835	StCh
Howard, Abram to Scyotha J. Means 19 July 1838	Clin

111

Howard, Arrey B. to Annjalenah Ray 6 Jan. 1831	Coop
Howard, Charles to Elizabeth Mulkey 26 Apr. 1820	Coop
Howard, Charles to Mariah Killmore 29 Oct. 1829	Perr
Howard, David to Rebeccah McCutchin 15 Apr. 1838	Warr
Howard, Edmond to Polly Robinson 10 June 1824	Coop
Howard, Hamilton C. to Polly Elliot 24 Jan. 1833	Cole
Howard, Henry to Annis Nanse 12 Feb. 1828	Fran
Howard, Henry F. to Lucinda Sinclair 11 Mar. 1836	Rall
Howard, Hiram to Lucinday McKenney 3 June 1830	Coop
Howard, Isham to Polly Moon 11 May 1828	Cole
Howard, Jackson to Mary Nurenhaus 8 June 1839	Ripl
Howard, James to Elizabeth Rowland 21 Dec. 1822	Char
Howard, James to Elinda Bradley 14 Nov. 1839	Cole
Howard, James B. to Mary Watts 28 Dec. 1837	CG-A
Howard, Jesse to Francis Cunningham 19 Sept. 1839	John
Howard, John to Sarah Roark 8 Oct. 1835	Cole
Howard, Joseph B. to Sarah Cunningham 24 May 1827	Boon
Howard, Leroy to Penelopy Wood 27 Dec. 1833	Coop
Howard, Leven to Nancy M. Howard 13 Feb. 1837	Clar
Howard, Martin to Frances Woodey 11 Jan. 1838	Warr
Howard, Mordichi to Elizabeth Hughes 23 Aug. 1831	Wash
Howard, Ozedekiah to Jane English 13 Dec. 1808	CG-1
Howard, Richard to Louisa Jameson 5 Apr. 1832	Rall
Howard, Seth to Hannah Ingram 18 Feb. 1831	Cole
Howard, Seth to Lydia Bond 7 May 1835	Cole
Howard, Seth B. to Margart Alexander 30 Jan. 1834	Gree
Howard, Sirus to Ruth Giles 27 Sept. 1838	Rand
Howard, Stephen to Sarah Stinson 18 Oct. 1838	Morg
Howard, Thomas to Altazard Morgan 12 Mar. 1835	CG-B
Howard, Wm. to Rosmary Roberts 14 July 1827	Char
Howard, Wm. to Elenor McGuire 27 July 1837	CG-A
Howdershell, David to Mary Cannon 13 Nov. 1834	Linc
Howdershell, Henry to Elizabeth Baxter 13 Aug. 1826	Rall
Howdeshell, John to Margaret McElwee 14 May 1829	Clay
Howdeshell, Wm. to Elizabeth Groshong 29 Jan. 1817	StCh
Howe, Harvy to Rachel Steel 4 Dec. 1830	Coop
Howe, James M.G. to Anne C. Baker 20 Nov. 1834	Call
Howe, Wm. to Charlotte Jones 6 Dec. 1820	Coop
Howell, Benj. to Mahala Costley 28 Sept. 1815	StCh
Howell, Eli to Nancy D. Luck 7 Aug. 1838	Pk-B
Howell, Francis Jr. to Mary Ramsey 29 Dec. 1816	StCh
Howell, Francis to Mary Pratt 13 June 1833	Warr
Howell, James F. to Isabell Morris 13 May 1827	StCh
Howell, John to Grace Baldridge 21 Feb. 1805	StCh
Howell, John to Polly Wilson -- Sept. 1821	Howa
Howell, John to Joanna Evans 10 Apr. 1828	StCh
Howell, John C. to Lucinda Stewart 20 Dec. 1838	Warr
Howell, John E. to Katharine Kippers 9 Mar. 1837	Monr
Howell, Larkin to Martha Baugh 10 Feb. 1831	StCh
Howell, Pirives W. to Mary A. Howell 29 Dec. 1836	Warr
Howell, Riley to Jane Reeves 28 Nov. 1835	StCh
Howell, Samuel to Eliza Stokes 4 Feb. 1835	Lafa
Howell, Wm. to Martha Cason 9 Jan. 1827	Howa
Howell, Wm. to Elizabeth Bailey 6 Mar. 1831	CG-A
Howell, Wm. J. to Maria L. Smith 11 Feb. 1836	Mari
Howell, Wm. M. to Mary Byrd 31 Mar. 1831	CG-A
Howell, Young to Kathryn Welty 3 Dec. 1831	Linc
Howerton, Henry T. to Sarah Brookin 18 June 1835	Lewi
Howerton, Jefferson to Jane Casteel 24 Apr. 1838	Coop
Howerton, Jeremiah to Elizabeth Casteel 24 Apr. 1838	Coop
Howgin, Henry to Dicy Underwood 19 Nov. 1835	Md-B
Howland, Daniel to Gunilda Hays 4 July 1821	StCh
Howzon, Christfer to Betsey Clarke 3 Oct. 1809	CG-1
Hubbard, Adolph to Polly Gaines 2 Jan. 1817	Howa
Hubbard, Albert G. to Francis M. Austin 18 Mar. 1835	Call

Hubbard, Asa R. to Martha Owens 27 Sept. 1838	Rand
Hubbard, Charles to Margaret Cannon 20 Dec. 1829	Linc
Hubbard, Daniel C. to Elizabeth Holman 24 June 1828	Char
Hubbard, Eli to Kesiah Cannon 23 July 1826	Linc
Hubbard, Eli to Margaret Myers 30 Oct. 1828	Linc
Hubbard, Eli to Elizabeth Buchanan 6 May 1836	Linc
Hubbard, James to Betsy Rees 17 Nov. 1831	Coop
Hubbard, Joseph to Lucinda Luis 25 Dec. 1827	Linc
Hubbard, Thomas J. to Paulina Hays 17 Jan. 1837	Howa
Hubbard, Wm. to Josephine Stevens 29 Oct. 1835	Char
Hubbard, Wm. to Elizabeth Barnes 28 Dec. 1836	Boon
Hubbel, Ebeneasor to Rebeca Foster 19 Nov. 1807	CG-1
Hubble, Daniel to Alafair Meek 26 Apr. 1830	CG-A
Hubble, Jhames to Eleanor Patterson 22 Nov. 1835	CG-B
Hubble, Mathew to Pegge Walters 15 Feb. 1811	CG-1
Hubble, Mathew to Caty Perkil 11 July 1815	CG-1
Hubbles, Ebeneazar to Ruthey Crump 18 Mar. 1818	CG-1
Huber, Wm. to Rebecca Frances 14 Aug. 1834	Warr
Hubert, Joseph to Elizabeth Marichalle 2 Mar. 1829	StCh
Huck, Joseph to Frances Graidy 8 Nov. 1829	Char
Huddleston, Anthony to Mrs. Sarah Keith 28 Oct. 1838	StFr
Huddleston, Jessey to Harriet Huddleston 17 Sept. 1835	Ripl
Huddleston, John to Sarah Austmass 19 Apr. 1833	Mari
Huddleston, John C. to Sarah Bunch 13 June 1835	Wash
Huddleston, Joseph to Elizabeth Perkins 13 Aug. 1837	Ripl
Huddleston, Miliner to Peggy Smith 9 Aug. 1838	Ripl
Hudgins, Prince S. to Nancy Logan 26 Feb. 1835	Ray
Hudson, Calvin to Elizabeth Hinksons 5 Mar. 1826	Wash
Hudson, Charles to Frances M. Litton 2 Oct. 1834	Linc
Hudson, Enock to Polly Bollinger 23 Aug. 1818	CG-1
Hudson, James to Ann Hudson Jr. 9 Apr. 1835	Monr
Hudson, Joseph to Sally Andrews 27 Feb. 1838	Howa
Hudson, Pleasant to Polly Mase 4 Jan. 1827	Pk-1
Hudson, Samuel to Malinda W. Bevins 28 May 1829	Clay
Hudson, Thomas to Polly Hammond 23 Oct. 1828	Pk-1
Hudson, Thomas to Emeline Johnson 24 Nov. 1836	Lafa
Hudson, W.D. to Jane Anderson 21 Nov. 1839	Lewi
Hudson, Wm. to Sally L. Litton 21 July 1825	Linc
Hudson, Wm. to Susan Smyth 12 Oct. 1834	Lafa
Hudson, Wm. to Mary Jackson 17 Mar. 1837	Rand
Hudson, Wm. P. to Martha Irwin 29 Dec. 1839	Cass
Hudspeth, Abijah to Sarah Gray 30 Oct. 1833	StFr
Hudspeth, Geo. W. to Mary E. Ward 27 Mar. 1831	Lafa
Hudspeth, Lewis to Sally Gauge 29 Nov. 1832	Cr-1
Hudspeth, Thomas to Synthy Hambright 31 Mar. 1829	Jack
Hues, Edward to Nancy Hues 9 Jan. 1839	Clar
Hueston, Robt. to Caroline Taylor 7 Oct. 1835	Warr
Huett, Wilkerson to Sally Robison 2 July 1833	Wash
Hufaker, Walter to Minerva Bartee 30 Jan. 1838	Clay
Huff, Absalom to Newrary Mullin 20 Jan. 1820	Coop
Huff, Bartholomue to Polly Gwinn 28 Apr. 1836	Sali
Huff, David to Rebecca Parsons 27 Aug. 1829	Jack
Huff, David to Sarah Horton 6 Mar. 1836	Cass
Huff, Harrison to Hannah Miller 25 Dec. 1834	Cole
Huff, I.Y. to Elizabeth Hardin 14 Mar. 1839	Howa
Huff, Montraville to Amanda Thorton 3 Mar. 1836	John
Huff, Noah to Hetta Cooper 9 July 1835	Cole
Huff, Peter to Frances Martin 19 Sept. 1824	Coop
Huffaker, Washington to Mrs. Sally Shackleford 1 Nov. 1832	Clay
Huffender, John to Barbary Sterguin 18 Nov. 1838	StCh
Huffet, Geo. to Elizabeth Horton 27 May 1837	Cass
Huffet, Jacob to Nancy Hays 16 Jan. 1838	StFr
Huffman, ---- to Sarah Childers 18 July 1830	Fran
Huffman, Alfred to Sarah Jones 1 Sept. 1835	Cr-1
Huffman, David P. to Jane Agee 14 Apr. 1834	Gasc

```
Huffman, Geo. Jr. to Mary McConnell 13 Dec. 1830          StCh
Huffman, Geo. to Nancy Mason 15 June 1837                 StCh
Huffman, Isaac to Elizabeth Burris 8 Jan. 1825            Howa
Huffman, Isaac to Polly A. Wilds 22 Mar. 1829             Howa
Huffman, James to Jane Smyth 18 Nov. 1832                 Fran
Huffman, James to Leanner Criswell 19 Jan. 1837           Polk
Huffman, Jesse to Nancy Bennet 27 Nov. 1834               Clay
Huffman, Jesse to Mourning Estes 7 Nov. 1836              Clay
Huffman, John G. to Agness Pryor 23 June 1831             Gasc
Huffman, Wm. T. to Martha Smith 10 Jan. 1839              Plat
Huffstutter, Levi to Mary Gregory 25 Feb. 1836            Wash
Hufft, Jacob to Dala M. Smith 27 Apr. 1839                Cass
Hufman, Jacob to Sally C. Sides 25 Oct. 1831              CG-A
Hufman, Peter to Sarah McConnell 13 Apr. 1834             StCh
Hughes, Abraham Sr. to Mary Smith 13 Nov. 1813            StGe
Hughes, Allen to Malvina D. Hughes 20 Dec. 1825           Howa
Hughes, Andrew to Polly Morrow 18 Nov. 1832               Linc
Hughes, Bela M. to Catharine Neal 9 Jan. 1838             Clay
Hughes, Berry to Susan Campbell 26 Oct. 1830              Clay
Hughes, Daniel G. to Elizabeth Woods 13 Jan. 1825         Coop
Hughes, David B. to Mariah Griffith 13 Oct. 1836          Lewi
Hughes, Elijah to Rachel Dale 2 Nov. 1826                 Boon
Hughes, Elisha to Susan McMurtry 8 Nov. 1838              Call
Hughes, Geo. K. to Rhody Boyle 30 Nov. 1838               Coop
Hughes, Hays to Sarah Boyd 23 Mar. 1826                   Wash
Hughes, Hugh H. to Margaret Moyer 28 Feb. 1836            Wash
Hughes, James to Elvira Sharp 3 Apr. 1834                 Warr
Hughes, James to Rebecka Brown 18 Aug. 1839               Davi
Hughes, Jeremiah to Purlina Burrus 25 Jan. 1837           Howa
Hughes, John to Jane A. West 7 Feb. 1828                  Boon
Hughes, John to Mary E. Peyton 7 Dec. 1837                Call
Hughes, John H. to Deborah B. Lawrence 19 June 1838       Ray
Hughes, Joseph to Rhodia Riggs 2 Sept. 1818               Howa
Hughes, Mahlon to Eveline McFarland 21 Sept. 1837         StFr
Hughes, Mark to Elaine Campbell 12 Oct. 1826              Wash
Hughes, McKenny to Lavina Davidson 11 June 1835           Gasc
Hughes, Roland to Mary A. Hughes 31 July 1832             Howa
Hughes, Rolly to Elizabeth Harper 20 Aug. 1826            Coop
Hughes, Samuel to Tatha Gwinn 3 Jan. 1836                 Sali
Hughes, Stephen to Jane Helton 19 Sept. 1833              Gasc
Hughes, Taylor to Elizabeth Sebree 21 Mar. 1839           Howa
Hughes, Thomas C. to Tillithi Eastin 12 Mar. 1839         Mari
Hughes, Van C. to Mary Head 13 Sept. 1837                 Rand
Hughes, Washington to Sarah S. Williams 22 Mar. 1838      Wash
Hughes, Wm. to Isabellah Howard 2 Nov. 1826               Linc
Hughes, Wm. to Mitalda Oldham 9 Jan. 1834                 Jack
Hughes, Wm. to Mary Williams 7 July 1835                  Howa
Hughes, Wm. to Bathiar Neberry 22 July 1835               Cr-1
Hughes, Wm. to Martha Hyden 23 July 1838                  Cr-1
Hughes, Wm. H. to Mahala DuVall 11 Mar. 1838              Barr
Hughey, Miles to Sativa R. Parker 20 Oct. 1837            Perr
Hughhart, Joseph T. to Ann Henderson 30 Aug. 1827         Call
Hughlett, Geo. to Syrena Duncan 3 Aug. 1830               Pk-1
Hughlett, John to Mrs. Diannah Willis 17 Oct. 1833        Pk-1
Hughlett, Solomon to Parthenia Willis 1 Nov. 1835         Pk-1
Hughs, Benj. to Euphemia Ewing 29 Aug. 1839               Pk-B
Hughs, Drury to Violet Lovin 7 Aug. 1836                  Gasc
Hughs, Graham to Sarah L. Chauncey 4 Apr. 1837            StCh
Hughs, John to Sally C. McNew 21 Feb. 1836                Pett
Hughs, Micajah to Caroline Seats 14 Dec. 1834             Morg
Hul, John to Sally Mitchel 7 Mar. 1839                    Clay
Hulen, John to Nancy Hulett 18 Dec. 1834                  Boon
Hulett, John to Eliza Loret 2 Oct. 1834                   Howa
Hull, Albert G. to Elizabeth Ashcraft 6 July 1833         Howa
Hull, Henry I. to Mary A. Alkire 10 Jan. 1828             Gasc
```

114

```
Hull, Jesse C. to Mahala Drace 26 Sept. 1839                          Fran
Hull, John to Sarah E. Tucker 3 Nov. 1836                             Call
Hull, John to Rebecca Pemberton 27 June 1839                         Sali
Hull, Joseph to Constincy Alley 18 Dec. 1834                         Fran
Hulse, Wm. to Sarah Strange 12 Feb. 1837                             John
Hulsey, James to Sarah Bryan 17 Sept. 1833                          Wash
Hulsey, Wm. to Elizabeth Horine 18 May 1833                         Wash
Hults, Duke to Margaret Love 23 Oct. 1827                           Call
Hultz, Lorenzo D. to Melissa Vanbibber 12 Jan. 1837                 Call
Hume, John to Nancy Sharp 3 Feb. 1831                               Boon
Hume, Thornton to Louisa Sharp 12 Jan. 1827                         Boon
Humes, Geo. to Harriet McBain 24 June 1824                          Boon
Humphrey, Henry to Elizabeth Ashby 13 Aug. 1837                    Char
Humphrey, Jesse to Hannah McMillen 2 Nov. 1828                     Pk-1
Humphreys, John to Susanah Crawford 5 June 1836                    Call
Humphries, Azariah to Margaret Pitzer 5 Sept. 1839                 Pk-B
Humphries, John to Nancy Skaggs 5 Sept. 1822                        Gasc
Humphries, Jonathan to Livinia Bass 1 Feb. 1839                    Mill
Humphries, Nathan to Latitia Jamison 27 Mar. 1827                  Gasc
Humphries, Robt. to Lucy Williams 12 Feb. 1824                     Call
Humphries, Samuel to Louisa G. Smart 3 Mar. 1833                   Call
Humphries, Wm. to Frances Muir 3 Mar. 1835                         Call
Humphry, Nathanial to Jane Arhart 23 July 1839                     Mill
Humpreys, Thomas to Mildred McDavitt 26 Dec. 1830                  Rand
Hun, Conrad to Walburge Metzshingereen 26 Aug. 1833               StCh
Hungate, John to Lezertha Gray 23 Nov. 1837                        Monr
Hunner, Robt. to Rhoas Patton 5 Apr. 1838                          Ray
Hunsucker, Thomas to Elizabeth Guinn 12 July 1826                 Lafa
Hunt, David to Rebecca Boggs 18 Mar. 1821                          Howa
Hunt, David to Ann Todd 1 Aug. 1839                                Plat
Hunt, Frederick to Helna Palmer -- -- 1837                         Boon
Hunt, Henry to Elizabeth Frazier 10 May 1831                       Ray
Hunt, James to Margaret Hunt 10 Nov. 1825                          Coop
Hunt, Jesse to Anna Norris 10 Feb. 1831                            Lafa
Hunt, John to Lucinda Alexander 2 June 1839                        StFr
Hunt, John G. to Sarah A. Elliott 16 May 1837                      CG-A
Hunt, Johnson to Marcha Covey 18 Feb. 1836                         Sali
Hunt, Jonthan to Catharine Emberson 21 Apr. 1834                   Rand
Hunt, Nathan to Isabella Wright 20 Mar. 1823                       Howa
Hunt, Umphrey to Nancy Burriss 9 May 1834                          Jack
Hunt, Wesley to Malissa Callaway 24 Oct. 1833                      Warr
Hunt, Wm. to Sophia J. Keele 5 Sept. 1835                          Call
Hunter, Andrew to Ann Rock 14 Feb. 1822                            Call
Hunter, Enoch R. to Judith Wade 13 May 1828                        Boon
Hunter, Henry to Martha Morray 4 Nov. 1833                         Cole
Hunter, Ira to Martha Bowers 15 Oct. 1835                          Jack
Hunter, John to Martha Talbot 10 -- 1833                           Warr
Hunter, Joseph S. to Sally Martin 4 May 1834                       Cole
Hunter, Overton to Elizabeth Huff 21 Dec. 1837                     Call
Hunter, Samuel to Elizabeth Depart 15 Jan. 1839                    Call
Hunter, Wm. to America Fry 13 Apr. 1834                            Pk-1
Hunter, Wm. to Sarah Talbot 21 Jan. 1836                           Call
Hunter, Wm. to Mariah Spurnhoward 11 July 1839                     Cass
Huntsaker, Bradford to Dicey Stice 30 Apr. 1835                    Shel
Huntsman, Edward to Maryann Orr 26 Sept. 1833                      Pk-1
Huntsman, Isaac to Martha Rutherford 4 Dec. 1838                   Rand
Huntsman, John to Nancy Brooks 19 Jan. 1837                        John
Hurl, Rich S. to Emerine Dale 22 Nov. 1832                         Clay
Hurley, John to Louise Dooly 21 Mar. 1833                          Rall
Hurley, Moses to Catherine Roberson 22 Oct. 1805                   CGRA
Hurly, Wm. to Nelly Doris 1 July 1830                              Cole
Hurry, Joseph F. to Nancy Cunningham 7 Dec. 1823                   StFr
Hurst, Absalom to Orlean Dobbs 10 Oct. 1839                        Polk
Hurst, John to Mary Wright 26 Mar. 1837                            Boon
Hurt, Allen to Leona J. Robinson 27 Aug. 1839                      Boon
```

Hurt, Archy B. to Polly Ward 12 Apr. 1829   Cr-P
Hurt, Gilford to Sarah McKinney 13 Aug. 1029   Fran
Hurt, John to Ann Stout 1 Mar. 1839   Polk
Hurt, Joshua to Anna Denny 20 Sept. 1821   Howa
Hurt, Judbel to Martha Clark 5 July 1827   Howa
Hurt, Miner to Emely Kellion 8 Oct. 1835   Char
Hurt, Moses to Eliza Hays 26 Feb. 1834   Char
Hurt, Wm. to Catherine Robertson 12 Sept. 1837   Coop
Hurt, Wilson D. to Judith Barnes 28 Dec. 1826   Fran
Hurt, Wilson D. to Mary J. Jeffries 8 June 1837   Fran
Hurt, Zachaus to Jane Wardrup 18 June 1837   Polk
Huse, Joseph to Eliza Read 4 Oct. 1827   Boon
Huskey, D. Lafayette to Maria Jones 10 Nov. 1838   Jeff
Huskey, Silas to Martha S. Northcraft 8 Sept. 1833   Jeff
Huskey, Stephen to Judith Hensley 1 Dec. 1836   Jeff
Huskey, Wm. to Martha Hensley 1 Dec. 1836   Jeff
Huskey, Wm. to Martha Hensley 1 Dec. 1837   Jeff
Huskey, Wm. Sr. to Mrs. Dicy Willhight 5 Aug. 1839   Jeff
Hust, Wm. to Elizabeth Saling 27 Apr. 1828   Rall
Huston, Jahugh to Sarah Dillen 22 Dec. 1839   Md-B
Huston, Joseph to Elizabeth Lawless 30 Apr. 1826   Sali
Huston, Shelton to Martha Harris 24 Jan. 1833   Coop
Hutcherson, John to Keziah Anson 6 Oct. 1836   Lewi
Hutcherson, John to Isabel Meteer 21 Sept. 1837   Call
Hutcherson, Levi to Mary Pitman 16 May 1839   StCh
Hutcheson, Benj. to Polly Gordan 3 Sept. 1835   Warr
Hutchings, Allin S. to Eliza Reed 14 Aug. 1834   Wash
Hutchings, Green to Zorada G. Nash 20 Dec. 1820   StCh
Hutchings, Moses to Matilda Odell 12 Feb. 1825   Ray
Hutchings, Thomas to Frances A. Johnson 20 Nov. 1833   Wash
Hutchins, Ignatius to Charlotte Layton 22 Sept. 1835   Perr
Hutchins, John to Susanna Mattingly 16 Jan. 1830   Perr
Hutchinson, Cyrus to Eliza A. Lock 15 Sept. 1835   Char
Hutchinson, John H. to Sally Moore 13 Aug. 1822   Coop
Hutchinson, Nathan to Polly Crismon 31 May 1818   Howa
Hutchison, Daniel to Alvira Telmon 22 Jan. 1839   Barr
Hutchison, Greenville to Buthema Allison 3 Oct. 1839   Monr
Hutchison, James to Mary A. Gibson 12 Apr. 1838   CG-A
Hutchison, James M. to Jamima A. Gilliland 3 Feb. 1836   Henr
Hutchison, Jeremiah to Elizabeth Penrod 13 Mar. 1837   CG-A
Hutchison, Wm. to Nancy H. Biggs 3 Apr. 1833   Pk-1
Hutchison, Wm. to Lucinda Cahall 10 Jan. 1838   Linc
Hutson, Giles to Eliza A.C. Bess 10 Nov. 1839   Cass
Hutson, Martin to Elizabeth McAlroy 24 May 1832   Lafa
Hutson, Samuel P. to Catherine D.W. Cole 3 Feb. 1831   Wash
Hutson, Wm. to Minerva Brown 28 Dec. 1820   CG-1
Hutson, Wm. H. to Lena Hatton 23 May 1839   Perr
Hutt, Thomas G. to Judith Armstead 18 Oct. 1838   Linc
Hutten, Matthew to Mary Johnson 25 May 1836   Cr-1
Hutton, Jonathan to Levina Gordon 25 July 1839   Fran
Hutton, Samuel to Elizabeth Adams 9 Aug. 1838   Fran
Hutton, Willis to Cassandra Humphrey 16 Aug. 1827   Pk-1
Hyatt, Milton to Rosannah Adams 16 Apr. 1835   Gasc
Hyatt, Robt. B. to Lusinday Wood 17 Jan. 1832   Cr-1
Hyden, Alexander to Ellender Glenn 11 Sept. 1837   Cr-1
Hymes, Isaac to Margarette Francis 16 Mar. 1834   Lafa
Hynes, Mathias to Elizabeth Smith 20 Sept. 1827   Howa
Hynes, Wesley to Elizabeth Davis 19 July 1818   Howa

Igo, Lewois to Elvirey Allen 23 Jan. 1838   Gree
Igo, Wm. to Mary C. Montgomery 20 Dec. 1832   Pk-1
Ikard, Geo. to Nancy Williams 10 Mar. 1831   CG-A
Iler, Stephen H. to Elenor Burkleo 6 Jan. 1829   StCh
Iler, Stephen H. to Vergain Roberts 8 Nov. 1832   StCh

116

```
Iler, Wm. to Rebecca Wilson 25 Feb. 1838                              Rall
Iles, James T. to Margret Morrows 21 Jan. 1836                       Md-B
Inge, Braxton J. to Meriam Brickey 5 July 1832                       Wash
Inge, Chesly B. to Avee V. Powell 30 Apr. 1835                       Wash
Inge, Elijah S. to Mary C. Henderson 14 Jan. 1830                    Wash
Ingersoll, Joseph W. to Cynthia Atchinson 4 Aug. 1835               Lewi
Ingland, John M. to Jane Carnahan 6 Oct. 1836                        Wash
Ingle, Petter to Sally Riddles 18 July 1839                          Polk
Inglebaret, Geo. to Elizabeth Hudson 13 June 1831                   Boon
Inglish, Amon to Helena Martin 5 Feb. 1829                           Cole
Inglish, Campbell to Elizabeth Crisp 28 Apr. 1833                    Gree
Inglish, Hutchins B. to Katherine Routen 29 Jan. 1832               Cole
Inglish, James to Polly Vivion 25 Aug. 1823                          Cole
Inglish, John to Mary E. Hughes 23 Oct. 1837                        Cole
Ingram, Elisha to Priscilla Henderson 24 Dec. 1835                  Pk-1
Ingram, James S. to Jane Gorham 28 Oct. 1830                        Rand
Ingram, John to Elviry Smiley 23 Aug. 1827                          Coop
Ingram, John to Hulday Oden 11 Apr. 1833                            Warr
Ingram, John to Verbena A. Brown 12 Mar. 1839                       Barr
Ingram, Jonathan to Elizabeth Uptegrove 15 June 1837               Linc
Ingram, Sidney to Jane Canneax 2 Apr. 1834                          Gree
Ingram, Wm. to Mary Walless 29 Dec. 1810                            CG-1
Inks, Samuel to Polly Huffman 11 July 1839                          Polk
Inlow, Wm. M. to Elizabeth Roberts 9 Oct. 1836                      Pk-1
Inman, James to Letitia Howard 3 Aug. 1826                          Cole
Inskeep, Soloman to Julia Gallaher 14 Mar. 1839                     Shel
Ion, Thomas to Elizabeth Nickolson 21 Nov. 1835                     Md-B
Irons, Wm. to Mary Huffstutter 30 July 1837                         Carr
Irvin, Alexander to Elizabeth Rice 4 Mar. 1834                      Md-A
Irvin, Samuel to Alpha Ingledow 7 Feb. 1832                         Wash
Irvin, Samuel to Mary Andrew 13 Oct. 1836                           Ripl
Irvin, Samuel H.O. to Spicy L.G. Dunkin -- -- 1838                  Davi
Irvin, Wm. to Kitty House 18 Jan. 1827                              Pk-1
Irvine, Albert P. to Mrs. Ann Brown 9 Jan. 1835                     StCh
Irvine, Alexander to M. Dunnica 19 Mar. 1833                        Call
Irvine, Robt. to Evaline Scott 10 Mar. 1836                         Call
Irvine, Samuel to Nancy G. Cole 22 Jan. 1839                        Wash
Isaacs, David to Dicey Lawless 25 Mar. 1826                         Howa
Isbell, John to Katharine Hall 14 Aug. 1837                         Polk
Isbell, John to Nancy Wormington 30 May 1839                        Barr
Isbell, Thomas to Martha Hill 29 Dec. 1838                          CG-B
Isbull, Jason to Emily Ellis 22 June 1823                           Howa
Isgrigg, Wm. to Violet Silvers 8 Mar. 1832                          Wash
Ish, Carroll to Mary B. Baldridge 14 Feb. 1836                      Sali
Ish, Wm. to Martha Huklin 7 June 1819                               Coop
Isles, Peter to Elizabeth M. Hibler 29 June 1834                    Char
Isom, Wm. to Odeal Kelly 13 Feb. 1825                               Md-A
Itson, Wm. to Eliza Snow 6 Oct. 1835                                Wash
Ivens, John to Fanny Yount 20 May 1832                              CG-A
Ives, Wm. to Annis Kilgore 3 Dec. 1821                              Boon
Ivy, Joseph to Betsy Locklear 9 Dec. 1832                           CG-A
Ivy, Martin to Nelly Thomas 7 Dec. 1835                             Ripl


Jack, Alfred to Emeline E. Stapp 13 May 1830                        Lafa
Jack, Lamanzy to Statia Owen 2 Oct. 1828                            Lafa
Jack, Nathanial to Seeny Seebow 27 Sept. 1838                       Pett
Jackman, Porter to Polly Arnold 14 Jan. 1819                        Howa
Jackman, Thomas to Dicey Potter 6 Sept. 1832                        Call
Jacks, Elias to Polly Warden 11 Feb. 1823                           Howa
Jacks, John to Pelina Williams 21 Nov. 1826                         Howa
Jacks, Richard to Catherine Powell 17 Oct. 1839                     Plat
Jackson, ---- to Parthena Lee 4 Feb. 1837                           Ray
Jackson, Aaron to Rachel Morlan 10 Feb. 1831                        StCh
Jackson, Abraham W. to Milicia Hartgrove 28 Aug. 1834              Lafa
```

```
Jackson, Alford to Murfree Tarwater 16 Sept. 1829              Ray
Jackson, Alpheus to Elizabeth Woods 3 Oct. 1839               Monr
Jackson, Andrew to Catherine Bird 18 Jan. 1837               Cole
Jackson, Asia to Mary Handley 30 Jan. 1839                   Clay
Jackson, C.F. to Jane B. Sappington 17 Feb. 1831            Sali
Jackson, Calburn F. to Eliza W. Pearson 27 Nov. 1838        Sali
Jackson, Caleb to Mary A. Brockman 18 Dec. 1834            Howa
Jackson, Clayborn to Nancy Vaugh 16 July 1835              Fran
Jackson, Elijah to Sally Taylor 24 July 1838               Clay
Jackson, Gabriel to Louisa Doke 22 Dec. 1836              Howa
Jackson, Gaines to Lidyia Linville 12 Apr. 1832            Ray
Jackson, Geo. to Crissy Handcock 7 Oct. 1813              StCh
Jackson, Geo. to Malinda Jacks 6 Nov. 1828                Pk-1
Jackson, Gypson P. to Elizabeth Cooper 7 July 1831        Md-A
Jackson, Haden to Louisa Williams 28 Mar. 1838            Ray
Jackson, Israel to Sophronia Y.A.G. Campbell 25 Sept. 1838   Pk-B
Jackson, Jacob to Nancy Burdyne 6 July 1837              StCh
Jackson, James to Edy Hand 18 Mar. 1821                   StGe
Jackson, James to Abby A. Jackson 13 May 1834            Boon
Jackson, James to Lucy Turner 14 Oct. 1834               Boon
Jackson, Jerry to Susan Rice 22 Mar. 1827                Howa
Jackson, John to Abaline Anderson 23 Mar. 1834           Coop
Jackson, John to Rachel Boosinger 16 Mar. 1838           Ray
Jackson, John to Emeline Jameson 27 Oct. 1839            Howa
Jackson, Josiah to Mary McClelland 13 June 1839          Rall
Jackson, Lewis to Elizabeth Seedmon 8 Sept. 1836         John
Jackson, Milton G. to Milly Carson 13 Mar. 1838          Howa
Jackson, Oliver I. to Mary A. Livingston 22 Aug. 1833    Clin
Jackson, Philip to Catherine Hamilton 7 Apr. 1836        Wash
Jackson, Robt. to Sarah A.A. Roan 19 Feb. 1829           Wash
Jackson, Rucker to Polly Calloway 21 Dec. 1824           Md-A
Jackson, Smith to Susan Horine 18 Nov. 1834              Wash
Jackson, Solomon B. to Susannah Gifford 2 Mar. 1831      CG-A
Jackson, Thomas to Mary Marshall 20 Jan. 1824            Howa
Jackson, Thomas to Julian Mifford 2 Aug. 1827            Pk-1
Jackson, Thomas to Mary Baker 31 May 1838                Gasc
Jackson, Thomas A. to Margaret South 10 Nov. 1839        Gasc
Jackson, Tryal E. to Margaret Boils 21 Mar. 1839         Polk
Jackson, Wesley to Elizabeth Waddell 9 Nov. 1834         Pk-1
Jackson, Wm. to Margaret Harrison 23 Sept. 1823          Howa
Jackson, Wm. J. to Jane Shelby 21 Aug. 1834              Howa
Jackson, Wm. J. to Sarah E. Wren 31 Oct. 1839            Call
Jackson, Wm. T. to Mahaly Garret 14 June 1835            Wash
Jackson, Yearly to Adeline Ervin 7 May 1835              Linc
Jacoba, Francis to Telitha Bonderant 31 Oct. 1833        Pk-1
Jacobs, Clayton to Mary A. Hardwood 22 Mar. 1836         Ray
Jacobs, James to Polly A. White 2 May 1839               Boon
Jacobs, John W. to Auri J. Hix 29 Mar. 1837              Morg
Jacobs, Joseph to Jane Dailey 1 Sept. 1839               Boon
Jacobs, Thomas to Lydia Dawson 9 Nov. 1834               Call
Jacobs, Thomas W. to Elizabeth A. Lomax 5 May 1835       Clay
Jacobs, Willis to Lucy A. White 6 Aug. 1839              Boon
Jacoby, Samuel to Ann Givens 21 Dec. 1837                Pk-B
Jacson, John J. to Emily Pain 6 Mar. 1837                Wash
Jamerson, Willis to Fanny Stone 20 Nov. 1827             Rall
James, ---- to Mary Boyd 17 Jan. 1839                    Call
James, Allen to Elizabeth Daniel 9 May 1837              John
James, Berry to Piety Ross 25 Sept. 1831                 Lafa
James, Calvin to Nancy Smith 9 Oct. 1837                 Clin
James, Calvin to Mahala Leatherston 27 Nov. 1839         Warr
James, Calvin C. to Perlina Tucker 26 Mar. 1839          Cass
James, David to Eleanor Horton 26 May 1833               Rand
James, Henry to Elizabeth A. Sensebaugh 22 Dec. 1825     Lafa
James, Jacob to Katherine Yount 6 Oct. 1812              CG-1
James, Jacob to Nancy Bridges 1 Jan. 1837                CG-A
```

```
James, James Jr. to Caroline Pendleton 12 Mar. 1835          Clay
James, James to Lavica Taylor 28 Jan. 1838                   Gree
James, Joseph to Barbery Bullinger 7 Feb. 1828              CG-A
James, Morris to Mary Beasley 5 Sept. 1830                   Pk-1
James, Lewis to Mary Vail 19 Feb. 1829                       Pk-1
James, Nelson to Mary Fields 7 Dec. 1839                     Buch
James, Nicholas to Nancy Hamilton 4 Oct. 1833               Lafa
James, Phineas to Rhodian Delany 6 Dec. 1827                 Fran
James, Thomas W. to Adeline Crooks 22 Nov. 1838             Lewi
James, Wm. to Reliance Booth 21 Aug. 1834                    Carr
James, Wm. to Evaline Blackburn 24 May 1838                 Call
Jameson, Geo. M. to Nancy Jordon 31 Oct. 1839              Cr-1
Jameson, Harris to Nelly Barnes 1 Mar. 1818                 Howa
Jameson, James to Susan E. Buckner 20 Nov. 1835            Monr
Jameson, James C. to Mary Jameson 1 Apr. 1832               Linc
Jameson, Newton to Pamela Smith 21 Jan. 1836               Call
Jameson, Samuel to Caroline Sherwood 13 Oct. 1836          Pk-1
Jamison, Durret H. to Elizabeth Ausburn 29 Dec. 1825       Fran
Jamison, James Jr. to Easter Brown 23 Apr. 1835            Pk-1
Jamison, James to Mrs. Elizabeth Steele 27 May 1835        Pk-1
Jamison, James W. to Martitia Eller 7 Apr. 1836            Coop
Jamison, John to Susan Power 27 Apr. 1823                   Boon
Jamison, John to Susan Harris 16 Feb. 1837                  Boon
Jamison, John to Margaret Hodges 6 Jan. 1839               Fran
Jamison, Samuel to Malinda Harris 10 Aug. 1826            Boon
Jamison, Webster to Nancy Peyton 22 Feb. 1833             StFr
Jamisson, Adam to Nancy Sherwood 8 Apr. 1830              Pk-1
Janis, Anthony to Felicita Bogy 14 Nov. 1826              StGe
Janis, Antoine to Marguerite Lebeau 19 Nov. 1817          StCh
Janis, John B. to Louisa Lacroix 18 Sept. 1832            StCh
Janis, Maximilian to Marguerite Lauraint 22 Jan. 1833     StCh
Janis, Nicholas to Mary Beauchemin 15 Jan. 1827           StCh
January, John to Margaret Catlet 31 July 1838             Clin
Jarete, Isaac to Eloyser Bruer 30 Apr. 1829               Perr
Jarrell, John to Elizabeth A. Dawson 14 June 1839         Bent
Jarvais, Joseph to Josephine Joyong 16 Apr. 1811          StCh
Jarvis, Wm. to Laney Boalding 21 Jan. 1827                Fran
Jarvis, Wm. to Jane Poynter 11 May 1834                   Gasc
Jarvis, Wm. F. to Rebecca R. Vanlandingham 7 Nov. 1839    Mari
Jasper, Herman H. to Catharina B. Freeman 1 Jan. 1838     StCh
Jasper, Herman H. to Catharine B. Tieman 1 Jan. 1838      Warr
Javnes, Louis to Delindy Hayes 21 Mar. 1815               StCh
Jawan, David to Amy Philips 30 May 1833                   Call
Jefferies, Matthew to Eliza Moss 19 Jan. 1832             Boon
Jeffers, Geo. to Elizabeth Poteet 19 Oct. 1820            Howa
Jeffers, Hughah to Lucy A. Knole 8 Sept. 1836             Mari
Jefferson, James to Sally Palmer 6 May 1832               Boon
Jeffries, Achilles to Elizabeth Bell 14 Mar. 1833         Fran
Jeffries, Cuthbert S. to Susannah Williamson 13 Sept. 1827  Fran
Jeffries, Dixon to Rachel E. Hoover 13 July 1838          Gree
Jenkins, Aaron to Mary J. Fristoe 4 Feb. 1836             Pett
Jenkins, Eliab to Esther Burnam 26 Jan. 1837             StCh
Jenkins, Elijah to Mary McCray 1 Aug. 1838                Clin
Jenkins, Geo. to Mary Hughes 7 Oct. 1838                  Boon
Jenkins, James L. to Nancy Tuly 2 July 1835               Lewi
Jenkins, James M. to Polly A. Armstrong 27 Oct. 1839      Davi
Jenkins, John to Elizabeth Woodson 8 Dec. 1836            Pk-1
Jenkins, John H. to Silvy Whitlock 4 Jan. 1837            Gree
Jenkins, Solomon to Jane Wells 15 Jan. 1838               StCh
Jennings, Allen to Lucinda Whitsell 20 Jan. 1828          Lafa
Jennings, Benj. to Lucinda Jennings 2 Apr. 1838           Barr
Jennings, James to Polly Roberts 27 Jan. 1820             Howa
Jennings, James to Elizabeth Sanders 11 Nov. 1829         Howa
Jennings, James to Caroline Fletcher 28 Oct. 1838         Lafa
Jennings, John to Sarah McAlroy 19 June 1823              Lafa
```

Jennings, John to Elmira Hopper 3 Jan. 1836 — Lafa
Jennings, Moses to Mary Standiford 9 Nov. 1827 — Howa
Jennings, Thomas to Pottly Coats 22 Jan. 1826 — Boon
Jennings, Tipton to Elizabeth Robinson 1 Nov. 1838 — Lafa
Jennings, Wm. to Elizabeth Hopper 9 Mar. 1828 — Lafa
Jennings, Wm. O. to Mary M. Nave 12 Nov. 1835 — Lafa
Jentery, Westly to Susan Estes 5 Nov. 1839 — Clin
Jeragar, Bucklon to Polly Gawsin 3 Aug. 1820 — Howa
Jesse, James to Margaret Price 5 Oct. 1833 — Call
Jesserton, Jesse to Dolly Houx 23 June 1834 — Coop
Jeter, Benj. F. to Mary J. Burkhart 5 Oct. 1837 — Howa
Jeter, Lloyd to Mary M. Masterson 24 Aug. 1837 — Mari
Jett, Stephen to Patsy Parker 1 Apr. 1834 — Pk-1
Jewel, Jasper to Mrs. Mary Williams 18 Feb. 1835 — Pk-1
Jewel, Robt. to Mary Galliway 18 Dec. 1831 — Gasc
Jewell, Robt. to Elvira Shivers 14 July 1839 — Gasc
Jewell, Wm. L. to Patience Thomas 29 May 1838 — Linc
Jewett, Nathan to Ann E. Graham 30 May 1839 — Bent
Jimerson, Allen to Katherine Savage 13 Sept. 1838 — Polk
Jimerson, John to Polly Gillerland 12 Nov. 1825 — Linc
Jinkens, Ephraim to Margrat McDowel 16 Dec. 1830 — Pk-1
Jinkerson, Geo. to Elizabeth Copling 1 Mar. 1820 — Howa
Jinkins, Richard P. to Sarah E. Mahan 7 Jan. 1836 — Mari
Jinkinson, Geo. to Jane Simpson 31 Aug. 1828 — Wash
Job, Abraham to Margaret Reeves 13 Oct. 1822 — Coop
Job, Bartholmew to Morgan Williams 21 Nov. 1833 — Coop
Job, Jacob to Parthena Hinch 13 Nov. 1817 — Howa
Jobe, Abraham to Matilda Crum 7 Jan. 1836 — Cole
Jobe, Abram to Clarinda Chandler 26 Dec. 1838 — Cole
Jobe, Elisha to Elizabeth Williams 25 Mar. 1827 — Cole
Jobe, Logan to Mary Sailing 16 Sept. 1825 — Cole
Jobe, Robt. to Margaret Atkins 11 Feb. 1838 — Davi
John, Samuel to Mary Cave 16 Sept. 1838 — Boon
Johns, ---- to Hannah Lasly 12 Sept. 1830 — Fran
Johns, Caleb to Nancy Woodland 24 Nov. 1831 — Fran
Johns, Christopher to ---- ---- 6 Dec. 1832 — Coop
Johns, Curtus to Melby Taylor 26 Jan. 1831 — Howa
Johns, Geo. W. to Nancy J. Pritchett 30 Apr. 1837 — Fran
Johns, James to Julia Martin 25 June 1820 — StCh
Johns, Samuel to Louisa Robnett 27 May 1830 — Fran
Johns, Thomas to Agnes Boyd 9 Jan. 1834 — Fran
Johns, Wm. to Matilda Shookman 23 Feb. 1835 — Gasc
Johnson, Abner to Lucinda Green 13 Mar. 1837 — Char
Johnson, Alexander to Mary Logan 5 Nov. 1839 — Coop
Johnson, Alfred to Huldah Sandford 11 Mar. 1821 — Howa
Johnson, Barry to Rachel Cheaney 9 Dec. 1829 — Boon
Johnson, Bazle to Nancy Campbell 29 Sept. 1836 — StCh
Johnson, Benj. to Eliza Murle 12 Oct. 1828 — Wash
Johnson, Berryman to Sally Norris 23 Feb. 1834 — Lafa
Johnson, Billington to Nancy Sally 14 Mar. 1834 — Pett
Johnson, Calvin to Nancy Bailey 22 Dec. 1831 — Wash
Johnson, Charles to Kiriah Trapp 18 Oct. 1827 — Jack
Johnson, Clark to Barbary Millsap 1 Jan. 1826 — Coop
Johnson, Clasbourn to Sarah Bartlett 16 June 1836 — Morg
Johnson, D. to M.A. Petty 8 Aug. 1833 — Call
Johnson, David to Mournin Kelly 15 Jan. 1827 — Coop
Johnson, David to Anna Johnson 24 Jan. 1830 — Lafa
Johnson, David to Jane Bradley 26 Nov. 1835 — Howa
Johnson, David to Mary A. Johnson 22 Feb. 1837 — Clay
Johnson, David to Frances E. Cook 12 Dec. 1839 — Jack
Johnson, Edward to Sally Young 30 Nov. 1821 — CG-A
Johnson, Edward to Margaret Routh 8 Jan. 1839 — Plat
Johnson, Eli B. to Amelia Patton 3 Jan. 1837 — Warr
Johnson, Elijah to Sarah Douglas 11 Apr. 1838 — Boon
Johnson, Enos M. to Mahala Isenhaur 27 Feb. 1831 — CG-A

```
Johnson, Ettel to Elizabeth Travis 23 Dec. 1821                          Coop
Johnson, Evans to Angelique LeFevre 28 May 1834                          StCh
Johnson, Gabriel to Ruthie Morris 10 May 1827                           Wash
Johnson, Geo. A. to Jane McDow 4 Apr. 1827                              Boon
Johnson, Henry to Isabela Stuart 28 May 1829                           Cr-P
Johnson, Henry to Judith Haghn 5 Oct. 1837                             CG-A
Johnson, Irvin to Elizabeth A. Maggard 2 Mar. 1836                     Rand
Johnson, Jacob to Mary A. Davidson 14 Nov. 1839                        Fran
Johnson, James to Nancy Becket 1 July 1827                             Coop
Johnson, James to Maryan Taylor 9 Feb. 1830                            Coop
Johnson, James to Mary A. Boulware 4 Jan. 1831                         Mari
Johnson, James to Ruth Catch 18 May 1831                               Wash
Johnson, James to Rebecca Christman 16 May 1833                        Jack
Johnson, James to Melvina Parmer 12 Apr. 1836                          Carr
Johnson, James to Katharine McGee 28 Feb. 1839                         Jack
Johnson, James B. to Dorinda Stone 18 Dec. 1836                        Linc
Johnson, James R. to Hannah Baker 1 Aug. 1839                          CG-B
Johnson, Jefferson to Martha Thompson 11 July 1830                     Cr-P
Johnson, Jesse to Becky Von 18 Nov. 1827                               Coop
Johnson, John to Elizabeth Wilkinson 22 Oct. 1805                      CGRA
Johnson, John to Sarah Moore 24 Dec. 1820                              Coop
Johnson, John to Mrs. Mary Moring 21 Feb. 1828                         StCh
Johnson, John to Mary Johnson 26 Sept. 1833                            Jack
Johnson, John to Catharine Clodfelter 30 Apr. 1835                     CG-B
Johnson, John to Milly Moore 16 June 1836                              Md-B
Johnson, John to Eave Bollinger 3 Aug. 1837                            CG-A
Johnson, John to Elizabeth A. Mahony 1 Apr. 1839                       Warr
Johnson, John Bte. to Celeste Levry 27 Nov. 1826                       StGe
Johnson, John C. to Rebecca Trotter 17 May 1831                        Mari
Johnson, John C. to Hannah Nave 22 Nov. 1838                           Sali
Johnson, John E.T. to Elizabeth A. Robertson 17 Dec. 1835             Coop
Johnson, John H. to Judith A.C. Shores 17 Oct. 1830                    Wash
Johnson, John M. to Polly Edinger 27 Sept. 1831                        CG-A
Johnson, John M. to Elizabeth Watson 7 May 1839                        CG-B
Johnson, John N. to Elizabeth Beaty 7 Aug. 1834                        Carr
Johnson, John W. to Pamelia Cheaney 30 Dec. 1836                       Boon
Johnson, Joseph to Sally A. Brower 26 June 1836                        Mari
Johnson, Joseph to Elizabeth Anderson 30 Dec. 1838                     Lewi
Johnson, Larkin Jr. to Judah Johnson 19 Dec. 1839                      Jack
Johnson, Lewis to Cynthia Johnson 15 Nov. 1836                         Lafa
Johnson, Luther to Francis Wall 27 Oct. 1831                           Wash
Johnson, Martin to Comfort Drace 26 Dec. 1837                          Fran
Johnson, Mathew to Artimissa Buis 12 June 1831                         CG-A
Johnson, Milas to Mary Dooley 6 Dec. 1838                              Monr
Johnson, Moses to Nancy Cole 4 Dec. 1823                               Lafa
Johnson, Nevil to Catherine Hammons 17 July 1833                       Coop
Johnson, Perry to Mary J. Limbrick 26 Mar. 1835                        Pk-1
Johnson, Reuben to Hezeah Givens 10 Oct. 1837                          Howa
Johnson, Robt. to Elender Prowel 6 Apr. 1824                           Cole
Johnson, Ruben to Peney Hicks 10 Nov. 1836                             Wash
Johnson, Samuel to Sally Travis 1 Mar. 1818                            Howa
Johnson, Samuel to Margaret Hanna 18 Oct. 1828                         Boon
Johnson, Samuel to Elvira Morrison 19 July 1830                        Wash
Johnson, Samuel to Elizabeth Freeman 28 Dec. 1834                      Rand
Johnson, Samuel A. to Sarah Wilson 23 June 1831                        StCh
Johnson, Shelby to Emellina Stivers 16 Oct. 1834                       Boon
Johnson, Snelling to Prudence Hackney 21 May 1826                      Cole
Johnson, Solomon to Dianah Hinshaw 19 Feb. 1839                        Howa
Johnson, Tabin to Rebecca OBannion 28 Aug. 1833                        Coop
Johnson, Thomas to Liddy Keeney 9 June 1827                            Coop
Johnson, Thomas to Jane Lubbastose 21 Jan. 1830                        Fran
Johnson, Rev. Thomas to Sarah T. Davis 7 Sept. 1830                    Pk-1
Johnson, Thomas to Elvira Newel 23 Apr. 1834                           Cole
Johnson, Thomas to Margaret A. Craddock 8 May 1836                     Md-B
Johnson, Thomas to Catharine Heyde 7 Mar. 1837                         Cr-1
```

Johnson, Thomas M. to Eleanor Steel 28 Dec. 1837   Gree
Johnson, Uriah to Clara Frizell 15 Jan. 1830   Md-A
Johnson, Valentine M. to Susan Husley 1 Apr. 1838   Wash
Johnson, Vincent to Lucy Allison 2 Oct. 1823   Coop
Johnson, Wiley to Caroline Johnson 30 Nov. 1837   Fran
Johnson, Wm. to Mahala Varel 14 July 1828   Boon
Johnson, Wm. to Margaret Ennis 8 Apr. 1829   Lafa
Johnson, Wm. to Eleanor Clement 16 Aug. 1829   Cr-P
Johnson, Wm. to Sarah L. Gholson 25 Aug. 1829   Md-A
Johnson, Wm. to Elizabeth Russell 27 June 1830   Cole
Johnson, Wm. to Elizabeth Smith 10 June 1833   Boon
Johnson, Wm. to Eleanor S.J. Robinson 8 May 1834   Boon
Johnson, Wm. to Mary J. Chick 28 May 1834   Howa
Johnson, Wm. to Sally Stockston 8 Dec. 1836   Fran
Johnson, Wm. to Luson Riggs 15 May 1837   Cole
Johnson, Wm. to Rebecca S. Adams 4 Dec. 1837   Clay
Johnson, Wm. to Michell Dill 15 Nov. 1838   Cr-1
Johnson, Wm. to Lucille Caulin 12 June 1839   StCh
Johnson, Wm. to Masinai Gordon 28 July 1839   Linc
Johnson, Wm. B. to Mary J. McGirk 9 Aug. 1827   Howa
Johnson, Wm. G. to Eliza Greenee 15 Oct. 1835   Rall
Johnson, Wm. M. to Polly Grayham 24 Dec. 1837   Md-B
Johnson, Whiting to Mary Wilson 22 Feb. 1836   Lewi
Johnston, B. Jr. to Charlotte Tyler 30 Sept. 1834   Jeff
Johnston, Dison to Malinda Dent 5 Mar. 1829   Fran
Johnston, Gabriel to Elizabeth Humphreys 17 July 1828   Char
Johnston, Isaac to Margaret Reed 3 Dec. 1833   Boon
Johnston, Jacob to Prudence Story 23 Dec. 1825   Coop
Johnston, John to Milandy Lambert 21 Nov. 1824   Howa
Johnston, John to Polly Bacon 10 May 1826   Fran
Johnston, John to Charlotte Clark 6 Sept. 1827   Jeff
Johnston, John H. to Eliza Wise 6 Apr. 1827   Jeff
Johnston, Joseph to Louisa Williams 23 June 1836   StFr
Johnston, Julius D. to Neville Christy 10 Dec. 1834   StCh
Johnston, Noble to Peggy Pinkerton 31 Jan. 1829   Perr
Johnston, Thomas to Synthis Jackson 20 Nov. 1825   Md-A
Johnston, Thomas T. to Margaret Watson 14 June 1836   Pk-1
Johnston, Wesley to Mary Bruffee 17 Mar. 1831   Coop
Johnston, Wm. to Sary Rawlings 5 Aug. 1826   Howa
Johnston, Wm. to Sally Cartmill 30 Jan. 1831   Lafa
Joliff, James to Lusinday Burriss 18 Apr. 1838   Ripl
Jollin, Charles to Pelagia Larose 9 Oct. 1833   Wash
Jolly, Joseph to Rebecca Cathey 8 Dec. 1836   Coop
Jolly, Wm. to Sally Nanney 12 Mar. 1826   Coop
Jones, Ambrose to Mrs. Elizabeth A.J. Brown 5 July 1836 Clay
Jones, Augustus to Agnes W. Hunter 13 Oct. 1826   Wash
Jones, Benj. to Sarah Hinson 12 Aug. 1822   Gasc
Jones, Benj. to Jane Jones 28 Mar. 1827   Coop
Jones, Benj. A. to Maria J. Cross 22 May 1822   CG-1
Jones, Berry to Sally Titus 1 Dec. 1839   Carr
Jones, Berry W. to Orpah P. Cross 5 Feb. 1835   Char
Jones, Calvin to Eliza Scott 13 Jan. 1833   Mari
Jones, Clende to Sarah C. Truman 10 June 1839   Livi
Jones, David Jr. to Elizabeth Flood 3 May 1832   Md-A
Jones, David N. to Martha A.L. Townson 30 Mar. 1837   Coop
Jones, Elijah to Elizabeth R. Wills 19 Apr. 1836   CG-A
Jones, Elisha to Rachael P. Sharp 26 May 1839   Md-B
Jones, Fielding to Julia A. Keithly 19 Dec. 1839   StCh
Jones, Fountain to Mary Becket 16 Oct. 1831   Mari
Jones, Francis to Catherine Stover 25 Nov. 1839   Pett
Jones, Geo. to Nancy Hokell 5 Feb. 1835   Clay
Jones, Geo. W. to Jain Ward 17 Mar. 1831   Cr-P
Jones, Harrison to Sarah Upton 5 July 1837   Perr
Jones, Harrison to Paula Little 22 Jan. 1839   Boon
Jones, Heath to Artimissa Briscoe 5 Nov. 1835   Rall

```
Jones, Isaac D. to Mariah J. Dawson 11 Aug. 1836            Cole
Jones, Jabez to Martha Harris 20 Oct. 1831                 Coop
Jones, Jackson to Rebecca Jones 17 Jan. 1839               Barr
Jones, Jacob to Mary Simpson 12 Aug. 1828                  Jeff
Jones, James to Nancy Easten 28 July 1825                  Boon
Jones, James to Mary Dunn 17 Apr. 1831                     CG-A
Jones, James to Rosannah Morgan 4 Mar. 1833                CG-A
Jones, James to Nancy Jones 12 Dec. 1833                   Mari
Jones, James to Barthena Cross 19 Nov. 1835                Char
Jones, James to Nancy A. Self 11 Apr. 1839                 Morg
Jones  James H. to Ann Roades 20 Aug. 1835                 Fran
Jones, Jefferson to Jane Winkleblack 23 Nov. 1839          Buch
Jones, Jesse to Eliza Learue 28 Sept. 1834                 Cr-1
Jones, Jesse to Sarah Christian 21 June 1835               Rand
Jones, Jesse to Agnes J. Taylor 28 Mar. 1837              Coop
Jones, Jesse to Emma R. McMillan 27 May 1838               Cole
Jones, John to Barbery Cross 5 May 1818                    Howa
Jones, John to Frances Lee 3 June 1827                     Howa
Jones, John to Lydia Sidener 18 Dec. 1827                  Pk-1
Jones, John to Francis Anderson 31 Dec. 1829              Mari
Jones, John to Jane Sullens 3 Feb. 1830                    Jeff
Jones, John to Mary A. Landlin 19 Jan. 1834                Pk-1
Jones, John to Mrs. Margaret Kingston 1 Mar. 1837          Pk-A
Jones, John to Susan Ballew 24 Dec. 1837                   Polk
Jones, John C. to Maria Brinker 30 Oct. 1834               Wash
Jones, John J. to Rebecca Reynolds 13 May 1827             Call
Jones, John K. to Elizabeth Santee 1 May 1837              Md-B
Jones, John L. to Polly White 13 July 1828                 Char
Jones, Jonathan to Mary Robertson 1 Apr. 1827              StCh
Jones, Jonathan W. to Marietta Musick 27 Aug. 1837         Fran
Jones, Jordon to Nancy M. McMillen 22 May 1830             Cole
Jones, Judson to Maria Godman 29 Dec. 1831                 Mari
Jones, Lawson C. to Nancy Anderson 7 June 1829             Mari
Jones, Leander to Mrs. Sarah Potter 9 Sept. 1830           Clay
Jones, Lewis to Elizabeth McKinney 16 Jan. 1820            Howa
Jones, Lewis to Mary Christison 13 Nov. 1831               Jack
Jones, Lewis to Mary Willbarger 28 June 1837               Pk-A
Jones, Lewis C. to Mary McCrary 18 Aug. 1837               Coop
Jones, Lewis G. to Nancy Pepper 26 Sept. 1839              Mari
Jones, Martin M. to Elizabeth Wallace 24 Jan. 1836         Rand
Jones, Marvel M. to Barshewy Potter 9 Nov. 1828            Clay
Jones, Maryland to Sally Anderson 22 Dec. 1825             Pk-1
Jones, Michael I. to Emily Alford 27 Mar. 1838             Rall
Jones, Oliver to Jane Brown 8 Feb. 1827                    StFr
Jones, Quiller to Matilda Brown 13 Aug. 1837               Polk
Jones, Reason to Ruth E. Montgomery 24 Dec. 1835           Polk
Jones, Reese to Elizabeth Bevins 21 Mar. 1837              Howa
Jones, Richard to Eliza Michael 9 Jan. 1839                Ripl
Jones, Richard R. to Eliza C. Chambers 22 Feb. 1838        Fran
Jones, Richard R.W. Jr. to Rulina Dean 23 Feb. 1832        Mari
Jones, Robt. to Susannah Teetore 10 May 1823               StCh
Jones, Robt. to Fellacinda Sympson 10 June 1830            Call
Jones, Robt. to Alcy C. Whitledge 5 Mar. 1835              Pk-1
Jones, Robt. H. to Mariah Ramsay 5 June 1828               Cole
Jones, Samuel N. to Mrs. Frances Love 3 Jan. 1839          Pk-B
Jones, Singleton to Agnes Neale 12 Nov. 1838               Boon
Jones, Stephen to Louisa Dodge 31 Dec. 1837               Clin
Jones, Thomas to Sarah Young 20 Oct. 1836                  Call
Jones, Thomas to Margaret Duley 8 June 1837                Call
Jones, Thomas to Mrs. Sarey Dale 15 July 1837              Rand
Jones, Wesley to Matilda Patrick 10 Feb. 1831              Rand
Jones, Wiley to Mart Proctor 5 Oct. 1833                   Cole
Jones, Wilkinson to Mary Johnson 25 Apr. 1831              Howa
Jones, Wm. to Rebecca Walkup 15 Nov. 1825                  Boon
Jones, Wm. to Polly Henderson 8 Nov. 1826                  CG-A
```

Jones, Wm. to Martha A. Davis 10 Dec. 1826   Perr
Jones, Wm. to Margaret Stephenson 17 June 1828   Howa
Jones, Wm. to Sally Sadler 23 June 1831   Monr
Jones, Wm. to Nancy Bess 9 Jan. 1834   Cole
Jones, Wm. to Amanda Miller 20 Feb. 1834   Call
Jones, Wm. to Emily Ford -- Feb. 1837   Boon
Jones, Wm. to Nancy Morgan 8 Aug. 1837   Char
Jones, Wm. to Elizabeth Jones 1 Mar. 1838   Call
Jones, Wm. to Mary Bridges 28 Apr. 1838   Clay
Jones, Wm. to Ann Drennen 2 May 1838   Jeff
Jones, Wm. to Jane Rausdale 12 Aug. 1838   Monr
Jones, Wm. to Susan Lang 1 Dec. 1838   Char
Jones, Wm. H. to Mary J. Williams 3 Feb. 1831   Pk-1
Jones, Wm. J.W. to Rachel Tolly 31 May 1836   Polk
Jonston, Elijah to Delila Hunsaker 22 Nov. 1829   Mari
Jonston, James to Hester A. Tailor 13 Mar. 1829   Rall
Jonston, James to Elvina Hughs 28 Jan. 1836   Gasc
Joolley, John to Kiziah Waddle 19 Oct. 1837   Gree
Joplin, Harris G. to Holly Sims 23 Jan. 1834   Gree
Joplin, Wm. to Mary Clark 24 Nov. 1836   Pett
Jopson, Samuel to Mary Toomey 26 Mar. 1834   Jack
Jordan, Elisha H. to Jane Boggs 6 Jan. 1839   StCh
Jordan, Harris to Lucy A. Darvies 30 Oct. 1839   Monr
Jordan, James A. to Julian Smith 29 Apr. 1830   Pk-1
Jordan, James D. to Malissa Barnes 16 Apr. 1839   Coop
Jordan, John to Elizabeth Underwood 17 Aug. 1830 Pk-1
Jordan, John C. to Nancy Underwood 23 Mar. 1830   Pk-1
Jordan, John M. to Sarah Jones 22 June 1826   Pk-1
Jordan, John R. to Mrs. Laura Parks 22 Jan. 1835 Pk-1
Jordan, Robt. to Clarissa Sears 31 Mar. 1838   Howa
Jordan, Robt. B. to Isipheny Allison 24 Aug. 1826 Pk-1
Jordon, John H. to Nancy Waggoner 11 Feb. 1830   CG-A
Josli, Wm. to Sophia Anders 22 July 1834   Perr
Joster, Ellison to Edy Byrd 19 July 1836   CG-A
Jott, Denis to Margaret Adams 29 Nov. 1828   Fran
Jourdain, Andrew to Hellene Lucien 15 Feb. 1831   StCh
Jourdan, Calbert to Catharine Denton 14 Jan. 1836 Monr
Jourdon, Wm. H. to Mary Garland 12 May 1833   Lewi
Journey, Andrew J. to Ann E. Tagert 15 Dec. 1836 StCh
Journey, Joseph to Polly Zumwalt 11 Aug. 1814   StCh
Jovnes, John to Minerva Callaway 22 Oct. 1818   StCh
Juden, G.W. to Ellenor Shackleford 27 Mar. 1832   CG-A
Juden, John to Abby Block 23 Oct. 1828   CG-A
Julian, Alfred M. to Susanna Owen 16 May 1839   Gree
Julian, R.C. to Polly Wilson 5 Sept. 1839   Gree
Jump, James to Rebecca Gibson 31 Oct. 1839   Gasc
Junifer, John S. to Jemima Mase 30 July 1829   Rall
Jurdon, John B. to Elizabeth Gilbert 1 Sept. 1836 Mari
Justice, Stewart to Lucinda Lovel 20 Mar. 1838   Mari

Kahal, Thomas to Mary Allen 10 Mar. 1834   Gree
Kanada, Charles C. to Sarah A. Jones 28 Aug. 1837 Fran
Kanox, Ezekiel to Mary Hughes 10 Nov. 1829   Perr
Kare, Thomas to Mariah Fristoe 23 Feb. 1830   Howa
Karn, Geo. to Regina Beil 15 July 1838   StCh
Karrick, Geo. O. to Amanda Goza 8 July 1823   StGe
Kase, John H. to Catherine Engel 1 May 1836   StCh
Kavanaugh, Archibald to Mary A. Ewing 11 July 1821 Coop
Kavanaugh, Patrick to Margaret Munday 12 Dec. 1839 Wash
Kavanaugh, Wm. M. to Polly Hancock 16 Nov. 1818   Howa
Kavenaugh, Charles C. to Tabitha C. McLean 15 Dec. 1830 Coop
Kaylor, Wm. M. to Emeline G. Manning 13 Oct. 1836 Lewi
Keach, John to Polly Lake 29 Mar. 1832   Mari
Keatchlen, Geo. to Anna Austin 6 June 1811   StCh

124

```
Keath, Judson M. to Sarah Hammer 6 Sept. 1831                          Pk-1
Keathley, Absolom to Sina Costley 14 Jan. 1819                         StCh
Keathley, Obedia to Hermacinthia Scott 28 Apr. 1836                   StCh
Keathly, Eli to Nancy Aulman 9 Aug. 1832                              Pk-1
Keathly, Levi to Elenor Bell 5 Apr. 1836                              Rall
Keaton, Henry to Cyan Reed 21 Mar. 1833                               Call
Kee-s, Obadiah to Mary A. Carter 1 Jan. 1826                         Gasc
Keel, Wm. to Susan Barker 8 Aug. 1839                                 Ripl
Keen, Henry to Sarah William 31 Aug. 1837                            Boon
Keene, James to Sarah Johnson 2 Feb. 1832                             Boon
Keeney, Isbey to Elizabeth Keeney 29 Jan. 1832                       Sali
Keenough, Frederick to Sinderella Marshall 15 Aug. 1839               Lewi
Keeny, James to Modest Keeny 19 Mar. 1832                             Coop
Keeny, Joseph to Winny Chesney 27 Dec. 1827                          Jack
Keeny, Joseph to  Susan Trowley 17 June 1836                          Ray
Keepey, Lewis to Parrylee Chandler 10 Oct. 1839                       Jeff
Keeth, Wm. to Elizabeth Brewer 9 Apr. 1834                            Wash
Keeton, Thomas to Sarah Reed 28 June 1827                            Boon
Kefer, Joseph to Kitty Stafford 10 July 1828                          Lafa
Keiffer, John to Nancy B. Fugate 14 Sept. 1839                       Audr
Keill, Christian to Mary Sheppard 4 Apr. 1833                         Howa
Keiser, Christopher to Rebecca Holding 19 May 1828                   Mari
Keiser, John to Matilda Bird 11 May 1826                             Rall
Keith, James to Catherine Manning 8 May 1831                          StFr
Keith, Pleasant G. to Clarinda Baker 18 Aug. 1831                     StFr
Keithley, Abraham to Lucretia Derwit 2 Apr. 1830                      Linc
Keithley, Isaac to Elizabeth Northcutt 23 Oct. 1834                  Warr
Keithley, Jonathan to Ella Robertson 16 Mar. 1834                    Linc
Keithley, Joseph to Palina Barshears 23 Apr. 1835                    Pk-1
Keithly, Daniel to Elizabeth Hostetter 18 Dec. 1832                  StCh
Keithly, Nathaniel to Mary Northcut 31 Jan. 1839                     Warr
Keithly, Wm. to Lottie Costly 23 Nov. 1815                           StCh
Keithly, Wm. R. to Julia A. Haizlip 19 May 1836                      StCh
Kelison, John to Margaret B. Lockridge 8 Apr. 1830                   Call
Kell, John to Nancy Martin 7 Feb. 1826                               Coop
Keller, John to Nancy Zumwalt 22 June 1837                           StCh
Kelley, Geo. to Elizabeth Hipkins 30 Sept. 1838                      Mari
Kelley, Wm. to Susan A. Shannon 26 June 1838                         Mari
Kellison, Absalom to Mary Palmer 31 Aug. 1837                        Morg
Kellogg, Silvester to Elizabeth A. Calvert 5 Apr. 1832              Coop
Kelly, Alexander to Margaret Mansker 6 July 1834                     CG-B
Kelly, Benj. to Mary Bennet 17 Nov. 1825                             Md-A
Kelly, Jacob to Ann Hayden 9 May 1826                                Perr
Kelly, James to Elizabeth Mullins 17 Aug. 1839                       Coop
Kelly, John to Bitha Lawless 27 Mar. 1821                            Howa
Kelly, John to Sally S. Ray 20 Aug. 1832                             Lafa
Kelly, John to Nancy Davis 26 Jan. 1837                              Sali
Kelly, Joseph to Nancy Guthrie 29 Aug. 1839                          Monr
Kelly, Joshua to Catharine A. Martin 25 Jan. 1835                    Cole
Kelly, Moses to Louisa Block 23 Oct. 1828                            CG-A
Kelly, Richard to Eliza Smith 27 May 1838                            Barr
Kelly, Stephen to Mary McSy 6 Apr. 1837                              Md-B
Kelly, Thomas to Nancy Zumwalt 7 Dec. 1821                           StCh
Kelsey, James to Margaret Kelsey 16 Dec. 1831                        Coop
Kelsey, Samuel to Lucretia Applegate 5 Mar. 1835                     Cole
Kelso, Edward to Nancy Byrd 13 Sept. 1838                            CG-A
Kelsy, Andrew to Mary Kelsy 18 June 1839                             Henr
Kelsy, Benj. to Nancy Roberts 25 Oct. 1838                           Henr
Kemp, Jourdan to Mary Dunlap 19 May 1831                             Call
Kemp, Robt. M. to Nancy P. Craghead 22 Jan. 1839                     Call
Kemp, Wm. to Lizean Gardener 16 Oct. 1834                            Call
Kemper, Enoch to Mary A. Holsclaw 28 Sept. 1830                      Howa
Kemper, Enoch to Sarah A. Pilcher 13 Aug. 1835                       Howa
Kemper, John to Jane Bowyer 20 Apr. 1832                             Howa
Kemper, John H. to Angel C.D. Meyor 25 Dec. 1839                     Gasc
```

Kemper, Octavus to Eliza A. Palmer 25 July 1839   Linc
Kemper, Wm. to Rachel Mattock 28 Feb. 1839   Shel
Kenada, Greenberry to Demerius Bruk 7 Feb. 1839   Boon
Kenard, Jesse to Rachel Cheaney 8 Oct. 1839   Boon
Kendel, S.F. to Catherine Sumner 2 May 1833   StCh
Kenedy, John to Ann Cayce 8 May 1834   StFr
Keneer, John to Rebecca Berry 31 Oct. 1833   Monr
Kennada, Charles to Lucy Williamson 15 Sept. 1838   Fran
Kennan, Samuel to Harriet Rogers 5 Sept. 1833   Boon
Kennan, Thomas to Ann Cave 10 Mar. 1821   Boon
Kennedy, Asa to Harriet Hopkins 17 Dec. 1839   Polk
Kennedy, Housen to Lucinda Mahan 24 Dec. 1833   Monr
Kennedy, James to Sarah Lisles 10 Jan. 1816   StCh
Kennedy, John to Martha Donagair -- -- 1832   Coop
Kennedy, John to Nancy Brockman 18 July 1838   Sali
Kennedy, Josephus to Rachel Griffith 29 May 1824   StFr
Kennedy, Shelton to Catharine Hays 27 Aug. 1834   Pk-1
Kennel, Archibald W. to Phebe A. Smith 12 Nov. 1839   Cole
Kennett, L.M. to Martha Boyce 15 Sept. 1832   StFr
Kenney, Azariah to Manima Dunnicah 22 Dec. 1825   Cole
Kenney, James to Fanny Vivion 30 Nov. 1818   Howa
Kenney, John to Mary A. O'Brien 23 July 1833   Rall
Kenney, Robt. to Hannah Miller 18 Mar. 1827   Cole
Kenny, John to Lamira Yount 9 Oct. 1828   Call
Kenny, Micle to Luncell Backus 26 Dec. 1839   Gasc
Kenny, Nicholas to Polly Herrington 10 Jan. 1834   Rall
Kenny, Richard to Polly Cooper 24 Apr. 1828   Cole
Kent, Dozier to Nancy Collard 21 Jan. 1834   Warr
Kent, John to Catherine Zumwalt 21 Sept. 1817   StCh
Kenyon, James to Sindareler Hubble 2 Sept. 1825   CG-A
Kenyon, John to Mary Brooks 29 Mar. 1832   CG-A
Kerby, Asa to Elvira Blue 14 June 1826   Char
Kerby, David to Nancy Johnson 16 May 1825   Char
Kerby, Overton J. to Ann E. Cheatham 19 Mar. 1839   Sali
Kerby, Solomon to Rhoda Duncan 15 June 1832   Rand
Kerby, Wade to Emuld Blue 23 Feb. 1832   Rand
Kerby, Wm. to Matilda Sears 17 July 1823   Char
Kerby, Wm. to Polly Bartee 20 Dec. 1832   Howa
Kerby, Yewen to Sally Rowland 17 Dec. 1834   Rand
Kerforth, Geo. A. to Lousindia Fretwell 2 May 1838   Lewi
Kerkendoll, Wiat to Vashti Glover 2 Oct. 1834   Cole
Kerkindol, Jeffry to Mary Saling 14 Sept. 1830   Rall
Kerley, Henry to Elizabeth Daniel 30 Mar. 1833   Gasc
Kerley, Henry to Nancy Miller 14 Jan. 1838   Gasc
Kerley, Wm. to Margaret Colvin 23 July 1835   Gasc
Kerney, Peter to Francis Cheaney 8 Aug. 1830   Boon
Kerr, D. James A. to Martha M. Bell 16 July 1827   Char
Kerr, John to Sally Wells 13 June 1833   Pk-1
Kerr, Wm. to Patsy Draper 19 Jan. 1826   Linc
Kester, John to Dorette Huhne 29 Oct. 1837   StCh
Kester, Samuel H. to Sarah Simpson 11 Feb. 1838   Call
Ketchum, John to Pheby Dunn 16 June 1839   Howa
Ketchum, Joseph to Sophia Parsons 5 Apr. 1835   Clay
Kethley, James to Susannah Hodges 21 May 1835   Gree
Ketton, James to Nancy Card 1 Mar. 1833   Coop
Key, Lewis to Edy Wood 9 July 1837   Cr-1
Key, Wm. to Lovina Stafford 27 Feb. 1831   Cr-P
Keys, Francis to Nancy Miller 23 June 1831   Ray
Keys, John to Mary A. Woolard 14 Apr. 1836   Ray
Keyton, John to Margaret Briscoe 10 Oct. 1828   Coop
Keyton, Wm. E. to Nancy D. Cole 29 June 1826   Coop
Kibbey, Alfred to Cynthia Harrison 9 June 1831   Call
Kibler, ---- to Mary Armstrong 4 Apr. 1828   Call
Kibler, Christian to Elizabeth Hahs 22 Sept. 1838   CG-A
Kibler, David to Sally Statler 6 Oct. 1836   CG-A

```
Kidd, Benj. to Rachail Creasman 16 July 1839                    Mari
Kidd, Thomas to Edy Speed 14 Feb. 1836                         Gree
Kidd, Wm. to Minerva Hopkins 18 July 1835                      Mari
Kidd, Wm. to Elizabeth Lester 29 June 1837                     Mari
Kidwell, Henry to Nancy Mullins 16 Sept. 1830                  Mari
Kidwell, Wm. M. to Elizabeth A. Odell 17 Dec. 1835            Lewi
Kiell, Henry to Hannah M. Cross 22 July 1824                   StGe
Kierley, James to Mary Flatt 7 Jan. 1830                      Gasc
Kies, Harrison to Eliza Herreck 12 Apr. 1834                  Clay
Kilby, Abraham E. to Rhoda Parsons 22 Mar. 1832              Pk-1
Kilby, Caswell to Patsy Standford 6 Oct. 1832               Pk-1
Kile, John to Delilah Bilford 12 Dec. 1822                   Boon
Kilgore, Charles to Catherine Cockran 18 Feb. 1836          Shel
Kilgore, John to Margaret Willingham 28 June 1831           Call
Kilgore, John to Patsey Williams 11 Dec. 1835               Call
Kilgore, John H. to Pamela D. Kilgore 25 Feb. 1836          Call
Kilgore, Samuel to Dicy Boon 20 Oct. 1836                    Lewi
Killebrew, John to Sally Dearst 18 Aug. 1806                StCh
Killeon, John to Lydia Conley 25 Aug. 1818                   Howa
Killian, Philip to Polly Bivens 14 May 1837                 CG-A
Killibrew, John to Cynthia Bryan 11 Nov. 1813               StCh
Kim, John to Elizabeth Brokehoff 5 July 1838                Gasc
Kimberling, Nathaniel to Nancy Birchfield 27 Oct. 1825      Wash
Kimble, David to Sarah A. Cooper 3 July 1838                Howa
Kimbrough, James to Rhoda Hannah 21 July 1836               Rand
Kimbrough, John to Lucinda Hamilton 5 Dec. 1833             Rand
Kimbrough, Thompson C. to Nancy W. Jackson 15 Aug. 1839     Rand
Kimmel, Joseph S. to Caroline M. Manning 16 Feb. 1830       Perr
Kimmell, Cyrus F. to Malinda Reed 2 Nov. 1831               Perr
Kimsey, James to Susannah O. Walker 9 Apr. 1836             Henr
Kimsey, John to Susannah Brock 30 June 1833                 Jack
Kimsey, Samuel to Emily Conner 7 Mar. 1832                  Jack
Kimson, Landers to Nicy Kimson 17 Nov. 1839                 CG-B
Kincade, John to Caroline Campbell 22 July 1828             Pk-1
Kincaid, Andrew to Elizabeth Barnes 24 Feb. 1835            Boon
Kincaid, John P. to Elizabeth Robertson 8 May 1838          Ray
Kincaid, Joseph to Nancy Kincaid 12 Jan. 1824              Boon
Kincaid, Lewis to Elizabeth Abbott 18 Dec. 1823            Boon
Kincaid, Wm. to Rebecca McDonald 28 May 1824               Boon
Kincaid, Wm. M. to Jane Woolery 11 Feb. 1836               Mari
Kinder, Adam to Hannah Hill 25 Nov. 1827                    CG-A
Kinder, Adam to Sally Devore 22 Oct. 1837                   CG-A
Kinder, Eli to Elizabeth Duncan 8 June 1834                CG-B
Kinder, Jacob to Rachel Ramsey 6 May 1830                   CG-A
Kinder, Jacob to Elizabeth Moyers 23 May 1837              CG-A
Kinder, Joel to Syrena Thompson 11 Sept. 1828             CG-A
Kinder, Joel to Mary Devore 10 Mar. 1836                   CG-A
Kinder, John to Rachel Moiers 16 Feb. 1832                 Md-A
Kinder, Michael to Margerate Meyers 29 Mar. 1832           Md-A
King, Aaron to Elizabeth Gross 4 Dec. 1838                 Char
King, Abel to Cynthia E. Tilford 9 Nov. 1837              Clay
King, Abraham B. to Harriet Stonebreaker 1 July 1834       Linc
King, Benj. to Sarah J. Riley 1 Feb. 1838                  Clay
King, Carson to Nancy Humphry 20 Dec. 1832                 Pk-1
King, David to Beulah Webb 17 Jan. 1828                    Howa
King, David to Nelly Pierson 19 Apr. 1829                  Char
King, Edward to Elizabeth Hafter 1 Dec. 1839               Rand
King, Enoch to Sarah Brown 16 Oct. 1839                    Clay
King, Harrison to Mary Spires 25 July 1833                 Warr
King, Isaac to Polly A. Haynes 14 Feb. 1839                Clin
King, James to Elizabeth Haun 31 Jan. 1828                 StCh
King, John to Elizabeth McKinney 4 Apr. 1811               StCh
King, John to Polly Clay 1 Mar. 1829                       StCh
King, John to Narcissus Conger 29 Oct. 1835                Call
King, John S. to Harriet Oden 5 Apr. 1833                 Pk-1
```

127

King, Moses to Manerva Titus 8 Apr. 1834   Howa
King, Richard to Eleanor Cline 10 Nov. 1839   Linc
King, Samuel to Eunice Wilcox 28 Aug. 1828   Mari
King, Samuel to Ann Willbarger 13 Apr. 1837   Pk-A
King, Samuel M. to Paulina Guinn rec. 8 Mar. 1834   Mari
King, Stephen to Cynthia Cheaney 28 Oct. 1830   Boon
King, Thomas to Elizabeth Hall 11 May 1828   Howa
King, Thomas A. to Elizabeth A. Jacobs 19 Dec. 1837   Ray
King, Thomas H. to Sarah A. McWilliams 25 Oct. 1838   Mari
King, Wm. to Polly Haines 6 Sept. 1832   Coop
King, Wm. to Polly Young 31 Jan. 1836   Fran
King, Wm. to Lucy King 8 Mar. 1836   Char
King, Wm. D. to Margaret Thomson 3 Sept. 1834   Lafa
King, Wm. Z.D. to Mira B. Bone 7 Aug. 1834   Lafa
Kingery, Andrew to Elizabeth Degraffenreid 26 Feb. 1837   Mill
Kingkaid, John to Sarah McDando 6 Apr. 1820   Howa
Kingry, Greenbury to Jane Barlow 14 Dec. 1838   Cole
Kingsbury, Ira to Melcena Gibson 5 Jan. 1835   Linc
Kingsbury, Noah to Nancy Hughes 24 Dec. 1835   Howa
Kingston, John to Harriet Holland 27 July 1837   Pk-B
Kinion, Benj. Jr. to Polly Early 20 Oct. 1831   Linc
Kinion, Lemuel to Sarah Hall 10 Nov. 1831   Linc
Kinizer, Geo. to Amanda Yeates 11 Oct. 1838   Rand
Kinkead, Allen to Mary Price 14 June 1838   Call
Kinkead, Andrew B. to Rebecca Elgin 2 Nov. 1837   StFr
Kinkead, James to Susanna Hughes 15 Sept. 1835   Wash
Kinnard, Beverly to Emely Scott 6 Nov. 1834   Wash
Kinneman, Erasmus to Wineford Brock 10 June 1827   Fran
Kinney, James to Jane Williams 20 Dec. 1829   Pk-1
Kinney, Nathan to Margaret Saunders 13 Apr. 1836   StFr
Kinnison, Lewis to Charity Devore 13 Oct. 1839   CG-B
Kinnison, Presley to Mary Richardson 29 Dec. 1829   Perr
Kinnison, Stephen B. to Nancy Mahan 12 June 1836   Perr
Kinnon, Wm. to Rachel Cox 21 July 1831   Linc
Kinsey, Alvis to Casey Simpson 29 May 1839   Plat
Kinsey, Benj. to Betsy Morris 2 Jan. 1820   Howa
Kinsey, Soloman to Mary Bradley 25 July 1821   Howa
Kirby, Jesse to Elizabeth Brashear 23 Feb. 1834   Howa
Kirby, Wm. to Polly Finnell 6 Aug. 1835   Howa
Kirk, Joseph to Nancy Jepson 30 Jan. 1831   Mari
Kirk, Milan to Ruth Boyd 26 July 1835   Coop
Kirkendall, Moses to Susan Brown 13 Jan. 1833   Jack
Kirkendall, Wiette to Jane Stone 24 Apr. 1832   Coop
Kirkendell, Wm. to Malvina Amick 28 Feb. 1833   Coop
Kirkepatrick, Joseph to Patsey Ross 4 Dec. 1822   CG-1
Kirkham, Thomas J. to Louisianna Wills 12 Sept. 1838   Pk-B
Kirkindoll, Benj. to Matilda Self 9 Oct. 1831   Lafa
Kirkpatrick, David to Machael Wright 28 Mar. 1827   Boon
Kirkpatrick, Finnis E. to Margart Gott 20 Feb. 1827   Coop
Kirkpatrick, John to Jane Mainer 4 Sept. 1839   Plat
Kirkpatrick, Marcus to Sarah A. Christian 3 May 1832   Rand
Kirkpatrick, Robert to Jane Morris 9 Jan. 1821   Howa
Kirkpatrick, Robert to Catherine Blag 12 Apr. 1838   Wash
Kirkpatrick, Wm. to Matilda Wooton 16 Dec. 1827   StCh
Kirkpatrick, Wm. to Mary Winifree 20 Nov. 1837   Carr
Kirney, John to Sarah Scaggs 18 Dec. 1828   Jeff
Kistler, Frederic to Sally McCoy 24 Dec. 1822   StCh
Kitchen, Wm. to Angelina Yates 15 May 1839   Buch
Kitching, Wm. to Sally Wahhul 18 June 1838   Fran
Kizer, Peter S. to Eliza A. Fegines 28 Sept. 1837   Mari
Klain, Wm. to Vinecea Massey 20 June 1837   Perr
Kling, Wm. to Eliza A. Allen 8 June 1837   Pk-A
Klinger, Ludwig to Louisa E. Knupper 9 Jan. 1838   StCh
Klinghammer, Andrew to Mary Reel 18 Nov. 1838   StCh
Knaus, Henry to Elizabeth Monroe 16 Mar. 1821   Howa

```
Knaus, Henry Jr. to Nancy Maxwell 18 Dec. 1828                          Howa
Knaus, Jacob to Catharine Maxwell 12 Apr. 1832                          Howa
Knave, John to Elizabeth Kelly 24 Dec. 1823                            Sali
Knight, Jonathan to Aley Sanders 22 Dec. 1839                          Ripl
Knight, Mathew M. to Sophrenia Moore 28 Feb. 1833                      Md-A
Knight, Simeon to Sally Sollars 14 Dec. 1831                          Clay
Knot, Henry to Elizabeth Brewer 26 Nov. 1839                          Perr
Knott, David to Louise Barada 5 Sept. 1833                            StCh
Knott, Hilary to Mariah Brewer 12 Feb. 1833                           Perr
Knott, J.A. to Virginia Block 17 Aug. 1837                            CG-A
Knott, Lloyd W. to Martha A. Allen 26 June 1834                       Lewi
Knott, Wm. B. to Martha A. McClellande 11 Sept. 1834                  StCh
Knowel, John to Malinda Jackson 23 Feb. 1836                          Jack
Knox, Geo. to Amanda Gaw 3 May 1834                                   Boon
Knox, Henry to Lucinda Hunter 11 Feb. 1830                            Linc
Knox, Joseph A. to Nancy Allen 12 Nov. 1835                           Henr
Knox, Mathen to Nancy Gallaway 19 Dec. 1833                           Linc
Knox, Thomas to Elizabeth Benson 23 July 1837                         Howa
Knox, Washington to Ellen Gain 13 Sept. 1836                          Boon
Knuckles, Garland to Lavina Glove 26 Feb. 1828                        Wash
Knust, Albrecht to Albertina Kayser 16 Apr. 1837                      StCh
Koch, Ferdinand to Louisa Pfeifer 15 Nov. 1836                        StCh
Kolly, James W. to Nancy Taylor 9 June 1837                           Morg
Konig, F. Ernest to A. Elizabeth Weinrich 18 Sept. 1837              StCh
Konyon, John to Elizabeth Cantrell 24 Sept. 1829                      Linc
Koons, Eanos to Margaret Akens 1 Feb. 1835                            Wash
Kosters, Bernadus J. to Margaret A. Kostens 10 Apr. 1837             Cole
Krichbaum, John G. to Anna M. Muller 28 July 1839                     StCh
Krigbaum, Jacob to Maria Brandon 6 Aug. 1826                          Rall
Kritzmeyer, Fredolin to Adelaide Hoskins 18 Mar. 1839                Cole
Kruger, Adolphus to Emelie Rathge 15 Apr. 1837                        Fran
Kruze, Tolamich to Elizabeth Koster 28 Sept. 1839                     StCh
Kunce, Henry to Margaret Welker 6 June 1828                           CG-A
Kuntze, Charles A. to Elizabeth Cumton 9 Apr. 1835                    Warr
Kunzel, Edward to Catharina Gallingharst 14 Feb. 1837                 Warr


Laberge, Charles to Marguerite LeBeau 15 Jan. 1827                    StCh
Labuyer, Julien to Eulalie Buatte 5 Sept. 1826                       StGe
Lacey, Charles C. to Sarah J. Maupin 22 Jan. 1835                     Jeff
Lacey, John L. to Almyra Church 1 Oct. 1832                           Mari
Lachance, Francis Jr. to Mary L. Lachance 6 Feb. 1826                Md-A
Lachance, Francis to Francious LaComb 6 Jan. 1827                    Md-A
Lachance, Francis C. to Magdalena Griford 11 May 1837               Md-B
LaChance, Lewis to Margaret LaChance 8 Jan. 1833                     Md-A
Lachance, Nicholas to Jane Crawford 23 Mar. 1837                     Md-B
Lack, John A. to Martha A. Crowder 13 Jan. 1836                       Fran
Lackey, James to Susan Ashby 19 Mar. 1836                            Clay
LaComb, Nicholas to Elleanor Rober 21 Aug. 1834                      Md-A
Lacroix, Auguste to Brigitte Saucier 3 Nov. 1835                     StCh
Lacy, Cravenor to Mary Patrick 24 Aug. 1837                          Coop
Lacy, John K. to Susan A. Massie 29 Sept. 1835                       Coop
Lacy, Richard D. to Margaret E. Nelson 30 Apr. 1835                 Mari
Lacy, Richard E. to Sophia Tucker 12 Mar. 1838                        Ray
Ladd, Thomas to Sarah Lloyd 18 Mar. 1835                             Gasc
Lady, Joseph to Martha Doke 27 Jan. 1835                             Jack
Laffaun, Preston P. to Eliza J. Miller 25 June 1835                 Clay
Lafferty, Lawson V. to Hester A. Martin 2 Dec. 1834                 Pk-1
Laffoon, Alexander to Hatty Ellis 28 Dec. 1837                       Jeff
Laffoon, Peyton to Mary J. Church 16 May 1839                       Clin
Lafon, Atwell to Margaret Fisher 15 May 1834                         Mari
LaFour, Charles to Martha Baradas 11 Apr. 1837                       StCh
Lafune, Geo. to Malinda Averett 28 Sept. 1828                        Clay
Laghin, Samuel to Nancy Doty 5 Jan. 1830                             Linc
Lain, Joseph to Mahala Newberry 17 Apr. 1831                         Cr-P
```

```
Lair, John to Margaret Looney 20 Mar. 1834                          Monr
Lair, Robt. to Elizabeth Culberson 11 Dec. 1834                     Mari
Lair, Thomas to Catherine Anderson 3 Oct. 1830                      Mari
Lair, Wm. to Mrs. Eliza A. Bradley 23 Aug. 1836                     Mari
Lair, Wm. W. to Elizabeth L. Bradley 8 Nov. 1838                    Mari
Lake, Charles to Betsy Schofield 17 Jan. 1822                       Rall
Lake, Daniel to Mary Turpin 18 Aug. 1831                            Mari
Lake, Enoch to Nancy Scofield 20 Jan. 1825                          Rall
Lake, Geo. W. to Lucinda Swift 9 June 1830                          Lafa
Lake, Thomas to Barbary Whaley 1 Dec. 1825                          Rall
Lakey, Joshua to Polly Brown 20 Aug. 1819                           Coop
Laliberty, Peter to Liner Revaux 11 Feb. 1833                       Jack
Lally, Daniel W. to Jane S. Sims 8 May 1828                         Boon
Lally, Geo. to Ally Brown 12 Oct. 1828                              Gasc
Lamb, James to Elizabeth Crow 5 Dec. 1833                           Pk-1
Lamb, Talbert to Elizabeth Coy 22 Sept. 1829                        Howa
Lamb, Talbot to Action Bunch 1 Feb. 1834                            Char
Lamb, Thomas to Lucindy Nickerson 28 Apr. 1836                      Howa
Lamb, Wm. to Missouri A. George 30 Nov. 1837                        Howa
Lambert, Augusta to Joanna Rhodes 19 Nov. 1837                      Call
Lambert, Eli to Peggy Bolin 7 July 1832                             Howa
Lambert, Elisha to Nancy Wilson 1 Sept. 1836                        Boon
Lambert, Geo. to Sarah Hubble 21 May 1829                           CG-A
Lambert, Gilbert to Eliza Walls 3 Apr. 1831                         CG-A
Lambert, Samuel to Clerindy Garner 19 Aug. 1832                     CG-A
Lambert, Wm. to Susannah Burnett 13 Apr. 1828                       Call
Lambreth, Daniel to Nancy Miller 30 Oct. 1838                       Gasc
Lamkins, Edward to Lucinda Wharton 9 Jan. 1834                      Boon
Lamm, John to Caroline Pusely 26 May 1838                           Coop
Lampkin, Daniel to Nancy Michel 27 June 1819                        Howa
Lampkin, James C. to Phebe M. Fishback 15 Dec. 1835                 Mari
Lampkin, Robt. to Sarah Hurt 11 Dec. 1836                           Howa
Lampkins, John to Ruth Minter 13 Sept. 1822                         Boon
Lampton, John W. to Marilda A. Bruce 20 Feb. 1838                   Coop
Lampton, Wm. to Polly Fountain 30 Nov. 1830                         Boon
Lance, Isaac B. to Violett Baker 21 Feb. 1822                       Clay
Lance, Moses to Zerpha Graham 12 Sept. 1826                         Md-A
Land, Joshua to Elizabeth Moore 30 Apr. 1837                        Boon
Land, Thomas to Jane McCullough 23 Mar. 1833                        Jack
Landers, Benj. to Mary Pendergras 27 Sept. 1818                     StCh
Landers, James to Margaret Lewis 23 July 1839                       Buch
Landers, Wm. to Betsy Tate 30 Aug. 1810                             StCh
Landers, Wm. to Nancy Hoover 26 Feb. 1839                           Barr
Landingham, Wm. to Rebecca K. Landingham 24 Nov. 1838              Ray
Landrum, Wm. to Polly Mulkey 1 Jan. 1822                            Cole
Lane, Benj. to Charity Huntsucker 25 Aug. 1833                      Jack
Lane, Lewis to Mildred Westerfield 9 Sept. 1831                     Boon
Lane, Martin to Jane Caldwell 23 Mar. 1826                          Fran
Lane, Mordeca to Rebecca Rice 8 June 1829                           Char
Lane, Peter to Nancy Rice 14 Feb. 1838                              Mari
Lane, Washington F. to Mary N. Daugherty 6 Nov. 1838               Pk-B
Laneheart, Wm. to Mary Ritchie 14 Sept. 1828                       Clay
Lanford, James to Amanda R. Fort 20 Mar. 1839                       Rand
Langley, Archibald to Lucinda Freeman 24 Mar. 1839                 Call
Langley, James to Matilda Haynes 22 Jan. 1824                      Call
Langley, James N. to Ruth A. Newton 9 Aug. 1838                    Call
Langley, John to Elizabeth Rose 25 May 1829                        Call
Langley, Joseph to Martha A. Beasley 12 Sept. 1837                 Boon
Langly, Rile to Malinda Taylor 4 Nov. 1830                         Boon
Langly, Thomas to Elizabeth Savage 25 July 1829                    Jack
Langston, Martin to Tempy Swan 18 May 1828                         Boon
Lanier, Edward R. to Jane M. Luckett 3 Nov. 1836                   StCh
Laniers, Jacob to Nancy Long 23 July 1839                          Md-B
Laning, Joseph to Eliza Fleming 22 Apr. 1821                       CG-1
Lankford, Daniel to Hildah C. Young 15 Mar. 1826                   Lafa
```

```
Lankford, Jesse to Nancy Garrett 24 Apr. 1828                        Sali
Lankford, Laurence to Polly McCann 14 July 1836                     Warr
Lankford, Wm. to Lucinda Burton 27 Apr. 1837                        Lafa
Lanms, David to Sophia Hickman 24 Mar. 1829                         Boon
Lanpher, Geo. to Elizabeth Nifong -- Nov. 1832                      Md-A
Lansdown, Geo. W. to Mary A. Dixon 24 Feb. 1835                     Cole
Lanters, Asa to Nancy Wright 4 Mar. 1836                            Howa
Lapp, David to Permelia A. Armstrong 8 Mar. 1832                    Linc
Lapp, Isaac to Jemina Hubbard 9 Feb. 1832                           Linc
Lapp, Samuel to Malinda Lapp 27 July 1826                           Linc
Lapoch, David to Zalanna Clayton 14 Dec. 1838/9                     Perr
Lapton, Samuel to Sary Mattuck 30 Oct. 1830                         StCh
Lard, Hezekiah A. to Mary C. Cheatwood 23 Apr. 1835                 Rall
Laremore, James to Orpha Greenstreet 29 Nov. 1827                   Fran
Laremore, Pinkney to Ann Cheek 4 Jan. 1838                          Fran
Larne, Felix G. to Nancy McDaniel 2 Mar. 1834                       Cole
Larose, Antoine to Marie Maurice 31 Jan. 1826                       StGe
Larose, Felix to Emelie Thomur 30 Jan. 1827                         StGe
Larsh, Worthington to Priscilla R. Yantis 27 Oct. 1836             Lafa
Larue, Aaron to Maria Sitton 31 Aug. 1834                          Call
Larue, Anthony to Phebe Shoemate 17 Dec. 1835                       Cr-1
Larue, Isom to Elizabeth Shoemate 18 June 1834                      Cr-1
Larue, Jabez to Sally Laugherty 14 Aug. 1814                        CG-1
Larue, John R. to Charlotte Barnes 1 Apr. 1832                      Howa
Lasater, Hezekiah Jr. to Lavena Harris 7 June 1836                  StFr
Lashment, Wm. D. to Mary C. Martin 5 Sept. 1838                     Clay
Lasity, Hezekiah to Mary Holt 27 Aug. 1835                          StFr
Lasley, John to Esther Ray 4 Feb. 1830                              CG-A
Lasource, Louis to Odille Bives 15 Jan. 1833                        Md-A
Lassley, Thomas to Mary A. Graves 3 Aug. 1837                       StCh
Latham, Wm. K. to Elvira C. Bunch 15 Jan. 1836                      Polk
Lathlin, Bailey to Salina Agee 3 Dec. 1835                          Call
Lathlin, Samuel to Franky Coats 22 Oct. 1829                        Call
Lathrope, John to Elizabeth Coffin 17 Jan. 1827                     Howa
Latimer, Milton to Susan Kinsworthy 19 June 1826                    StFr
Latimore, Robt. to Eliza Houk 12 Mar. 1837                          Wash
Latour, Joseph to Francois Goudin 30 Apr. 1830                      StCh
Latraille, Louis to Judith Brugiere 22 Jan. 1838                    StCh
Latreille, Gabriel to Mary L. Perau 18 Nov. 1835                    StCh
LaTrielle, Antoine to Mrs. Mary Tayon 18 Nov. 1834                  StCh
Laughlin, Henry to Rachel Reed 17 Jan. 1838                         Ripl
Laughlin, James to Nancy McCoy -- Aug. 1836                         Linc
Laughlin, John M. to Magdalene Alkire 6 Mar. 1823                   Gasc
Laughlin, Robt. R. to Elizabeth McNight 29 Nov. 1836               Gasc
Laughlin, Samuel to Sally Agee 18 Oct. 1832                         Gasc
Laughlin, Stephen to Margaret Kimbro 14 Jan. 1836                   Rand
Laughlin, Wm. to Mary Eddz 30 Sept. 1823                            Gasc
Laughnberg, John H. to Lotta Wehr 5 Sept. 1839                      Fran
Lauk, Aloys to Juliane Fisher 9 Jan. 1837                           Perr
Laune, Joseph to Jane Davis 7 Nov. 1835                             Coop
Laurain, Louis to Odille Denney 5 Oct. 1829                         StCh
Laurain, Peter to Florance Martinau 21 Sept. 1829                   StCh
Lavalette, Pierre to Catherine Uno 30 July 1807                     StCh
Law, Green to Elizabeth Pinkerton 13 Apr. 1837                      Perr
Lawler, Timothy to Mary Brian 4 Mar. 1827                           Coop
Lawless, Bird to Elizabeth G. Scott 9 Dec. 1824                     Howa
Lawless, Burton to Nancy Humphreys 27 Aug. 1818                     Howa
Lawless, John to Sophia Ikard 20 Dec. 1835                          CG-B
Lawless, Mastin to Susannah Pipes 8 Nov. 1821                       Boon
Lawrence, Benj. F. to Emeline Shaw 26 Sept. 1836                    StFr
Lawrence, Edward to Evey Murdock 21 June 1839                       Call
Lawrence, Greenville C. to Deborah January 1 July 1835             Ray
Lawrence, Martin to Maria Davis 12 Jan. 1823                        CG-1
Lawrence, Ratia to Frances Neale 24 Aug. 1834                       CG-A
Lawrence, Wm. F. to Mary S. Mills 13 Feb. 1839                      Coop
```

131

```
Laws, Alfred to Pernela I. Epperson 20 Dec. 1838            Jack
Lawson, Jeremiah S. to Matha Hieronymus / Mar. 1839         Howa
Lawson, Samuel to Polly Miller 25 Mar. 1835                 Cole
Lawson, Wm. F. to Sally Anderson 15 June 1836               Cole
Lay, Alfred to Letty Litnel 4 Feb. 1830                     Howa
Lay, Daniel to Sarah A. Neal 1 Mar. 1836                    Howa
Lay, Jesse to Fanny Horton 24 June 1829                     Jack
Layne, Ayres to Polly Sidener 8 Jan. 1828                   Pk-1
Layne, John to Ann Porter 5 Apr. 1827                       Pk-1
Layson, Josiah to Mary Young 13 Dec. 1832                   Call
Layton, Adair to Edith Summers 28 Mar. 1833                 Morg
Layton, Andrew to Cecily Tucker 3 Jan. 1837                 Perr
Layton, Anselm to Elizabeth Miles 25 Nov. 1834             Perr
Layton, Austin to Theressia Duvall 4 Sept. 1832            Perr
Layton, Austin to Lucinda Riney 4 July 1837               Perr
Layton, Bede H. to Mary Duvall 25 July 1837               Perr
Layton, Edward C. to Emely C. Foley 11 Jan. 1838          Lewi
Layton, Ignatius to Cecilia Miles 5 Oct. 1830            Perr
Layton, Ignatius to Mary D. Brewer 25 July 1837          Perr
Layton, James to Mary Maddock 31 July 1832               Perr
Layton, John to Marcella Maddock 11 June 1832            Perr
Layton, Joseph to Catherine Moore 30 Oct. 1827           Perr
Layton, Joseph to Melany A.E. Moore 25 Nov. 1834         Perr
Layton, Leo to Mary M. McAttee 17 Oct. 1827              Perr
Layton, Lewis to Perneleanna Miles 7 May 1838            Perr
Layton, Sylvarum to Juliane Tucker 22 Apr. 1839          Perr
Layton, Vincent to Mrs. Clotilday Manning 22 Apr. 1839   Perr
Lea, Geo. to Melinda Garner 13 Oct. 1828                 Mari
Lea, James to Mahala Clay 4 Sept. 1834                   Cole
Leach, Adlai to Mary A. Ramsey 8 Sept. 1839              CG-B
Leach, Frederick to Matilda Giboney 16 May 1827          CG-A
Leach, John to Louisa Snell 15 Dec. 1831                 Howa
Leach, Presley to Paulina Crews 23 Aug. 1832             Howa
League, Christopher to Jane Holmes 26 Mar. 1835          Wash
League, Wesley to Emily Richards 5 Oct. 1836             Linc
League, Wm. to Agnes Head 15 Feb. 1822                   Boon
Leake, Gravil to Elizabeth Riddle 10 July 1838           Rall
Leake, James to Verlindie A. Hardy 13 Oct. 1831          Rall
Leake, James to Mrs. Ann Carter 28 Mar. 1837             Rall
Leake, James to Mary Leake 24 July 1839                  Rall
Leake, Robt. to Ellenor Elliott 10 Apr. 1834             Rall
Leake, Wm. to Mary Z. Pierceall 5 Dec. 1837              Monr
Leaky, Jeremiah to Ann Burch 25 Mar. 1838                Howa
Leaky, John to Ailsey Huit 18 Mar. 1821                  Howa
Leaky, Wm. to Cynthia Burton 16 Nov. 1826                Howa
Lear, Adison to Nancy Wood 6 Oct. 1836                   Mari
Lear, Henry to Mary Reed 26 Nov. 1835                    Mari
Lear, John to Nancy Becket 24 Apr. 1834                  Mari
Lear, Martin to Matilda Kerby 16 Dec. 1821               Char
Lear, Thomas to Julia A. Nichols 4 Feb. 1836             Mari
Lear, Wm. to Elizabeth Ingraham 14 Mar. 1839             Mari
Leaton, Reuben to Editha Leaton 8 Apr. 1834              Lafa
Leaton, Wm. to Elizabeth Thompson 22 Dec. 1835           Linc
Leavenworth, Ralph to Polly Hinch 11 Nov. 1819           StGe
LeBeau, Ambrose to Victoire Beauchemin 15 Feb. 1835      StCh
LeBeau, John B. to Felicite Janis 20 Jan. 1829           StCh
Lebō, Samuel to Sally Wilson 20 Apr. 1833                Ray
Lebo, Wm. H. to Caroline McFarland 24 Apr. 1838          Morg
LeClari, Francis to Mary Noval 8 Nov. 1830               StCh
Leclere, Francios to Elizabeth Hoff 28 July 1829         Wash
LeCompte, Hilarie to Emelie Janis 23 Jan. 1827           StGe
Ledford, Daniel to Margaret White 12 Jan. 1837           Lewi
Ledford, James to Mary Rice 31 July 1838                 Rall
Ledford, John to Emily Adkins 22 Aug. 1839               Rall
Ledgerwood, John to Matilda George 19 Mar. 1829          Clay
```

Lee, Archillus to Rebecca Null 3 Jan. 1828   Jeff
Lee, Burrell to Ann M. Smith 1 Sept. 1833   CG-A
Lee, Francis to Jane V. Johnson 4 Oct. 1835   Clay
Lee, Giles to Ara Graham 28 Oct. 1838   Jeff
Lee, Hiram to Elizabeth Cheek 23 Mar. 1826   CG-A
Lee, Jacob to Elizabeth Mills 11 Jan. 1838   Barr
Lee, James to Elizabeth Brazel 2 Aug. 1837   Ripl
Lee, James to Mrs. Margaret Garnett 14 Dec. 1837   Rall
Lee, John to Stacy Phillips 20 Apr. 1833   Ray
Lee, Lilbernk to Fanney Estes 6 Dec. 1838   Barr
Lee, Noah to Rebecca Lacey 18 Oct. 1838   Pett
Lee, Permount to Caroline Roberts 18 Oct. 1839   Livi
Lee, Richard to Nancy Harvey 8 Jan. 1818   Howa
Lee, Richard to Elizabeth Burns 30 Nov. 1834   Perr
Lee, Robt. to Malinda T. Brown 5 Mar. 1829   Ray
Lee, Washington to Amanda Lee 17 Aug. 1836   Sali
Lee, Wm. to Margaret Davis 14 Dec. 1837   Mari
Lee, Wm. B. to Susanna Bradley 16 Dec. 1819   Howa
Leech, David to Mary C. Riggs 5 Sept. 1833   Boon
Leech, John to Elizabeth Drybread 11 Jan. 1821   StGe
Leeney, James to Anny Ramsey 8 Feb. 1821   Lafa
Leeper, Guian to Malinda Murry 28 Apr. 1839   Gree
Leeper, Henry A. to Elenor Campble 7 Nov. 1836   Char
Leeper, James A. to Florence McPheeters 28 Oct. 1825   Call
Leeper, John to Mahala Hobbs 9 June 1831   Pk-1
Leeper, John to Amanda Bayles 27 Feb. 1834   Char
Leeper, John to Catharine Craig 16 June 1836   Gree
Leer, Jacob to Catharine Ewing 9 Apr. 1835   Pk-1
Lefaivre, Auguste to Mary Labelle 25 Jan. 1831   StCh
LeFevre, Alexir to Louise Saucier 2 Mar. 1835   StCh
LeFevre, Alexis to Georgine St. Louis 18 Sept. 1834   StCh
LeFevre, Charles to Poupone LePage 6 Jan. 1835   StCh
LeFevre, Louis to Genevieve Chancellier 11 Feb. 1839   StCh
Leffler, John to Jane Rummons 23 July 1835   Boon
Leffler, John to Larutha March 15 Oct. 1835   Boon
Leffler, Joseph to Polly Brumman 9 Feb. 1832   Boon
Lefler, Elisha to Elizabeth Cannon 4 Dec. 1832   Mari
Lefler, Jacob to Katharine Lindmares 7 June 1838   Warr
Leflet, Augustus to Elizabeth Shobe 19 Dec. 1829   Mari
Lefore, John J. to Martha Inglish 9 Mar. 1837   Polk
Legerwood, Wm. to Delia Parsons 11 Nov. 1838   Clay
Leget, Wm. to Dowy Wilson 2 Oct. 1836   CG-A
Legg, Wm. to Elizabeth Bogarth 11 Nov. 1834   Mari
Leggate, Geo. to Patsy Davis 12 Oct. 1826   CG-A
Leggit, Enoch to Rebecca Robut 31 Feb. 1839   Howa
Leggit, James to Nancy Douglas 3 Sept. 1818   Howa
Leggit, John to Nancy Simson 24 Feb. 1828   Howa
Leggit, Jonathan to Mary Stepp 25 Nov. 1838   Howa
Leggit, Joseph to Rachel Leaky 11 Mar. 1827   Howa
Leiper, David to Martha Scott 25 Jan. 1832   Call
Leiper, James to Elizabeth Edwards 26 July 1838   Warr
LeJeunesse, Baptiste to Mrs. Emilie Gueril 9 Feb. 1835   StCh
Leking, James to Elizabeth Rogers 8 Mar. 1839   Jeff
Lemasters, Wm. to Jenitia Tyler 5 Nov. 1837   StFr
Lemey, Patrick to Jane Hogg 20 Dec. 1819   Coop
Lemmas, John to Elizabeth Harrison 7 Aug. 1821   Boon
Lemmon, Wm. to Ben Farley 29 June 1828   Jeff
Lemmons, John to Elizabeth Holcomb 31 Mar. 1836   Lewi
Lemmons, John to Spice South 10 Dec. 1838   Barr
Lemon, Robt. to Amanda Marrs 24 Jan. 1839   Boon
Lemons, Lemuel to Sally Mitchell 27 Jan. 1835   Jack
Lemons, Thaddeus to Sarah Grayham 19 Jan. 1834   Howa
Lenard, Joseph to Sara Grant 10 Dec. 1826   Call
Lenon, David to Elizabeth Brown 18 May 1826   Gasc
Lenox, Hamilton to Mariah Harrison 4 Sept. 1834   Cr-1

Lenox, Wilson to Susannah Brown ? Oct. 1827   Gasc
Leonard, Christian to Priscilla Conrad 19 Feb. 1832   Perr
Leonard, Joseph to Mary Perdum 26 Nov. 1838   Clar
Leonard, Richard to Annthorett Bruce 10 Nov. 1836   Boon
Leopold, Charles to Freemelda Runge 18 Apr. 1838   StCh
LePage, Andrew to Julia Hebert 22 Nov. 1830   StCh
LePage, Etienne to Louisa Renolds 26 Feb. 1838   StCh
Ler, James to Sarah Wood 18 Nov. 1832   Monr
Leroy, Isaac to Athaliah Huff 15 Mar. 1839   Sali
Lesage, Jean Bte. to Francoise Roy 5 Nov. 1833   StCh
Lesieur, Ferdinand to Lucille Saucier 8 Nov. 1830   StCh
Lesley, Alexander to Lucy Williams 14 July 1833   Jeff
Lesly, Andrew to Lucy A. Robb 13 Nov. 1831   Howa
Lesly, Geo. to Mary Neale 1 Mar. 1831   CG-A
Lessley, John W. to Elizabeth Hill 20 Jan. 1837   Rand
Lester, Jesse to Jane Russell 14 Jan. 1819   Howa
Lester, John to Katharine King 24 Mar. 1835   Ripl
Lester, John to Sarah Timmons 1 Sept. 1835   Cr-1
Lester, John C. to Jane Scott 27 Sept. 1838   Lafa
Letbetters, Pleasant to Elizabeth Baker 3 July 1832   CG-A
Letchworth, Thomas to Polly Chisholm 5 Apr. 1821   Coop
Letchworth, Thomas to Margaret Robinson 25 Sept. 1833   Morg
Letney, Lewis to Polly Lowe 15 Feb. 1829   Cr-P
Level, Harvey to Milly Boone 14 Nov. 1833   Call
Level, Wm. H. to Elizabeth Gouge 25 Dec. 1838   Char
Leverage, Reubin L. to Rebecca Monroe 14 Dec. 1826   Howa
Levingston, Samuel to Hannah Maccoun 3 Jan. 1830   Clay
L'Evique, John to Josette Bourdeaux 2 Jan. 1832   StCh
Lewallen, John to Martha A. Pritchett 7 July 1836   Pk-1
Lewell, Thomas to Mary Ridge 16 Sept. 1823   Lafa
Lewellen, Owen to Margaret E. Pritchett 9 Mar. 1837   Pk-A
Lewellen, Robt. to Dicy Benham 10 Oct. 1833   Monr
Lewis, Aaron J. to Nancy Loveless 20 Feb. 1830   Mari
Lewis, Abner to Susan McCoy 14 Jan. 1838   Linc
Lewis, Abram to Elizabeth Cleavenger 5 Feb. 1827   Ray
Lewis, Albert to Rhoda Brickey 12 Apr. 1829   Wash
Lewis, Angrew M. to Mary A. Leer 1 May 1838   Mari
Lewis, Chester to Elizabeth Clair 6 Dec. 1832   Linc
Lewis, Chancy to Elizabeth Lewis 31 Dec. 1837   Wash
Lewis, Comedore C. to Marthyan Hily 18 Feb. 1833   Wash
Lewis, Daniel to Mary Pain 18 Feb. 1821   Boon
Lewis, Elias to Darley Philips 6 Apr. 1834   Call
Lewis, Enos to Sarah A. Andrews 26 Sept. 1837   Wash
Lewis, Ethelbert W. to Rebecca Randolph 31 July 1839   Sali
Lewis, Fielden to Martha Smith 8 Nov. 1838   Pk-B
Lewis, Firnig to Nancy Perringer 21 Jan. 1838   Md-B
Lewis, Francis to Sarah Teasly 3 Feb. 1839   StCh
Lewis, Geo. W. to Mary J. Eidson 13 Mar. 1832   Md-A
Lewis, James to Mary Gregg 20 Nov. 1827   Jack
Lewis, James to Elizabeth Gress 9 Dec. 1830   StCh
Lewis, James to Anna James 10 May 1833   Jack
Lewis, James to Nancy Montgomery 1 Feb. 1838   Char
Lewis, Jesse to Eliza McClain 6 Mar. 1830   Boon
Lewis, John to Susan Houx 17 Mar. 1831   Coop
Lewis, John to Delany Hitt 21 Apr. 1831   CG-A
Lewis, John to Ellen Gilliam 2 July 1835   Clay
Lewis, John to Elizabeth Miles 13 Oct. 1837   Pk-B
Lewis, John W. to Hannah Palmer 27 June 1836   Ripl
Lewis, Joshua to Dicy Stone 8 Feb. 1823   Coop
Lewis, Limon E. to Mary Hardin 20 Dec. 1835   Linc
Lewis, Milton to Sally Huchins 4 Oct. 1813   StCh
Lewis, Moses to Delialah Jamison 7 Mar. 1833   Call
Lewis, Nathaniel to Minerva McClain 29 Apr. 1830   Boon
Lewis, Nelson to Pethany Eakins 21 Feb. 1833   Call
Lewis, Stone to Susannah Gibson 15 Jan. 1833   Jack

```
Lewis, Stuart to Mary Fulkerson 24 July 1823                        Boon
Lewis, Thomas to Frances Bohannon 5 June 1828                       CG-A
Lewis, Thomas to Cathy Fugate 10 Feb. 1834                          Rall
Lewis, Thomas H. to Virginia Whitelow 17 May 1836                  CG-A
Lewis, Valentine L. to Dicy Thomas 3 Jan. 1830                      Mari
Lewis, Wm. to Catherine Travis 21 Feb. 1815                        StCh
Lewis, Wm. to Phebe Hynes 23 Dec. 1837                             StFr
Lewis, Wm. C. to Nancy Fitzhugh 14 Sept. 1837                      Jack
Lewis, Wm. W. to Mahala Young 27 Mar. 1834                         Linc
Lewis, Wilson to Martha A. Bevins 10 Feb. 1836                     Jack
Lewright, Wm. P. to Mary E. Crowder 5 Mar. 1839                    Fran
Liberge, Peter to Julie Martinou 25 July 1836                     StCh
Liggen, Samuel S. to Eleanor Hall 10 Sept. 1839                   Clay
Ligget, Thomas to Elizabeth Lemons 29 Sept. 1825                  Clay
Ligget, Wm. to Lucinda Elgin 6 Aug. 1839                          Howa
Liggett, John to Eliza A. Barron 11 Feb. 1837                     Ray
Lighter, Christian to Matilda Keithley 8 Sept. 1825               Pk-1
Lightner, Abia T. to Jemima Snelling 1 July 1830                  Lafa
Lightner, Jeremiah to Jane White 10 Mar. 1835                     Lafa
Ligon, Wm. to Charity Gilliland 21 Oct. 1833                      Linc
Like, Christopher to Fanny Gunnels 26 Jan. 1832                   CG-A
Like, Jacob to Drussilla Strong 15 Apr. 1832                      CG-A
Lile, Alin P. to Mary Cox 7 July 1833                             Ray
Lile, Charles P. to Purnacy Black 14 Feb. 1826                    Ray
Lile, Henry to Jane Andrews 13 Nov. 1825                          Ray
Lile, Henry to Lydia Conner 23 Oct. 1828                          Ray
Liles, Daniel W. to Matilda McHill 9 Feb. 1837                    Linc
Liles, Wm. to Lotty Parmer 27 Nov. 1815                           StCh
Lillard, Hamilton to Susan A. ---- 27 Dec. 1838                   Lewi
Lillard, Walker to Mary A. Stansfer 27 Sept. 1838                 Lewi
Lillig, Carl to Charlotte Seelen 11 May 1837                      CG-A
Lillis, Calvin W. to Isebella B. Black 20 Sept. 1833              Mari
Lilly, John to Susan P. Howland 3 July 1834                       StCh
Lilly, Zachariah to Agatha L. Nash 31 May 1837                    Henr
Limbaugh, ---- to Mary Simmons 30 Apr. 1835                       CG-B
Limbaugh, Frederic to Catey Statler 15 June 1824                  CG-A
Limbaugh, Jacob to Mary Shell 6 Jan. 1814                         CG-A
Lime, Love to Sophia Potter 8 Feb. 1838                           Morg
Limpaugh, Geo. F. to Katherine Edinger 4 May 1830                 CG-A
Lincecum, Harmon to Lucinda Thompson 6 July 1825                  CG-A
Linch, David to Nancy Joiner 29 May 1837                          CG-A
Linch, Isiah to Jane Turner 10 Aug. 1826                          Lafa
Linch, James to Mary Smith 1 May 1828                             Jack
Linch, Wm. to Elizabeth Casy 3 Sept. 1832                         Jack
Linckhon, John to Luvina Fletcher 18 Aug. 1834                    Md-A
Lincoln, Absalom to Mary Baker 22 Dec. 1831                       CG-A
Lincoln, John to Nancy Holtzclaw 12 Apr. 1827                     Clay
Lincon, Lazer to Catherine Compton 18 Sept. 1839                  Ripl
Lindley, Jacob to Matilda Hembree 9 Dec. 1838                     Polk
Lindly, John to Sally Lindly 3 Jan. 1836                          Polk
Lindly, Pitman to Malinda Williams 29 Dec. 1836                   Polk
Lindsay, James to Carline C. Frier 4 Oct. 1838                    Md-B
Lindsay, John to Polly Plummer 13 Oct. 1829                       Linc
Lindsay, Nimrod B. to Mary A. Bowles 2 Sept. 1839                 Pk-B
Lindsay, Thomas to Margaret Garvin 28 Jan. 1830                   StCh
Lindsey, Jacob L. to Nancy E. McPherson 20 June 1837             Mari
Lindsey, James to Emily Lindsey 21 Feb. 1833                      StCh
Lindsey, Leasel to Adiline Edwards 4 July 1837                    Boon
Lindsey, Robt. to Elizabeth Ford 30 July 1835                     Pk-1
Lindsey, Wm. to Christiana Greer 22 Jan. 1829                     CG-A
Lindsey, Wm. to Harriet Humphrey 8 Feb. 1838                      Pk-B
Liney, Geo. to Margaret Colliver 9 Mar. 1836                      Rall
Lingenfelter, Geo. B. to Cynthia S. Evans 18 Mar. 1828           Clay
Link, Aaron to Katherine Slinkard 4 Nov. 1834                     CG-B
Link, Daniel to Elena Peters 21 Dec. 1819                         CG-1
```

135

```
Link, Henry to Sally C. Philips 21 Dec. 1837            Fran
Link, John to Nancy Taylor 15 Sept. 1825               CG-A
Linkter, Samuel to Nancy Swaford 22 June 1826          Gasc
Linley, Jayha to Ruth Linley 16 Apr. 1834              Gree
Linn, Hines C. to Hester A. Caton 18 Feb. 1836         Warr
Linn, Isaac to Ann Shipp 7 Jan. 1838                   Linc
Linn, Luther M. to Matilda Perkins 15 Apr. 1834        Linc
Linn, Simeon to Irena Madden 10 Oct. 1837              CG-A
Linn, Wm. to Seralda Pearson 4 Dec. 1839               Plat
Linnville, Wm. to Paulina Hensley 24 Dec. 1839         Buch
Linsey, Wm. N. to Elizabeth Henslee 8 Sept. 1839       Polk
Linson, Nathan to Susannah Keith 30 July 1826          StFr
Linvil, David to Sofiah Bates 1 May 1838               Clay
Linville, Abraham to Nancy Trap 4 Mar. 1824            Lafa
Linville, Andrew to Ealenor Elison 15 Aug. 1822        Lafa
Linville, Geo. H. to Sarah Burris 21 Feb. 1839         Lafa
Linville, Harrison to Nancy Bounds 20 Nov. 1837        Clin
Linville, John to Polly Vanderpool 30 Oct. 1830        Ray
Linville, John to Nancy Smith 14 Jan. 1836             Ray
Linville, Lewis to Nancy Stone 19 Feb. 1824            Ray
Linville, Thomas to Charity Wadkins 16 Feb. 1824       Howa
Linville, Thomas to Martha A. Stone 20 Nov. 1833       Ray
Linville, Thomas to Rebecca Cole 29 Apr. 1834          Lafa
Linville, Wm. to Mary Mayberry 22 Mar. 1832            Ray
Linville, Wm. to Leah Bowers 3 Oct. 1834               Jack
Lions, Umberson to Cynthy Brassfield 2 May 1833        Clay
Lippo, Thomas D. to Luiza Mattock 16 Aug. 1838         Polk
Lipscomb, Wade to Mary Baker 18 Sept. 1839             Gree
Liscomb, Samuel S. to Mrs. Margaret Carter 17 Mar. 1836  Jeff
Lisdell, Wm. to Elizabeth Hunt 27 Jan. 1836            Ray
Lisle, Benj. L. to Margaret Jacoby 11 Oct. 1837        Cole
Lisle, Samuel V. to Jurusla Willis 9 May 1836          Clin
Liston, Samuel to Elizabeth Thompson 7 Sept. 1837      Polk
Liter, John to Susan Clark 14 Jan. 1827                Pk-1
Literal, Geo. F. to Amanda Z.T. Brown 5 Feb. 1837      Audr
Litle, Gabriel to Lucinda Ashabran 1 June 1832         CG-A
Litle, Wm. P. to Mary A. Young 15 Mar. 1831            CG-A
Litrell, John to Polly Biswell 10 Feb. 1831            Rand
Litter, Abraham to Rebecka Bonham 14 Mar. 1837         Pk-A
Little, Alexander to Mahala Short -- July 1828          Boon
Little, Benedict to Eliza J. Elder 13 Nov. 1837        Rall
Little, Calvin to Margaret Bryant 21 Dec. 1838         Boon
Little, Hiram W. to Eleanor Berry 5 Oct. 1825          Boon
Little, John B. to Minerva Fowler 16 Jan. 1839         Boon
Little, Joseph to Winford Short 15 Oct. 1823           Boon
Little, Josua to Emely Scanthee 8 Mar. 1832            Md-A
Little, Martin to Eliza Owings 14 Nov. 1839            Howa
Little, Oliver to Jane Trimble 7 Dec. 1833             Call
Little, Wm. to Margaret Crews 17 Oct. 1833             Howa
Littlejohn, James to Elvia Neal 5 July 1838            Linc
Litton, Brice M. to Nancy Shaw 3 Sept. 1835           Linc
Litton, Henderson R. to Mary A. Stephens 15 Sept. 1833  Linc
Litton, Isaac to Sally Cantwell 17 May 1828            Linc
Litton, J. Winston to Mary Buchannon 14 Mar. 1832      Linc
Litton, James J. to Nancy J. Huston 1 Dec. 1825        Boon
Litton, John A. to Jane Cannon 14 Feb. 1838            Linc
Litton, John G. to Mary A. Fisher 2 Apr. 1835          Linc
Litton, Joseph W. to Kathryn Wilson 15 Sept. 1829      Linc
Litton, Lawrence B. to Nancy Martin 27 Aug. 1837       Linc
Litton, Lawrence D. to Patsy Thompson 27 May 1830      Linc
Litton, Patrick to Angelisy Horine 4 June 1835         Wash
Litton, Samuel G. to Rebecca Porter 23 Feb. 1826       Linc
Litton, Wm. B. to Polly Irgim 21 Dec. 1826            Linc
Littrel, John to Ann Woods 27 Apr. 1826                Howa
Littrel, Robt. to Matilda Reed 6 Feb. 1834             Howa
```

Littrell, Geo. to Eliza Hawker 5 Dec. 1833   Howa
Littrell, James to Malvina Harvey 4 Aug. 1828   Howa
Lively, Daniel to Mrs. Mildred E. Harrison 2 May 1839   Mari
Lively, Jesse to Sarah Wrattles -- Sept. 1823   Gasc
Livingston, John to Susannah Collins 23 Sept. 1819   Howa
Livingston, Smith to Nancy Higgins 19 Sept. 1833   Clin
Livingston, Thomas to Elizabeth Higgins 1 Mar. 1832   Clay
Livingston, Wm. to Hannah McKown 13 June 1831   Clay
Lizenby, Cyrus to June C. Garner 16 Sept. 1834   Mari
Lizenby, Thomas to Susan Rush 21 June 1831   Mari
Lock, Abram N. to Mildred H. Linnet 5 Jan. 1836   Char
Lock, David to Cynthia Gibson 7 Aug. 1823   Howa
Lock, David to Nancy Carter 22 Sept. 1839   Barr
Lock, Wm. to Nancy Smith 16 Dec. 1838   Rand
Lock, Wm. W. to Elizabeth Gibson 18 Sept. 1834   Gree
Lockhard, Samuel to Elizabeth Hempstead 11 July 1836   CG-A
Lockwood, James to Anna M. Hill 3 Mar. 1835   Jeff
Loe, James to Maria S. Hindi 5 Nov. 1829   Rand
Loe, John to Rachel Gross 15 June 1830   Rand
Loe, Martin to Theollis White 4 Apr. 1827   Howa
Loe, Paul to Elizabeth Arnold 30 Apr. 1837   Lewi
Loe, Thomas to Margaret Hackley 6 Mar. 1836   Howa
Loe, Thomas to Lydia Lyle 3 Feb. 1837   Lewi
Lofton, James to Elizabeth Dill 28 Sept. 1837   Cr-1
Lofton, Samuel to Elizabeth King 19 Feb. 1832   Wash
Lofton, Wm. to Mrs. Sally Robnett 12 Jan. 1837   Fran
Logadore, Wm. to Sarah Switzler 19 Jan. 1836   Sali
Logan, Alexander S. to Sarah Easley 4 Apr. 1839   Lafa
Logan, David to Servillity Rubottom 1 Feb. 1812   CG-1
Logan, Hulets to Zerilda West 24 Oct. 1833   Boon
Logan, James to Elizabeth Talbott 12 May 1836   Call
Logan, John to Mary Lorimier 13 Feb. 1814   CG-1
Logan, John to Frances Reavs 18 Feb. 1830   Linc
Logan, John to Harriet Mallow 13 Dec. 1832   Wash
Logan, John to Annie C. Hulen 17 Nov. 1833   Boon
Logan, Phillip P. to Elizabeth J. Hanshaw 26 June 1831   Clay
Logan, Preston to Nancy Cochrell 15 Dec. 1836   John
Logan, Robt. to Mary Rubottom 7 Mar. 1816   CG-1
Logan, Wm. to Rebecca Havens 5 Sept. 1838   Clay
Logan, Wm. to Sarah Collins 13 Sept. 1838   Lewi
Logsdon, John to Annatisia Simson 24 Aug. 1832   Gasc
Logston, Albion to Sarah Simon 8 Mar. 1827   Gasc
Lollers, Elisha to Jane Snowden 18 Jan. 1821   Ray
Lomax, John W. to Elizabeth Peterson 23 Oct. 1838   CG-A
Lomons, John to Sarah Person 3 Jan. 1836   Clin
Lonceford, Littleton to Nancy Strain 6 Feb. 1839   Henr
Long, Allen to Cathorein Armstrong 11 Feb. 1838   Mill
Long, Belitha G. to Margret Thomas 28 Mar. 1831   Pk-1
Long, Benj. S. to Mary Burnett 30 May 1837   Clay
Long, Beverly G. to Sarah Hawthorn 12 Feb. 1837   Clar
Long, Caleb to Sarah Lewis 4 Dec. 1825   CG-A
Long, David J. to Rhoda Dutton 1 May 1826   Cole
Long, Foreman to Harriett Crow 27 Nov. 1832   Pk-1
Long, Francis R. to Dowilla E. Branham 20 Aug. 1839   Clay
Long, Gabriel to Elizabeth Brookins 13 Dec. 1835   Lewi
Long, Harrison L. to Kezia Kendall 11 Oct. 1838   Jeff
Long, Horace M. to Harriet Tong 21 June 1838   Md-B
Long, James to Crecy Oder 20 July 1815   StCh
Long, James to Mildred Bales 10 Oct. 1830   Perr
Long, James to Nancy Patterson 21 Jan. 1838   Ripl
Long, James H. to Rebecca Story 12 Feb. 1829   Clay
Long, John to Lisa A. Grymes 25 Jan. 1831   Pk-1
Long, Joseph to Aretta Zumwalt 30 June 1839   Pk-B
Long, Lawrence to Malvine Huchins 4 Mar. 1830   StCh
Long, N.J.F. to Caroline Hutchings 8 Sept. 1836   StCh

```
Long, Philip S. to Isabella Murphy 15 Jan. 1833            StFr
Long, Reuben to Nancy Hawker 9 Nov. 1825                   Howa
Long, Robt. to Mahala Litte 16 Oct. 1832                   Boon
Long, Wm. to Elizabeth Hectar 17 Nov. 1818                 CG-1
Long, Zadock to Sarah Liles 8 Feb. 1837                    Linc
Longan, Augustin K. Jr. to Evaline McDaniel 19 Dec. 1837   Cole
Longan, Benj. A. to Sally Jones 24 Oct. 1824               Coop
Longan, John B. to Elizabeth Reavis 2 Sept. 1827           Coop
Longan, Lewis L. to Polly Randolph 20 Dec. 1835            Coop
Longan, Philip to Mahala Vivion 11 Sept. 1825              Cole
Longan, Spotswood to Mahalia Linsey 2 July 1826            Coop
Longmire, Joseph to Harriet Culbertson 22 Mar. 1832        Mari
Longmire, Wm. to Mary Thomas 7 Mar. 1833                   Mari
Lonlau, Wiley to Elizabeth Smith 2 Mar. 1834               Mari
Looney, Madan J. to Elizabeth Collins 15 Feb. 1838         CG-A
Looney, Wm. to Elmyria McClure 23 July 1838                Polk
Loor, Peter to Eliza Cowie 30 Dec. 1830                    Wash
Loper, Samuel to Mariah Vessels 7 July 1834                Perr
Lopp, Alexander to Mary A. Rutherford 31 May 1838          Polk
Lord, Jesse to Elenora Spencer 20 Nov. 1832                Howa
Lord, John to Richanah Whitesides 23 Jan. 1838             Char
Lorimier, Lewis to Margaret Penney 4 Oct. 1816             CG-1
Lorimier, Louis to Polly Berthireaume 4 June 1810          CG-1
Lorimier, Wm. Jr. to Nancy Patterson 26 Dec. 1830          CG-A
Loring, Francis to Elizabeth Slaughter 20 May 1830         Mari
Loring, John to Elizabeth Lewis 12 Feb. 1828               Mari
Lorrance, John to Hanah Baker 2 July 1805                  CG-1
Lorton, Joseph D. to Nancy Williams 10 Sept. 1835          Call
Lott, Wm. H. to Sarah J. Duncan 22 Aug. 1839               Clay
Loudermilk, Joseph to Nancy Baily 3 Mar. 1833              Lewi
Loudon, Wm. T. to Priscilla Dickin 24 Mar. 1839            Lewi
Louis, Elisha to Jane Hagewood 5 Nov. 1834                 Pk-1
Louis, Lunsford L. to Eliza J. Louis 4 Nov. 1832           Pk-1
Loutern, Richard to Elender Maupin -- Nov. 1821            Howa
Love, Andrew Jr. to Mary A. Muir 29 Sept. 1836             Pk-1
Love, Augustus to Julia Chaunchagrin 8 Jan. 1833           Wash
Love, Charles to Catherine Martin 24 May 1827              Call
Love, Harvey to Martha Sands 10 Sept. 1835                 Cr-1
Love, James to Matilda Scholl 4 Mar. 1836                  Call
Love, James to Polly Bennett 25 Aug. 1836                  Pk-1
Love, James H. to Polly Jimison 26 Jan. 1837               Ripl
Love, John to Ruth Hobbs 7 Sept. 1837                      Pk-B
Love, Louis to Yacent Placet 28 Nov. 1826                  Wash
Love, Louis to Louise Blais 16 Nov. 1829                   Wash
Love, Peter W. to Tresa Tobeaux 1 June 1811                StGe
Love, Robt. to Frances Swain 2 Jan. 1833                   Rall
Love, Samuel to Jane Morris 24 May 1838                    Pk-B
Love, Wm. to Elizabeth Eoff 12 July 1838                   Pk-B
Loveall, Stephen to Thurzy McKay 8 Mar. 1836              Cole
Loveall, Zeblin to Elizabeth Roberts 22 Feb. 1838         Cole
Lovejoy, Elijah P. to Celia A. French 4 Mar. 1835          StCh
Lovel, James to Clarinda Colier 6 Aug. 1834                Jack
Lovel, Timothy to Elizabeth Fowler 11 Mar. 1819            CG-1
Lovelace, Nelson to Emily Turpin 19 Aug. 1832              Mari
Lovelace, Zachariah to Mary Lovel 8 Oct. 1835              Pk-1
Lovelady, James to Elizabeth Lewis 5 Apr. 1838             Clin
Lovell, John to Elizabeth Lovelace 29 Sept. 1836           Pk-1
Lovell, Thomas to Letty Wilkins 10 July 1832               Cole
Lovering, Lawson to Barbara A. Rice 31 Dec. 1826           StCh
Lovet, Asa to Elizabeth Ellis 11 Dec. 1823                 Howa
Lovick, Nicholas to Mary Ginst 10 Sept. 1835               StCh
Loving, Gabriel to Sarah Phelin 27 May 1838                Cole
Loving, Howard F. to Charity F. Bouldin 5 Apr. 1838        Cole
Loving, Wm. to Sally Kingery 12 Apr. 1835                  Cole
Loving, Wm. R. to Malinda Brown 16 Nov. 1837               Cole
```

Low, Isaac to Amanda Blue 2 June 1830   Rand
Lowe, Wm. to Mary Kelsay 29 Aug. 1833   Morg
Lowell, Elisha to Lucy Jones 14 -- 1838   Fran
Lowen, David B. to Frances R. Collier 28 May 1837   Howa
Lowery, David to Susannah Weir 25 Jan. 1839   Gasc
Lowery, Wm. to Mary Fitzhugh 26 May 1836   Morg
Lowrey, Russel to Larany Merril 25 June 1836   Ripl
Lowry, John J. to Harriett Hubbard 2 Mar. 1818   Howa
Lowry, John J. to Nancy M. Gorham 1 May 1821   Howa
Lowthrain, John to Pimecia McKirk 14 Feb. 1839   Howa
Loyd, Owen to Lucy Chapman 5 Mar. 1838   Ray
Loyd, Samuel to Lavina Chapman 23 Sept. 1827   Ray
Luallen, Enoch to Delphia Muse 28 Aug. 1839   Pk-B
Lubblefield, Robt. to Polly Cannon 3 Apr. 1828   Linc
Lucas, Allen B. to Jane Burdyne 19 Apr. 1835   StCh
Lucas, Washington to Sarah Rogers 23 Dec. 1828   Howa
Luck, Asa to Lucy Fitsue 27 Dec. 1832   Pk-1
Lucket, Thomas to Elizabeth C. Edwards 24 Jan. 1839   StCh
Luckett, Gipson B. to Martha O. Edwards 14 Aug. 1838   Warr
Luckett, Wm. H. to Catherine L. Campbell 23 Dec. 1838   StCh
Luellen, Richard to Kitty Brice 11 Aug. 1833   Pk-1
Lunceford, Wiley to Katharine Hoge 18 Nov. 1838   Gree
Lund, Jacob to Sally Prather 7 Oct. 1838/9   Wash
Lunsford, Amos to Fanny Barton 23 May 1839   StFr
Lunsford, Wm. to Rachel Walker 2 Oct. 1839   Cr-1
Lupton, Jonathan to Gracie J. Hays 31 Aug. 1834   Wash
Lupton, Richard to Elvira Manning 3 July 1832   Wash
Lurby, Thomas to Fanny Bigs 7 Feb. 1806   StCh
Lusby, Elliott to Avis Lewis 13 Sept. 1827   StCh
Luse, Daniel to Elisabeth Oakes 19 Apr. 1835   Ripl
Lusher, Jacob to Ann Florey 13 June 1837   Char
Lusk, Cyrus to Amalia Collier 20 Nov. 1838   Boon
Luster, John to Charity Kell 9 Nov. 1825   Coop
Luster, Loid to Sally Prine 30 Aug. 1838   Polk
Luster, Robt. to Polly Scott 4 Mar. 1830   Cole
Lute, Phillip to Paulina Wills 17 Oct. 1833   Rall
Lutes, Geo. to Eve Crites 20 Apr. 1826   CG-A
Luther, Eliphalet to Visey Allen 30 Oct. 1825   Clay
Lyle, John J. to Martha Greathouse 27 Dec. 1834   Rall
Lyle, Martin J. to Emily Bolware 27 Nov. 1834   Rall
Lyman, Rolland to Mary L. Lentze 31 Oct. 1839   Boon
Lynch, Aaron to Ann Reece 9 Dec. 1838   John
Lynch, Benj. to Rebecca Smith 23 Mar. 1833   Jack
Lynch, Cornelius to Elizabeth Nichols 20 July 1830   Boon
Lynch, Cornelius to Sarah Johnson 5 Apr. 1836   Boon
Lynch, David to Nancy Turner 28 Feb. 1839   Buch
Lynch, Geo. to Nelly Talbard 1 Dec. 1836   StCh
Lynch, Jeremiah to Julia Lewis 30 Aug. 1832   Jack
Lynch, John to Mary Bush 10 Sept. 1817   Howa
Lynch, John to Elizabeth Cushing 10 Mar. 1821   Boon
Lynch, John to Betsy Eichelberger 12 Feb. 1828   Jeff
Lynes, Harrison to Mary A. Gray 28 Aug. 1833   Boon
Lynes, Madison to Hannah Victor 15 Aug. 1833   Boon
Lynes, Washington to Susan Suggett 28 July 1836   Call
Lynn, Charles to Melcena C. Bryan 30 Jan. 1834   Warr
Lynn, John H. to Isabella Y. Anderson 7 Dec. 1837   Clay
Lynn, Joseph to Rachel Allen 26 Nov. 1829   StCh
Lyon, Daniel to Martha Barnett 25 July 1839   John
Lyon, Jefferson to Catherine Suggett 9 Nov. 1829   Boon
Lyons, James to Nancy Rice 28 June 1838   Maco
Lyons, Nathaniel to Permelia Maden 21 Apr. 1839   CG-B
Lyons, Wm. to Sarah Brasier 5 Sept. 1839   Rall
Lytle, James S. to Lucinda Davis 1 Aug. 1839   Monr
Lytle, Luke to Margaret Johnson 16 Aug. 1838   Cole

McAfee, John to Emily Dickerson 7 June 1837   Shel
McAfee, Phillip T. to Mary A. Shelby 27 May 1834   Call
McAfee, Robt. to Mary Gladden 18 -- 1821/22   Lafa
McAfee, Thomas to Elizabeth Mattson 2 July 1837   Shel
McAfee, W. to Mrs. Fine Perkins 28 Feb. 1836   Fran
McAfee, Wm. to Rebecca Richards 20 Jan. 1831   Clay
McAlister, Brightberry to Mary A. Walker 15 Oct. 1833   Howa
McAllister, David to Ann Hawkins 10 Apr. 1838   Pk-B
McAllister, Harvey to Rachel McKiney 17 May 1836   StFr
McAllister, John to Frances Feek 29 Mar. 1837   Coop
McAlroy, David B. to Gula E. Howel 18 Aug. 1832   Clay
McAttee, Henry to Catherine Vessels 14 Jan. 1836   Perr
McAttee, Patrick to Mary A. Dorsey 28 Feb. 1832   Perr
McBain, Ignatius to Sally Park 18 Feb. 1830   Boon
McBride, Ebenezer to Juliana Snell 16 Dec. 1830   Boon
McBride, I.H. to Milly Barns 14 Dec. 1837   Lewi
McBride, J. H. to Lettis Tate 25 Apr. 1834   Lewi
McBride, James to Mahala Miller 20 June 1830   Fran
McBride, P.A. to Mary Snell 6 Feb. 1827   Boon
McBride, Patrick to Lucy Furguson 19 Nov. 1831   Perr
McBride, Robt. to Prisilla Han 21 Feb. 1836   Lewi
McBride, Wm. to Pauline Odey 25 Dec. 1837   Boon
McBroom, Wm. to Hannah Gist 1 Aug. 1839   Morg
McBryan, Soloman S. to Sarah A. Edwards 28 Feb. 1836   Ray
McCabe, Alpheus to Margaret A. Winch 18 Nov. 1838   Wash
McCabe, C.B.N. to Julia A.F. Block 22 Feb. 1837   CG-A
McCabe, Phillip to Martha Davidson 15 Apr. 1830   Wash
McCafferty, Wm. to Augusta Smith 12 Mar. 1837   Char
McCaleb, John to Elizabeth Smith 15 Aug. 1839   Coop
McCall, Adolphus to Susan Harriman 1 June 1837   Cole
McCall, James E. to Angelina Gilbert 7 Nov. 1839   Call
McCall, Samuel to Sinthy Lewis 7 Aug. 1830   Boon
McCampbell, Jesse to Agness Mitchell 1? July 1837   Boon
McCampbell, Jesse E. to Lucinda Congo 9 May 1824   Call
McCane, John to Sally Casey 1 June 1839   Bent
McCann, Henry to Polly Caldwell 23 Sept. 1830   Fran
McCann, James D. to Susan E. Shumate 31 Oct. 1839   Mari
McCann, Jesse to Thalba Williams 17 May 1836   Warr
McCansland, Mark to Sarah Branham 11 June 1839   Boon
McCarron, John to Lavena Whitely 7 Oct. 1832   StCh
McCartney, Thomas to Rachel L. Gilham 20 Sept. 1836   Lafa
McCarty, Dennis to Isabella Crane 3 Nov. 1839   Boon
McCarty, Ezekial to Dicey Thompson 27 Dec. 1834   Lewi
McCarty, James to Betsey Miller 31 Oct. 1822   Coop
McCarty, James to Nancy Lucas 9 July 1826   Lafa
McCarty, James to Polly Cole 9 May 1832   Coop
McCarty, James to Mary A. McFarland 2 Oct. 1838   Coop
McCarty, John to Rosanna Wilburn 11 Jan. 1824   Boon
McCarty, Michael P. to Artimacy A. Price 4 Oct. 1839   Howa
McCarty, Wm. to Nancy Brooks 16 May 1838   Cass
McCary, Hugh H. to Susan Davis 9 Feb. 1837   Call
McCaskie, Robt. L. to Amanda A. Nowlin 25 Dec. 1839   Ray
McCauley, Benit to Charlotte Tucker 6 Feb. 1837   Perr
McCauley, James to Rosanna Miles 19 Feb. 1836   Perr
McCauly, Hamilton to Narcisses Wiles 23 June 1833   Howa
McCausland, David to Mary S. Heald 10 Oct. 1832   StCh
McChord, John to Mariah Smith 16 Aug. 1832   Jack
McChord, Thomas to Rhoda Graham 8 Mar. 1832   Jack
McChrist, Wm. to Leah White 19 Oct. 1826   Howa
McClain, Charles to Ellin Phillips 12 May 1825   Boon
McClain, Ewen to Rebecca Mahan 13 May 1819   Howa
McClain, John to Racheal McClain 22 Nov. 1835   Boon
McClain, John T. to Iby J. Whittey 9 Oct. 1836   Call
McClain, Joseph to Elizabeth Legitt 17 Jan. 1839   Howa
McClain, Peter to Anna E. Cadwallader 3 Sept. 1835   Jeff

McClanahan, Andrew to Mariah Nelson 26 Dec. 1839 Coop
McClanahan, David to Elenor Rymal 26 June 1837 Coop
McClanahan, James to Keciah Rymal 28 Dec. 1837 Coop
McClanahan, John to Sarah Cunningham 27 July 1837 StFr
McClanahan, Thomas to Elizabeth Davis 26 May 1833 Coop
McClanahan, Wm. to Mary Williamson 18 Dec. 1839 Boon
McClane, Erastus to Ann Riggs 28 Mar. 1839 Clay
McClane, Franklin to Rebecca Counse 9 July 1834 Wash
McClary, Wm. to Martha Smith 25 May 1835 CG-B
McClay, Wm. to Elizabeth Killam 6 Aug. 1835 StCh
McClelan, John to Harriett Sullivan 14 Mar. 1839 Sali
McCleland, John A. to Sarah L. Kabler 18 Jan. 1838 Warr
McClellan, James to Elizabeth Grant 3 Jan. 1828 Pk-1
McClellan, Jordan to Marilla Burns 13 Dec. 1825 Pk-1
McClelland, Elisha to Betsey A. West 20 Mar. 1834 Call
McClelland, James to Widow Bryan 11 Dec. 1827 Boon
McClelland, Ross to Mary Talls 13 Jan. 1834 Rall
McClelland, Thomas to Sarah Robinet 1 May 1832 Call
McClelland, Wm. to Aveline Dickey 14 Mar. 1839 Cass
McClellen, Michael to Ann Hicklin 23 Mar. 1826 Lafa
McClenahan, John M. to Mildred T. McCord 5 Sept. 1839 Morg
McClendon, Asa to Louisa G. Anderson 30 Mar. 1830 Cr-P
McClendon, Bryan to Elizabeth Howard 23 Dec. 1832 Cr-1
McClendon, Jesse to Lavina Robins 1 July 1838 Clin
McClene, Wm. to Rerran Hooker 9 Aug. 1832 Perr
McClenny, John S. to Larany A. Biggs 4 Nov. 1837 StCh
McClenny, Robt. T. to Lucinda Keithly 16 Nov. 1837 StCh
McClenny, Wm. S. to Lucinda Clay 22 Jan. 1834 StCh
McCliney, Mekajah to Melinda Boone 7 Dec. 1828 StCh
McClintic, John to Eliza McBain 20 Jan. 1824 Boon
McClinton, Royl to Narceana E. Gill 21 Nov. 1833 Perr
McCloed, James to Sally Kelly 3 Jan. 1833 Pk-1
McClord, Adam to Mrs. Nancy Smith 27 Aug. 1815 StCh
McCloskey, John J. to Drucilla Turbit 20 May 1827 Pk-1
McCloskey, John J. to Olive Tolbert 21 Aug. 1833 Pk-1
McCloud, Daniel to Caroline Griffith 16 Dec. 1830 Mari
McClure, Charles to Hannah Hopper 15 Aug. 1824 Lafa
McClure, Harvey to Mary J. Davis 8 Oct. 1835 Call
McClure, James to Mary A. Lishlighter 28 July 1836 Rand
McClure, Wm. to Elizabeth M. McClure 16 Apr. 1833 Call
McCollister, James to Charollet Smith 13 May 1834 Boon
McCollum, Greenberry to Polly Williams 28 Mar. 1839 Linc
McCollum, Jackson to Polly McWilliams 22 May 1833 Lafa
McCollum, Wm. to Polly Pitts 8 Dec. 1831 Ray
McCombs, Robt. to Mary Wallace 17 Nov. 1831 CG-A
McCombs, Wm. to Saphrona Abernathy 24 Oct. 1839 Perr
McConnal, Wm. to Nancy Springer 8 Mar. 1839 Clay
McConnehue, Alexander to Catherine Hickenbotem 22 Oct. 1807 StGe
McConnel, Joel to Ann Thatcher 17 Dec. 1829 Call
McConnel, Joseph to Gaberillen Grimes 4 Sept. 1827 Clay
McConnel, Samuel to Elizabeth Wills 3 Feb. 1831 Boon
McConnell, James to Mary Feckley 7 Oct. 1832 StCh
McConnell, Wm. to Jane Hunter 14 Sept. 1831 Wash
McConnell, Zeppe to Lucinda Johnston 17 July 1834 Jeff
McCorcle, Jabez to Nancy Fristoe 19 Oct. 1826 Clay
McCord, Abijah S. to Susan D. Ritchie 3 Mar. 1837 Clin
McCord, Amos to Julia Cole 17 June 1837 Howa
McCord, Francis to Mary Weatherford 12 Mar. 1837 Pk-A
McCord, James to Edna Pepper 5 Sept. 1833 Pk-1
McCord, James N. to Elizabeth E. Lane 28 Feb. 1833 Gasc
McCord, John to Polly Adams 11 June 1837 Cass
McCord, John W. to Amely Grooms 29 Dec. 1822 Md-A
McCord, Wm. to Charlotte Ringo 18 Aug. 1828 Md-A
McCord, Wm. to Anna Bursley 24 Oct. 1837 Cass
McCork, John to Matilda Biven 12 Jan. 1837 Howa

McCorkle, Archibald to Zerelda Stone 22 Aug. 1833   Clay
McCorkle, Geo. to Matilda George 21 Feb. 1839   Clay
McCorkle, James to Mary A. Means 26 Sept. 1830   Clay
McCorkle, James F. to Sally Edwards 14 July 1831   Clay
McCorkle, John to Elizabeth Titus 4 Oct. 1826   Howa
McCorkle, Samuel to Malinda Camron 29 Nov. 1825   Clay
McCorkle, Samuel D. to Elizabeth Stoneham 9 Apr. 1839   Ray
McCormac, Fielding to Angeline Ray 30 Mar. 1836   StFr
McCormack, Wm. to Eliz. L. Jones 3 Jan. 1822   Call
McCormack, Wm. to Lavinia Gibson 30 Oct. 1837   Linc
McCormack, Wm. G. to Margaret M. Terrell 10 Mar. 1836   Mari
McCormic, David to Unice Jones 12 Mar. 1832   Call
McCormick, Enoch to Eliza Donnell 19 Mar. 1835   Jeff
McCormick, John R. to Eliza Zumault 7 Mar. 1839   Mari
McCormick, Marion W. to Elizabeth J. Muldron 21 Dec. 1838 Mari
McCormick, Peter to Eliza Alexander 25 Mar. 1824   StFr
McCormick, Wm. to Ann Bivens 11 Apr. 1839   Ripl
McCoun, Andrew to Mary Marshall 28 Feb. 1839   Howa
McCoun, James L. to Emily H. Dale 13 Dec. 1836   Clay
McCoun, Moses to Sarah Bagwell 24 June 1832   Howa
McCourt, James to Eliza Coonts 15 Jan. 1829   StCh
McCoy, James to Susanna Cope 28 Oct. 1827   Wash
McCoy, John to Martha Dunbar 1 Sept. 1808   StCh
McCoy, Joseph to Sulia Burklow 2 June 1808   StCh
McCoy, Martin to Elizabeth Crow 8 Jan. 1828   StCh
McCoy, Robt. to Malinda Logan 28 Oct. 1830   Clay
McCoy, Robinson to Elizabeth Amos 15 Dec. 1836   Pk-A
McCoy, Timothy to Susan Smethers 31 Mar. 1836   StCh
McCoy, Wm. to Temperson B. Harrilson 1 May 1828   Linc
McCracken, Alexander to Ann E. Culberson 9 Apr. 1839   Clay
McCracken, John C. to Rebecca Brown 25 Aug. 1837   Clin
McCrae, Alexander G. to Elizabeth Hendricks 11 Jan. 1838 Mari
McCraken, Anson to Mahala Pierson 27 Feb. 1834   Jack
McCraken, Nemerod to Effemine Simpson 26 Jan. 1829   Howa
McCrary, Charles to Catherine Jones 17 Mar. 1836   Coop
McCrary, Elijah to Hannah Edinger 6 June 1833   CG-A
McCrary, John to Lucinda Splawn 22 Mar. 1838   Davi
McCrary, Wm. to Sally Wills 10 Sept. 1835   Clay
McCraw, Edmund to Louisa Bynum 20 Oct. 1836   Jack
McCraw, Wm. G. to Emily Dehony 2 Aug. 1836   Jack
McCray, Geo. to Elizabeth Ranney 25 Dec. 1834   CG-B
McCray, Massey to Mrs. Sarah Proops 13 Aug. 1836   Cr-1
McCreary, Benj. to Frances A. Proctor 17 Dec. 1835   Clay
McCreary, Gilead to Fanny Hackley 26 Mar. 1835   Howa
McCreary, Wm. to Catherine Safferins 2 Jan. 1833   Howa
McCredie, Geo. P. to Sarah A. McKinsey 12 Oct. 1830   Call
McCrery, James W. to Polly A. Vince 12 Feb. 1829   Wash
McCroskey, Levy to Susannah Rockhold 1 May 1828   Clay
McCroskey, Reuben to Betsey Benus 22 Jan. 1829   Pk-1
McCrurie, Samuel to Jane Brown 12 Sept. 1833   Pett
McCuistion, Newton to Calestian Boucher 2 Oct. 1836   Ray
McCulloch, D.D. to Julia Journey 15 Apr. 1837   StCh
McCulloch, Robt. Jr. to Katherine Robertson 27 July 1837 Coop
McCulloch, Thomas to Rebecca M. Craft 11 Dec. 1836   Call
McCullock, Allen to Susan Wicks 1 Jan. 1837   Wash
McCullom, Stephen to Elizabeth Slater 9 June 1825   Char
McCullough, James to Catharine Brown 11 July 1830   Jeff
McCully, John to Mary Litrell 13 Mar. 1834   Howa
McCully, Robt. to Louisa Arena 8 June 1837   Rand
McCune, Harvey L. to Mary Matson 24 Nov. 1836   Pk-1
McCune, John T. to Ruth A. Glasby 21 May 1839   Pk-B
McCune, Joseph to Martha Edwards 15 Feb. 1837   Pk-A
McCune, Wm. to Jane Guy 6 Nov. 1825   Pk-1
McCune, Wm. to Jane Edwards 30 Oct. 1834   Pk-1
McCuollough, G.W. to Unity Evans 2 Feb. 1837   Fran

```
McCurly, Henry to Nancy L. Harris 26 July 1826                          Coop
McCutchan, Walter to Sally A. Callason 20 Aug. 1835                     StCh
McCutchen, Dean to Patsy E. Sloan 27 Oct. 1829                         Coop
McCutchen, James E. to Sarah A. Williams 4 Oct. 1832                   Coop
McCutchen, Robt. to Nancy Young 28 Dec. 1831                          Coop
McCutchens, Thomas to Mary Mulligan 29 Sept. 1831                     Boon
McCutcheon, James to Zerilda Darst 5 Apr. 1832                        StCh
McDaniel, Edward to Nancy Jordan 4 Apr. 1833                          Cole
McDaniel, David to Patsey Morgan -- -- 1834                          Char
McDaniel, David to Catharine Goins 2 Apr. 1835                       Char
McDaniel, Geo. to Charlott Brewer 22 Feb. 1825                       Rall
McDaniel, Harvey to Egley A. Boulton 19 Oct. 1835                    Coop
McDaniel, Henry to Elisa Cowin 28 Aug. 1828                          Howa
McDaniel, James to Susannah Blackwell 9 Mar. 1837                    Cr-1
McDaniel, Jeremiah to Sarah Abbott 23 July 1823                      Boon
McDaniel, John to Cynthia Alexander 5 Aug. 1824                      Call
McDaniel, John to Nancy Harris 11 Dec. 1825                          Cole
McDaniel, Joseph to Jane Edwards 21 Apr. 1836                        Pett
McDaniel, Martin to Henrietta Landrum 8 Aug. 1833                    Cole
McDaniel, Samuel to Susannah R. Johnson 12 Sept. 1830               Coop
McDaniel, Thomas to Hannah Moore 8 Aug. 1837                         John
McDaniel, Wm. to Caty Fisher 16 Mar. 1820                            Coop
McDaniel, Wm. to Belinda Wise 15 Jan. 1828                           Jeff
McDaniel, Wm. to Mary Conner 8 Feb. 1835                             Coop
McDaniel, Wm. to Sarah McDaniel 1 Aug. 1839                          Jeff
McDaniel, Wm. J. to Elizabeth Ground 19 May 1836                     Md-B
McDavitt, James F. to Malinda R. Kerby 28 Jan. 1830                  Rand
McDermott, Nelson to Nancy B. McFarlin 22 June 1837                  Cass
McDermott, Thomas to Ann Logsden 4 Apr. 1837                         Lewi
McDole, Henry to Elizabeth Maddox 21 Dec. 1834                       Mari
McDonald, Abraham to Sally Parker 16 Aug. 1825                       Coop
McDonald, Alexander to Marian Kelly 19 July 1836                     StCh
McDonald, Allen B. to Lucinda G. Robnett 4 Jan. 1831                 Mari
McDonald, Augustus to Samantha Pinson 8 July 1838                    Wash
McDonald, Cash to Drusilla Davis 20 June 1833                        Call
McDonald, Darias to Agnes Gladney 19 Dec. 1833                       Linc
McDonald, Hiram to Susan Parker 16 Aug. 1825                         Coop
McDonald, Hiram to Lisa A. Tilford 1 Feb. 1833                       Linc
McDonald, Hiram to Nancy Buchanan 7 Apr. 1836                        Livi
McDonald, J. to Mary Crump 11 Nov. 1827                              CG-A
McDonald, James to Margaret Quick 2 Sept. 1830                       Jeff
McDonald, James to Jane Caldwell 9 Jan. 1831                         Fran
McDonald, Jessee to Polly R. Caldwell 6 Nov. 1817                    Fran
McDonald, John K. to Jane Burnett 11 July 1833                       Call
McDonald, Joseph  to Jane Boyd 17 Oct. 1835                          Call
McDonald, Pink to Elizabeth Wainscot 26 Sept. 1839                  Clar
McDonald, Thomas to Nancy Presley 25 June 1839                       Linc
McDonald, Wm. H. to Orrency Armstrong 10 Nov. 1839                   Mill
MacDonals, Jerrel to Mary Davis 28 Apr. 1839                         Audr
McDonell, Joseph to Nancy Harison 1 July 1835                        John
McDouglas, John to Hannah Barnes 15 Aug. 1835                        Boon
McDow, John to Alpha Nash 22 July 1819                               Howa
McDowan, Wm. to Demaris Bradley 23 Dec. 1832                         Pk-1
Macdowel, John to Mary Allen 20 May 1837                             Md-B
Mackdowel, Joseph W. to Elizabeth Allen 10 Dec. 1837                 Md-B
McDowel, Wm. to Mary Gilmore 3 Aug. 1837                             Clay
McDowell, Benj. S. to Mary Burch 14 Jan. 1838                        Pk-B
McDowell, David to Polly --hite 18 Oct. 1821                         Lafa
McDowell, James to Rachel McGee 7 June 1827                          Coop
McDowell, John to Jermima Wells 21 July 1822                         Howa
McDowell, John B. to Lettitia Birch 26 Oct. 1837                     Pk-B
McDowell, Wm. to Jane Hughs 7 Apr. 1836                              Pk-1
McDowl, Henry to Elizabeth Keach 22 June 1837                        Mari
McElhaney, Robt. J. to Cordelia Bunch 15 Feb. 1838                   Polk
McEllmury, John to America Sullinger 31 Aug. 1834                    CG-A
```

McElmurry, Charles G. to Leah M. Hayden 21 Nov. 1838   CG-A
McElroy, Farlar to Margaret Baker 5 Feb. 1830   Md-A
McElroy, Hugh to Catharine McAfee rec. 30 Dec. 1835   Mari
McElroy, Wm. C. to Lucy J. Pointer 3 Sept. 1839   StCh
McElwee, Dan to Nancy Bradley 20 Nov. 1834   Pk-1
McElwee, James D. to Mary Mills 3 Jan. 1833   Pk-1
McElwee, Wm. to Sarah M. Barr 24 Nov. 1836   Lewi
McEven, Wilson C. to Nancy Easter 29 Apr. 1830   Fran
McEwen, Robt. to Mary M. Speed 21 July 1831   Jeff
McFaddin, Jacob to Sarah Hijot 24 Feb. 1828   Md-A
McFaddon, ---- to Sarah E. Sage 8 Dec. 1832   Mari
McFarland, Alexander to Sary Hix 10 Aug. 1821   Coop
McFarland, Arthur to Louisa Morrow 3 Oct. 1834   Md-A
McFarland, Benj. F. to Sary Richardson 3 Dec. 1830   Coop
McFarland, Daniel to Letitia Taylor 1 Dec. 1836   Warr
McFarland, David to Susan Ross 26 Jan. 1828   Coop
McFarland, Eli N. to Ann M. Samuels 14 Dec. 1837   StFr
McFarland, Elijah to Frances Hix 8 Mar. 1821   Coop
McFarland, Geo. to Malinda Randol 25 Dec. 1832   CG-A
McFarland, Green to Katharine Organ 8 Oct. 1839   Rall
McFarland, Hustand to Susan Davis 29 Aug. 1839   Coop
McFarland, Huston to Eliza Crawford 7 Jan. 1835   Coop
McFarland, Huston C. to Elizabeth R. Robinson 19 Oct. 1837 StFr
McFarland, I. to Sarah Talbot 5 Sept. 1839   StCh
McFarland, Jacob to Polly McFarlin 4 July 1822   StFr
McFarland, Jacob H. to Mary A. Barnett 31 Dec. 1835   Morg
McFarland, James to Polly Jones 16 Oct. 1832   Coop
McFarland, John to Nancy Morris 1 July 1824   Coop
McFarland, John to Mary A. Frizzel 22 Sept. 1831   Wash
McFarland, John to Katherine Sebow 21 Apr. 1838   Pett
McFarland, John to Eliza Sloan 9 June 1839   Wash
McFarland, John to Louisa Shook 31 Oct. 1839   StFr
McFarland, Joseph to Polly E. McFarland 12 Jan. 1834   StFr
McFarland, Reuben to Alvirah George 13 Sept. 1827   Coop
McFarland, Ruben to Martha Benton 15 Feb. 1835   Gasc
McFarland, Samuel to Jane Morrow 15 Sept. 1824   Coop
McFarland, Walter to Harriet Matson 21 Nov. 1839   Pk-B
McFarland, Walter L. to Pennelia Barrett 6 Oct. 1835   Morg
McFarland, Wm. to Juliann Easton 26 Aug. 1828   Mari
McFarland, Wm. to Lucinda Riggs 3 Jan. 1830   Coop
McFarland, Wm. A. to Elizabeth Vance 31 Oct. 1838   StFr
Macfarlen, Hissikiah to Jensey Pinnel 12 Aug. 1832   Wash
McFarlin, Geo. to Abigal Carthey 19 Dec. 1816   Howa
McFarlin, Reuben to Unicy Rice 17 Jan. 1828   Howa
McFarling, John to Emerien Noland 25 Feb. 1835   John
McFathrich, Wm. to Deborah May 1 Nov. 1837   Pett
McFerren, James to Susan Hardy 21 Nov. 1836   Rall
McFerron, Joseph to Eve Tyler 6 Feb. 1810   CG-1
McFinen, James to Tabitha Ashby 24 Dec. 1834   Char
McGary, Strother to Huldah Benning 16 May 1839   Mari
McGaugh, John to Mrs. Jane Evans 8 Nov. 1821   Ray
McGaugh, Robert Jr. to Sally Davis 7 Nov. 1832   Ray
McGaugh, Thomas to Margaret Wall 2 June 1836   Ray
McGaugh, Thomas to Sarah Amos 25 Dec. 1839   StCh
McGavock, Robt. to Ann Hickman 9 Mar. 1819   Howa
McGee, Alney T. to Peggy Lee 9 July 1833   Ray
McGee, Charles to Mahaly Poteete 8 Aug. 1821   Clay
McGee, David to Elizabeth Boolen 14 July 1825   Coop
McGee, David to Mary J. Kertland 27 Oct. 1836   Monr
McGee, David D. to Eliza Lee 4 Sept. 1834   Ray
McGee, James to Polly Foreman 25 Oct. 1826   Rall
McGee, James H. to Mary Funk 13 Jan. 1839   Boon
McGee, James J. to Christiana Duley 2 June 1836   Monr
McGee, James L. to Elizabeth Bryant 22 Oct. 1829   Rall
McGee, John to Polly Smith 29 Jan. 1824   Howa

144

McGee, John to Mary A. Martin 26 Mar. 1833   Ray
McGee, John to Hannah Gest 3 Sept. 1837   Morg
McGee, Robt. to Caroline Miller 11 Mar. 1828   Ray
McGee, Robt. to Nancy Simpson 13 Mar. 1828   Rall
McGee, Robt. to Sarah McPerson 4 Jan. 1829   Coop
McGee, Robt. to Susan Smith 29 Oct. 1835   Monr
McGee, Samuel to Polly March 2 May 1837   Boon
McGee, Samuel K. to Agnes McDaniel 14 July 1831   Ray
McGee, Thomas to Susannah Donaldson 22 Oct. 1834   Morg
McGee, Wm. to Margaret Smith 23 Sept. 1832   Monr
McGeehe, Robt. to Elizabeth Bray 25 Mar. 1838   Barr
McGill, Henderson to Lucinda Long 8 Nov. 1832   Ray
McGilton, G. to Rachael Hudson 8 Aug. 1839   Sali
McGinnis, Achilles to Jane Briggs 28 Apr. 1822   Rall
McGinnis, Hardin to Cynthia A. Thurmond 20 Dec. 1836   Pk-A
McGirk, Matthias to Elizabeth Talbot 3 Mar. 1818   StCh
McGlochlin, Wm. to Jane Turnidge 8 Oct. 1833   Ray
McGowan, Leroy to Sarah Branson 14 Mar. 1834   Gasc
McGowen, Daniel to Susan Hinkson 20 Aug. 1838   Boon
McGowen, Geo. to Lucinda Gibs 15 Mar. 1837   Monr
McGrady, Israel to Lucy M. McIlvain 1 May 1831   Wash
McGready, Israel to Nancy Covington 24 Nov. 1825   Wash
McGready, John to Isabelle McIlvain 15 Dec. 1825   Wash
McGrew, Charles to Margaret Bozarth 29 Oct. 1824   Howa
McGrew, Geo. H. to Eliza M. Turley 7 Sept. 1837   Rall
McGrew, Wm. to Rebecca Donelson 5 Mar. 1834   Monr
McGrooder, Greenbury to Julia A. Whitelow 22 June 1834   CG-A
McGuess, Allen to Mary Oldham 11 Oct. 1831   Boon
McGuffin, Charles to Amanda Hust 5 May 1836   Sali
McGuire, Elams to Catherine E. Lewis 12 Apr. 1838   StCh
McGuire, James M. to Lucinda L. Farrar 2 Aug. 1832   CG-A
McGuire, John to Nancy Wheat 12 June 1827   Ray
McGuire, John W. to Hannah C. Ranney 7 Nov. 1832   CG-A
McGuire, Thom to Mira Pollard 3 Nov. 1835   Coop
McGuire, Wm. to Louiza Howard 6 Sept. 1838   CG-A
McGuire, Wm. E. to Elizabeth Farrar 4 Dec. 1834   CG-B
McGurd, John to Sarah McDaniel 8 Sept. 1824   Lafa
McHargue, John M. to M. Warmoth 31 Dec. 1839   Livi
McHarris, John to Sentha Steward 14 July 1836   John
McHaslain, M. Daniel to Jude Wade 13 Jan. 1838   Henr
McHenry, Elam to Nancy Poston 18 Jan. 1827   StFr
McHenry, James B. to Sidney Edgar 5 Feb. 1828   Wash
McIlvain, Jesse to Meaky Smith 17 Apr. 1834   StFr
McIlvain, Orville E. to Minerva Baker 22 Jan. 1835   StFr
McIntire, Charles W. to Margaret Harrison 10 Jan. 1828   Call
McIntosh, J.B. to Angelique Berribo 8 Oct. 1835   StCh
McKamey, James M. to Elizabeth Murray 8 Jan. 1829   Call
McKamey, Wm. H. to Angelina Scott 17 June 1836   Call
McKaroll, James to Manirvia Warren 25 June 1833   Gree
McKat, Wm. to Adeline Wilson 28 Jan. 1839   Jeff
McKay, Christopher to Jane Stewart 14 Oct. 1838   Linc
McKay, Jacob to Nancy Allen 23 Oct. 1828   Ray
McKay, Lewis to Susanna McKay 25 Sept. 1834   Clay
McKee, Andrew P. to Sarinda Boyd 15 Dec. 1836   Coop
McKee, Ewen to Rebecca Steele 17 July 1832   CG-A
McKee, Hiram to Nancy Truesdell 21 May 1833   Fran
McKee, James to Elizabeth Mulherron 9 June 1833   Pk-1
McKee, Joel Y. to Sarah A. Dodd 5 Apr. 1838   Rall
McKee, Michael to Louisa Gamble 19 Mar. 1835   Jeff
McKee, Peter to Caroline Ellis 9 May 1837   Clay
McKee, Seth G. to Auza M. Jones 10 May 1839   Jeff
McKee, Thomas to Rhoda ---- 20 Jan. 1831   StFr
McKee, Wm. to Emily Chandler 1 Dec. 1836   Linc
McKeen, Thomas to Clarinda Tindal 27 May 1829   Howa
McKenney, Henry to Nancy P. Dodson 5 Oct. 1837   StCh

145

```
McKenny, Francis to Elizabeth Jones 25 July 1832          Coop
McKenny, Nelson to Nancy Moad 21 Jan. 1838               Cole
McKenny, Seth to Cordely Baul 7 Nov. 1839               Cole
McKenny, Stephen to Louisa Anderson 23 Nov. 1826         Boon
McKenny, Wilson to Lavinia Hughes 27 Mar. 1832           Boon
McKensey, Elexander to Marthay Mayhan 17 Sept. 1838      Barr
McKensey, Kenneth to Eliza Smith 13 Jan. 1828            Coop
McKenzie, Havington to Elizabeth Russell 21 Nov. 1833    CG-A
McKenzie, Isaac to Sarah Tipton 28 Nov. 1837             Boon
McKenzie, Kenethen to Ann Welch 13 Oct. 1831             CG-A
McKenzie, Kenneth to Rachel Tabor 3 Jan. 1819            Howa
McKey, Cyrus to Malinda Jones 23 Nov. 1830               Pk-1
McKiney, Henry to Susannah Gouge 26 Apr. 1827            Cole
McKinney, Abner W. to Celeste Connoyer 23 Apr. 1835      StCh
McKinney, Caswell to Anna Murry 10 Aug. 1831             Cole
McKinney, Charles to Mary A. Craig 10 Feb. 1830          Call
McKinney, David to Maria Massey 21 May 1834              Gasc
McKinney, David to Nancy Wade 27 Aug. 1837               Cole
McKinney, Henry to Nancy P. Dodson 5 Oct. 1837           Warr
McKinney, James to Rhoda Berdon 23 Feb. 1834             Gree
McKinney, Jessee to Eliza Lancaster 23 Aug. 1835         CG-B
McKinney, John to Anna Keshler 13 June 1819              Howa
McKinney, John to Juda Landrum 9 Jan. 1834               Cole
McKinney, John to Anna E. Hill 21 Sept. 1837             Call
McKinney, Matthew to Nancy Godsey 30 Aug. 1829           CG-A
McKinney, Phillip to Jane Neel 25 Apr. 1839              Ray
McKinney, Robt. to Elizabeth Brigs 19 Mar. 1837          Gasc
McKinney, Samuel L. to Artenisia P. McLean 20 Mar. 1833  Rand
McKinney, Seth to Jane Patterson 15 Sept. 1834           Cole
McKinney, Wm. to Sarah West 13 Aug. 1829                 Mari
McKinny, Alexander to Nancy Bryant 31 Mar. 1814          StCh
McKinny, Colvin to Roena Gilmore 7 Jan. 1838             Cole
McKinsey, Wm. to Elizabeth Sheppard 22 July 1830         CG-A
McKiny, Robt. to Nancy Carter 29 Sept. 1831              Cr-1
McKinzie, Allen to Helene Randoll 22 Oct. 1805           CGRA
McKinzie, Daniel to Martha A. Lewis 11 Jan. 1829         Cole
McKinzie, Nelson to Martha A. Dunicky 5 Oct. 1833        Cole
McKirk, Geo. to Mary J. Bowman 12 Feb. 1822              Howa
McKissick, John to Jane English 10 Feb. 1835             Clay
McKnight, John F. to Sarah J. Griffith 29 June 1828      StCh
McKnight, John F. to Abigail Robbins 1 Apr. 1833         StCh
McKnight, Wm. to Mahaly Laughten 1 Jan. 1839             Gasc
McKorkle, Robt. to Manervy Forrest 20 Oct. 1825          Char
McKoun, Lawrence to Elizabeth McKoun 7 May 1832          Clay
McKown, James to Olive Butler 12 Feb. 1839               Clin
McKown, Jeremiah to Adeliada Livingston 13 June 1836     Clin
McKown, Jesse to Sarah J. Finch 7 Feb. 1839              Plat
McKoy, James to Patsy Hardwick 3 June 1833               Clay
McLane, Alfred to Clarissa Steeley 12 Oct. 1837          Perr
McLane, David D. to Elizabeth Devenport 27 July 1830     CG-A
McLane, John A. to Mary Hayden 29 Nov. 1832              Perr
McLard, Daniel to Rachel Pierce 18 June 1835             CG-B
McLard, Henry to Nancy Minton 3 Mar. 1830               CG-A
McLard, Joseph to Eleanor Abernathie 9 Jan. 1838         CG-A
McLaughlain, John to Martha A. Sidwell 28 Feb. 1833      Pk-1
McLaughlin, Abraham to Mary A. Turnidge 14 Nov. 1834     Ray
McLaughlin, Cornelius to Mary Niece 9 July 1837          Cole
McLaughlin, Daniel to Julia Logston 8 Mar. 1832          Cole
McLaughlin, Daniel to Sarah Bilyeu 24 Dec. 1838          Mill
McLaughlin, James to Frances Burford 13 Apr. 1826        Wash
McLaughlin, Joseph to Polly Raglin 1 Jan. 1837           StFr
McLaughlin, Michael to Mary Hase 28 Feb. 1832            Perr
McLaughlin, Wm. to Leny Callaway 19 Feb. 1829            Call
McLean, David H. to Nancy Clay 13 May 1837               Warr
McLean, Elijah D. to Judith Rule 23 June 1831            Fran
```

146

```
McLean, Jeremiah to Mary Donnell 19 July 1838                        Jeff
McLelland, John F. to Caroline M. Dutch 21 Nov. 1833                 CG-A
McLenny, John C. to Sarah J. Welch 28 June 1838                      Warr
McLoskey, Archibald to Nancy Sumner 6 Jan. 1836                      StCh
McLure, Samuel to Ann Masterson 3 Nov. 1831                         CG-A
McMahan, Isham to Elizabeth Duncan 6 Jan. 1831                       Call
McMahan, James to Nancy Young 5 July 1821                            Sali
McMahan, Jesse to Polly McMahan 16 Mar. 1822                         Sali
McMahan, Jesse to Susan Vaughn 19 Jan. 1837                          Sali
McMahan, Moses to Sarah Groom 4 Feb. 1836                            Clin
McMahan, Richard to Louisa J. Love 1 Nov. 1832                       Call
McMahan, Samuel to Martha Miller 3 Dec. 1833                         Coop
McMahan, Samuel W. to Harriett Riddle 17 Mar. 1833                   Coop
McMahan, Thomas Jr. to Lucy Riddle 25 Mar. 1830                      Coop
McMahan, Wm. to Sarah Huston 5 Jan. 1826                             Coop
McMahon, Jesse to Emily Cunningham 12 Apr. 1835                      Carr
McMahon, John to Polly Millsap 27 Oct. 1836                          Coop
McMahon, John M. to Elzira Turley 19 Apr. 1832                       Coop
McMannus, Charles to Susan C. Pointer 12 Aug. 1837                   Gasc
McMannus, John to Elizabeth Sparks 24 Apr. 1828                      Wash
McMay, Jackson to Maria Johnson 17 Nov. 1835                         Cole
McMeans, John to Ruth Green 5 Jan. 1827                              Jeff
McMillan, Charles B. to Mary A. Hunter 3 Nov. 1839                   Plat
McMillan, Robertson to Polly M. Martin 28 June 1836                 Cole
McMillen, James to Tabitha Unsel 26 Aug. 1830                        Pk-1
McMillen, John M. to Coanza Howell 29 Aug. 1827                      StCh
McMillen, Thomas to Ursula Humphrey 25 Sept. 1828                   Pk-1
McMillin, Aaron to Sarah Zumwalt 19 Jan. 1826                        Call
McMinn, Nicholas to Pena Culbertson 1 Oct. 1834                      Mari
McMinn, Nicholas to Camelia S. Clark 10 Jan. 1839                    Polk
McMinnis, Lawrence W. to Elizabeth Roggers 13 Jan. 1838             Clay
McMullen, Joseph L. to Elizabeth Kinney 6 May 1827                   Jeff
McMullen, Robt. to Rebecca Mullen 10 Nov. 1827                       Jeff
McMullen, Wm. to Sally Phares 25 June 1833                           Howa
McMullin, James to Mahala Wise 4 May 1837                            Jeff
McMullin, James H. to Kitty Flemming 31 Mar. 1836                    Jeff
McMullin, John F. to Eliza M. Jameson 21 Apr. 1835                   Jeff
McMuntry, Thomas to Charlotte Maupin 6 Nov. 1836                     Carr
McMurtrey, James to Polly McMurtrey 25 July 1826                     Md-A
McMurtrey, John to Clementine McMurtrey 11 Nov. 1830                Md-A
McMurtrey, Joseph to Mariah Morris 21 July 1829                      Wash
McMurtry, Alexander to Emily McPherson 14 Nov. 1838                 Rall
McMurtry, Wm. to Eleanor Kabler 17 Feb. 1835                         Warr
McMurty, James to Serelda Hays 10 Oct. 1832                          Call
McMurty, Levi to Fanny Chick 5 May 1831                              Call
McNair, Alexander to Dincy McCoy 21 Oct. 1834                        Pk-1
McNally, John to Mary Murphy 29 May 1833                             Wash
McNamee, Laurence V. to Errelia Cole 25 Mar. 1829                    StCh
McNay, Howard to Harriet Rowland 18 Sept. 1836                       Boon
McNeal, Benj. to Laviny Stout 12 Sept. 1837                          Wash
McNeal, John to Sarah Willoughby 8 Nov. 1839                         Pett
McNeal, Joseph R. to Rachel Long 1 Sept. 1835                        Ripl
McNeely, Ezekial to Mary A. Wilson 31 Oct. 1837                     CG-A
McNeely, Wm. B. to Elizabeth McPherson 17 Sept. 1839               CG-B
McNees, John C. to Margaret Meadew 24 Oct. 1837                     Howa
McNeily, John to Salina Tuttle 30 May 1839                          Linc
McNew, Frederick to Charlotte Box 28 Feb. 1837                      Pett
McNight, Abel to Polly Trotter 25 Jan. 1829                          Jack
McNight, Wm. to Zephore Block 29 Dec. 1835                          CG-B
McNutt, John to Margaret Wells 27 Nov. 1832                          StCh
McOdell, Thomas to Betsy Clemmons 26 July 1832                       Ray
McPeake, Matthew to Ruth Hobson 19 Jan. 1836                         Jeff
McPhatridge, James to Sarah Scott 18 July 1833                       Boon
McPheeter, Wm. to Lidia A. Boggs 11 Apr. 1839                        Mari
McPheeters, James S. to Caroline L. Redd 22 Jan. 1837               Mari
```

McPheeters, Joseph H. to Nancy Rodd 31 Jan. 1838   Mari
McPheeters, Wm. to Ruthy M. Reed 27 Nov. 1827   Boon
McPherson, Benj. to Sarah A. Woods 8 Dec. 1839   Coop
McPherson, John to Sarah Newkirk 11 Sept. 1838   Morg
McPheters, Charles W. to Mary C. Berry 6 July 1835   Monr
McPheters, Jacob B. to Julia A. Nall 2 May 1833   Lewi
McPike, Jesse to Nancy Boydston 28 Aug. 1834   Clay
McQuie, E.J. to E. Yale 24 Feb. 1834   Linc
McQuie, Edwin to Margaret Smith 8 Oct. 1837   Pk-B
McQuie, John W. to Elizabeth E. Rowland 24 Sept. 1839   Pk-B
McQuiston, Jarmin to Rebecca McClintock 4 Apr. 1830   Ray
McQuitty, Andrew to Mary Crain 24 June 1832   Boon
McQuitty, Daniel to Susan Whitesides 24 Mar. 1835   Boon
McQuitty, David to E. Copher 17 Apr. 1823   Boon
McQuitty, Geo. to Elizabeth A. Roland 29 July 1824   Boon
McRae, John to Mary Cook 20 June 1836   Mari
McRae, Stephen to Isabella Thrasher 22 Sept. 1825   Rall
McRees, John to Jane M. Jordan 5 Nov. 1837   Pk-B
McReynolds, John to Sarah Henry 14 Feb. 1828   Mari
McReynolds, Nelson to Ann Craig 28 June 1836   Lafa
McRoberts, Preston to Fannie Waid 1 Dec. 1831   Linc
McSwain, Wm. M. to Frances Walker 8 July 1832   Pk-1
McVicker, James to Mahala Dickerson 23 Apr. 1839   Shel
McWard, Francis to Nancy Wilson 20 Oct. 1831   CR-1
McWaters, James M. to Rhoda Woodlan 10 Dec. 1829   StCh
McWaters, John to Lydia Wingfield 14 Apr. 1831   StCh
McWilliams, Andrew to Mrs. Catharine Powell 29 Nov. 1838   Mari
McWilliams, Geo. W. to Levina B. McKinney 10 Dec. 1835   Warr
McWilliams, James to Cynthia Norris 24 Apr. 1827   Lafa
McWilliams, James to Patsy Mitchell 2 Apr. 1835   Lewi
McWilliams, James H. to Mary K. Bunds 15 Jan. 1832   Clay
McWilliams, John to Lousinda Carter 13 Mar. 1828   Clay
McWilliams, John to Elizabeth Wathen 4 May 1835   CG-B
McWilliams, Joseph to Jedidah Perkins 20 Nov. 1831   Lafa
McWilliams, Presly to Eliza J. McCoy 9 Apr. 1836   Fran

Mabe, James to Nancy Murdock 4 Mar. 1831   StCh
Maberry, Cornelius to Mary J. Sanders 6 Aug. 1833   Lafa
Maberry, David to Elizabeth McDaniels 10 Apr. 1837   CG-A
Mabery, Phillip to Mary Uptegrove 21 Nov. 1834   Linc
Mabray, Pleasant to Barshaba Ingram 1 Mar. 1832   Pk-1
Maccord, Robert to Mary A. Tailor 29 May 1834   Monr
Maccoun, John to Peggy Livingston 7 Feb. 1828   Clay
Mace, Solomon to Clary Sutton 1 Sept. 1839   Boon
Machett, Charles C. to Margaret Bruin 21 Mar. 1834   StCh
Mackey, John A. to Sarah Sinclair 7 Oct. 1834   Pk-1
Mackey, Thomas J. to Sarah Griffith 11 Aug. 1831   Pk-1
Mackmillen, Samuel to Ann Calwell 12 Mar. 1835   Pk-1
Macmahale, James to Almeda Pigg 3 June 1837   Pk-B
Madding, Thomas to Elizabeth Jeans 4 Apr. 1835   Linc
Maddox, Alfred to Susan Rupe 20 Mar. 1834   Lafa
Maddox, Joseph to Melinda Forrest 28 Oct. 1824   Char
Made---, Geo. to Katherine Schneider 14 Feb. 1837   StCh
Madison, Geo. to Elizabeth McFarland 16 Oct. 1825   StFr
Madison, Thomas to Caroline Griffith 3 Jan. 1830   StFr
Madison, Wm. to Sarah M. Taylor 14 Apr. 1831   StFr
Madkins, Leroy to Sally Chasteen 27 Apr. 1831   CR-1
Magdaline, Baptiste to Margarite Tiercerau 1 Oct. 1827   StCh
Magee, Henry to Rosanna Reed 10 Feb. 1833   Gasc
Magee, John to Matilda Martin 15 May 1823   Char
Magers, David to Nancy Johnson 29 Jan. 1835   Monr
Maggard, Henry to Elizabeth Skinner 29 Jan. 1832   Rand
Magill, David P. to Sally Gragg 10 Mar. 1825   Clay
Magill, David P. to Elizabeth Roberts 20 Sept. 1835   Clay

```
Magill, John to Phoebe Head 7 Aug. 1815                          StCh
Magill, John to Saray Groom 4 Jan. 1827                          Clay
Magill, Samuel to Milly Campbell 24 Dec. 1822                    Clay
Magill, Samuel to Eliza Huffman 19 Aug. 1824                     Clay
Magill, Samuel to Margarett Owens 4 Jan. 1831                    Clay
Magill, Samuel to Elvina McGaugh 29 Jan. 1835                    Ray
Magnor, Jeremiah to Susan E. Searcy 7 Oct. 1829                  Clay
Mahan, Anthony to Zilpha Jennings 29 May 1834                    Clay
Mahan, David P. to Susan Letchworth 17 Sept. 1820               Coop
Mahan, James to Nancy Miller 8 Feb. 1829                         Coop
Mahan, Porter to Jean Turner 23 July 1818                        Howa
Mahon, James to Polly Scruggs 2 Aug. 1832                        Cole
Mahoney, Andrew to Sally A. Moxley 21 Aug. 1828                  Call
Mahonny, Daniel to Malinda Leach 1 Nov. 1835                     Call
Maier, Joseph to Ann Schneider 9 Feb. 1839                       CG-B
Mainiss, Ephriam to Sally Mainiss 25 July 1836                   Wash
Major, Samuel C. to Elizabeth Daly 5 Mar. 1829                   Howa
Majors, Alex to Katherine Stalkup 6 Nov. 1834                    Jack
Mal-jnger, Geo. to Margaret Carter 27 Sept. 1837                 StCh
Malett, Philip to Sally Webb 9 Dec. 1830                         Mari
Malicoat, Daniel to Malinda Whitenburg 6 Mar. 1838              Gree
Malicotes, Mooney to Effy Johnson 21 May 1837                    Polk
Mallert, John E. to Ruby Waterman 29 Dec. 1839                   Ray
Mallin, Jesse to Margaret McNair 20 Apr. 1834                    Linc
Mallinckrodt, Wm. J. to Mary McCurry 15 July 1832               StCh
Mallinkrodt, Emil to Eleanor Lucky 10 Feb. 1833                  StCh
Mally, Matthew to Kitty Peyton 26 July 1838                      Maco
Malone, Anderson to Malissa Davis 4 Jan. 1838                    Livi
Malone, Andrew to Ann McLain 21 Oct. 1832                        CG-A
Malone, Galvin to Julietta Smith 23 May 1839                     CG-B
Malone, Jonathan to Nancy Hammon 5 Sept. 1833                    CG-A
Malone, Richard to Elizabeth Constible 25 Dec. 1830             Jack
Malone, Robt. to Matilda Arthur 17 Apr. 1830                     Wash
Malott, Hardin to Sally A. Collins 7 Nov. 1838                   Jack
Malott, Joseph to Polly Smith 27 Oct. 1831                       Clay
Malott, Thomas to Mahala Munkres 12 Apr. 1832                    Clay
Malott, Wm. to Christena Moore 28 Dec. 1823                      Clay
Maloy, Bartholomew to Mrs. Brigett Moore 25 Apr. 1830          Clay
Maloy, Wm. to Sarah Glaze 1 Sept. 1839                           Carr
Man, Finas to Deanna Duncan 5 Mar. 1835                          Md-A
Man, Isaac to Milley Lester 1 Mar. 1832                          Wash
Manchester, David to Jinney Rawlings 7 Feb. 1822               Howa
Manes, Lewis to Elizabeth Brown 1 Jan. 1839                      Coop
Maniru, Jonas to Nancy Dunlap 1 Jan. 1836                        Ray
Manley, John to Ozzhague Papin 11 Apr. 1809                      StCh
Mann, Alfred to Juliet Wilson 4 Sept. 1838                       Howa
Mann, Charles H. to Magadorah McWilliams 26 Apr. 1838          Fran
Mann, Jacob to Elizabeth Cavit 4 Sept. 1828                      Md-A
Mann, Marshall to Mrs. Permelia Allen 2 May 1831               Mari
Mann, Thomas to Mrs. Mildred Jones 22 Sept. 1836               Linc
Mann, Wm. to Lucinda Carter 27 June 1837                         Linc
Mann, Wm. to Sarah Stearns 7 Sept. 1838                          Carr
Manning, Cornelius to Anna Moore -- Oct. 1825                    Perr
Manning, Geo. to Nancy Hargrove 5 Feb. 1837                      Sali
Manning, Hiliariah to Mary Moore 10 Aug. 1830                    Perr
Manning, John to Ann Windfield 22 Nov. 1825                      Perr
Manning, Joseph Sr. to Sarah Shurtley 12 May 1834              Perr
Manning, Pius to Reney Perdy 13 Sept. 1836                       Perr
Manning, Robt. to Ann Mattingly 18 Apr. 1826                     Perr
Manning, Sidney to Eliza Williams 18 June 1837                  Wash
Manning, Wm. to Sarah A. Layton 6 Oct. 1829                      Perr
Mansfield, Allen to Martha A. Turpin 28 Sept. 1837             Lafa
Mansfield, Geo. to Malvina Banks 11 Oct. 1837                    Lafa
Manship, Geo. to Sally Stokes 28 July 1822                       Lafa
Mansker, Lewis to Jane Smith 24 June 1826                        CG-A
```

149

```
Mapes, ---- to Harriett Williams 8 Jan. 1835                          Jeff
Mappin, Mathew to Eliza McGee 26 Oct. 1826                            Rall
Marais, Augustin to Cecilia Degagne 21 May 1827                      Wash
Marble, Jeames to Lewyze Love 15 Apr. 1828                           Wash
March, Charles to Ann Frost 27 Oct. 1835                             Boon
March, John to Polly A. Smith 28 Mar. 1838                           Boon
March, Robt. to Nancy C. Anderson 6 Nov. 1836                        Coop
March, Tyre to Agness Still 21 Jan. 1830                             Boon
March, Wm. to Hannah Winn 16 Jan. 1833                               Boon
Marchal, Baptist to Christian Voisard 2 Feb. 1829                    StCh
Marechalle, Francis to Mary Dubeaut 25 Aug. 1830                     StCh
Margrave, Wm. L. to Matilda Decker 16 Aug. 1838                      Fran
Marhen, Thomas to Katherine Fields 14 May 1827                       Boon
Marie, Francis to Cecile Deschamps 2 Aug. 1817                       StCh
Marinier, Jaque to Catherine Joffre 4 May 1819                       StCh
Markle, Charles Jr. to Elizabeth E. Lippincott 16 Dec. 1824         Rall
Markle, Charles to Catherine McFarland 22 Feb. 1838                  Rall
Markle, John to Susan Inskeep 27 Oct. 1835                           Mari
Markle, Richard B. to Nancy Barnett 28 July 1839                     Rall
Markle, Wm. to Mary Thomas 17 Mar. 1836                              Monr
Markley, John M. to Mary A. Robison 17 Sept. 1839                    Pk-B
Marklin, Cyrus C. to Eliza D. Morris 23 Sept. 1836                   Howa
Markrom, Thomas to Sally Jones 13 Sept. 1825                         Clay
Marks, John N. to Mary C. Brown 14 Oct. 1838                         Lewi
Marksworth, Christoph to Federeki R. Muller 25 Aug. 1839             Perr
Markum, Meddon to Nancy Collett 28 Feb. 1828                         Boon
Marler, Joseph to Mary Massy 25 May 1834                             Wash
Marler, Levi to Ruth Williams 18 Nov. 1838                           Wash
Marley, Abel to Catherine Cockrell 21 Jan. 1821                      Howa
Marley, Eli to Sarah Boyles 5 Mar. 1833                              Coop
Marlin, Daniel to Matilda Allen 21 Aug. 1834                        Pett
Marlin, Spencer to Susan Patterson 20 Dec. 1835                      Gree
Marlin, Thomas to Sevesee Lee 23 May 1839                            Pett
Marlin, Wilson to Nancy Allen 1 Dec. 1836                            Pett
Marlow, Gabriel to Julie Chancellier 23 Jan. 1834                    StCh
Marlow, James to Jane Doren 1 Mar. 1827                              StFr
Marmaduke, Meredith M. to Levinia Sappington 4 Jan. 1826            Sali
Marmaduke, Wm. D. to Elmira Johns 6 Apr. 1838                        Mari
Marquiss, Geo. W. to Mary Duncan 29 Mar. 1832                        Ray
Marr, Almond to Emily Greer 10 Apr. 1834                             Lafa
Marr, Daniel P. to Tabitha Martin 11 Oct. 1838                       Clay
Marr, Jesse to Catharine Parkison 18 Nov. 1829                       Lafa
Marr, John to Sally Braly 17 Jan. 1828                               Clay
Marr, Rickson to Matilda Green 4 Dec. 1834                           Howa
Marr, Thomas to Mary Jeffries 23 Feb. 1822                           Sali
Marr, Wm. to Mary E. Faulkner 17 Jan. 1838                           Clay
Marrow, Andrew to Theresa Peyton 28 Oct. 1836                        StFr
Marrow, Wm. to Onia Branam 20 Feb. 1835                              Ripl
Marrs, Andrew J. to Martha Danley 10 Oct. 1837                       Barr
Marrs, Franklin to Juliann Havens 5 Oct. 1837                        Barr
Marrs, Jeremiah R. to Margaret Shannon 8 May 1834                    Gree
Marsey, Frederick to Minna Bock 7 Dec. 1834                          Warr
Marsh, Jonathan to Nancy J. Bradley 9 Oct. 1834                      Howa
Marshal, Flemming to Frances Frey 28 Feb. 1837                       Howa
Marshall, Isham to Polly Barns 24 Apr. 1831                          Lafa
Marshall, James to Sarah McClure 19 Dec. 1830                        Howa
Marshall, James J. to Elizabeth J. Henshaw 9 Feb. 1837              Clay
Marshall, Rhodes to Mary Finley 2 Nov. 1837                          Sali
Marshall, Richard to Patcy Bennett 28 Oct. 1830                      Md-A
Marshall, Richard F. to Marget Bennett 29 July 1838                 Md-B
Marshall, Samuel to Sarah Covert 13 Oct. 1834                        Pett
Marshall, Thomas J. to Martha A. Wyatt 9 Aug. 1838                   Warr
Marshel, John to Berthena Smith 18 July 1833                         Cole
Martain, Andrus to Sally Farrar 7 Jan. 1817                          StGe
Martan, James to Sarah Balsha 31 Aug. 1837                           Perr
```

150

```
Martenon, Francois to Julia Lepage 9 Jan. 1831                          StCh
Martin, Amos to Mahala Williams 8 Nov. 1835                             Boon
Martin, Anderson to Margaret Rees 24 Sept. 1829                         Ray
Martin, Bughlberry to Elizabeth Willis 22 Feb. 1835                     Clay
Martin, Bughwell to Nancy Lessley 16 Feb. 1832                          Rand
Martin, Caleb to Louisa Crowder 28 Nov. 1833                           Coop
Martin, Caleb to Frances Woods 19 Feb. 1835                            Howa
Martin, Christian to Elizabeth Hornman 24 Mar. 1839                    CG-B
Martin, Christopher to Pemela Job 19 Jan. 1824                         Lafa
Martin, Daniel to Mrs. Elizabeth Morning 5 Jan. 1830                   StCh
Martin, Daniel to Sarah M. Barker 18 Oct. 1831                         StCh
Martin, Evin C. to Mrs. Audrey Davis 19 June 1810                      StCh
Martin, Geo. to Catharine Matthews 14 Nov. 1833                        CG-A
Martin, Geo. to Polly Cowin 17 Jan. 1836                               Gasc
Martin, Geo. W. to Isabella McKay 2 Apr. 1835                          Cole
Martin, Geo. W. to Nancy J. Liggett 19 Nov. 1835                       Carr
Martin, Gill E. to Tabitha Thorp 21 July 1834                          Clay
Martin, Greenberry to Eliza Bones 1 June 1834                          Ray
Martin, Hardin D. to Avolina Cearcy 1 Nov. 1838                        Clay
Martin, Henry to Mary Thompson 2 Sept. 1838                            Monr
Martin, Henry to Lanny Reavis 24 Apr. 1839                             Mari
Martin, Hugh to Elizabeth T. Bright 23 May 1829                        Ray
Martin, Hugh to Hester A. Brewer 6 Mar. 1834                           Ray
Martin, Isaac to Mary Smith 22 Feb. 1827                               Coop
Martin, James to Margaret George 23 Mar. 1830                          Coop
Martin, James to Celia A. Patterson 15 May 1834                        Howa
Martin, James to Patsy Hardin 3 Nov. 1839                              Rand
Martin, James F. to Sarrie Rudissel 6 June 1837                        Perr
Martin, James L. to Zerilda Bainbridge 10 May 1832                     StCh
Martin, John to Margery Miller 26 Apr. 1818                            Howa
Martin, John to Sarah Harrington 4 Feb. 1830                           Clay
Martin, John to Catharine Friend 9 Jan. 1834                           Gree
Martin, John to Ruth Howard 23 July 1835                               Cole
Martin, John to Rosannah Ross 23 Oct. 1836                             CG-A
Martin, John to Elizabeth Bowling 24 Dec. 1839                         Monr
Martin, John A. to Margaret Willingham 20 Dec. 1838                    Audr
Martin, John B. to Mary A. Loring 28 Mar. 1833                         Mari
Martin, John W. to Elizabeth A. Folwell 26 July 1835                   Perr
Martin, Jonathan P. to Polly Inglish 4 July 1822                       Cole
Martin, Jonathan P. to Margaret Shipley 6 Apr. 1828                    Coop
Martin, Joseph to Rebecca Carson 11 Oct. 1821                          Howa
Martin, Joseph to Malinda McKinzie 1 May 1838                          Cole
Martin, Joseph to Lucinda Cotton 12 July 1838                          Mill
Martin, Joshua to Elizabeth Edwards 4 Oct. 1832                        Coop
Martin, Julius to Elizabeth McPherson 19 Feb. 1839                     Lafa
Martin, Noah to Virginia Closby 11 Feb. 1835                           Call
Martin, Noah to Judith P. Oliver 12 Apr. 1836                          Rand
Martin, Osimus A. to Nancy Warner 8 Oct. 1828                          Wash
Martin, Robt. to Ann Baker 22 Feb. 1827                                Call
Martin, Robt. to Nancy Herd 3 Nov. 1831                                Linc
Martin, Robt. A. to Margaret Spence 17 Oct. 1833                       Gree
Martin, Robt. B. to Rebecca Wood 26 Dec. 1830                          Rall
Martin, Samuel to Judith Wright 21 May 1829                            Call
Martin, Thomas to Lydia Hendricks 3 Aug. 1823                          Ray
Martin, Thomas to Louisa Kinsey 17 Apr. 1834                           Lafa
Martin, Thomas to Julia A. Elliott 2 Jan. 1838                         Howa
Martin, Thomas to Martha Creason 11 Mar. 1838                          Ray
Martin, Thomas to Elizabeth Boon 12 Nov. 1838                          Gasc
Martin, Tiry to Elvira Thompson 26 Mar. 1834                           Pk-1
Martin, Valentino to Catherine Inglish 25 Oct. 1832                    Cole
Martin, Wm. to Phebe Foly 5 July 1825                                  Boon
Martin, Wm. to Catharine Wise 5 Jan. 1827                              Jeff
Martin, Wm. to Margaret McKay 15 Dec. 1836                             Cole
Martin, Wm. to Eliza Davis 9 Aug. 1838                                 Linc
Martin, Wm. B. to Mary Shirkey 24 Jan. 1839                            lewi
```

Martin, Wm. H. to Sophronia McLanahan 26 Dec. 1835   Call
Martin, Wm. H. to Sarah True 6 Oct. 1836   Mari
Martin, Wm. J. to Harriet Crobarger 22 Aug. 1839   Plat
Martin, Wm. N. to Eliza Kilgore 9 Aug. 1838   Audr
Martin, Zadoc to Sarah McElwee 15 May 1823   Clay
Martinau, Charles to Catherine Loise 23 Mar. 1829   StCh
Martindale, Howard to Elizabeth Eaton 9 Aug. 1838   Wash
Martineau, Pierre to Adrienne LePage 13 Jan. 1834   StCh
Marvin, Edmund to Lory Sherwood 12 Oct. 1834   Clay
Mase, John to Louisa Harris 8 Mar. 1832   Pk-1
Masengill, Samuel to Nancy Wilhite 30 June 1836   Clay
Mason, Albert to Susana Spires 26 Dec. 1833   Warr
Mason, Albert to Sarah King 27 Nov. 1834   Jack
Mason, Andrew J. to Juliet Olba 27 Nov. 1831   StCh
Mason, David to Hannah Hays 19 Dec. 1824   Howa
Mason, Geo. G. to Elizabeth Carter 19 July 1838   Monr
Mason, Glaswell to Nancy Edwards 29 Apr. 1835   Warr
Mason, James to Nancy Wood 12 Sept. 1830   Coop
Mason, John to Polly Paul 24 July 1825   Howa
Mason, John W. to Sarah H. Lewis 15 May 1835   Ripl
Mason, Nimrod to Latty Baldwin 23 Feb. 1835   Ripl
Mason, Perry L. to Catharine A. Barnard 20 July 1838   Monr
Mason, Samuel G. to Mary Andrew 22 Feb. 1839   Call
Mason, Samuel T. to Susannah Burns 18 Sept. 1839   Plat
Mason, Stephen to Rebecca Robertson 24 May 1832   Gasc
Mason, Thomas to Mary Sampson 10 Feb. 1834   Gasc
Mason, Vestel W. to ---- Prather 19 Dec. 1838   Maco
Mason, Wm. to Nelly Richardson 16 Feb. 1830   Howa
Mason, Wm. to Celia Simpson 27 Sept. 1835   Gasc
Mason, Wm. M. to Sarah Goodrich 1 Aug. 1839   StCh
Masquirter, Alfred to Emilee O'Bryan 28 Feb. 1837   Coop
Massey, Ephriam to Eliza Warren 7 July 1836   Gree
Massey, Henry A. to Nancy D. Massey 22 June 1829   Cr-P
Massey, James to Nancy Keeny 24 May 1827   Sali
Massey, James to Martha Anderson 10 July 1838   Gree
Massey, Nathanial to Nancy Ellison 9 Mar. 1837   Gree
Massey, Tarleton to Caroline Ward 3 Sept. 1835   Gasc
Massie, Charles to Luiza Rowarth 15 Feb. 1827   Gasc
Massie, D. to T. Petty 22 Apr. 1830   Gasc
Massie, Geo. to Margaret Branson 29 Dec. 1833   Gasc
Massie, Peter to Charlotte Rodney 3 Mar. 1814   CG-1
Massie, Thomas to Betsy Cooly 28 July 1815   StCh
Massie, Wm. to Elizabeth Hill 10 Jan. 1828   Gasc
Masters, Henry to Susan Moyers 13 July 1837   CG-A
Masters, Michael to Jamima Spencer 20 Nov. 1834   Gree
Masters, Wm. to Ann Turner 19 May 1829   Howa
Masterson, Elijah to Rebecca Hall 17 Feb. 1829   CG-A
Masterson, John A. to Nancy James 9 Sept. 1837   Pk-B
Masterson, Samuel to Nancy Brooks 9 Nov. 1826   CG-A
Mathens, Thomas to Maryan Adams 15 Jan. 1838   John
Matheny, Daniel to Susan Ewell 22 Feb. 1836   Carr
Mathes, Thomas to Katharine Mathes 12 Feb. 1835   Gree
Mathew, Diego C. to Azila J. Ligon 19 June 1834   Linc
Mathew, John to Nancy Dale 4 Mar. 1833   Boon
Mathew, Joseph to Nelly Bittle 14 Nov. 1837   Boon
Mathew, Presley T. to Lutty Hickman 5 Oct. 1838   Rand
Mathews, Andrew to Elizabeth Burton 22 Oct. 1835   Fran
Mathews, Benj. to Catharine Keykendoll 8 Mar. 1818   Howa
Mathews, Benj. to Elizabeth Dyer 13 Apr. 1834   Lafa
Mathews, James to Jane Belcher 2 Jan. 1823   Boon
Mathews, John to Catherine Jefferson 20 Sept. 1833   Boon
Mathews, John to Elizabeth Alberson 26 Sept. 1836   Lafa
Mathews, Overton to Tabitha Campbell 13 July 1837   Wash
Mathews, Rufus to Eliza J. Jones 14 Mar. 1839   Mari
Mathews, Wm. to Eleanor Greenhalgh 2 Feb. 1825   Boon

```
Mathews, Willis to Elizabeth Barrett 7 Jan. 1830                          Boon
Mathis, Hyram to Mary Blevins 12 Feb. 1835                                Gree
Mathis, Littleton to Luther J. Todd 18 Feb. 1838                          Clin
Mathus, Thomas to Rebecah Herley 15 June 1833                             Gree
Matkin, Benj. to Matilda Matkin 4 Apr. 1839                               StFr
Matkin, Wm. to Betsey A. Ritter 8 Nov. 1838                               StFr
Matkin, Wm. S. to Elizabeth Hunt 13 July 1837                            StFr
Matkins, James D. to Martha Dorse 9 July 1835                            StFr
Matlock, Elias to Mary Flynn 30 Mar. 1833                                Cr-1
Matlock, Isaac to Prudence Sanders 25 Mar. 1837                          Gree
Matlock, James to Ester A. Wright 28 May 1839                            Cr-1
Matlock, John to Emily Nobles 9 May 1839                                 Cr-1
Matson, Abraham to Phoebe A. Coshen 14 Sept. 1839                        StCh
Matson, L.L. to Mary Crul 28 Feb. 1836                                   Shel
Matson, Valentine to Dulrena Vardeman 17 Dec. 1833                       Rall
Matson, Valentine P. to Dolly Miller 11 Jan. 1838                        Rall
Matteer, Wm. to Sally Hunter 27 Aug. 1829                                Call
Mattews, John to Mary Williams 9 Sept. 1834                              Jack
Matthens, James to Elizabeth Buff 4 Feb. 1836                            John
Matthews, Bartley to Minerva Baker 11 Jan. 1838                          Gasc
Matthews, Briten to ---- Zumwalt 28 Apr. 1831                            Call
Matthews, Elijah B. to Sarah B. Powell 5 July 1832                       Wash
Matthews, Greenfield to Nancy Newby 13 Dec. 1837                         Clin
Matthews, James to Jinncy Murry 29 Dec. 1831                             Cr-1
Matthews, John Jr. to Nancy Smith 15 Dec. 1822                           Md-A
Matthews, John to Elizabeth Butler 20 June 1830                          Fran
Matthews, John to Sally Walker 22 Aug. 1833                              Mari
Matthews, Thomas A. to Mary Blocker 11 Jan. 1827                         CG-A
Matthews, Wm. to Nancy Barnes 11 Oct. 1825                               Boon
Mattingly, Jacob to Mary Duvall 8 Nov. 1825                              Perr
Mattingly, Lewis to Nancy Griffiths 25 Apr. 1838                         Perr
Mattock, Henry to Matilda Cox 19 July 1835                               Call
Mattock, Wm. to Milla Nobles 22 July 1829                                Cr-P
Maughers, Mordecai M. to Dorothy Stephenson 22 Dec. 1829                 StCh
Mauphet, Wm. to Catherine Martin 22 Oct. 1805                            CGRA
Maupin, Amos to Rebecca Heatherly 24 Apr. 1828                           Fran
Maupin, Archibald to Rebekah Adams 26 June 1832                          Howa
Maupin, Clifton to Margaret Woods 17 Sept. 1829                          Boon
Maupin, Daniel to Rebecca Nix 11 Nov. 1832                               Fran
Maupin, John to Polly A. Taylor 18 Nov. 1838                             Fran
Maupin, John M. to Martha Harris -- Sept. 1839                           Boon
Maupin, Levi to Juda Hall 15 Sept. 1838                                  Howa
Maupin, Lewis to Mary Salyers 7 Sept. 1828                               Fran
Maupin, Milton to Mary A. Maupin 30 Aug. 1836                            Boon
Maupin, Moses to Nancy Patton 18 Dec. 1836                               Fran
Maupin, Wm. to Isabella Lemon 29 Mar. 1832                               Boon
Maupin, Wm. to Margaret A. Stapleton 18 Oct. 1838                        Howa
Maw, Henry to Caroline Lile 3 Aug. 1837                                  Ray
Mawd, Eppe to Mary McAfee 10 Nov. 1832                                   Ray
Mawd, Jesse Jr. to Elizabeth Linville 5 Sept. 1831                       Ray
Mawd, Robt. to Heffsabe Prine 20 Dec. 1821                               Ray
Maxey, Elisha A. to Ann Spencer 24 Oct. 1839                             Monr
Maxey, Joel to Margaret Kipper 24 Mar. 1836                              Monr
Maxey, Patrick to Honery Hounseler 7 July 1835                          Cole
Maxey, Radford to Nancy Logan 27 Dec. 1838                               Warr
Maxey, Wm. H. to Sebbella Glazebrooks 5 June 1835                        Cole
Maxwell, B. to Martha J. Denwooddy 15 Feb. 1838                          Howa
Maxwell, Bluford to Matilda Anderson 3 Mar. 1836                         Polk
Maxwell, Jefferson to Rhoda Campbell 8 Dec. 1836                         Coop
Maxwell, John to Ann Garner 27 Apr. 1828                                 Mari
Maxwell, Joseph to Louisa Williams 3 Mar. 1835                           Monr
Maxwell, Robt. G. to Elizabeth Igart 4 Sept. 1836                        Polk
Maxwell, Samuel to Permelia Moon 27 Dec. 1829                            Coop
Maxwell, Samuel T. to Polly Garner 17 May 1829                           Mari
May, Beecom to Adeline Cirom 22 Oct. 1835                                Linc
```

```
May, Gabriel to Elizabeth Craghead 4 Dec. 1823                          Call
May, James to Patience Wells 16 Aug. 1836                               Pk-1
May, James B. to Emily Prine 5 Apr. 1838                                Cass
May, John to Delea Boon 20 Feb. 1834                                    Call
May, John to Emelia Turner 14 Oct. 1835                                 Carr
May, Pinkney M. to Mary E. Chambers 15 Dec. 1836                        StCh
May, Richard to R. Crump 17 Dec. 1829                                   Call
May, Robt. A. to Martha D. Pulliam 7 Feb. 1839                          StCh
May, Silas to Polly Jones 2 Mar. 1834                                   Morg
May, Thomas to Mary A. Wallace 15 Apr. 1830                             CG-A
May, Ware S. to Elizabeth A. Burnett 28 Feb. 1828                       Clay
May, Wm. to Mary Haun 20 Sept. 1834                                     CG-B
Mayberry, John to Sally Chaley 28 Sept. 1826                            Ray
Mayberry, Wm. to Mary Wilkison 19 Feb. 1837                             Livi
Mayers, John to Nancy Eaker 12 Dec. 1839                               CG-B
Mayers, Robt. to Louisana Blanstel 26 Jan. 1839                        Maco
Mayfield, Elisha to Susanna Hawk 7 May 1829                            CG-A
Mayfield, Elisha to Mahala Miller 1 Aug. 1833                          CG-A
Mayfield, Ezariah to Ady Lee 4 Feb. 1827                               CG-A
Mayfield, Geo. to Polly Check 19 Dec. 1839                             CG-B
Mayfield, Jacob to Katherine Bollinger 19 Dec. 1833                    CG-A
Mayo, Alan to Fraytchea Finnell 25 Apr. 1823                           Char
Mayo, Archibald to Jane Frost 16 June 1832                             Boon
Mayo, James to Nancy Sexton 22 Feb. 1830                               Boon
Mayo, John to Polly Pendergreass 25 Mar. 1819                          Howa
Mayo, John to Martha A. Robinson 9 Feb. 1838                           Boon
Mayo, Valentine to Margaret McCullough 29 Aug. 1822                    Howa
Mayors, James to Isce Dunham 22 Oct. 1838                              Jeff
Mays, Drury to Polly Barns 17 July 1832                                Boon
Mays, Hamilton to Kitty Shepherd 18 Dec. 1831                          Mari
Mays, James to Malinda Boice 12 Oct. 1821                              Boon
Mays, John to Margaret Trotter 16 Dec. 1834                            Lewi
Mays, Martin to Cordelia Palmer 7 Apr. 1836                            Pk-1
Mays, Signor to Martha Ridgway 18 Sept. 1835                           Call
Mays, Wm. to Elizabeth Barnes 3 Jan. 1839                              Boon
Meacham, Christopher to Baersheba Neille 22 Oct. 1835                  Call
Mead, Adam to Sally Clay 25 Apr. 1832                                  Call
Mead, Davis to Hester Bosarth 20 July 1824                            Howa
Mead, Davis to Fanny Gutherie 29 Dec. 1837                            Howa
Mead, John to Mintey Punnels 15 Aug. 1833                             Call
Mead, Joseph to Levina Thomas 27 Sept. 1832                          Call
Mead, Stephen C. to Sarah Flannagan 11 Mar. 1823                     Clay
Mead, Wm. to Lucinda Cave 28 June 1838                               Clay
Meader, Fleming to Sally Hughs 9 Nov. 1837                           Morg
Meador, Bannister W. to Charlotte Hendrix 28 Mar. 1839               Cass
Meadow, John to Lucinda Lemon 10 Aug. 1834                           Jack
Meadows, Jeremiah to Anne Music 28 June 1819                         Coop
Meadows, Lewis to Ivannah Robertson 7 Mar. 1839                      Rand
Meadows, Thomas to Adeline Claybrook 13 July 1834                    Cole
Meaks, John to Loucinda Jones 18 Jan. 1832                           Clay
Meals, James P. to Rebecca Woodward 29 Nov. 1832                     Howa
Meals, John N. to Susan Calloway 13 Feb. 1834                        Howa
Meanea, Francis to Ellen Gallitan 15 Jan. 1834                       Jeff
Means, Adam to Penelope Jones 9 Dec. 1838                            Clay
Means, Benj. to Caroline Massy 9 Jan. 1827                           Mari
Means, Geo. W. to Sylvina Brown 8 Feb. 1836                          Clin
Means, James to Sally Murphy 7 Aug. 1827                             Howa
Means, James to Elva McWilliams 1 Feb. 1833                          Lafa
Means, John to Eliza Marr 30 Dec. 1832                               Clay
Means, Joseph to Maria Osburn 21 Dec. 1837                           Henr
Means, Joseph B. to Susan A.M. Bradley 20 Mar. 1834                  Mari
Means, Robt. to Alsey A. Hurt 12 Dec. 1839                           Henr
Means, Wm. to Nancy Gentry 1 Apr. 1830                               Boon
Means, Wm. C. to Anna Irwin 5 Mar. 1837                              Clin
Mears, Lewis to Salome Eppler 29 Jan. 1833                           Carr
```

```
Meason, Geo. M. to Elizabeth Hay 16 Nov. 1837                      Clar
Medcalf, Hiram to Elizabeth Upton 29 Dec. 1835                     Morg
Medders, Jeremiah to Eleanor Wilson 24 Apr. 1828                   Cole
Meddlers, John H. to Jane Allen 4 May 1832                         Sali
Mede, John to Polley Ellice 3 Apr. 1829                            Call
Media, Henry to Edy Taylor 29 Aug. 1816                            Howa
Medley, Daniel to Sarah McGuire 18 July 1833                       Jeff
Medlin, Lewis to Clarinda Eades 3 Dec. 1835                        Cole
Medlock, Elijah to Lucy Morris 25 Oct. 1835                        Cr-1
Medlock, Isom to Kesiah Shoemate 6 Dec. 1835                       Cr-1
Meek, Hiram C. to Rachel Lightner 24 Dec. 1826                     Lafa
Meek, James H. to Elizabeth Riddle 30 June 1831                    Ray
Meeks, Meriet to Sarah Burden 2 Sept. 1834                         Gree
Mefford, John to Frances Bailey 28 Feb. 1839                       Pk-B
Mefford, Noah to Indiana Schofield 5 Oct. 1830                     Mari
Meganz, John L. to Elizabeth Gray 5 Aug. 1830                      Perr
Mehafey, Andrew to Mary McClendon 1 Mar. 1832                      Cr-1
Meines, Josephus to Polly Greyum 10 July 1834                      Cole
Melhollan, Levi to Sally Lindley 28 Mar. 1839                      Polk
Mellidge, Henry to Mary Garmon 3 Apr. 1839                         Ray
Mellon, Henry L. to Catharine Forst 23 Feb. 1837                   Char
Mellon, Wm. to Ann Lettrall 29 July 1831                           Howa
Melone, John to Jane Ray 10 Mar. 1831                              Cr-P
Melton, James to Eleanor Charlton 20 Oct. 1829                     Cole
Melton, Thomas to Elizabeth Myer 23 Sept. 1836                     Henr
Melton, Yelvaton to Susan Taylor 3 July 1823                       Cole
Menage, Louis to Ester Viale 5 July 1836                           StCh
Menard, Joseph to Louise Martineau 21 Jan. 1828                    StCh
Menas, Jacob to Emilin Evans 27 Feb. 1835                          Gasc
Menifee, Alfred to Mary H. Mason 25 Nov. 1830                      Call
Menon, Joshua M. to Ellen Bate 9 Apr. 1839                         StCh
Mense, John F. to Sarah S. Owen 10 Oct. 1838                       Fran
Menteer, James to Delilah Estes 19 Dec. 1822                       StFr
Menteer, Joseph to Elizabeth Estes 25 May 1823                     StFr
Meral, Charles to Sarah Finley 12 Oct. 1834                        Mari
Mercer, John D. to Judea Pemberton 27 Dec. 1838                    Pett
Mercer, Reuben to Cynthia Bun 18 Aug. 1836                         Jack
Merchant, Blueford to Susan ---- 21 Mar. 1837                      Warr
Meredith, Charles L. to Sarah Gordon 23 Apr. 1835                  Cole
Meredith, Daniel to Sarah Long 29 Aug. 1809                        StGe
Meredith, Thomas to Susanna Wooldridge 23 Aug. 1832               Coop
Merick, Daniel to Sally Lawson 14 Oct. 1838                        Ripl
Merida, Wm. to Nancy Faubian 27 Oct. 1836                          Clay
Meridith, Daniel to Mary Hogard 24 Aug. 1837                       Perr
Meriel, Antoin to Susann Davre' 15 Feb. 1836                       Wash
Merill, Abner to Sarah May 18 Sept. 1834                           Lewi
Meris, Jewett to Sarah E. Peery 26 Nov. 1837                       Livi
Merit, Zedekiah to Caroline Smith 10 Dec. 1835                     Pk-1
Meriteer, Wm. to Caty Ovizon 2 Jan. 1825                           Gasc
Merrell, Eli to Susannah Laytham 18 Sept. 1831                     Mari
Merrell, Wm. to Martha Mays 17 Apr. 1838                           Mari
Merril, Nicholas to Jane Short 6 Nov. 1839                         Buch
Merrill, Eli to Mary A. McCoy 24 Aug. 1837                         Mari
Merrill, John C. to Sarah Patison 14 July 1836                     Ripl
Merrit, Thomas to Susan J. Suddeth 6 Oct. 1836                     Linc
Messersmith, Barnabus to Nancy Ray 17 June 1838                    Cole
Messimore, Geo. to Margaret Taylor 26 Jan. 1836                    CG-B
Meyer, Frederick to Catharina W. Moass 22 Apr. 1839               Fran
Michel, Louis J. to Marguerite DePatie 6 Feb. 1827                 StCh
Michel, Wm. to Susanna Craig 28 Dec. 1834                          Linc
Mickel, Jonathan to Mary Bowlin 19 Aug. 1835                       Coop
Middlecalf, Thomas to Sarah Harris 28 June 1836                    Gasc
Middlekamp, John H. to Margaret Slater 25 Nov. 1838               Warr
Middleton, John H. to Meichael Scott 14 Sept. 1839               Audr
Midett, Benj. D. to Elizabeth Barbee 9 Apr. 1839                  Carr
```

```
Midlin, Hardy to Winney Scott 27 Nov. 1833               Coop
Midlin, Jarot to Rebeka Allee 1 Aug. 1833                Cole
Miers, Geo. to Milley Anderson 20 Mar. 1831              Pk-1
Miers, Henary to Sally Yount 16 Aug. 1818                CG-1
Mifflin, John H. to Nancy Waters 5 Oct. 1810            CG-1
Mifford, Alfred to Betsey Pritchard 10 July 1828        Pk-1
Mifford, Caleb to Mary Pritchett 11 Feb. 1830           Pk-1
Mileham, Richard to Rachael Shepherd rec. 23 Aug. 1827  Clay
Miles, J. to Elizabeth Layghten 3 Sept. 1836            Perr
Miles, John J. to Susan McCune 1 Dec. 1836              Pk-1
Miles, Joseph to Elizabeth Moore 20 Sept. 1836          Perr
Miles, Joseph to Hamona R. Addley 13 Nov. 1838          Perr
Miles, Robt. M. to Caroline A. Gibbons 29 Dec. 1836     Mari
Miller, Abraham to Nancy Ranney 20 July 1834            CG-A
Miller, Alexander S. to Polly Cathey 1 Mar. 1829        Coop
Miller, Allen to Mariah Reed 22 Oct. 1828               Call
Miller, Allison E. to Dorothy Glascock 10 June 1830     Rall
Miller, Bailey to Susan Jones 20 Oct. 1831              Call
Miller, Benj. to Eva Blevins 29 Apr. 1827               Call
Miller, Benj. to Sally Jamison 4 Dec. 1831              Fran
Miller, Boyd to Isabella Mulkey 10 Mar. 1825            Cole
Miller, Daniel to Polly Moman 5 June 1827               Call
Miller, Daniel to Nancy Ferguson 22 Oct. 1829           CG-A
Miller, Daniel B. to Araminda Dunn 19 Dec. 1839         CG-B
Miller, David to Elizabeth Welton 15 Feb. 1827          Gasc
Miller, Dickson to Olteny J. Stephens 4 Feb. 1838       Polk
Miller, Edward to Catharine Coutis 17 Aug. 1837         Gasc
Miller, Elijah to Hannah Gartin 12 June 1836            Cole
Miller, Finis to Melvina Young 1 Aug. 1839              Pett
Miller, Fleming to Susan Simonds 15 Aug. 1825           StCh
Miller, Francis to Fany Phillips 20 Mar. 1836           Fran
Miller, Frederick to Sarah Mullinix 7 May 1839          Rand
Miller, Geard to Nancy Nesbit 2 Aug. 1832               Boon
Miller, Geo. to Elizabeth Williams 19 June 1829         Md-A
Miller, Geo. to Betsy Adams 10 Dec. 1829                Pk-1
Miller, Geo. to Louisa Bosye 3 May 1832                 Boon
Miller, Geo. to Sarah Huffman 7 Nov. 1832               Fran
Miller, Geo. to Grisenda Kathey 19 July 1837            Rall
Miller, Gidson B. to Elizabeth Jenkins 24 Oct. 1833     Pett
Miller, Harry to Isabel Warner 5 Dec. 1838              Livi
Miller, Henry to Sally Richison 2 July 1837             Rall
Miller, Henry to Louisa S. Richards 9 Jan. 1838         Howa
Miller, Henry to Mary Likes 5 July 1838                 CG-A
Miller, Isaak to Catey Bulinger 22 Jan. 1805            CG-1
Miller, Isaac to Katharine James 10 Sept. 1829          CG-A
Miller, Isaac to Narcissa Shockley 1 Nov. 1837          Gasc
Miller, Isaac to Elizabeth Cope 15 Nov. 1838            Davi
Miller, Jacob to Luffy Bullinger 8 Jan. 1805            CG-1
Miller, James to Polly Harris 1 Sept. 1820              Howa
Miller, James to Elizabeth Clay 15 Jan. 1824            Cole
Miller, James to Margaret Flatt 18 June 1829            Gasc
Miller, James to Mahalah Cason 20 Oct. 1829             Howa
Miller, James to Hannah Lorshel 4 Oct. 1830             Wash
Miller, James to Sarah Coffelt 26 Sept. 1833            Cole
Miller, James to Polly Kimsey 28 May 1835               Jack
Miller, James Jr. to Lucindy Whitest 27 Aug. 1835       Cole
Miller, James to Margarett M. White 12 Sept. 1837       StFr
Miller, James to Margaret Permon 15 July 1838           Jack
Miller, James to Martha Woodson 18 June 1839            Char
Miller, James C. to Belinda Kirby 26 Jan. 1826          Rall
Miller, James D. to Constantine Burnet 8 Aug. 1820      Howa
Miller, James R. to Polly Rhea 18 Dec. 1834             Morg
Miller, Jefferson to Hannah Simpson 9 Sept. 1827        Fran
Miller, Jerry W. to Jenac Roberts 7 Jan. 1832           Coop
Miller, Jesse to Mitilda Ormes 1 Mar. 1835              Gasc
```

156

```
Miller, Jesse to Lucy Miller 19 Nov. 1839                          Cg-B
Miller, John to Elizabeth Rogers 7 May 1829                        Coop
Miller, John to Elizabeth Hendricks 23 Nov. 1830                   CG-A
Miller, John to Malinda Mullinick 15 May 1834                      Rand
Miller, John to Hannah Deck 23 July 1835                           CG-B
Miller, John to Margret Mathews 24 Jan. 1836                       Md-B
Miller, John to Mary Holman 28 Jan. 1836                           Ray
Miller, John to Elizabeth Spotswood rec. 8 July 1836              Rall
Miller, John to Sarah Sewell 8 Sept. 1838                          Cr-1
Miller, John to Mary Clevenger 25 Oct. 1838                        Ray
Miller, John C. to Mary M. Shell 10 Apr. 1831                      CG-A
Miller, John H. to Sarah Gabriel 23 Nov. 1828                      Coop
Miller, John H. to Sally Mallicate 10 Apr. 1836                    Gree
Miller, John N. to Narcissa Patterson 4 Oct. 1832                  CG-A
Miller, John S. to Patsy Smith 24 June 1817                        StGe
Miller, John W. to Louisiana Coons 3 Nov. 1836                     Call
Miller, Joseph to Polly White 26 Feb. 1826                         Pk-1
Miller, Joseph to Sarah Hartle 24 Aug. 1829                        CG-A
Miller, Joseph to Elizabeth Conrad 15 Feb. 1830                    Perr
Miller, Joseph P. to Manervy J. Springer 11 Nov. 1832             Wash
Miller, Josiah to Hetty Logan 10 Aug. 1837                         Lafa
Miller, Martin A. to Jane Miller 4 Feb. 1830                       Call
Miller, Mathew to Jane Colvin 10 Oct. 1835                         Gasc
Miller, Matison to Mary Hunter 13 May 1838                         Cole
Miller, Milton to Lydia Caldwell 6 Jan. 1831                       Coop
Miller, Moses L. to Louisa Ferguson 15 June 1836                  Call
Miller, Octavius A. to Elizabeth Ousley 14 Apr. 1837             Lewi
Miller, Philip to Lucy McIntire 30 Jan. 1823                      Fran
Miller, Preston N. to Mrs. Jean Travillier 21 Nov. 1833          StFr
Miller, Richard to Margaret Stanton 5 Jan. 1824                   Howa
Miller, Robt. to Selia Young 27 Aug. 1837                         CG-A
Miller, Robt. B. to Susan Smith 21 May 1837                       John
Miller, Robt. W. to Mary J. Paten 3 Mar. 1837                     Call
Miller, Samuel to Sarah Kerby 11 Jan. 1827                        Mari
Miller, Samuel to Bethabara Mulkey 8 Mar. 1832                    Cole
Miller, Samuel to Julia E. Francisco 1 May 1838                   Sali
Miller, Smiley to Eleanor Gentle 15 Dec. 1833                     Pk-1
Miller, Thomas to Margaret Kenny 23 July 1822                     Cole
Miller, Thomas H. to Mary J. Houx 8 Jan. 1832                     Coop
Miller, Thomas S. to Mary B. McKamey 17 Oct. 1833                Monr
Miller, Tobias to Kitteann Brawner 6 Nov. 1839                   Clay
Miller, Valentine to Elizabeth Hughs 6 Feb. 1831                 CG-A
Miller, Wikeliff to Louisa Jones 19 Feb. 1834                    Call
Miller, Wilcon to Elizabeth Highsmith 22 Nov. 1827               Linc
Miller, Wm. to Nancy Boyce 2 Dec. 1813                           StGe
Miller, Wm. to Susannah Loe 18 Dec. 1817                         Howa
Miller, Wm. to Sally Mulkey 31 Aug. 1820                         Coop
Miller, Wm. to Polly Carpenter 14 July 1827                      Coop
Miller, Wm. to Nancy Allen 23 Apr. 1829                          Cole
Miller, Wm. to Nancy Howard 16 Feb. 1832                         Gasc
Miller, Wm. to Nelly Smith 10 June 1832                          Jack
Miller, Wm. to Emily Foster 2 Aug. 1832                          Linc
Miller, Wm. to Lucyann Oliver 19 Mar. 1835                       Gasc
Miller, Wm. to Sally Eaker 11 Feb. 1838                          CG-A
Miller, Wm. A. to Agnes C. Mitchell 21 Jan. 1823                 Coop
Miller, Wm. C. to Eliza Fry 27 Aug. 1829                         Clay
Miller, Young E. to Emily Barnes 31 Aug. 1831                    Coop
Millhiser, John to Hester C.D.D.A. Hampton 24 Sept. 1835        Rall
Million, Herman to Eliza J. Wiley 1 Jan. 1836                    Howa
Mills, Albert W. to Elizabeth Arrowsmith 16 Apr. 1839           Shel
Mills, Benj. M. to Susannah Murphy 8 Aug. 1839                  Clar
Mills, Caleb W. to Catharine Runkle 22 Dec. 1834               Monr
Mills, David to Temperence Benn 14 July 1836                   Rall
Mills, Geo. W. to Emeline Johnson 28 Apr. 1836                 Wash
Mills, Ignatius W. to Angeline Gaty 1 Jan. 1828               StCh
```

```
Mills, Isaac L. to Eliza A. McDowell 4 Dec. 1836                    Pk-1
Mills, James to Rosanah Henry 10 Sept. 1839                        Pk-B
Mills, James M. to Mary Kelly 21 Aug. 1838                         Rall
Mills, John to Jane Pennington 29 Nov. 1838                        Barr
Mills, John V. to Mary Watters 25 June 1835                        Rall
Mills, Simon W. to Jemima Stanley 25 Dec. 1839                     Rand
Mills, Washington to Mary J. Nelson 24 Nov. 1836                   Boon
Mills, Wm. to Eliza Teague 8 Sept. 1836                            Jack
Millsap, Hiram to Lucy Cooper 26 June 1836                         Rand
Millsap, James to Margaret Firl 2 Apr. 1829                        Howa
Millsap, Manuel to Katy Baker 25 May 1826                          Coop
Millsap, Riley to Nancy J. Campbell 22 Nov. 1836                   Coop
Millsap, Robt. to Zulley Moon 10 Dec. 1830                         Coop
Millsaps, Hiab to Milly Parsons 10 Jan. 1839                       pk-B
Millsaps, Nelson to Martha Nowlin 25 Oct. 1838                     Jack
Millsaps, Thomas to Matilda Chesney 14 Jan. 1828                   Jack
Milroy, Wm. L. to Elizabeth Johnson 28 Mar. 1839                   Pk-B
Milsap, Caleaway to Sarah Handley 1 May 1834                       Clay
Milsap, Job A. to Mehala Sprigg 30 May 1839                        Sali
Milsap, Wm. to Elizabeth Clevinger 9 Apr. 1835                     Clay
Milstead, Camel to Narcissa Maw 8 Apr. 1838                        Ray
Milton, Frederick to Sarah Merchant 26 Aug. 1834                   Warr
Milum, Jacob to Elizabeth Burgen 22 Oct. 1829                      Jack
Minchels, Ira to Isabel Decker 17 Jan. 1839                        Fran
Minkley, Daniel to Clarissa Perry 10 Dec. 1837                     Clin
Minor, James to Elizabeth Tooley 19 July 1826                      Char
Minor, John to Mary Cook 22 Nov. 1837                              Rand
Minor, John to Lucy Ford 9 Dec. 1838                               Ray
Minor, Joshua M. to Ellen Bates 9 Apr. 1839                        StCh
Minor, Louis S. to Eliza Clark 9 Nov. 1837                         Linc
Minter, John to Polly Williams 24 Dec. 1833                        Howa
Minter, Harrison to Eliza Williams 12 Oct. 1835                    Howa
Minton, John to Sarah Hobbs 15 June 1837                           CG-A
Minton, Smith to Emeline McClary 5 Apr. 1832                       CG-A
Minton, Smith to Rebecca Poe 30 Aug. 1838                          CG-A
Minx, Hugh to Caty Tetherow 14 Apr. 1822                           Boon
Miot, Willson to Abigail Cabashia 19 Oct. 1828                     Wash
Mires, Geo. to Malinda McDaniel 20 Aug. 1835                       Call
Mires, Jacob to Mary Teter 24 Feb. 1831                            StCh
Mires, James G. to Mary A. Sandlan 8 May 1834                      Perr
Mires, John to Elizabeth Ruth 11 Oct. 1838                         StCh
Mires, John R. to Nancy Patterson 31 Mar. 1839                     Wash
Mirm, Wm. to Susan Pepper 20 Sept. 1838                            Pk-B
Misee, Robt. to Julia Wilsie 8 Sept. 1835                          Cole
Misplay, Bartholomew to Susan Neeves 10 Aug. 1832                  Wash
Misplay, Bazile to ---- Sullivan 18 Sept. 1832                     Wash
Misplay, James E. to Sally Randall 1 Oct. 1835                     Wash
Misset, Pierre to Margaurete Pru_hommer 27 Jan. 1835              Wash
Missletcalf, Isaac G.M. to Sally Carr 25 June 1835                 StCh
Mister, Gayhart H. to Feliciana Stegitmire 15 Aug. 1836           StCh
Mitchel, Benj. to Matilda Loony 2 Feb. 1836                        Polk
Mitchel, Isaac to Nancy Hunt 28 Mar. 1827                          StGe
Mitchel, J.B. to Caroline McCollough 28 Apr. 1838                  Mari
Mitchel, Jesse to Susannah N. Thompson 5 Jan. 1837                CG-A
Mitchel, Wm. to Eliza Carrell 24 Dec. 1829                         Coop
Mitchell, Alfred to Iris Pinson 4 Mar. 1830                        Wash
Mitchell, Daniel to Sally A. Wilhite 25 Feb. 1839                  Pk-B
Mitchell, David to Cyntha Newby 7 Apr. 1836                        Clin
Mitchell, E.L. to Sarah Violette 14 July 1835                      Clay
Mitchell, Frederick to Mrs. Elizabeth Warren 9 July 1833          Clay
Mitchell, Harvey to Harriett Hendrick 8 Aug. 1833                  Pk-1
Mitchell, Heninger to Frances Johnson 7 July 1839                  Polk
Mitchell, James to Elizabeth McKee 20 Mar. 1834                    StFr
Mitchell, John to Patsey Watson 9 Mar. 1828                        Pk-1
Mitchell, John to Sarah Prichard 11 Sept. 1831                     Pk-1
```

```
Mitchell, Moses to Elizabeth Switzer 15 Jan. 1825                Howa
Mitchell, Nathaniel C. to Eliza T. Gleaves 10 Feb. 1825         Lafa
Mitchell, Newman T. to Priscilla Hughes 4 Sept. 1828            Howa
Mitchell, Richard to Nancy Jeffries 26 July 1821                Howa
Mitchell, Robt. S. to Polly Long 19 Sept. 1828                  Ray
Mitchell, Stephen to Martha Bond 26 Nov. 1839                   Polk
Mitchell, Thomas to Malinda Robers 29 May 1836                  Mari
Mitchell, Wm. to Mary Pound 29 Mar. 1821                        Fran
Mitchell, Wm. to Polly McKee 22 Apr. 1833                       StFr
Mitchell, Wm. to Elizabeth Slavens 10 May 1838                  Mari
Miyers, Abraham to Ann E. Leake 8 Nov. 1836                     Rall
Moad, Calvin to Mary Polly 19 July 1835                         Cole
Moad, John T. to Mary A. West 27 Aug. 1835                      Cole
Moad, Ludewick to Senith Rustin 26 June 1831                    Cole
Moberly, Joab to Elizabeth Crul 25 Dec. 1839                    Shel
Mobley, John to Anna Enyart -- June 1823                        Howa
Mobley, Wm. to Sophia Burman 2 Dec. 1822                        Howa
Mock, Eijah to Mary Shackleford 12 June 1824                    Coop
Mock, Robt. to Polly Blassengame -- Aug. 1839                   Morg
Mockbee, Thomas to Eliza A. Chiles 23 Aug. 1836                 Jack
Mode, James to Rebecca Pauly 14 Nov. 1820                       Ray
Moiers, Martin to Mary Cotner 15 Aug. 1839                      Md-B
Moirs, David to Nancy Yant 27 Dec. 1838                         Md-B
Molen, Joel to Caty Martin 20 June 1817                         Howa
Monbeau, Charles to Maria March 21 Sept. 1808                   StCh
Moncil, Samuel to Rebecca Davis 13 Aug. 1829                    Jack
Monday, Wade H. to Ruth M. ---- -- Nov. 1835                    StCh
Monroe, Daniel to Elizabeth Baronet 10 June 1819               Howa
Monroe, Geo. to Mary Mourning 14 Apr. 1829                      Howa
Monroe, James to Minerva Gearhart 18 Apr. 1839                  Howa
Monroe, John to Mrs. Sarah S. Stewart 26 Sept. 1837            Fran
Monroe, Joseph J. to Huldah Hubbard 19 July 1821               Howa
Monroe, Thomas to Elizabeth Garret 10 Sept. 1818               Howa
Monroe, Wm. B. to Martha A. Tuttle 30 Apr. 1838                Call
Monrow, Thomas to Louisa Vaughn 17 Sept. 1826                  Clay
Monteer, John to Susanna Bryan 21 Dec. 1837                    Call
Montgomery, David to Nancy Milsap 15 May 1827                  Howa
Montgomery, James to Alcey Smith 24 Mar. 1812                  CG-1
Montgomery, James to Jane Elliott 26 June 1822                 Howa
Montgomery, James to Celeste Russ 3 Jan. 1827                  Wash
Montgomery, James to Eliza J. Bryant 22 Nov. 1836             Rand
Montgomery, James G. to Mary Porter 19 Apr. 1818              Howa
Montgomery, Jefferson to Nancy Anderson 31 Oct. 1831          Cr-1
Montgomery, John to Elisah Layton 22 Apr. 1828                Perr
Montgomery, John to Elizabeth Ravenscraft 27 Mar. 1831        Pk-1
Montgomery, John L. to Matilda Campbell 31 Jan. 1839          Lafa
Montgomery, Joseph to Elizabeth Spraull 15 Feb. 1835         Lafa
Montgomery, Robt. to Malinda Duff 15 June 1832                Cr-1
Montgomery, Wm. to Elizabeth Schabano 7 Jan. 1838            Fran
Montroy, Michael to Cordelia Cockran 16 Sept. 1828          Perr
Moodie, John W. to Agness Weston 7 Mar. 1832                Jack
Moody, Daniel to Anna Haun 20 Feb. 1834                      Warr
Moody, Esquire to Nancy A. Thomas 30 July 1838               Boon
Moody, Isaac to Rebecca Guin 4 June 1820                    Fran
Moon, Jake to Phebe Wigham 15 Feb. 1838                     Boon
Moon, Jasper to Nancy Cathey 11 Sept. 1831                  Coop
Moon, Jesse to Mary Gillum 2 Mar. 1828                      Coop
Moon, Job to Katherine Allen 7 May 1835                     Morg
Moon, Joseph to Elizabeth Willson 21 Jan. 1830             Jack
Moon, Perry B. to Cornelia Kendrick 23 Jan. 1834          Mari
Moon, Thomas to Lucany Proctor 25 Apr. 1826               Cole
Moon, Wm. to Catherine Roundtree 19 June 1833             Jack
Mooney, James to Polly Hanna 3 June 1824                   Boon
Monney, James to Pelena Cheaney 26 May 1830               Boon
Moony, Joseph to Rachel Dedrick 11 Nov. 1838              Ripl
```

159

Moonyham, Ervin to Jane Herd 12 Mar. 1837   Lafa
Moonyham, Wm. to Rachel Barns 3 July 1836   Lafa
Moor, Curtis to Fanny Twitty 24 Jan. 1833   Cr-1
Moor, Daniel B. to Mrs. Celia Tate 17 July 1836   Fran
Moor, James to Amanda Williams 16 Sept. 1827   Wash
Moor, Samuel W. to Nancy Huff 26 Sept. 1837   Mari
Moor, Willis R. to Matilda Tidwell 10 Mar. 1833   Md-A
Moore, Albert A. to Melissa Stapp 28 Feb. 1839   Lafa
Moore, Alexander to Jane S. Boyce 27 Sept. 1836   StFr
Moore, Alfred to Polly Morgan 24 May 1838   Polk
Moore, Augustus to Catherine Matier 22 Sept. 1831   Call
Moore, Austin to Emily Manning 27 Apr. 1830   Perr
Moore, Benj. to Martha M. Hughes 8 Jan. 1839   Clay
Moore, Clairborn to Eliza A. Payton 6 Apr. 1828   Howa
Moore, Daniel to Elizabeth Adams 24 Feb. 1833   Fran
Moore, David to Betsey Burnam 7 Nov. 1819   Howa
Moore, David to Rebeccah English 21 July 1825   Clay
Moore, David to Rebecca Burris 24 Dec. 1825   Clay
Moore, David to Martha Lampton 19 Mar. 1835   Cole
Moore, David C. to Clementine S. Ellis 4 Jan. 1838   Morg
Moore, Drury to Elizabeth J. Gibson 8 Nov. 1838   Clin
Moore, Elisha to Jane Gillet 24 Dec. 1818   StCh
Moore, Geo. to Frances Stephens 24 May 1822   Coop
Moore, Geo. W. to Burlinda Brockman 21 May 1825   Howa
Moore, Henry E. to Maria Dunn 30 Sept. 1836   Coop
Moore, Henry F. to Adaline B. Bennett 31 July 1834   Cole
Moore, Houston to Unisey A. Miller 13 Sept. 1838   Char
Moore, Isaac to Lidia White 10 Jan. 1833   Coop
Moore, Isaac to Rebecca Hart 24 Dec. 1834   Call
Moore, Isidor to Catharine Cissell 2 Mar. 1835   Perr
Moore, Isidore to Mary Hagan 19 Jan. 1836   Perr
Moore, J.W. to Eleanor Holliday 30 Nov. 1837   Shel
Moore, James to Viey A. Smith 10 May 1827   Call
Moore, James to Cecily Manning 22 May 1832   Perr
Moore, James to Ann Patrick 13 Dec. 1832   Coop
Moore, James to Polly Deakin 24 Dec. 1833   Coop
Moore, James to Catharine Malott 3 Nov. 1836   Clay
Moore, James to Dellia E.A. Michell 13 July 1837   Monr
Moore, Jesse to Corden Gnash 11 July 1828   Clay
Moore, Joel T. to Polly Malot 19 May 1836   Jack
Moore, John to Nancy Forrest 12 Sept. 1822   Char
Moore, John to Betsy Sherron 14 Mar. 1829   Rand
Moore, John to Lenna McKay 22 Nov. 1832   Cole
Moore, John to Sarah Delosure 29 Apr. 1838   Gree
Moore, John B. to Elizabeth Nash 20 Jan. 1831   Call
Moore, John L. to Agnes Trale 25 Apr. 1839   Linc
Moore, Jonah to Nancy Montgomery 28 June 1836   Howa
Moore, Joshua to Ione R. Delazier 15 July 1838   Henr
Moore, Leo to Ann M. Cissell 16 Apr. 1833   Perr
Moore, Martin L. to Susann Hagan 23 Oct. 1832   Perr
Moore, Mastin to Margaret Parsons 8 Mar. 1832   Pk-1
Moore, Matthew B. to Amanda Lain 14 Nov. 1830   Pk-1
Moore, Merriman to Permelia E. Farmer 31 Aug. 1831   Pk-1
Moore, Milton to Semira Paton 15 Oct. 1839   Howa
Moore, Milton L. to Louisa P. Perry 6 Apr. 1837   Livi
Moore, Perry to Nancy Clay 30 Jan. 1834   StFr
Moore, Pleasant to ---- Mathews 19 June 1834   Md-A
Moore, Robt. to Matilda Smith 16 Feb. 1836   Md-B
Moore, Robt. to ---- Scrivner 27 Oct. 1836   Char
Moore, Robt. Sr. to Mrs. Margaret Graham 8 Apr. 1838 Char
Moore, Robt. to Polly Forrest 19 Dec. 1839   Char
Moore, Squire to Ceily Curtis 27 Jan. 1836   Char
Moore, Stephen T. to Sarah Cissell 7 Nov. 1837   Perr
Moore, Surdane to Nancy Thomas 15 July 1838   Carr
Moore, Thomas to Lucinda Derrill 3 July 1829   Coop

```
Moore, Thomas J. to Louisa Grubb 14 Feb. 1834                    Ray
Moore, Wharton H. to Mariah Ferguson 16 June 1831               Call
Moore, Wm. to Mary Miars 21 Oct. 1827                           Md-A
Moore, Wm. to Margaret Henderson 12 Apr. 1832                   CG-A
Moore, Wm. to Margaret Gillingham 1 Sept. 1833                  Linc
Moore, Wm. to Eliza J. Ellison 12 Sept. 1833                    CG-A
Moore, Wm. to Mrs. Mary Keller 19 Oct. 1834                     Perr
Moore, Wm. to Matilda Smith 30 June 1836                        Coop
Moore, Wm. to Nancy Hagan 1 Sept. 1837                          Monr
Moore, Wm. to Elizabeth Wilson 4 July 1839                      Plat
Moore, Wm. to Elizabeth Collins 27 Aug. 1839                    Linc
Moore, Wm. to Lucinda Wingfield 21 Nov. 1839                    Cass
Moore, Wm. G. to Elizabeth H. Long 1 May 1838                   Call
Moore, Wm. J. to Rebecca T. Bull 11 Oct. 1836                   Howa
Mopin, Thomas to Elizabeth Austin 5 Feb. 1837                   Livi
Morais, Louis to Marguerite Roy -- Nov. 182_                    StCh
Moran, Joseph to Catherine Limbaugh 4 Jan. 1838                 CG-A
Mordecai, Soloman to Ibby Kincade 20 Apr. 1817                  Howa
Mordock, John to Louisa Grider 27 Dec. 1829                     StCh
More, Edward to Agness Waldin 30 June 1831                      Cr-P
More, Ezekial to Sarah Morris 29 Apr. 1830                      Cr-P
More, Green to Elizabeth Deakins 13 Mar. 1835                   Morg
More, John to Mehalig Lea 18 Jan. 1838                          Cole
Morehead, Armsted B. to Nelly Shuck 23 June 1831               Rall
Morehead, John H. to Elizabeth Hughes 12 Nov. 1834             Ray
Morehead, Thomas to Martha M. Locket 2 Nov. 1837              Mari
Morehouse, Philimon to Maryann Perry 13 May 1831               Cr-P
Moreland, Chestley to Matilda Toffelmire 2 Feb. 1837          Clay
Moreland, James to Katherine Smiley 7 July 1828                Coop
Moreland, John to Ann Farris 10 Feb. 1825                      Coop
Moreland, Wm. A. to Eleanor Noblet 8 Aug. 1839                 Gasc
Morely, John J. to Matilda Doyle 28 Oct. 1837                  Coop
Moreor, Isuau to Ophelia Livingston 4 Feb. 1838               Call
Morer, Edward to Nansey Erven 3 Dec. 1837                      CG-A
Morgan, Alexander to Milly Winkler 12 Jan. 1837               Rand
Morgan, Archibald to Abigail Kunes 27 June 1808               StGe
Morgan, Carrel to Jane McKee 22 Feb. 1834                     Howa
Morgan, Charles to Matildy Holmes 3 Feb. 1830                 Mari
Morgan, Charles to Sarah Gilliland 16 Jan. 1838              John
Morgan, Daniel to Matilda Browning 1 Mar. 1835               Warr
Morgan, Elijah to Permelia Tribble 30 Apr. 1836              Lafa
Morgan, Enis to Patsy Warhurt 11 July 1824                    Char
Morgan, Henry to Elizabeth Netherton 16 Dec. 1839           Davi
Morgan, John to Elizabeth Blize 9 Sept. 1828                  Cole
Morgan, Joseph to Elizabeth Stepp 17 Mar. 1822               Howa
Morgan, Joseph to Elmina Morgan 31 Oct. 1834                 Coop
Morgan, Joseph F. to Elizabeth Landrum 25 Aug. 1831         Md-A
Morgan, Nathan R. to Anne Mapinyill 26 Oct. 1837            Ray
Morgan, Ruddy to Lizey Fields 13 Mar. 1832                   Ray
Morgan, Russell to Catharine Keeny 24 Sept. 1833            Lafa
Morgan, St. Clair to Sarah Seat 3 Oct. 1834                  Coop
Morgan, Wm. to Elizabeth Thornton 23 Aug. 1832              Ray
Morgan, Wm. to Eleanor Morgan 28 Aug. 1832                   Jeff
Morgan, Wm. to Caroline Hayden 16 Jan. 1838                 CG-A
Morin, Jesse to Zarilda Hughes 18 Aug. 1831                 Howa
Morland, Geo. to Ann Lewis 9 Apr. 1835                       Rall
Morning, Burel to Catherine St.Arnoud 10 Mar. 1836         StCh
Morrell, Edward to Hariete M.A. Hall 12 Nov. 1835          Perr
Morris, Abner to Elizabeth Ramsey 29 Dec. 1836             Lafa
Morris, Archibald to Polly A. Whitenberg 11 Oct. 1835     Gree
Morris, Caleb to Polly A. Kinnedy 15 Mar. 1838            Cr-1
Morris, Charles to Polly Wadkins 12 May 1834              Jack
Morris, Daniel to May Stephens 31 Oct. 1839               Lewi
Morris, David to Lucy Smith 16 Aug. 1835                   Coop
Morris, David to Permelia Threlkeld 16 Feb. 1837          Monr
```

161

```
Morris, Edward T. to Ann Spalding 2 Feb. 1832                        StCh
Morris, Elisha to Helen M. Rudolph 21 Oct. 1839                     Clin
Morris, Frederick M. to Susan R. Verdier 1 May 1838                  Linc
Morris, Geo. to Elizabeth McClelland 17 Mar. 1827                   Call
Morris, Geo. to Nancy Harris 16 Oct. 1828                          Wash
Morris, Henry S. to Nancy McCormick 20 Sept. 1839                   Mari
Morris, Hosea to Amy Dickson 30 Jan. 1834                          Lafa
Morris, Jacob to Elizabeth Claypole 17 Aug. 1837                    Boon
Morris, James to Sarah Gibson 26 Mar. 1832                         Cr-1
Morris, Joel W. to Rachel Creason 6 Apr. 1837                      Howa
Morris, John Jr. to Elizabeth Howell 28 Jan. 1830                   StCh
Morris, John to Elizabeth Matthens 24 Jan. 1837                     John
Morris, John to Nancy J. Bright 5 Feb. 1838                         Ray
Morris, John L. to Permelia K. Hinkle 16 Oct. 1834                 Fran
Morris, John P. to Mary I. Hughes 14 Nov. 1823                     Howa
Morris, John R. to Lucinda Adams 25 June 1837                      Pk-A
Morris, Joseph to Mrs. Sarah Rutledge 26 Oct. 1837                 Gree
Morris, Joshua to Narcissa Vanlandingham 11 Oct. 1825             Rall
Morris, Joshua to Luvey Hyatt 18 Feb. 1838                         Ripl
Morris, Moses to Polly McMurtrey 12 Mar. 1835                      Wash
Morris, Preston to Adaline Miller 6 Aug. 1829                      Wash
Morris, Richard to Hannah Bradley 31 Jan. 1832                     Howa
Morris, Robt. W. to Nancy Greathouse 24 May 1817                   Howa
Morris, Samuel to Hannah Johnson 11 Jan. 1835                      Howa
Morris, Smith to Margaret A. Mordoc 16 Oct. 1839                   Bent
Morris, Thomas to Elizabeth Warren 15 Apr. 1835                    Howa
Morris, Thomas J. to Jane Scott 8 Sept. 1831                       Coop
Morris, Thomas J. to Elizabeth Wright 7 Mar. 1839                  Howa
Morris, Warner to Mary Teeter 18 Oct. 1834                         Boon
Morris, Wm. to Eunice Short 12 Mar. 1826                           Md-A
Morris, Wm. to Elizabeth Morris 31 Dec. 1835                       StCh
Morrison, Albert to Ann Griggs 8 Nov. 1838                         Mari
Morrison, Alfred M. to Minerva Jackson 15 Mar. 1825               Howa
Morrison, Clarington to Elizabeth McGee 19 June 1834              Wash
Morrison, John to Elizabeth Groom 12 Nov. 1835                     Clay
Morrison, Joseph to Elizabeth Washburn 5 June 1834                Gree
Morrison, Nathaniel to Rode Blasgame 13 Dec. 1828                  Coop
Morrison, Stubblefield to Elizabeth Dinwiddie 12 Dec. 1830         Coop
Morrison, Thomas P. to Jane Steward 16 Sept. 1838                  Morg
Morrison, Wm. to Elizabeth Harrison 11 May 1838                    Cr-1
Morriss, Robt. to Elizabeth McPherson 16 Mar. 1837                 Morg
Morrow, Alexander M. to Mary E. Bullock 7 June 1835               Lewi
Morrow, Benj. to Martha Robirds 19 Sept. 1839                      Mari
Morrow, David to Rachel McFarland 23 Jan. 1834                     Lafa
Morrow, James to Elizabeth Tigert 11 Nov. 1832                     Cr-1
Morrow, James to Margaret Crocket 30 Sept. 1834                    Boon
Morrow, James to Selesa Agee 26 Jan. 1837                          Call
Morrow, James W. to Elizabeth Kyle 14 July 1839                    Howa
Morrow, Jefferson to Manerva Summers 29 Dec. 1836                  Rand
Morrow, Jesse V. to Lucinda Brannun 20 May 1835                    Ripl
Morrow, John B. to Jane Crockett 7 Feb. 1826                       Boon
Morrow, Richard to Polly Tomlinson 23 Aug. 1831                    Cole
Morrow, Robt. to Louvecy Lawrence 9 Mar. 1834                      Howa
Morrow, Robt. to Sylphianer Enlow 29 July 1836                     Cole
Morrow, Robt. D. to Elizabeth Ray 23 Nov. 1820                     Howa
Morrow, Samuel to Sarah Smith 13 Apr. 1834                         Boon
Morrow, Thomas to Charlotte Williams 19 Jan. 1832                  Cole
Morrow, Wm. to Polly Hughes 29 Nov. 1832                           Pk-1
Morrow, Wm. to Louanna Summers 10 Sept. 1839                       Maco
Morse, Louis to Elizabeth N.  25 Nov. 1826 (free negros)           StGe
Morse, Mathew to Sarah A. McKay 17 Mar. 1836                       Cole
Morse, Thomas to Nancy Carleton 31 Aug. 1837                       Barr
Morten, Charles to Cyntha Walls 10 Apr. 1838                       Fran
Morton, Benj. R. to Sarah J. Hunt 19 June 1839                     Plat
Morton, John C. to Frances Morrison 20 Nov. 1838                   CG-A
```

Morton, Robt. to Elizabeth Murphy 26 Apr. 1838	Boon
Morton, Wm. M. to Mary A. Delazier 15 July 1838	Henr
Mosby, Wm. to Elizabeth Jonson 26 Feb. 1839	Clay
Moseing, Jesse to Alice Johnson 9 Nov. 1837	StCh
Moseley, Fielding to Sarah Adams 15 Mar. 1819	Howa
Moseley, John to Sophia Mahan 24 Sept. 1833	Call
Moseley, Thomas to Susan Yancey 22 Feb. 1838	Monr
Mosely, Geo. to Eveline Cooper 31 Mar. 1839	Clar
Mosier, Seneca to Matilda Marvin 4 Nov. 1835	Ray
Mosley, James to Elizabeth Figgins 2 Mar. 1838	Rall
Moss, Ambrose to Lucinda Maxwell 8 Jan. 1829	Howa
Moss, Edward Y. to Mary Stone 14 Oct. 1834	Linc
Moss, Geo. W. to Mary E. Maupin 29 Aug. 1839	Monr
Moss, John to Mary Hunt 28 Sept. 1826	Call
Moss, John to Margaret Lear 29 Aug. 1833	Mari
Moss, Joseph to Catherine Garner 29 Apr. 1832	Mari
Moss, Joseph L. to Marin L. Johnson 14 May 1834	Perr
Moss, Matthew to Jane Mackey 2 Nov. 1826	Pk-1
Moss, Middleton to Hannah Fanning 22 June 1834	Rall
Moss, Oliver P. to Caroline M. Thornton 21 Dec. 1837	Clay
Moss, Richardson to Almeda Cukerdall 17 Jan. 1837	Clay
Moss, Samuel to Lucinda Camron 15 Dec. 1834	Clay
Moss, Samuel to Zerelda Perry 8 Aug. 1839	Monr
Moss, Wm. to Louisa Mackey 11 Apr. 1837	Pk-A
Moss, Woodson I. to Sarah A. Brookie 21 Dec. 1834	Boon
Mostiller, Geo. to Caroline Chapman 14 Mar. 1839	StFr
Motaw, Joseph to Catharine McGuire 14 June 1839	Jeff
Mothershead, Charles to Susannah Long 26 Oct. 1832	Jeff
Mothershead, Whitaker to Ellen Long 2 Jan. 1834	Jeff
Mouche, Wm. to Rebecca Lynch 15 Dec. 1823	Howa
Moudy, Martin to Emily Arnett 11 Feb. 1830	Md-A
Mounce, Henry H. to Edith Davidson 21 Feb. 1836	StCh
Mount, Hugh to Rebecca Tennison 9 Oct. 1831	CG-A
Mouser, Benj. to Rachel Moiers 17 Feb. 1833	Md-A
Mouser, Benj. to Katharine Moirs 16 May 1839	Md-B
Mouser, Daniel to Barbera Kinder 17 July 1828	CG-A
Mouser, Michael to Elizabeth Moiers 9 June 1836	Md-B
Mouzer, John to Hanah Kinder 13 Jan. 1820	CG-1
Moxey, Benj. to Louisa Scott 16 Nov. 1837	Howa
Moxley, Hardy to Lurany Freeman 16 Oct. 1838	Char
Moxley, Solomen R. to Maria S. Verdier 1 May 1838	Linc
Moyers, Isaac to Polly Grayham 4 May 1834	Md-A
Muchany, John B. to Jane E. McCleur 25 June 1835	StCh
Mudd, John F. to Eliza S. Scott 2 Mar. 1826	Wash
Mueller, Leonard R. to Barbara Ramlieter 14 May 1839	Fran
Muhlfield, Michael to Susanna Sutterah 23 Apr. 1838	Perr
Mulanthy, John to Hester Masterson 1 Oct. 1827	Wash
Muldron, Geo. G. to Eliza McElroy 20 Dec. 1838	Mari
Muldrow, James to Minerva Grundy 1 Jan. 1823	Rall
Mulenbrough, Nicholas F. to Sarah Davidson 8 Aug. 1839	Warr
Muler, Christian A. to Helena J.P. Bock 9 Nov. 1837	Warr
Mulherren, John to Jane Griffith 25 Oct. 1832	Pk-1
Mulherrin, John D. to Theodosia Beauchamp 15 Oct. 1835	Pk-1
Mulherrin, Wm. to Ann McCoy 25 Feb. 1836	Pk-1
Mulholland, Edward to Patsy Keeney 10 Feb. 1827	Ray
Mulkey, Charles to Sally Eads 27 Oct. 1821	Cole
Mulkey, Charles to Lavinia Reece 14 Oct. 1832	Jack
Mulkey, John to Charity Vernon 26 July 1829	Cole
Mulkey, John to Mary Evans 19 Dec. 1837	Barr
Mulkey, John H. to Mary H. Venable 13 Sept. 1836	Char
Mulkey, Luke to Ruthy Reed 18 Dec. 1834	Lafa
Mulkey, Robt. to Betsey Welch 2 Dec. 1832	Jack
Mulkey, Wesley to Polly W. Black 15 Nov. 1838	Jack
Mulky, Christopher to Jane Haslip 26 Apr. 1835	John
Mulky, Daniel to Nancy Gan 25 Sept. 1823	Lafa

Mulky, Elijah to Jane McAdams 29 July 1833   Lafa
Mulky, John L. to Amanda Carpenter 21 Aug. 1836   John
Mulky, Johnson to Susanna Roberts 17 Feb. 1836   John
Mulky, Thomas to Sarah Carpenter 15 Apr. 1829   Lafa
Mullens, Joshua to Sally Becket 1 Oct. 1822   Boon
Mullens, Leroy to Elizabeth Woods 1 Aug. 1830   Call
Mullens, Patrick to Mahala McKinzie 14 Aug. 1838   Morg
Muller, Carl G. to Ameline F. Ruhn 18 Aug. 1839   Perr
Mullin, Geo. M. to Katherine Sailor 18 June 1839   Shel
Mullin, Geo. W. to Sarah Harvey 4 May 1833   Carr
Mullinix, Jesse to Borilla Jones 31 Jan. 1837   Pk-B
Mullinix, John to Mary Grimes 15 June 1837   Rand
Mullins, Byrum to Susan Thompson 13 Mar. 1831   Boon
Mullins, David to Nancy Rollins 20 Sept. 1821   Howa
Mullins, Moses to Julian Gavenor 12 Dec. 1837   Howa
Mullins, Richard A. to Elizabeth Strode 16 Aug. 1829 Mari
Mullins, Thompson to Catherine Stewart 2 Nov. 1831   Howa
Mullins, Wm. to Nancy Ringo 9 Jan. 1823   Howa
Mullins, Wm. to Elizabeth Stewart 20 Sept. 1838   Ray
Mullins, Wm. M. to Polly Roberts 2 Aug. 1819   Howa
Mullory, Edward H. to Mary J. Carson 12 Sept. 1839   Mari
Muncel, Channey to Mariah Lechbider 1 Jan. 1826   Howa
Mundy, Benj. to Mary Foster 25 Dec. 1834   Clay
Mundy, Philip to Mary Goveranau 11 Sept. 1828   Wash
Munkers, Absalom to Elizabeth Crocket 18 Mar. 1836   Clay
Munkres, Redman to Mary George 19 Dec. 1839   Clay
Munroe, Daniel to Polly Thorp 19 Jan. 1826   Clay
Munson, Alonzo to Mary Ford 28 June 1832   StCh
Munson, Lewis to Sarah McNew 8 July 1838   Perr
Murdock, James to Susannah Dodson 13 July 1818   StCh
Murdock, James to Lydia Bell 6 Jan. 1835   Fran
Murdock, Robt. to Carolina Fleeke 5 Nov. 1834   StCh
Murfy, Wm. S. to Nancy Jones 10 Sept. 1839   Plat
Murkress, Benj. to Polly Crawley 12 July 1818   Howa
Murphy, Absalom to Lucy Steers 14 Apr. 1836   Rall
Murphy, Augustus to Nancy Curry 28 Nov. 1833   Call
Murphy, Charles C. to Melinda Osborne 26 Dec. 1837   Fran
Murphy, David to Mrs. Rachel Whittenburgh 15 Feb. 1827 CG-A
Murphy, David Jr. to Elviny Whitinburg 5 Feb. 1829   StFr
Murphy, David H. to Lucretia Cundiff 26 Aug. 1832   StFr
Murphy, Dubart to Elizabeth Anthony 10 Nov. 1835   Md-B
Murphy, Enoch to Mary Geiger 9 July 1839   Linc
Murphy, Gilbert W. to Calfirna M. Lemaster 31 Oct. 1839 Polk
Murphy, Isaiah T. to Rebecca Clark 24 Aug. 1837   Fran
Murphy, James to Lucinda Holbut 22 June 1820   StGe
Murphy, James G. to Cynthia Pursly 6 Apr. 1826   Fran
Murphy, Jesse to Polly Hines 16 June 1820   Howa
Murphy, Jesse to Caroline P. Johnson 18 May 1836   Wash
Murphy, John to Betsy Robinson 11 Apr. 1824   StFr
Murphy, John to Lucretia Vawn 10 Feb. 1833   Gasc
Murphy, John to Mary A. Shaw 19 July 1834   Gasc
Murphy, John to Margaret Harris 9 Mar. 1837   Boon
Murphy, John A. to Sally E. Pringle 27 Apr. 1838   Warr
Murphy, Lewis to Elvira Alexander 10 Mar. 1839   StFr
Murphy, Richard to Sarah Murphy 10 Jan. 1819   StFr
Murphy, Robt. P. to Keziah Bennon 20 Oct. 1826   StCh
Murphy, Samuel to Polly Bennon 20 Oct. 1826   StCh
Murphy, Wm. to Mrs. Frances Johns 15 Mar. 1829   StFr
Murphy, Wm. to Nancy Nelson 29 Jan. 1832   Cole
Murphy, Wm. to Mary Boas 10 Oct. 1838   Wash
Murray, Absalom to Polly Tailor 19 July 1835   Cole
Murray, Andrew R. to Nancy Sheley 28 Dec. 1837   Call
Murray, Berryman G. to Maryan K. Stephens 16 Aug. 1827 Wash
Murray, Ephraim D. to Malvina Jacobs 11 Oct. 1836   Ray
Murray, Hiram to Mary D. Puckitt 28 Feb. 1830   Coop

164

Murray, John to Isabelle Leabe 27 Oct. 1830   Ray
Murray, John to Mary Grooms 31 Aug. 1834   Boon
Murray, Peyton to Elizabeth Lenran 7 Mar. 1826   Cole
Murray, Thomas to Elizabeth Durham 31 May 1832   Cole
Murray, Westly to Sarah B. Johnson 15 Aug. 1833   CG-A
Murray, Wm. to Mary Cox 12 Dec. 1833   Lafa
Murray, Wm. D. to Sally W. Renick 24 Oct. 1820   Coop
Murrel, Elias to Jane Perkins 12 Sept. 1833   Wash
Murroh, Louis to Sarah A. Crossman 28 June 1825   Clay
Murrow, Nicholas Sr. to Mrs. Mary Owens 22 Aug. 1832   Pk-1
Murry, Adam to Mrs. Polly McCoy 22 Sept. 1831   Howa
Murry, John P. to Hester McGinnes 10 Nov. 1836   John
Murry, Joseph to Aba Croley 25 Dec. 1837   Henr
Murry, Nicholas to Hester Owens 3 July 1839   Pk-B
Murry, Samuel to Sarah Thomas 7 July 1839   Wash
Murry, Shadwick to Elvira K. Wilhite 8 Sept. 1831   Cole
Mury, Joseph to Mary Pinkerton 5 Sept. 1827   Perr
Musgrove, Henry B. to Margaret Burdet 3 Nov. 1831   Mari
Musgrove, John to Susan Birditt 22 Dec. 1835   Monr
Music, John to Rebeka Scobee 24 Dec. 1827   Rall
Musick, Colly to Sarah Johnson 30 Oct. 1836   Mari
Musick, John R. to Elizabeth Suddeth 15 Aug. 1837   Mari
Musick, Lafranier C. to Jane D. Haden 4 Nov. 1832   Pk-1
Musick, Lauson T. to Irena Middleton 4 July 1837   Pk-A
Musser, Jacob to Jane Williams 3 Jan. 1838   Linc
Mussett, Alvin to Sarah Phillips 9 Mar. 1837   Boon
Myers, Daniel F. to Malvina Crews 3 Sept. 1835   Howa
Myers, David to Lucretia M. Jones 2 Mar. 1830   Call
Myers, Elias T. to Nancy Brendenburgh 28 Nov. 1839   Lafa
Myers, Geo. to Lucy Adams 1 June 1831   Howa
Myers, Henry to Judith Scrader 16 June 1839   Rand
Myers, James to Thirsa Walker 20 Mar. 1823   Howa
Myers, John to Elizabeth Adams 16 Feb. 1826   Howa
Myers, John to Eve Rutenbiller 6 Mar. 1828   StCh
Myers, John to Catherine Grounds -- Oct. 1834   Md-A
Myers, Joseph to Mary Boyles 5 Jan. 1832   Gasc
Myers, Michael to Mary Haley 27 Nov. 1839   Rand
Myers, Robt. to Martha Lynch 30 Aug. 1829   Howa
Myers, Wm. Jr. to Margaret Maggard 30 Mar. 1830   Rand
Myres, Fredric to Caty Shrum 20 Oct. 1835   CG-B
Myrtle, Johnson M. to Sally Hardin 4 Dec. 1818   Howa
Myrtle, Reuben to Elizabeth Bozarth 29 May 1826   Howa

Nailor, John to Rebecca Payne 12 Nov. 1832   Boon
Nailor, John to Mary Thomas 7 Apr. 1836   StCh
Nale, Benj. to Ann Walker 14 Nov. 1830   Call
Nally, Bennet to Jane Anderson 15 June 1830   Pk-1
Nance, Drury C. to Martha Abernathy 29 Dec. 1831   Perr
Nance, John to Peggy Howard 9 Aug. 1827   Gasc
Nance, John to Elizabeth Simons 29 Apr. 1829   Fran
Nance, John to Susanna Shearley 31 Dec. 1835   Cole
Nanson, John to Jane Cartner 11 June 1822   Coop
Napier, Hiram to Winny Mornan 16 Feb. 1839   Gasc
Napton, Wm. B. to Malinda Williams 27 Mar. 1838   Sali
Nash, Alfred to ---- Conger 11 Jan. 1831   Call
Nash, Hardin to Sarah Adair 26 Feb. 1836   Call
Nash, Ira to Martha Hill 26 July 1834   Boon
Nash, Ira P. to Ann Smith 18 Dec. 1827   Call
Nash, Joseph to Peggy Chaney 4 June 1829   Clay
Nash, Noah to Elizabeth Johnson 9 June 1836   Jack
Nash, Samuel to Ann Williams 12 Jan. 1834   Clin
Nash, Wm. to Mary Aldridge 31 May 1830   Perr
Nashions, David to Hannah P. Panick 4 Aug. 1826   CG-A
Natherly, Sherard to Jane Stephens 12 Oct. 1831   Linc

Nations, Bannister to Keziah Barren 4 Dec. 1831   CG-A
Nations, Geo. to Mrs. Matilda Stroup 28 Jan. 1834   CG-A
Nations, James to Frances E. Brown 20 Nov. 1834   CG-B
Nations, John to Elizabeth Malone 18 Sept. 1825   CG-A
Nations, Richard to Ann Lewis 8 Oct. 1835   CG-B
Nations, Thomas to Elizabeth Hinkle 16 Feb. 1836   CG-B
Nations, Wm. to Lucinda Mattingly 4 May 1838   Perr
Nave, Abraham to Mary J. Trimble 13 July 1836   Gree
Nave, Geo. to Nancy Jobe 31 May 1821   Sali
Nave, Hardin to Rebeckah Shipton 6 May 1827   Sali
Nave, Jacob to Elizabeth Spalden 28 June 1835   Ripl
Nave, James to Ebby Collector 14 Aug. 1817   Howa
Nave, Wm. to Mahalia Trapp 22 Feb. 1827   Lafa
Naylor, Geo. to Thirza A. Hutchinson 10 May 1831   Howa
Naylor, Geo. T. to Peggy Helton 8 Nov. 1838   Howa
Naylor, John to Margaret Smith 26 Feb. 1835   Howa
Neacl, Valentine to Polley Sumpter 21 Feb. 1835   Wash
Neal, Clabourn to Louisa C. Gibson 5 Dec. 1839   Clin
Neal, Nathan to Elizabeth Stone 23 Mar. 1826   Coop
Neal, Pallis to Mary A. Dowell 20 July 1837   Pk-A
Neal, Robt. to Eliza Hammers 22 Dec. 1836   Pk-1
Neal, Sytte to Elizabeth Winchester 27 Mar. 1837   StCh
Neal, Wilbourn to Susan Butler 2 Oct. 1834   Pk-1
Neale, Daniel to Mary Collins 13 Oct. 1829   Boon
Nealy, Calaway to Esther Carpenter 9 May 1839   Boon
Nealy, Jacob to Sarah Walls 31 May 1827   CG-A
Neel, David to Mary J. Blackaby 12 Jan. 1838   Linc
Neel, David H. to Elyrilla Casper 13 Jan. 1839   Ray
Neel, John to Ellender Vanderpool 19 Nov. 1830   Ray
Neel, John to Clemency Casper 31 Dec. 1837   Ray
Neele, Lewis to Polly Lindly 5 Feb. 1832   Cr-1
Neely, Pallis to Lucinda Hopkins 22 Oct. 1839   Polk
Neely, Wm. to Mary M. McClanahan 5 Sept. 1833   Coop
Neese, James to Lewsindy Allen 4 Jan. 1836   Cole
Neighfong, Geo. to Cate Baker 2 Feb. 1806   CG-1
Neil, Uriah to Sarah Calvin 21 Dec. 1837   Pk-B
Neill, Joseph to Elizabeth Hays 1 Dec. 1836   Wash
Neisbit, John T. Jr. to Lucretia Lyon 7 Dec. 1837   Monr
Nelson, Alexander P. to Rebecca M. McNeal 23 Dec. 1839 Cole
Nelson, Benj. F. to Nancy Guest 19 May 1834   Mari
Nelson, Elijah to Lucinda Staples 6 Oct. 1833   Jeff
Nelson, Geo. to Margaret Crawford 16 Mar. 1825   Lafa
Nelson, Hiram to Eliza Anderson 6 Apr. 1834   Mari
Nelson, James to Mary White 7 June 1836   StCh
Nelson, James to Eliza Pathon 24 Dec. 1837   Ripl
Nelson, Josiah F. to Cynthia McFarland 8 June 1828   Lafa
Nelson, Samuel to Cynthia Head 3 Apr. 1820   Howa
Nelson, Thomas to Pamelia Parrish 1 Mar. 1832   Lafa
Nelson, Thomas H. to Mary L. Wyan 12 Dec. 1837   Coop
Nelson, Wm. to Susan Collins 19 Nov. 1834   Boon
Nesbit, Geo. A. to Eliza Hayden 15 July 1830   Mari
Nesbit, John to Catharin Waller 21 July 1836   Monr
Nesbit, Samuel to Mary Thompson 18 Apr. 1826   Fran
Nesbitt, Samuel to Polly A. Meredith 14 June 1838   Call
Nester, Jacob to Elizabeth Hopper 4 May 1837   Howa
Nesunger, Manuel to Polly Baker 22 Dec. 1836   CG-A
Neswanger, Peter to Elizabeth James 1 Sept. 1831   CG-A
Netherton, Moses to Sarah Grant 25 Nov. 1838   Lafa
Netherton, Wm. to Nancy Holland 3 Dec. 1835   Clay
Nettle, Geo. to Hannah Belcher 3 May 1837   Barr
Nettle, Shadrack to Ann Burlison 23 June 1831   Cr-1
Nettleton, Gilbert to Juliette Pratt 20 Nov. 1839   Perr
Nevet, Hugh to Mrs. Soults 6 Aug. 1839   Fran
Nevil, Samuel E. to Charlotte Boon 7 June 1832   Pk-1
Neville, Presley to Delila Keithley 30 Apr. 1835   Pk-1

```
Nevins, John D. to Mary J. Fisher 5 Sept. 1838             Call
Nevins, Robt. to Mary A. Ridgeway 25 May 1837              Boon
Nevins, Samuel to Mahala Adams 18 June 1837               Boon
Nevins, Thomas to Kitty Randolph 26 Sept. 1835            Call
Nevins, Wm. to Ellen Teeters 1 Aug. 1833                  Boon
Newberry, Cyrus to Lenna Brandwaters 19 June 1831         Cr-P
Newberry, Henry to Nancy Swift 27 Oct. 1836              Cr-l
Newberry, Henry to Catharine Ganes 26 Sept. 1837         Md-B
Newberry, Thomas to Margaret Martin 8 June 1830          Perr
Newberry, Wm. to Gabrela Frier 4 Sept. 1834              Md-A
Newberry, Wm. to Mahala Palmer 12 Nov. 1835              Linc
Newbill, Fanklin I. to Marian Eckert 3 Dec. 1835         StCh
Newbill, Nathanial A. to Sarah Swope 28 Mar. 1833        Pett
Newchurch, Andrew to Rebecca Smithers 27 Sept. 1832      Linc
Newcom, James to Julia A. Crocket 13 June 1837           Rall
Newcom, Wm. T. to Margaret Dale 19 June 1836             Lewi
Newcom, Wm. to Sarah Myrtle 1 Mar. 1829                  Howa
Newel, Leroy to Elizabeth Haley 17 June 1834            Cole
Newfield, Abraham to Eleanor Tong 4 July 1813            StGe
Newkirk, Charles to Disa Boian 30 May 1839               Morg
Newkirk, David to Semirah Devault 5 Oct. 1837           CG-A
Newkirk, Stephen to Elizabeth Garner 7 Nov. 1833         CG-A
Newland, Isaac to Hannah Hicks 15 Feb. 1827             Boon
Newland, Samuel to Mary W. Martin 12 Dec. 1839          Call
Newlin, Geo. to Polly A. Searcy 11 Feb. 1836            Boon
Newlin, John to Minerva Hardwick 31 Oct. 1839           Carr
Newlin, Keelin T. to Cyntha Barnes 5 Oct. 1837          Howa
Newman, Albert to Minerva Hays 26 Feb. 1839             Plat
Newman, James M. to Jane S. Clark 18 July 1839          Pk-B
Newsome, Allen T. to Martha Johnson 5 July 1837         Monr
Newton, Asa to Angelina Ashby 14 Aug. 1836              Char
Newton, Isrel to Rachael Jenkins 12 July 1836           Cole
Newton, James to Experience Newton -- -- 1835           Char
Newton, James to Polly Maggard 1 Dec. 1836              Rand
Newton, Wm. to Polly Witt 29 June 1822                  Howa
Newton, Wm. to Jane Rucker 29 Dec. 1839                 Rand
Nichlin, Wm. H. to Mary J. Nelson 1 May 1838            Linc
Nicholas, Evins M. to Judith Crowder 8 Sept. 1839       Buch
Nicholas, John to Sarah Ross 10 Aug. 1830               Howa
Nichols, Felix to Ruth Cunningham 26 Mar. 1832          Linc
Nichols, Felix G. to Elizabeth A. Renoe 12 Feb. 1833    Call
Nichols, Frederick to Angeline Crump -- -- 1832         Call
Nichols, Garland to Maria Winterbower 26 Jan. 1837      Boon
Nichols, Geo. to Hannah Brite 29 June 1826              Call
Nichols, James to America Vancamp 25 Mar. 1838          Lafa
Nichols, James to Frances Smith 14 Feb. 1839            Buch
Nichols, Jesse to Eby Persinger 8 Mar. 1822             Howa
Nichols, John to Ila Broadhush 4 Apr. 1822              Howa
Nichols, John to Nancy Gilliam 23 Jan. 1831             Clay
Nichols, John to Maryann Brown 5 Feb. 1832              Pk-l
Nichols, John to Julia Lewis 10 Oct. 1839               Call
Nichols, John F. to Sarah Blythe 30 June 1836           Call
Nichols, Julius to Margaret Davidson 26 Sept. 1837      Mill
Nichols, Larkin to Polly Stark 28 July 1824             Cole
Nichols, Lorenso D. to Amanda M. Boyce 28 May 1839      Mari
Nichols, Robt. to Priscilla Wren 28 Feb. 1836           Boon
Nichols, Robt. to Eliza A. Williams -- Dec. 1836        Sali
Nichols, Robt. to Mary J. Slanen 9 Aug. 1838            Boon
Nichols, Samuel to Elizabeth Worthington 26 May 1838    Clar
Nichols, Sydney to Sarah Grant 19 Sept. 1834            Boon
Nichols, Thomas to Amanda Lewis 20 Feb. 1838            Call
Nichols, Wm. to Hannah J. Muir 22 Oct. 1829             Call
Nichols, Wm. to Mahala J. Worthington 22 May 1838       Clar
Nicholson, Geo. to Anna Zumwalt 11 Dec. 1824            Call
Nicholson, Joseph to Zerelda Allen 24 May 1836          Mari
```

```
Nickerson, James to Melvina Herriford 31 Jan. 1839          Char
Nickerson, Wm. to Elizabeth Herryford 6 Feb. 1838           Char
Nickles, Thomas to Mrs. Jane Hall 18 Oct. 1838              Barr
Nicklin, Jonathan to Malinda Young 6 Apr. 1825             Lafa
Niell, Thomas to Demshea Miller 12 Oct. 1834               CG-B
Niell, Wm. to Frankky Henson 23 Aug. 1832                  CG-A
Nifong, Alexander to Alvy Arnot 2 Oct. 1832                Md-A
Nifong, Jacob to Letty Sims 3 Apr. 1825                    StFr
Night, Benj. to Amanda Goddard 1 June 1839                 Rand
Night, Hiram to Harriet Robinson 7 Jan. 1833               Md-A
Niswanger, David to Polly Starnes 5 Mar. 1835              CG-B
Nixcon, Robt. R. to Catharine Evear 27 Sept. 1809          CG-1
Nixon, Geo. to Phebe Boonard 4 Aug. 1836                   Morg
Nixon, Lorenzo to Mary Williams 24 July 1830               Cole
Nixon, Moses A.J. to Lucinda Wooten 30 Dec. 1832           Coop
Noble, Ignatius to Eleanor Skinner 17 Aug. 1831            Rand
Noble, James to Priscilla Standerford 22 Dec. 1825         Howa
Noble, Lemuel to Morgan Harris 15 Sept. 1833               Boon
Noble, Liberty to Syntha Pipes 3 Apr. 1834                 Rand
Noble, Liberty to Mildred A. Henderson 4 Aug. 1839         Rand
Noble, Thomas to Nancy Williams 25 Dec. 1832               Monr
Nobles, Elijah to Malissa Hudson 7 May 1833                Jeff
Nobles, James to Mary Burgain 30 Oct. 1832                 Cr-1
Noe, James to Rachel Turner 1 Aug. 1833                    Boon
Noe, Sidney to Mrs. Lucinda Ruggles 5 Apr. 1829            Wash
Noel, Benj. S. to Ann E. Martin 23 July 1835               Rand
Noel, Jackson to Elizabeth Wilson 18 Feb. 1838             Monr
Noel, Leroy to Amanda Davis 15 Apr. 1827                   Rall
Noel, Reuben to Polly Zumwalt 15 Mar. 1812                 StCh
Noell, Thomas to Matilda Atterberry 1 Apr. 1832            Monr
Noell, Wm. to Elizabeth A. Cox 2 Feb. 1836                 Md-B
Noell, Wm. to Mary Gregoire 27 Apr. 1836                   Perr
Noland, Andrew J. to Sarah Pitcher 13 Mar. 1834            Jack
Noland, Ervin to Frances Hill 26 Apr. 1835                 Lafa
Noland, Henry to Elizabeth Pitcher 11 Jan. 1826            Clay
Noland, Martin to Sarah Lampkins 2 Mar. 1826              Call
Noland, Wm. Jr. to Polly Braden 7 Mar. 1833                Jack
Noland, Woodford to Milly Creason 9 Oct. 1826              Lafa
Nonval, Joseph to Catharine Laise 1 Feb. 1836             StCh
Nordister, Benj. to Jane Jackson 2 May 1829                Rand
Norfleet, Abraham to Margaret Campbell 16 Aug. 1832        Call
Norman, Joseph to Eliza Gwynn 2 July 1835                  Monr
Norman, Ruben to Ellender Patterson 15 Dec. 1805           CG-1
Norris, Abner to Jane Evans 14 July 1825                   Lafa
Norris, Charles to Cinthy Davis 12 Oct. 1837               Clar
Norris, Hosea to Sintha A. Allen 24 Dec. 1837              Clay
Norris, James to Evira Odle 7 Mar. 1834                    Lafa
Norris, John to Dicy Dodson 27 Dec. 1825                   Howa
Norris, John to Polly Burris 15 Mar. 1831                  Lafa
Norris, Wm. to Rebecca Gragg 23 Aug. 1818                  Howa
Norris, Wm. to Nancy Farley 13 Nov. 1835                   Jeff
North, Flavins J. to Francis C. Goode 27 Nov. 1834         Fran
North, James to Mary F. Martin 11 Aug. 1837                Fran
North, Thomas L. to Martha Barnett 19 Dec. 1839            Maco
North, Wm. to Nancy Williamson 19 Feb. 1835                Fran
North, Wm. T. to Mary A. Owens 8 Dec. 1834                 Fran
Northcutt, Dudley A. to Polly Fuqua 2 Nov. 1837            Rall
Northcutt, Geo. to Catharine Welch 4 Oct. 1838             Warr
Northcutt, Lewis C. to Clarissa M. Shahoney 16 Dec. 1838   Rall
Norton, James to Mrs. Hannah Frost 27 Dec. 1831            Clay
Norton, Jesse O. to Mrs. Phebe A. Shelton 25 Dec. 1837     Wash
Norton, John A. to Ellen A. Haff 1 Oct. 1837               Pk-B
Norton, Marvel H. to Druzilla Coontz 31 July 1838          Rall
Norton, Melzor to Mildred A. Haff 14 Sept. 1837            Pk-B
Norton, Whitfield to N.M.S. Massey 9 Oct. 1836             Rand
```

Norvell, James M. to Nancy L. Ashby 6 Sept. 1838   Char
Nottleman, J.B. to Ulie Go 21 Oct. 1829   StCh
Nousse, Thomas to Adelina Collins rec. 25 May 1836   StCh
Novaille, Francis to Louise Proux 3 Nov. 1827   StCh
Novalle, Joseph to Ursalle Dumond 12 Aug. 1830   StCh
Novel, Geo. to Levisa Boyd 14 May 1839   Coop
Novel, Parker to Ann Seely 9 Aug. 1837   Rall
Nowel, Hardin to Martha J. Eckert 16 May 1825   StCh
Nowell, Garret to Isabella Galbreath 14 Aug. 1828   Rall
Nowlin, Brian W. to Lucy N. Davis 3 Nov. 1837   Clay
Nowlin, John N. to Adaline Buford 23 Jan. 1838   Lafa
Nowlin, John S. to Attalanta Harris 15 Feb. 1828   Sali
Nuese, Geo. to Belinda Steerman 28 Dec. 1828   Wash
Null, Geo. W. to Martha A. Cravens 1 Feb. 1838   Linc
Null, John to Lency Hyet 4 Nov. 1833   Fran
Null, John S. to Eliza M. Baxter 10 May 1835   Warr
Null, Josiah to Lucretia Naton 20 Aug. 1835   Jeff
Null, Wm. to Phebe Koontz 27 Dec. 1829   Linc
Null, Wm. Jr. to Sarah Metz 1 Sept. 1831   Jeff
Null, Wm. to Martha Boyd 31 Jan. 1839   Jeff
Nun, Catton to Eliza Elmore 1 Aug. 1833   Pk-1

Oakes, Joshua to Matilda Williams 12 Nov. 1829   CG-A
Oakly, Harry to Mrs. Susanna Millson 25 Dec. 1825   Linc
Oatman, John to Polly Chapman 21 May 1839   StFr
Obanion, Briant W. to Nancy Liles 7 Aug. 1834   Pk-1
O'Bannon, Geo. W. to Margaret Willson 8 Nov. 1836   CG-A
O'Bannon, Jefferson to Margate McDowel 15 Nov. 1835   Md-B
O'Bannon, John B. to Mary Wilson 10 Aug. 1833   CG-A
O'Bannon, Welton to Rebecca Russell 9 Oct. 1838   CG-A
O'Bannon, Yelverton to Melvina Burdette 18 Apr. 1830   Md-A
Oberdalhoff, Frederick to Mariana Obermaier 5 Dec. 1834   Warr
O'Brien, M. to Rebecca M. Hause 16 Apr. 1827   Jeff
O'Bryan, John to Mary Reavis 14 Aug. 1834   Coop
O'Bryan, Jorden T. to Amelia Reavis 1 Oct. 1835   Coop
Obouchon, Napoleon to Mary Valle 20 Sept. 1837   Md-B
OBuchon, Francis to Judith DeGuire 6 Feb. 1833   Md-A
Obuchon, Lewis to Lewise Magdaline 6 Jan. 1829   StCh
Obuchon, Napoleon to Elizabeth Goza 15 Jan. 1835   Md-A
Obushon, Baryl to Louise Papin 10 Apr. 1839   StFr
Ocket, John to Catherine Hall 27 July 1837   Mari
Odd, Nehemiah to Nancy McGuire 8 Oct. 1818   Howa
Odear, John to Mary A. Thompson 13 Dec. 1838   John
Odell, Abraham to Lucinda Smith 2 Jan. 1837   Lewi
Odell, Caleb to Jane Odell 21 Feb. 1828   Ray
Odell, Edward to Katty Clevenger 25 Jan. 1823   Ray
Odell, Evan to Rhody Clark 16 Mar. 1825   Ray
Odell, Francis to Rachel Clevenger 29 Feb. 1828   Ray
Odell, Isaac to Elizabeth Adams 10 Mar. 1828   Ray
Odell, Isaac to Ellendor Riggs 7 June 1832   Ray
Odell, James to Polly Riggs 4 May 1832   Ray
Odell, James to Susanna Cates 7 June 1838   Ray
Odell, Job to Elizabeth Row 12 Feb. 1829   Ray
Odell, John to Catharine Riggs 16 Mar. 1829   Ray
Odell, John to Mary Shelton 7 June 1837   Ray
Odell, Samuel to Polly Rowland 26 July 1832   Ray
Odell, Simeon to Perellen Lewis 7 Apr. 1832   Ray
Odell, Soloman to Mary Coats 19 Nov. 1836   Ray
Odell, Wm. to Peggy Odell 20 Mar. 1831   Clay
Odell, Wm. to Mary Odell 29 Jan. 1832   Ray
Oden, Alfred to Frances A. Brown 23 May 1833   Pk-1
Odenull, Levi to Elizabeth Johnson 24 Dec. 1821   Cole
Odle, Jeremiah C. to Margaret Blythe 21 Apr. 1829   Howa
Odle, Jonathan C. to Emily Boyd 21 May 1832   Coop

Odum, John to Lydia Spalding 28 Nov. 1839   StFr
Offe, Peter to Lucy Kelly 24 Nov. 1825   Pk-1
Officer, James to Evalina G. Cooley rec. 5 Mar. 1828   Clay
Officer, Robt. to Rebecca Shackleford 23 May 1833   Clay
O'Flaherty, Thomas to Catherine Reilhe 25 Nov. 1839   StCh
Ogden, James to Priscilla McLaughlin 4 June 1839   Cole
Oge, Luc to Hortense A. Misse' 2 Feb. 1836   Wash
Ogelive, Lorenzo B. to Sophrina Cottle 22 Feb. 1835   Linc
Ogg, Geo. to Harriet Howard 29 May 1830   Linc
Ogle, James to Mary Williams 7 June 1829   Jeff
Ogle, John to Elvira Wright 8 Aug. 1839   Jeff
Oglesby, Nimrod to Mary J. McClean 26 Mar. 1839   Coop
Oglesby, Pleasant G. to Milly Woolery 24 Jan. 1833   Coop
Oglisby, Richard H. to Mary Simms 23 Aug. 1833   Wash
O'Haver, Francis to Sarah J. Garvin 20 Apr. 1836   Wash
Ohlhousen, Edmond C. to Ann M. Elis 1 Feb. 1838   Clay
Ohmore, Jacob H. to Sophia Bomker 14 Mar. 1834   Warr
O'Howell, Stephen to Partheny Moon 23 Oct. 1836   Coop
Ola, Berry to Mary Meng 4 Feb. 1838   Call
Oldacre, Wm. to Fanny Brockman 15 Feb. 1835   Clay
Oldham, Alexander to Lydia Williams 1 Mar. 1827   Pk-1
Oldham, Elias Jr. to Susan Bratton 30 Dec. 1838   Barr
Oldham, Jackson to Polly Jackson 23 Feb. 1833   Boon
Oldham, Leonard to Elizabeth Hughes 12 Mar. 1835   Howa
Oldham, Richard to July Williams 25 Oct. 1831   Pk-1
Oldham, S.C. to S.A. Shortridge 26 Dec. 1839   Jack
Oldham, Wm. B. to Margaret Frye 19 July 1838   Mari
Oldken, Nicholas R. to Fidilian Richards 8 Aug. 1839   CG-B
Oliver, Archibald to Elizabeth Vallens 13 Sept. 1827   StCh
Oliver, Dixon to Elizabeth McKnight 5 Sept. 1838   Mari
Oliver, James to Nancy Brotten 13 Dec. 1832   Call
Oliver, James to Louisiana Yarnall 28 Aug. 1834   StCh
Oliver, John to Elizabeth Brown 9 Sept. 1830   StCh
Oliver, John to Elender Carpenter 6 Jan. 1833   Pk-1
Oliver, John to Frances Archy 20 Jan. 1836   Gree
Oliver, Mathew to Elizabeth Moore 29 Sept. 1831   Rand
Oliver, Miles to Melinda Crater 22 Feb. 1830   StCh
Oliver, Mordica to Frances A. Pollard 30 Aug. 1836   Ray
Oliver, Thomas to Elizabeth Perrimen 15 July 1807   StGe
Olson, Jacob to Martha Lendland 20 June 1839   Shel
Olverson, Nelson to Dicy Evans 23 Sept. 1830   Howa
Olverson, Sidney P. to Mary Padgett 19 Feb. 1835   Howa
Omara, Eugene to Mrs. Terrance Brown 6 Nov. 1827   Wash
O'Meara, Daniel to Elizabeth Maddock 31 July 1832   Perr
O'Neal, Absolem to Mary Parks 9 Sept. 1838   Wash
Oneal, Charles to Patsey Hillhouse 25 Feb. 1830   Cr-P
Oneal, Charles to Nancy Annis 10 Nov. 1836   Clay
Oneal, Joseph to Martha Watson 16 Feb. 1826   StGe
O'Neal, Joseph to Nancy Baldrige 23 Aug. 1837   Pk-A
O'Neal, Stanley to Amanda Chiles 20 Jan. 1835   Boon
Onsley, Willice Y. to Tempy Brown 26 Jan. 1826   StGe
Onstat, Marville to Charlotte Hayes 3 June 1830   Pk-1
Onstot, David to Katharine Gibson 12 Apr. 1832   Pk-1
Onstott, Solomon to Maryann Fugate 13 Nov. 1828   Pk-1
Orberts, Martain to Margarett Hutchison 7 Aug. 1836   CG-A
Orchard, Alexander to Elizabeth Ramsey 28 Sept. 1837   Fran
Orchard, John to Rosanna Ashbrook 13 Apr. 1828   Wash
Orear, Enoch to Mary Hadin 5 Jan. 1835   Boon
O'Rear, John to Elizabeth Talbot 22 May 1834   Boon
O'Rear, Trussey to Betsy J. Davis 14 May 1835   Coop
Orme, Robt. to Elizabeth Shobe 16 Dec. 1834   Gasc
O'Roarc, Damster to Elizabeth Simpson 22 Aug. 1839   Ray
Orr, Isaac to Joanah Campbell 16 Mar. 1826   Pk-1
Orr, Isaac to Susan Darby 20 Oct. 1831   Pk-1
Orr, Wm. to Malvina Glenn 25 July 1838   Monr

```
Orrick, Campbell to Sarah L. Munion 31 Jan. 1839          StCh
Orrick, John to Elizabeth Taylor 6 June 1837              StCh
Orrick, Wm. D. to Eliza P. Mills 4 May 1837              StCh
Orton, Nestil to Lucinda Spradling 13 Aug. 1833          StFr
Osborn, Amzi to Esther Perrine 10 Apr. 1835             Perr
Osborn, Geo. to Catherine Colvin 25 Aug. 1835           Boon
Osborn, Jephthah to Eliza Grant 12 Nov. 1825            Boon
Osborne, Hyrum to Drusilla Sappington 14 Feb. 1838      Fran
Osburn, John to Rachel Lemmon 13 Aug. 1825              Boon
Osgood, Aaron to Mary Icenhower 17 Nov. 1836            StCh
Oslin, James L. to Mary A. Jesse 27 Aug. 1839           Audr
Osmon, Joniah to Rosetta Busby 10 May 1816              Howa
Osten, John to Rachel Freeman 17 Dec. 1835              Gree
Osterwald, Charles to Mary Miller 6 Dec. 1838           Fran
Ostrander, Nathaniel to Eliza J. Yantis 11 Apr. 1838    Lafa
O'Toole, James R. to Sophia Hickman 9 Aug. 1836         Howa
Otry, Wm. to Tabitha McBride 15 July 1833               CG-A
Ousley, Burdine to Catharine Shropshire 14 Oct. 1834    Mari
Ousley, Jephtha to Eunice Brown 12 Mar. 1829            Pk-1
Ove, James to Ellender Splawn 3 Apr. 1829               Ray
Overall, Wilson to Caroline M. Gould 5 Oct. 1836        StCh
Overby, Wm. to Mrs. Jane Hardester 31 Oct. 1839         Rand
Overfelt, Eli to Sarah Parker 18 Nov. 1833              Call
Overstreet, John to Laura Williams 1 June 1836          StCh
Overton, Benj. to Ann Holt 15 July 1830                 Call
Overton, Dudley to Dulcena Naul 24 Nov. 1829            Mari
Overton, James F. to Harriet A. Baynham 11 Oct. 1832    Call
Overton, Richard to Anna Byrd 17 Dec. 1837              CG-A
Overton, Waller H. to Mary J. Shackleford 28 Sept. 1837 Mari
Overton, Wm. G. to Avaline Nall 17 Nov. 1829            Mari
Owen, Davis to Jane Seggatt 13 Mar. 1838                Pett
Owen, James to Susan Wells 16 Oct. 1828                 Jeff
Owen, James T. to Emily Paul 23 Aug. 1838               Ray
Owen, Jonathan to Elizabeth Murphy 5 Dec. 1839          Plat
Owen, Mosby N. to Evelina Jack 7 Apr. 1831              Ray
Owen, Thomas to Sally Pointer 11 May 1830               Gasc
Owen, Thomas J. to Sarah S. Chapman 10 Feb. 1831        Rand
Owen, Thomas J. to Sarah Mourning 4 May 1837            Howa
Owen, Wm. M. to Delila Rupe 15 Mar. 1832                Lafa
Owen, Wm. M. to Sarah Grooms 26 Sept. 1838              Clay
Owenby, Canady to Lucinda Walker 17 July 1834           Rand
Owenby, John to Polly Hutchinson 10 June 1835           Rand
Owenby, Joseph P. to Nancy Garrett 20 Apr. 1837         Maco
Owenby, Powell to Lucy Davis 9 May 1837                 Monr
Owens, Alvin to Sarah Davidson 8 May 1836               Clay
Owens, Fleming to Nancy Thompson 2 May 1838             Polk
Owens, Gibson T. to Louisa Duncan 26 Jan. 1837          Clay
Owens, Henry to Missouri Smith 7 Mar. 1833              Clay
Owens, James H. to Eliza J. Johnson 16 May 1839         StCh
Owens, John to Patsy King 7 Feb. 1820                   Howa
Owens, John to Nancy Thorp 12 Aug. 1834                 Clay
Owens, Richard to Elizabeth Lindsey 28 Nov. 1833        Pk-1
Owens, Robt. C. to Hester Bogghess 14 Apr. 1833         Clay
Owens, Samuel to Fanny Brumley 22 Jan. 1832             Gasc
Owens, Wm. to Sarah Hall 22 Sept. 1836                  Polk
Owens, Wm. to Mary Grooms 11 Sept. 1838                 Clay
Owens, Willis to Erusa Baker 5 Apr. 1832                Jeff
Owesley, Moses to Mahala Gooden 28 May 1833             Lafa
Owings, Henry to Margaret Galbreath 26 June 1823        Rall
Owings, John to Nancy Gash 13 Mar. 1834                 Rand
Owings, Richard to Mary E. Fant 25 Sept. 1839           Warr
Owins, Isom to Casander Indicut 3 May 1838              Clay
Owsley, John H. to Amanda Francis 19 Dec. 1833          Mari
Oxford, Wm. to Malinda Clark 18 May 1832                CG-A
Ozburn, John P. to Agnes Oliver 29 Jan. 1838            Barr
```

Pace, Geo. to Reyrinda F. Finks 6 Sept. 1838	Howa
Pace, Dr. H. to Lucretia Hart 11 July 1833	Coop
Pace, Hiram to Matilda Woods 29 Feb. 1824	Call
Pace, James to Zerilda Wayne 24 Mar. 1836	Call
Pace, John C. to Eliza A. McCulum 3 Mar. 1831	Rall
Pace, Thomas to Wilhemina Howard 3 Sept. 1839	Sali
Pace, Wm. to Hester Kidwell 24 June 1836	Call
Packwood, Samuel W. to Mary A. Heartatch 11 June 1835	Wash
Padget, Hardin to Susan E. Ramsey 9 Mar. 1836	Howa
Padget, Washington to Rebecca Jones 7 Apr. 1833	Call
Padget, Washington to Martha Carter 24 June 1838	Call
Page, Ancel to Sally Richey 14 Mar. 1831	Lafa
Page, Andrew to Elizabeth Jewel 24 June 1824	Howa
Page, Granville R. to Mary Ridge 22 July 1835	Lafa
Page, James to Emily Bentley 19 Oct. 1837	Howa
Page', Jean B. to Hermoine Collman 7 Oct. 1834	Wash
Page, Jeremiah to Manetta Perkins 29 Oct. 1835	Warr
Page, John to Bashua Morton 28 Nov. 1833	Howa
Page, John to Nancy O'Dell 30 Mar. 1837	Davi
Page, Joseph H. to Elizabeth Coats 7 Jan. 1836	Lafa
Page, Loren to Eliza Clark 14 Sept. 1834	Clay
Page, Marble W. to Nancy Johnson 22 Dec. 1836	Lafa
Page, Rachel F. to Margaret Richey 17 Jan. 1834	Lafa
Pain, Benj. F. to Martha Johnson 23 Nov. 1828	Wash
Pain, Edward to Mary A. Randall 19 May 1838	Wash
Pain, Wm. to Elizabeth Williams 17 Feb. 1828	Cole
Painter, Lewis to Harriet Ramsey 14 Apr. 1829	CG-A
Palardie, Peter to Eulalie Serre 3 May 1830	StCh
Pallardie, Bazil to Agnes Lucier 26 Sept. 1836	StCh
Pallardy, Antoine to Josephine Hiutt 6 Jan. 1832	StCh
Palmer, David K. to Rebecca Thomas -- June 1837	Sali
Palmer, Henderson to Louisa Williams 21 Jan. 1838	Boon
Palmer, Henry to Nancy McGowan 14 Apr. 1835	Pk-1
Palmer, James to Emily Munday -- -- 1831	Linc
Palmer, Peraguin to Nancy Blevin 19 Dec. 1834	Boon
Palmetary, James to Eliza Johnson 8 May 1831	Howa
Palmetary, Thomas to Harriet Bozarth 27 Dec. 1832	Howa
Pancost, Wm. H. to Darcus Loe 15 Jan. 1826	Howa
Paneck, Alfred to Polly Statler 6 Nov. 1831	CG-A
Panick, John to Sally Kunce 2 Mar. 1826	CG-A
Panick, John to Sally Wise 28 Sept. 1837	CG-A
Pannells, Wm. B. to Oleavia Loveall 4 Oct. 1832	Perr
Panton, Joseph to Julie Lacroix 2 Feb. 1829	StCh
Papin, Louise to Louise Clairmont 7 Jan. 1828	StCh
Paragett, Francis to Letitia Ruder 30 Oct. 1836	Henr
Parent, David to Jane Collier 30 Mar. 1825	Boon
Parent, Peter to Mary A. Frazier 5 May 1839	Fran
Parish, Benj. to Nancy C. Hendley 1 Sept. 1831	Clay
Parish, Levi to Elizabeth Reed 2 Oct. 1839	Pett
Parish, Price to Jane Patterson 1 Jan. 1826	CG-A
Park, Isaiah to Catherine Grant 1 Feb. 1827	Boon
Park, Wm. to Susan Leffler 17 Apr. 1824	Boon
Park, Wilson to Nancy Frazier 6 July 1833	Fran
Parke, Josiah to Barbary Ingram 11 Oct. 1838	Pk-B
Parker, Agrippa to Caty Cox 10 June 1838	Wash
Parker, Azarich to Amy Wilkerson 10 Dec. 1835	Carr
Parker, David to Sarah Lefton 2 Jan. 1837	Fran
Parker, James to Eliza Williams 11 Aug. 1833	Lewi
Parker, James to Elvira Davis 24 Sept. 1837	Coop
Parker, Jesse to Mary A. Parker 16 Jan. 1839	Carr
Parker, Jesseit to Sally Bay 26 Dec. 1830	Fran
Parker, John to Sarah Rayfield 2 Jan. 1832	Wash
Parker, John to Margaret McGuire 23 Dec. 1836	Coop
Parker, Jonathan to Sarah Ewell 17 May 1838	Ray
Parker, Lemun to Rebecca Knox 16 Nov. 1826	Howa

Parker, Nathan to Temperance O. Briant 29 July 1838	Polk
Parker, Nathanial H. to Elizabeth Johns 9 July 1837	Fran
Parker, Oliver to Mary L. Theall 11 May 1825	Boon
Parker, Robt. W. to Margaret Wear 10 Sept. 1828	Coop
Parker, Sidney to Cordelia C. Dosier 27 Oct. 1836	Linc
Parker, Thomas to Catharine Hamet 27 Oct. 1825	Howa
Parker, Thomas to Susanna Riggsby 11 Jan. 1835	Rand
Parker, Thomas B. to Martha A. Nelson 25 Oct. 1835	Mari
Parker, Thomas J. to Melissa A. Almond 10 Nov. 1836	Pk-1
Parker, Wm. to Emily Bell 20 Aug. 1835	Coop
Parkey, Francis to Sarah Cochran 25 Sept. 1833	Linc
Parkins, Joseph to Mary Millin 19 Jan. 1826	Wash
Parkinson, John to Susanna Higgenbotham 4 Mar. 1830	Wash
Parks, Alen to Emily Bratten 4 July 1827	Boon
Parks, Alfred L. to Delilah E. Hogard 10 June 1834	Perr
Parks, Anderson to Susannah Stites 9 May 1839	Fran
Parks, Daniel to Jenny Jones 28 Apr. 1831	CG-A
Parks, Gabrel L. to Joanna Hale 5 Feb. 1837	Morg
Parks, James to Franky Hariford 5 Sept. 1824	Char
Parks, James to Alizar Benning 3 June 1836	Pk-1
Parks, Jehiel to Margaret Parks 9 Oct. 1827	Howa
Parks, Madison to Polly Hess 20 Feb. 1839	Ray
Parks, Peterson to Elender Hurt 22 Jan. 1834	Howa
Parks, Samuel to Nancy Moore 25 Dec. 1824	Char
Parks, Samuel to Nancy Jones 16 Nov. 1826	Coop
Parks, Samuel to Christiana Clark 7 Feb. 1833	Coop
Parks, Thomas to Sally Hart 2 July 1830	Coop
Parks, Wm. to Ann Page 26 Dec. 1823	Char
Parks, Wm. to Lewra Moore 29 Nov. 1827	Pk-1
Parks, Wm. to Polly Stites 4 Aug. 1830	Fran
Parmer, Charles to Betsy Colvin 30 Aug. 1807	StCh
Parmer, Charles to Anna Estes 28 July 1833	Clay
Parmer, Claiborn to Elizabeth Holoway 14 Aug. 1828	Ray
Parmer, Clifton to Elvina Johnson 26 Oct. 1834	Carr
Parmer, Geo. to Elizabeth Cooley 4 Apr. 1837	Carr
Parmon, Gilbert to Olive Gumpstock 31 Dec. 1835	Carr
Parrick, James to Elizabeth Moad 11 Oct. 1838	Polk
Parrick, Thomas to Lucy Marlow 13 July 1828	StFr
Parris, Anthony to Mary Smith 10 Jan. 1826	Perr
Parrish, Nathanial H. to Martha J. Willson 25 Aug. 1836	Mari
Parrish, Thomas to Elvira Owens 4 Dec. 1839	Mari
Parriss, James M. to Polly A. Lear 19 Oct. 1836	Mari
Parsons, Hugh to Nancy Smith 25 May 1828	Jack
Parsons, Jacob to Jane E. Smith 29 June 1837	Linc
Parsons, James to Elizabeth Shobe 12 Aug. 1821	StCh
Parsons, James to Elizabeth Foster 27 Apr. 1826	Lafa
Parsons, Lewis to Louisa Moore 1 Aug. 1833	Pk-1
Parsons, Richard to Frances Fuqua 16 July 1837	Rall
Parsons, Samuel W. to Margaret Hinton 7 Aug. 1828	Pk-1
Parstch, Godfrey to Anna M. Huffender 18 Nov. 1838	StCh
Partin, Wm. to Elizabeth Bozarth 11 Mar. 1819	Howa
Partney, Amiable to Sarah McCullough 8 Nov. 1838	Jeff
Parvy, Wm. to Polly Everson 3 Jan. 1820	Coop
Patchin, Paul to Mary Lesage 16 Mar. 1837	StCh
Pate, Minor to Sally Mays 12 Dec. 1833	Call
Pate, Thomas to Rebekah Calvert 4 Apr. 1824	Coop
Pate, Thomas to Hetty Lewis 28 Sept. 1834	Boon
Paterson, Mathew to Loretty Boyd 24 May 1838	Ripl
Patlett, Wm. to Elenor Barnett 12 Dec. 1833	Lafa
Patrick, Arthur to Martha Cole 4 Dec. 1827	Coop
Patrick, Elias to Susan Collins 19 Jan. 1837	Coop
Patrick, James to Mary J. Ponty 29 May 1828	Coop
Patrick, James to Sally McDonald 23 May 1830	Howa
Patrick, Larkin C. to Elizabeth A. Cross 1 Feb. 1838	Howa
Patrick, Robt. to Ann Thomas 5 Aug. 1822	Sali

```
Patrick, Samuel to Lucy Thomas / Oct. 1827                        Lafa
Patrick, Thomas to Catherine Peters 31 May 1836                   Coop
Patten, Charles to Elizabeth Brown 25 Dec. 1839                   Jack
Patten, Francis to Elizabeth Jackson 16 July 1837                 Boon
Patterson, Albert G. to Mary Paine 7 Mar. 1839                    Gree
Patterson, Andrew to Elizabeth Hitchock 25 Dec. 1829              Jack
Patterson, Cyrus to Elizabeth Mooney 8 Aug. 1828                  Gasc
Patterson, David to Mary Danngilder 27 May 1838                   CG-B
Patterson, James to Mary Hutchinson 13 Sept. 1827                 CG-A
Patterson, James to Sarah A. Thompson 9 Aug. 1838                 StFr
Patterson, James to Jurusha Kinnison 31 Jan. 1839                 Perr
Patterson, James to Polly Compton 31 Oct. 1839                    John
Patterson, Jesse to Elizabeth McQuester 26 Nov. 1838             Morg
Patterson, Rice to Cordella G. Martin 15 Apr. 1838               Howa
Patterson, Rufus to Violett Patterson 8 May 1834                  Wash
Patterson, S.G. to Elizabeth Paxton 10 Dec. 1834                  Linc
Patterson, Wm. to Susan Gallaway 21 Feb. 1828                     Linc
Patterson, Wm. to Elizabeth Reed 20 Dec. 1838                     Gree
Pattie, T.E. to Sarah McNight 27 Nov. 1838                        Gasc
Patton, Aron F. to Mary P. Gunnell 21 June 1838                   Ray
Patton, Daniel to Nancy Ewing Tilford 23 Dec. 1839                Ray
Patton, Geo. to Nancy Yarnall 13 Apr. 1837                        StCh
Patton, Geo. R. to Lucy A. Melton 13 Apr. 1839                    Rand
Patton, Hans to Sally Hatton 23 Mar. 1826                         Call
Patton, Hugh to Nancy Crabtree 19 May 1833                        Jack
Patton, Hugh to Isibel Ridgeway 9 Jan. 1834                       Jack
Patton, James to Elizabeth Jamison 14 Dec. 1825                   Pk-1
Patton, James to Mary E. Stephenson 4 Feb. 1834                   StCh
Patton, John to Margaret Maupin 8 Oct. 1835                       Fran
Patton, Mathew C. to Melcena Phillips 6 Feb. 1839                 Howa
Patton, Nathanial to Eliza A. Holeman 27 Feb. 1831               Boon
Patton, Nathaniel H. to Rebecca Roush 26 Sept. 1837              Rand
Patton, Robt. to Cinthy Baker 23 Aug. 1832                        Rand
Patton, Thomas to Elenor Lupton 10 Sept. 1835                     Wash
Patty, John to Polly McNight 31 July 1832                         Gasc
Patty, Roland H. to Nancy McNight 1 Nov. 1838                     Gasc
Paul, James A. to Matilda Campbell 12 July 1827                   Howa
Paul, John to Mary Devenport 9 Feb. 1837                          John
Paul, John to Margaret Boyer 27 Feb. 1838                         Wash
Paul, Zachariah N. to Katherine Phillips 18 Mar. 1835            Ray
Paulgel, Jacob to Sarah Smith 27 Aug. 1835                        Call
Paxton, Pascal to Milly Reavis 6 May 1832                         Sali
Pay, Uri to Huldah Potts 4 Nov. 1833                              Jeff
Payne, Ballenger to Mary Hobs 26 Jan. 1826                        Boon
Payne, Daniel to Elviry Smiley 6 July 1838                        Gree
Payne, James to Louisa Elston 16 Nov. 1823                        Boon
Payne, James to Margaret Young 29 Oct. 1829                       Boon
Payne, James R. to Lucy P. Chandler 6 Dec. 1837                   Coop
Payne, Nehemiah to Nancy Westlake 18 Sept. 1828                   Boon
Payne, Nehemiah to Elizabeth Anderson 21 Jan. 1832               Boon
Payne, Oliver to Elizabeth Payne -- July 1839                     Pk-B
Payne, Wm. to Mary A. Robinson 4 May 1837                         Howa
Paynter, Reece to Martha E. Freeman 13 Nov. 1839                  Carr
Payton, Samuel to Sarah Cabel 20 Jan. 1834                        Morg
Peacher, James to Jane Wilson 7 May 1837                          Howa
Peake, Wm. H. to Nancy Glascock 22 Aug. 1838                      Rall
Pearce, John to Polly Burdyne 26 Nov. 1834                        StCh
Pearce, John to Palen J. McCarman 24 Jan. 1839                    Mari
Pearce, Samuel to Sarah Baker 15 Jan. 1828                        Gasc
Pearce, Thomas to Nancy Hirsh 25 Sept. 1836                       Boon
Pearce, Wm. to Eve Baldridge 25 July 1833                         StCh
Pearciful, Thomas W. to Margaret I. Dunn 9 Jan. 1838             CG-A
Pearson, Benj. to Livina Jack 16 Jan. 1834                        Lafa
Pearson, Charles to Polly Colfer 6 Nov. 1836                      Cole
Pearson, E. to Eliza Sappington 22 Oct. 1821                      Howa
```

```
Pearson, Edward L. to Eliza J. Brady 22 July 1835                        StCh
Pearson, James to Axah Pearson 15 Jan. 1837                              Clin
Pearson, John to Emdiah Whitten 30 Oct. 1834                            Howa
Pearson, John to Mary Pearson 21 Dec. 1837                             Audr
Pearson, Pinkston to Eliza A. Lewis 22 July 1839                       Plat
Pearson, Richmond to Elizabeth Allen Brown 15 Mar. 1832               Call
Pearson, Thomas H. to Lucy Cartner 4 Aug. 1831                        Coop
Pearson, Valentino J. to Julia Clark 14 June 1827                     Linc
Pease, Augustus to Sarah A. VanDoren 12 June 1839                      Md-B
Peaton, John to Mrs. Lucy Mark 11 Oct. 1824                          Boon
Pebler, Michael to Fanny Jacks 27 July 1830                          Howa
Pebley, John to Dosha Millham 8 Apr. 1829                            Jack
Peebler, Samuel to Polly Ford 15 Sept. 1822                          Howa
Peebly, Elijah to Hannah Brown 8 Apr. 1838                           Clay
Peenix, Wm. to Nancy Thompson 19 Feb. 1829                           Pk-1
Peerly, Ashford to Elizabeth Hoover 19 Dec. 1838                     Henr
Peers, Edward J. to Mrs. Lytha Reynolds 27 Oct. 1839                 Linc
Peery, Crockett to Mary George 9 Apr. 1839                           Ripl
Peery, Edward to Mary Peery 13 Jan. 1832                             Wash
Peery, John to Mrs. Mary Cartman 17 Feb. 1839                        Monr
Peery, Jos. A. to Harriet Tally 19 Sept. 1837                        Audr
Pegg, John A. to Elizabeth Lampton 23 Dec. 1830                      Boon
Pegg, Raymond to Frances Simms 24 July 1823                          Boon
Pehrle, Joseph to Francisca Ernst 17 Apr. 1832                       Perr
Peler, John to Elenor Johnson 25 Jan. 1821                           Howa
Pell, Lewis to Francoise Prevalle 18 Jan. 1830                       StCh
Pelo, Peter to Lucretia Phelps 2 June 1828                           Clay
Pelo, Peter to Sally Kirkendol 10 Oct. 1833                          Clay
Pemberton, Geo. to Malissa Pemberton 15 Aug. 1839                    Pett
Pemberton, John U. to Kathern Hunter 6 Oct. 1836                     Call
Pemberton, Merrimon to Frances Hay 21 Dec. 1830                      Howa
Pemberton, Tilford to Sally Lee 18 Dec. 1838                         Howa
Pen, Wm. to Matilda Fowler 4 Apr. 1839                               Shel
Penake, John to Margaret Winson 27 Feb. 1828                         CG-A
Penal, Richard to Artimisa A. Williams 27 June 1833                  Wash
Pence, Adam to Elizabeth Snell 26 Mar. 1837                          Clay
Pence, Henry to Lourena Snell 12 Jan. 1827                           Clay
Pence, Jackson to Olive Rule 11 Jan. 1835                            Clay
Pence, Richard H. to Elvina Rowlings 2 Sept. 1825                    Clay
Pendleton, Robt. to Martha Pratt 21 Feb. 1839                        Warr
Pendleton, Samuel to Margaret Tracy 22 June 1837                     Howa
Penick, Charles I. to Martha A. Elliott 30 July 1839                 Char
Penick, Jacob to Sarah Clubb 24 Jan. 1836                            CG-B
Penland, Wm. to Nancy Stephens 4 Apr. 1824                           Coop
Penn, Gabriel to Lucinda Glascock 3 Jan. 1839                        Rall
Penn, Geo. to Sarah B. Chambers 5 Nov. 1831                          Sali
Penn, Lewis to Clarissa Parriot 25 May 1837                          Rand
Penn, Wm. to Emerine Carter 12 Oct. 1831                             Rall
Pennell, Jeremiah to Ann Crow 26 July 1836                           Cr-1
Pennington, Asa B. to Polly Wannister -- Oct. 1837                   Sali
Pennington, Henry to Emily Cowen 17 Apr. 1838                        Boon
Pennington, Royal to Christena Rimell 3 Jan. 1837                    Clay
Pennix, Wm. to Patsey Kelly 4 Aug. 1831                              Monr
Penny, Isaac to Mary Walker 4 June 1826                              CG-A
Penny, Wm. to Rachel Renfroe 17 Mar. 1830                            CG-A
Penny, Wm. to Mariah D'Lashmutt 28 Jan. 1834                         CG-A
Pentzer, Valentine to Ann Owen 10 Mar. 1838                          Mari
Penrod, Daniel to Queen Short 16 Aug. 1836                           Fran
Penrod, James to Mary A. Mallow 23 Jan. 1834                         Wash
Pentorf, Henry to Rose Murray 6 Sept. 1827                           CG-A
Peoples, Robt. to Margaret Howard 20 Dec. 1822                       Howa
Pepper, Elijah to Elizabeth Calvert 12 Apr. 1832                     Mari
Pepper, John to Lucinda Wilson 21 Nov. 1836                          Fran
Pepper, Wm. to Sarah Lair 27 Aug. 1835                               Mari
Percell, Abraham to Marthy A. Smith 7 Feb. 1838                      Clay
```

Percival, Thomas to Eliza J. Burnam 6 Oct. 1836   Howa
Pergro, Charles to Louise Deaudir 30 May 1833   StCh
Peringer, John to Polly Dunken 11 July 1819   CG-1
Perkins, Ambros to Jane Goodwin 14 Feb. 1830   Linc
Perkins, Avington to Winna A. Stallard 2 Jan. 1834   Linc
Perkins, Charles E. to Louiza Bailey 1 Jan. 1835   Linc
Perkins, Christopher to Elizabeth Fulkerson 6 Mar. 1831   Boon
Perkins, Constantine to Thursa Trusdel 13 Oct. 1836   StFr
Perkins, Edward T. to Cinthy Brunt 1 Sept. 1829   Howa
Perkins, Elihu H. to Avis Riggs 15 Nov. 1838   Linc
Perkins, Enoch to Huldah A. Pringle 15 Oct. 1835   Warr
Perkins, Ephrain to Olive Smith 6 Aug. 1837   Fran
Perkins, Ephriam to Luisa Strien 2 June 1833   Gasc
Perkins, Haslin to Parthena Ball 16 June 1839   Polk
Perkins, Isaac to Nancy Bell 8 Dec. 1836   Morg
Perkins, Isaac to Nancy Davis 4 Apr. 1839   Ripl
Perkins, John to Emeline Fuget 17 July 1827   Boon
Perkins, John to Juliett Leake 4 Jan. 1829   Rall
Perkins, John to Eliza Burgess 31 Aug. 1837   Gasc
Perkins, John F. to Sarah Tarpley 16 July 1837   StFr
Perkins, Joseph to Mrs. Emily Lacey 26 Jan. 1834   StFr
Perkins, Martin to Peggy Wiley 28 May 1829   CG-A
Perkins, Michael to Jane Quisenberry 17 Mar. 1836   Howa
Perkins, Thomas to Sarah Perkins 6 Dec. 1838   Howa
Perkins, Walton to Louisanna Green 25 May 1834   Linc
Perrier, Joseph to Mrs. Neville Obuchon 10 Feb. 1834   StCh
Perrigeau, Samuel to Ann Dunham 30 Aug. 1827   CG-A
Perrin, Aythman L. to Julian S. Morton 15 Nov. 1838   Mari
Perrin, Caleb H. to Mary Meredith 24 Dec. 1829   Perr
Perringer, Adam to Margaret Johnson 20 Dec. 1821   Howa
Perry, Allen G. to Elizabeth Parsons 19 Aug. 1836   Cass
Perry, Ephriam to Lucinda Ramsey 25 July 1839   Plat
Perry, James to Elizabeth Lamb 25 July 1839   Mill
Perry, John to Polly Harris 20 May 1819   Howa
Perry, John to Mary Tillman 20 Sept. 1827   Sali
Perry, Montgomery to Mrs. Celia Robans 28 Dec. 1826   StCh
Perry, Moses to Eliza Ritchie 8 Aug. 1827   Clay
Perry, Wm. to Ellender Maccary 26 July 1827   Howa
Perry, Wm. to Margaret Hutchinson 22 Nov. 1838   Howa
Perryman, David E. to Mariah Blackwell 18 Jan. 1838   Wash
Perryman, Thomas to Lydia Wallis 21 Dec. 1837   Gree
Persinger, Alexander to Elizabeth Spence 24 Feb. 1831   Boon
Persinger, Joseph to Eliza Branin 3 Jan. 1832   Boon
Persinger, Lewis to Mary Jennings 1 Oct. 1829   Howa
Pervant, Peter to Creasy Stevans 20 June 1836   Lafa
Perves, Henry to Sally A. Vanland 24 Aug. 1837   Shel
Perwitt, Samuel to Nancy Strong 15 Feb. 1838   Cass
Peter, John to Mary Boring 1 Sept. 1836   Wash
Peterman, Geo. to Morning Smith 2 Dec. 1838   Md-B
Peters, David to Lucy Kelly 25 July 1825   Coop
Peters, Ira to Elizabeth A. Stevenson 11 Apr. 1830   Clay
Peters, Silas to Ann Powell 21 Feb. 1839   Lafa
Peters, Wm. to Sarah A. Long 19 Mar. 1835   Clay
Peterson, John to Martha Wall 16 July 1835   CG-B
Peterson, John to Mary Cheek 25 Nov. 1838   Polk
Peterson, John to Rachel Youngblood 2 Aug. 1839   CG-B
Peterson, Zeby to Rebecca Hopper 11 Aug. 1831   Lafa
Petitt, Wm. to Lucinda Cramer 8 Sept. 1839   Coop
Petree, Hiram to Mary Carr 31 Mar. 1831   Pk-1
Pettibone, Levi to Martha Rouse 14 June 1831   Pk-1
Pettigrew, Mathew to Cynthia Vivion 30 Nov. 1818   Howa
Pettis, Larkin to Martha Williams 26 Dec. 1837   John
Pettit, Geo. to Elizabeth Shaw 10 July 1832   StFr
Pettit, James to Sally Donahue 9 Feb. 1806   StGe
Pettit, John L. to Sarah Williams 5 Mar. 1826   Md-A

```
Pettit, Wm. to Melinda Morrice 24 May 1820                        StCh
Pettitt, Wm. to Ann Cook 22 May 1828                             CG-A
Pettus, Wm. G. to Caroline Morrison 31 Dec. 1826                 StCh
Petty, Alfred to Synthia Howard 15 May 1831                      Call
Petty, Joel H. to Penelope Haddock 7 Dec. 1837                   Barr
Petty, John to Patsey Bunch 16 Apr. 1833                         Call
Petty, Wm. to Peggy Sennet 20 Nov. 1831                          Cr-1
Petty, Zachariah to Mary J. Bryant 7 Aug. 1833                   Call
Petyon, James H. to Sarah Mateer 14 Sept. 1837                   Call
Peure, John to Elizabeth Majers 11 Sept. 1839                    StCh
Pewterbaugh, David to Elizabeth Anderson 13 Apr. 1837            Pk-A
Peyton, Samuel to Elizabeth Hanes 11 Aug. 1836                   Rall
Peyton, Thomas to Charlotte Smyth 28 Mar. 1817                   CG-1
Phar, James to Lucy P. Fortune 21 Apr. 1829                      Pk-1
Phares, James P. to Catharine Johnson 6 June 1833               Howa
Phares, Wm. to Eliza Murphy 24 Oct. 1833                        Howa
Pharis, Martin to Deberough Bradley 23 Mar. 1826               Howa
Phelen, Wm. to Nancy C. Loving 25 Sept. 1839                    Cole
Phelps, Ezekiel to Matilda Stice 12 July 1827                   Rall
Phelps, James to Polly Abbot 26 Apr. 1832                       Monr
Phelps, James to Sarah Longboth 29 Sept. 1835                   Monr
Philebert, Joseph to Peninah Yoacham 26 Feb. 1833              Gree
Philipin, Absolam to Emelia Fugit 7 Aug. 1826                   Cole
Philips, Hiram R. to Emily T. Wilkerson 10 Nov. 1836           Call
Philips, Israel to Rebecca Kam 24 Aug. 1838                     Monr
Philips, James to Elizabeth Applegate 17 Aug. 1813             StGe
Philips, James A. to Emily Hollingsworth 12 Dec. 1835         Rall
Philips, John to Elizabeth Bailey 20 July 1835                  Fran
Philips, Robt. W. to Elizabeth E. Gardner 10 Jan. 1839        Char
Philips, Samuel to Nancy Robertson 13 Jan. 1838                Fran
Phillip, ---- to Mary Cutter 3 June 1838                        Boon
Phillip, Henry to Nancy Gentry 10 Jan. 1827                     Boon
Phillips, Bennett to Frances Crouch 7 Aug. 1834               Boon
Phillips, Bethel to Darly Estes 2 Jan. 1828                     Call
Phillips, Charles W. to Azuriah Robbins 17 Sept. 1830         StCh
Phillips, Geo. to Mary Mason 8 Apr. 1829                        Boon
Phillips, James to Mary Phillips 10 Mar. 1833                   Carr
Phillips, Jeremiah to Jemima Lay 4 July 1833                   Howa
Phillips, Jeremiah A. to Martha Hackley 7 Mar. 1825           Howa
Phillips, John to Lucy A. Tittsworth 13 June 1839             Coop
Phillips, Martin G. to Susan Huff 24 Dec. 1835                Morg
Phillips, Moses to Anay Agey 26 Feb. 1829                      Call
Phillips, Richard to Sarah Morris 10 Jan. 1833                Howa
Phillips, Ridmon to Elizabeth Bishop 6 May 1834               Perr
Phillips, Wm. to Sarah Dodge 29 Sept. 1833                     Cr-1
Philph, Campbell to Elizabeth Lynch 16 Feb. 1834             Jack
Philpot, Edward to Rebecca Ward 21 Nov. 1832                  Howa
Phine, Wm. to Uln Roques 8 Mar. 1835                           Jeff
Phye, Nicholas to Margaret Roy 7 Oct. 1827                     Call
Picket, Alexander A. to Mary Clark 5 Dec. 1839               Clay
Pickett, James M. to Nancy Goldsberry 22 Feb. 1838          Pk-B
Piedcock, Jry to Melinda Shoemate 19 Apr. 1835               Cr-1
Pieler, David to Sarah Wilcoxson 4 Oct. 1821                  Howa
Pierce, Andy to Priscilla Brown 10 Oct. 1833                  Ray
Pierce, Geo. to Nancy Fields 1 June 1838                      Mari
Pierce, Ira to Mary A. Shohoney 7 Jan. 1836                   Rall
Pierce, James to Susan Davison 13 -- 1835                     Linc
Pierce, John to Mary Casey 21 Apr. 1835                       Wash
Pierce, John to Sarah Nash 26 Jan. 1839                       Clin
Pierce, Melvin to Mary Wallis 8 Jan. 1835                     Jack
Pierce, Nathaniel T. to Harriet Roberts 30 Oct. 1834        Pk-1
Pierce, Thomas to Kesziah Napper 10 Oct. 1839                Fran
Pierceall, James to Maria Murphy 25 June 1839                Monr
Pierceall, Josyah to Rose A. Leake 5 Apr. 1837               Rall
Piercy, Geo. to Levina Whitlow 27 Dec. 1836                   Monr
```

177

Pierson, Lemuel to Elizabeth Masters 28 Aug. 1836   Jack
Pigg, Laban to Catherine Parks 23 Nov. 1835   Coop
Piggott, James A. to Lucinda McDowell rec. 25 Feb. 1836   StCh
Piles, Byrd to Gabriella Pemberton 18 Dec. 1827   Howa
Piles, John to Polly Douglass 25 Dec. 1838   Ripl
Piles, Wm. H. to Catherine M. Keeper 30 Apr. 1837   Jeff
Pilkington, Levi to Margaret Jones 25 Aug. 1839   Plat
Pinckley, John H. to Agness Byrne 29 Jan. 1838   CG-A
Pinkerton, Adam to Ann Saddler 3 July 1831   CG-A
Pinkerton, David to Margaret Powers 20 May 1832   Perr
Pinkerton, Henry to Elizabeth Pinkerton 15 Jan. 1835   Perr
Pinkerton, John to Dizy Sadler 9 Mar. 1830   Perr
Pinkerton, Wesley D. to Mariah J. Boid 24 June 1832   Cole
Pinkston, Giliston to Malindy Burdett 23 Mar. 1837   Mari
Pinkston, Joshua to Polly McKinney 2 Nov. 1835   Fran
Pinkston, Wm. to Eliza Sparks 5 May 1836   Mari
Pinnell, Augustus to Emelia E. Shepard 1 Nov. 1838   Cr-1
Pinnell, Wesley to Eliza M. Marquiss 23 Jan. 1831   Wash
Pinter, Joseph to Susannah Garner 13 Sept. 1832   Wash
Pinter, Wm. to Elizabeth Mason 18 Sept. 1834   Clay
Piper, John to Adeline Huston 16 Apr. 1829   Coop
Piper, John C. to Susan McLaughlin 26 Apr. 1835   Cole
Piper, Louis A. to Sarah McKinney 14 Feb. 1837   Cole
Piper, Thomas to Sally H. Stuart 10 Jan. 1834   Gasc
Piper, Wm. G. to Sarah R. Butler 4 July 1838   Fran
Pipes, David to Mildred Williams 20 Dec. 1832   Boon
Pipes, Harrison to Sary Agin 23 Oct. 1831   Boon
Pipes, James to Nancy Johnson 21 Feb. 1822   Howa
Pipes, Washington to Polly Pipes 2 July 1830   Boon
Pipkin, Isaac to Ann Evans 13 July 1838   CG-A
Pireson, Charles to Sarah Calffee 25 Apr. 1837   Morg
Pishford, Wm. A. to Abigail Weldon 3 Apr. 1823   Perr
Pit, John to Patsey True 23 Nov. 1834   Pk-1
Pitcher, Berry to Elizabeth Harrington 8 Dec. 1827   Clay
Pitcher, James M. to Angeline L. Noland 20 Jan. 1834   Jack
Pitcher, Thomas to Nancy Parish 3 Jan. 1828   Jack
Pitman, Barry to Jane Morris 2 Dec. 1828   StCh
Pitman, Cullan to Mahaly Hall 12 Feb. 1839   Ripl
Pitney, Simeon to Eliza J. Turner 26 Dec. 1839   Howa
Pitt, Joseph to Rachel Hinton 24 Mar. 1831   Linc
Pitts, Govey to Phebe A. Woolsey 28 June 1837   Carr
Pitzer, Robt. to Alias Pitman 31 July 1833   Warr
Plank, Henry to Mariah Kearns 14 Apr. 1839   Clar
Plant, Massenello W. to Elizabeth J. Staples 24 Dec. 1836   Lewi
Pledge, John A. to Miriam Warren 14 Feb. 1831   Call
Pledge, Thomas to Florence C. Luper 22 Feb. 1838   Call
Plemmons, James G. to Renea Gilbreath 10 Mar. 1836   Coop
Plemmons, Thomas to Polly Calvert 28 Sept. 1829   Coop
Plummer, Joseph to Katherine Young 25 Mar. 1830   Linc
Plummer, Philamon to Polly Gordon 24 Dec. 1826   StCh
Plummer, Wm. to Elizabeth A. Mackney 7 Nov. 1839   Cole
Poage, Andrew M. to Nancy Grooms 29 July 1822   Clay
Poage, Greenbury to Hannah Victor 18 Mar. 1838   Clin
Poage, Munn to Anne Keeton 8 June 1825   Boon
Poe, Madison to Eliza Backus 14 Jan. 1830   Gasc
Poe, Simon to Tabitha Randol 2 Jan. 1834   CG-A
Poe, Stephen to Rebecca Randol 11 Dec. 1834   CG-B
Poe, Terry to Elizabeth McLain 19 June 1837   Perr
Poe, Wm. to Nancy Flannery 10 May 1832   Jack
Poe, Wm. to Nancy Mulky 2 Feb. 1834   Jack
Pogue, Grattin E. to Ann S. Price 30 Apr. 1837   Monr
Pogue, Thomas to Mary M. Maxey 12 Dec. 1833   Monr
Poindexter, Edmund to Margaret Morris 29 Dec. 1835   Monr
Pointer, Geo. to Ruth Butler 14 May 1826   Gasc
Pointer, Isam to Elizabeth McMannus 28 Sept. 1837   Gasc

```
Pointer, James to Sarah Miller 12 Feb. 1834                        Gasc
Pointer, James to Nancy Branson 10 Jan. 1836                       Gasc
Pointer, John to Evelina Capehart 8 Apr. 1827                      Gasc
Pointer, Wm. to Vecinda Daniel 8 Jan. 1835                         Gasc
Pointer, Wm. to Elizabeth Morrison 31 May 1835                     Pk-1
Pointer, Wm. to Mary Jones 21 Apr. 1836                            Fran
Pointer, Wm. to Elizabeth Tony 14 Dec. 1839                        Fran
Polite, Paul to Lydia Turley 17 Jan. 1826                          Wash
Polk, John to Christina Yount 20 Jan. 1820                         CG-1
Polk, Thomas to Lucinda Younger 23 Nov. 1837                       Gree
Polk, Wm. to Mary A. Sharp 25 Aug. 1831                            Md-A
Pollard, Bartemous to Angelina ---- 21 Dec. 1837                   Linc
Pollard, Brocton to Harriett Jamison 18 Dec. 1835                  Jeff
Pollard, Henry to Kessiah Clark 13 Aug. 1835                       Linc
Pollard, Perry to Bettie Henderson 17 Oct. 1834                    Call
Polleck, John to Mary Lindsay 21 July 1828                         Coop
Pomeroy, E.M. to Maria Aull 18 June 1835                           Lafa
Ponder, Bla_ins to Francisca Myer 15 Feb. 1836                     Perr
Ponton, Joel to Sally Reavis 4 Jan. 1827                           Coop
Pool, James to Phebe Holcombe 8 Aug. 1824                          StGe
Pool, James J. to Jane Thompson 26 Mar. 1835                       Cole
Pool, Thomas to Diana Pool 17 Feb. 1829                            Howa
Poor, James to Ellen Britt 3 Apr. 1838                             Linc
Poor, James to Amanda Britt 3 Dec. 1839                            Linc
Poor, John to Jacquthe Smith 3 Mar. 1835                           Mari
Poor, Thomas to Ann E. Lockett 17 Nov. 1836                        Mari
Poorman, John to Nancy Bancroft 29 May 1836                        Clay
Porrel, Joseph to Zelia Brinck 8 Mar. 1838                         Linc
Portais, Francois to Marie L. Mercil 2 Feb. 1830                   Wash
Portais, Joseph to Marie L. Boyer 24 Oct. 1826                     Wash
Portais, Pierre to Therese Vilmere 18 Nov. 1834                    Wash
Portay, Pierre to Marie Vilmere 18 Nov. 1834                       Wash
Porter, Allen to Louisa Harvey 17 Nov. 1821                        Sali
Porter, Andrew to Frances Walts 18 Sept. 1834                      Boon
Porter, Andrew H. to Lucy L. Coppedge 5 July 1836                  Cr-1
Porter, Edwin K. to Susan O. Collier 21 June 1835                  Md-A
Porter, Geo. W. to Eleanor Taylor 4 Oct. 1838                      Warr
Porter, Green to Lucinda Morris 22 Dec. 1836                       Coop
Porter, Henry to Eliza Jacoby 21 Nov. 1832                         Cole
Porter, Hezekiah to Harriett Williams 1 Jan. 1835                  Jack
Porter, James to Sarah Walker 5 Mar. 1829                          Howa
Porter, James to Lydia L.L. Litton 17 Mar. 1829                    Linc
Porter, James to Frances Keer 14 Feb. 1839                         Jeff
Porter, John to Eliza J. Brooks 9 Dec. 1838                        Jeff
Porter, John to Mary Crabtree 14 July 1839                         Bent
Porter, Joseph to Mary Gragg 20 Dec. 1822                          Ray
Porter, Nathaniel to Lucinda Baily 18 May 1830                     Rall
Porter, Samuel T. to Ann Winn 18 Oct. 1836                         Rand
Porter, Thomas D. to Tabitha B. McFerron 29 Sept. 1836            Cass
Porter, Warren to Amy Sumner 6 Dec. 1833                           Jack
Porter, Wm. J. to Rachel Blevins 18 May 1838                       Clin
Posey, Allison to Caroline Kimbrough 16 Feb. 1837                  Rand
Posey, Ambrose H. to Elizabeth A. Southworth 29 June 1834          Fran
Posey, Andrew to Patsy Harrison 22 Aug. 1839                       Polk
Posey, Dulaney to Mary A. Wright 22 Jan. 1837                      Howa
Posey, Leaden to Sary Campbell 20 Mar. 1838                        Gasc
Posse, James P. to Julean Singleton 27 July 1837                   Clay
Post, Pleasant to Sarah Allred 11 Feb. 1836                        Cr-1
Postin, Martin to Polly Litteral 5 Aug. 1839                       Maco
Poston, Richard to Martha Hill 22 Jan. 1835                        StFr
Poteet, James to Lovey Crockett 5 Mar. 1826                        Clay
Poteet, Samuel to Synthyann Willis 12 July 1832                    Clay
Poteet, Samuel to Elizabeth Burkhart 10 Jan. 1833                  Cr-1
Poteet, Thomas to Lidia McCorkle 5 July 1827                       Clay
Potter, David to Mary Creason 12 Apr. 1835                         Char
```

```
Potter, David to Mary Ettleman 13 May 1838                          Ray
Potter, Elijah to Rhoda Ham 24 Jan. 1837                           Call
Potter, Greenbury to Huldah Johnson 5 Jan. 1830                    Wash
Potter, James to Polly Upshaw 7 Sept. 1837                         Polk
Potter, John to Clency Batty 26 Mar. 1829                          Char
Potter, John to Ann Baxter 3 Apr. 1834                             Clay
Potter, Joseph to Elizabeth Guyer 1 Sept. 1825                     Coop
Potter, Joseph to Ann Anderson 6 Oct. 1832                         Lafa
Potter, Nathaniel to Matilda Gaithis 3 June 1827                   Howa
Potter, Richard to Martha Staton 21 Sept. 1834                     Ray
Potter, Samuel to Rhoda L. Ellis 9 Dec. 1839                       Cass
Potter, Wm. to Nancy Dillard 18 Nov. 1819                          Coop
Potter, Wilson to Sally Stone 8 Jan. 1835                          Clin
Potts, Alfred to Cherry Pipes 11 Oct. 1838                         Boon
Potts, Frederick to Martha Pendleton 18 Oct. 1838                  Boon
Potts, Jeremiah to Mary Goodin 3 Jan. 1830                         Cr-P
Potts, Joel to Sarah A. Blizzard 25 July 1834                      StCh
Potts, John to Margaret Spence 13 Dec. 1837                        Boon
Potts, John W. to Mary A. Kring 15 Oct. 1839                       Howa
Potts, Samuel C. to Teresa Gray 27 July 1826                       Howa
Pougiole, Andrew to Mary L. Roi 25 Oct. 1830                       StCh
Pougole, Francis to Louise Petit 15 June 1830                      StCh
Poujole, Andrew to Victoire Champagne 27 Feb. 1838                 StCh
Pound, Newman to Lucinda Graham 15 Aug. 1833                       Jeff
Pound, Richard to Patsy Baidston 8 Sept. 1833                      Cr-1
Pound, Thomas S. to Mrs. Lucretia Turner 26 Apr. 1836             Jeff
Pounds, Joseph to Mary Wideman 7 Jan. 1836                         Jeff
Pounds, Wm. to Margery White 26 Sept. 1839                         Fran
Powe, Wm. R. to Ann E. Karns 24 Nov. 1838                          Clin
Powel, Cyrus to Seery McCinsey 31 Oct. 1833                        Gree
Powell, Alexander to Eliza Headen 19 Jan. 1832                     Wash
Powell, Alvin to Julia A. Underwood 13 July 1838                   Rall
Powell, Brown to Jane Gipson 13 Nov. 1834                          Cole
Powell, Charles to Ann Crockett 30 Sept. 1839                      Carr
Powell, Harrison to Sarah Mann 17 July 1834                        Linc
Powell, J.M. to Harriet Griffith 17 Aug. 1834                      Perr
Powell, James to Myra Newel 3 Mar. 1833                            Cole
Powell, John to Nancy Gentry 27 May 1834                           Boon
Powell, Joseph M. to Lucy A. Skinner 5 May 1836                    Warr
Powell, Ludwell to Ann B. Shaw 7 Jan. 1830                         StCh
Powell, Martin to Elizabeth Shinter 5 Feb. 1838                    Cole
Powell, Richard to Barbary McClellan 6 Mar. 1829                   Jack
Power, Alexander to Patsy Ferrier 25 Dec. 1827                     Call
Power, Milton to Martha Orley 13 June 1839                         StCh
Power, Samuel to Cyntha Hill 8 Dec. 1831                           Wash
Powers, Andrew to Louisa Furguson 17 Nov. 1839                     Perr
Powers, David to Mary Mitchell 16 June 1821                        Boon
Powers, James to Nancy Whoopaugh 24 Feb. 1819                      CG-1
Powers, Moses to Jain Boyd 6 Mar. 1838                             Barr
Powers, Richard D. to Judith Shortridge 19 June 1838              Rand
Powers, Wm. to Susanna Edwards 4 May 1823                          Coop
Powers, Wm. E. to Nancy Bryan 14 Dec. 1837                        Monr
Prat, Jonathan to Caroline Martin 31 Aug. 1837                    StCh
Prather, Baruch to Nancy Roberts 23 Aug. 1838                      Clay
Prather, Daniel to Nancy Short 15 Mar. 1827                        Fran
Prather, James to Mary Hawkins 7 July 1839                         Morg
Prather, John to Cinthy Green 24 July 1828                         Howa
Prather, Wm. to Hetty Bay 8 May 1834                               Fran
Pratt, John to Amy Barker 11 Jan. 1821                             Call
Pratt, John to Elizabeth Miller 23 Jan. 1830                       CG-A
Pratt, Thomas to Lucinda Patty 19 Sept. 1839                       Call
Pratt, Virgil to Patsy Wood 24 Aug. 1835                           Mari
Pratt, Wm. to Polly Eaken 18 Apr. 1822                             Call
Pratte, Francis to Cora Cox 6 Nov. 1838                            Md-B
Pratte, Jean B. to Aspasie Duclos 17 June 1834                     Wash
```

Pratte, John B. to Marcellite DeGuire 26 Dec. 1832   Md-A
Pratte, Sabestian B. to Margar-- Guignon 5 May 1835   Md-A
Preasey, Baptiste to Delile Capeler 1 Jan. 1827   Wash
Presley, Anthony to Sally A. Walker 17 Feb. 1831   Linc
Presley, David to Mahalia Ulelly 5 Aug. 1827   Linc
Presley, Jacob to Clarissa Holcomb 24 Aug. 1828   Linc
Presseau, Francois to Mary Godifrois 5 Jan. 1829   StCh
Preston, John N. to Lundry Barnes 9 Apr. 1835   Boon
Preston, Sandford to Cassandra Robinson 20 Sept. 1836   Boon
Preston, Wm. E. to Sarah A. Rundlett 4 Apr. 1837   StCh
Prewett, Noel to Catharine Dykes 18 June 1839   Mari
Prewit, Austin to Mrs. Mathilda Thompson 23 May 1839   Jeff
Prewitt, John to Mahala McAlister 23 Dec. 1834   Gree
Prewitt, John to Permelia Pemberton 13 Oct. 1836   Howa
Prewitt, Joseph to Sarah Prewitt 27 Apr. 1834   Wash
Prewitt, Mosby to Mary Fisher 28 Jan. 1836   Jack
Prewitt, Moss to Nancy Johnson 9 May 1828   Boon
Prewitt, Pleasant to Hannah Kinchlow 9 Nov. 1817   Howa
Prewitt, Wm. to Rebecca Brown 19 Aug. 1824   Ray
Prewitt, Wm. to Michal Dickson 4 Nov. 1835   Ray
Price, Allen to Jane McGuire 17 July 1836   Ray
Price, Calvin I. to Frances A. Lankford 8 Aug. 1838   Clar
Price, Columbus to Lydia Swan 1 Dec. 1836   CG-A
Price, Cyrus to Adeline Dickerson 2 Nov. 1837   Call
Price, Edward to Hannah Brown 22 July 1830   Gasc
Price, Evans to Martha S. News 20 Dec. 1832   Howa
Price, Fontly R. to Gilly Simpson 25 Feb. 1836   John
Price, James to Elizabeth Decker 6 July 1832   Fran
Price, James to Mary E. Elliott 24 Jan. 1837   Clay
Price, John W. to Hannah Baldridge 8 Mar. 1838   StCh
Price, Joseph to Polly Temple 9 Apr. 1835   Char
Price, Joseph to Mary B. Hill 24 June 1835   Gree
Price, Lesley to Nancy Neisbit 27 Dec. 1833   Monr
Price, Michael to Nancy Bransfield 14 Aug. 1806   StCh
Price, Miles to Luannah Baxter 22 May 1834   Pk-1
Price, Napoleon I. to Artimesa A. Scott 1 Feb. 1826   . Howa
Price, Robt. to Matilda Cox 3 Oct. 1838   Monr
Price, Samuel to Sally Couch 16 Sept. 1828   Jeff
Price, Sterling to Martha Head 14 May 1833   Rand
Price, Thomas to Nancy Norris 31 July 1837   Lewi
Price, Thomas to Rosanna Lard 24 Aug. 1837   Pk-B
Price, Wm. to Mary Simpson 21 Apr. 1831   Jack
Price, Wm. B. to Lucy Stepp 18 Nov. 1832   Howa
Price, Wm. W. to Esther Odell 19 May 1836   Ray
Prier, Abel to Saree Vorous 31 May 1836   Clay
Prier, Linsey W. to Jane Renfro 17 Apr. 1826   Wash
Priest, Madison J. to Sarah A. Vandever 29 Sept. 1836   Mari
Priest, Zenas to Anne Severs 19 June 1816   CG-1
Prigman, Daniel to Mary Sears 17 Jan. 1836   Henr
Prigmore, Joseph to Mahalah Dixon 7 May 1827   Lafa
Prigmore, Wm. to Mary Dixon 19 Mar. 1825   Lafa
Prill, David to Francis Dillard 13 Mar. 1839   Gree
Prime, Mastin to Polly Daily 15 May 1831   Jack
Prince, Thomas to Mary A. Bradley 9 Sept. 1837   Howa
Prine, Daniel to Catharine Bryant 11 Dec. 1827   Jack
Prine, Francis to Sarah Prine 25 Nov. 1824   Clay
Prine, Francis to Elizabeth Dailey 15 Feb. 1827   Jack
Prine, John to Lydia Prine 29 Dec. 1824   Clay
Prine, Sylus to Sally Spears 15 Aug. 1838   Polk
Prine, Wm. to Elizabeth Spreer 27 Feb. 1832   Cole
Prior, John to Ann Stringer 30 Apr. 1835   Gasc
Prior, Stephen to Cenith McDaniel 8 May 1836   Cole
Prior, Walton to Dolly Dowel 17 Jan. 1831   Clay
Pritchard, Jesse to Sarah McHugh 25 June 1837   Pk-A
Pritchet, Joshua M. to Emily C. Edwards 11 Sept. 1837   StCh

Pritchett, Bird to Desdamona Bennings 15 Oct. 1835   Mari
Pritchett, John to Sophronia Mitchell 29 Mar. 1838   Pk-B
Pritchett, John to Mariah Martin 11 Apr. 1839   Pk-B
Probst, Daniel to Elizabeth Crites 9 Nov. 1819   CG-1
Probts, Geo. to Hannah Critz 13 Jan. 1829   CG-A
Prock, Henry to Elizabeth Cordil 1 Jan. 1835   Lafa
Proctor, Benj. to ---- ---- 1831   Coop
Proctor, Columbus to Eleanor Wood 17 Jan. 1833   Mari
Proctor, Francis to ---- Perkins 6 May 1827   Cole
Proctor, John to Lidy Westbrook 5 Nov. 1820   Coop
Proctor, Joseph to Sussannah Proctor 4 Aug. 1832   Cole
Proctor, Moses to Susanna Brown 15 Apr. 1838   Polk
Proctor, Reuben to Lennet Lay 28 July 1829   Howa
Proffer, David to Mary J. Hutchings 8 Feb. 1838   CG-A
Proffer, Peter to Elinor M. Hanly 11 Feb. 1836   CG-B
Proffit, David to Polly Bradley 14 Nov. 1827   Char
Proffit, Robt. to Sevrinah Fauks 27 July 1836   Rand
Proffitt, Wm. to Rebecca Linville 26 July 1827   Ray
Propes, John to Kanzado Cheek 15 Mar. 1832   CG-A
Prophet, David W. to Eliza Waldon 24 Apr. 1834   Wash
Prosson, Washington to Margaret Gilmore 26 June 1838   StCh
Proupher, Moses to Sally Courtner 1 Sept. 1836   CG-A
Prowell, Robt. to Charlotte Bishop 5 Jan. 1838   Boon
Prowfer, Geo. to Elizabeth Marnay 11 Aug. 1829   CG-A
Prowfer, Jacob to Dinney Crump 30 Oct. 1834   CG-A
Prueit, Geo. to Mahalay Ruggles 11 July 1834   Wash
Pruett, --rafford to Margaret Johnson 30 June 1835   Md-A
Pruex, Joseph to Mary A. Robinson 2 Dec. 1823   StGe
Pruit, Francis to Jincy Clinton 15 Sept. 1831   Cr-1
Prvort, Thomas to Mahala M. Hendrick 25 July 1839   Henr
Pryor, Charles to Katherine Baldwin 31 July 1834   Clin
Pryor, Daniel to Cintha A. Massie 5 May 1833   Gasc
Pryor, John to Patsy Edmundson 23 Mar. 1823   Gasc
Pryor, John to Patsy Hughs 14 Feb. 1833   Gasc
Pryor, John Jr. to Mary A. Griffey 3 Oct. 1837   Gasc
Pryor, Wm. to Eliza Newby 28 Dec. 1837   Clin
Pugh, Silas B. to Emmeline Davis 16 June 1825   Call
Pugiett, Louis to Louisa Lacroix 30 Jan. 1832   StCh
Pulaim, John to Zeznlda Hodges 15 Nov. 1838   Fran
Pulaskay, Elifelett to Betsy Kane 30 Dec. 1834   Pk-1
Pulis, Reuben to Nancy McDonald 13 Dec. 1838   Audr
Pulket, Paul to Polly Prine 3 Feb. 1824   Clay
Pullam, Richard to Ann Smith 13 May 1834   Boon
Pullam, Robt. to Hycinthia Elliott 11 Nov. 1835   Boon
Pulley, Lorenzo D. to Demonas Cruse 22 Apr. 1834   Coop
Pulliam, Asa to Angeline Miller 7 Jan. 1837   Call
Pulliam, John C. to Catharine Chambers 27 Apr. 1836   Sali
Pulliam, John W. to Elizabeth Heart 18 Apr. 1833   Call
Pulliam, Nathan to Frances Austin 18 Mar. 1835   Howa
Pulliam, Richard P. to Melissa Thomas 30 Oct. 1839   Mari
Pulliam, Wm. to Nancy Mitchell 6 Apr. 1820   Howa
Pullian, Benj. G. to Sarah M. Head 26 May 1835   Rand
Pulling, James R. to Mrs. Rebecca Ferguson 20 May 1824 Cole
Pullum, John to Sinthia Spencer 20 Sept. 1832   CG-A
Pullum, Milton O. to Susan Moore 25 Dec. 1834   Clay
Pulush, Conrad to Susan Gardner 10 Sept. 1835   Rall
Pummel, Sampson to Deborah Morrow 23 June 1831   Gasc
Purcell, Richard to Penelopy Cromwell 26 Dec. 1836   CG-A
Purdin, Caleb B. to Eliza A. Rector 22 June 1831   Coop
Purdom, John to Catharine J. Weatherford 11 Aug. 1831   Pk-1
Purdom, Thomas to Frances Buford 28 Apr. 1831   Rall
Purdue, Wm. to Elizabeth Anderson 11 July 1839   Gree
Purkin, John to Sally Tally 14 Dec. 1835   Pk-1
Purkins, Richard to Sally Wylie 6 Feb. 1831   CG-A
Purkins, Thomas to Muluny Turner 10 Nov. 1836   Rand

Purse, Samuel N. to Elizabeth M. Davidson 7 Nov. 1839   Pk-B
Purseley, David C. to Elizabeth Zumalt 1 Oct. 1833   Pk-1
Pursinger, Obidiah to Rebecca Elliott 8 Mar. 1837   Clin
Purvis, Geo. to Unity Pattrick 15 Sept. 1831   Rall
Pybourn, David to Abigail Odell 20 Mar. 1836   Ray
Pyburn, Edward to Elizabeth Robins 24 Dec. 1832   Cr-1
Pyburn, Jacob to Catharine Pettyjohn 12 Nov. 1832   Cr-1
Pyburn, John to Nancy Logan 14 July 1835   Clay
Pyburn, Joseph to Elizabeth Marr 24 Mar. 1836   Clay

Quarles, Steven to Annette Cross 7 Aug. 1834   StFr
Quean, John to Rachel Chandler 19 Jan. 1823   CG-1
Quebeck, Pierre to Lulalle Lamarche 15 Apr. 1811   StCh
Queen, John to Mahala Chandler 3 Aug. 1834   CG-A
Queener, Wm. to Elizabeth Blevins 4 July 1839   Henr
Querry, M. Newton to Sarah Hope 9 Aug. 1831   CG-A
Query, Newton to Nancy Blair 19 Sept. 1839   CG-B
Quesenberry, David to Lucinda Warder 9 Oct. 1828   Lafa
Quick, Aonmon to Jane Wray 21 Mar. 1833   Warr
Quick, Geo. W. to Bernitte Reece 23 Jan. 1838   Coop
Quick, Jacob to Polly Beckett 1 Jan. 1828   Coop
Quick, Jacob to Lucy Allen 10 Apr. 1836   Ray
Quick, James to Ellen Murphy 15 Jan. 1836   Wash
Quick, John W. to Lydia Burns 14 July 1835   Perr
Quick, John W. to Julia Gregoire 17 Mar. 1836   Perr
Quick, Richard B. to Elizabeth Clevenger 7 Mar. 1839   Ray
Quick, Thomas to Rachel Johnson 8 Nov. 1827   Coop
Quigley, Thomas to Mrs. Laviney C. Chronister 2 Dec. 1838 Ripl
Quinley, Richman to Margaret J. Ginnings 12 Nov. 1835   Howa
Quinn, Goldsbury to Lucy Roberts 18 Aug. 1836   Howa
Quisenberry, Jackson to Louisa A. Graham 1 Dec. 1838   Howa
Quisenberry, Wm. to Joanna Henderson 21 Feb. 1839   Boon
Quisenburg, Geo. to Martha Kinnier 4 Jan. 1839   Sali
Quisenbury, James to Ann Palmer 25 Jan. 1835   Boon

Raburn, Hodge to Sarah Reid 22 Nov. 1822   Coop
Radford, Charles to Polly Stillwell 1 Nov. 1838   Wash
Radford, Milender to Lovey Parker 22 July 1830   Wash
Radican, Elisha to Cena King 2 Mar. 1837   Call
Raffity, Thomas to Elizabeth Compton 3 Apr. 1832   Wash
Ragan, Greenbury to Miss Tate 29 Sept. 1839   Jack
Ragan, Timothy to Patsy Moore 1 Mar. 1835   Md-A
Ragan, Wm. to Thizziah O'Dell 9 July 1822   Howa
Ragland, Elvis to Maria Brewer 20 May 1830   Perr
Ragsdale, Anthony to Nancy Hutson 19 Sept. 1833   Md-A
Ragsdale, Charles to Zeriaha Underood 28 Nov. 1833   Md-B
Ragsdale, Edward to Sarah Noonon 30 May 1839   Monr
Ragsdale, James to Sarah Dever 29 Apr. 1832   Monr
Ragsdale, James to Mahala Stout 8 July 1834   Linc
Rainey, Allen to Nancy Earickson 9 Apr. 1824   Ray
Rainey, James W. to Mrs. Elizabeth Ross 17 May 1836   StFr
Rains, James to Rachel Vanderpool 3 Oct. 1835   Ray
Rains, Joab to Elizabeth Dondly 2 Dec. 1834   Gree
Rains, John to Sarah Troth 27 May 1838   Polk
Rains, Laurence Jr. to Mary Troth 20 Jan. 1839   Polk
Raker, Joseph to Mary A. Mullens 16 June 1836   Monr
Ralls, John to Lucinda Silvers rec. 22 May 1835   Rall
Ralls, Morgan to Linda Abbott 5 Apr. 1838   Shel
Ralls, Wm. S. to Margaret Suddeth 2 Sept. 1830   Rall
Ramberger, Henry to Elizabeth Shelton 1 Mar. 1838   Wash
Ramey, Jacob to Rebecca Wilkison 20 Sept. 1838   Gree
Ramey, James to Permeley Woolf 24 Aug. 1834   Pett
Ramey, Wm. to Elen Wason 1 Mar. 1832   Sali

Ramley, Adam to Mahala Artman 13 Jan. 1831   Ray
Ramley, Jacob to Matilda Artman 14 May 1834   Ray
Ramsay, B.A. to Martha C. Ramsay 27 Apr. 1826   Cole
Ramsay, John T. to Elizabeth Moore 3 Apr. 1837   Cole
Ramsay, Samuel to Selinda Fuller 29 Jan. 1835   Pett
Ramsay, Thomas to Catharine Ashabran 4 June 1826   CG-A
Ramsey, Abselam to Katherine Barks 8 Feb. 1838   CG-A
Ramsey, David to Mary Hale 9 Nov. 1830   CG-A
Ramsey, Geo. R. to Hessa Burrus 4 Oct. 1835   Lafa
Ramsey, Hon. Higginbothum to Manerva McAlister 23 May 1839   Sali
Ramsey, Jewel to Caroline Conger 31 Jan. 1828   Call
Ramsey, John to Mary Meek 28 Mar. 1805   StCh
Ramsey, John to Rachel Ramsey 10 Dec. 1836   Boon
Ramsey, John to Agnes Briton 7 Dec. 1837   Cr-1
Ramsey, John to Sarah Hall 30 Dec. 1838   CG-B
Ramsey, John A. to Maraine Miller 14 Aug. 1834   Fran
Ramsey, John A. to May T. Tompson 5 Jan. 1836   Howa
Ramsey, Lycurgus L. to Jane Fenton 8 Feb. 1837   Audr
Ramsey, Robt. L. to Elizabeth Sullivant 3 Oct. 1833   Cr-1
Ramsey, Samuel to Elizabeth Frye 17 Aug. 1837   Mari
Ramsey, Thomas to Sarah J. Gillum 15 Oct. 1837   John
Ramsy, Lewis to Elizabeth Hetherly 22 Aug. 1833   Fran
Ramsy, Wm. to Malinda Collins 11 Apr. 1833   Fran
Ramy, Daniel L. to Eliza G. Rice 28 Sept. 1836   Coop
Randol, Abm. to Sarah Poe 26 Jan. 1837   CG-A
Randol, David to Leanner Malone 22 July 1838   CG-A
Randol, Ellison to Sarah Hill 12 June 1832   CG-A
Randol, Harrison to Serilda Stout 15 Oct. 1835   CG-B
Randol, Hiram to Polly Masterson 8 Dec. 1830   CG-A
Randol, James H. to Lucinda Dowty 1 Mar. 1827   CG-A
Randol, Medard to Debora Waller 22 Oct. 1805   CGRA
Randol, Samuel to Matilda Randol 23 Dec. 1827   CG-A
Randol, Samuel to Belranetta Golliher 29 Jan. 1831   CG-A
Randol, Samuel to Cynthia Whiting 28 Nov. 1837   CG-A
Randol, Thomas to Sarah Masterson 3 Nov. 1826   CG-B
Randol, Thomson W. to Evaline Malone 18 Sept. 1836   CG-A
Randol, Wm. G. to Emily Green 29 Sept. 1831   CG-A
Randol, Wilson to Nancy Hayden 11 Aug. 1836   CG-A
Randolls, James to Ann Dowly 22 Oct. 1805   CGRA
Randolph, Daniel H. to Betsy A. Young 28 June 1838   Clin
Randolph, Edmund to Patsy McClelland 4 Dec. 1832   Call
Randolph, Francis M. to Rebecca Ruth 31 Oct. 1838   Clin
Randolph, Robt. to Amanda J. Humphries 14 Jan. 1836   Call
Randolph, Thomas to Frances Britton 20 Dec. 1832   Cr-1
Randolph, Wm. to Nancy Holleman 4 July 1830   Mari
Raney, David to Catharine Baimbrick 17 Sept. 1836   Sali
Rankin, Charles S. to Sarah R. Bryant 10 Jan. 1839   Jeff
Rankin, R. to Margaret Whitsell 3 Jan. 1822   Lafa
Ranner, Michael to Magdalen Fisher 29 Dec. 1839   Perr
Ranney, Johnson to Mary Gayle 21 June 1832   CG-A
Ranney, Johnson to Emily Neale 11 June 1835   CG-B
Rapsuck, Peter to Ellen Lee 30 July 1835   Jeff
Rash, Wm. to Lusina Tompkins 21 Jan. 1839   Lewi
Ratekin, Edmond W. to Susan Cheatham 8 May 1838   Call
Rathburn, Edmund to Elizabeth Gibbs 28 Nov. 1819   Howa
Rathburn, Robt. to Roena Chapel 28 Apr. 1839   Pk-B
Ratliff, Commach to Elizabeth Brock 22 Jan. 1835   Gree
Ratliff, Jonathan to Delany Rowland 15 Dec. 1829   Rand
Ratliff, Jonathan to Susany Rowland 20 Sept. 1831   Rand
Rattles, Wm. to Polly Reed 3 July 1838   Gasc
Raune, Geoffray to Aspasie Villemer 31 Jan. 1832   Wash
Rauschaelbeck, Frederick to Maria Schuchart 8 Mar. 1838   Cole
Ravenscroft, Milton to Frances Luck 19 Sept. 1833   Pk-1
Rawlins, Dudly to Elizabeth Hoskins 3 Jan. 1836   Howa
Rawlins, John Jr. to Nancy Burk 4 Feb. 1832   Howa

```
Rawlins, John to E. Emerson 2 Apr. 1835                        Howa
Ray, Benj. to Hanna Warren 12 Mar. 1839                        John
Ray, Bonapart to Elizabeth Keithly 10 Aug. 1836               StCh
Ray, Elsey to Nancy Graham 11 Jan. 1838                        John
Ray, Geo. N. to Margaret Carter 21 Sept. 1838                  Cole
Ray, James to Mary Greer 8 July 1832                           Lafa
Ray, James M. to Elizabeth Brown 28 Dec. 1837                  Lewi
Ray, John to Polly Hall 12 Feb. 1832                           Lafa
Ray, Jon to Sidney Abington 25 Oct. 1832                      StCh
Ray, Matthew to Sarah Brown 29 Sept. 1833                      Lewi
Ray, Samuel Jr. to Nancy Caton 30 Aug. 1832                    Howa
Ray, Stephen to Jane Richardson 11 July 1819                   Howa
Ray, Thomas to Phebe I. Johnson 2 Nov. 1837                    Howa
Ray, Wm. to Emily Walker 27 Mar. 1834                          Cole
Rayle, Wm. to Sarah McCullouch 15 Dec. 1835                    Coop
Read, Andrew to Emely Baley 7 Apr. 1836                        Howa
Read, John to Matilda Fanning 5 May 1837                       Ray
Read, Michael to Louiza M. Tilford 30 May 1839                 Linc
Read, Robt. to Mary A. Castleman 22 Aug. 1839                 Mill
Read, Samuel to Mary J. Phillips 16 May 1830                   Mari
Reading, Thomas to Elizabeth Beauchamp 6 Oct. 1836            Pk-1
Reagan, Joseph D. to Elizabeth E. Adams 27 July 1835           Call
Ream, Abraham to Eunaty Ramsey 24 Oct. 1819                    Howa
Reanolds, Geo. to Sarah A. Harper 17 Feb. 1833                 Call
Rease, Isam to Malinda Furgason 6 Apr. 1837                    John
Reason, Wm. to Matilda Norrice 28 Jan. 1838                    Barr
Reaves, John to Eda Taylor 12 Apr. 1838                        Gree
Reaves, Wm. to Reachel Johnson 26 July 1825                    CG-A
Reavis, Anderson to Sarah Berkley 4 Aug. 1836                  Coop
Reavis, Ashley L. to Catherine Bowles 20 Oct. 1835            Coop
Reavis, Fenton G. to Mary I. Dickson 18 Apr. 1839             Coop
Reavis, Henry I. to Sally McCullough 6 Nov. 1831              Coop
Reavis, Jackson J. to Zerilda H. Levins 24 May 1838           Coop
Reavis, James to Elizabeth Berry 13 Feb. 1823                 Boon
Reavis, Joseph P. to Frances W. Briscoe 3 Jan. 1839          Coop
Reavis, Lewis D. to Mary Hunt 23 June 1836                    Coop
Reavis, Light H. to Susannah Anderson 11 Sept. 1831          Sali
Reavis, Warren to Polly Box 10 Apr. 1834                      Pett
Reavs, Samuel to Permelia Scott 6 Mar. 1836                   Polk
Record, John to Mary A. Read 24 July 1839                     Mill
Rector, Enoch J. to Parthena Jones 14 Feb. 1839              Coop
Rector, Henry to Elizabeth L. Allen 26 Oct. 1833             Call
Rector, James to Sally A. Loveland 23 Sept. 1839             Linc
Rector, Jesse H. to Cynthia Strother 18 Feb. 1838           Pk-B
Rector, Lewellen to Amanda Mattingly 18 Oct. 1838           Coop
Red, Norsley to Pamelia I. Read 15 Jan. 1831                 Coop
Redd, Edward to Rebecca Colvin 15 July 1830                  Fran
Redd, John F. to Elizabeth A. Francis 12 Apr. 1838          Mari
Redd, Joseph D. to Polly White 19 Dec. 1833                 Pett
Reddick, James to Ann M. Manning 28 Apr. 1829               Perr
Reddick, Peter to Rachel Wilds 1 Feb. 1831                  Howa
Redding, James to Eliza Williamson 25 Apr. 1839            Mari
Redding, Lewis to Lydia Ivers 28 May 1830                   Fran
Reddish, John B. to Caroline F. Asbury 5 Mar. 1839         Lewi
Reden, Elijah B. to Patsy Bray 16 May 1831                  Cole
Redes, Lewis to Rachel Sercy 6 Jan. 1839                    Gasc
Redford, Wm. to Abby Morgan 21 Sept. 1826                   Perr
Reece, Wm. H. to Elizabeth Alexander 22 Dec. 1836          John
Reed, ---- to Sarah Thompson 17 June 1834                   Monr
Reed, Allen G. to Lucinda Adkins 1 Nov. 1837               Clay
Reed, Aloysius to Charity Layton 6 Feb. 1826               Perr
Reed, Archibal to Feba Dun 24 Jan. 1830                     CG-A
Reed, Archibald to Elizabeth Wallace 23 Oct. 1834          SG-A
Reed, Archibald to Louisa A. Creed 5 Mar. 1835             Monr
Reed, Archibald to Elizabeth Wills 5 Dec. 1837             CG-A
```

Reed, Charles to Patsy Potts 22 Jan. 1833   Boon
Reed, Daniel to Frances Patterson 25 Sept. 1825   Cole
Reed, David to Tiny Brock 1 Apr. 1827   Jack
Reed, David to Elizabeth Messersmith 20 Aug. 1829   Cole
Reed, Edward to Delitha Shivers 19 Apr. 1832   Gasc
Reed, Edward to Nancy Biticks 30 May 1833   Gasc
Reed, Elijah to Delila Martin 6 Dec. 1835   Cole
Reed, Farloe to Nancy Horton 20 Oct. 1836   Cass
Reed, Henry J. to Zelinda Owens 11 Feb. 1837   Rand
Reed, James to Elizabeth Harlow 25 Dec. 1825   Pk-1
Reed, James to ---- Nickols -- July 1833   Boon
Reed, James to Nancy Pitts 6 Nov. 1834   Ray
Reed, James W. to Elizabeth Boulware 29 Nov. 1835   Monr
Reed, Jesse to Margaret Henchlow 13 Aug. 1833   Coop
Reed, John to Margaret Wolfskill 8 July 1820   Howa
Reed, John to Sarah Kirkpatrick 20 Mar. 1823   Coop
Reed, John to Marie L. Bouchard 16 Nov. 1829   Wash
Reed, John to Nancy Lay 28 Oct. 1830   Howa
Reed, John to Elizabeth Jones 4 July 1833   Cole
Reed, John to Malinda Searcy 12 Nov. 1833   Jack
Reed, John to Sally Moxley 31 Oct. 1835   Call
Reed, John to Casandria A. McIlhenny 13 Sept. 1836   Jack
Reed, John to Sally Jones 19 Feb. 1837   Cr-1
Reed, John to Elizabeth Jones 7 May 1839   Md-B
Reed, John to Henrietta Mead 8 Dec. 1839   Clay
Reed, John A. to Eliza A. Weir 9 Feb. 1837   Boon
Reed, Joseph to Hannah Shobe 8 Oct. 1826   Gasc
Reed, Leonard to Rhoda Veach 11 Jan. 1827   Gasc
Reed, Leonard to Rebecca Branson 29 Mar. 1832   Gasc
Reed, Lewis to Sally Barnes 17 Aug. 1838   Boon
Reed, Nathan R. to Sealy Reed 10 Mar. 1839   Gasc
Reed, Robt. to Harriet Haydon 9 Oct. 1834   Mari
Reed, Samuel to Grezel Reed 13 Jan. 1825   Coop
Reed, Silvester to Elizabeth Ware 19 July 1837   Fran
Reed, Solomon to Elizabeth Fuller 12 Mar. 1826   Coop
Reed, Solomon to Roza Fitzhugh 20 Apr. 1836   Pett
Reed, Stewart to Eliza Spott 19 Dec. 1837   Sali
Reed, Thomas to Amilia Buford rec. 22 May 1835   Rall
Reed, Wm. to Ruth Allson 15 July 1830   Lafa
Reed, Wm. to Elizabeth Ridenhour 30 Dec. 1832   Fran
Reed, Wm. to Hannah Stealey 13 Dec. 1836   Md-B
Reed, Wm. to Sarah Woolrich 23 Mar. 1837   Mari
Reed, Wm. to Margaret A. Gaines 17 Apr. 1838   Clar
Reed, Wm. A. to Mahala Collier 22 Jan. 1833   Coop
Rees, Amos to Judith Trigg 15 July 1830   Clay
Reese, Addison to Margaret Hunter 22 Dec. 1835   Lewi
Reever, Martain to Leddadah Mullins 22 Feb. 1837   Sali
Reeves, Absalom to Mary L. Ross 25 Feb. 1838   StFr
Reeves, Albert to Mary Patterson 27 Feb. 1837   Wash
Reeves, Benett A. to Hortentia Johnson 13 Jan. 1826   CG-A
Reeves, Caswell to Matilda Weeks 25 Feb. 1836   Md-B
Reeves, Isaac to Ruth Reed 14 Sept. 1828   Md-A
Reeves, Jesse J. to Susannah Innman 16 July 1839   Cr-1
Reeves, Wm. to Martha Brown 29 Oct. 1829   Howa
Reeves, Wm. to Hannah A. Givens 13 Dec. 1831   Howa
Reid, David to Sarah R. Reid 19 May 1836   Linc
Reid, Granville to Nancy Black 21 Feb. 1837   Call
Reid, James to Patsey Abernithie 19 Feb. 1829   CG-A
Reid, James to Sarah B. Pulliam 25 Aug. 1836   Sali
Reid, Thomas S. to Adeline Reid 24 Oct. 1838   Linc
Reiney, David to Parneaty Jackson 15 Feb. 1830   Ray
Remby, John to Nancy Tarwater 5 Jan. 1832   Ray
Remey, Wm. B. to Eliza S. Howland 11 May 1837   StCh
Remingham, Enoch to Jane Risley 2 Dec. 1839   Bent
Renalette, Pierre to Mrs. Lewezy Roi 10 Sept. 1828   Jack

```
Rencontre, Emilien to Eulalie Frudelle 25 Aug. 1830          StCh
Renfro, James C. to Susan Thrailkill 29 Aug. 1839            Livi
Renfro, John to Elizabeth Wilds 13 Mar. 1834                 Ray
Renfro, Joseph to Sinthy Rolin 28 May 1826                   Wash
Renfro, Mark to Nancy Ridgeway 18 Sept. 1825                 Call
Renfro, Mark to Cynthia Murphy 4 July 1833                   StFr
Renfro, Ratio to Malinda Saberfield 14 Mar. 1833             Gasc
Renfro, Thomas to Eliza Inge 3 Feb. 1839                     Wash
Renfroe, David to Elizabeth English 26 Feb. 1835             CG-B
Renfroe, Jackson to Nancy Cracraft 2 Apr. 1839              CG-B
Renfroe, John to Matilda Rodney 16 June 1831                 CG-A
Renfrow, Wade to Elizabeth Phillips 30 Sept. 1832            Cr-1
Renick, Burton L. to Susan Galbreath 3 Nov. 1825            Sali
Renick, Cyrus to Mrs. Josie Clouda 1 July 1839              Lewi
Renick, James to Milly A. Warder 20 June 1839               Lafa
Renick, Leonard H. to Jane Steward 19 Apr. 1832             Ray
Renick, Strother to Rebecca H. Levisay 19 Nov. 1839         Lafa
Renick, Wm. H. to Sally A.F. Ewing 29 Mar. 1832             Lafa
Renick, Wm. H. to Sally Wallace 12 Mar. 1835               Lafa
Renison, John to Anna Weeden 23 May 1822                    Howa
Renn, James to Rebecca Whitley 18 Mar. 1821                 Boon
Rennick, Henry to Eliza L. King 29 Nov. 1827               Clay
Rennison, Geo. to Sally Stow 2 Jan. 1834                    Coop
Rennison, Joseph to Aristine Seat 15 Dec. 1836             Coop
Renno, Wm. C. to Malinda Hoover 3 Sept. 1838               Gree
Rennols, Richard to Nancy Chapel 28 Sept. 1836             Call
Renny, Felix to Hannah Duckworth 3 Feb. 1834               Wash
Renny, James to Rosanah Brown 4 Feb. 1830                  Pk-1
Renoe, R.D. to Jane Davis 9 Aug. 1838                      Call
Renolds, Allen to Polly B. Martin 2 June 1833             Call
Renphroe, Wm. to Lucy Reeves 15 Oct. 1832                 Fran
Renshaw, John W. to Margaret A. Martin 12 Oct. 1835       Coop
Renshaw, Peter to Peggy Fields 22 Apr. 1830               Ray
Repato, Ephriam to Vicindarilla McMillon 26 Feb. 1835     Cole
Rephlo, John B. to Mary Heland 8 July 1838                Gasc
Reserosh, August to Wilh. Kruse 24 Jan. 1833              StCh
Reshnar, Samuel to Permelia Cook 13 Jan. 1832             Wash
Revel, John to Nancy Thacker 7 Dec. 1837                  CG-A
Revell, James to Celia Gregory 27 Aug. 1824               CG-1
Revell, King B. to Leuame McCain 19 Dec. 1839             Howa
Revensbill, Christian to Eve Wolf 3 Dec. 1825             StCh
Revey, Lewis to Mahala Owens 18 Feb. 1836                 Clay
Revis, Edward to Lucy Berry 9 Feb. 1837                   Sali
Revis, Warren to Margaret Smelser 5 Jan. 1823             Sali
Reviz, Geo. to Mary Reed 6 Aug. 1829                      Gasc
Rew, John to Jane Hughes 9 Jan. 1831                      Coop
Rey, Isaiah to Julia Captain 4 Oct. 1830                  Gasc
Reynolds, Andrew J. to Catherine Wilson 26 Apr. 1835      Perr
Reynolds, Cornelius to Evelina Thornton 16 Oct. 1827      Howa
Reynolds, Geo. to Emily Roderoque 7 Apr. 1839             Wash
Reynolds, Hedgeman to Judith H. Williams 10 Mar. 1838     Cass
Reynolds, Henry to Lavina Comstock 10 Nov. 1836           Carr
Reynolds, James to Eliza Daniwood 14 Jan. 1834            Jack
Reynolds, John to Letha Stona 11 Jan. 1821                StCh
Reynolds, John to Nelly Woods 10 Jan. 1832                Monr
Reynolds, Joseph W. to Elizabeth McIntyre 25 Oct. 1838    Call
Reynolds, Noel to Susan Robertson 29 July 1838            Rand
Reynolds, Robt. to Sarah Payne 27 Aug. 1834               Howa
Reynolds, Shadrick to Nancy Wood 15 Apr. 1835             Call
Reynolds, Thomas to Louisa Guthrie 15 July 1819           StGe
Reynolds, Thomas C. to Mary Tribble 7 Apr. 1829           Boon
Reynolds, Whitfield to Malinda Turley 30 Dec. 1838        Coop
Reynolds, Wm. to Sarah Lewis 2 Aug. 1832                  Boon
Reynolds, Wm. to Polly A. Day 1 Jan. 1835                 Call
Reynolds, Wm. J. to Darcus M. Wisdom 25 July 1839         Polk
```

Reys, John to Martha Farris 24 Mar. 1839   Rand
Rhea, Nicholas to Amanda Phillips 15 Feb. 1838   Howa
Rhinehart, Alfred to Catherine Cunningham 11 Feb. 1838   CG-A
Rhines, Jonas to Jane McCormick 28 July 1839   Ripl
Rhoads, Goree to Jane Hull 23 May 1839   Sali
Rhoads, Samuel to Sarah Pace 27 June 1824   Call
Rhodes, Alexander to Martha Tomison 26 Aug. 1838   CG-A
Rhodes, Barna to Polly McMillen 4 Apr. 1839   Pk-B
Rhodes, Cornelius to Mary Reily -- Oct. 1830   Perr
Rhodes, Cornelius to Mary Suton 22 Jan. 1839   Perr
Rhodes, Geo. W. to Sally Kinder 15 Oct. 1829   CG-A
Rhodes, Henry to Rachel Abbott 6 Jan. 1837   Shel
Rhodes, James to Mary Musgrove 9 Feb. 1837   Shel
Rhodes, John to Elizabeth Lorance 24 Nov. 1825   CG-A
Rhodes, Joseph to Elisabeth Burdet 11 May 1832   Mari
Rhodes, Joseph to Mary B. Morris 19 Oct. 1834   Perr
Rhodes, T. Hantley to Sarah Stice 7 Apr. 1836   Shel
Rhodes, Thomas to Minerva J. Jones 17 Aug. 1837   Mari
Rhodes, Wm. to Rosannah Dougherty 3 Dec. 1821   Call
Rhodes, Wm. to Martha Lewis 31 Mar. 1831   Mari
Rhosberry, Nathaniel to Nancy M. Williams 16 July 1835   Monr
Rhyne, Daniel to Sally Hofman 10 June 1838   Perr
Rice, Alfred to Nancy James 20 Mar. 1830   Clay
Rice, Caleb to Nancy D. Bacon 10 Oct. 1839   StCh
Rice, Colton to Mary Griffen 26 Sept. 1833   StCh
Rice, Franklin to Elizabeth McCarther 12 Oct. 1834   Gree
Rice, Geo. to Sally Fisher 4 Nov. 1835   Pett
Rice, Jacob to Polly Weeden 2 Nov. 1834   Coop
Rice, Jacob to Margaret Ford 26 Dec. 1839   Bent
Rice, Jefferson to Lavina Banning 2 Dec. 1836   Rand
Rice, John W. to Martha Kerby 17 May 1835   Rand
Rice, Joseph to Euphema Brown 31 Jan. 1836   Rall
Rice, Lewis to Jane Patrick 29 Oct. 1838   Coop
Rice, Martin to Mary Lynch 3 Apr. 1836   Lafa
Rice, Michel to Nancy Gillet 28 Aug. 1821   Howa
Rice, Pleasant to Verlinda Ray 2 Aug. 1826   Lafa
Rice, Rassel to Coley Sherrin 20 Sept. 1835   Rand
Rice, Samuel to Patsy Coyl rec. 28 June 1819   StCh
Rice, Samuel O. to Sally Tice 23 Jan. 1834   Warr
Rice, Thomas to Mahala Hatten 16 Aug. 1838   Monr
Rice, Walter to Margueritte McRay 19 Aug. 1833   StCh
Rice, Westley to Susan Cheaney 26 Mar. 1835   Boon
Rice, Wm. to Sally Dunkin 14 Feb. 1836   Monr
Rice, Wm. B. to Dorothy Hutchings 13 Sept. 1836   StCh
Rice, Wm. C. to Mary Arnule 14 Feb. 1839   Warr
Rice, Wm. H. to Elizabeth Drinkhart 17 Dec. 1835   Rand
Richard, Merret to Dicy Paine 19 Oct. 1826   Boon
Richards, Gilford to Elizabeth Whorton 1 Oct. 1835   Clay
Richards, Gilford to Lucy Wharton 14 Jan. 1838   Clay
Richards, John to Jane Young 5 May 1839   CG-B
Richards, Lewis to Mrs. Jane Tynnell 13 May 1823   Char
Richards, Lewis to Hiscey Goza 5 June 1826   CG-A
Richards, Mathew to Susan Evans 16 July 1829   Howa
Richards, Noah to Nancy West 24 Jan. 1828   Clay
Richardson, Aaron to Nancy Brown 10 Jan. 1822   Fran
Richardson, Alexander to Lucy J. Shaw 27 Sept. 1837   Call
Richardson, Allen to Polly Christopher 27 Oct. 1835   Wash
Richardson, Clayton to Nancy Adams 1 Nov. 1829   Fran
Richardson, Daniel to Dorcas Dougherty 25 Jan. 1838   Fran
Richardson, Edward F. to Elizabeth Sidenbender 26 Aug. 1838   Clar
Richardson, James to Eliza A. West 23 Dec. 1839   Rand
Richardson, James E. to Elizabeth Mars 16 Nov. 1820   Howa
Richardson, John to Britanny Multon 6 Mar. 1835   Fran
Richardson, John M. to Jane Heriford 12 July 1838   Lewi
Richardson, Joshua to Polly Stafford 28 Oct. 1827   StFr

188

```
Richardson, Larking to Jane Jones 13 Aug. 1834                    Boon
Richardson, Nathan to Lidia Kelly 24 May 1827                     Howa
Richardson, Richard to Jincy Brock 9 Aug. 1822                    Fran
Richardson, Richard to Charlotte Cooper 20 Nov. 1831             Gasc
Richardson, Robt. to Cinderella Estes 4 Jan. 1835                Morg
Richardson, Schuyler to Manerva Patterson 13 Feb. 1834           Howa
Richardson, Wm. to Nancy Summers 7 Feb. 1839                     Morg
Richardson, Wm. S. to Martha Morgan 8 Nov. 1839                  StFr
Richart, Christones to Polly A. Harget 26 June 1836              StCh
Richey, Samuel to Nancy McCarty 19 Dec. 1824                     Coop
Richie, John to Delitha McNite 24 Dec. 1837                      Gasc
Richmond, Samuel W. to Susan T. Bold 24 June 1830               Rand
Rickey, Powers to Amanda Letts 23 May 1839                       Howa
Rickman, Robt. to Sarah Flourney 8 Oct. 1835                     Jack
Riddales, Thomas to Nancy J. Akin 6 Mar. 1837                    Gree
Riddle, Samuel to Mary Kencheloo 24 Dec. 1839                    Coop
Riddle, Wm. to Betsy Dunlap 8 Sept. 1836                         Lewi
Riddles, Abner to Lucinda Smith 12 Nov. 1837                     Polk
Ridenhour, John S. to Isabel Hiliard 21 Jan. 1837               Fran
Rider, Henry to Rebecca Hendricks 27 Feb. 1835                   Jack
Rider, Wm. to Cinthy Hendrix 13 Feb. 1838                        Cass
Ridgeway, Benj. to Minerva Simmons 5 Oct. 1833                   Coop
Ridgeway, Enoch to Aley Barnes 27 Dec. 1828                      Boon
Ridgeway, John D. to Saphira Wigginson 9 June 1831               Call
Ridgeway, Zecheriah to Martha Gay 22 Nov. 1838                   Boon
Ridgway, Charles to Ibby Head 5 Jan. 1826                        Howa
Ridgway, James to Mary Prince 14 Sept. 1837                      Howa
Ridgway, Jesse to Ann Wiley 27 Dec. 1836                         Howa
Ridgway, Reason to Harriett Reede 17 Sept. 1835                  Call
Ridgway, Thomas to Sally Standford 28 Dec. 1820                  Howa
Ridgway, Wm. to Hannah Price 17 Nov. 1835                        Howa
Ridie, James to Elizabeth Duncan 12 Feb. 1824                    Howa
Ridings, Robt. to Elizabeth Swift 20 Dec. 1838                   Henr
Ried, Zachariah to Susan Richardson 31 Mar. 1839                 Fran
Rieles, Joseph to Frances Cochran 7 Oct. 1832                    Monr
Riendeau, Francis to Mealaney Boyer 6 Sept. 1830                 Wash
Riens, Patrick to Catharine Byrd 29 Mar. 1827                    CG-A
Riffe, Jacob to Sarah Shannon 28 Apr. 1836                       Carr
Riffee, Jacob to Ruth Martin 15 Feb. 1821                        Ray
Riffee, Thomas to Elizabeth Taylor 3 Sept. 1831                  Ray
Riffle, Lewis to Casandra Holmes 10 Dec. 1835                    Linc
Rigeway, Thomas to Elizabeth Stephens 30 June 1832               Boon
Rigeway, Wm. to Paulina Renfro 19 Apr. 1831                      Boon
Rigg, Noah L. to Elizabeth Johnson 27 Jan. 1836                  Lafa
Riggins, James to Elizabeth Haynes 2 Sept. 1830                  Call
Riggins, John to Rebecca Stokes 15 Apr. 1838                     Clay
Riggins, Powell to Polly Waggenton 21 Oct. 1828                  Boon
Riggins, Thomas B. to Nancy Wyatt 23 Nov. 1837                   Cole
Riggs, Daniel to Mahaly Chapman 28 Oct. 1827                     Ray
Riggs, David to Jane Gostings 26 June 1834                       Perr
Riggs, Enoch to Ann Littlefield 27 May 1838                      Davi
Riggs, Isaac to Polly Henson 12 Oct. 1826                        Boon
Riggs, Jonathan to Mary Burton 12 May 1825                       Rall
Riggs, Lenoir to Elizabeth Lampton 24 Dec. 1826                  Call
Riggs, Reuben to Rachel Riggs 3 Dec. 1828                        Ray
Riggs, Rubin to Nancy Riggs 11 Jan. 1832                         Monr
Riggs, Samuel to Roady Belcher 23 Aug. 1825                      Howa
Riggs, Samuel to Nancy Robinson 22 Aug. 1826                     Boon
Riggs, Samuel to Nancy Dollins 2 Feb. 1837                       Audr
Riggs, Samuel to Margaret Ridgeway 28 May 1838                   Boon
Riggs, Silas to Sary Hicks 18 Mar. 1819                          Howa
Right, Isaac to Agaline Amick 7 Apr. 1831                        Howa
Right, Joseph to Elisa Yount 23 Mar. 1834                        Howa
Right, Lewis to Frances Kitchens 1 Oct. 1835                     Cr-1
Right, Townsend to Lucy Barnes 10 June 1834                      Boon
```

Rigsby, Isaac to Catharine Anson 20 Dec. 1833   Pk-1
Riley, Cleaveland to Sarah Loviall 11 Apr. 1839   Ripl
Riley, James to Susan Smith 24 Feb. 1833   Rand
Riley, James to Minerva More 24 Apr. 1835   Cr-1
Riley, James M. to Adeline Benoise 20 Sept. 1832   Clay
Riley, John to Elizabeth Hubbard -- -- 1837   Boon
Riley, Richard to Patience Simon 17 July 1838   Clar
Riley, Wm. to Janira McBride 17 Sept. 1835   Boon
Riley, Wm. to Marial Waller 16 May 1839   Clay
Rillian, Jacob to Pricilla Haghn 26 Oct. 1837   CG-A
Rimmer, Samuel to Emaline Vallandingham 5 Nov. 1839   Ray
Rines, Evaristus to Nancy Hagan 4 Apr. 1837   Perr
Riney, James F. to Ann D. Durbin 21 May 1836   Lewi
Riney, Simon to Louisa Manning 14 May 1838   Perr
Ringer, Abraham to Barbary Norwine 13 Oct. 1827   StFr
Ringer, Abraham to Aluntdear Norwine 22 Dec. 1833   Wash
Ringer, David to Rachael W. Downing 8 Aug. 1838   Mari
Ringer, Mathias P. to Eliza Capehart 23 Dec. 1824   Md-A
Ringer, Wm. to Sarah A. Downing 23 Sept. 1836   Mari
Ringo, Andrew H. to Margaret L. Wert 9 Sept. 1830   Clay
Ringo, Henry to Maria Tulbert 23 Apr. 1829   StCh
Ringo, John to Jane Hood 5 Apr. 1827   Howa
Ringo, Peter to Edy Jones 8 Jan. 1822   Howa
Ringo, Samuel Jr. to Elizabeth A. Wirt 6 Apr. 1826   Clay
Rinsay, Thomas to Elizabeth Fetter 7 Aug. 1837   StCh
Ripley, Richard to Alcy Baugh 23 July 1829   StCh
Rippy, James F. to Emeline Harr 20 Sept. 1828   Perr
Risher, Samuel to Rosina Bennett 24 Jan. 1828   CG-A
Risk, Wm. to Polly Wilcox 24 Dec. 1820   Howa
Ritchie, Austin to Mahala Lofton 2 Mar. 1839   Gasc
Ritchie, John D. to Catherine Yates 11 Jan. 1829   Clay
Ritchie, Wm. H. to Jane McCord 3 Sept. 1837   Clin
Ritter, Daniel to Chrishiana Clap 6 June 1808   CG-1
Rix, Adolph to Helen Fute 7 Aug. 1834   Perr
Rix, Matthew to Barbara Fiox 5 Mar. 1832   Perr
Roach, James to Pauline Frier 4 June 1829   Pk-1
Roads, Alexander H. to Dollie M. Tutt 7 Feb. 1837   Coop
Roark, John to Polly M. Garton 11 July 1830   Cole
Roark, Malachy to Mary N.C. Hutchins 16 Nov. 1839   Perr
Robards, Jesse to Barthena Smith 22 June 1837   Audr
Robards, Josiah to Elizabeth Thompson 24 May 1837   Clar
Robberson, Allen to Mary Montgomery 2 Oct. 1834   Gree
Robberson, John to Nancy Luny 29 Jan. 1834   Gree
Robbins, C.A. to Kiturah V. Overfelt 28 Apr. 1835   Call
Robbins, Prospect R. to Elizabeth Evans 7 Mar. 1816   StCh
Roberd, Charles to Celest Uno 1 Sept. 1835   Wash
Roberson, James to Hannah Wilson 17 Mar. 1828   Howa
Roberson, John to Phany Catron 12 June 1820   Coop
Roberson, Mathew to Myranda Fergason 5 Feb. 1837   John
Robert, Alexis to Margaret Page' 1 Feb. 1838   Wash
Robert, Francois to Odelia Archambo 28 Nov. 1826   StGe
Robert, James to Sally Foster 18 Aug. 1833   Gree
Robert, John B. to Celeste Auge' 28 Apr. 1828   Wash
Robert, Joseph to Marie Courtois 2 Feb. 1836   Wash
Robert, Louis to Eugenie Bouchard 9 Feb. 1830   Wash
Robert, Louis to Cecile Beauchamp 9 Sept. 1834   Wash
Robert, Michel to Celeste Brurassas 1 Jan. 1832   Wash
Robert, Perin to Matilda Govero 20 Feb. 1827   StGe
Roberts, Burrel to Sarah Steele 9 Apr. 1834   CG-A
Roberts, David to Dinah Roberts 2 Sept. 1830   Boon
Roberts, David to Abigal Reed 12 Dec. 1830   Howa
Roberts, David to Sarah A. Atkins 19 Sept. 1838   Clay
Roberts, David A. to Rachel Lee 19 Dec. 1838   Howa
Roberts, Edward to Nancy Masters 2 Jan. 1834   Jack
Roberts, Edward to Elizabeth Scott 11 June 1839   Pett

```
Roberts, Elisha to Claresy Byrd 24 Nov. 1830                        CG-A
Roberts, Geo. W. to Elizabeth Frazer 1 Nov. 1825                    CG-A
Roberts, Isam to Catherine F. Conner 13 Nov. 1828                   Jeff
Roberts, Isham to Susannah Wolfskill 1 Jan. 1824                    Howa
Roberts, James to Nancy Williams 21 Feb. 1821                       Howa
Roberts, James to Sarah Wainscott 6 Jan. 1825                       Boon
Roberts, James to Katharine Fisher 28 Jan. 1830                     Sali
Roberts, James to Elizabeth George 22 Nov. 1835                     Clay
Roberts, James M. to Elizabeth J. Hall 13 Sept. 1838               Clay
Roberts, Jesse to Vatilla Johnson 23 Apr. 1830                      Boon
Roberts, Jesse to Araminta Liles 26 May 1835                       Clin
Roberts, Joel to Matilda Gelvin 22 Aug. 1822                        Howa
Roberts, John to Anna Bradley 21 Oct. 1821                          Howa
Roberts, John to Theodotia H. Cunningham 4 Oct. 1829               Howa
Roberts, John to Dorus Loyston 9 July 1837                         Cole
Roberts, John to Nancy Johnson -- Oct. 1838                        Boon
Roberts, John to Sarah Martin 3 Jan. 1839                          Boon
Roberts, John to Quittency Thompson 7 Nov. 1839                    Lewi
Roberts, John J. to Mrs. Catharine Dickson 12 Sept. 1837          Monr
Roberts, John W. to Lucinda Summers 26 Nov. 1834                   Gree
Roberts, Jonathan to Frances Holmes 11 Sept. 1836                  Clin
Roberts, Joseph to Susan Davis 9 Nov. 1837                         Clay
Roberts, Joshua to Agnes Davis 25 Feb. 1838                        Lewi
Roberts, Joshua to Nancy Clark 19 June 1839                        Sali
Roberts, Nicholas to America George 21 Dec. 1829                   Clay
Roberts, Obediah to Elizabeth Edward 24 June 1833                  Clay
Roberts, Parker to Armerica P. Mitchell 2 Mar. 1837               Clar
Roberts, Redding to Elizabeth Tate -- Sept. 1838                   Lewi
Roberts, Richmond to Polly Roberts 29 Dec. 1831                    Howa
Roberts, Samuel to Mary Holland 10 Mar. 1836                       Clay
Roberts, Samuel to Eliza Hoskins 15 Feb. 1838                      Cole
Roberts, Silas to Hannah Johnson 28 Aug. 1828                      Boon
Roberts, Thomas to Mary Belew 5 Nov. 1828                          Howa
Roberts, Thomas to Tabitha H. Crowden 26 Nov. 1839                Fran
Roberts, Tillmon to Diadema Nelson 4 Sept. 1828                    Mari
Roberts, Wm. to Ann Finnell 1 Jan. 1827                            Char
Roberts, Wm. to Amanda Thompson 21 Aug. 1834                       Cole
Roberts, Wm. to Mary Whitney 9 Jan. 1839                           Howa
Roberts, Wm. to Manerva Edwards 7 Feb. 1839                        Pett
Roberts, Wm. H. to Sarah Sexton 18 Feb. 1830                       Boon
Roberts, Wm. K. to Jane W. Collins 9 Nov. 1837                     Mari
Roberts, Wm. P. to Mary Goode 31 Jan. 1833                         Fran
Robertson, Andrew to Katharine Shirley -- Dec. 1829              Coop
Robertson, Andrew J. to Polly McGee 27 Dec. 1835                  Gasc
Robertson, Archibald to Nancy Medlin 9 Nov. 1828                  Cole
Robertson, Charles to Lucinda Fort 7 Nov. 1822                    Coop
Robertson, Daniel to Patey VanCleave 3 Sept. 1828                Call
Robertson, Geo. to Peggy Rowe 25 Oct. 1830                        Coop
Robertson, Herdin to Lydia Hensley 14 Jan. 1830                   Gasc
Robertson, Hiram to Elizabeth Coyle 9 Apr. 1826                   Gasc
Robertson, Hiram to Sidney Wayland 18 Feb. 1834                   Rand
Robertson, Isaac to Barbara Roller 7 Nov. 1835                    Rall
Robertson, James A. to Susannah Perkins 26 May 1839              Fran
Robertson, Jesse to Fany Hutson 17 July 1838                      CG-A
Robertson, John to Mary McClure 22 July 1821                      Coop
Robertson, John to Elvinea McMurtrey 30 Jan. 1835               Wash
Robertson, John to Rebecca Farmer 28 May 1839                    Cass
Robertson, Joseph to Lydia Lankford 11 Mar. 1826                 Lafa
Robertson, Joseph to Felicia Gaines 9 Jan. 1839                  Rand
Robertson, Michael to Mary Phillips 3 Apr. 1838                  Boon
Robertson, Robt. to Cordelia Phillips 29 Dec. 1833              Boon
Robertson, Wiley to Jane Collins 11 Dec. 1838                    Rand
Robertson, Wm. to Barbery Probst 6 Mar. 1817                     CG-1
Robertson, Wm. to Mary Lizzenby 9 Aug. 1831                      Mari
Robertson, Wm. to Caroline Masters 22 Mar. 1832                  Coop
```

```
Robertson, Wm. to Jane Kennady 8 Feb. 1838                          Shel
Robertson, Wm. A. to Malinda Brock 19 Oct. 1834                     CG-n
Robertsto, Wm. to Rebecca Reece 9 Dec. 1836                         John
Robeson, Jehu to Julien Ogresby 9 Dec. 1836                         John
Robey, Hezekiah to Magdaline Tillet 7 Oct. 1833                     Pk-1
Robinet, Pleasant to Catherine Hunt 10 Feb. 1829                    Call
Robinson, Abram to Frances Fristoe 28 Dec. 1837                     Pett
Robinson, Alexander to Katherine Hughes 5 Dec. 1833                 Boon
Robinson, Alonzo C. to Daphne McCloud 20 Jan. 1833                  StCh
Robinson, Alvis to Mary Gross 19 Oct. 1834                          Ray
Robinson, Arthur C. to Kansas Bradford 19 Dec. 1839                 Call
Robinson, Benj. to Frances McClanahan 14 Nov. 1833                  Boon
Robinson, Benj. to Marinthia McCrary 28 Oct. 1835                   Wash
Robinson, Benj. B. to Elizabeth Long 27 June 1834                   Linc
Robinson, Charles to Martha A. Redding 10 Dec. 1829                 Boon
Robinson, Charles S. to Jane Becket 1 Mar. 1821                     StCh
Robinson, Edward to Lydia McCoy 20 Feb. 1827                        Coop
Robinson, Geo. to Lorenly Stinson 20 July 1837                      Coop
Robinson, Hardy to Manerva Riggins 11 Aug. 1833                     Cole
Robinson, Isaac to Kiziah Sanders 24 Apr. 1815                      CG-1
Robinson, Jeremiah to Nancy Bryant 14 Oct. 1834                     Md-A
Robinson, James to Sinthy Deakin 15 Jan. 1829                       Coop
Robinson, James to Tabitha Chalbourne 7 Sept. 1831                  Wash
Robinson, James to Catherine Handcock -- Aug. 1836                  Boon
Robinson, John to Polly Howard 30 Dec. 1832                         Cole
Robinson, John to Mrs. Susan Calaway 22 Dec. 1835                   Md-B
Robinson, John to Jane Bray 25 Oct. 1838                            Gasc
Robinson, John B. to Sarah M. Rownels 13 Sept. 1828                 StFr
Robinson, John L. to Sarah Bryan 11 Dec. 1823                       StGe
Robinson, Joseph to Margaret Thomas 10 Nov. 1836                    Howa
Robinson, Lawson to Sarah Hampton 13 May 1835                       Cole
Robinson, Phillip to Winniford Cain 17 July 1833                    Howa
Robinson, Sidney to Marie Callahan 11 Dec. 1832                     Boon
Robinson, Thomas to Mary Cox 21 Nov. 1838                           Boon
Robinson, Wm. to Sally Winegan 20 Apr. 1833                         Ray
Robison, Daniel to Mary Luis 19 Apr. 1838                           CG-A
Robison, Kinsay to Elizabeth Ordway 3 Mar. 1811                     CG-1
Robison, Thomas to Aggatha Risher 9 Dec. 1831                       CG-A
Robison, Wm. to Nancy Colvin 30 Dec. 1829                           Fran
Robnet, John to Polly Powell 1 Feb. 1832                            Lafa
Robnete, Samuel F. to Mary A. Ritchey 9 June 1836                   Mari
Robnett, Wm. to Hannah Powell 17 Sept. 1834                         Lafa
Roch, Wm. to Louisa Poppelman 27 Sept. 1837                         StCh
Roche, Hugh to Franky Sharp 2 Aug. 1830                             Ray
Rochester, John C. to Nancy Kelley 28 Feb. 1821                     Coop
Rock, Alexander D. to Mary A. Herndon 24 Dec. 1839                  Howa
Rockhold, Alfred to Eliza Fisk 3 Mar. 1836                          Carr
Rockhold, Lloyd to Jane Connor 8 Mar. 1827                          Clay
Rockwell, Aron P. to Luand Belle 16 Feb. 1832                       Jack
Rodgers, Elisha to Susannah Wallace 17 Dec. 1835                    Gasc
Rodgers, Jacob S. to Elizabeth Talbert 5 June 1834                  Carr
Rodgers, Jeremiah to Thursey Hubbard 3 May 1836                     Howa
Rodgers, John to Katharine G. Mason 26 Nov. 1836                    Mari
Rodgers, Joseph to Pasha Rattler 14 Dec. 1837                       Gasc
Rodgers, Joseph B. to Nancy Burleson 18 Apr. 1822                   Howa
Rodgers, Levi to Morning Hains 18 Feb. 1834                         Gasc
Rodgers, Thomas to Leuvica Hubbard 12 Dec. 1833                     Howa
Rodgers, Valentine to Malinda Durbin 29 Nov. 1839                   Gasc
Rodney, John to Rachel Ramsey 3 Aug. 1815                           CG-A
Rodney, Thomas J. to Maria L. Rodney 14 May 1834                    CG-A
Roe, Alexander to Louiza Casady 13 Aug. 1832                        Coop
Roe, James to Martha Rosser 14 May 1835                             Coop
Roe, John to Susan Thompson 22 Dec. 1835                            Cole
Roebuck, Henry K. to Rosy Jenkins 7 Dec. 1837                       Rand
Roger, Thompson to Clerissa Hodges 21 Nov. 1837                     Fran
```

```
Rogers, Benj. to Matilda Manion 7 Feb. 1822                          StCh
Rogers, Chambers to Cynthia Shipman 15 Dec. 1831                     Cole
Rogers, Druey to Elizabeth Hilderbrand 21 Nov. 1839                  Jeff
Rogers, Elisha to Deborah Cowie 13 Dec. 1832                         Wash
Rogers, Francis to Nancy Collins 18 Sept. 1834                       Boon
Rogers, Geo. to Everanna Egman 28 Sept. 1837                         Cass
Rogers, Isaac to Mahala Brown 26 Oct. 1828                           StFr
Rogers, John to Susan Hunter 12 Feb. 1839                            Pk-B
Rogers, John R. to Ann Stephens 29 Dec. 1824                         Md-A
Rogers, Joseph to Mrs. Emeline Hunt 26 June 1838                     Wash
Rogers, Leonard to Eliza J. Gooch 24 July 1838                       Pk-B
Rogers, Rufus W. to Elizabeth A. Ford 23 May 1838                    Pk-B
Rogers, Thomas to Margaret Galliway 3 May 1832                       Gasc
Rogers, Thomas M. to I. James 3 Mar. 1833                            Fran
Rogers, Wm. to Mariah Fletcher 27 Feb. 1834                          Rand
Rogers, Wm. to Mary Steers 24 Apr. 1838                              Rall
Rogers, Wm. to Louisa A. Creasy 16 Dec. 1838                         Lewi
Rogers, Wm. M. to Polly Lillard 1 May 1820                           Coop
Rogers, Wm. M. to Sarah Watts 28 Mar. 1838                           Gree
Roi, Julian to Marguerite Degrarier 18 May 1835                      StCh
Rolan, Jesse to Nancy M. Isbel 29 Oct. 1835                          Wash
Rolan, Wm. to Nancy Coplan 11 Feb. 1818                              Howa
Roland, John to Ellen Phillips 26 Oct. 1837                          Boon
Roland, Peter to Matilda Reed 8 Mar. 1839                            Howa
Roland, Samuel to Emeline Schooling 25 Oct. 1832                     Boon
Roland, Thomas to Jane Hogue 9 Apr. 1833                             Lewi
Rolens, James to Susan M.F. Cole 24 Apr. 1839                        Clay
Rolinne, John to Purmelia A. Johnson 19 June 1834                    Wash
Rollin, Wm. to Susan Norman 10 Apr. 1831                             Boon
Rollin, Wm. to Lucetta Nealy 12 Feb. 1837                            Boon
Rollins, James to Mary Hickman 6 June 1837                           Boon
Rollins, Wm. to Sarah A. Rule 29 July 1832                           Clay
Rolls, James to Martha Woods 21 May 1838                             Barr
Rolls, John to Celia Cockram 25 July 1833                            Mari
Romane, Lewis to Adolphia Penman 6 Mar. 1835                         Jeff
Romine, Thomas to Phoebe Baker 17 Jan. 1826                          Jeff
Ronick, Robt. A. to Mary B. Ewing 9 Oct. 1823                        Lafa
Rood, Wm. E. to Caroline McQueen 18 Apr. 1839                        Buch
Roof, Henry to Rachel Wilkison 23 Apr. 1839                          Livi
Rook, David to Elizabeth Malicoat 17 Sept. 1839                      Polk
Rooker, Wm. G. to Elizabeth Hutchinson 12 Oct. 1830                  Howa
Rookwood, Thomas to Fidelida Dickerson 17 Dec. 1839                  Shel
Roop, David to Polly Hancock 28 June 1835                            Clay
Roque, Andre to Mme. DeBoushomme 11 Feb. 1809                        StCh
Rose, Bassel to Rebecca Ones 20 Sept. 1833                           Gree
Rose, Bluford to Violet Chapman 3 Jan. 1838                          Lafa
Rose, Bozele to Sarah Bryan 30 Mar. 1822                             Call
Rose, Ezra to Julyann McKay 14 Mar. 1833                             Clay
Rose, Freeland W. to Mary Collard 14 July 1831                       Linc
Rose, James to Deleria Zumwalt 30 Oct. 1824                          Call
Rose, John H. to Eleanor Holman 11 Nov. 1832                         Rand
Rose, Samuel to Margaret Daniel 19 May 1839                          Ripl
Ross, Alexander to Manerva Campbell 24 Mar. 1835                     Coop
Ross, Clolum to Hannah Fawbush 6 Dec. 1820                           Coop
Ross, David to Polly Houx 1 Nov. 1832                                Coop
Ross, David to Louisa Robberson 12 Mar. 1834                         Gree
Ross, David to Elizabeth Weeden 15 Feb. 1835                         Coop
Ross, David to Sarah Lemons 21 Sept. 1836                            Polk
Ross, Geo. A. to Phebe Hall 13 Apr. 1835                             Perr
Ross, Henry to Lucinda Crow 25 Dec. 1839                             StCh
Ross, James Jr. to Currilla Lewis 4 Aug. 1829                        Jack
Ross, James C. to Joanna Lowery 5 June 1839                          Coop
Ross, James F. to Mary Thompson 19 Sept. 1833                        CG-A
Ross, John to Mrs. Rachel Smith 4 May 1834                           Gree
Ross, John to Sarah A. Jones 23 Feb. 1836                            Jack
```

Ross, Lawrence to Sarah Taylor 11 Apr. 1823   StCh
Ross, Peter to Susan A. Duncan 14 May 1836   Coop
Ross, Robt. to Minerva Potter 15 Apr. 1832   Coop
Ross, Robt. S. to Rebecca Matkins 1 Dec. 1836   StFr
Ross, Shapley to Catherine Fulkerson 4 Nov. 1830   StCh
Ross, Thorret to Mary Carter 10 May 1825   Char
Ross, Wm. to Luanna Apperson 28 Dec. 1836   Cole
Ross, Wm. to Caroline Leestin 6 Aug. 1839   Maco
Rosser, Wm. to Elizabeth Sneed 8 Nov. 1838   Linc
Rosson, John to Margaret Daniel 25 June 1839   Call
Roundtree, Edwin C. to Mary Arlington 3 Oct. 1839   StCh
Rountree, Jonison M. to Marthy J. Miller 7 Aug. 1831   Cr-P
Rouse, Uriel to Nancy Tanner 30 Aug. 1838   Rall
Roussin, Charles to Ann Lore 22 Nov. 1831   Wash
Rout, Elbert G. to Ann M. Ross 13 Sept. 1838   Mari
Routh, Levin to Viletty Brown 12 Aug. 1838   Gree
Rovland, John to Martha Keeny 4 Apr. 1833   Jack
Row, Geo. to Kitty Smith 20 Feb. 1834   CG-A
Row, James to Patsy Garner 27 Feb. 1826   Ray
Row, John to Luticia Fletcher 24 Aug. 1834   Md-A
Row, Thomas to Jane Odell 12 Apr. 1830   Ray
Row, Wm. to Susannah Newkirk 7 Sept. 1837   CG-A
Rowan, John L. to Catherine Spalding 27 May 1828   Wash
Rowden, Wm. H. to Malinda C. Bailey 1 Mar. 1838   Gree
Rowhuff, James to Margaret Sharp 3 Dec. 1839   Jack
Rowland, David to Elizabeth Lee 5 Jan. 1834   Ray
Rowland, David B. to Elizabeth N. Mothershead 6 Nov. 1825   Boon
Rowland, Fredrick to Anna Kirby 28 Jan. 1823   Char
Rowland, Geo. W. to Letticia S. Walts 26 Dec. 1839   Boon
Rowland, James to Rodah Hickman 1 May 1831   Rand
Rowland, James to Elizabeth Dunaway 2 July 1839   Ray
Rowland, Jesse D. to Mary P. Lemon 21 Mar. 1839   Ray
Rowland, Rhyley C. to Catherine Areteman 16 Jan. 1834   Ray
Rowland, Robt. to Jane Turner 7 Sept. 1824   Boon
Rowland, Thomas to Clarissa A. Schooling 15 Sept. 1839   Boon
Rowland, Wm. to Elizabeth Holdman 28 Jan. 1823   Char
Rowland, Wm. to Sindy Bozwell 26 Feb. 1829   Rand
Rowland, Wm. to Mary C. Roush 26 Feb. 1837   Monr
Rowland, Winburn to Emeline Hammett 9 Jan. 1834   Rand
Rowland, Y.W. to Elizabeth Rowland 29 Nov. 1839   Rand
Rowson, Jeremiah to Mahala Walker 8 Feb. 1827   Cole
Roy, Andrew to Temperance Shivers 15 June 1831   Call
Roy, Andrew to Margaret Dunica 4 May 1835   Gasc
Roy, Charles to Mary M. Mattingly 14 May 1833   Perr
Roy, Francis to Lucille Degranier 27 Jan. 1839   StCh
Roy, James to Jane Summers 20 Mar. 1834   CG-A
Roy, Jean Bte. to Cecile R. Tayon 29 June 1807   StCh
Roy, John to Jane Peterson 16 Mar. 1837   CG-A
Roy, Louis to Julie Rogers 4 July 1807   StCh
Rubey, Henry to Winifred W. Ewing 28 Feb. 1822   Coop
Rubey, Henry H. to Mary A. Carson 15 Oct. 1839   Coop
Rubey, Phillip to Ann Burnett 22 Sept. 1838   Henr
Rubey, Samuel G. to Elizabeth Alison 6 Nov. 1827   Pk-1
Rubey, Thomas B. to Elizabeth A. Hannah 1 Dec. 1835   Rand
Rubey, Urban E. to Catherine Cockrel 18 Feb. 1830   Coop
Rubey, Wm. to June J. Ewing 6 Sept. 1821   Coop
Ruble, Thomas B. to Charlotte M. Fulton 6 Sept. 1838   Clin
Rubottom, Pleasant to Jeane Robinson 6 June 1815   CG-1
Rucker, Anthony G. to Temperance Sharp 25 Feb. 1836   Monr
Rucker, Jeremiah to Elizabeth Burris 12 Oct. 1837   Howa
Rucker, Wm. to Verinda Tayler 30 Mar. 1831   Howa
Rucker, Wilton to Martha Lively 14 Nov. 1839   Pett
Rudd, Thomas to Elizabeth Kelly 4 Jan. 1838   Mari
Rudd, W.H. to Elizabeth Snead 12 Apr. 1838   Mari
Ruddel, Stephen to Rachel Wood 6 Apr. 1834   Linc

194

Rudeloff, John M.F. to Mrs. Juliane Schnidit 28 Aug. 1839   Perr
Rudisel, David to Lydia Sydes 15 Aug. 1833   CG-A
Rudolf, Charles to Margaretta Miller 14 Oct. 1839   StCh
Ruffner, J.P. to Jenetta Wiseman 13 Oct. 1835   Boon
Ruggles, Benj. to Ann Kennedy 4 Mar. 1832   Wash
Ruggles, Edmund L. to Rebecky Smith 27 Feb. 1835   Ripl
Ruggles, Elijah S. to Lora L. England 3 Apr. 1832   Wash
Rul, Deniel G. to Elizabeth Boone 9 June 1836   Pk-1
Ruland, John to Ann F. Wells 28 Dec. 1818   StCh
Rule, Nelson to Eliza Loony 5 Aug. 1833   Gree
Rule, Press G. to Judith Stanton 18 May 1826   Fran
Rule, Thomas to Clerissa Pence 13 Sept. 1832   Clay
Rule, Wm. to Caroline Donly 12 June 1831   Rall
Rummons, James to Polly Evans 27 Oct. 1828   Boon
Rummons, John to Juliet Pringle 24 Dec. 1833   Warr
Rummons, Samuel to Elizabeth Turner 14 Nov. 1833   Boon
Rummons, Samuel to Parmelia Corlin 25 June 1836   Boon
Rummons, Stephen to Susan Eastin 31 Mar. 1831   Boon
Rummons, Wm. to Matilda Donohoe 30 Sept. 1833   Boon
Runkle, Mathew to Elisa J. Miner 4 July 1838   Char
Runkle, Wm. to Elizabeth McKamey 19 Dec. 1831   Monr
Runnels, Hue B. to Frances Harlis 23 Nov. 1837   Clay
Runnels, Levi W. to Elizabeth Harlis 7 Dec. 1837   Clay
Runnels, Michael to Nancy Taylor 30 June 1822   Cole
Runnels, Russel to Fanny Monroe 23 Nov. 1817   Howa
Runnels, Wm. to Elizabeth Smith 1 Oct. 1835   Clay
Runnolds, Alfred to Elizabeth Heather 22 May 1834   Morg
Runols, Richard to Rachel Zumwalt 24 Apr. 1823   Call
Rupe, David to Phebe Demasters 27 Mar. 1825   Lafa
Rupe, Gilead to Jane Maxwell 31 Dec. 1826   Lafa
Rupe, John to Katherine Kelly 8 Apr. 1824   Lafa
Rupe, Wm. to Sally Horn 1 Aug. 1822   Lafa
Rupert, Thomas to Rebecca Newsom 17 Apr. 1838   Call
Ruple, Henry to LoBina Clay 31 Mar. 1818   StCh
Russ, John to Eliza Paterson 5 Apr. 1838   Wash
Russel, Miles M. to Sarah Fannon 25 Aug. 1836   Gree
Russel, Nathan Sr. to Elizabeth Guinn 25 May 1826   Lafa
Russel, Robinson to Minerva A. McCombs 27 Dec. 1836   CG-A
Russel, Wm. H. to Harriott E. Warder 9 June 1835   Lafa
Russell, Abraham F. to Jane A.M. Boice 9 Nov. 1834   Cole
Russell, Adam to Avena Bramel 19 Feb. 1835   Fran
Russell, Andrew to Morman Martin 8 Aug. 1819   Coop
Russell, Andrew to Amarinto Maize 2 Oct. 1839   CG-B
Russell, John to Nancy Allee 2 Sept. 1830   Coop
Russell, John to Rebecca Griden 22 May 1838   Polk
Russell, Joseph to Elizabeth Gray 17 Mar. 1821   Boon
Russell, Joseph to Permelia A. Clark 11 Feb. 1830   Cole
Russell, Levi to Nancy Bledsoe 18 Jan. 1828   Jack
Russell, Levi to Percilla Rookard 19 Feb. 1839   Barr
Russell, Patterson to Sarah Hirsh 15 Apr. 1824   Boon
Russell, Wm. S. to Sarah White 26 Oct. 1826   Jeff
Rustin, Jacob to Lucinda Shurlay 23 Apr. 1837   Cole
Ruth, Hugh to Elizabeth Brown 25 July 1839   Polk
Rutherford, Hayden to Casandria Goggin 30 Aug. 1836   Rand
Rutherford, Joseph to Sabree Posey 13 May 1838   Rand
Rutherford, Merriman to Nancy Orr 22 Oct. 1835   Pk-1
Rutherford, Wm. to Jane Jahs 4 May 1822   Call
Rutherford, Wm. to Phebe J. Dameron 19 July 1838   Rand
Rutherford, Wm. P. to Phoebe Dillard 29 Dec. 1835   Coop
Rutledge, Isaac to Elizabeth Lynch 1 Aug. 1831   Jeff
Rutledge, Isam to Ann Drybread 23 Apr. 1829   Jeff
Rutledge, James to Margaret Scott 18 Aug. 1839   Lafa
Rutledge, James A. to Frances Farrar 26 Feb. 1835   Perr
Rutluf, Geo. to Cecilia Winkler 24 Dec. 1838   Perr
Rutter, Chambers to Nancy Hornback 27 Dec. 1834   Rall

Rutter, John to Matilda McCarty 18 Apr. 1819   CG-1
Ruyle, Gideon to Polly Looney 3 Aug. 1837   Polk
Ryan, John to Susan Botts 26 Sept. 1837   Livi
Ryburn, Lewis to Ann M. Graves 5 Sept. 1837   Boon

Sadler, Henry F. to Adeline Davis 26 Aug. 1830   CG-A
Sadler, Labon to Elvira Dunlap 13 May 1830   CG-A
Safferins, John to Matilda Bevel 1 Jan. 1833   Howa
Safford, John to Huldah Shropshire 15 Mar. 1832   Mari
Sagers, Harrison to Lucinda Madison 22 Dec. 1834   Clay
Sago, John to Sally Crump 19 July 1827   StFr
Sailing, ---- to Esther Coil 14 Nov. 1824   Cole
Sailing, Clark to Mary Poster 13 Dec. 1835   Cole
Sailing, John to Polly Padget 2 Oct. 1829   Cole
St. Eber, Noel to Eliza McCoy 21 July 1828   StCh
St. Gemme, Bartholmew to Mary A. DeGuire 15 Apr. 1831   Md-A
St. Marie, Samuel to Felicit_ Bourassas 6 Feb. 1837   Wash
Saky, Joel J. to Elizabeth Stapp 4 Aug. 1836   Howa
Salier, John B. to Therese Morain 30 Oct. 1827   StCh
Saling, James to Elizabeth Rice 10 Oct. 1839   Monr
Saling, Jefferson to Catherine Hust 27 Apr. 1828   Rall
Saling, Liggett S. to Mary A. Rigsby 18 Jan. 1838   Maco
Saling, Richmond to Frances Burton 12 May 1825   Rall
Saling, Rumsey to Matilda Snow 3 May 1829   Rall
Saling, Wm. to Nancy Snow 22 Feb. 1824   Boon
Saling, Wm. to Mary Williams 3 May 1824   Coop
Salisburry, Samuel to Milly Wallace 2 Sept. 1832   Cole
Sallee, Benj. to Susan Cooley 14 Dec. 1835   Pk-1
Sallee, Thomas to Margaret Games 9 July 1834   Call
Sallens, Sterling to Elizabeth Penn 17 Mar. 1837   Polk
Sallie, Isaac to Lucinda Baugh 20 Apr. 1828   StCh
Sally, Wm. to Emily Bowles 13 Aug. 1839   Bent
Salnis, John to Sarah Kaisy 9 Dec. 1839   Gree
Salor, John to Virginia Pirkins 17 Oct. 1833   Call
Sampson, Benj. to Elizabeth Mansfield 2 Apr. 1830   Clay
Sampson, Geo. to Emeline E. Fry 18 Sept. 1832   Wash
Sams, Burdit to Sarah Lockett 8 May 1831   Mari
Sams, Joseph to Nancy A. Yater 6 July 1837   Mari
Samuel, Geo. to Rebecca Todd 13 Mar. 1838   Boon
Samuel, Priestly to Sarah Morrison 19 Nov. 1828   Howa
Samuel, Richard to Lucy Marrs 17 Mar. 1825   Boon
Samuel, Robt. to Martha Overton 5 Nov. 1829   Call
Samuel, Willis to Adelia Hansborough 7 Apr. 1831   Mari
Samuels, James to Margaret Jefferson 22 July 1828   Boon
Sander, Wm. to Elizabeth Wells 30 Aug. 1839   Ray
Sanders, Bryant to Sally Byram 13 Sept. 1838   Lafa
Sanders, Daniel to Mary Numan 18 Jan. 1830   Howa
Sanders, David to Alesey Sikes 23 Nov. 1837   Shel
Sanders, Drury to Elizabeth Colvin 4 Jan. 1834   Boon
Sanders, James to Mary Williams 30 Dec. 1832   Wash
Sanders, James to Martha A. Todd 22 Mar. 1835   Clay
Sanders, James to Mary A. Zankey 29 Apr. 1837   Pett
Sanders, Lewis to Susan R. Gough 8 Feb. 1838   Monr
Sanders, Reece to Hannah White 29 Dec. 1830   Howa
Sanders, Stephen to Narcissa Brooks 15 Feb. 1832   Perr
Sanders, Thomas to Letitia Breckenridge 25 May 1837   Call
Sanders, Wm. to Saly Moore 2 Dec. 1835   Monr
Sanders, Wm. to Elizabeth Gaines 11 Dec. 1838   Monr
Sanders, Wm. to Juliann Matlock 6 June 1839   Cr-1
Sanderson, Benj. to Tempay Fay 21 Jan. 1838   Char
Sanderson, Edward to Rosanna Graham 12 Feb. 1835   Ray
Sandford, Joel to Elizabeth Williams 12 Jan. 1834   Clay
Sandlin, Barnet to Cyntha Sandlin 5 May 1839   Perr
Sandlin, John to Sarah McDelany 10 Aug. 1833   Gree

Sandusky, Luderick to Narcissa Taylor 17 Oct. 1838 Wash
Sanford, Callinthenes to Mary Thompson 28 Dec. 1830 Linc
Sanford, Charles O. to Mary Taylor 31 Mar. 1836 Lewi
Sangster, Arbuckle S. to Eliza J. Hamilton 6 June 1839 Call
Sansberry, Wm. H. to Elizabeth Estes 18 Apr. 1832 Cole
Sansouci, Joseph to Elesie Maryotte 5 Jan. 1836 Wash
Santee, Geo. to Elizabeth Sebastian 21 Sept. 1830 StFr
Santee, Joseph to Charlotte Williams 5 Jan. 1837 StFr
Sap, Peater to Patience Wells 22 Nov. 1831 Pk-1
Sap, Thomas to Nancy Sap 30 Sept. 1827 Boon
Sapaugh, Jesse to Polly Bullinger 25 Feb. 1830 CG-A
Sapp, Wm. to Martha Lile 21 Sept. 1836 Ray
Sappington, Fielding to Anna Cahill 14 Oct. 1829 Fran
Sappington, John to Rebecca Wilcoxen 8 Feb. 1830 Boon
Sappington, James to Nancy Cooper 22 Mar. 1821 Howa
Sargent, Philip M. to Margaret Hicklin 13 Jan. 1822 Rall
Sarsey, John to Mary May 27 Sept. 1827 Perr
Sartar, Peter to Martha Enoch 27 Jan. 1839 Mill
Sarters, Henry S. to Nancy Bass 12 June 1835 Coop
Sartin, Wright to Milly M. Wilson 9 May 1839 Howa
Satterfield, John to Esther L. Hill 2 Apr. 1839 Polk
Saucier, Charles to Placide DeLisle 24 Apr. 1817 StCh
Saucier, Frederick to Pelazie Roussin 16 June 1835 Wash
Saucier, Henry A. to Tabitha Ranney 1 Jan. 1828 StCh
Saucier, J. Bte. to Marguerite LePage 28 Dec. 1828 StCh
Saulsbury, Samuel to Christianna Wilson 19 July 1836 Call
Saunders, Henry to Nancy Heathman 26 Oct. 1837 Monr
Saunders, Joseph to Mrs. Elizabeth McClay 1 Feb. 1838 StCh
Saunders, Robt. to Sally Magill 26 Sept. 1839 Clin
Sausse, Christopher to Euphrosyne Kreig 3 Jan. 1836 StCh
Savage, Britton to Mrs. Rachel Linch 22 Sept. 1828 Jack
Savage, James to Mary Stephens 30 Jan. 1817 Howa
Savage, James R. to Louisa Jamison 11 Mar. 1838 Polk
Savage, John to Casander Stephens 29 Jan. 1825 Coop
Savage, John M. to Cinthy J. Crawford 2 Apr. 1830 Coop
Savage, Samuel C. to Elizabeth L. Brown 5 June 1836 Pk-1
Sawyer, Richard to Jemima Fletcher 7 Sept. 1834 Jack
Saxbe, Peter to Mary Obuchon 16 Aug. 1830 StCh
Saybaugh, Daniel to Elizabeth Stadler 15 Apr. 1827 CG-A
Saybaugh, Jesse to Susanna Yount 3 July 1831 CG-A
Saylor, Sydney H. to Louisa A. Ragsdale 29 Mar. 1838 Clar
Scags, Thomas to Elizabeth C. Cunningham 14 June 1836 Gree
Scalf, John to Malinda Wood 17 Jan. 1837 Lewi
Scarburough, James to Emily Ellis 8 Feb. 1835 CG-B
Schaberg, Gerhard H. to Maria E. Vonderhasse 25 Aug. 1833 StCh
Schawless, Thomas to Dicy Dale 20 Dec. 1821 Boon
Schemme, J.H. to Catherine M. Wieligman 16 July 1836 StCh
Schmattz, Lewis to Elizabeth Cambren 10 Feb. 1835 Perr
Schmedding, John to Lucetta Wolbert 16 Nov. 1839 Henr
Schmettgens, Franz to Margretha Wannch 27 Feb. 1839 StCh
Schofield, Thomas to Margaret Reed 31 Jan. 1833 Mari
Schofield, Wm. to Belinda Shobe 25 Dec. 1835 Mari
Scholl, Joseph to Eliza Broughton 24 Feb. 1831 Call
Schooling, Drury to Ivy Fountain 6 Mar. 1834 Boon
Schooling, James to Mary Lason 24 Jan. 1836 Howa
Schools, Francis to Lisabeth Isaak 1 May 1829 Perr
Schoppenhorst, Wilh. to Alaria Peterjohans 5 Apr. 1835 StCh
Schoultz, Jesse to Ann Hickman 14 Dec. 1826 CG-A
Schrivner, Elcand to Mrs. Sarah Walden 19 June 1839 Rand
Schrump, Nicholas to Mary A. Klump 10 Feb. 1835 Perr
Schulse, Wm. F.W. to Catharine Wisthabe 18 Aug. 1839 Gasc
Schulz, Andraes to Angelike Perschlacher 4 Mar. 1838 StCh
Scobee, Lewis to Nancy Dale 15 Jan. 1828 Rall
Scobee, Robt. to Mary Upton 20 Aug. 1835 Rall
Scobee, Stephen to Frances Wood 1 Sept. 1829 Rall

Scoby, John to Polly Haynes 25 Dec. 1832   Call
Scoby, Wesley to Lydia Orr 30 Mar. 1837   Pk-A
Scofield, Henry to Betsy Green 27 Apr. 1823   Rall
Scoggin, Nathaniel to Sally Love 28 July 1836   Pk-1
Scoly, Stinson to Hannah Haynes 28 Dec. 1837   Boon
Sconce, John to Rachel Ramley 12 Jan. 1826   Ray
Scot, John to Nancy Burgan 24 Aug. 1837   John
Scott, Andrew to Jane Rackerby 2 Sept. 1824   Rall
Scott, Archibald M. to Eliza A. Orr 7 Nov. 1833   Howa
Scott, Arthur to Sally Fuqua 21 May 1839   Rall
Scott, Asa to Polly Pepper 3 Nov. 1836   Fran
Scott, David to Caty Woods 9 July 1820   Howa
Scott, David to Lucretia Jobe 26 June 1828   Cole
Scott, Davis to Nancy Embree 24 Apr. 1828   Howa
Scott, Geo. W. to Nancy Dodge 28 Dec. 1822   StGe
Scott, Isaac C. to Jane Camplin -- Sept. 1839   Boon
Scott, James to Elizabeth Purdom 23 June 1829   Pk-1
Scott, James to Susan Kinne 19 Apr. 1835   Clay
Scott, James to Nancy Stricklen 4 Feb. 1836   Warr
Scott, James to Rachel Clark 19 Aug. 1839   Char
Scott, John to Hannah Brady 20 Sept. 1824   StGe
Scott, John to Charlotte Meek 26 Jan. 1825   Ray
Scott, John to Margaret Givens 20 Jan. 1831   Pk-1
Scott, John to Sarah A. Durbin 24 Apr. 1838   Lewi
Scott, John to Mary Shrigby 3 Dec. 1839   Livi
Scott, John B. to Evaline Campbell 27 June 1833   Wash
Scott, John C. to Louisaney Fisher 3 May 1826   StFr
Scott, Joshua B. to Permelia Phepher 15 May 1831   StCh
Scott, Leonard to Eliza Clark 16 June 1836   Lafa
Scott, Matthew to Elizabeth J. Burns 11 Feb. 1836   Call
Scott, Merrit to Elizabeth Prewitt 21 May 1833   Howa
Scott, Milton to Betsey Richardson 1 Oct. 1835   Rall
Scott, Samuel to Sarah Thompson 22 Feb. 1821   Howa
Scott, Thomas to Nancy Sailing 15 Apr. 1824   Cole
Scott, Thomas P. to Emily Boone 11 June 1839   StCh
Scott, Walker B. to Louisianna Moody 13 Sept. 1827   StCh
Scott, Wm. to Frances Ormsby 13 Jan. 1830   Cr-P
Scott, Wm. to ---- Anderson 16 June 1833   Pett
Scott, Wm. to Elizabeth Dixon 25 June 1835   Cole
Scraggs, Hank to Louisa Mahan 20 Mar. 1834   Coop
Scritchfield, Garlan L. to Permalia Boyd 22 Aug. 1833   Coop
Scritchfield, Lewis to Nancy Rout 6 June 1839   Rand
Scritchfield, Samuel to Nancy Henderson 3 Apr. 1834   Rand
Scroghum, Thomas to Susan Harryford 28 Mar. 1839   Call
Scruggs, Lewis to Ann Stubblefield 24 July 1828   Cole
Seabaugh, Allen to Barbary Statler 25 June 1835   CG-B
Seabaugh, Christopher to Mary Hartle 11 Aug. 1818   CG-1
Seals, John K. to Thursey Chase 5 Jan. 1836   Gasc
Sealy, David J. to Melissa Land 4 May 1837   CG-A
Sealy, Wm. to Smithy Williams 13 May 1829   CG-A
Seaman, John to Unicy I. Crooks 2 Feb. 1837   Lewi
Seamon, Harrison to Louisa Bates 21 Nov. 1839   Lewi
Searcigran, Wm. to Angeline C. Olive 20 Feb. 1833   Wash
Searcy, Edward to Judith Gibbony 7 July 1831   Mari
Searcy, Gallatin to Margaret M. Robertson 19 July 1836   Clay
Searcy, John to Mrs. Elizabeth Witt 10 July 1838   Rall
Searcy, John M. to Elizabeth J. Empson 27 Sept. 1837   Rand
Sears, Henry to Patsy Fullington 6 July 1831   Rand
Sears, Jacob to Christy Slagle 7 Jan. 1836   Polk
Sears, John to Polly Jacks 12 Sept. 1822   Howa
Sears, John to Dorcus Prigman 3 Dec. 1835   Henr
Sears, Joseph to Elizabeth Loe 23 Oct. 1817   Howa
Sears, Joseph to Elizabeth Kerby 17 June 1821   Howa
Sears, Washington to Susanna Rowland 29 Nov. 1835   Rand
Sears, Wiley to Elizabeth Grace 10 Feb. 1825   Char

198

```
Sears, Wiley to Nancy Beals 28 Mar. 1830                       Rand
Sears, Wm. to Sally Kerby 13 Apr. 1823                         Char
Sears, Willis to Elizabeth Jackson 5 Nov. 1839                 Rand
Seavers, Adamiram to Jane DeLashmutt 3 Feb. 1831              CG-A
Seavers, Nicholas to Arramitta Howard 20 Jan. 1831           CG-A
Sebastian, Edwin C. to Artimesia E. Pettit 4 Dec. 1836        StFr
Sebastian, Jeremiah V. to Harriet Green 2 Mar. 1837          StFr
Sebastian, Moses to Peggy Santee 6 Oct. 1829                  Md-A
Sebaugh, Henry to Matilda Hahn 12 July 1839                   CG-B
Sebaugh, Levi to Sarah Hahn 17 Mar. 1839                      CG-B
Sebery, Edmon to Laticha Caps 26 Apr. 1838                    Clay
Sebo, Jacob to Elizabeth Petree 24 Jan. 1836                  Ray
Sebough, Joseph to Elizabeth Ferguson 30 July 1839           Pett
Sebree, John P. to Louisa Daly 21 Nov. 1839                  Howa
See, Benj. to Ann West 5 Jan. 1826                            Rall
See, Henry to Esther A. Burditt 25 Apr. 1839                  Monr
See, James to Lear Culbertson 26 June 1839                    Mari
See, Wm. to Elizabeth Martin 10 Oct. 1839                     Rall
Seely, Geo. to Betsy Shelby 17 Feb. 1814                      StCh
Seely, Isaac to Rebecca White 9 Jan. 1827                     Rall
Seely, Samuel G. to Ann E. Prim 17 Jan. 1833                 CG-A
Seeth, John to Polly Walker 17 June 1827                      Coop
Segraves, Custis to Emily Forbes 6 Sept. 1837                 Coop
Segraves, Marshall to Lucinda Glass 18 June 1827             Lafa
Seignor, David to Betsy Tilford 10 Feb. 1829                  Boon
Seignor, Samuel to Susan Matthews 4 Oct. 1827                Boon
Seinor, John R. to Nancy Rapp 7 Sept. 1834                    Gree
Seitz, W. Eli to Vicey Seitz 5 May 1828                       Md-A
Selby, Charles to Polly Phillips 11 Nov. 1837                Gasc
Selby, Jesse to Elizabeth Hereford 5 Nov. 1828               Call
Selby, Thomas to Elizabeth Collins 29 Mar. 1832             Boon
Selby, Wm. P. to Amanda P. Anderson 12 Mar. 1836            Call
Self, David to Patsey Cotner 11 Jan. 1829                    CG-A
Semino, Francis to Elizabeth Campbell 29 June 1824           StGe
Senor, Peter to Hannah Frost 10 Apr. 1825                     Clay
Sensebaugh, Robt. to Elizabeth Blevins 18 Apr. 1830         Lafa
Seoct, Slement to Julia Roi 13 June 1829                      Jack
Sepaugh, Peter to Sarah Hartle 7 Feb. 1828                   CG-A
Sercy, Francis D. to Nancy Dotey 17 Mar. 1836               Howa
Settlemyers, David to Katharine Bess 2 Oct. 1827            CG-A
Sevenenger, Joseph to Nancy Short 2 Mar. 1824              Boon
Sevier, Henry C. to Frances Mason 22 May 1825              Howa
Sevier, Robt. to Ann H. Sibley 24 Mar. 1831                  StCh
Sewell, Joshua A. to Patsy Poage -- Sept. 1822             Boon
Sewell, Newton to Nancy Stringfellow 15 Sept. 1829         Boon
Sewell, Wm. to Sarah Beasley 15 Sept. 1829                  Boon
Sexton, Charles E. to Elizabeth Gentry 29 Nov. 1835        Boon
Sexton, Geo. to Ann Orear 15 Apr. 1834                      Boon
Sexton, Ishar to Louisa Abbey 1 May 1827                    Boon
Sexton, James to Perlina Hulen 11 Feb. 1830                 Boon
Sexton, James to Sarah Faucher 9 Oct. 1839                  Barr
Sexton, Jonathan to Margaret Orr 29 Aug. 1839              Clar
Sexton, Samuel to Ann Turner 10 Feb. 1831                   Boon
Sexton, Thomas to Vidilla Roberts 1 June 1839              Boon
Seymour, Wm. to Elizabeth Alexander 29 Oct. 1839           Boon
Shackleford, James to Eliza Miller 4 Sept. 1837            CG-A
Shackleford, Jas. to Mary Arnold 20 Aug. 1838               Clay
Shackleford, Ryland to Alley McGinness 25 Dec. 1832         Clay
Shackley, Isaiah to Nancy Clark 11 Oct. 1821                Char
Shadden, John to Polly Elkins 20 Jan. 1839                  Rand
Shafer, Joseiah to Mary Crumet 22 Mar. 1838                 Clay
Shaffet, Jacob to Keziah Smallwood 15 Dec. 1836            Lewi
Shahoney, James to Fanny Carter 8 Mar. 1832                Rall
Shanklin, Jefferson to Zanippa Lampton 6 Apr. 1837         Coop
Shanks, Hanible W. to Sarah E. Philips 19 Aug. 1834        Mari
```

Shanks, Joseph to Patsy Davis 9 Aug. 1832   Pk-1
Shannon, Andrew to Nancy Maggard 17 Feb. 1838   Rand
Shannon, John to Alcey J. Nelson 2 June 1836   Mari
Shannon, John to Elizabeth Oens 30 Aug. 1837   Polk
Shannon, Robt. M. to Maria J. Sleed 21 Mar. 1833   Md-A
Shannon, Samuel to Elizabeth Little 3 Jan. 1828   Boon
Shannon, Thomas J. to Eliza Short 23 Sept. 1835   Mari
Sharer, Willis to Sally Vaughn 6 July 1832   Clay
Sharp, Andrew to Sarah Calvert 3 Sept. 1835   Coop
Sharp, Anthony to Charlot Walker 17 Aug. 1825   Md-A
Sharp, James H. to Hannah Austin 11 Jan. 1827   Boon
Sharp, John to Susan Shortridge 23 May 1839   Monr
Sharp, Josiah to Sally Walker 28 Apr. 1830   CG-A
Sharp, Lewis to Jane Callaway 6 Mar. 1832   Boon
Sharp, Lewis to Sarah Anthony 8 Dec. 1833   Boon
Sharp, Richard to Mary Safford 6 Mar. 1832   Mari
Sharp, Wm. to Sally Jeffries 1 Sept. 1836   Clay
Sharp, Willis to Elizabeth Mitchell 20 Nov. 1836   Clay
Shattock, Hiram to Elizabeth Stark 4 Jan. 1824   Howa
Shave, John to Elizabeth Norton 24 Dec. 1835   Linc
Shaver, John to Sally Utterback 20 Dec. 1832   Rall
Shaver, John to Eleanor F. Lipp 30 May 1839   Rall
Shaver, Peter to Sarah W. Johnson 1 Oct. 1835   Wash
Shaver, Washington to Eliza Lincoln 13 Mar. 1834   Clay
Shaw, Bethuel to Susanna Smith 10 Mar. 1832   Linc
Shaw, David to Susan Cook 31 Jan. 1839   Morg
Shaw, Geo. to Narcissa Smith 14 Mar. 1839   Clin
Shaw, Geo. W. to Cynthia A. Minor 20 Dec. 1832   Howa
Shaw, Gidiun to Elizabeth Bess 4 Nov. 1838   Perr
Shaw, James to Polly Higgins 14 Oct. 1827   Clay
Shaw, James to Eliza Bevins 24 May 1836   Shel
Shaw, James to Nancy Riggs 15 Aug. 1837   Linc
Shaw, John to Jane Hood 14 Feb. 1832   Coop
Shaw, John to Elizabeth Davis 12 Sept. 1833   Pk-1
Shaw, Robt. to Polina Noble 8 Nov. 1832   Howa
Shaw, Robt. to Catharine Reed 12 Oct. 1837   Linc
Shaw, Samuel to Ann Thomson 17 July 1819   StCh
Shaw, Scott to Mary J. Thompson 12 Jan. 1836   Pk-1
Shaw, Wm. to Sarah Gilliam 14 June 1822   Clay
Shaw, Wm. to Nancy Potter 10 Sept. 1835   Clay'
Shawner, Alexander to Narcissa Kerby 13 May 1837   Maco
Shearer, Hysam to Eliza Creek 27 May 1827   Jack
Shearl, Daniel to Rebeckah Drummonds 23 Aug. 1834   StCh
Shehonney, Wm. P. to Verlinda Benn 19 Jan. 1837   Pk-1
Sheilds, John G. to Elizabeth Emmerson 29 Jan. 1835   Pk-1
Shelby, Geo. to Margaret Tunage 23 Feb. 1821   Lafa
Shelby, John to Nancy Berry 2 Dec. 1830   Linc
Shelby, Joshua to Ann Shelby 4 Mar. 1832   Boon
Shelby, Peter to Adaline H. Adams 25 Feb. 1839   Coop
Shelby, Reuben to Mary Beavios 13 Oct. 1839   Perr
Shelby, Ruben to Sarah A. Flynn 3 Sept. 1836   Perr
Shelby, Thomas C. to Nancy H. Gordon 18 Jan. 1838   Lafa
Sheley, James to Mary A. Smart 8 Nov. 1837   Call
Sheley, Singleton to Jane Christwell 18 Feb. 1834   Call
Shell, Benj. to Elizabeth Bollinger 13 Apr. 1807   CG-A
Shell, Daniel to Betsy Banks 10 Dec. 1829   CG-A
Shell, Frederick to Mary Deck 23 Feb. 1837   CG-A
Shell, Geo. H. to Mary Cravens 7 Jan. 1834   CG-A
Shell, Henry to Sarah Welker 20 Jan. 1831   CG-A
Shell, John to Fanny Hahn 12 Sept. 1819   CG-1
Shellhorse, Wm. to Betsey Griffith 20 Jan. 1835   Pk-1
Shelton, Absalom to Nancy Alexander 27 June 1839   CG-B
Shelton, Afgey to Nancy Shooman 14 Oct. 1836   Fran
Shelton, Albert to Eliza Gardner 25 Dec. 1839   Henr
Shelton, David to Elizabeth Greenup 15 Apr. 1832   Cole

200

```
Shelton, David to Frances Wilson 30 May 1837                          Clin
Shelton, Fillmon to Elizabeth Rodes 12 June 1839                      Buch
Shelton, Griffith D. to Levina Parris 7 Apr. 1825                     Rall
Shelton, James to Jane Carter 6 Dec. 1832                             StCh
Shelton, John to Nancy Doggett 3 May 1838                             Fran
Shelton, Levi to Christina Rhoads 30 Aug. 1838                        Clin
Shelton, Merryman to Elizabeth Holman 28 July 1831                    Ray
Shelton, Peter to Martha Cockran 7 Nov. 1831                          Linc
Shelton, Peter R. to Martha R. Wade 19 Dec. 1839                      Linc
Shelton, Samuel to Prudy Miller 25 Jan. 1831                          Fran
Shelton, Solomon to Judith Nichols 19 Mar. 1839                       Buch
Shelton, Willis to Nancy Elston 30 Aug. 1821                          Call
Shelton, Zebedee to Lavina Miller 11 Oct. 1829                        Fran
Shemy, Amassa to Susannah Collans 28 July 1834                        Gasc
Sheperd, Elijah to Rebecca Yates 22 Mar. 1829                         Jack
Shepherd, Craven to Susan Mitchell 15 Dec. 1836                       Mari
Shepherd, Jasper to Matilda Weimer 8 Sept. 1839                       Mill
Shepherd, Samuel to Charity Swartout 7 June 1835                      Clay
Sheppard, James R. to Sally James 2 Mar. 1818                         Howa
Sherell, Joel to Jincy Thornton 2 Oct. 1836                          Cr-1
Sherman, Daniel to Sylvia J. Bewly 11 Jan. 1838                       StCh
Sherman, John to Martha Fray 22 Jan. 1835                             Howa
Sherman, Thomas to Mildred Buchly 5 Feb. 1839                         Warr
Sherman, Wm. S. to Eliza Heath -- -- 1836                             Coop
Shernwell, Thomas to Nancy Bone 6 Jan. 1835                           Coop
Sherrer, Jacob to Elisabeth Seibert 11 June 1829                      Perr
Sherrer, Wm. to Rebecca Spurgeon 26 Mar. 1838                         Barr
Sherron, Aaron to Mary Summers 29 Oct. 1835                          Rand
Sherry, John to Clare F. Hamilton 12 Jan. 1823                        Perr
Shestri, Joseph to Marie L. Uno 13 July 1808                          StCh
Shevers, Stephen to Susan Hicks 28 July 1822                          Howa
Shewk, Jacob to Elisibeath Ashabraner 18 Feb. 1806                    CG-1
Shibley, Henry to Eliza A.M. Boyd 12 Feb. 1839                        Rall
Shickett, Henry to Marcia Lowacol 22 Nov. 1830                        Jack
Shidders, James to Tempy Rogers 5 Mar. 1827                           Wash
Shields, Francis to Lucinda Deatherage 12 Oct. 1826                   Howa
Shields, Henry to Caroline Morris 7 Aug. 1838                         StCh
Shields, Hugh to Nancy Todd 12 Oct. 1826                              Howa
Shields, James to Mariah Cirkpatrick 22 Nov. 1832                     Wash
Shields, John to Louisa Talbot 1 Apr. 1837                            Boon
Shiflett, Coalby to Peggy Benge 28 Aug. 1834                          Howa
Shiflett, Thomas to Ale Hines 23 July 1839                            Howa
Shiflett, Wallis to Nancy Standley 5 Aug. 1838                        Howa
Shin, Wm. to Mary J. Altman 15 Apr. 1834                             Rand
Ship, Richard to Sarah J. Gates 27 Jan. 1832                          Rand
Shipley, Esquire to Calista P. South 15 Nov. 1838                     Boon
Shipley, Geo. to Elizabeth Ellice 25 Mar. 1830                        Coop
Shipley, Robt. to Charlotte Mulkey 17 Nov. 1836                       Cole
Shipman, Abraham to Hetty Garrison 7 May 1835                        Cr-1
Shipman, Calvin to Nagoney Brannans 2 Nov. 1837                       Ripl
Shipman, Geo. to Clarinda Perkins 14 June 1832                        Cole
Shipman, Matthew to Matilday Brickley 16 Apr. 1835                    Cr-1
Shipp, Benj. H. to Silvey Baloo 24 Aug. 1822                          Howa
Shipp, John R. to Louisa Irwin 27 Mar. 1839                           Linc
Shipp, Wm. to Lydia Knaus 12 July 1832                                Howa
Shirley, James to Maria Sexton 10 Feb. 1831                           Boon
Shirley, James A. to Martha J. Hayden 21 Nov. 1833                    Howa
Shirley, Jesse to Elizabeth Miller 17 Dec. 1835                       Coop
Shirley, John to Louisa Kent 5 Sept. 1837                             StCh
Shirley, Wm. to Ann Hoof 17 Dec. 1829                                 Coop
Shivers, Wm. to Nancy Perry 10 Jan. 1829                              Gasc
Shives, Daniel to Margaret Mayberry 17 Feb. 1836                      Carr
Shobe, Archibald to Susannah Bryan 9 Sept. 1830                       StCh
Shobe, Jonas to Elizabeth Hughes 26 Dec. 1824                         Gasc
Shobwall, Albert to Catharine Greery 13 Feb. 1836                     Howa
```

Shock, Hector to Sarah A. Jackson 15 Mar. 1826   Boon
Shock, Henry to Polly Jackson 12 Sept. 1825   Boon
Shock, Henry to Hannah Cox 6 Sept. 1838   Boon
Shock, Wm. to Rebecca Evan 6 Sept. 1838   Boon
Shockley, Henry to Mahaly Christman 20 Feb. 1834   Gasc
Shockley, Isaiah to Malinda Campbell 23 Nov. 1837   Gasc
Shockley, Richard to Elizabeth Burgess 14 Oct. 1830   Gasc
Shockley, Thomas to Rachel Crider 26 Mar. 1829   Gasc
Shockley, Uriah to Matilda Barbrake 6 May 1830   Gasc
Shockley, Westley to Bestsy Curtis 25 Jan. 1835   Gasc
Shockley, Wm. to Rebecca Copeland 15 Aug. 1833   Gasc
Shoe, Michael to Amy Mallerson 27 Feb. 1839   StCh
Shoemake, Geo. to Mary Peyton 26 Sept. 1825   StFr
Shoemaker, Alva to Sally Mullinick 29 Nov. 1829   Rand
Shoemaker, Calvin to Tabitha Shoemaker 22 Jan. 1836   Rand
Shoemaker, Charles to Hariet Humphreys 1 Feb. 1827   Coop
Shoemaker, Geo. to Neely Edwards 27 Dec. 1821   Howa
Shoemaker, John to Mrs. Lucinda Patrick 9 Sept. 1830   Howa
Shoemaker, Miles to Lucinda Shoemaker 8 Jan. 1836   Rand
Shoemaker, Rufus to Eliza A. Hungerford 28 Aug. 1823   Coop
Shoemaker, Westley to Dicey Gibson 29 Dec. 1836   Rand
Shoemaker, Wm. to Barbary Cory 7 Mar. 1837   Rand
Shoemate, Geo. to Sinthy Wines 10 Jan. 1836   Cr-1
Sholan, Whitan to Mary A. Neeves 3 Apr. 1833   Wash
Shoot, Wm. to Mary J. Pavey 17 Jan. 1836   Monr
Shotterback, John to Sarah A. Miller 21 Aug. 1838   Rall
Shores, John to Eliza Burch 20 Mar. 1836   Pk-1
Shores, Wm. to Susan R. Johnson 3 Sept. 1829   Howa
Short, Aaron to Harriet King 7 Oct. 1839   Fran
Short, Aron to Mariah Wall 4 Oct. 1823   Fran
Short, Cornilius to Sarrah Wisdom 14 Jan. 1834   Boon
Short, Elhanan to Ann Riley 18 Oct. 1838   Char
Short, Glover to Rebecca Hodge 5 June 1826   Boon
Short, Isaac C. to Jane Cary 5 Nov. 1835   Boon
Short, James G. to Susan Taler 13 Feb. 1839   Barr
Short, Jesse to Rebecca Lewis 31 Mar. 1839   Fran
Short, John to Lovey A. Relso 6 Mar. 1838   Mari
Short, Joseph to Jency Boyd 4 Feb. 1827   Fran
Short, Samuel W. to Jemima Dollarhide 29 Mar. 1838   Fran
Short, Wm. to Ann Douglass 10 Apr. 1829   Boon
Short, Wm. A. to Jane Campbell 23 Oct. 1838   Perr
Shortridge, Albert to Catharine A. Rucker 6 Sept. 1839   Monr
Shotwell, Nathan to Catherine Geery 22 May 1834   Rall
Shoult, John to Hanner Clay 3 Sept. 1839   CG-B
Shoults, Jacob to Mary Burns 16 Feb. 1834   Perr
Shoults, Micajah to Nancy S. Martin 23 July 1835   Perr
Shoutts, Joseph to Elizabeth Boyd 25 Sept. 1827   Perr
Shoutts, Joseph to Eliza Dickinson 1 Mar. 1835   Perr
Shretrant, Lawrence to Lavenia Thompson 31 Aug. 1837   Cole
Shrewsberry, Charles to Mary Morris 10 Oct. 1839   Ray
Shrieve, Wilson to Barbara Mock 2 Jan. 1834   Cole
Shropshir, John E. to Martha Withen 30 Jan. 1834   Mari
Shuckman, Michael Sr. to Mrs. Elizabeth Brown 4 Dec. 1838   Fran
Shull, Henry to Elizabeth Yoakum 17 Oct. 1835   Gree
Shull, Samuel to Sophia Davison 29 Dec. 1829   Perr
Shuls, Jacob to Polly Young 29 May 1828   Linc
Shults, John to Frankey Whitledge 19 Dec. 1830   CG-A
Shuman, David to Martha Kelsy 24 Aug. 1837   Morg
Shumard, Wm. to Enfield Ammarrian 14 Apr. 1839   Gasc
Shumate, James to Julia A.S. Taylor 5 May 1827   Wash
Shumate, James to Susana Adams 5 July 1835   John
Shumate, John to Eliza Merril 3 May 1838   Mari
Shumate, Samuel to Nancy Baskett 24 Apr. 1831   Cr-P
Shurley, Daniel to Mary Gilmore 30 Oct. 1835   Morg
Shutts, Lewis to Polly Green 9 Jan. 1834   Jeff

Shy, Samuel to Sarah A. Stadley 11 Apr. 1839   Pk-B
Siddon, John to Martha Maupin 21 Apr. 1833   Ray
Sides, Henry to Elizabeth Miller 8 Jan. 1839   CG-B
Sides, Jacob to Elizabeth Welty 9 Dec. 1832   CG-A
Sides, John to Rebecca Green 17 Dec. 1826   CG-A
Sides, Michael to Malinda Brinkle 17 Jan. 1833   CG-A
Sidner, Martin to Louisa A.M. Buckner 19 Jan. 1837   Monr
Sidwell, Elijah to Martha Todd 7 Aug. 1834   Pk-1
Sidwell, Moses to Amanda Dunn 31 Dec. 1835   Pk-1
Sidwell, Willis to Eliza Brown 10 Jan. 1833   Pk-1
Siegnor, Michael to Rebecca Head 10 Jan. 1833   Boon
Siffard, Henry to Christina Braucher 13 Apr. 1817   CG-1
Sifford, Lewis to Mrs. Betsy Ross 4 Feb. 1834   CG-A
Sights, John I. to Bethiah Hays 11 Jan. 1837   Char
Silbert, Abraham to Maria E. Gardner 10 Feb. 1837   Rall
Silver, Gersom to Mary Brown 31 July 1832   Rall
Silver, James E. to Sally A. Kemper 7 Feb. 1839   Howa
Silvers, Golden to Polly Turner 1 Mar. 1839   Buch
Silvers, Hiram to Tabbitha McKiney 14 Sept. 1826   Lafa
Silvers, Jourdin to Cinthy A. Turner 3 Jan. 1836   Cass
Silvers, Washington to Susan Shore 2 Oct. 1836   Wash
Silvers, Wm. to Lucinda Hush 4 Dec. 1827   Boon
Silvers, Wm. to Louisa Daulton 21 Feb. 1839   Rall
Silvey, Derias to Lucy Boon 13 June 1837   StCh
Silvey, Gabriel to Matilda Larue 2 Feb. 1823   Howa
Silvey, James H. to Mary A. Yager 21 Feb. 1839   Howa
Silvey, John to Elender Waldren 9 Feb. 1837   Howa
Silvey, John to Malcina Stewart 5 Oct. 1837   StCh
Siman, Lewis to Elizabeth Graves 15 Dec. 1835   Mari
Simery, Joseph to Elizabeth Fyffe 30 July 1838   Linc
Simm, John C. to Winfred Redman 11 Dec. 1836   Rall
Simmerman, Levi to Nancy Davis 14 Aug. 1837   Perr
Simmerrill, Samuel to Matilda Wood 11 Feb. 1836   Coop
Simmons, Geo. W. to Cynthia S. Mahan 25 Oct. 1838   Coop
Simmons, Noah to Lucy P. Vivion 20 Apr. 1837   Cole
Simmons, Thomas P. to Nancy McHaney 6 Oct. 1836   Jack
Simmons, Tilman H. to Sarah S. Wilcoxson 29 Mar. 1832   Howa
Simms, Armsted to Nancy Fanning 5 Sept. 1839   Rall
Simms, Felix to Ann Maddock 31 Mar. 1834   Perr
Simms, James to Ann Benson 13 Dec. 1827   Howa
Simonds, Oliver to Lucy Wilkison 23 Sept. 1834   Linc
Simons, John to Nancy Crow 23 June 1833   StCh
Simons, Wm. to Keren Jeringen 1 July 1838   Coop
Simonton, Adam to Cynthia Cropper 30 Oct. 1828   Coop
Simonton, Adam to Rebecca Clarke 12 Dec. 1839   Coop
Simpson, Benj. to Ann Branson 14 Apr. 1839   Gasc
Simpson, Benj. to Eliza J. Wisdom 28 May 1839   Plat
Simpson, Charles to Evaline Fretwell 21 Oct. 1836   Lewi
Simpson, Daniel to Elizabeth Pryor 23 May 1836   Gasc
Simpson, Geo. to Zora Ashabran 26 Apr. 1835   Md-A
Simpson, Greenbury to Elizabeth Thompson 10 May 1839   Clar
Simpson, Henry to Parthenia Martin 14 Mar. 1839   Warr
Simpson, Ignatius to Charlotte McLain 27 Nov. 1827   Perr
Simpson, James to Fannie Hill 26 Mar. 1833   Linc
Simpson, James B. to Sarah J. Dickson 13 Oct. 1836   Boon
Simpson, James B. to Polly Cantly 22 Feb. 1838   Fran
Simpson, James M. to Frances E. Cummins 1 Dec. 1831   Jack
Simpson, James W. to Susanna A. Gillum 29 Aug. 1833   Warr
Simpson, John to ---- McGee 31 Jan. 1828   Rall
Simpson, John to Sarah Enloe 13 Jan. 1835   Fran
Simpson, John to Martha Vanible 13 Nov. 1837   Livi
Simpson, Joseph to Lovey Coats 27 Dec. 1823   Boon
Simpson, Joseph D. to Mary Cissell 13 Sept. 1830   Perr
Simpson, Moses to Nancy Dodds 3 Apr. 1834   Gasc
Simpson, Moses to Elizabeth Vinson 30 Mar. 1837   Gasc

                            203

Simpson, Samuel to Sarah Prior 6 July 1834   Gasc
Simpson, Thomas to Betsy Gallaway 18 Mar. 1826   Linc
Simpson, Thomas to Rosannah Buff 14 Mar. 1839   John
Simpson, Walker D. to Ann C. Dickson 14 Nov. 1833   Monr
Simpson, Wm. to Pamelia Burns 7 May 1826   Pk-1
Simpson, Wm. H. to Elizabeth M. Allen 11 July 1833   StCh
Sims, Elias to Cynthia Pemberton 4 Sept. 1834   Boon
Sims, Enoch to July Gregory 26 Oct. 1828   Mari
Sims, Folton to Pemelia Rawlings 21 Dec. 1837   Boon
Sims, Henry to Nancy Crafford 31 July 1832   Rall
Sims, Henry to Susan J. Sims 7 Nov. 1837   Monr
Sims, Irvine to Elizabeth Turner 24 Jan. 1838   Boon
Sims, Jacson to Laviny Cummins 17 Apr. 1834   Wash
Sims, James to Patsy Beden 24 Feb. 1833   Call
Sims, James to Margaret Isham 22 May 1834   Call
Sims, Nathaniel to Polly Cahoon 1 Dec. 1839   Clay
Sims, Zachariah to Eliza Adams 7 Mar. 1839   Gree
Simson, Christopher G. to Lucind Courtney 19 Jan. 1826   StCh
Sinclair, Alexander to Lucinda Boling 3 July 1831   Pk-1
Sinclair, Charles to Polly Hines 27 Dec. 1829   Md-A
Sinclair, Elias to Eliza Rossitter 3 July 1834   Lewi
Sinclair, Soloman to Sarah J. Meville 28 Dec. 1837   Lafa
Sinclear, Christopher to Nancy Bowling 30 June 1829   Rall
Sinclear, John to Polly Bramlet 5 July 1831   Rall
Single, John S. to Mary Fox 18 May 1836   Howa
Singleton, Charles S. to Julian M. Poessey 24 Mar. 1836   Clay
Singleton, Jackaman to Sally A. Burton 21 May 1839   Boon
Singleton, John B. to Sarah J. Vandiver 28 Nov. 1839   Shel
Singleton, Samuel to Sarah Darr 8 June 1834   Mari
Singleton, Wm. to Martha Peter 15 May 1833   Rall
Sintacoms, John to Sarah Caldwell 25 Oct. 1835   Fran
Sipes, Henry to Mary A. Stites 25 Oct. 1838   Fran
Sipes, John to Saly Srum 18 Oct. 1829   CG-A
Sirk, Layton to Patsey Newton 2 Aug. 1831   Howa
Sisemore, Jourdon to Mary Fox 25 June 1826   Rall
Sissell, John to Charlotte Faught 8 Dec. 1822   StFr
Sissom, Francis to Lucinda Mundy 11 Sept. 1834   Clay
Sissom, Jackson to Maryann Felps 9 July 1837   Clay
Sitter, Samuel A. to Malinda Fisher 8 Dec. 1836   Coop
Sitton, Benj. to Patsy Holaday 25 Aug. 1835   Pett
Sitton, Benj. F. to Rebecca Austin 7 Jan. 1823   Call
Sitton, James to Ann Flood 25 Mar. 1827   CG-A
Sitton, John to Sally Jamison 11 Nov. 1825   Call
Sitton, Joseph T. to Preciller May 17 May 1821   Call
Sitton, Martin to Harriet Allen 24 Aug. 1826   Call
Sitton, Silas to Martha F. Crump 10 Aug. 1837   Wash
Sitton, Thomas H. to Melinda Allen 22 Apr. 1838   Pett
Sitton, Vincent to Amilly Fisher 18 Aug. 1833   Pett
Sitton, Wm. to Rebecca Bell 8 Oct. 1826   Rall
Sitz, Lawson to Catherine Bess 11 Oct. 1831   CG-A
Size, John to Cintha Fergusen 8 Sept. 1833   Lafa
Skaggs, Andrew to Sarah Morrison 21 May 1826   Gasc
Skaggs, Benj. to Sally Burk 26 Feb. 1837   Boon
Skaggs, Jesse to Elizabeth Combs 21 Aug. 1834   Md-A
Skaggs, Jonathan to Polly Estes 8 May 1834   Clay
Skaggs, Samuel to Susan Miller 1 Feb. 1835   Md-A
Skaggs, Shadrack to Ferby Branson 29 June 1832   Cr-1
Skaggs, Stephen to Martha J. Shipton 26 Mar. 1834   Pett
Skaggs, Wm. to Elizabeth Smith 15 July 1832   CG-A
Skean, Alexander to Polly Blevin 29 Apr. 1834   Jack
Skeggs, Henry to Elizabeth Momon 29 June 1834   Fran
Skelton, Isaac D. to Nancy Stooky 16 June 1825   Char
Skidmore, Elexander to Mary Boon 28 Dec. 1837   Perr
Skidmore, James to Deliah Eastes 8 Mar. 1828   Cole
Skidmore, John to Mary Thomas 11 Apr. 1833   Cole

204

Skidmore, Peyton to Milly Vanlandingham 13 Jan. 1830   Boon
Skiel, Samuel to Sarah Cosby 12 Apr. 1838   Jeff
Skinner, Alexander to Jane Davis 20 Mar. 1835   Warr
Skinner, Benj. F. to Ann Bishop 27 Aug. 1838   Warr
Skinner, Charles A. to Lascen Stewart 22 Aug. 1833   Linc
Skinner, Charles S. to Mary A.S. Cashman 15 Mar. 1838   Lewi
Skinner, James to Mary Turner 1 Apr. 1832   Linc
Skinner, Narves to Sarah A. Mothershead 13 Oct. 1836   Boon
Skinner, Richard to Ann E. Dent 1 Mar. 1833   Fran
Skinner, Robt. to Nancy Skinner 7 Nov. 1839   Rand
Skinner, Stephen P. to Eliza Burton 22 Apr. 1838   Maco
Skinner, Wm. to Marinda Richardson 6 Dec. 1835   Fran
Slack, James to Caroline Humphrey 1 Feb. 1838   Char
Slack, John to Elizabeth Pipes 30 Jan. 1834   Boon
Slack, Lewis to Ametes I. O'Daniel 2 Oct. 1838   Mari
Slagle, Abel to Marthew Lunsford 24 Dec. 1833   Gree
Slagle, James to Hannah Cantwell 30 Apr. 1837   Polk
Slaten, Thomas to Melinda Luke 24 Dec. 1838   Mari
Slater, Daniel to Anna Wilson 13 July 1834   Char
Slater, Wm. to Martha Montgomery 25 Feb. 1827   Char
Slaughter, Francis T. to Elizabeth Conner 25 Apr. 1826   Clay
Slaughter, Jessee to Elizabeth Slaughter 10 Mar. 1839   Clay
Slaughter, John to Eliza E. Brown 11 May 1837   Polk
Slaughter, Robt. to Elizabeth Bradshaw 18 Apr. 1837   Lewi
Slaughter, Robt. to Nancy Kendrick 15 Jan. 1839   Lewi
Slavens, James H. to Louisa Rountree 17 June 1832   Cr-1
Slayback, A.L. to Ann M. Minter 30 July 1837   Mari
Slenslan, James to Martha Martin 30 July 1837   Coop
Slingolin, John to Sabry Wilcox 7 Aug. 1836   Clay
Slinkard, Daniel to Eve Morrison 10 Apr. 1836   CG-A
Slinkard, Geo. to Elizabeth Bollinger 5 Aug. 1832   CG-A
Slinkard, Jacob to Phebe Hubble 26 Jan. 1837   CG-A
Slinkard, John to Viney Strader 8 Dec. 1839   CG-B
Slinkard, Joseph to Alley Shrum 11 Dec. 1836   CG-A
Slinker, Frederic to Rebecca Smith 10 Jan. 1828   CG-A
Sloan, Amos to Malissa Henderson 15 Mar. 1827   CG-A
Sloan, Ellis R. to Nancy Armstrong 7 Aug. 1834   Call
Sloan, Joseph to Irena Wilcockson 11 Apr. 1o33   Call
Sloan, Robt. to Margaret D. Ewing 13 Dec. 1826   Coop
Sloan, Wm. to Jane B. Allcorn 21 Aug. 1821   Howa
Sloan, Wm. to Milla A. Breckenridge 29 Aug. 1839   Wash
Sloane, James E. to Matilda Crowley 28 Jan. 1836   Clay
Slone, Moraad to Doshean Rogers 21 Feb. 1837   Gree
Slusher, Christopher to Susan Houck 14 June 1837   Lafa
Slusher, Henry to Rebecca Robinson 11 Apr. 1839   Lafa
Slusher, Rowland to Lockey T. Jennings 3 Mar. 1833   Lafa
Small, Geo. to Malinda Hinch 16 Mar. 1830   Sali
Small, Henry to Nancy Moseby 14 Apr. 1836   Pett
Smallwood, Russell to Peggy Briscoe -- June 1820   Coop
Smarr, John to Mary A. Field 6 Dec. 1838   Mari
Smart, Armstead to Elizabeth Smith 19 Oct. 1826   Char
Smart, Bryce M. to Amy Cox 14 Feb. 1837   Gree
Smart, Buckner to Nancy Gentry 14 Mar. 1833   Carr
Smart, Elisha to Patsey Brown 16 Aug. 1838   Gree
Smart, Glover to Elvira Day 5 Feb. 1834   Call
Smart, James to Rachel C. Ewing 15 Feb. 1838   Call
Smart, John to Polly Cooly 27 Jan. 1826   Howa
Smart, John T. to Virginia L. Smart 5 Mar. 1837   Call
Smart, Landy to Isabela Kimberling 31 Mar. 1833   Gree
Smart, Stephen to Margaret Trotter 27 Mar. 1838   Carr
Smart, Wm. to Elizabeth Thomas 3 Nov. 1836   Carr
Smart, Wm. to Nancy Garrison 6 May 1838   Gree
Smiley, Geo. W. to Isabella Small 17 Aug. 1826   Coop
Smiley, Wm. B. to Ann Hall 13 Sept. 1835   Pett
Smily, Samuel E. to Emily Nickoll 25 June 1829   Linc

Smirl, Aaron to Sally Stewart 23 Oct. 1828   Jeff
Smith, Abner to Mrs. Elizath Baker 16 Nov. 1823   Clay
Smith, Abraham W. to Deanner Merfrey 22 Jan. 1835   Md-A
Smith, Abram to Elizabeth Anthony 9 Mar. 1837   Boon
Smith, Absolem to Hilley Kinzey 1828/29   Jack
Smith, Adam to Sary Hogan 4 Apr. 1827   Gasc
Smith, Addam to Elizabeth Haustatter 24 July 1834   StCh
Smith, Adison to Catharine Alfrod 28 Feb. 1839   CG-B
Smith, Albert G. to Milly Pepper 15 Aug. 1832   Mari
Smith, Alexander to Nancy Martin 26 Apr. 1829   Wash
Smith, Alexander W. to Susanna Fox 1 Apr. 1824   Rall
Smith, Alford to Mary A. Hoops 20 Aug. 1835   Gasc
Smith, Alvis to Mary E. Picket 21 Mar. 1839   Clay
Smith, Aly to Sarah Collett 6 June 1838   Cole
Smith, Anderson to Sintsey Braley 5 Jan. 1832   Clay
Smith, Anderson to Mahala A. Henderson 20 Mar. 1833   Clay
Smith, Anderson to Ann Enyart 10 July 1837   Clin
Smith, Andrew to Nancy Sanders 3 Apr. 1839   Ripl
Smith, Anthony to Mary E. Reed 13 Apr. 1831   Coop
Smith, Archibald to Caroline Powel 4 Aug. 1839   Pett
Smith, Augustin G. to Marrian Panyme 13 Aug. 1835   Mari
Smith, Austin G. to Mary G. Moffitt 16 Nov. 1837   Shel
Smith, B. to Sarah Ferguson 19 Sept. 1833   Call
Smith, Benj. to Martha Hoops 24 Sept. 1833   Gasc
Smith, Benj. to Margaret Jones 28 Sept. 1834   Clay
Smith, Benj. D. to Martha J. Robison 23 July 1839   Linc
Smith, Birdon G. to Sally Simpson 9 Dec. 1839   Buch
Smith, Cardwell to Nancy Wilkerson 20 Dec. 1827   CG-A
Smith, Charles to Rebecca Hood 27 Oct. 1829   Coop
Smith, Charles to Nancy Ferguson 22 May 1833   Lafa
Smith, Charles to Elizabeth Clark 5 Dec. 1837   CG-A
Smith, Charles to Honora Rielly 23 Apr. 1839   Wash
Smith, Columbus to Susan Myers 25 Dec. 1829   Howa
Smith, Daniel to Mary Drummonds 19 Oct. 1828   Linc
Smith, Daniel to Emily Ringo 8 Sept. 1836   Ray
Smith, Darling to Winny Clay 4 Mar. 1824   StCh
Smith, David to Elizabeth Hinkle 22 July 1819   CG-1
Smith, David to Adaline Bess 12 July 1827   CG-A
Smith, David to Sophia McMickle 3 Apr. 1834   Boon
Smith, Davud to Oney Woods 5 Sept. 1829   StCh
Smith, Dixon to Nancy Taylor 30 May 1823   Boon
Smith, Doctor to Nancy Wisdom 10 Feb. 1825   Howa
Smith, Doctor to Malinda Morgan 23 July 1837   Clay
Smith, E. to Sarah Green 1 Jan. 1829   Call
Smith, Edward to Alcey Best 1 Apr. 1830   Clay
Smith, Edwin H. to Amanda J. ---- 20 Oct. 1836   Cole
Smith, Elijah to Milly L. Keach 19 Nov. 1833   Mari
Smith, Elijah to Meriah Pulliam 7 July 1837   Clay
Smith, Elisha to Cintha G. Runnuls 29 July 1830   Clay
Smith, Enos to Arilla Miller 14 Feb. 1834   Jack
Smith, Ephraim to Polly Bryant 27 Dec. 1829   Rall
Smith, Ephriam to ---- Powers 19 July 1838   Monr
Smith, Felix to Barbary Dismukes 18 July 1833   Pk-1
Smith, Franklin to Sarah Clark 4 Dec. 1832   Jack
Smith, Gabriel to Susanna Head 21 Dec. 1834   Boon
Smith, Geo. to Mahala Hawkins 14 Dec. 1827   Boon
Smith, Geo. to Elvina Tinnin 7 July 1832   CG-A
Smith, Geo. to Mary Hughes 8 Nov. 1835   Wash
Smith, Geo. to Malinda Brown 27 Mar. 1836   Clay
Smith, Geo. to Margaret Rochester 29 Oct. 1837   StCh
Smith, Geo. to Elizabeth Sutton 9 Jan. 1838   Boon
Smith, Geo. R. to Ann McCabe 21 Sept. 1829   Wash
Smith, Geo. W. to Elizabeth R. Basket 9 Feb. 1834   Call
Smith, Geo. W. to Orlina Bunch 8 May 1838   Polk
Smith, Geo. W. to Sally Gentry 27 Dec. 1839   Plat

Smith, Henry to Elizabeth Gillet 20 Sept. 1820 Howa
Smith, Henry to Pheobe Strickland 3 May 1827 Jeff
Smith, Henry to Jane Horton 6 July 1837 Rand
Smith, Henry to Mary Pierce 23 Oct. 1838 CG-A
Smith, Hezekiah to Polly Bates 11 Dec. 1815 StCh
Smith, Hiram to Rebecca Cole 14 Feb. 1832 Wash
Smith, Hiram to Margarett Coffman 14 July 1832 Clay
Smith, Hiram to Mary Crump 8 Aug. 1833 Boon
Smith, Hiram to Emily Shultz 4 Oct. 1837 Jeff
Smith, Hiram M. to Priscilla Vaughn 20 May 1830 Cole
Smith, Hugh R. to Harriet W. Hart 26 Jan. 1837 Clay
Smith, Isaac to Sabria Fisher 6 Jan. 1822 Coop
Smith, Isaac W. to Lavina Tarleton 20 Apr. 1827 CG-A
Smith, Jackson to Mary Owens 7 June 1835 Char
Smith, Jacob to Perlina Y. Darr 2 Aug. 1831 Rall
Smith, James to Jinsy Ramsy 1 Feb. 1824 Fran
Smith, James to Alizer Findley 10 July 1828 Pk-1
Smith, James to Jane Possee 12 June 1831 Clay
Smith, James to America Webb 5 Aug. 1833 Lewi
Smith, James to Jane McLard 4 Sept. 1834 CG-A
Smith, James to Marthew Williams 4 Jan. 1835 Gree
Smith, James to Sally McPherson 14 July 1836 Rall
Smith, James to Jane Easten 24 Jan. 1837 Boon
Smith, James to Elizabeth Daugherty 27 May 1838 CG-A
Smith, James to Rebecca J. Delap 26 June 1838 CG-A
Smith, James to Eliza Daniel 17 Aug. 1839 Plat
Smith, James H. to Rosey A. McKeammy 12 May 1831 Monr
Smith, James H. to Emely P. Allen 23 Sept. 1838 Char
Smith, James H.M. to Mary A. Looney 16 July 1829 Rall
Smith, Jephtha S. to Elizabeth Moseley 19 Apr. 1838 Clar
Smith, Jeremiah to Sarah A. McKenney 15 Feb. 1838 Mari
Smith, Jesse to Nancy Haley 30 June 1835 Howa
Smith, Jesse B. to Sarah G. Martin 2 Dec. 1830 Wash
Smith, John to Sally McMahan 3 May 1819 Coop
Smith, John to Polly Blackwell 27 Sept. 1825 Howa
Smith, John to Nancy Roberts 5 -- 1827 Boon
Smith, John to Sarah Fristow 20 Nov. 1827 Jack
Smith, John to Unity Gilliam 6 Aug. 1829 Clay
Smith, John to Widow Johnson 17 Nov. 1829 Perr
Smith, John to Mary Knott 21 Jan. 1830 StCh
Smith, John to Dicey Rhodes 7 Nov. 1833 CG-A
Smith, John to Katharine Genesse 28 Feb. 1834 Gree
Smith, John to Marthew Luny 2 Nov. 1834 Gree
Smith, John to Malinda Ballard 30 Apr. 1835 Howa
Smith, John to Pauglena Day 10 Mar. 1836 Jack
Smith, John to Mary Bass rec. 3 June 1837 Rall
Smith, John to Martha Yeater 19 Oct. 1837 Pk-B
Smith, John to Sarah Weatherford 7 July 1839 Gasc
Smith, John to Polly Comstock 12 Nov. 1839 Ripl
Smith, John B. to Sally Yates 4 June 1829 Rall
Smith, John C. to Margarett Bradley 10 Apr. 1836 Mari
Smith, John D. to Susan Geiger 23 May 1839 Linc
Smith, John H. to Mary Edes 29 Sept. 1839 Warr
Smith, John L. to Lean Suddeth 12 Oct. 1833 Marr
Smith, John O. to Mary L. Mattingly 18 Nov. 1839 Perr
Smith, John T. to Susan Reynolds 17 May 1836 Howa
Smith, John W. Jr. to Margaret Clark 21 Aug. 1838 Gree
Smith, Jonathan to Eliza A. Drip 22 Dec. 1827 Jack
Smith, Jonathan to Eliza Brown 13 Sept. 1832 Linc
Smith, Joseph to Nancy Beck 12 Jan. 1834 Lafa
Smith, Joseph to Sarah Phillips 31 Dec. 1837 Howa
Smith, Joseph to Mary C. Nichols 24 Feb. 1839 Gasc
Smith, Joshua to Lavica Keeney 20 Oct. 1833 Jack
Smith, Joshua to Eleanor Huft 20 May 1838 Cass
Smith, Josiah to Elizabeth Pierce 2 Oct. 1832 CG-A

207

Smith, Josiah to Alley Oens 24 Sept. 1838	Polk
Smith, Julis H. to Barbery Bollinger 24 May 1836	CG-A
Smith, Lawrence to Maria C. Schichken 12 May 1836	Warr
Smith, Lisbourn to Melvina Barnes 6 Feb. 1834	Char
Smith, Mackey to Mary Cheatham 10 Oct. 1833	Call
Smith, Marshall to Mary Reed 22 May 1831	Boon
Smith, Matthew to Susanna Layne 25 Sept. 1827	Pk-1
Smith, Michael to Emeline Barnhart 3 Sept. 1839	Mill
Smith, Montellian to Cassandra West 20 Mar. 1828	Boon
Smith, Moses to Rebecca Manuel 4 Apr. 1826	StCh
Smith, Nathaniel to Archange Palen 5 Feb. 1835	Lewi
Smith, Noah to Betsey Phillips 3 Sept. 1837	CG-A
Smith, Obadiah to Katharine Harkman 30 Mar. 1826	Howa
Smith, Owen to Eliza P. Pace 16 June 1835	Call
Smith, Peter to Jane Rine 6 Oct. 1835	CG-B
Smith, Pleasant to Thursa Means 6 Mar. 1837	Clin
Smith, Posy N. to Margaret A. Smith 14 Feb. 1836	Rall
Smith, Ralph to Patsy Easton 9 Sept. 1834	Mari
Smith, Reddind to Sarah Williams 29 May 1834	CG-A
Smith, Reuben to Giddida Hall 4 Jan. 1829	Coop
Smith, Richard to Jane Blake 16 Nov. 1834	Jack
Smith, Richard to Eliza Waggener 15 Mar. 1835	Call
Smith, Richard S. to Elizabeth Shaw 29 June 1837	Pk-A
Smith, Robt. to Martha Wedding rec. 25 Feb. 1836	StCh
Smith, Robt. to Susan H. McIlvain 8 Dec. 1836	Wash
Smith, Ruben to Catharine Slinker 9 Jan. 1828	CG-A
Smith, Samuel to Patsey Yates 11 Dec. 1828	Rall
Smith, Samuel to Frances Norris 21 Jan. 1834	Linc
Smith, Samuel to Orra Culbertson 7 Aug. 1834	Mari
Smith, Samuel to Sary Boon 24 June 1838	Clin
Smith, Sanford to Mary Colvin 2 Jan. 1838	Cole
Smith, Simon to Sarah Mitchel 31 Dec. 1833	Boon
Smith, Simon to Polly Holland 21 Dec. 1837	Clay
Smith, Stephen to Sarah Bast rec. 16 Feb. 1839	Rall
Smith, Terriath to Peggy Henceley 29 Nov. 1818	Howa
Smith, Thomas to Eliza Dearst 25 Sept. 1806	StCh
Smith, Thomas to Catherine Craig 29 Jan. 1828	Call
Smith, Thomas to Mary Huddleston 16 Aug. 1829	Call
Smith, Thomas to Jane Ainsworth 8 Sept. 1829	Howa
Smith, Thomas to Lorrinda Silvers 11 Dec. 1830	Jack
Smith, Thomas to Mahala Caststeel 18 Nov. 1832	Pk-1
Smith, Thomas to Nancy Hickason 3 Jan. 1833	Pk-1
Smith, Thomas to Charlotte Risher 24 Mar. 1833	CG-A
Smith, Thomas to Elizabeth Nicoles 30 Nov. 1837	Gasc
Smith, Thomas to Mrs. Rebecca Shepherd 12 Mar. 1839	Lewi
Smith, Thomas to Nancy A. Turman 14 Apr. 1839	Cass
Smith, Thomas B. to ---- Edwards 15 Oct. 1829	Boon
Smith, Thomas F. to Talitha Foley 25 -- 1837	Morg
Smith, Thomas R. to Mary A. Hutchinson 25 July 1839	Coop
Smith, Wm. to Elizabeth Bradley 5 Feb. 1811	CG-1
Smith, Wm. to Ann Yaakhom 14 Nov. 1812	CG-1
Smith, Wm. to Patsy McMickle 5 Dec. 1822	Boon
Smith, Wm. to Mary Tetherow 7 Aug. 1826	Boon
Smith, Wm. to Malinda Lewis 21 Jan. 1831	Boon
Smith, Wm. to Elizabeth Hedrick 20 Nov. 1831	Howa
Smith, Wm. to Martha Clark 22 Jan. 1832	Jack
Smith, Wm. to Amanda Emmerson 4 Mar. 1834	Rand
Smith, Wm. to Cinthia Camplin 18 May 1834	Boon
Smith, Wm. to Martha E. Staples 24 Nov. 1836	Lewi
Smith, Wm. to Martha Frasier 31 Aug. 1838	Ray
Smith, Wm. to Susanna Bittle 4 July 1839	Boon
Smith, Wm. A.D. to Melinda Hoozer 24 Sept. 1835	Coop
Smith, Wm. C. to Elizabeth Lard 24 Sept. 1835	Clin
Smith, Wm. D. to Jane Holt 7 Feb. 1839	Clin
Smith, Wm. H. to Nancy Jennings 28 Feb. 1827	Howa

208

```
Smith, Wm. H. to Mary Edwards 27 Dec. 1837                          Pk-B
Smith, Wm. L. to Mrs. Constantia D. Miller 16 July 1823             Clay
Smith, Wm. S. to Mary A. Hood 4 Oct. 1827                           Boon
Smith, Wm. W. to Harriet Stone 25 June 1822                         Rall
Smith, Wm. W. to Isabella Burt 18 July 1830                         Wash
Smith, Wm. W. to Katey Riley 13 Sept. 1839                          Rand
Smith, Wollondine to Mrs. Mary Wonderly 3 Feb. 1834                 StCh
Smithers, John to Nancy Bilyew 2 Oct. 1838                          Mill
Smoot, Abraham to Lucinda Bozarth 24 Dec. 1837                      Maco
Smoot, James to Nancy Arnold 19 Feb. 1837                           Barr
Smoot, John to Mary Morris 2 Oct. 1828                              Perr
Smoot, John to Elizabeth Morris 31 May 1829                         Perr
Smoot, John to Catharine Griffin 19 Apr. 1838                       Maco
Smoot, Thomas to Sally Hatten 1 Mar. 1829                           Perr
Smoot, Warren to Mary Dale 31 Jan. 1832                             Rand
Smoot, Wm. to Rachel Block 25 Dec. 1832                             CG-A
Smyth, Baxter to Jane Laremore 10 Oct. 1822                         Fran
Smyth, John to Lucinda Peyton 5 Oct. 1815                           CG-1
Smyth, Ruffis M. to Sinu Edgman 6 Mar. 1832                         Cole
Smyth, Scudder to Elizabeth Miller 8 Oct. 1826                      Fran
Smythie, John to Hannah Nash 13 June 1833                           Clin
Snapp, Lawrence M. to Hannah F. Jennings 22 Jan. 1839              Lewi
Snavely, Joseph to Catherine Williams 20 Dec. 1838                 Howa
Snedegar, Robt. Jr. to Melinda J. Orea 9 July 1837                 Rall
Snedegar, Wm. to Lucilla S. Cox 9 July 1837                        Rall
Sneed, ---- to Catharine Boocher 6 Nov. 1832                       Ray
Sneed, Finley to Luiza Engle 24 Oct. 1838                          Polk
Sneed, Henry P. to Elizabeth Leurand 29 Jan. 1839                  StFr
Sneed, Hesekeah to Elizabeth Mercer 15 Sept. 1831                  Cr-P
Sneed, Hiram to Elizabeth Malott 5 Jan. 1832                       Clay
Sneed, Richard to Sarah A. Lyon 1 Feb. 1835                        Jack
Sneed, Wm. to Caroline Davis 9 Feb. 1837                           Linc
Snedigar, Francis to Abigal Lewellen 29 Sept. 1833                Rall
Sneid, Geo. M. to Mary Clark 10 May 1836                           Jeff
Snell, Ephraim to Louisa Hamlet 26 Sept. 1826                      Howa
Snell, Geo. B. to Sarah A. Turpin 4 Oct. 1839                      Lewi
Snell, Granville to Emily Poage 6 Jan. 1836                        Monr
Snell, Greenup to Sarah A. Mackentire 14 Dec. 1837                Call
Snell, Lewis N. to Ann M. Vanlandingham 18 Apr. 1839              Mari
Snell, Richard D. to Alithia Dickens 23 Aug. 1839                 Howa
Snell, Wm. to Susan Woods 16 July 1834                            Boon
Snelling, Vinson to Adeally Tandy 1 Apr. 1829                     Lafa
Snelson, Isaac to Sarah Grisham 27 Mar. 1836                      Cr-1
Snelson, Levi to Hannah Gardner 28 Sept. 1837                     Cr-1
Snelson, Thomas to Nancy A. Atkinson 17 Feb. 1837                 Cr-1
Snethen, Abraham to Malinda Howard 12 Nov. 1839                   Warr
Snider, Aaron to Synthy Young 9 Mar. 1826                         CG-A
Snider, Andrew to Mary Miller 4 July 1833                         CG-A
Snider, Gabriel to Trecy Shuck 13 Mar. 1831                       Rall
Snider, Henry to Elizabeth Hilton 23 July 1835                    Rall
Snider, Jacob Jr. to Mary A. Cross 16 Mar. 1837                   CG-A
Snider, John to Elizabeth Young 16 Nov. 1837                      CG-A
Snider, Martin to Margaret Eaker 10 Oct. 1826                     CG-A
Snider, Michael H. to Menervy McCully 23 Aug. 1838               Howa
Snider, Nathanil D. to Elizabeth E. Rous 31 Aug. 1837           Rall
Snider, Wm. to Ellen King 4 Jan. 1827                            CG-A
Snidicor, Parker to Eliza P. Ware 19 Aug. 1830                    Wash
Snoddy, James to Polly Smith 30 May 1819                          Howa
Snoddy, Joseph W. to Narcissa Foster 7 Mar. 1819                  Howa
Snoddy, Wm. to Mary Harrison 22 June 1834                         Howa
Snodgrass, Andrew I. to Salina Burgher 22 July 1834              Coop
Snodgrass, Archibald to Nancy McGee 21 June 1832                 Cr-1
Snodgrass, Edward to Nancy Harris 19 Dec. 1830                    Coop
Snodgrass, Edward to Lucy Harris 21 Feb. 1836                     Coop
Snodgrass, James to Oliver Yeats 6 Dec. 1829                      Cr-P
```

Snodgrass, Joseph to Sally Hooser 1 Dec. 1825	Coop
Snodgrass, Reuben to Nancy Martin 5 Oct. 1826	Coop
Snodgrass, Wm. to Dorcas Huff 29 Dec. 1836	Coop
Snodgrass, Wm. to Rebecca Banks 26 Dec. 1839	Livi
Snow, Edward to Hannah Riggs 9 June 1827	Boon
Snow, Bird to Sindy Compton 6 June 1833	Md-A
Snow, Isah to Nancy Hopper 27 Aug. 1818	Howa
Snow, Lacy to Lucinda Barton 8 Mar. 1827	Rall
Snowden, Jacob to Elizabeth M. Waller 16 Aug. 1832	Ray
Snowden, James to Mahala Sollers 2 Apr. 1838	Clin
Snowden, James Jr. to Hannah Slaighter 13 Oct. 1839	Ray
Snowden, Jonathan to Cyrene Hudgins 7 Oct. 1830	Ray
Snowden, Samuel to Polly Write alias Brewer 6 Apr. 1829	Ray
Snyder, Frederick to Eveline Weldy 18 Mar. 1838	Pk-B
Snyder, Geo. to Martha Seely 26 Nov. 1829	CG-A
Snyder, Joseph to Augusta Poucher 10 June 1832	StCh
Soane, James to Eliza Peyton 12 Feb. 1835	Cole
Socier, Francis to Pelagie Robidoux 6 Nov. 1837	StCh
Sohlimput, John T. to Maria R. Poppity 30 June 1839	Perr
Sollers, Henry to Polly Hufft 28 Mar. 1829	Jack
Sollers, Saber T. to Mary Rhoades 6 Oct. 1839	Buch
Sollers, Thomas to Margaret Huff 6 Aug. 1832	Clay
Somers, Geo. M. to Sally Scott 16 Aug. 1836	CG-A
Son, James to Margaret Trotter 26 July 1829	Coop
Son, John to Isabel McClure 20 July 1821	Coop
Son, John to Angelina E. Hubble 21 July 1839	Buch
Son, Wm. to Lavanna Burger 7 Dec. 1826	Coop
Sone, John F. to Polly H. Doke 21 Apr. 1839	Henr
Sonsee, Francis to Mary DeCleose 13 Apr. 1839	Wash
Sorrell, John to Elizabeth Cornett 27 Dec. 1839	Rand
Sorrell, Napoleon B. to Ruth B. Jamison 24 Dec. 1829	Wash
Soudder, Jacob to Rebecca Melton 4 May 1823	Cole
South, Benj. to Janie Meek 7 Dec. 1835	Boon
South, Samuel to Redonia Irvin 11 Apr. 1837	Pk-A
South, Seneca to Elizabeth Evans 5 Oct. 1835	Boon
South, Thomas to Margaret South 26 Jan. 1830	Pk-1
South, Thomas B. to Elizabeth Summers 31 Jan. 1837	Pk-B
Souther, Thomas to Sarah Enoch 30 Dec. 1832	Cole
Southerland, Huckleberry to Sarah Bridgewater 5 Mar. 1835	Coop
Southworth, James B. to Exony Reeves 23 July 1836	Fran
Sower, John H. to Pennella Powell 27 Jan. 1838	Shel
Spain, James to Eliza Tansey 28 Nov. 1838	Fran
Spain, James M. to Lydia Holt 28 Jan. 1838	Md-B
Spain, Lewis to Marthew Poor 12 Jan. 1834	Gree
Spain, Wm. to Malinda Odom 7 Apr. 1833	Md-A
Spalding, Ignatius to Susan Frazier 20 Nov. 1836	Rall
Spalding, Michael to Eulilia Hagan 9 June 1835	Perr
Spalding, Michael to Louisa Taylor 13 Sept. 1836	Perr
Spalding, Pius to Clatilda Layton 10 Feb. 1834	Perr
Spalding, Thomas to Maria Rindesbacher 10 July 1836	StCh
Spalding, Thomas to Mary A. Boskett 16 Nov. 1836	StCh
Spalding, Thomas to Catherine Donnally 27 Aug. 1839	Rall
Spalding, Wm. to Elizabeth Oberry 4 May 1828	StCh
Spalding, Wm. to Betsy Aubrey 4 May 1828	StCh
Spann, Wm. J. to Caroline Miller 19 Mar. 1839	Polk
Sparks, Milton to Amanda Howell 14 Mar. 1835	Monr
Sparks, Wm. to Mary Delany 6 May 1831	Monr
Sparlin, Benj. to Ann Twitty 24 May 1838	Barr
Sparlin, Wm. to Susan Lee 7 June 1838	Barr
Sparrow, Wm. to Ann D. Coleman 24 Dec. 1839	Shel
Spaulding, Joseph to Melvina Parmer 25 Jan. 1835	Carr
Speaks, John to Rachel Payne 13 Jan. 1834	Char
Spears, Edward to Catherine Saxton 26 Sept. 1810	CG-1
Spears, Henry D. to Letitia Criddle 21 Feb. 1839	CG-B
Spears, Samuel to Nancy Stafford 28 Sept. 1834	Cr-1

```
Spence, Elija to Nancy Estes 29 Nov. 1830                        Coop
Spence, Wm. to Rebecca Hays 16 Apr. 1836                         Char
Spencer, Alexander to Ruth Crum 23 Feb. 1836                     Cole
Spencer, Alexander to Mary H.A. Calvin 13 Oct. 1836             Wash
Spencer, Andrew to Christena James 21 Sept. 1837               CG-A
Spencer, Charles G. to Malinda Gibson 27 Nov. 1839            Linc
Spencer, Geo. to Sally McConnell 14 Apr. 1807                   StCh
Spencer, Geo. to Amanda Foster 29 July 1834                    StCh
Spencer, Israel to Elizabeth Bess 11 Feb. 1838                CG-A
Spencer, Jeremiah to Eliza J. Ronald 18 June 1835             Md-A
Spencer, Jesse to Catherine Cabeen 20 Oct. 1835               Char
Spencer, John to Amanda M. Brice 19 June 1834                 Pk-1
Spencer, John to Nancy Crowley 5 Nov. 1837                    Clay
Spencer, Robt. to Eliza Cayce 10 Nov. 1831                    StCh
Spencer, Sebert to Katharine James 3 Oct. 1837               CG-A
Spencer, Wm. to Elizabeth Decamp 23 Sept. 1832               Pk-1
Spencer, Wm. to Hannah Croft 26 Oct. 1834                     Fran
Spenser, Robt. to Magdelaine Denis 9 Sept. 1833              StCh
Sperry, Harlow W. to Rebecca C. Lovell 23 Aug. 1838          Pk-B
Sperry, James M. to Elizabeth Bybee 8 Oct. 1837              Monr
Spilman, Hezekiah to Elizabeth Journey 14 Jan. 1819          StCh
Spilman, Michael E. to Nancy A. Price 12 Feb. 1839           Lewi
Spiva, Elisha to Frankey Thacker 23 June 1822                Cole
Spiva, Elza to Mariah Craddock 30 Oct. 1834                  Md-A
Spiva, James to Tabitha Henderson 10 May 1835                Md-A
Spivey, Elisha to Alhay Guyn 28 Aug. 1822                    Coop
Spivey, Jonas to Polly Cain 19 Mar. 1836                     Ripl
Splawn, Isaac to Isabella Atkison 31 Aug. 1835               Ray
Splawn, John Jr. to Nancy McHeny 4 Mar. 1830                 Ray
Splawn, Mayberry to Bertheny McHeny 20 Oct. 1826            Ray
Splawn, Mayberry to Frances Brassfield 20 Dec. 1838         Davi
Splawn, Moses to Ann Riggs 14 Ap. 1825                       Ray
Splawn, Wm. to Patsy Splawn 22 July 1828                     Ray
Sponhimore, Wm. to Polly Green 22 Apr. 1824                  Coop
Spooner, Geo. to Patsy Pipes 10 Jan. 1838                    Howa
Sportsman, James to Sarah Turpin 5 Dec. 1835                Char
Sportsman, John to Elizabeth Turpin 9 Aug. 1823             Char
Spradlin, Joseph to Matilda Snodgrass 4 Oct. 1832           Cr-1
Spradling, Wm. to Kissiah Baidsten 5 July 1832              Cr-1
Spratt, W.A.H. to Emily B. Crafford 4 Sept. 1835            Lafa
Spring, Harvey to Polly Poteet 12 Sept. 1833                Clay
Springer, Gershum to Catherine Gee Collins 4 Sept. 1834     Clin
Sproule, Joseph to Elizabeth McGee 8 Dec. 1836              Monr
Srum, Joseph to Polly Jones 3 Dec. 1835                     Perr
Stacy, Albert to Jane Baker 5 Jan. 1836                     Wash
Stacy, Wm. to Josy Land 14 Aug. 1830                        Jack
Stafford, Levi to Mary Linville 22 Nov. 1835                Lafa
Stafford, Richard to Eliza A. Key 26 Mar. 1837              Cr-1
Stafford, Wm. to Sarah O'Haver 19 Oct. 1837                 Wash
Staggs, Joshua to Betsey James 3 May 1816                   StCh
Stagner, Wm. to Elizabeth Throgmarton 9 Nov. 1838           Cole
Stalcup, Soloman to Mary Saunders 15 Oct. 1831              Jack
Stallard, Randolph to Mary A. Biscoe 20 July 1837           StCh
Stamm, Christian to Lucinda Myers 27 Dec. 1829              Wash
Stamm, Geo. Sr. to Mary Delany 13 Jan. 1823                 StFr
Stamp, Charles L. to Caroline Boone 13 Aug. 1835            StCh
Stamps, Wm. to Mary Reed 9 Nov. 1826                        Md-A
Standefer, Thomas to Jane Q. Penrod 28 Sept. 1839          Fran
Standifer, Wm. to Keziah Haydon 21 Dec. 1838               Monr
Standiford, Dodson to Elizabeth Pharis 7 Jan. 1834         Howa
Standiford, John to Sarah A. Bradley 30 June 1836          Howa
Standiford, Scelton to Peggy Wadkins 19 Sept. 1825         Howa
Standiford, Thomas to Rhoda Ginnings 9 Apr. 1835           Howa
Standley, Davis to Betsey Strel 2 Nov. 1819                Howa
Standley, Elihu to Minerva Ralph 22 Sept. 1831             Ray
```

```
Standley, John to Elizabeth Llewellyn 20 Nov. 1834          Char
Standley, Larkin to Elizabeth Goode 17 July 1827            Ray
Standley, Minard to Nancy Wilson 20 Oct. 1825              Howa
Standley, Rheuben to Luthy Pulliam 18 Mar. 1835            Call
Standley, Robt. to Hannah Ashby 28 Aug. 1834              Char
Standley, Thomas to Evelina Llewellyn 21 Apr. 1836        Char
Standley, Thomas to Mary Atterberry 28 Apr. 1836          Howa
Standley, Uriah to Harriet Lukus 15 Feb. 1829             Ray
Standly, Page to Mary Casteel 9 Mar. 1837                 Clin
Stanfield, James to Frances Adams 6 Sept. 1837            Polk
Stanford, Joseph to Fanney Williams 20 Mar. 1834          Pk-1
Stanley, Amza to Mahaly Bristoe 2 Sept. 1838              Polk
Stanley, Harrison to Elizaseth Shelton 1 Mar. 1836        Clin
Stanley, Hugh to Delila Ashby 24 Jan. 1826               Char
Stanley, Jeremiah to Polly Wilson 9 Sept. 1827            Howa
Stanley, John to Lovace Sartin 1 Mar. 1838               Howa
Stanley, Jonathan R. to Mrs. Jane Bigham 30 Nov. 1828     Coop
Stanley, Page to Catherine Williams 24 Mar. 1839          Buch
Stanley, Wm. to Nancy J. Holt 28 Apr. 1836               Call
Stanley, Wright L. to Sarah Elgin 5 Dec. 1833            Howa
Stanly, Wm. to Polly Burris 13 Aug. 1838                 Coop
Stansbury, Thomas to Sarah Crawford 19 Mar. 1839          Lewi
Stanton, Benj. to Matilda Baldwin 13 Mar. 1836           Clay
Stanton, Bledford to Malinda Munkers 18 Jan. 1827        Clay
Stanton, Jeremiah to Mary Smith 16 Apr. 1832             Clay
Stanton, Thomas to Margaret Ledgerwood 8 Feb. 1827       Clay
Staples, Nelson C. to Ann E. Staples 14 Mar. 1839        Lewi
Stapleton, Robt. to Melinda Bradburry 9 Apr. 1837        Fran
Stapleton, Thomas to Elizabeth Spencer 2 Mar. 1837       Fran
Stapleton, Wm. to Evaline Kingsbury 19 Feb. 1835         Howa
Stark, Charles to Sally Amos 12 June 1823                Cole
Stark, Isaac to Peggy Howard 8 Jan. 1826                 Cole
Stark, Jeremiah to Mary A. Jones 30 July 1836            Pk-1
Stark, John to Racheal Casbolt 27 Nov. 1828              Gasc
Stark, John to Elizabeth Todd 2 Feb. 1832                Cr-1
Stark, Madison to Elizabeth Barton 21 Apr. 1836          StFr
Stark, Thomas to Leah Vernon 24 Aug. 1823                Cole
Starke, Daniel to Eliza M. Cambel 6 Oct. 1832            Pk-1
Starke, John B. to Betsy Gray 2 Sept. 1813               StCh
Starkes, Charles to Elizabeth Manner 13 June 1836        Morg
Starks, Rowlen to Sarah McCorkle 19 Aug. 1824            Howa
Starky, Joel to Frances Wyatt -- -- 1825                 Gasc
Starn, Peter to Nancy Palmer 24 May 1830                 Perr
Stateler, Learner B. to Malinda S. Purdom 26 Jan. 1836   Pk-1
Statler, Abraham to Margaret Brown 9 Apr. 1831           CG-A
Statler, Christian to Susannah Bollinger 18 Sept. 1834   CG-B
Statler, Conrad to Elizabeth Leonard 24 Nov. 1836        CG-A
Statler, Peter Jr. to Peggy Masters 24 Mar. 1816         CG-1
Statler, Peter to Sally Fulbright 7 Nov. 1830            CG-A
Statler, Wiley to Mary Hart 19 Jan. 1834                 CG-A
Staton, Charles C. to Mary Adkins 13 Apr. 1834           Carr
Staton, James M. to Nancy Adkins 24 Jan. 1838            Carr
Stauns, Thomas to Sarah McCray 1 Aug. 1833               CG-A
Stazle, John to Christiane W. Rothe 2 Aug. 1839          Perr
Stean, John Y. to Frances Collins 13 Oct. 1825           Char
Steaples, John T. to Minerva Lucket 3 Apr. 1838          Mari
Stearman, Thomas J. to Polly Roberson 15 Dec. 1832       Wash
Steel, Alexander G. to Eveline S. Lewellen 24 Jan. 1839  Pk-B
Steel, Benj. to Mary J. Gilmore 13 Nov. 1838             Sali
Steel, Chester to Elizabeth Edwards 6 Nov. 1836          Lafa
Steel, David to Alcinda Leaton 20 Aug. 1835              Linc
Steel, David to Elizabeth Cannefax 15 Aug. 1837          Gree
Steel, Henry P. to Sarah Walker 26 Apr. 1835             Fran
Steel, Jesse to Elizabeth March 15 July 1829             Howa
Steel, John to Polly Davidson 30 May 1831                Howa
```

Steel, Joseph to Abby C. Morrison 15 Oct. 1827   Coop
Steel, Robt. to Osa Stout 14 Nov. 1833   Linc
Steel, Samuel to Rachael Richard -- Apr. 1827   Boon
Steel, Wm. to Margaret Simpson 24 July 1834   Monr
Steel, Wm. to Mary Kerr 28 Aug. 1834   Pk-1
Steel, Wm. I. to Martha Finch 26 Sept. 1838   Coop
Steel, Wm. W.B. to Sarah Hedrick 18 Feb. 1836   Coop
Steele, Andrew to Mary C. Campbell 24 Nov. 1839   Gree
Steele, Henry F. to Elizabeth Young 21 Jan. 1830   CG-A
Steele, James to Celia Green 29 Jan. 1826   CG-A
Steele, Samuel to Dosha Copher 28 Mar. 1821   Boon
Steely, James to Cynthia Cowan 31 Nov. 1837   Cole
Steen, John to Mary Mitchel 17 July 1838   Pett
Steen, Wm. to Narcissa Burns 30 Oct. 1830   Jeff
Stegall, Martin to Nancy Jones 6 Apr. 1823   StFr
Steigert, Urbain to Wallinge Sipoos 26 Aug. 1833   StCh
Steinbeck, Daniel to Agatha Lorimier 3 Dec. 1809   CG-1
Steinbeck, Wm. to Zilphey Poe 9 Jan. 1832   CG-A
Steines, Frederick to Bertha Herminghanz 1 Jan. 1835   Fran
Stemmons, John to Ann Copeland 10 Mar. 1822   Boon
Stephens, Absaleum W. to Eliza J. Hull 15 Mar. 1838   Monr
Stephens, Absalom to Elizabeth Haney 28 Feb. 1833   Coop
Stephens, Augustus to Nancy C. Fretwell 22 Apr. 1838   Sali
Stephens, Benj. to Cary Ryan 31 May 1827   Boon
Stephens, Beverly to Amanda Owings 3 Nov. 1836   Howa
Stephens, Charles to Margaret Valley 11 Oct. 1834   Jack
Stephens, Charles H. to Lucinda Williams 21 Dec. 1837   Lewi
Stephens, Clark to Sally Groom 13 July 1820   Howa
Stephens, Christopher to Mary A. Bourne 24 Mar. 1834   Lewi
Stephens, Dodge to Mary Cropper 4 Sept. 1834   Coop
Stephens, Gabriel to Virginia Williams 6 Feb. 1834   Md-A
Stephens, Geo. to Anne Brown 30 Dec. 1822   Clay
Stephens, Geo. to Leuisa Duvall 1 June 1826   Clay
Stephens, Geo. W. to Elizabeth Powell 20 May 1827   Md-A
Stephens, Henson to Elizabeth Gasperson 10 Apr. 1839   Fran
Stephens, Jacob to Nancy T. Egans 4 Apr. 1824   Cole
Stephens, Jacob to Nancy Deez 26 June 1836   Md-B
Stephens, Joseph to Ann McNee 17 Feb. 1825   Coop
Stephens, Joseph to Sarah Patterson 16 Dec. 1838   John
Stephens, Joseph to Polly A. Brenegan 22 Aug. 1839   Boon
Stephens, Joseph J. to Katherine Kavanaugh 29 Nov. 1832   Coop
Stephens, Joseph L. to Loueza Wiatt 24 Mar. 1836   Wash
Stephens, Lawrence to Margaret Moore 24 Sept. 1820   Coop
Stephens, Lusford to Emily Swindell 16 June 1835   Monr
Stephens, Nathan to Luise M.M.J. Old 3 Jan. 1833   Md-A
Stephens, Peter to Elizabeth Dollis 14 Mar. 1839   Coop
Stephens, Stephen Jr. to Marth J. Gilmore 16 June 1839   Linc
Stephens, Thomas to Sally Williams 17 July 1828   Cole
Stephens, Thomas to Lucretia Liegon 3 Aug. 1830   Linc
Stephens, Thomas to Betsy Leek 12 Jan. 1837   Wash
Stephens, Thomas to Jane Hoozer 11 Aug. 1839   Coop
Stephens, Thomas N. to Mary A. Swindel 11 Feb. 1834   Monr
Stephens, Wm. to Rebecca Amos 13 Nov. 1823   Cole
Stephens, Wm. to Emaline Glenn 5 Apr. 1826   Howa
Stephens, Wm. to Eliza Trotter 26 Apr. 1829   Mari
Stephens, Wm. to Pemelia Renfro 13 Mar. 1834   Boon
Stephenson, Alexander to Margaret Hill 17 Oct. 1839   CG-B
Stephenson, Augustus to Sarah Cave 9 Aug. 1827   Boon
Stephenson, Edward to Nancy Massie 17 Aug. 1815   StCh
Stephenson, Garret to Affia A. Blue 19 Sept. 1833   Monr
Stephenson, James to Katharine Hope 22 Sept. 1836   CG-A
Stephenson, John to Margaret Bennet 23 Oct. 1821   Boon
Stephenson, John to Martha Allen 17 Feb. 1830   Boon
Stephenson, John Y. to Phebe Baxter 21 Feb. 1833   Clay
Stephenson, Joseph M. to Emily Montgomery 13 Jan. 1839   Md-B

Stephenson, Levi to Polly Crowley 27 Jan. 1831   Clay
Stephenson, Marcus to Catherine Hancock 23 Sept. 1830   Howa
Stephenson, Marius to Elizabeth B. Allin 24 June 1830   Rall
Stephenson, Mark to Rachel Finnel 1 Jan. 1833   Howa
Stephenson, Samuel to Elizabeth See 5 Mar. 1833   Rall
Stephenson, Samuel F. to Elvira A. Whitledge 23 Jan. 1838   Pk-B
Stephenson, Wm. to Mary Whitson 22 Dec. 1835   Clin
Stephenson, Wm. E. to Matilda Eliot 11 Apr. 1837   Clin
Stepp, Akejah to H. Brawley 3 Oct. 1823   Howa
Stepp, James to Hannah Legitt 12 Jan. 1832   Howa
Stepp, John to Martha Leggitt 8 Dec. 1826   Howa
Stepp, Levi to Elizabeth Farris 3 Apr. 1835   Howa
Stepp, Wm. to Sarah Thomas 28 June 1839   Howa
Steppar, Peter to Marie Blockmann 30 Sept. 1839   StCh
Steregill, David to Emily Patton 2 Sept. 1828   Fran
Sterling, Jeremiah C. to Nancy McSpadden 9 Nov. 1837   John
Sterling, John to Elizabeth Keeny 21 Nov. 1837   John
Sterling, Travis to Cloe Dunkin 30 Jan. 1838   Livi
Sterman, Alfred A. to Pauline Fry 22 May 1838   Mari
Sterman, James H. to Catharine W. Roberts 28 Aug. 1838   Mari
Sternes, Wm. to Elizabeth Shrum 10 June 1838   CG-B
Sterrett, Washington to Margaret Graffort 7 Oct. 1832   Pk-1
Stevens, Frederick M. to Mrs. Ellen Cox 10 Feb. 1836   Md-B
Stevens, Jackson W. to Polly Green 22 Dec. 1839   Lewi
Stevens, Jacob to Elizabeth James -- -- 1820   CG-1
Stevens, James to Mary Love 23 Aug. 1832   Pk-1
Stevens, James to Rodd Cooper 1 Dec. 1836   Cole
Stevens, John to Mary McQuitty 4 Nov. 1834   Boon
Stevens, John to Lavenia Cooper 13 Mar. 1838   Cole
Stevens, Phillips to Sarah Howard 6 Aug. 1839   Morg
Stevens, Robt. to Elizabeth Mad 22 Jan. 1828   Cole
Stevenson, Archibald C. to Elizabeth D. Runnels 16 Jan. 1838   Clin
Stevenson, Barton to Harriet Parks 10 Apr. 1839   Henr
Stevenson, James to Martha J. Scott 8 Mar. 1836   Monr
Stevenson, Samuel to Polly Rigeway 29 Nov. 1832   Boon
Steward, Garret N. to Sarah B. Goodrich 6 June 1837   Morg
Steward, Geo. to Virginia Solivan 17 Jan. 1834   Wash
Steward, Hamilton to Sarah Patty 2 Aug. 1832   Call
Steward, Jacob to Lucinda Lampkins 27 Feb. 1820   Howa
Steward, John to Rebecca Cronester 15 Apr. 1838   CG-A
Steward, John to Sarah A. Ellison 24 Nov. 1839   Gree
Steward, Steven to Henrietta Hensley 28 Feb. 1838   Clin
Steward, Thomas to Isabella T. Winfield 8 May 1832   Perr
Steward, Thomas to Janean Donaldson 30 June 1836   Morg
Stewart, Charles to Mary J. McCauly 31 Dec. 1833   Perr
Stewart, Henry to Rachel Edes 30 Sept. 1830   Gasc
Stewart, Henry G. to Malinda Rhoads 23 Mar. 1839   Clar
Stewart, Isaac N. to Malinda Nunn 23 Feb. 1833   Rall
Stewart, James to Edith Boman 14 July 1834   Lafa
Stewart, James H. to Mary H. Young 20 Jan. 1833   Pk-1
Stewart, Jesep to Lucinda Gilliland 26 Feb. 1839   John
Stewart, John to Mary Wofort 1 Jan. 1832   Wash
Stewart, John to Relief Riffle 15 Sept. 1836   Linc
Stewart, John to Judith Harrison 26 Aug. 1838   Mill
Stewart, John K. to Gabrilla Watts 11 Mar. 1830   Linc
Stewart, Joseph to Mary McHaddan 3 Aug. 1837   Maco
Stewart, Joseph to Sarah A. Marshall 7 Aug. 1838   Pett
Stewart, Joshua to Melissa Pidcock 8 July 1838   Cr-1
Stewart, Pleasant S. to Judy Boughton 22 Mar. 1829   Jeff
Stewart, Reuben to Nancy Stewart 29 May 1831   Call
Stewart, Robt. to Lucy Lowen 4 Dec. 1832   Mari
Stewart, Robt. N. to Caroline M. Smith 23 Feb. 1839   Call
Stewart, Taylor to Tabetha Medlin 1 Oct. 1835   Cole
Stewart, Warren V. to Mary E. Buxton 20 Sept. 1838   Warr
Stewart, Wm. to Sarah Marchand 11 May 1832   Jeff

```
Stice, Abraham to Elizabeth Turpin 11 Oct. 1838          Lewi
Stice, Peter to Matilda Phelps 12 July 1827             Rall
Stice, Shelby to Jane Phelps 27 Sept. 1827              Rall
Stigmyer, Henry to Katherine H. Jacobs 10 Aug. 1834     StCh
Stiles, David to Rutha Rutherford 15 Aug. 1839          Gasc
Stiles, Simeon to Rebecca A. Hanna 13 Sept. 1838        Howa
Still, Bluford to Salina Hill 13 Oct. 1831              Boon
Still, Josiah to Emily Estes 22 Feb. 1827               StFr
Still, Joshua to Louisa Mordecai 11 Aug. 1836           Boon
Still, Moses to Elizabeth March 7 Feb. 1825             Boon
Still, Samuel to Elizabeth Fox 31 Jan. 1839             Clay
Stilwell, Abraham to Lydda Parker 1 Mar. 1839           Wash
Stimson, Chester to Louisa Bowen 18 Dec. 1838           Lewi
Stinet, Wm. to Susanah Hicks 14 Feb. 1810               CG-1
Stinett, Henry to Melinda Brown 13 July 1839            Barr
Stinnet, John to Elizabeth Hildebrandt 25 May 1837      CG-A
Stinson, James H. to Sarah Robertson 7 Feb. 1833        Morg
Stinson, Stephen to Nancy Martin 2 Feb. 1832            Coop
Stirvant, John to Elizabeth Bryan 6 May 1832            StCh
Stites, David to Sarah Murphy 9 Apr. 1820               Fran
Stites, Isaac to Susan Williams 19 June 1825            Call
Stites, James to Mary Mosbay 20 Sept. 1838              Fran
Stites, Joel to Catharine Decker 4 May 1829             Fran
Stits, Wm. to Polly Perkins 25 Mar. 1826                Fran
Stockstill, Thomas to Nancy Jones 11 June 1832          Coop
Stockton, Isac D. to Hilda Smith 18 Dec. 1834           Gree
Stockton, John to Eliza Smith 23 July 1834              Gree
Stockton, Newberry to Sally Mills 2 July 1838           Barr
Stockton, Thomas to America Jacobs 16 Apr. 1839         Boon
Stofer, John W. to Martha M. Bruffic 25 Sept. 1836      Wash
Stogden, John to America Roundtree 12 Aug. 1833         Boon
Stogden, John H. to Louisianna Caldwell 3 Jan. 1838     Fran
Stogden, Davidson to Elizabeth Rhodes 26 June 1834      Mari
Stokes, Henry W. to Elisa Bailey 28 Nov. 1839           Call
Stokes, John to Elizabeth Turnidge 2 June 1823          Ray
Stokes, Leroy to Sarah A. Johnson 26 Oct. 1837          Lafa
Stollings, Jacob to Binsey Estes 28 Mar. 1830           Clay
Stollings, Jesse to Racheal Estes 24 Feb. 1825          Clay
Stolt, Barry to Mary A. McCarty 9 Apr. 1839             Boon
Stone, Alexander to Nancy McFarland 1 Dec. 1829         Coop
Stone, Alexander to Louisa Tilford 25 Mar. 1834         Linc
Stone, Blueford to Jane A. Hansly 26 Jan. 1837          Warr
Stone, Caleb to Mary G. Woods 2 Dec. 1830               Boon
Stone, Caleb to Ann Wilson 15 May 1832                  Boon
Stone, Chilton A. to Rachel Burrass 5 Apr. 1838         Ripl
Stone, Elijah to Jane Mooney 24 Aug. 1833               Gree
Stone, Hardin to Judith Mann 22 Apr. 1832               Ray
Stone, Henderson to Terrissa Wilkinson 22 Feb. 1835     CG-B
Stone, Isaac to Rebecca Huff 23 July 1835               Wash
Stone, James to Elizabeth McHeney 29 Apr. 1829          Ray
Stone, James to Charlotte Cosner 27 Feb. 1834           Carr
Stone, Jeremiah to Jane Barnes 18 Aug. 1822             Howa
Stone, John to Sarah C. Hill 31 Jan. 1837               Clin
Stone, John H. to Catherine R. Grant 22 Feb. 1838       Call
Stone, Joseph to Ruth Armstrong 23 Dec. 1836            Clin
Stone, Joseph B. to Nancy Chilton 24 Feb. 1833          Md-A
Stone, Madison to Sarah Woods 25 Sept. 1834             Boon
Stone, Oliver to Mary Vancamp 25 Apr. 1839              Lafa
Stone, Orlington L. to Polly Cresbongy 25 Oct. 1827     Linc
Stone, Pendleton P. to Nancy Cliss 10 Nov. 1836         Linc
Stone, Radeford to Hannah R. Adams 28 Mar. 1839         Howa
Stone, Robt. to Betsy Barker 17 June 1832               Lafa
Stone, Samuel P. to Mary Powell 2 Dec. 1838             Wash
Stone, Theophelus to Elizabeth Nash 1 Apr. 1838         Mari
Stone, Wm. to Elizabeth Stinnett 23 Sept. 1837          Barr
```

Stone, Wm. to Elizabeth Buckner 21 Dec. 1037   Cole
Stone, Wm. to Fanny McTabb 22 Mar. 1838   Mari
Stone, Wm. B. to Elizabeth V. Gray 10 Aug. 1837   Call
Stone, Wm. H. to Martha Meazle 6 Feb. 1839   Barr
Stonebreaker, David to Eloisa Homes 1 Aug. 1833   Linc
Stoner, James Griffeth to Jaming Williams 12 July 1835   Fran
Stoner, Isaac to Nancy J. Roberts 21 Jan. 1836   Fran
Stonum, Samuel to Elizabeth Rockhold 12 Mar. 1832   Clay
Stonum, Wm. to Hannah J. Mathis 12 Oct. 1837   Clin
Stookey, John to Julian Rucker 24 Sept. 1835   Howa
Stookey, John D. to Patsy Stone 8 Oct. 1819   Howa
Stool, John to Belindah Twitty 18 Nov. 1828   Jeff
Stoppel, Henry to Juliann Leuwekamp 7 Aug. 1839   Fran
Storer, Raleigh D. to Huldy Lile 15 Dec. 1830   Ray
Story, Cornelius to Prudence Schrichfield 8 Feb. 1829   Coop
Story, Isaac to Rebecca Larke 8 Jan. 1829   Cole
Story, James to Rebecca Randol 4 Feb. 1827   CG-A
Story, James to Mary Poe 4 Aug. 1833   CG-A
Story, John to Mary Randol 20 Apr. 1827   CG-A
Story, Macijah to Dewey Walker 15 Mar. 1827   CG-A
Story, Wm. to Elizabeth Randol 15 Oct. 1835   CG-B
Stotler, John to Patsy Brown 6 Mar. 1827   CG-A
Stouck, John to Sarah Miller 17 June 1830   CG-A
Stoud, John to Mary A. Young 21 Jan. 1834   Boon
Stout, Anderson to Emily Hayden 7 Jan. 1831   CG-A
Stout, Daniel M. to Patsy Tharp 25 July 1815   StCh
Stout, Francis B. to Anna M. Stowers 28 Dec. 1837   Rall
Stout, Jacob to Sinthy Fortenberry 25 Aug. 1839   Ripl
Stout, James to Mary Craig 27 Jan. 1833   Linc
Stover, John to Jane Goin 5 Apr. 1838   Pett
Stow, Cephas to Amantha Richey 27 Jan. 1828   StCh
Stowe, John to Lucinda Hilderbrand 4 Oct. 1835   Jeff
Stowe, Richard to Lucinda Johnston 19 May 1834   Jeff
Stowers, Samuel to America J. Whaley 17 Nov. 1831   Mari
Strain, John to Jane McGee 31 Oct. 1830   Rall
Strange, John B. to Mary J. Shaw 5 Oct. 1836   Pk-1
Stranghan, Jacob to Milly Skidmore 1835   Boon
Straper, Mathias to Maria Miller 25 June 1839   Mari
Stratton, Daniel to Alisabeth Mayden 3 Mar. 1839   Ray
Street, Antoney to Salle Wallis 1 Apr. 1812   CG-1
Street, Corlen I. to Martha Bentley 25 Apr. 1839   Howa
Street, Presley B. to Amanda A. Wingate 22 Jan. 1835   Howa
Strewhern, Wiley to Nancy Hudgens 19 Aug. 1834   Cr-1
Strickland, Henry to Jane Hurt 31 Dec. 1835   Ripl
Strickland, James to Nancy Wilson 20 Feb. 1812   CG-1
Strickland, James to Margaret Sherrer 9 July 1837   Perr
Strickland, John to Nancy Blackwell 8 May 1830   Wash
Strickland, John to Mary A. Lamkin 1 Apr. 1833   Jeff
Strickland, John to Mrs. Sally Bounds 16 Aug. 1835   StFr
Strickland, Jonathan to Jane Williams 27 Sept. 1829   Jeff
Strickland, Titus to Celesta Semino 5 Dec. 1826   StGe
Strickland, Wm. to Rachel Stout 5 Dec. 1833   Ripl
Strickland, Wm. P. to Eliza T. Egleberger 8 Aug. 1837   Jeff
Stricklin, Abial to Isabella Henderson 27 Mar. 1834   Wash
Stricklin, Thomas to Eliza Shock 8 June 1826   Boon
Strode, Charles to Susan Bennett 30 July 1835   Jack
Strode, Jeremiah Jr. to Nancy Forman 1 Oct. 1822   Rall
Strode, Malor to Liddy Ragsdale 22 Feb. 1827   Boon
Strode, Wm. to Jane Ely 18 Jan. 1827   Rall
Strode, Wm. to Jane E. Johnson 4 June 1837   Mari
Stroder, Alexander to ---- ---- 7 Apr. 1836   CG-B
Stroder, Magnus to Sinthy Young 10 Nov. 1839   CG-B
Stroder, Thomas to Sealy Bolin 11 Mar. 1834   CG-A
Strodes, Jacob to Frances May 20 July 1826   Call
Strong, John to Mary Thompson 12 Jan. 1826   CG-A

```
Strothmann, John L. to Katherine Apins 13 Nov. 1839            Fran
Strotter, Thornton to Catharine Cooper 23 Mar. 1826            Howa
Stroud, Anderson to Mary White 11 June 1837                    Polk
Stroup, John to Elizabeth Flemming 5 May 1833                  Jeff
Stroup, Lawsin to Sally Bradshall 10 Apr. 1830                 CG-A
Struckhoff, Herman to Catherine Koopman 22 Apr. 1834          StCh
Stuart, Jacob C. to Elizabeth Bristo 11 July 1827             Gasc
Stuart, James to Hannah Philips 29 July 1830                   Gasc
Stuart, James to Sarah Decker 21 Mar. 1839                     Fran
Stuart, Joel F. to Addeline Casbaugh 12 Nov. 1839             Jack
Stuart, John H. to Ann Lindsay 25 Dec. 1833                   StCh
Stuart, Samuel to Nancy Throckmorton 12 Jan. 1829            Gasc
Stuart, Wm. to Sarah Duvall 27 Nov. 1827                       Perr
Stubblefield, Geo. W. to Nancy Briggs 22 Nov. 1821            Rall
Stubblefield, Jeremiah to Matilda C. Harrison 3 Oct. 1833     Cole
Stubblefield, Robt. to Rachel Pollard 15 Sept. 1831          Linc
Stubblefield, Robt. to Elizabeth Kenady 21 Feb. 1833         Morg
Stublefield, Wiatt to Vivey Shelton 1 July 1830               Cole
Studevant, Geo. to Maryan Morrison 18 Feb. 1835              Cr-1
Studevant, John R. to Malissa Shannon 10 July 1838          Gree
Stufflefield, Henry to Mrs. Ann Marlow 15 Nov. 1838          Lewi
Stufman, Jacob to Poly Stovers 23 Feb. 1830                   CG-A
Stunut, Reuben to Ruthy Mincher 8 May 1831                    Fran
Sturd, Charles J. to Elizabeth Simmonds 16 Oct. 1832         Coop
Stute, Taylor S. to Eliza Leaton 2 June 1836                  Linc
Stuthus, John to Sarah Cane 25 Jan. 1835                      Fran
Stuts, John to Orba Greenstreet 7 Oct. 1834                   StFr
Sucket, Frederick to Angeline Martin 14 May 1838             Linc
Sudduth, Ira to Molly I. Davis 24 Sept. 1839                 Linc
Suel, James to Polly Poage 11 Dec. 1825                       Clay
Suggett, Eagecorub to Zerilda Maupin 7 Mar. 1827             Boon
Suggett, Mentor to Louisa Petty 21 Dec. 1837                 Call
Suggett, Pope to Mary ORear 9 Feb. 1838                       Boon
Suggett, Thomas to Polly Patton 23 Nov. 1830                 Boon
Suggett, Volney to Mary H. Shortridge 23 May 1836            Call
Suggs, Charles to Elizabeth Ganter 22 Oct. 1837              Henr
Sulica, Joseph to Patsy Hughes 11 Aug. 1836                  Wash
Sulivan, James to Patsy Jacson 3 Feb. 1837                    Wash
Sullavan, James to Ruth Smelser 23 Dec. 1826                 StCh
Sullens, Nathan to Cynthia Medley 30 July 1837               Jeff
Sullins, Jefferson to Margarett Crow 19 Mar. 1829            Fran
Sullins, John to Sarah Goodin 22 June 1827                    Boon
Sullins, Peter to Sinthy Peper 22 May 1826                    Fran
Sullins, Wm. to Dorshey Gunn 26 June 1824                     Howa
Sullivan, Daniel to Mary Bonne 18 Nov. 1835                   Wash
Sullivan, Samuel to Polly Gibson 24 Mar. 1831                 CG-A
Sullivan, Samuel W. to Elizabeth Reifer 11 Apr. 1839         Sali
Sullivan, Tempest to Prunella C. Keiffer -- May 1839         Sali
Sullivan, Wm. to Mary Bone 18 Nov. 1834                       Wash
Sullivant, John to Poly Copland 5 Mar. 1837                  Cr-1
Sullivant, Joseph to Elizabeth Bolen 5 Feb. 1837            Cr-1
Sullivant, Mark to Merry Benton 8 Nov. 1834                  Cr-1
Sulson, John to Keturah Matlock 4 Apr. 1839                  Shel
Summers, Andrew to Melissa Shoemaker 24 Oct. 1838            Maco
Summers, Austin to Matilda Mattock 6 Nov. 1836               Wash
Summers, Barclay to Rebecca Hopper 21 Nov. 1837              Mari
Summers, Berkley to Sarah Wilcoxen 16 Dec. 1832              Mari
Summers, Hiram Jr. to Mary Patrick 13 Nov. 1836             Rand
Summers, Isaac Jr. to Fanny Wooldridge 21 May 1834          Rand
Summers, James to Mary Henary 6 July 1809                    CG-1
Summers, James to Rhoda Barger 15 Oct. 1834                  Morg
Summers, John Jr. to Julian Patrick 13 Feb. 1832            Rand
Summers, Joseph to Martha Green 4 May 1828                   Char
Summers, Moses to Sarah Wooldridge 4 Aug. 1832              Rand
Summers, Morris to Lucinda K.J. Patrick 3 Mar. 1833         Rand
```

Summers, Nathan to Betsy Johnson 23 Aug. 1833	Jack
Summers, Ninevah to Jane Gilstrap 7 Nov. 1832	Rand
Summers, Preston to Betsy A. Rutherford 30 July 1835	Rand
Summers, Samuel R. to Jane Isgrig 28 May 1828	Wash
Summers, Valentine to Nancy Pellers 5 Oct. 1834	Wash
Summers, Wm. to Sarah A. Pierce 13 Mar. 1834	CG-A
Summers, Wm. to Eliza Barnes 1839?	Cass
Summers, Wm. H. to Marinda A. Pinson 7 Nov. 1833	Wash
Sumner, Demps to Lucinda Lacquin 28 Feb. 1826	Cole
Sumner, Jesse to Charlotte McDermid 19 Feb. 1817	StCh
Sumner, Joseph L. to Mary A. Hall 19 May 1833	Rall
Sumner, Josiah to Betsy Ireland 13 June 1838	Davi
Sumolt, Ivy to Sally James 18 Sept. 1831	Pk-1
Sumpter, Edmunster to Mary Parker 17 Aug. 1837	Monr
Sumpter, Isaac A. to Darkes Rice 28 Dec. 1834	Rand
Sumpter, James to Ibba Hardister 2 Jan. 1834	Rand
Sumpter, John to Malinda Prather 29 May 1834	Fran
Sumpter, Robt. to Martha Parker 24 Dec. 1835	Monr
Sumpter, Urbin to Eliza Hargis 18 Mar. 1839	Wash
Surer, Wm. O. to Margaret Gorman 23 Aug. 1838	Cr-1
Surgen, I. to I. League 18 July 1839	Jeff
Sutherland, James to Sarah Riddle 24 Jan. 1836	Cr-1
Sutherland, John M. to Jane E. Huston 25 Dec. 1838	Rall
Sutherland, John N. to Oraminta McMahan 22 Mar. 1838	Coop
Sutliff, Anson to Elizabeth Vaughn 13 Dec. 1834	Cole
Sutten, John to Elisa Rackerby 3 July 1823	Rall
Sutter, Geo. to Virginia Martin 19 Nov. 1837	Rand
Suttin, Jeremiah to Sally Adkins 14 July 1839	Wash
Sutton, Hezekiah E. to Lucy C. Thomas 21 Feb. 1836	Monr
Sutton, Jonas to Sarah Martin 14 Feb. 1834	Clay
Sutton, Joseph Jr. to Elizabeth Strickland 7 Aug. 1831	Md-A
Sutton, Nathan to Syntha A. Brown 25 Aug. 1829	Md-A
Sutton, Robt. E. to Peggy A. Randel 19 Jan. 1830	Wash
Sutton, Roland to Elizabeth McCullough 2 Feb. 1823	Howa
Sutton, Valentine to Eliza Peterson 1 May 1837	Wash
Sutton, Wm. to Hannah Duff 8 Nov. 1832	StFr
Swafford, James J. to Rebecca Hethorn 26 Apr. 1837	Wash
Swan, Alfrod to Chloe Colbert 19 Nov. 1839	Linc
Swan, James F. to Nancy Dodson 6 Feb. 1835	Perr
Swaney, Daniel to Elizabeth Boli 6 Dec. 1827	Jeff
Swanson, Joseph W. to Mary Hendricks 15 Jan. 1835	Jack
Swanson, Thomas to Elizabeth St. Leager 23 July 1820	StCh
Swaringen, Alfred to Amanda McCloar 15 Sept. 1831	Pk-1
Swayze, Joshua W. to Nancy Clyce 19 Nov. 1835	Warr
Swearingen, David P. to Lydia M. Woolery 20 June 1839	Coop
Swearingen, James M. to Susan A. Scruggs 5 Sept. 1839	Cole
Swearingen, John R. to Polly Baxter 4 Sept. 1818	Howa
Swearingen, Mides to Mary Mahon 5 Feb. 1818	Howa
Swearingen, Obediah to Sophia McClain 17 Aug. 1820	Howa
Swearingen, Samuel to Amanda Wiles 12 Nov. 1830	Howa
Swearingen, Thomas to Leary Calloway 24 Jan. 1828	Howa
Swearingen, Wm. to Lucy Mahon 28 May 1818	Howa
Swearingen, Wm. to Polly Hinley 2 Sept. 1819	Coop
Swearingen, Wm. to Rebecca Johnson 29 Mar. 1832	Coop
Swearinger, Thomas to Polly Ashcraft 3 Jan. 1839	Monr
Sweeny, Louis to Euphrosine Barribo 14 Aug. 1836	StCh
Sweet, Samuel to Rebecca Patterson 13 Sept. 1832	Jack
Sweezy, Peter to Malinda Hayes 7 May 1836	Call
Swetman, John to Mary A. Belmear 16 July 1835	Howa
Swetman, Sydney to Susanna Hardin 21 Jan. 1830	Howa
Swezer, David to Nancy Roberts 5 Oct. 1826	Howa
Swift, Henry to Absneth Selby 8 July 1830	Boon
Swift, Nathan to Sally Campbell 24 Nov. 1825	Pk-1
Swift, Washington to Betsy A. Taber 15 Sept. 1836	Cr-1
Swimmer, John to Jane McQuary 3 May 1836	Pk-1

```
Swindel, John to Vianna Cruse 23 Jan. 1834                        Monr
Swinney, Chesley to Jane Burton 17 Jan. 1830                      Rall
Swinney, Fountain to Martha Dent 1 Apr. 1838                      Monr
Swinney, James to Ann Smith 10 Dec. 1831                          Rand
Swinney, Preston to Rebina Hull 29 Sept. 1835                     Monr
Swinney, Thomas to Polly Andrews 24 Apr. 1828                     Howa
Switzler, Greenvill to Catharine Spott 8 Sept. 1839              Sali
Swoot, Armstead to Elizabeth Smith 19 Oct. 1826                  Char
Swope, Charles to Melissa Wilds 3 Apr. 1837                      Howa
Swope, Medeth to Sarah Greer 19 Dec. 1839                        Pett
Sydes, Daniel to Lydia Miller 12 Mar. 1839                       CG-B
Sydes, Elisha to Sicy Welker 25 Jan. 1833                        Perr
Symes, Wm. to Polly Gay 24 Oct. 1839                             Boon
Symms, John to Martha A. Huffman 29 Jan. 1835                    Clay
Sympson, Hubbard to Sarah Greenstreet 28 Oct. 1838              Fran
Sype, Eli to Christenah Rhyne 28 Apr. 1835                       Perr
Sytes, Alexander to Anna Sytes 26 Aug. 1837                      CG-A


Tabor, Solomon to Susan Harman 26 Nov. 1835                      Cr-1
Tacket, Wm. to Sariann Chapple 8 Oct. 1837                       Gasc
Tackett, Geo. to Mary Pryor 14 Aug. 1828                         Gasc
Tackett, John to Sally Hensley 30 July 1829                      Gasc
Tagart, Abner to Audrey Lamasters 22 Mar. 1837                   StCh
Tagart, Rezen S. to Nancy A. Baldridge 9 Nov. 1837             StCh
Taggart, Archibald to Mary Henson 21 Dec. 1826                   Howa
Tailor, David P. to Mary Dowty 21 Apr. 1831                      CG-A
Tailor, Geo. W. to Mary A. Estes 4 May 1829                     Lafa
Tailor, John to Nancy Walker 21 Dec. 1831                        CG-A
Talbot, John A. to Alice W. Daly 13 June 1833                    Howa
Taler, Francis to Susanna Young 9 July 1839                      Clay
Taler, John L. to Martha Wilkerson 31 Aug. 1835                 Call
Tally, David C. to Mary A. Fristow 6 Sept. 1839                 Jack
Tally, Henderson to Mary A.C. Taylor 15 Dec. 1836              Coop
Tally, Wiley to Sally Wilkerson 13 Jan. 1831                     Rall
Tally, Wm. to Louisa Watkins 16 Jan. 1833                        Boon
Tally, Wm. J. to Rachael Harmon 24 Nov. 1836                    Monr
Tandy, Wm. to Elizabeth Spence 15 Sept. 1835                    Mari
Tankersly, James to Agnes Calloway 23 May 1838                 Coop
Tankersly, Levi to Eve Kinder 19 Oct. 1828                       CG-A
Tankersly, Lorenzo to Nancy Sides 29 Jan. 1835                  Md-A
Tansy, Levi to Nancy Mitchell 5 Mar. 1826                        Fran
Tapley, Green to Hannah Parker 1 Mar. 1825                       Rall
Tapley, Joseph D. to Jemima C. Matson 13 May 1830              Pk-1
Tapley, Thomas to Patty Cole 21 Sept. 1830                       StFr
Tapp, Pendleton W. to Martha Dycke 22 Oct. 1839               Clay
Tarick, Peter to Elizabeth Jones 10 Jan. 1833                   StFr
Tarlton, James to Ann Murphy 25 Dec. 1825                        CG-1
Tarpley, Peterson to Mary Boring 12 June 1839                   StFr
Tarrant, Erasmus to Mrs. Ann Huffaker 2 May 1833              Clay
Tarwater, Jacob to Diana Rowland 22 Apr. 1836                   Ray
Tarwater, John to Ruth Odle 13 Sept. 1820                        Sali
Tarwater, John to Sarah Loid 31 May 1826                        Ray
Tarwater, John to Louisa Robertson 25 June 1835                Ray
Tarwater, Lewis to Martha A. McHeney 26 June 1831             Ray
Tarwater, Louis to Mary McGuire 1 May 1825                      Ray
Tarwater, Samuel to Mary Broadhurst 8 Sept. 1825              Ray
Tarwater, Steven to Rachel Rowland 11 Sept. 1830              Ray
Tary, Simeon to Elizabeth A. Adams 11 Oct. 1838               Howa
Tate, Allen to Cerilda Banus 4 Dec. 1832                        Howa
Tate, Caleb W. to Emily Hamblin 8 Oct. 1839                     Call
Tate, Calvin H. to Elizabeth H. Allen 11 Feb. 1835           Call
Tate, Geo. to Mary E. Early 21 Mar. 1838                        Pk-B
Tate, Isaac to Jane Henderson 14 July 1830                      Call
Tate, John to Nancy Donaldson 10 June 1826                      Rall
```

```
Tate, Leonard to Malinda Keathley 7 Aug. 1838              Linc
Tate, Nathanial to Sarah Bailey 17 Mar. 1833               CG-A
Tate, Richard C. to Elizabeth Hamblin 17 Oct. 1839         Call
Tate, Thomas to Mary Keathley 14 June 1838                 Linc
Taylor, Airs to Mary J. McAtee 26 May 1836                 Rall
Taylor, Andrew to Barbary Murray 20 Nov. 1834              Cole
Taylor, Archibald to Sonorie E. Carr 1 Dec. 1836           Linc
Taylor, Benj. to Temperance Ashebranner 15 May 1830        CG-A
Taylor, Caleb to Margaret McCoy 4 May 1837                 Mari
Taylor, Carter P. to Minerva Collett 30 July 1829          Howa
Taylor, Charles to Mary Mathews 4 May 1815                 CG-1
Taylor, Christopher to Darkey Fields 24 June 1823          Ray
Taylor, Creed to Margaret Harris 15 July 1832              Jack
Taylor, Daniel to Hannah Creason 28 Dec. 1837              Ray
Taylor, David to Eliza Packwood 23 Dec. 1838               Barr
Taylor, Felix to Rebecca Nickols 23 Mar. 1837              Fran
Taylor, Fountain to Delilah McCann 12 Sept. 1839           Warr
Taylor, Francis to Polly Morris 3 Mar. 1831                Rand
Taylor, Francis to Sarah Ross 29 Dec. 1831                 StCh
Taylor, Geo. to Rhody Elliott 25 Apr. 1836                 Ray
Taylor, H.H. to Sarah Pritchett 1 Nov. 1838                Clar
Taylor, Harry R. to Ellen E. McClean 23 Aug. 1839          Rand
Taylor, Henry to Lydda Brickey 7 Apr. 1832                 Wash
Taylor, Isaac to Sally Holman 17 Mar. 1818                 Howa
Taylor, Isaac to Mary Asherbranner 10 Mar. 1832            CG-A
Taylor, Jacob to Julia N. Birkhear 21 Nov. 1839            Linc
Taylor, James to Caty Robertson 20 July 1826               Ray
Taylor, James to Sarah Huffman 25 Oct. 1831                Clay
Taylor, James to Louisa Farris 22 May 1834                 Coop
Taylor, James to Catharine Dunn 5 Aug. 1835                Perr
Taylor, James to Clarinda Gibson 26 May 1836               Ripl
Taylor, James to Sarah Lindley 16 June 1838                Polk
Taylor, James to Pamelia Woggener 25 Sept. 1839            Linc
Taylor, James B. to Elizabeth A. Lilly 27 Oct. 1836        Mari
Taylor, James W. to Sarah C. Ruder 21 Oct. 1838            Warr
Taylor, Jeremiah Jr. to Clara Luvless 25 Apr. 1833         Mari
Taylor, John to Elizabeth Laytham 8 Apr. 1830              Mari
Taylor, John to Elizabeth Calvert 12 Apr. 1832             Coop
Taylor, John to Mrs. Mary Couples 27 Mar. 1834             CG-A
Taylor, John to Nancy Burkel 3 Apr. 1834                   Clay
Taylor, John to Louisa McDonald 20 Dec. 1835               Ray
Taylor, John to Mrs. Precilla Thompson 6 June 1836         Perr
Taylor, John to Margaret C. Farr 23 May 1837               CG-A
Taylor, John to Cleopatra Fraizer 18 Dec. 1838             Lewi
Taylor, John H. to Lemisey Seat 11 Jan. 1835               Morg
Taylor, John H. to Mary A. Clark 10 Sept. 1839             CG-B
Taylor, Joseph to Caty Senor 4 Sept. 1819                  Howa
Taylor, Joseph M. to Emily Findley 6 Aug. 1839             Morg
Taylor, Josiah to Jinsey Loveall 12 Apr. 1832              Ray
Taylor, Larkin to Mary A. Kitchum 3 Nov. 1835              Boon
Taylor, Levy to Menerva Bone 20 June 1831                  Coop
Taylor, Martin to Elizabeth Usher 29 July 1835             Cole
Taylor, Michael F. to Luceal Rodney 14 June 1832           CG-A
Taylor, Nathan to Patience Wade 8 Sept. 1824               Cole
Taylor, Perry Y. to Elizabeth Murray 27 Aug. 1833          Cole
Taylor, Reuben to Kezia Watson 18 May 1836                 Ripl
Taylor, Robt. to Jane Joenes 21 Jan. 1819                  StCh
Taylor, Robt. to Mary Trotter 31 May 1834                  Lewi
Taylor, Samuel K. to Hetty Smoot 4 Feb. 1836               Lewi
Taylor, Thomas to Ann Simpson 29 Nov. 1832                 Cole
Taylor, Thomas to Barbara Tucker 25 Aug. 1835              Perr
Taylor, Thomas to Lydia Dearing 5 Mar. 1837                Call
Taylor, Tilford to Catharon Johnston 20 Mar. 1833          Warr
Taylor, Vincent to Mary McCann 6 Nov. 1839                 Warr
Taylor, Warren to Catherine Gilliam 29 Jan. 1839           Clin
```

```
Taylor, Washington to Patience Step 16 Mar. 1826                    StCh
Taylor, Wm. to Susy Crow 2 Nov. 1828                               StCh
Taylor, Wm. to Polly Sumolt 27 Nov. 1828                           Pk-1
Taylor, Wm. to Ann Fisher 20 Jan. 1829                             Perr
Taylor, Wm. to Lucy Ham 29 Sept. 1831                              Call
Taylor, Wm. to Mary Wintfield 3 Nov. 1835                          Perr
Taylor, Wm. to Ibby Fields 3 Nov. 1835                             Ray
Taylor, Wm. to Elizabeth Taylor 14 Nov. 1835                       Wash
Taylor, Wm. to Jane Barnett 1 Oct. 1838                            Morg
Tayon, Benedict to Senorada Marischalle 26 Sept. 1826             StCh
Tayon, Charles to Charlotte Ganscom 12 Aug. 1812                   StCh
Tayon, Ignace to Mary Cote 22 Jan. 1834                            StCh
Tayon, Ignatious to Mary Tiercero 4 Feb. 1833                      StCh
Tayon, Joseph to Julie Marechal 7 June 1805                        StCh
Tayon, Joseph to Catherine Martinall 12 Nov. 1832                  StCh
Teage, Elder to Hannah Silvers 23 Mar. 1826                        Lafa
Teague, David to Polly Williams 16 Sept. 1829                      Jack
Teague, James to Lydia Silvers 6 Sept. 1832                        Jack
Teal, Charles to Sarah Dillon 5 July 1827                          Md-A
Teal, John to Rebecca Bombaugh 22 June 1828                        Md-A
Teale, James to Polly C. Clare 26 Dec. 1837                        Linc
Teas, Geo. W. to Sarah A. Younger 1 July 1832                      Boon
Teas, Samuel to Evaline Blackwell 20 Apr. 1830                     Wash
Tedford, Samuel to Rachel E. Graham 9 Dec. 1834                    Rand
Teeter, Garrard to Polly Brason 2 Sept. 1823                       Boon
Teeter, Geo. to Polly Ridale 30 Dec. 1821                          Boon
Teeter, Peter A. to Mary S. Greer 4 Sept. 1833                     Boon
Teeters, Geo. to Nancy Farrar 16 Apr. 1832                         Boon
Teeters, Lewis to Polly Mays 24 June 1819                          Howa
Teeters, Michael to Mrs. Catherine Kelly 21 Apr. 1834             StCh
Teeters, Robt. to Catherine Hicum 14 Jan. 1820                     Howa
Tegg, Archabal C. to Ann C. Copel 25 Dec. 1834                     Lafa
Telford, Samuel to Athalia Smith 3 June 1836                       Lafa
Temberlake, James to Lavina Holden 1 Feb. 1838                     Warr
Temple, Andrew B. to Mary Hoges 2 Oct. 1836                        Wash
Temple, Geo. to Mariah Thornton 4 Feb. 1827                        Howa
Templeton, Mijaman to Mary Mackey 5 Jan. 1832                      Pk-1
Tena, Ambrose to Peggy McCoy 30 Oct. 1828                          StCh
Tenell, John to Amanda Rickey 24 Sept. 1835                        Fran
Tenison, Joseph to Elvira Cooper 24 Dec. 1835                      Cr-1
Tennerson, John to Honor Holden 9 Aug. 1836                        Gasc
Tennille, Geo. to Sally Davis 21 Nov. 1819                         Coop
Tennison, Harrison to Elizabeth Newberry 19 Jan. 1837             Cr-1
Tennison, John to Rebecca Clankey 7 Jan. 1828                      CG-A
Tennison, Samuel to Polly B. Wiley 18 Aug. 1837                    Cr-1
Terlamond, Jacob to Elizabeth Powers 9 May 1834                    Gree
Ternia, John A. to Polly A. Eads 1 Mar. 1832                       Wash
Terrell, Benj. to June Stoga 26 Jan. 1834                          Mari
Terrell, Cornelius D. to Elizabeth Wilson 21 Apr. 1835            Gree
Terrell, James A. to Hester A.R. Kelso 24 Jan. 1833               Call
Terrell, Wm. H. to Cyrenaann Sams 29 June 1836                     Mari
Terril, Herry to Patsy Jones 29 Jan. 1819                          Howa
Terril, Josephus to Mary Pepper 18 May 1837                        Mari
Terrill, James A. to Rebecca Wright 2 Feb. 1837                    Rand
Terrill, Wm. to Virginia Sorell 15 Oct. 1839                       Gasc
Terry, David to Elizabeth Williams 16 May 1839                     Linc
Terry, Green to Elizabeth Childers 8 Jan. 1834                     Gasc
Terry, John B. to Elizabeth Bounds 16 Aug. 1836                    Lafa
Terry, Lewis to Catrean Armen 17 Mar. 1835                         Fran
Tessereau, Bernard to Polly Green 25 Apr. 1830                     Md-A
Tesson, Abraham to Anne McDonald 24 Aug. 1837                      Jeff
Tesson, John B. to Isabella Hunt 5 Sept. 1839                      Jeff
Teters, Benj. to Mary Holmes 12 May 1834                           StCh
Teters, Wm. to Mary A. Culver 19 Apr. 1829                         StCh
Tetherford, Wm. to Rachel Stevens 4 June 1835                      Ripl
```

Tetherow, James to Polly Smith 16 July 1837   Clin
Tevault, Jesse to Elizabeth McGaw 17 Aug. 1820   Ray
Tevis, John W. to Sarah C. Thurston 22 Dec. 1836   Morg
Thacker, Joel to Mariah Brumly 9 June 1839   Mill
Tharp, Jackson to Harriett Barton 26 Aug. 1823   Howa
Tharp, James to Rebecca Jones 10 Oct. 1816   Howa
Tharp, Jeremiah to Mary W. Kelsoe 5 Oct. 1837   Call
Tharp, Joel to Susannah Hough 17 Oct. 1833   Call
Tharp, John to Lucy Embree 23 July 1818   Howa
Tharp, John C. to Mariah Mozun 28 May 1833   Jack
Tharp, Obediah to Margit March 25 Feb. 1836   Gree
Tharp, Tiny to Nancy Burnham 8 Feb. 1827   Howa
Thatcher, Elijah N. to Nancy S. Griffith 11 Aug. 1839   Call
Thatcher, John to Ann Hase 18 Dec. 1828   Call
Thatcher, John to Virginia B. Wells 25 Sept. 1839   Pk-B
Thatcher, Wm. S. to Charlotte Westbrook 9 May 1839   Call
Thaxton, James to Polly Stoker 12 Sept. 1839   Call
Theague, John R. to Lutitia Silvers 21 Mar. 1839   Buch
Therman, Robt. P. to Any Tilford 13 Dec. 1832   Boon
Thermon, Claybourn M. to Rebecca Mackey 14 Mar. 1833   Pk-1
Thibault, Louis to Louise Robert 15 May 1827   Wash
Thibeau, Antoin to Briget Robert 6 Feb. 1838   Wash
Thibeau, Etienne to Marie L. Collman 26 Nov. 1833   Wash
Thiemann, Frederick to Caroline Leever 27 Oct. 1839   Lafa
Thinsey, Thomas to Patsy Hill 20 Dec. 1821   Howa
Thirman, John to Lucy Shelton 10 Jan. 1833   Linc
Thomas, Rev. ---- to Jane Spiva 28 July 1835   Md-A
Thomas, Abraham M. to Lucinda Munday 7 May 1835   Pk-1
Thomas, Andrew to Alesy Renfrow 23 Aug. 1835   Ripl
Thomas, Barnett to Elizabeth Caldin 7 Feb. 1839   Boon
Thomas, Benj. to Elizabeth Sipple 17 Mar. 1831   Rand
Thomas, Benj. to Maria Hans 24 Apr. 1836   Wash
Thomas, Claiborne to Ann A. Braley 31 July 1828   CG-A
Thomas, Daniel to Elizabeth Canada 14 Feb. 1832   Wash
Thomas, Daniel C. to Martha J. Pearson 6 May 1838   Clay
Thomas, David to Mary A. Smith 10 Dec. 1835   StCh
Thomas, Edmond to Sarah Martin 25 June 1834   Lafa
Thomas, Elisha W. to Ailsey McKinney 15 May 1838   Carr
Thomas, Henry to Mary A.S. Bryant 28 Jan. 1834   Monr
Thomas, Henry to Elizabeth B. Donalson 15 July 1838   Monr
Thomas, Henry M. to Mary Robberts 28 Jan. 1838   Clay
Thomas, Hiram H. to Elizabeth Meredith 1 Feb. 1835   Call
Thomas, Ira to Malisa Fox 18 May 1824   Call
Thomas, Isaac to Harriet Goodno 9 Apr. 1829   Coop
Thomas, Jackson to Sarah McGee 11 May 1837   Monr
Thomas, Jacob to Catherine Woolsey 27 Apr. 1820   Coop
Thomas, Jacob W. to Jane Thomas 7 Mar. 1830   Pk-1
Thomas, James to Polly Cleaveland 17 Jan. 1828   Wash
Thomas, James to Hannah J. Waters 5 Oct. 1836   Boon
Thomas, James H. to Sarah E. Fisher 6 Jan. 1836   Jack
Thomas, James P. to Elizabeth Rochester 4 Dec. 1828   StCh
Thomas, John to Elizabeth Bradley 6 Jan. 1819   Howa
Thomas, John to Nancy Murry 28 Jan. 1834   Ray
Thomas, John to Darcus Munday 13 Nov. 1834   Pk-1
Thomas, John to Theresa C. Green 29 Jan. 1839   Rall
Thomas, John to Safrania Harrison 9 Apr. 1839   Ripl
Thomas, John D. to Mary Knaus 20 June 1838   Howa
Thomas, John M. to Elizabeth Rutledge 6 July 1834   Lafa
Thomas, Jonas to Isella Woolery 8 Feb. 1835   Coop
Thomas, Jonathan to Mary A. Stuttress 24 Aug. 1836   StCh
Thomas, Jonathan G. to Mary T. Smith 28 May 1837   Morg
Thomas, Joseph to Rachel Ham 9 Mar. 1837   Call
Thomas, Joseph H. to Sallyan Sidwell 27 Jan. 1831   Pk-1
Thomas, Larkin to Louisa Addar 12 Feb. 1833   Call
Thomas, Lewis B. to Polly Robertson 26 Aug. 1823   Call

```
Thomas, Marten to Polly Faurbis 20 Oct. 1833              CG-A
Thomas, Massey to Phebe Bain 7 May 1837                   Lewi
Thomas, Matthew to Rebecca Williams 23 May 1829           Jeff
Thomas, Napoleon B. to Sarah Faubian 18 Sept. 1834        Clay
Thomas, Nelson to Susan Edmonds 19 Feb. 1835              Wash
Thomas, Peter to Martha Maupin 19 Nov. 1835               Monr
Thomas, Phillips J. to Verlinda Duncan 24 Feb. 1831       Pk-1
Thomas, Porter to Paulina Andrews 17 Aug. 1837            Clar
Thomas, Randolph to Mary Fauks 29 Dec. 1836               Rand
Thomas, Robt. to Louisa Herill 5 Dec. 1838                Lewi
Thomas, Samuel to Elizabeth Wells 13 May 1830             Pk-1
Thomas, Thomas to Melinda Hann 24 Oct. 1837               Boon
Thomas, Thomas T. to Nancy Curl 6 Dec. 1829               Ray
Thomas, Wm. to Amanda Wood 28 Feb. 1830                   Rall
Thomas, Wm. to Ann Stanton 7 Sept. 1833                   Clin
Thomas, Wm. to Patsy Morgan 25 Nov. 1835                  Ray
Thomas, Wm. to Elizabeth Behurst 17 July 1838             CG-A
Thomas, Wm. H. to Cindrilla Tevis 29 Jan. 1836            Coop
Thomas, Wm. L. to Polly Lane 11 Jan. 1835                 Char
Thomas, Young to Sally Davis 15 Mar. 1836                 Sali
Thomason, Andrew to Matilda Webb 7 Jan. 1830              CG-A
Thomasson, Gabriel to Sarah Orton 3 Jan. 1837             StFr
Thomasson, Richard to Fanny Williams 25 May 1837          StFr
Thompkins, Geo. to Elizabeth Lientz 9 Sept. 1824          Boon
Thompkins, James B. to Sarah Edwards 3 Mar. 1834          Perr
Thompson, Alexander to Sarah Craig 29 Mar. 1828           Wash
Thompson, Allen to Susan Miller 25 Jan. 1838              Clay
Thompson, Andrew J. to Lucy A. Holloway 7 July 1833       Cole
Thompson, Asa to Peggy Wallace 13 Mar. 1821               Howa
Thompson, Benj. W. to Martha Wilkerson 6 Dec. 1838        CG-A
Thompson, Calvin to Elizabeth Looving 7 July 1839         Gasc
Thompson, David to Ann Dorting 12 July 1827               Call
Thompson, Elmore to Patsy Smith 25 Feb. 1830              Boon
Thompson, Geo. to Nancy O'Bannion 29 Jan. 1818            Howa
Thompson, Geo. to Elcey Greenstreet 8 Feb. 1833           Fran
Thompson, Geo. C. to Eleanor Leeper 29 July 1830          Call
Thompson, Hezekiah to Martha Stow 26 July 1838            Polk
Thompson, Hiram to Elisabeth Daile 2 June 1822            Rall
Thompson, Isaac to Mary J. Sorrell 25 Dec. 1836           Rand
Thompson, James to Hester Estes 22 Feb. 1834              StFr
Thompson, James to Nancy Danford 12 Mar. 1835             Gasc
Thompson, James to Lonesa Clay 22 Nov. 1835               Cole
Thompson, James to Rebecca Mathews 21 Oct. 1838           Ripl
Thompson, James to Emeline Dickey 13 Dec. 1838            Cass
Thompson, James to Eliza Little 7 May 1839                Rall
Thompson, James H. to Mary A. Jones 26 Dec. 1837          Shel
Thompson, James S. to Martha J. Ogel 17 Apr. 1834         Linc
Thompson, Jesse to Mahala Gibson 17 Feb. 1836             Linc
Thompson, John to ---- Munkres 28 June 1818               Howa
Thompson, John to Sarah Richards 23 Mar. 1823             Clay
Thompson, John to Mary Cain 28 Sept. 1826                 Wash
Thompson, John to Mary Holliway 2 May 1832                Gasc
Thompson, John to Mary A. Knott 18 Sept. 1832             Perr
Thompson, John to Catherine Delaney 9 Nov. 1835           StFr
Thompson, John to Martha A. Saunders 29 Nov. 1836         Pk-1
Thompson, John to Mrs. Mary I. Hall 18 Apr. 1837          Mari
Thompson, John to Francis Jackson 25 Jan. 1838            Monr
Thompson, John A. to Jane Morton 17 May 1838              CG-A
Thompson, John D. to Lucretia E. Boyd 28 Nov. 1839        Polk
Thompson, John W. to Polly Campbell 13 Apr. 1826          Fran
Thompson, Joseph to Patsy Baker 13 Jan. 1831              Call
Thompson, Joseph to Hannah M. Vanderpool 12 Nov. 1837     Ray
Thompson, Leonard to Elizabeth Hog 15 Mar. 1832           Coop
Thompson, Madison to Eliza Anderson 15 May 1835           Gasc
Thompson, Micajah to Elizabeth Mefford 20 Nov. 1832       Pk-1
```

Thompson, Napoleon to Matilda L. Lindsey 9 Apr. 1829   Pk-1
Thompson, Patrick H. to Letitia Shelby Thompson 24 Aug. 1835   Carr
Thompson, Phillip M. to Brunette Lawless 4 Oct. 1818   Howa
Thompson, Robt. to Lucy T. Nowlin 11 Apr. 1826   Sali
Thompson, Robt. to Mary Howdershell 10 Sept. 1835   Linc
Thompson, Samuel to Amanda Crump 27 July 1828   CG-A
Thompson, Smith to Mary A. Jackson 25 Jan. 1838   Monr
Thompson, Walter to Martha Hickaby 29 Aug. 1830   Rand
Thompson, Wm. to Nancy Petty 23 Aug. 1819   StCh
Thompson, Wm. to Lucinda Douglass 20 Nov. 1828   CG-A
Thompson, Wm. to Jane E. Kincaid 18 Dec. 1832   Clay
Thompson, Wm. to Sarah A. Sheilds 1 Oct. 1835   Pk-1
Thompson, Wm. to Martha Moman 8 Sept. 1836   Gasc
Thompson, Wm. J. to Susan E. Wood 13 Dec. 1838   Fran
Thompson, Wm. P. to Sarah J. Moss 18 July 1839   Howa
Thomson, Geo. F. to Mary J. Pulliam 24 June 1829   Sali
Thomson, Jesse Q. to Mrs. Nancy M. Legue 8 Feb. 1838   Mari
Thomson, Mathew to Elizabeth Lick 2 Jan. 1834   Perr
Thomson, Milton to Midred Scroggins 21 Sept. 1837   Pett
Thomson, Morton to Sarah Powel 22 Dec. 1839   Pett
Thomson, Wm. to Mary Ramsey 2 Jan. 1838   Gasc
Thomure, Francious to Celeste Deguire 4 Oct. 1826   StGe
Thorice, Louis to Marguret Grandby 17 Aug. 1826   StGe
Thorn, Samuel to Ann Walker 3 Nov. 1831   CG-A
Thornhill, Duford to Elizabeth A. Burkhead 6 Sept. 1836   Linc
Thornhill, Leonard to Elizabeth Ewell 25 Dec. 1834   Ray
Thornhill, Wm. to Sarah A. Jones 22 Aug. 1839   Fran
Thornton, David to Nancy Alexander 22 May 1836   CG-A
Thornton, Hiram to Sophia Turley 16 Apr. 1835   Coop
Thornton, Isaac to Rachel Chappell 2 Feb. 1837   Sali
Thornton, John to Katherine House 7 Dec. 1820   Coop
Thornton, John to Sally Morgan 24 July 1823   Ray
Thornton, John to Sarah Oldham 7 Apr. 1836   Sali
Thornton, Peter to Elizabeth Snider 16 Sept. 1824   Char
Thornton, Wm. to Hannah Todd 10 Oct. 1837   Howa
Thorp, Dodson H. to Rebecky Adams 20 Mar. 1822   Clay
Thorp, Green B. to Nancy Linville 14 Oct. 1830   Clay
Thorp, Joseph to Dorothy M. Vaughn 9 Feb. 1826   Clay
Thorp, Joseph to Nancy Monroe 21 Sept. 1834   Clay
Thorp, Lamech to Sarah A. Hughes 19 Aug. 1832   Wash
Thorp, Orval W. to Milly Fugate 3 Apr. 1826   Boon
Thorp, Owen to Elizabeth Hiett 10 June 1821   Ray
Thorp, Owen to Nancy McGee 25 Oct. 1831   Clay
Thorp, Wm. to Elizabeth Rowley 31 Mar. 1825   Clay
Thorp, Zachariah to ---- Ellis 22 Aug. 1834   Clay
Thorpe, Robt. to Elender Hays 23 July 1835   Boon
Thraeldkild, Geo. to Eveline Sexton 11 June 1835   Boon
Thrailkill, Jacob to Eleanor A. Harvey 6 July 1831   Sali
Thrailkill, James to Mary A. Winkler 16 Apr. 1838   Sali
Thrailkill, John to Emily Moore 28 May 1834   Ray
Thrasher, Elias to Fanny Lear 19 Dec. 1826   Rall
Thrasher, Stephen to Lucinda Mullins 13 Nov. 1828   Mari
Thrasher, Stephen F. to Sarah Rush 23 Feb. 1837   Mari
Thrasher, Stephen F. to Mary Wine 8 Nov. 1838   Rall
Thrasher, Wm. to Mary Miller 25 Jan. 1838   Mari
Thro, Casper to Catherine Bobenreid 15 Nov. 1838   StCh
Thro, Melchoir to Catherine Crater 10 May 1838   StCh
Thrombugh, Loland to Polly Andrews 19 May 1832   Lafa
Throop, Thomas J. to Mary Throop 17 Oct. 1839   Clar
Thruston, Richard to Mary J. Walker 11 May 1837   Sali
Thurman, Bennet to Fleny Calvert 14 Nov. 1839   Wash
Thurman, Daniel to Sintha Hill 28 Mar. 1839   Morg
Thurman, John to Jane Ally 7 May 1837   Cole
Thurman, John to Margaret Cantley 29 July 1838   Fran
Thurman, Wm. to Martha Adkinson 30 Sept. 1836   Morg

```
Thurmon, Joseph to Mrs. Dicy A. McAnry 23 Sept. 1838          Pk-B
Thurmond, Geo. to Frances Shaw 21 Aug. 1838                   Pk-B
Thurston, John B. to Nancy R. Walton 29 June 1837            Morg
Thurston, Wm. R. to Mary A. Walton 7 Nov. 1839              Morg
Tibbits, Andrew to Mary R. Swain 27 Sept. 1838              Pk-B
Tice, John to Analia Conrades 4 Dec. 1834                   Warr
Tidwell, Garret to Lean Miers 17 Nov. 1829                  Md-A
Tiege, Pearson to Delila Whitehead 19 July 1838            Clin
Tiercero, Louis to Catherine Tayon 4 Feb. 1833            StCh
Tigert, Josiah to Nancy Span 7 Mar. 1830                   Cr-P
Tilford, John to Sarah Hanna 23 Jan. 1834                  Ray
Tilford, Samuel to Eliza Proctor 25 Mar. 1828             Boon
Tilford, Thomas to Eleanor M. Haynes 16 Nov. 1832         Ray
Tiller, Richard A. to Elizabeth Shipley 25 Apr. 1839      Cole
Tillery, Clayton to Mary J. Ligon 29 June 1826            Clay
Tillery, Clayton to Ann M. Vaughn 6 Apr. 1837             Clay
Tillery, Eppy to Malianda Vaughn 6 July 1824              Clay
Tillery, Reuben to Mary Adkins 5 Sept. 1825               Clay
Tillery, Wm. to Susan J. Powe 31 Oct. 1838                Clin
Tillery, Wm. W. to Susan L. Poave 30 Oct. 1838            Clay
Timberlake, Benj. E. to Eliza M. Overstreet 20 Dec. 1836  StCh
Timberlake, John M. to Elizabeth Mason 3 Nov. 1835        Jack
Timmonds, John to Sarah Harris 14 July 1831               Cr-1
Tinan, Antwine to Syntha Moore 10 Dec. 1829               Md-A
Tindel, Thomas to Emmerly Kingsbury 18 Apr. 1839          Howa
Tiner, Jesse to Sophia Mitchell 23 May 1834               Gree
Tinker, Charles to Luceta Roberts 19 Nov. 1835            Pk-1
Tinker, John to Delila Harris 16 Oct. 1828                Wash
Tinnen, Hugh to Elizabeth Harris 30 Jan. 1814             CG-1
Tinnen, Hugh to Sarah Bollinger 25 Mar. 1832              CG-A
Tinnin, Azeriah to Susanah Yount 13 Feb. 1817             CG-1
Tinnisson, John to Mary Armstrong 18 Apr. 1830            Md-A
Tipet, James to Ann Bells 13 Dec. 1836                    Carr
Tipton, John to Lucinda Everett 1 Jan. 1838               Clay
Tipton, Michel to America Mothershead 15 Apr. 1838        Monr
Tipton, Samuel to Syntha Richardson 12 Dec. 1839          Clay
Tisdel, Samuel to Almeta Riggs 2 Aug. 1838                Clay
Tisdele, Aimable to Mary P. Savar 4 Nov. 1834             StCh
Tisdell, John to Mary A. Cardinal 3 Nov. 1834             StCh
Tisdell, James D. to Martha A. Boxley 7 June 1832         Pk-1
Tishon, Jean B. to Mary Barrada 27 Jan. 1836              StCh
Tittsworth, David to Lavinia May 14 July 1831             Coop
Titus, Abraham to Jane Finney 8 Apr. 1836                 Rand
Titus, John Jr. to Celia A. Harvey 15 May 1839            Howa
Titus, Joseph to Mary Titus 29 Dec. 1829                  Howa
Titus, Leander to Rebecca Wright 14 Sept. 1824            Boon
Titus, Mathias to Sally Thomas 22 Nov. 1829               Char
Tnble, Dudly to Mary J. Lanton 30 Jan. 1838               Clay
Toaly, Geo. to Eliza Foard 29 Oct. 1831                   Monr
Tod, Geo. to Mary Lewis 25 May 1837                       Mari
Tod, Peter to Polly Anderson 23 May 1838                  Boon
Todd, A. to Mary A. Bridges 23 Dec. 1839                  Howa
Todd, Asa to Elizabeth Whitledge 11 Apr. 1833             Pk-1
Todd, Asa C. to Rebecca Bennett 30 Dec. 1824              Boon
Todd, Charles R. to Ester Fisher 15 Sept. 1833            Fran
Todd, F.C. to Mary A. Buford 23 Aug. 1833                 Pk-1
Todd, Isaiah to Elizabeth Prather 7 Jan. 1833             Fran
Todd, James to Martha Snowden 7 July 1836                 Ray
Todd, Joab to Mary Atterbury 8 Oct. 1839                  Howa
Todd, John to Betsy Gall 15 Oct. 1829                     Fran
Todd, John to Polly Searcy 24 Dec. 1835                   Wash
Todd, John W. to Nancy Chance 22 May 1836                 Clay
Todd, Joseph to Susanna Tribble 10 Apr. 1831             Lafa
Todd, Joseph to Susan Harrison 27 Nov. 1837              Livi
Todd, Lindsay to Viletta Beardsley 16 June 1836          Pk-1
```

Todd, Moses to Maria Carnes 25 Feb. 1830	Wash
Todd, Nemiah to Manervy Hawker 15 Dec. 1829	Howa
Todd, Robt. to Ann Mullins 25 Aug. 1826	Howa
Todd, Tillman to Kiziah Harryman 4 Sept. 1832	Cole
Todd, Wm. to Perlina Fugitt 2 Nov. 1818	Howa
Todd, Zehemiah to Sally Stephens 5 Sept. 1839	Call
Tofflemire, John to Anne James 19 Mar. 1818	Howa
Tolbert, Nathanial to Susanna Richards 2 Sept. 1828	Boon
Toliver, Samuel A. to Betsy Peters 23 Nov. 1838	Clay
Tolly, Berry to Martha Sims 28 Oct. 1832	Boon
Tolly, Isaac to Elizabeth Wardouf 7 Apr. 1839	Polk
Tolly, Nathan to L. Minor 8 Dec. 1833	Char
Tolman, John to Mary Duque 21 May 1834	Lewi
Tolson, Fountain to Sarah Fauter 16 Aug. 1824	Boon
Tolson, Franklin to Charlotte Goslin 4 Feb. 1829	Boon
Tolson, James to Angeline Goslin 3 July 1834	Boon
Tolson, Thomas to Polly Brown 11 Nov. 1824	Howa
Tolson, Wm. to Polly Smith 29 Oct. 1829	Howa
Tomason, Nicholas to Amanda Braughman 2 June 1831	Md-A
Tomkins, May B. to Elizabeth Barton 11 June 1829	Rall
Tomkins, Richard W. to Mary A. Howland 14 Mar. 1839	Pk-B
Tomlin, James to Lucy Yancy 10 Feb. 1829	Howa
Tomlin, Wm. to Susan McCrary 4 Sept. 1826	Howa
Tomlis, Jefferson to Leusindy Steward 17 Oct. 1830	Cole
Tompkins, Wm. to Patsy Gilbert 25 May 1814	StCh
Tompson, John to Jane Munn 25 Mar. 1827	Rall
Toms, David to Polly Franklin 12 Jan. 1834	Lafa
Toney, Little Berry to Nancy McMurtrey 17 Nov. 1833	Md-A
Tong, James to Elizabeth Thompson 15 Sept. 1816	StGe
Tonge, Henry D. to Elizabeth Wood 2 Jan. 1838	StFr
Torick, Louis to Helen Chartrand 2 Jan. 1838	StCh
Towles, Stockley W. to Mary W.W. Ellis 25 July 1839	Rand
Towner, Minor M. to Ann V. Shackles 11 Apr. 1837	Mari
Townley, Geo. to Almedia Parsons 20 June 1839	Cass
Townley, John M. to Perinna Alkire 26 Sept. 1833	Gasc
Townsend, Wm. to Eliza Anderson 27 Feb. 1834	Call
Townsend, Winford to Sousan Buchanan 2 Aug. 1839	Barr
Townsend, Winford G. to Evaline Shannon 7 Sept. 1835	Gree
Townson, James to Hannah Smith 23 May 1828	Jack
Toy, Wm. to Mary Doolin 29 June 1837	Jeff
Tracy, Benj. N. to Frances Cornelius 27 June 1839	Rand
Tracy, Erasmus to Judith Hughs 27 Dec. 1838	Mill
Tracy, Geo. to Eleanor Duncan 12 Sept. 1839	Clay
Tracy, John to Sarah M. Smith 29 Aug. 1831	Rall
Tracy, Lewis to Sally Krigbaum 27 Dec. 1826	Rall
Trail, John H. to Eliza A. Kenion 24 Jan. 1836	Linc
Trail, John H. to Polly Welty 21 July 1839	Linc
Trammell, James to Polly Foster 26 June 1817	Howa
Trammell, James M. to Elizabeth Spiva 22 Jan. 1835	Md-A
Trapp, John to Cynthia Travis 27 Oct. 1831	Jack
Trapp, Wm. to Mary Garner 18 Jan. 1838	Lafa
Trask, Marvin W. to Mrs. Olla Steene 18 Nov. 1827	Wash
Trask, Putnam to Polly Campbell 28 June 1828	Wash
Trass, Terry to Elizabeth Jennings 24 July 1824	Howa
Travis, Wm. to Polly Drinkwater 27 Dec. 1821	Coop
Treasher, James to Permelia Nesbit 6 Nov. 1832	Monr
Trent, Garrard to Elizabeth Bartlett 27 June 1839	Morg
Trent, Thomas A. to Mary Dalton 2 July 1839	Char
Treplett, Martin to Marietta Boyce 16 -- 1837	Mari
Trewitt, John to Margaret Hayden 8 Nov. 1827	Pk-1
Tribble, James S. to Eliza Hargus 30 July 1837	Howa
Tribble, Joseph to Jane Demastors 3 Nov. 1822	Lafa
Tribble, Samuel to Polly Munne 28 May 1824	Boon
Tribble, Silas to Kasander Gunn 8 Apr. 1824	Lafa
Tribble, Thomas to America Winn 1 June 1837	Boon

```
Tribue, Edward to Lydia Nevill 23 May 1835                          Pk-1
Trien, Absolom H. to Elizabeth McCullough 25 Apr. 1838             Coop
Trigg, Jos. to Julian McClelland 9 May 1828                        Boon
Trigg, Thomas to Mary A. West 13 June 1838                         Boon
Trigg, Wm. H. to Sarah Wyan 17 Mar. 1835                           Coop
Triller, John to Edee Cartner 1 Nov. 1835                          CG-B
Trimble, Benj. F. to Lucretia Boyd 9 Nov. 1830                     Rall
Trimble, David to Katherine Henly 22 Feb. 1838                     Cole
Trimble, James to Ruth Wells 5 Jan. 1832                           Pk-1
Trion, Truman to Rebecca Conner 2 July 1835                        Clay
Triplet, James C. to Frances Crucher 21 May 1834                   Monr
Triplett, Francis E. to Luiza A. Hall 1 Nov. 1838                  Pk-B
Triplett, John to Sarah J. Buckner 7 May 1837                      Fran
Triplett, Thomas to Jane E. Bradley 13 Feb. 1831                   Pk-1
Triutly, John P. to Margaret Berncer 3 May 1832                    StCh
Troll, Joseph to Adeline Heberly 21 May 1837                       Md-B
Troll, Joseph to Theresa Ziegler -- Nov. 1837                      CG-A
Troque, Joseph to Judith Millhomme 17 Feb. 1832                    Wash
Trosper, Elisha to Margaret Trosper 17 Nov. 1837                   Davi
Trosper, Thomas I. to Susan Fox 18 Jan. 1838                       Ray
Trotter, Geo. to Catherine Clay 9 Dec. 1835                        Henr
Trotter, James to Cynthia Carey 16 Apr. 1837                       Carr
Trotter, John to Marian Standley 22 Nov. 1824                      Ray
Trotter, John to Lucinda Cannada 10 May 1827                       Coop
Trotter, Robt. to Polly Busby 7 Dec. 1823                          Lafa
Trower, Henry to Matilda A. Keyth 10 Apr. 1836                     Pk-1
Truck, John to Barbara Berthold 30 May 1836                        StCh
True, Lewis to Patsy Floyd 30 Oct. 1836                            Howa
True, Willis to Mary Young 8 June 1832                             Boon
Truesdell, John to Elizabeth Ebenns 10 Oct. 1839                   Fran
Truitt, Charles W. to Jane Herrin 7 May 1829                       Rall
Truitt, Geo. W. to Emaline Realing 18 May 1837                     Rall
Truitt, James to Polina Hostetter 27 Feb. 1834                     Rall
Truitt, Wm. L. to Ellen Brammin 24 Dec. 1829                       Howa
Trummul, Lee to Susan Becket 10 Apr. 1828                          Ray
Trussell, Pendelton to Mary Comley 28 Dec. 1837                    Monr
Trusty, Ransom H. to Mary A. Muzingo 23 May 1839                   Buch
Tucker, Appollo N. to Elizabeth J. Taylor 27 Feb. 1838            StFr
Tucker, Benj. to Clarrissa Noland 24 Aug. 1828                     Jack
Tucker, Cullen to Polley A. Biggs 27 May 1832                      Pk-1
Tucker, David to John Elliott's dtr. 10 Nov. 1836                  Ray
Tucker, Edmon to Betsy Colwell 24 Mar. 1831                        Pk-1
Tucker, Henry H. to Elizabeth Williams 24 July 1834               Jack
Tucker, Isaiah to Sally Ellis 1 Jan. 1826                          Perr
Tucker, James to Mezelar Reed 6 Jan. 1828                          Md-A
Tucker, James to Ann Powell 16 Aug. 1831                           Wash
Tucker, James to Polly Dunbar 14 Jan. 1835                         Boon
Tucker, James to Mary A. Powers 6 June 1836                        Perr
Tucker, John to Fany Smith 12 Apr. 1804                            CGRA
Tucker, John to Mary Moran 11 Oct. 1829                            Md-A
Tucker, John Jr. to Anna Garner 25 Feb. 1830                       CG-A
Tucker, John to Elizabeth Overton 19 Feb. 1832                     Jack
Tucker, John to Christine Hagan 15 Jan. 1833                       Perr
Tucker, John T. to Mary Dean 20 Jan. 1834                          Perr
Tucker, Joseph to Sarah A. Steward 14 May 1833                     Perr
Tucker, Joseph to Lucinda Taylor 13 Sept. 1836                     Perr
Tucker, Joseph to Elizabeth Robertson 28 Feb. 1837                Coop
Tucker, Josephus to Nancy Keener 8 Oct. 1826                       StGe
Tucker, Josephus to Elizabeth Johnston 9 May 1833                  Perr
Tucker, Leo to Susan M. Knott 12 Feb. 1838                         Perr
Tucker, Martin to Elinda Adlin 21 Nov. 1837                        Perr
Tucker, Michael to Mary Johnson 26 Oct. 1829                       Perr
Tucker, Michael to Elizabeth Cissell 22 Apr. 1833                  Perr
Tucker, Michael to Susanna Holster 16 Apr. 1839                    Perr
Tucker, Milton to Eliza Chandler 9 Dec. 1834                       Linc
```

227

Tucker, Nathaniel B. to Eliza Naylor 11 Oct. 1828   StCh
Tucker, Nathaniel B. to Lucy A. Smith 13 Apr. 1830   Howa
Tucker, Nicholas to Sarah Moore 15 Jan. 1833   Perr
Tucker, Peter to Mary Steward 11 Apr. 1826   Perr
Tucker, Peter to Elizabeth Rhodes 27 Aug. 1828   Perr
Tucker, Raymond to Mary M. Cissell 25 Nov. 1834   Perr
Tucker, Robt. to Madam Margaret Simpson 16 Oct. 1829   StCh
Tucker, Robt. to Ellen Moore 9 July 1834   Perr
Tucker, Robt. to Margaret Amen 30 Dec. 1837   Lewi
Tucker, Robt. to Margaret Adams 10 Jan. 1839   Coop
Tucker, Stephen to Agnes West 10 May 1829   Perr
Tucker, Thomas to Betsey Harper 2 May 1823   Call
Tucker, Thomas to Elizabeth Thompson 22 July 1833   Perr
Tucker, Thomas to Sarah Ellis 22 Mar. 1837   Perr
Tucker, Wm. to Elly McFarland 31 Aug. 1826   Coop
Tucker, Wm. to Ruth Reed 18 Feb. 1827   Md-A
Tucker, Wm. to Mary Woodruff 3 Dec. 1833   Boon
Tuder, Cornelius to Polly Morse 20 Mar. 1839   Rand
Tudor, Joseph to Elvina Harris 4 Dec. 1838   Howa
Tuggel, Wm. to Alba Smith 1 Sept. 1836   Howa
Tuggle, Geo. to Elizabeth Gregory 22 Aug. 1834   Mari
Tuggle, Thomas to Ann Coulter 31 Oct. 1837   Maco
Tull, Wm. to Margaret Lewis 17 Jan. 1837   Mari
Tullock, Samuel to Mary J. Boyd 24 Feb. 1839   Jeff
Tullock, Wm. W. to Jane Cherry 21 Feb. 1838   Wash
Tully, Allen to Mary Giboney 24 Aug. 1831   CG-A
Tully, Britton to Sarah Hall 7 July 1831   CG-A
Tumblin, John to Milly Clark 12 Jan. 1832   Howa
Tunley, Robt. L. to Elizabeth Majors 15 Feb. 1835   Jack
Tunnell, Francis A.D. to Elizabeth Houston 25 Apr. 1839 Ray
Turbin, Daniel to Catherine Massey 18 Apr. 1837   Wash
Turley, Aaron to Maria Westover 21 Mar. 1830   Wash
Turley, Aaron P. to Frances L. Smith 9 July 1835   StFr
Turley, Ephriam to Gabella Marquess 28 Oct. 1826   Wash
Turley, Geo. to Sarah Spires 4 Jan. 1835   Boon
Turley, Giles to Margaret Montgomery 1 June 1826   Wash
Turley, James to Harriett Miller 24 Dec. 1834   Call
Turley, Jesse to Jutitia Riddle 14 Feb. 1822   Coop
Turley, Jesse L. to Lucy Horndon 12 Sept. 1833   Coop
Turley, Rolly to Lucinda Smith 12 Mar. 1833   StFr
Turley, Zadok to Margaret Vineyard 9 Nov. 1828   Wash
Turmon, Robt. I. to Margaret A. Smith 4 June 1839   Cass
Turnage, Michael to Jeremiah Rawling 12 Jan. 1828   Lafa
Turnborg, John to Ruth McLane -- Jan. 1834   Pk-1
Turnbow, John to Jane Turnbow 8 May 1831   Wash
Turnbow, Sted to Jane Ashley 22 Apr. 1832   StCh
Turnbow, Wm. to Elizabeth Chism 6 Jan. 1830   Rall
Turnbull, Geo. to Sarah Smith 6 Sept. 1832   Linc
Turner, Abraham to Nancy O'Neal 25 Aug. 1833   Boon
Turner, Alexander S. to Elizabeth Anderson 19 Dec. 1839 Clar
Turner, Alfred to Susan Gibson 2 Feb. 1837   Linc
Turner, Alonzo to Nancy A. Greening 24 Oct. 1839   Mari
Turner, Archibald to Mary A. Stone 14 June 1836   Boon
Turner, Asa to Sarah Parker 25 June 1837   Md-B
Turner, Charles to Susannah Lear 4 Jan. 1824   Rall
Turner, Clinton to Caroline Foowler 16 Feb. 1836   Boon
Turner, Eaton to Nancy Weldy 23 Oct. 1834   Pk-1
Turner, Edward to Susannah Collins 29 Mar. 1832   Howa
Turner, Edward M. to Mary A. Snoddy 2 Sept. 1834   Howa
Turner, Elias to Mary A. Herring 4 July 1838   Char
Turner, Ephraim to Sally Russell 9 Feb. 1823   Howa
Turner, Elza to Margaret Thompson 15 Aug. 1838   Gasc
Turner, Geo. S. to Margaret F. Staples 20 Dec. 1836   Lewi
Turner, Graham to Scithe A. Meyers 14 May 1836   Call
Turner, Henry to Mary Hook 12 Aug. 1830   Call

```
Turner, Henry H. to Sarah A. Menifee 7 Feb. 1839              Mari
Turner, Jackson to Jane Davis 10 Aug. 1837                   Boon
Turner, James to Tabitha Billingsly 4 Jan. 1822              Coop
Turner, James to Verlinda Hocker 16 June 1825                Howa
Turner, James to Sary A. Connelly 2 May 1833                 Boon
Turner, James to Patsy Gillard 23 Oct. 1835                  Cr-I
Turner, James to Nancy Jones 27 July 1836                    Morg
Turner, James to Jemima Turner 15 Dec. 1839                  Boon
Turner, James J. to Sarah Clark 12 Apr. 1835                 Ray
Turner, Jesse to Ann Maupin 11 Jan. 1820                     Howa
Turner, John to Nancy Campbell 11 Feb. 1819                  Coop
Turner, John to Elizabeth Hutson 18 Dec. 1828               Rall
Turner, John to Zelphia Jackson 19 Jan. 1830                 Boon
Turner, John to Margaret Gordon 11 May 1830                  Pk-I
Turner, John to Nancy Street 29 July 1830                    Howa
Turner, John to Rhonda A. Prewitt 11 Feb. 1836              Boon
Turner, John to Patsy Shy 21 Mar. 1839                       Pk-B
Turner, John to Susan McGaw 21 Nov. 1839                     Ray
Turner, John D. to Elizabeth Strode 1 Aug. 1822             Boon
Turner, John P. to Emily E. Todd 7 Aug. 1838                 Wash
Turner, Jonas to Lienhetta Gillum 16 Aug. 1832              Lafa
Turner, Levi to Nancy Keithley 18 Aug. 1831                 Rall
Turner, Levy to Louisianna Newton 5 June 1833               Howa
Turner, Littleton W. to Mareah Price 15 Oct. 1835           Clay
Turner, Manley to Nancy Phillips 1 Dec. 1836                Carr
Turner, Mathew to Lucinda Warrick 29 Dec. 1836              Howa
Turner, Miles to Polly Hatfield 22 Aug. 1810                StCh
Turner, Moses to Eliza McClanahan 30 July 1828              Coop
Turner, Nicholas to Kezeh McClure 19 July 1825              Lafa
Turner, Nicholas N. to Polly A. Phelps 19 Aug. 1838         Monr
Turner, Reuben to Mary Culbertson 4 Feb. 1829               Mari
Turner, Richard to Ann Horine 26 May 1832                   Wash
Turner, Samuel to Elizabeth Scobee 12 Apr. 1825             Rall
Turner, Samuel to Malinda Cooley 23 June 1827               Ray
Turner, Stephen B. to Ann C. Shobe 20 Dec. 1834             Mari
Turner, Sterling to Lydia Allchon 24 Dec. 1835              Pk-I
Turner, Steven B. to Martha H. Gardner 3 Jan. 1839          Mari
Turner, Talton to Sarah Erickson 1 Feb. 1820               Howa
Turner, Thomas to Jemima Bowing 19 Jan. 1807                StGe
Turner, Thomas to Catherine Rees 1 July 1830                Coop
Turner, Thomas to Elender Turner 27 Sept. 1838              Boon
Turner, Thomas G. to Susan E. Settle 22 Nov. 1838           Rall
Turner, Thomas J. to Ruth Gordon 14 Sept. 1837             Linc
Turner, Walker to Nancy Linginfelter 22 Feb. 1827          Clay
Turner, Washington to Mary A. Lynch 21 Jan. 1838           Clin
Turner, Wm. to Mahaly Scobee 4 Nov. 1831                    Rall
Turner, Wm. to Lucy Whitlow 18 Oct. 1832                    Mari
Turner, Wm. to Sarah Tull 15 Mar. 1838                      Mari
Turner, Wm. H. to Susan Elliott 23 July 1839                CG-B
Turner, Wm. M. to Nancy J. Cobbs 28 Aug. 1834              Mari
Turner, Wm. W. to Louisian Mitchell 13 Dec. 1839           Rand
Turner, Winslow to Sarah Palmer 21 Aug. 1835               Clay
Trupen, Jeremiah to Lydia Young 15 Jan. 1829               Mari
Turpin, Achillis B. to Telitha Banks 8 Oct. 1837           Mari
Turpin, Asa to Kesiah Person 24 June 1838                  Char
Turpin, Benj. to Jane Craig 28 Feb. 1836                    Wash
Turpin, Francis C. to Mildred P. Emerson 4 June 1833       Mari
Turpin, Henry to Celena Young 20 Mar. 1834                 Mari
Turpin, James to Susannah Carter 1 Mar. 1838               Char
Turpin, John to Nancy Wisdom 2 June 1830                    Cr-P
Turpin, John to Betsey Moore 3 June 1830                    Pk-I
Turpin, John J. to Cynthia Madison 23 Oct. 1837            Pk-B
Turpin, John L. to Susannah White -- -- 1835               Char
Turpin, Martin to Louisa Webb 21 July 1839                  Cr-I
Tusand, Percy to Patsey Wideman 11 Jan. 1834               Jeff
```

Tuttle, Henry S. to Mary A. Ray 5 Apr. 1838   Howa
Tuttle, Pleasant to Silan Green 18 Oct. 1830   Rand
Tuttle, Samuel R. to Exceline Gray 4 July 1839   Polk
Tuttle, Thomas to Jane Cooley 16 Apr. 1833   Rand
Twentyman, John to Polly Howard 7 June 1830   Cole
Twiddy, Allen to Anna Tigare 15 May 1834   Gree
Twindemann, Fidelis to Ebrosina Boessheart 2 Mar. 1835   StCh
Twitty, Allen to Patsy Cowis 29 July 1830   Fran
Twitty, Ambrose to Sarah Booke 12 July 1838   Fran
Twitty, John R. to Elira Patton 22 July 1835   Fran
Tygert, Jonah to Elizabeth Walden 17 Jan. 1828   Gasc
Tyler, Berry J. to Cyarina E. Dickey 16 June 1835   Jack
Tyre, Frederick to Polly Ray 13 May 1832   Howa
Tyre, James H. to Margaret McCullough 29 Jan. 1829   Howa
Tyre, John to Nancy Turner 28 Mar. 1833   Howa
Tyre, Lewis to Mary Wilson 1 Feb. 1838   Howa
Tyre, Pearson to Fanny Street 28 May 1833   Howa
Tyre, Thomas to Phebe Riggs 10 Aug. 1825   Howa
Tyser, Alen to Pernina Freeman 21 Oct. 1837   Char

Ullery, Samuel to Lavina E. Johnson 10 Oct. 1837   Perr
Ult, Herod to Mary Bailey -- Aug. 1836   Boon
Umpers, John to Lydia Stanfield 6 Nov. 1823   Char
Underhill, Wm. to Catharine Mayhan 6 Sept. 1838   Barr
Underwood, Alexander S. to Elizabeth Potter 17 Oct. 1839   Md-B
Underwood, David to Olive Potter 6 June 1839   Md-B
Underwood, John to Polly Ely 10 Feb. 1831   Rall
Underwood, John to Lucy Eleanor McAtee 7 Feb. 1837   Linc
Underwood, Reuben to Nancy Fry 10 Oct. 1833   Pk-1
Underwood, Thomas to Eliziah Huchison 1 Jan. 1839   Polk
Underwood, Wesley to Martha Fletcher 3 Feb. 1839   Lafa
Underwood, Wm. to Malissa Brown 17 Mar. 1830   Md-A
Underwoods, Joseph to Louisa Dunkin 2 July 1839   CG-B
Uno, Louis to Elizabeth Surrat 22 Oct. 1830   Call
Uppergrove, John to Nancy Boian 25 Aug. 1836   Morg
Upshaw, Asle B. to Lecifeth Macky 12 July 1835   Gree
Upshaw, John S. to Jane Woods 19 Dec. 1833   Gree
Uptegrove, Isaac to Elizabeth A. Ingram 9 Oct. 1834   Pk-1
Upton, Joseph to Sarah Clark 12 Jan. 1832   CG-A
Upton, Wm. to Cinderella H.E. Monroney 18 Oct. 1838   Monr
Utterback, Henry to Benuda Rouse 7 Feb. 1839   Monr

Valle, Charles B. to Ann Eidson 14 May 1839   Md-B
Valle, Jean to Josette Demarais 26 May 1807   StCh
Valle, Joseph C. to Felicite Robert 16 Jan. 1827   Wash
Valle', Pierre to Mary Ferguson 24 Feb. 1829   Wash
Van, Wm. to Arrabella Williams 27 Dec. 1829   Fran
VanArsdall, Wm. K. to Rosanna M. Curry 19 Nov. 1829   Call
VanBibber, Joseph to Susan Boone 18 Mar. 1827   StCh
VanBurglow, Samuel to Eliza Ferry 24 Feb. 1833   StCh
VanBurkeloe, Samuel to Mary Gatty 11 Oct. 1810   StCh
Vance, Byrd to Prica Vanderpool 19 Oct. 1837   Ray
Vance, Handle to Mary Collins 18 Aug. 1833   Clay
Vance, John to Rachel Wilson 14 May 1836   Ray
Vance, John to Louisa Williamson 13 Aug. 1837   Gree
Vance, John to Elizabeth Carnahan 2 Nov. 1837   Md-B
Vance, John H. to Sally Vance 25 Mar. 1834   StFr
Vance, John P. to Martha A. Wilson 25 Feb. 1836   Monr
Vance, Joseph to Elizabeth Knaus 10 Jan. 1819   Howa
Vance, Joseph to Atlanta Jesse 20 June 1833   Clay
Vance, Joseph to Mary Thomas Given 23 Apr. 1837   Clay
Vandagraph, Jacob to Margaret Gilmore 12 Sept. 1833   Morg
Vandenburgh, Dan L. to Franky Cox 25 Oct. 1827   CG-A

Vanderpool, Anthony to Easther Stanley 1 Jan. 1837   Ray
Vanderpool, Daniel to Tabitha Fields 9 June 1834   Ray
Vanderpool, Holland to Leer Linville 30 July 1828   Ray
Vanderpool, John to Milly Mann 22 July 1828   Ray
Vanderpool, John to Polly Stanly 11 Nov. 1836   Ray
Vanderpool, Kimmon to Elizabeth Mann 9 July 1824   Ray
Vanderpool, Midder to Polly Linville 10 Apr. 1830   Ray
Vanderpool, Tilford to Barbara Petree 23 Oct. 1836   Ray
Vanderveer, Eli to Rebecca Marlow 2 Aug. 1837   Wash
Vanderver, Geo. to Cisiah Turley 26 July 1832   Wash
Vandeventer, Wm. to Sarah A. Cowherd 31 Oct. 1838   Monr
Vandipool, Thomas to Elizabeth Coots 14 Jan. 1830   Clay
Vanduson, Jacob to Mary Vancurk 20 Jan. 1828   Howa
Vanhern, Simeon to Eliza White 17 June 1819   Howa
Vankirk, James to Nancy McDaniel 10 Apr. 1823   Char
Vankirk, John to Polly Tooly 14 Sept. 1823   Boon
Vanlandingham, Holland W. to Margaret A. Soule 28 Mar. 1839   Mari
Vanlandingham, Lewis P. to Mary Hawkins 16 Mar. 1837   Mari
Vanlandingham, Samuel to Catharine Mitchel 12 Mar. 1839   Mari
Vanlandingham, Wm. to July Woolery 7 Mar. 1833   Mari
Vanlin, Geo. to Sarah Terry 28 Oct. 1838   Fran
Vanmeter, James to Mary Plyman 25 Aug. 1839   Davi
Vannort, Wm. H. to Sarah A. Creel 24 Dec. 1839   Shel
Vannoy, Wm. to Nancy Mackey 11 Sept. 1834   Pk-1
Vanter, Wm. to Amanda Poage 26 Sept. 1839   Monr
Vanvickel, Aaron to Catharine Mase 23 Oct. 1832   Pk-1
Vanwinkle, Napoleon B. to Sarah Crow 27 Nov. 1832   Pk-1
Vapar, Benj. to Mrs. Rachael Brown 20 July 1829   Clay
Varum, Justus B. to Sarah A. Dixon 31 Oct. 1830   Jeff
Vassar, Samuel to Arbela Lisle 22 Apr. 1838   Clin
Vaughan, Elisha to Lear Davis 10 Nov. 1839   Mill
Vaughan, Peter T. to Mary I. Jeans 4 Sept. 1834   Pk-1
Vaughan, Rebeye to Polly Wall 13 Jan. 1831   Fran
Vaughan, Thomas R. to Lucy L. Edmunds 2 May 1832   Pk-1
Vaughan, Wm. H. to Nancy Washam 12 Mar. 1835   Gasc
Vaughn, Aaron to Maria Terrill 22 Sept. 1836   Coop
Vaughn, Albert to Minerva Gibson 21 Jan. 1836   Jack
Vaughn, Aleay to Martha Relph 30 Aug. 1836   Ray
Vaughn, Alexander to Nancy Davis 5 Aug. 1838   Gasc
Vaughn, Anderson to Lucy Brock 10 Feb. 1831   Fran
Vaughn, David to Leny McConnel 10 June 1827   Clay
Vaughn, Harrison to Polly Tansy 29 July 1830   Fran
Vaughn, Harrison to Martha Poague 26 July 1838   Monr
Vaughn, Jackson to Nancy Davis 20 Jan. 1835   Clay
Vaughn, James to Libina Painter 24 July 1836   Gree
Vaughn, James to Charity Hill 4 Nov. 1837   Coop
Vaughn, John to Nancy Man 15 May 1826   Coop
Vaughn, John to Eliza Trick 7 Dec. 1827   Perr
Vaughn, John to Mahala Johnson 24 July 1828   Coop
Vaughn, Joseph to Sarah A. Noonan 20 Nov. 1839   Monr
Vaughn, Joshua to Betsy Birdsong 2 Aug. 1827   Coop
Vaughn, Josiah J. to Betsy Duncan 8 Nov. 1827   Clay
Vaughn, Mastin to Caroline Wilburn 26 Nov. 1834   Call
Vaughn, Reuben to Maria D. Carter 24 Mar. 1831   CR-P
Vaughn, Samuel L. to Emily Horine 2 Jan. 1834   Fran
Vaughn, Singleton to Susannah Cooper 24 July 1828   Howa
Vaughn, Spencer S. to Mary F. Million 15 Oct. 1839   Lewi
Vaughn, Thomas to Sarah Hammons 14 Oct. 1829   Coop
Vaughn, Thomas to Martha Lampton 1 Feb. 1839   Monr
Vaughn, Thomas to Hannah A. Brown 10 Sept. 1839   Clay
Vaughn, Wesley to Belza Ellis 5 Dec. 1834   Clay
Vaughn, Westley to Rebecca Letchworth 4 Nov. 1830   Clay
Vaughn, Wm. to Eliza Pogue 6 Feb. 1834   Monr
Vaught, David to Sophony Combs 6 Apr. 1837   Morg
Vaugn, Joseph to Elvira Hill 29 July 1835   Coop

Veach, Thomas to Sarah Reed 11 Sept. 1832   Gasc
Venable, Robt. to Ann Hastings 25 July 1839   Howa
Verdier, James C. to Mary L. Clark 25 Apr. 1839   Pk-B
Vermillion, Josiah Sr. to Cintha A. Hosstetter 20 Jan. 1839   Pk-B
Vernon, Geo. to Rebecca Greenway 13 Nov. 1828   Cole
Vernon, Jeremiah to Betsy Stark 28 July 1824   Cole
Vesels, Clement to Catherine Miles 1 Feb. 1830   Perr
Vessel, Geo. W. to Mary Moore 20 Sept. 1836   Perr
Vessels, Geo. to Mary Burns 16 Feb. 1836   Perr
Vessels, Geo. W. to Mary M. Miles 23 Oct. 1832   Perr
Vessels, Henry to Monica Mills 17 Nov. 1835   Perr
Vessels, Thomas to Ann Melton 2 Aug. 1836   Perr
Vessells, Elisha to Varine Smith 3 Dec. 1835   Perr
Vest, Edward D. to Polly Decin 30 Dec. 1829   Rand
Vest, James to Mary J. Oslin 3 Mar. 1836   Call
Vestal, Daniel to Mary J. Snelling 7 Mar. 1839   Buch
Vestal, Jesse to Sarah Vestal 15 Aug. 1835   Rand
Vester, John F. to Louise Tingle 30 Aug. 1837   Shel
Vestzel, Joseph to Sarah Monhollon 15 Nov. 1832   Wash
Viant, Francis to Claris Denny 18 Feb. 1833   StCh
Victor, John to Aranetta McBride 14 June 1837   Boon
Viemann, Tan Wilhelm to Catherine Wesmeir 28 Apr. 1835   StCh
Vilet, Thomas to Evalina Fair 24 Nov. 1833   Carr
Vilmere, Alexis to Theresa Misplay 4 Feb. 1834   Wash
Vilmere, Louis to Celeste Bone 16 June 1829   Wash
Villemere, Michel to Marguarete Milhomme 24 Oct. 1826   Wash
Vincen, Bluffet to Rachel Earnest 26 July 1828   Linc
Vincent, Elisha to Nancy Heddleston 9 Apr. 1829   Call
Vincent, Isaac to Parthenia Orr 18 Aug. 1825   Boon
Vincent, Jesse to Jane Baker 11 Aug. 1825   Call
Vincent, Louis to Margaret Grahard 28 July 1830   Gasc
Vincent, Pierre to Seth Saurin 13 Feb. 1809   StCh
Vincent, Roy to Elizabeth Leaman 3 Jan. 1836   StCh
Vincin, A.W. to Polly Horine 30 Oct. 1834   Wash
Vinyard, Charles to Harriet Ogle 20 Mar. 1839   Jeff
Vinyard, Wm. to Stacy Cowen 23 Oct. 1831   Gasc
Vinyard, Wm. to Sarah Hammond 4 Oct. 1838   Jeff
Violet, Merit A. to Eliza A. Damrell 22 Sept. 1837   Monr
Violett, Joseph to Libby Murry 25 Apr. 1833   Clay
Viour, Peter to Nancy Lorean 26 Nov. 1837   Clin
Virgin, Jesse to Louisa Manker 19 Aug. 1832   CG-A
Virgin, Wm. to Betsey Brown 4 Aug. 1817   CG-1
Virus, Jesse to Elizabeth Bowan 15 Jan. 1837   Howa
Vivion, Adam to Exalina Alexander 23 Oct. 1825   Cole
Vivion, James to Mrs. Mary Brown 27 Dec. 1827   Howa
Vivion, John B. to Mariah A. Atkinson 21 Sept. 1836   Lafa
Vivion, Preston to Sally Stevens 22 Nov. 1832   Monr
Vocke, Ferdinand to Marie A. Gaskie 23 Apr. 1838   StCh
Vocklle, Benj. to Regina Vetsh 16 Apr. 1839   StCh
Voght, Wolfgang to Nancy Webb 15 Jan. 1833   Perr
VonderHeide, Casper H. to Lavina Layton 25 Nov. 1834   Perr
Voorhees, Geo. W. to Anna Sumner 8 July 1835   Clay
Vorderhause, Henry to Catherine H. Suhren 5 Apr. 1839   StCh
Vossel, Conrad to Maria Sutmoller 17 Apr. 1837   StCh
Voyard, Francis to Catherine Marie 2 May 1836   StCh

Waddle, John to Jane Bursley 30 June 1825   Lafa
Waddle, Wm. W. to Lois Goldsberry 1 Jan. 1835   Pk-1
Wade, Johnson to Sally Mead 25 Dec. 1823   Cole
Wade, Marlin to Judith Burnett 27 Feb. 1834   Lafa
Wade, Payton to Elizabeth Wilhoit 26 Oct. 1832   Clay
Wade, Reuben J. to Elizabeth Wings 5 Jan. 1837   Boon
Wade, Squire to Cecily Hudson 22 July 1834   Cole
Wade, Wm. to Elizabeth Carter 11 Feb. 1830   Rand

```
Wade, Wm. to Martha Dunbar 18 Sept. 1834                          Boon
Wade, Wm. D. to Elizabeth Stribling 14 Sept. 1837                Clay
Wadkins, John to Mahaley Hamby 4 May 1834                        CG-A
Wadkins, John to Jane McLard 5 May 1836                          CG-B
Wadley, David to Jane Conner 27 Jan. 1825                        Coop
Wadley, John to Susannah Howard 29 Dec. 1825                     Call
Wadley, John to Sophia Doyel 7 Dec. 1828                         Call
Wadley, John to Catherine Doyle 30 Sept. 1838                    Call
Wadsworth, Thabun to Rebecca Farrar 1 Jan. 1839                  Perr
Waggoner, David to Fanny Ronnalls 18 Sept. 1834                  Call
Waggoner, Jacob to Polly Sparks 26 Sept. 1830                    Coop
Waide, John to Nancy Watson 24 Jan. 1833                         Clay
Waidee, Wm. to Sally Toller 25 Sept. 1834                        Linc
Wainscot, Jourdan to Ana E. Roberts 17 Dec. 1832                 Boon
Wainscott, Daniel to Nancy McDaniel 14 Feb. 1839                 Audr
Wainscott, Jesse B. to Eliza Langley 16 Aug. 1838               Call
Walcott, Reuben to Elizabeth Freeman 25 Dec. 1839               Perr
Walden, Abednago to Telifa Warford 27 Oct. 1838                  Rand
Walden, James to Mary A. Hancock 26 Sept. 1833                   Howa
Walden, St. Clair to Emily Green 19 Jan. 1827                    Howa
Walden, Wm. to Susanna Piles 6 July 1837                         Rand
Waldo, Calvin to Francis North 12 Jan. 1837                      Fran
Waldo, Daniel to Malinda Lundsford 13 Mar. 1825                  Gasc
Waldo, John B. to Avarilla Turpin 23 Apr. 1826                   Gasc
Walke, Angus W. to Lisethe Holst 7 Dec. 1833                     Warr
Walker, Andrew I. to Frances M. Temple 14 Jan. 1827             Howa
Walker, Andrew J. to Elizabeth Murry 6 Mar. 1834                Morg
Walker, Benj. to Mrs. Abigail Fairwell 1 Jan. 1822              StCh
Walker, Benj. to Elizabeth Lilly 23 Jan. 1837                    CG-A
Walker, Ephriam to Louisa Patterson 29 Mar. 1838                CG-A
Walker, Gillum H. to Rodah Findley 27 Mar. 1834                  Howa
Walker, Green D. to Mary Hensley 28 Sept. 1823                   Cole
Walker, Griffin to Sally Roberson 3 Feb. 1831                    Call
Walker, Henry to Mary Garner 24 Mar. 1833                        CG-A
Walker, Henry R. to Sarah F. Read 18 Mar. 1829                   Coop
Walker, Jacob to Charlotte Jones 3 Jan. 1839                     Clin
Walker, James to Mahala James 18 Sept. 1834                      Linc
Walker, James G. to Louisa McClendon 23 July 1832               Cr-1
Walker, Jefferson to Ellender Pemberton 15 Mar. 1834            Pett
Walker, Jesse to Nancy Miller 29 Apr. 1835                       Howa
Walker, Jesse to Mary Gill 10 Apr. 1838                          Mari
Walker, Jesse R. to Elizabeth Cobb 18 Sept. 1838                Perr
Walker, Joel to Prudence Eldridge 7 Jan. 1811                    CG-1
Walker, Joel P. to Mary Young 17 Feb. 1824                       Lafa
Walker, John to Sarah Hill 6 Dec. 1832                           CG-A
Walker, John to Margaret Lorimier 19 Oct. 1834                   CG-B
Walker, John to Matilda Gann 16 Nov. 1837                        Livi
Walker, Johnson to Sophia Wainscott 5 Dec. 1830                  Boon
Walker, P. to Martha Montgomery 24 Mar. 1835                     Rand
Walker, Pleasant to Rebecca Lankford 4 Apr. 1830                 Lafa
Walker, Richard to Elizabeth Conway 15 Mar. 1838                 Mari
Walker, Richard to Elizabeth Hamilton 2 July 1839               Plat
Walker, Robt. to Ann Murray 2 Nov. 1829                          Cole
Walker, Rodney to Rachel Wyatt 6 Sept. 1829                      Gasc
Walker, Samuel to Kitty Townsend 31 Dec. 1835                    Call
Walker, Tandy to Susana Boger 8 Apr. 1833                        Mari
Walker, Thomas to Nancy Eades 11 July 1829                       Cole
Walker, Thomas to Polly Perry 19 Sept. 1830                      Linc
Walker, Washington to Mary Shin 26 Nov. 1833                     Rand
Walker, West to Rebecca Vestal 25 July 1836                      Rand
Walker, Wm. to Rachel Hendricks 23 Jan. 1825                     Ray
Walker, Wm. to Emily Moore 21 Dec. 1826                          Pk-1
Walker, Wm. to Sarah A. Stone 13 May 1834                        Boon
Walker, Wm. to Sophia Kerby 6 Mar. 1838                          Monr
Walker, Wm. A. to Mary Cobb 16 Jan. 1834                         CG-A
```

Walker, Wm. M. to Nancy Wills 8 Sept. 1835   CG-B
Walker, Wm. W. to Malinda Birch 7 June 1836   Rand
Walkup, John to Rebecca Ferguson 20 July 1820   Howa
Walkup, Robt. D. to Anna W. Cockran 21 Dec. 1820   Boon
Wall, Geo. W. to Sarah Gayle 29 Sept. 1831   CG-A
Wall, James to Malinda Jones 4 Feb. 1834   Howa
Wall, James to Elizabeth Nickerson 21 Mar. 1837   Howa
Wall, Jesse to Jantha T. Songbark 26 Jan. 1837   Ray
Wall, John to Lorinda Moor 27 Aug. 1838   Fran
Wall, Lorenso to Elizabeth Lowe 4 Apr. 1831   Cr-P
Wall, Robt. to Mary Cole 6 Mar. 1827   Fran
Wall, Van to Margaret Patton 26 Sept. 1839   Rand
Wall, Wade to Lavica Prichard 4 Aug. 1836   Ray
Wall, Samuel to Hannah Hart 18 July 1839   Boon
Wallace, David O. to Elender Wallace 16 Dec. 1837   Ray
Wallace, Geo. W. to Lucinda Jamison 1 May 1838   Coop
Wallace, Gordon H. to Margaret Fulkerson 19 Nov. 1835   StCh
Wallace, Hamilton to Elizabeth Smith 15 Nov. 1838   Carr
Wallace, Henry to Susan Martin 9 Apr. 1835   Lafa
Wallace, Heman to Sally Millheizer 28 Feb. 1826   Pk-1
Wallace, James C. to Sally Smith 14 June 1831   Lafa
Wallace, John to Ann Brown 22 June 1837   Clay
Wallace, John to Sally Turner 20 June 1839   Ray
Wallace, John B. to Nancy Collins 20 June 1819   Howa
Wallace, Mansfield to Delpha Lee 19 Oct. 1836   Ray
Wallace, Mansfield to Elizabeth Coats 19 Oct. 1839   Livi
Wallace, Reuben to Mary A. Strode 20 Aug. 1835   Jack
Wallace, Robt. to Margaret Steel 24 June 1824   Coop
Wallace, Robt. to Eliza Reed 23 Dec. 1834   CG-B
Wallace, Thomas B. to Rose A. Elliott 3 Apr. 1838   Coop
Wallace, Wm. to Nancy Dougherty 22 Oct. 1826   Cole
Wallace, Wm. to Martha J. Jones 10 May 1836   Rand
Wallace, Wm. to Mary J. Birch 22 Jan. 1839   Char
Wallace, Wm. to Sarah Ridenour 2 May 1839   Gasc
Wallen, David to Nancy Cravens 3 Mar. 1829   Cole
Waller, Lenard to Susanah Sanders 13 Nov. 1812   CG-1
Waller, Robt. to Maria Haigh 8 Mar. 1831   Wash
Wallice, Walter P. to Emeline Wills 22 Dec. 1833   Monr
Wallin, Bluford to Dulcena Hanly 15 Mar. 1831   CG-A
Walline, Alin to Nancy Smith 6 July 1828   CG-A
Walling, Nelson D. to Melinda Hayden 31 Jan. 1826   CG-A
Wallis, Jacob to Katherine Rice 2 Nov. 1836   Fran
Walls, Elias W. to Hellery Pearson 15 Dec. 1833   Gree
Walls, Hosea to Elizabeth Whitney 20 July 1836   Coop
Walls, Julius to Alay Langley 14 Nov. 1834   Call
Walls, Thomas to Frances Lambert 5 Oct. 1820   CG-A
Wallup, Samuel to Louise Roundtree 31 Mar. 1839   Buch
Wallz, Jacob to Charity Yount 8 Sept. 1839   Wash
Walner, John to Elizabeth Halter 21 Feb. 1839   CG-B
Walter, Lewis to Elizabeth Stacy 20 Nov. 1837   Lafa
Walther, Otto H. to Mrs. Agnes Bunger 15 Nov. 1839   Perr
Waltman, Armsteett C. to Lucretia Lafon 22 Oct. 1839   Lewi
Walton, Jacob to Sophia Jenkins 21 Aug. 1837   Barr
Walton, John to Eliza J. Ruley 1 Jan. 1835   Coop
Walton, Matthew H. to Martha J. Beaty 23 Apr. 1839   Audr
Walton, Robt. A. to Emily C. Bates 1 Sept. 1838   StCh
Walton, Wm. P. to Louisa J. Turley 7 May 1839   Coop
Wammock, Richard to Cintha Shirley 4 Nov. 1825   Linc
Wampler, Daniel to America Henry 24 Oct. 1839   Pk-B
Wamuck, Abraham to Lucinda Aikman 14 Feb. 1826   Lafa
Wangler, Wm. to Katherine Buddamen 21 Feb. 1835   Fran
Wanon, Joseph to Elizabeth Lesler 16 Sept. 1838   Howa
Ward, Alexander to Margaret Masterson 5 Mar. 1835   Lafa
Ward, Charles to Jane McCormick 21 Dec. 1826   Call
Ward, David to Nancy Holman 12 June 1829   Ray

234

```
Ward, Eli to Letitia Stephens 6 May 1823                              Md-A
Ward, Henry to Elizabeth Faust 1 Jan. 1835                            Warr
Ward, Hiram to Elizabeth Hughes 19 Sept. 1833                        Pk-1
Ward, James to Mary Long 29 July 1835                                Call
Ward, John to Elizabeth Bainbridge 27 May 1836                       Linc
Ward, John M. to Margaret Hunt 27 Dec. 1839                          Call
Ward, John S. to Marthy Cobbs 28 Apr. 1829                           Mari
Ward, Nicolas to Rodah Lenneus 14 Jan. 1839                          Ripl
Ward, Thomas to Mahala Horne 14 Mar. 1831                            Fran
Ward, Thomas M. to Glaphire Bowman 14 July 1834                      Lafa
Ward, Wm. to Elizabeth Toun 7 Feb. 1828                              CG-A
Ward, Wm. to Mary Reavis 31 Mar. 1835                                Boon
Ward, Wm. to Celia A. Stapp 17 Mar. 1836                             Lafa
Ward, Wm. to Eleanor Griffy 29 Sept. 1837                            Gasc
Ward, Wm. to Mary Lewis 14 Nov. 1839                                 Ripl
Ward, Wm. T. to Christiana McCoy 2 May 1833                          Jack
Warden, Elijah to Fanny Jackson 10 Oct. 1820                         Howa
Warden, Hezekiah to Sarah Butler 24 Dec. 1828                        Jack
Warden, Talton to Jane Byrd 7 Feb. 1838                              Pett
Warden, Wm. to Mahulda Butler 27 June 1827                           Jack
Wardlow, John W. to Maria Haston 24 July 1838                        Gree
Ware, Elias to Mary Miles 30 June 1825                               Howa
Ware, Geo. to Elizabeth Couch 8 Mar. 1827                            Jeff
Ware, Geo. to Mary Bowling 17 May 1834                               Jeff
Ware, Geo. to Furby Lewis 22 Oct. 1835                               Ripl
Ware, Henry to Rosanna Johns 29 Apr. 1830                            Fran
Ware, Robt. to Nancy M. Gray 21 Dec. 1835                            Pk-1
Ware, Wm. to Betsy Howard 21 Feb. 1831                               Rand
Waren, John to Docia Mills 1 Sept. 1839                              Maco
Warhurst, Archibald to Patsy Morgan 17 Oct. 1826                     Char
Warmack, Charles to Jane Marshall 4 Feb. 1833                        Lafa
Warmouth, Geo. W. to Sophia Runyon 9 Dec. 1834                       Char
Warmouth, Linder to Elizabeth Horton 16 May 1839                     Char
Warmouth, Phaddeus to Cyrene Lany 4 Sept. 1836                       Rand
Warmouth, Thaddeus to Elizabeth Mott 28 Dec. 1828                    Char
Warmuck, Allen to Eliza J. Snowden 10 Aug. 1835                      Lafa
Warner, Zachariah to Esther Champman 6 Dec. 1838                     Clay
Warren, Bushrod to Elizabeth Woody 13 Apr. 1834                      Clay
Warren, Clark M. to Mrs. Nancy Brown 3 Sept. 1835                    StFr
Warren, David to Rachel Burleson 3 May 1821                          Sali
Warren, Hugh C. to Manervy Morris 18 Feb. 1836                       Howa
Warren, James T. to Elizabeth H. Younger 25 Dec. 1836               Gree
Warren, Madison to Rhoda Granger 12 Apr. 1832                        Lafa
Warren, Martin D. to Elizabeth A. Dillingham 6 Oct. 1836           Lafa
Warren, Nelson to Lucinda Robertson 25 June 1834                     Jack
Warren, Robt. to Franklin Brasears 23 Sept. 1830                     Howa
Warren, Thomas to Lucy Ennis 10 Apr. 1831                           Lafa
Warren, Thomas to Sarah A. McDaniel 18 July 1837                     Henr
Warren, Thomas to Sarah A. McDaniel 5 Oct. 1837                      Henr
Warrick, Jacob to Martha A. Mathis 22 Apr. 1838                      Mari
Warrin, Samuel to Mary A. Morris 18 Sept. 1838                       Gasc
Wash, John to Sally A. Hodge 6 Jan. 1833                             Mari
Washam, Miles to Mary A. McQuarry 20 Aug. 1839                      Pk-B
Washburn, Leander to Sarah A. Darr 26 May 1830                       Mari
Wasson, Claiborne to Peggy Kimsey 17 Jan. 1825                       Howa
Wasson, John to Polly Ellison 15 Dec. 1818                           Howa
Waterfield, Fleming to Lucy Spicer 26 Aug. 1838                      Rand
Waterman, Wm. to Anne Lewis 24 May 1826                              StFr
Waters, David C. to Catherine Mathews 4 Aug. 1835                    Perr
Waters, Geo. to Eliza Spires 21 Mar. 1839                            Boon
Waters, Geo. W. to Letitia Israel 23 June 1831                       Clay
Waters, Isaac to Elizabeth Surnvey 16 Apr. 1824                      Boon
Waters, Isaac to Hannah I. Nichols 21 Nov. 1833                      Boon
Waters, James to Polly Wills 20 Nov. 1823                            Clay
Waters, Thomas P. to Sarah A. Garth 14 Nov. 1839                     Henr
```

Waters, Wilford to Ann Ward 14 June 1838	StCh
Wathen, Ignatius to Mary A. Waters 13 May 1810	CG-1
Wathen, Ignatius to Maud J. Wathen 16 Nov. 1831	CG-A
Wathen, J.R. to Maria R. Ellis 16 Aug. 1837	CG-A
Wathen, Richard to Mary A. Wathen 28 July 1829	CG-A
Watkin, Melborn to Eliza J. Thorp 22 Jan. 1839	Ripl
Watkins, Able to Mary Monnerger 1 Sept. 1839	Lewi
Watkins, Elisha to Elizabeth Baxter 28 June 1821	Howa
Watkins, Elisha to Catharine Stayton 12 Apr. 1836	Jack
Watkins, James D. to Vicy Coppege 24 Mar. 1826	Gasc
Watkins, James D. to Arthusia Brown 4 Oct. 1827	Clay
Watkins, Jesse to Mary Noble 20 Jan. 1822	Howa
Watkins, Joseph L. to Martha W. Dyer 22 Nov. 1837	Call
Watkins, Luke W. to Mahala Krigbaum 9 June 1837	Rall
Watkins, Wm. to Mary J. Stevenson 19 July 1838	Mari
Watkins, Wm. to Mary Hall 11 June 1839	CG-B
Wats, Ausker to Margaret Clark 2 Jan. 1838	CG-A
Wats, Lot to Maryanne Stockton 24 Nov. 1836	John
Watson, A.D. to Martha Christy 7 Nov. 1833	StCh
Watson, Archibald to Mrs. Jane Teazley 27 Sept. 1838	StCh
Watson, Cyrus to Betsy Mitchell 9 Apr. 1830	Pk-1
Watson, David to Nancy Brandon 10 Apr. 1827	Rall
Watson, David to Mary Edmunds 3 July 1834	Pk-1
Watson, Elihu to Elizabeth Watson 27 Nov. 1832	Pk-1
Watson, Geo. W. to Metelda Condry 22 June 1837	CG-A
Watson, James to Nancy Harris 8 May 1834	Boon
Watson, James to Emily A. Franklin 15 Oct. 1835	Pk-1
Watson, John to Nancy Hutton 7 Mar. 1826	Pk-1
Watson, John to Hester Morse 7 July 1834	Char
Watson, Joniah to Rhoda Watkins 27 Apr. 1817	Howa
Watson, Robt. to Elizabeth McQuie 13 Dec. 1832	Pk-1
Watson, Thomas to Mary O'Banion 11 Jan. 1814	StCh
Watson, Walter to Jane Vance 18 Oct. 1835	Cr-1
Watson, Wm. to Mary A. Blanton 26 Sept. 1837	Fran
Watson, Wm. F. to Amelia McQuie 30 Apr. 1834	Pk-1
Watson, Young to Jane Harryford 2 Jan. 1838	Char
Watson, Zenas H. to Louisa Carr 1 Dec. 1831	Pk-1
Watt, John to Catherine Sealy 12 Mar. 1829	Pk-1
Watts, Alford to Molynda Barry 22 Jan. 1835	Md-A
Watts, Anthony B. to Sally Dodson 11 July 1819	StCh
Watts, Francis to Ellen Todd 16 July 1835	Pk-1
Watts, Geo. to Elizabeth Hardin 23 Jan. 1827	Howa
Watts, Geo. to Patsey Mathews 4 July 1831	StCh
Watts, Geo. to Joanna Martin 20 Sept. 1838	Clin
Watts, Henry to Elizabeth Hill 18 Dec. 1838	StFr
Watts, Henry to Nancy G. Wilson 11 July 1839	Plat
Watts, J.H. to Frances Buchannon 14 Nov. 1833	Linc
Watts, Joseph to Susan Hulett 6 Feb. 1831	Howa
Watts, Ludwell to Sarah Bryan 21 Nov. 1839	StCh
Watts, Samuel to Patey Vie 14 Jan. 1836	Sali
Watts, Seneca H. to Frances Kemper 1 Feb. 1836	Linc
Watts, Stanford to Mary Throckmorton 20 Dec. 1838	Audr
Watts, Washington to Marietta Gray 17 May 1832	Pk-1
Watts, Wilkerson W.W. to Leones Jacoby 10 Sept. 1829	Pk-1
Watts, Wm. T. to Rebecca Clifton 20 Dec. 1838	Perr
Waugh, Abner to Elizabeth Bassa 24 Nov. 1836	Wash
Wauterback, Geo. to Ellenandrew Lesse 24 July 1838	Wash
Wayman, Jacob to Elizabeth Harrison 18 Apr. 1823	Howa
Wayman, Thomas to Rachel Throckmorton 10 Jan. 1833	Cr-1
Wayne, Temple to Elizabeth Gregg 12 Mar. 1835	Call
Weakley, Wm. to Naomi C. Snead 17 Apr. 1839	StFr
Wealch, David to Sally A. Anderson 25 July 1839	Polk
Wear, Alexander S. to Rachel Steel 19 Feb. 1833	Coop
Wear, Finis E. to Mary A. Oglesby 27 Nov. 1834	Coop
Wear, Geo. D. to Mary A. Cordry 27 Sept. 1838	Coop

```
Wear, Wm. G. to Sarah A. Yancy 2 Nov. 1837                       Coop
Wease, Elijah to Susanna Shoultz 15 Mar. 1821                    Jeff
Weatherford, Geo. to Susan Johnston 7 Jan. 1837                  Pk-B
Weatherford, Joel M. to Mary B. Standford 20 Apr. 1836           Pk-1
Weatherford, Wm. to Evaline Harper 23 Dec. 1829                  Call
Weatherford, Wm. to Laemay Sage 18 June 1835                     Gasc
Weathers, James to Rachel Roberts 27 Sept. 1821                  Howa
Weathers, James to Polly A. Tull 3 Aug. 1837                     Carr
Weaver, Adam to Nancy Gabriel 1 Nov. 1827                        Coop
Weaver, John B. to Jane A. Staats 30 May 1838                    Clay
Weaver, Larkin to Martha McCulah 27 Aug. 1835                    Morg
Weaver, Samuel to Rodah Fullbright 17 Jan. 1830                  Cr-P
Web, David to Malinda Reeder 3 Oct. 1832                         Jack
Web, Thomas to Polly Sevener 15 Nov. 1832                        Boon
Web, Wm. to Elizabeth Gillehan 30 June 1836                      Polk
Webb, Allen to Peggy Shelley 8 Oct. 1832                         Jack
Webb, Charles C.C. to Mary W. Philpot 2 Feb. 1837               Jack
Webb, Harrison to Emily Bricky 2 Sept. 1833                      Cr-1
Webb, Jacob to Elizabeth Wray 17 May 1838                        Cole
Webb, Joseph L. to Eleanor Goff -- Apr. 1823                     Howa
Webb, Wiley to Elizabeth Howard 24 Dec. 1835                     CG-B
Webb, Willis R. to Louisa Sitton 30 Nov. 1834                    CG-B
Webbert, Thomas to Lucretia Potter 16 Nov. 1837                  Call
Webster, Elezer D. to Polly Bradley 31 Mar. 1836                 Monr
Webster, Henry to Amanda McFarland 20 Apr. 1835                  Coop
Weed, Hampton to Mary Irvin 22 Oct. 1830                         Pk-1
Weeden, Benj. to Eliza Berry 3 Jan. 1828                         Coop
Weeden, Benj. to Catherine A. Fitten 27 Mar. 1837               Coop
Weeden, Hiram to Polly C. McKipick 14 Oct. 1830                  Clay
Weeden, Mathew to Margaret Kirkpatrick 15 Jan. 1837             Coop
Weese, Charles to Louiza Weese 20 Oct. 1839                      Clin
Weese, Geo. to Mary Culp 14 July 1839                            Clin
Wefel, Henry to Marie Myers 11 Mar. 1838                         StCh
Weiggle, Geo. to Susannah Clinginsmith 10 Sept. 1826            CG-A
Weir, John to Masey Branson 21 May 1837                          Gasc
Welch, David B. to Ketura A. Brink 13 Oct. 1836                  Monr
Welch, Henry R. to Elenor Hoozer 3 Apr. 1832                     CG-A
Welch, John to Jetdida Craft 6 Apr. 1826                         Fran
Welch, John Jr. to Frances Brown 9 Nov. 1826                     Clay
Welch, Joseph to Elizabeth Eastwood 15 May 1837                 Jeff
Welch, Michael to Leviney Rule 25 Dec. 1833                      Gree
Welch, Warren to Malissa Smith 3 Jan. 1839                       Warr
Welch, Wm. to LaFrancis Smith 28 Nov. 1833                       Warr
Welch, Wm. to Mary Inglish 12 June 1836                          Polk
Welch, Wm. D. to Mary Barks 7 Dec. 1837                          CG-A
Welch, Wm. W. to Amanda M. Dejarnatt 8 Feb. 1838               Monr
Welcher, Garrison to Patsy Brown 10 Feb. 1839                    Clin
Welcher, Steven to Hannah Hibbard 29 May 1834                    Boon
Welden, Abraham to Mary Carpenter 15 July 1838                   Boon
Welden, Milton A. to Jane M. Moss 15 Aug. 1837                   Lewi
Welden, Wm. H. to Martha A. Bain 16 Feb. 1839                    Lewi
Weldon, Abraham to Eliza Turner 20 June 1833                     Boon
Weldon, James to Polly Best 9 July 1819                          Howa
Weldon, James to Patsy Crump 23 Nov. 1833                        Boon
Weldon, Joseph to Mary C. Summers 13 Mar. 1823                   Char
Weldy, Henry to Lydia B. Taylor 11 Sept. 1836                    Rall
Weldy, Robt. to Elisabeth Ledford 4 Mar. 1832                    Rall
Welker, Daniel to Rebecca Row 9 Feb. 1826                        CG-A
Welker, Geo. A. to Mary H. Nance 15 Mar. 1835                    Perr
Welker, Jacob to Elizabeth Fulbright 5 Jan. 1826                 CG-A
Welker, Leonard to Patience Cheek 29 Mar. 1832                   CG-A
Welling, Charles to Elizabeth B. Frizel 5 July 1838            CG-A
Wellman, John H. to Sophie Brinkman 19 Sept. 1837              StCh
Wellman, Peter C.V. to Hannah Talbot 4 Nov. 1838               Clay
Wells, Andrew to Eveline Campbell 19 Mar. 1837                   Clay
```

237

Wells, Anthony to Keziah Pettitt 5 Apr. 1836   Rall
Wells, Dolfin to Nancy Carrell 11 Dec. 1825   Fran
Wells, Hugh to Mary R. Morrison 27 Oct. 1836   Perr
Wells, James to Polly Wheldon 24 Sept. 1817   StCh
Wells, John to Sarah English 3 June 1824   Ray
Wells, John to Lucinda Cummings 6 Oct. 1839   Davi
Wells, Jonothan B. to Elizabeth Shane 7 Dec. 1834   Jack
Wells, Joseph to Sally Bradley 28 Mar. 1820   Coop
Wells, Joseph to Mary Woods 7 June 1830   Ray
Wells, Joseph to Martha J. Daleney 14 June 1838   Lewi
Wells, Joseph to Elizabeth Foree 17 Nov. 1839   Clar
Wells, Nicholas to Mandy Williams 17 Nov. 1835   Pk-1
Wells, Peter to Nancy Simon 2 Apr. 1823   Gasc
Wells, Peter P. to Leficy McKean 7 July 1832   Ray
Wells, Phillip L. to Mary M. Hammond 25 Mar. 1834   Linc
Wells, Richard to Zerilda Kerr 30 June 1833   Pk-1
Wells, Robt. W. to Harriett A. Rector 20 Jan. 1830   Cole
Wells, Thomas C. to Susan Dawson 26 Apr. 1832   Pk-1
Wells, Wm. to Elizabeth Smart 25 Nov. 1836   Call
Welsh, David to Mrs. Sintheyn Mackey 18 July 1830   Wash
Welton, John to Perlina Thomas Mason Moore 18 Aug. 1833   Clay
Welton, Luis to Margy Hull 1 Feb. 1827   Gasc
Welton, Sandford to Elizabeth Brock 18 Dec. 1834   Clay
Welton, Washington to Jane Crosset 11 Jan. 1838   Clay
Welty, Hosea to Lavinah Link 21 Jan. 1836   CG-B
Welty, John to Susannah Caldwell 11 Sept. 1834   CG-B
Welty, John to Elizabeth McMahon 13 June 1839   CG-B
Wentworth, Stephen G. to Eliza J. Kindead 18 Apr. 1838   Sali
Wesley, Charles to Emily Cox 11 July 1831   Jeff
West, Daniel L. to Polly Armstrong 5 Apr. 1810   StCh
West, David to Bennety Brewer 7 Jan. 1837   Ray
West, Jack to Ruthy Lemon 14 Oct. 1828   Boon
West, James to Elizabeth Elliott 7 July 1836   Boon
West, James to Virginia McCracken 19 Dec. 1837   Lewi
West, John to Nancy Victor 9 Feb. 1826   Boon
West, John to Elizabeth Glaves 13 Feb. 1834   Call
West, John to Elizabeth A. Montgomery 4 Mar. 1834   Gree
West, Joseph to Maria Lemon 27 Aug. 1828   Boon
West, Joseph to Susannah Rogers 2 Sept. 1834   Gree
West, Josiah to Sarah J. Malery 23 Nov. 1839   Mari
West, Littleton to Faraha Compton 7 Sept. 1826   Howa
West, Morris to Elizabeth Davis 25 Dec. 1825   Fran
West, Nathan to Adaline L. Follett 13 Mar. 1836   Clay
West, Richard to Polly Snodgrass 16 Aug. 1829   Cr-P
West, Robt. to Salley Wilcocks 8 May 1825   Rall
West, Robt. M. to Susan E. Briggs 23 Aug. 1838   Monr
West, Samuel to Nancy Pointer 24 Sept. 1829   Fran
West, Samuel to Mary Vandeventer 20 Dec. 1838   Rall
West, Thomas G. to Mary A. Briggs 29 June 1836   Monr
West, Wm. to Viney Garten 3 Nov. 1834   Cole
West, Wm. to Margery Miller 21 Dec. 1834   Call
Westbrook, Wm. to Cynthia Jones 28 Mar. 1822   Coop
Westerfield, Wm. to Susan Cave 6 Aug. 1832   Boon
Westerman, Henry to Elizabeth Pierce 12 Oct. 1835   Linc
Westlake, Wm. to Ann Leonard 10 Apr. 1838   Boon
Westover, Isaac to Ann Atkinson 24 June 1831   CG-A
Wetherford, Burrell to Elizabeth Harper 25 June 1837   Monr
Wetherman, James to Sarah Laforce 25 Dec. 1834   Gree
Wethers, Enoch to Sarah Hughes 15 Mar. 1838   Coop
Wetmore, Diagnes to Sarah H--- 8 May 1836   Howa
Whaley, Albert to Polly Bird 21 Dec. 1826   Rall
Whaley, Geo. W. to Mary Vivion 7 Dec. 1837   Barr
Whaley, John to Nancy H. Forguson 23 Dec. 1830   Rall
Whaley, Wm. to Katherine Forman 2 Feb. 1827   Mari
Whaly, Daniel to Narcissa Mulkey 5 Aug. 1836   Jack

Whealing, James to Polly Web 10 Mar. 1831   Wash
Whealy, Wm. to Elizabeth Blain 27 July 1828   Wash
Wheat, Martin to Jeney Clark 21 Aug. 1828   Ray
Wheeler, Benj. to Mary E. Wathen 18 Mar. 1834   CG-A
Wheeler, Charles to Pamela Redman 11 Aug. 1835   StCh
Wheeler, Joseph to Caty A. Jackson 28 May 1833   Md-A
Wheeler, Mason to Nancy Wood 25 Apr. 1833   Mari
Wheeler, Oliver L. to Tilda Prather 11 Feb. 1827   Fran
Wheeler, Stephen to Nancy E. Monroe 1 Aug. 1837   Sali
Wheeler, Wm. to Manerva Thomas 19 Jan. 1836   Sali
Whet---, Washington to Salina Gash 25 July 1839   Henr
Whetstone, John to Jane Tucer 26 May 1829   Md-A
Whilley, Hobson to Esther Fugate 16 Sept. 1822   Boon
Whisenant, Robt. to Matilda Rosebury 5 Dec. 1837   Barr
Whiskinman, Soloman to Rachel Lundy 3 Jan. 1839   Maco
Whitacre, Newton to Maria Chomason 29 July 1839   Rall
White, Alexander to Laurinda Burbanks 24 Aug. 1830   StCh
White, Andrew to Phebe Cloff 15 Jan. 1828   Wash
White, Arnett D. to Sally Miers 30 Aug. 1838   Rand
White, Bartlett G. to Susan McPherson 24 Sept. 1835   Rall
White, Daniel D. to Lucy C. Cowherd 3 Sept. 1839   Jack
White, David to Nancy Maupin 29 Mar. 1821   Howa
White, David to Sally C.J. Crooks 31 Jan. 1833   Mari
White, David to Sarah A. Snelling 7 Sept. 1836   John
White, Edward to Gabriella Trotter 5 Sept. 1822   Rall
White, Edwin to Agnis Steinbeck 20 Mar. 1839   CG-B
White, Gearn to Sally A. McNeill 3 July 1838   Cole
White, Geo. to Barthena Herd 3 July 1832   Howa
White, Geo. W. to Mary A. Hobbs 24 Mar. 1831   Howa
White, Harrison to Bethany Gibson 14 May 1833   Rand
White, Hesikiah to Rody Howard 26 Apr. 1839   Monr
White, Hezekiah to Mariza Chappal 22 May 1835   Boon
White, Harrison P. to Bethania Smallwood 13 Nov. 1838   Howa
White, Hartley to Nancy Estes 31 Mar. 1833   Coop
White, Henry to Vienna Holman 21 Mar. 1839   Buch
White, James to Melinda Crooks 16 Dec. 1830   Mari
White, James H. to Cintha Johnston 8 Dec. 1837   Warr
White, James H. to Margaret Allison 17 July 1838   Coop
White, James W. to Joanna Root 14 Dec. 1830   StCh
White, Jesse to Lotty Morris 29 Oct. 1833   Coop
White, Jesse to Louisa Boon 8 Jan. 1836   Jack
White, John to Jemima Fowler 3 Mar. 1831   Boon
White, John to Polly Stinson 28 July 1831   Coop
White, John to Rueana Amon 22 Feb. 1838   Lewi
White, John to Mary A. Bayne 1 Dec. 1839   Lewi
White, John B. to Martha A. Towler 15 Aug. 1839   Mari
White, John D. to Rebecca Hovey 25 June 1829   Rall
White, John M. to Elizabeth Brown 19 Jan. 1839   Jack
White, John S. to Martha I. Bamy 16 Mar. 1836   Fran
White, Joseph to Elizabeth Carrico 7 Sept. 1826   StCh
White, Joshua to Ann Triplett 5 Dec. 1826   Pk-1
White, Joshua to Mary Hern 2 Oct. 1838   Boon
White, Josiah to Sarah Patton 27 July 1834   Howa
White, Julius to Hannah Macon 10 Dec. 1839   Clar
White, Lambert to Mrs. Esther Jenkins 3 Jan. 1839   StCh
White, Levi B. to Almira M. Harper 18 July 1834   Mari
White, Randolph to Betsy Riley 1 Sept. 1825   Char
White, Robt. R. to Amelia Rapp 6 Dec. 1835   Gree
White, Simon to Mahala Gibson 13 May 1830   Pk-1
White, Thomas to Jemima Cooley 21 Dec. 1817   Howa
White, Thomas to Clementin Billings 5 Jan. 1832   Mari
White, Wiley B. to Mary J. Rodgers 3 Jan. 1836   Cole
White, Wm. to Elizabeth Cooly 3 July 1813   StCh
White, Wm. to Nancy Nave 5 Mar. 1820   Coop
White, Wm. to Mary Tooley 23 May 1824   Char

White, Wm. to Rebecca Massie 23 Dec. 1830   Mari
White, Wm. to Mary Bounds 31 Dec. 1835   Lafa
White, Wm. to Laviny Morrow 18 May 1837   Boon
White, Wm. H. to Mary Miles 6 Nov. 1835   Perr
White, Wm. T. to Elizabeth Crabtree 5 Sept. 1839   Rand
Whitehead, James W. to Ann Rice 25 May 1835   Lafa
Whitehead, Thomas to Elizabeth R. Dowel 21 Mar. 1839   Plat
Whiteman, Samuel to Tetetha Strode 5 May 1837   Jack
Whitener, Daniel to Polly Clubb 11 Nov. 1827   Md-A
Whitener, Daniel to Margaret Bess 20 Aug. 1835   Md-B
Whitener, Henry Jr. to Adaline Sides 29 Jan. 1837   Md-B
Whitener, Soloman to Elizabeth Kinder 3 Jan. 1822   CG-1
Whiteness, Benj. to Elizabeth Rodes 3 Feb. 1828   Md-A
Whitenton, Harvey to Ann Story 30 Oct. 1838   Clay
Whitesearner, Joseph to Nancy Kuth 7 Nov. 1839   Boon
Whitesides, Jacob to Lydia Moss 14 May 1829   Linc
Whitesides, John to Ann E. Spellman 24 Dec. 1839   Boon
Whitesides, Joshua to Amanda Parker 30 June 1836   Linc
Whitesides, Wm. to Eliza Robinson 10 Dec. 1829   Linc
Whitfield, Eden A. to Nancy Griffen 22 Nov. 1833   Rand
Whiting, John to Nelly Morton 1 Jan. 1837   Howa
Whitledge, Thomas B. to Susan Jacoby 30 Aug. 1832   Pk-1
Whitledge, Wm. to Nancy Carr 2 Apr. 1829   CG-A
Whitledge, Wm. F. to Huldah Dempsey 8 Aug. 1838   CG-A
Whitlege, Persiokless to Rachel Wilson 24 Jan. 1839   CG-B
Whitley, Archibald to Sally Alfred 10 Dec. 1825   Boon
Whitley, Willis to Lucy Stear 4 Jan. 1838   Rall
Whitlock, John to Polly Wood 25 July 1837   StCh
Whitlock, Wm. to Sally Radford Ball 12 Jan. 1834   Clay
Whitmer, John to Sarah Jackson 2 Mar. 1833   Jack
Whitmer, Peter Jr. to Vastal Highley 14 Oct. 1832   Jack
Whitmire, John to Elisa Williams 25 Dec. 1828   Fran
Whitmire, Moses to Nancy Wheeler 30 Dec. 1832   Fran
Whitmire, Thomas to Mary Collins 28 Apr. 1833   Wash
Whitmire, Wm. to Catharine Wheeter 7 Feb. 1839   Fran
Whitney, Geo. H. to Elizabeth B. White 19 Mar. 1838   StCh
Whitney, Joshua to Julia Raundy 19 Sept. 1837   Carr
Whitsell, A. to Eliza A. Cull 12 Feb. 1835   Lafa
Whitsell, Isaac E. to Sarah A. Shackleford 5 Mar. 1837   Lafa
Whitsell, John to Martha Reed 8 Sept. 1835   Lafa
Whitsell, Wm. H. to Elizabeth Whitsell 25 Feb. 1838   Lafa
Whitsell, Wm. M. to Rachel Young 9 Oct. 1828   Lafa
Whitset, Alfred to Sarah Baxter 18 Aug. 1839   Clay
Whitsett, Samuel to Julia Windsor 4 Sept. 1838   John
Whitsitt, James to Nancy Horn 28 Apr. 1822   Lafa
Whitson, Thompson to Hannah Mar 26 Mar. 1820   Coop
Whitten, Jesse to Ann Swope 3 Aug. 1836   Howa
Whittenberg, Felix to Nancy Robberson 15 Oct. 1836   Gree
Whittenburg, Jacob to Sally Burkhart 1 Nov. 1821   Char
Whittenburg, John to Rachel Thompson 18 Oct. 1816   CG-1
Whittenburg, Solomon to Mahala Welty 24 Apr. 1837   CG-A
Whittle, John to Mary Whitty 23 Sept. 1832   StCh
Whittledge, Wm. to Rebecca Shoults 26 Aug. 1834   CG-A
Whitton, Henry to Rebecca E. Culbertson 23 June 1839   Mari
Whitworth, Stanford to Veny Dunkin 10 Dec. 1836   Fran
Whybark, Casper to Sally Grooms 20 Dec. 1827   Md-A
Whybark, Joshua to Mary Limpaugh 3 Apr. 1831   CG-A
Whybark, Samuel to Sophia Bollinger 8 Jan. 1828   CG-A
Wice, Jesse to Lydia Davis 20 Sept. 1839   Clay
Wickerham, Aquilla to Sarah Herrington 8 Jan. 1831   Jeff
Wickliff, Wm. N. to Ann Hertzog 14 Nov. 1831   Clay
Wicks, Einathan to Elizabeth Karr 16 Dec. 1827   Pk-1
Wideman, Jacob to Jemima Williams 30 Oct. 1830   Jeff
Wideman, Jacob Jr. to Eliza Thompson 25 July 1833   Jeff
Wideman, John H. to Mary Thompson 19 Oct. 1834   Jeff

Wideman, Leonard to Leathy Turner 30 Oct. 1830	Jeff
Wielgigmann, Henry to Maria E. Marquart 10 Nov. 1837	StCh
Wielpaut, John to Margaretta Crgel 5 May 1838	StCh
Wiet, Rubin to Rabeka Collet 13 Aug. 1835	Mari
Wiger, Robt. to Annie Hull 26 May 1832	StFr
Wiggan, Hiram to Sarah Haelt 20 Dec. 1837	Wash
Wiggenton, Townsend to Lucinda Maupin 19 Mar. 1829	Boon
Wiggins, Benj. to Ann McCoy 15 Feb. 1838	Howa
Wiggins, Ransom to Mournen Laws 2 Oct. 1838	StFr
Wiggins, Thilong Z. to Nancy Hickam 31 Dec. 1835	Boon
Wiggins, Zebulon to Elizabeth McCarty 7 Dec. 1828	Boon
Wigle, Jacob to Mary Vaneel 31 Mar. 1836	Perr
Wike, Joseph to Abigail Myers 16 Nov. 1837	Linc
Wilably, John to Peggy Elston 21 May 1820	Howa
Wilbarger, John W. to Lucy A. Anderson 26 May 1836	Pk-1
Wilbon, John to Catherine Delauney 9 Nov. 1835	StFr
Wilborne, James to Susanna G. Hall 13 Apr. 1830	CG-A
Wilbourn, Thomas J. to Elizabeth Gordon 9 Aug. 1835	Cole
Wilburn, Chipply to Elizabeth Bressie 20 Jan. 1834	StFr
Wilburn, Curtis to Ede Nettle 5 Dec. 1833	Call
Wilburn, Edward to Nancy Overton 18 Jan. 1830	Jack
Wilburn, Hiram to Phebe Williams 31 Jan. 1826	Lafa
Wilcocks, John to Mary Kinney 31 July 1824	Rall
Wilcockson, Harry S. to Rosa M. Crowson 18 Dec. 1838	Call
Wilcox, Abraham to Sarah Apperson 11 Sept. 1838	Mill
Wilcox, Daniel to Elizabeth Fillop 10 June 1822	Boon
Wilcox, Glenville to Lucretia A. McClean 7 June 1839	Rand
Wilcox, Henry to Sarah Pettus 2 Sept. 1829	Mari
Wilcox, Isaac to Prudence Smith 20 Oct. 1825	Rall
Wilcox, James to Mary A. Duly -- Sept. 1837	Boon
Wilcox, James to Ellendar McCullar 14 Apr. 1838	Gree
Wilcox, Peyton to Sarah Mitchel 13 Nov. 1839	Morg
Wilcox, Wm. L. to Susan Brockman 11 Aug. 1839	Mill
Wilcoxen, Daniel to Catherine Griggs 3 Apr. 1836	Boon
Wilcoxen, Newton to Margaret Dill 27 May 1838	Boon
Wilcoxson, David to Nancy Johnson 19 June 1821	Howa
Wilcoxson, Hiram to Sarah Marshall 7 June 1838	Howa
Wilcoxson, Joseph M. to Amanda Stapleton 8 Mar. 1832	Howa
Wiles, Wm. to Elizabeth Jones 4 Sept. 1834	Howa
Wiley, Enoch to Lydia Eagen 28 Feb. 1832	Lafa
Wiley, James to Martha Wilson 26 Dec. 1833	Lafa
Wiley, Jesse to Polly B. Walker 9 Apr. 1833	Cr-1
Wiley, John to Alzady Pharis 24 Feb. 1828	Howa
Wiley, Joseph D. to Agnes Stephens 8 Oct. 1839	StFr
Wiley, Joshua to Polly Ridgway 11 Dec. 1834	Howa
Wiley, Robt. to Elizabeth Thomas 30 May 1834	Lafa
Wiley, Thomas to Polly Grounds 3 Aug. 1826	CG-A
Wiley, Wm. to Nancy Ledford rec. 16 Feb. 1839	Rall
Wiley, Wm. C. to Missouri A. Raines 16 Aug. 1838	Lewi
Wilfley, James to Elizabeth Kelso 19 Aug. 1830	Call
Wilfley, Joseph to Sally Newland 27 Sept. 1838	Call
Wilfley, Samuel to Nancy Ellis 15 July 1824	Call
Wilfong, David to Jain Bess 29 Aug. 1833	CG-A
Wilhite, Elias to Nancy Baker 15 Feb. 1836	Sali
Wilhite, Fielding to Elizabeth McQuilly 4 Dec. 1819	Howa
Wilhite, Samuel to Nancy Benton 14 Aug. 1834	Clay
Wilhoite, Andrew to Jane Gentry 27 Sept. 1832	Clay
Wilhoite, Henry to Sally Floria 28 May 1829	Clay
Wilie, Samuel to Emily Bird 2 May 1839	Mari
Wilison, Charles to Elizabeth Hackty 21 Aug. 1828	Howa
Wilke, Samuel to Malinda Tate 1 June 1839	Call
Wilkenson, Laban to Martha Stone 13 Dec. 1835	Md-B
Wilker, Peter to Jane Robinson 28 June 1838	Wash
Wilkerson, Aaron to Sally Patrick 25 Oct. 1832	Howa
Wilkerson, Dien to Harriet Dunham 2 Aug. 1831	Call

Wilkerson, Harrod to Elizabeth Robertson 19 Jan. 1839	Linc
Wilkerson, Jeremiah to Nancy Stearman 12 Oct. 1826	Wash
Wilkerson, John M. to Ann Vance 13 Sept. 1832	Clay
Wilkerson, Major J. to Margaret J. Reed 18 July 1832	Coop
Wilkerson, Mason to Amelia Drydon 27 Aug. 1835	Monr
Wilkerson, Milton to Nancy Newsom 25 Oct. 1832	Monr
Wilkerson, Milton to Elvira J. Donaldson 9 Mar. 1835	Monr
Wilkerson, Moses to Amanda Duncan 9 Aug. 1838	Call
Wilkerson, Thomas to Mary Moore 10 July 1837	Livi
Wilkerson, Thomas J. to Margarett C. Young 10 Dec. 1839	Clay
Wilkerson, Wm. to Phebe Deen 4 Nov. 1830	Rall
Wilkerson, Wm. to Laura Young 29 Aug. 1833	Clay
Wilkeson, Jackson W. to Matilda Harper 10 Sept. 1836	Gree
Wilkey, Wm. to Elizabeth Potter 28 Dec. 1837	Polk
Wilkins, Isaac to Sarah Roe 26 Jan. 1832	Cole
Wilkins, Isaac to Delila Nouel 25 Jan. 1838	Mill
Wilkinson, Francis to Julia Brown 23 Jan. 1838	Perr
Wilkinson, Henry to Susannah Hines 13 Feb. 1829	Howa
Wilkinson, James to Polly Cole 19 Jan. 1826	Wash
Wilkinson, John L. to Nancy Howard 6 Dec. 1832	CG-A
Wilkinson, Livingston to Raney Granger 26 June 1832	Lafa
Wilkinson, Martin to Polly Lovell 19 Nov. 1830	Ray
Wilkinson, Morgan to Levina Dale 2 Jan. 1831	Rall
Wilkinson, Walter to Emily Pratte 16 Aug. 1838	Perr
Wilkison, Wm. to Polly Hoints 9 Dec. 1828	Howa
Wilkison, Wm. to Elizabeth Townsend 3 Apr. 1839	Clay
Wilkson, John to Ruth Hopson 27 Dec. 1838	Jeff
Willard, Henry to Sarah Garner 28 Apr. 1826	Rall
Willard, Martin to Mary Lindsey 8 Apr. 1821	CG-1
Willett, Wm. to Siney Suton 30 Dec. 1834	Md-A
Willett, Wm. F. to Irena Howard 23 May 1833	Morg
Willey, Samson to Hanner Bess 10 June 1832	CG-A
Willham, C.P. to Amelia Byrne 18 Aug. 1837	CG-A
Willhoite, James to Nancy Corum 3 July 1828	Clay
William, Wm. B. to Mary Munkers 6 Apr. 1837	Clay
Williams, Alexander to Lydia A. Sanford 2 Dec. 1830	Linc
Williams, Allen to Charlotte Williams 1 Nov. 1832	StFr
Williams, Allison to Winefred G. Weir 26 June 1828	Md-A
Williams, Alvin P. to Elizabeth Armer 21 Aug. 1831	Fran
Williams, Ames to Polly Scrivner 25 July 1835	Cole
Williams, Anderson to Lucina Pratt 25 July 1833	Warr
Williams, Anderson to Mary Welcome 17 July 1836	StCh
Williams, Andrew I. to Rachel Hickman 22 Feb. 1838	Davi
Williams, Benj. to Nancy Andrews 30 Mar. 1825	Howa
Williams, Benj. to Charlotte Scrivner 7 Jan. 1838	Polk
Williams, Benj. to Harriet Wingfield 14 Nov. 1838	Henr
Williams, Bluford to Elizabeth Lewis 5 Feb. 1832	Jack
Williams, Bradley to Polly Brummet 24 Apr. 1810	CG-1
Williams, Caleb to Sarah Updike 6 Oct. 1836	Cole
Williams, Calvin to Amaretta Adair 2 June 1833	Morg
Williams, Charles to Margaret Carpenter 12 Aug. 1828	Pk-1
Williams, Charles to Elvira Edmonson 18 June 1839	Cass
Williams, Charles W. to Mary S. Honey 12 Oct. 1837	Jeff
Williams, Colden to Margaret Evans 5 Sept. 1833	Howa
Williams, Daniel to Polly Wild 25 Oct. 1834	Ray
Williams, Daniel to Sally Jones 22 June 1836	StFr
Williams, Darling to Malinda Cary 19 Dec. 1824	Lafa
Williams, David J. to Mary Maxey 4 Apr. 1839	Shel
Williams, Elias to Margaret Holmes 3 Oct. 1839	Buch
Williams, Elijah to Polly Purdom 1 Mar. 1829	Pk-1
Williams, Ezekiel to Mary Jones 16 Jan. 1814	StCh
Williams, Geo. to Nancy M. Poage 23 June 1825	Clay
Williams, Geo. W. to Lavina Lawson 31 Oct. 1833	Warr
Williams, Geo. W. to Sarah Liles 20 Apr. 1837	Warr
Williams, Gideon P. to Elizabeth Goatley 21 Feb. 1839	Audr

Williams, Gipson A. to Anny Rule 8 Sept. 1831 — Cr-1
Williams, Graham to Louisa Fletcher 19 June 1836 — Mari
Williams, Grandison F. to Anna Wainscott 16 May 1839 — Clar
Williams, Green to Ruth Ballew 10 July 1828 — Gasc
Williams, Harrison to Alvira Hooper 30 Oct. 1836 — Jack
Williams, Henry to Jamima Carpenter 30 Apr. 1835 — Pk-1
Williams, Henry T. to Ann Graves 29 May 1827 — Char
Williams, Isaac to Elizabeth Gerry 21 Dec. 1826 — CG-A
Williams, J.W. to Nancy Michael 13 Jan. 1837 — Wash
Williams, Jacob to Sophia McCampble 1 May 1821 — StCh
Williams, Jacob to Catherine Hanly 2 Mar. 1826 — CG-A
Williams, Jacob to Cassandra Atchison 10 July 1835 — CG-B
Williams, James to Polly Savage 23 Feb. 1826 — Coop
Williams, James to Susannah Pepper 21 Aug. 1827 — Fran
Williams, James to Elizabeth Stone 11 Feb. 1836 — Boon
Williams, James to Hetty Son 14 Aug. 1839 — Buch
Williams, James M. to Artela Barker 18 July 1837 — Barr
Williams, James T. to Louisa Cecil 1 Mar. 1838 — Lewi
Williams, Jededeer to Polly Lewis 13 Nov. 1825 — Lafa
Williams, Jiles L. to Jane Burch 6 Apr. 1817 — Howa
Williams, John to Sally Foster 28 Dec. 1825 — CG-A
Williams, John to Margaret Wilson 13 June 1826 — Jeff
Williams, John to Eliza Graves 27 Sept. 1827 — Call
Williams, John to Ann Minter 11 June 1830 — Rand
Williams, John to Martha Skaggs 15 May 1831 — Md-A
Williams, John to Polly Potter 7 Feb. 1832 — Ray
Williams, John to Margret Rapp 15 July 1832 — Cr-1
Williams, John to Emily Bruffee 25 May 1837 — Coop
Williams, John to Rebecca Harris 20 Mar. 1838 — Gree
Williams, John to Sarah P. Meul 8 Dec. 1839 — Ray
Williams, John B. to Ann W.J. Bugg 1828 — CG-A
Williams, John E. to Melvina Hunter 10 Aug. 1837 — Polk
Williams, John P. to Mary Turner 1 Jan. 1827 — Linc
Williams, John P. to Amanda C. Williams 16 Oct. 1832 — Howa
Williams, John P. to Elizabeth A. Bradley 13 Sept. 1836 — Lewi
Williams, Joseph to Elizabeth Langley 6 Feb. 1825 — Call
Williams, Joseph to Rachael Laramore 15 May 1832 — Fran
Williams, Joseph to Sarah H. Farmer 17 Nov. 1836 — Mari
Williams, Joshua to Martha Swearingen 13 June 1839 — Coop
Williams, Josiah to Patsy Cooper 3 June 1832 — Howa
Williams, Levi A. to Elizabeth Finley 30 June 1836 — Polk
Williams, Lewis to Sarah Cornelison 25 Mar. 1837 — Gree
Williams, Lilburn to Jane Foster 12 Sept. 1839 — Jeff
Williams, Luke to Louisa Baty 14 July 1833 — Coop
Williams, Marcus Jr. to Mary J. Littlepage 14 Mar. 1839 — Coop
Williams, Mastin to Phoebe Williams 29 Nov. 1825 — Clay
Williams, Mathew to Rachel Ennis 4 Nov. 1829 — Lafa
Williams, Merrit to Elizabeth Lee 23 Dec. 1835 — Howa
Williams, Milliby to Susannah Turner 18 Sept. 1834 — Howa
Williams, Nathan to Harriet Phillips 8 Apr. 1834 — Jeff
Williams, Nathaniel T. to Naomi Jones 28 Apr. 1834 — Lewi
Williams, Noah to Polly Brant 27 May 1825 — Lafa
Williams, Price to Louisa Fauster 25 Aug. 1825 — Howa
Williams, Powell to Sally Gregg 29 Jan. 1829 — Howa
Williams, Reuben to Evaline Moore 17 Mar. 1836 — Call
Williams, Richard to Elizabeth Tuttle 24 Apr. 1836 — Howa
Williams, Richard to Margaret Whitsel 19 Aug. 1839 — Ray
Williams, Robt. to Frances May 30 Nov. 1824 — Call
Williams, Robt. to Amelia Beasley 15 Apr. 1827 — Pk-1
Williams, Robt. to Lina Williams 25 Dec. 1832 — Cole
Williams, Samuel to Sarah Johnson 2 Mar. 1824 — Cole
Williams, Samuel to Nancy Monroe 11 Aug. 1825 — Howa
Williams, Samuel to Patsy Morris 26 Sept. 1830 — Howa
Williams, Skillman to Demorris Morrison 11 Apr. 1830 — Jeff
Williams, Spencer to Dianna Makum 20 Dec. 1837 — Barr

Williams, Squire to Martha A. Barns 30 Sept. 1830 — CG-A
Williams, Thomas to Ruth Todd 6 Feb. 1828 — Jeff
Williams, Thomas to Caty Campbell 31 Oct. 1833 — Ray
Williams, Thomas to Elizabeth Todd 20 Jan. 1834 — Call
Williams, Thomas D. to Mrs. Elizabeth Odenel 22 Nov. 1839 — Buch
Williams, Washington to Franky Rule 8 Sept. 1831 — Cr-1
Williams, Wm. to Ann Titus 1 Dec. 1825 — Howa
Williams, Wm. to Elizabeth Mathes 26 Feb. 1826 — Wash
Williams, Wm. to Hannah Lewis 23 Mar. 1826 — Lafa
Williams, Wm. to Nancy Shookly 22 Oct. 1829 — Cole
Williams, Wm. to Sally Pain 6 Dec. 1831 — Cole
Williams, Wm. to Martha Murry 18 July 1833 — Cole
Williams, Wm. to Hannah Rupe 17 Feb. 1834 — Howa
Williams, Wm. to Matilda Williams 7 Sept. 1837 — Davi
Williams, Wm. to Louisa Poe 14 Dec. 1837 — CG-A
Williams, Wm. to Nancy Brunts 19 Dec. 1837 — Howa
Williams, Wm. to Melvina Sconover 29 July 1839 — Clar
Williams, Wm. A. to Elizabeth Watson 8 Nov. 1832 — CG-A
Williams, Wm. L. to Cordelius M. Kilgore 9 Feb. 1839 — Audr
Williams, Wilson to Clarissa Wilson 14 July 1831 — Jeff
Williams, Wilson to Trudy Wilson 18 Feb. 1837 — Clay
Williamson, Abraham to Elenor Cowick 4 Mar. 1835 — Wash
Williamson, James to Rebecca Housinger 5 Feb. 1826 — Gasc
Williamson, James to Diannia White 1 Feb. 1838 — Monr
Williamson, Jesse to Margaret Neisbit 17 Apr. 1834 — Monr
Williamson, Jesse to America Brundage 30 Dec. 1835 — Wash
Williamson, Thomas to Nancy Phillips 21 Dec. 1837 — Gree
Williamson, Wm. M. to Sarah A. Baker 8 Feb. 1839 — Clar
Williamson, Wm. W. to Mildred Armstrong 11 July 1839 — Monr
Williarts, John H. to Polly Williams 25 May 1831 — Cole
Willing, Wm. to Eliza C. Parker 8 Mar. 1838 — Call
Willingham, Delena to Malinda Winscott 23 June 1831 — Call
Willingham, Delaney to Sarah Hatten 12 May 1836 — Monr
Willingham, Geo. W. to Amanda M. Hatton 14 Oct. 1839 — Audr
Willingham, John to Polly Kilgore 14 Sept. 1823 — Boon
Willis, Henry to Jennett Seeber 21 Aug. 1839 — Lewi
Willis, Henry to Nahlcia Ryan 19 Sept. 1839 — Cole
Willis, James to Martha Felps 6 July 1837 — Mari
Willis, Terry to Sally Gatch 6 Jan. 1833 — Cr-1
Willis, Thomas to Eliza Owens 16 Aug. 1818 — Howa
Willock, Colo. David to Harriet Buckner 19 Jan. 1837 — Mari
Wills, Archibald to Nancy Huffman 28 Feb. 1828 — Clay
Wills, Cadandy to ---- ---- 13 July 1837 — Gree
Wills, Daniel to Christina Crites 15 Dec. 1833 — CG-A
Wills, David to Michael Smith 17 May 1836 — CG-A
Wills, Drury to Lelah E. Bauman 12 Feb. 1838 — CG-A
Wills, Hugh to Susannah Eddleman 21 Nov. 1837 — Perr
Wills, James to Jemine Trammell 19 Jan. 1817 — Howa
Wills, John to Sally Slinkle 10 Jan. 1830 — CG-A
Wills, John to Dizy Sydes 14 Sept. 1837 — CG-A
Wills, John to Mary Hughes 1 Dec. 1837 — Call
Wills, Richard to Lydia Cox 27 Nov. 1838 — Boon
Wills, Walton to Martha A. Rigby 28 Aug. 1832 — CG-A
Wills, Washington to Theodosha Hicks 18 Mar. 1828 — Boon
Willson, Geo. to Nancy Cunningham 1 June 1823 — StFr
Willson, John to Polly Lamb 30 June 1822 — Clay
Willson, Perletis to Mary E. Flake 22 Dec. 1835 — Perr
Willson, Robt. to Sally A. Walters 5 Dec. 1839 — Buch
Wilmott, Joseph to Frances Graves 2 Oct. 1838 — Boon
Wilson, A. to Elizabeth Oneal 27 Mar. 1836 — Boon
Wilson, Abner to Lucy McFarland 4 July 1838 — Barr
Wilson, Adam to Polly Williams 22 Dec. 1833 — Jeff
Wilson, Alexander to Mary Smith 1 Jan. 1828 — Coop
Wilson, Alexander to Elizabeth Porter 1 Mar. 1836 — Linc
Wilson, Alexander C. to Betsy Jones 16 July 1827 — Jeff

244

```
Wilson, Andrew to Elizabeth Douglas 12 Jan. 1835                          StCh
Wilson, Aquila to Lucinda Brickley 12 Dec. 1825                          Wash
Wilson, Armistead to Elizabeth Elliott 23 June 1835                      Rall
Wilson, Avington K. to Elizabeth Getz 13 Aug. 1828                       Jeff
Wilson, Benj. to Jane Anderson 3 Aug. 1829                               Perr
Wilson, Benj. to Mary S. Brown 10 July 1839                              Sali
Wilson, Berry A. to Elizabeth Thompson 23 May 1824                       CG-1
Wilson, Charles to Eliza Kinney 16 July 1835                            Clay
Wilson, David to Isaphana Collard 3 Dec. 1834                           Linc
Wilson, Edward to Leeny Burket 13 Oct. 1825                             Call
Wilson, Galbreath to Clarissa A. Foxworthy 31 Oct. 1839                 Call
Wilson, Geo. to Sarah Parsons 7 Nov. 1830                               Jack
Wilson, Geo. to Nancy Nichols 24 Mar. 1836                              Boon
Wilson, Geo. to Permela Benson 21 Aug. 1836                             Cr-1
Wilson, Giles to Nancy M.F. Williams 5 May 1831                         Cr-1
Wilson, Greenberry to Ann E. Parrish 18 Feb. 1834                       Mari
Wilson, Henderson to Mary Farmer 20 Dec. 1838                           Cass
Wilson, Hiram to Levina Ainesworth 1 Sept. 1831                         Howa
Wilson, Hiram to Susannah Jackson 7 Jan. 1838                           John
Wilson, Jacob to Jane Bridges 17 July 1834                             Gree
Wilson, James to Bitha Baley 18 Aug. 1829                               Perr
Wilson, James to Mary Bradley 12 July 1832                              Howa
Wilson, James to ---- Freeman -- Oct. 1833                             Boon
Wilson, James B. to Cynethia More 27 May 1833                          Jack
Wilson, James H. to Nancy McGaugh 11 Nov. 1828                          Ray
Wilson, James M. to Nancy Lewis 19 Apr. 1832                           Linc
Wilson, James W. to Martha Millhollan 14 Feb. 1833                      Cr-1
Wilson, Jeremiah to Elizabeth Wilhite 9 Oct. 1836                       Ray
Wilson, John to Sally Byrd 13 Oct. 1810                                CG-1
Wilson, John to Sarah Thorn 30 Jan. 1829                               Jeff
Wilson, John to Elizabeth Clark 5 Apr. 1830                            Howa
Wilson, John to Sena Winscot 18 Sept. 1833                            Howa
Wilson, John to Mary Owen 14 July 1834                                Howa
Wilson, John to Nancy J. Julian 15 Dec. 1839                          Gree
Wilson, John M. to Adeline Graham 7 Feb. 1839                         Jeff
Wilson, Johnson to Jane Farle 9 Mar. 1837                             Mari
Wilson, Jonah to Angeline Jewell 9 Nov. 1837                          Boon
Wilson, Joseph to Polly Millsap 8 Mar. 1821                           Sali
Wilson, Joseph to Polly Chamberlain 14 July 1832                      Jack
Wilson, Joseph G. to Sophia Weber 9 Nov. 1838                         Clar
Wilson, Joshua S. to Nancy Riley 19 July 1838                         Clay
Wilson, Marvin to Nancy Taylor 7 Feb. 1839                            Clar
Wilson, Peter to Nancy Williams 17 Aug. 1829                          Jack
Wilson, Ripley to Dorcas Devenport 27 Aug. 1835                       Gasc
Wilson, Robt. to Margaret Snoddy 13 May 1826                          Howa
Wilson, Robt. to Durna Gibson 28 Jan. 1836                            Linc
Wilson, Robt. to Martha A. Devaul 2 June 1839                         Davi
Wilson, Robt. A. to Mary Davis 8 Dec. 1839                            Coop
Wilson, Robt. W. to Martha I. Parish 5 July 1838                      Mari
Wilson, Samuel to Jane E. Anderson 21 Aug. 1834                       Fran
Wilson, Samuel to Rhodey Brooks 9 Apr. 1838                           Cass
Wilson, Samuel M. to Mary O. Jonicam 12 Dec. 1838                     Morg
Wilson, Simon H. to Matilda Collier 10 Apr. 1839                      Plat
Wilson, Tery to Rebeccah Seitze 24 Feb. 1829                          Md-A
Wilson, Thomas to Patsy Taylor 19 Mar. 1834                           Boon
Wilson, Thomas to Rebecca Reading 25 Aug. 1836                        Pk-1
Wilson, Thomas to Deborah A. Long 22 Nov. 1837                        Call
Wilson, Wiley to Amanda Nichols 15 Feb. 1838                          Boon
Wilson, Wm. to Hannah Cooley 17 July 1823                             Howa
Wilson, Wm. to Temperance Murphy 25 Sept. 1825                        StFr
Wilson, Wm. to Sarah Covey 13 Feb. 1834                               Ray
Wilson, Wm. to Lucinda McWilliams 31 Aug. 1834                        Clay
Wilson, Wm. to Polly Tincher 12 Dec. 1839                             Plat
Wilson, Wm. A. to Mary Reeves 4 June 1835                             Howa
Wilson, Wm. F. to Rebecca Griffith 14 June 1838                       Mari
```

Wilson, Wm. H. to Isabella J. Foxworthy 22 Jan. 1839   Call
Wilson, Wm. N. to Ally Boren 18 Nov. 1832   CG-A
Wilson, Willis to Nancy Pyburn 1 Nov. 1812   CG-1
Wilson, Willis to Elgerta Millhallen 10 Feb. 1831   Cole
Wilson, Zachariah G. to Elizabeth A. Pollock 14 June 1838   Coop
Wilt, John to Elizabeth Cave 19 Dec. 1818   Howa
Winbourne, Henry to Lucindy Jacobs 11 May 1828   Char
Windes, Jackson to Emily Drybread 20 Aug. 1834   Jeff
Windes, Robt. to Sarah Drybread 3 Jan. 1839   Jeff
Windser, Thomas F. to Verlinda A. Bowman 8 June 1834   Lafa
Windsor, Alfred to Elizabeth Mitchell 20 Feb. 1825   Boon
Windsor, John to Elizabeth Barnett 30 Aug. 1838   John
Winfield, Aryson to Mary E. Riley 25 Apr. 1837   Perr
Winfield, James to Patsey Staford 2 Apr. 1829   Perr
Winfield, Stephen T. to Badelia A. Staford 14 July 1829   Perr
Winfield, Wm. to Helena Miles 20 Jan. 1827   Perr
Winfrey, Nelson to Nancy Richards 22 May 1839   Polk
Wingate, Henry to Sarah Street 11 Jan. 1835   Howa
Wingfield, Owen to Mahala Holbert 26 Aug. 1838   Henr
Winhold, John H. to Mrs. Johane C. Walther 24 Nov. 1839   Perr
Winifrey, Israel to Catharine Dunn 25 Dec. 1834   Boon
Winifry, Samuel to Lucinda Waters 7 Dec. 1832   Boon
Winingham, Isom to Sarah Boon 8 June 1837   Clar
Winkler, Henry to Orvetta Ashbell 6 Aug. 1839   Maco
Winkler, Joseph to Rosina Helde 27 Apr. 1835   Perr
Winkler, Lewis to Elizabeth Cross 26 Oct. 1839   Rand
Winkler, Wm. to Rebecca Hardister 25 Mar. 1834   Rand
Winn, Charles to Eliza Hicks 7 Dec. 1827   Boon
Winn, Geo. to Susannah Hurd 19 June 1822   Howa
Winn, James to Rebecca Parks 30 Apr. 1823   Char
Winn, James to Sarah W. Duncan 13 Oct. 1825   Howa
Winn, James to Pamelia Palmer 16 Feb. 1834   Boon
Winn, John to Hannah Roberts 14 June 1819   Howa
Winn, John Jr. to Martha Hick 16 Feb. 1832   Boon
Winn, Martin to Elizabeth Jacobs 7 Aug. 1827   Char
Winn, Squire L. to Lucy Adams 28 Feb. 1828   Howa
Winn, Thomas to Nancy Brown 10 Dec. 1829   Howa
Winn, Thomas to Roxalina Day 25 Aug. 1839   Call
Winningham, John to Polly Yates 3 Jan. 1822   Boon
Winscot, Jeptha D. to Melinda Dingle 9 Oct. 1836   Mari
Winscot, Jirard to Alazara Winn 30 Dec. 1834   Boon
Winscott, Alfred to Asinia Bradley 14 June 1827   Howa
Winscott, Alfred to Ann Coats 6 Aug. 1835   Boon
Winscott, Dudley to Nancy Roberts 5 Oct. 1826   Boon
Winset, James to Oma Fowler 16 Sept. 1837   Perr
Winston, John H. to Elizabeth Tibbs 4 Dec. 1839   Plat
Winter, Samuel P. to Josephine J. Martin 25 Mar. 1838   Clay
Winter, Thomas to Salina Daulton 13 Jan. 1837   Rall
Winterbower, John to Elizabeth Zumwalt 11 Apr. 1839   Call
Winton, James C. to Margaret W. Duncan 10 Oct. 1839   Barr
Wisdom, Brusley to Bethenia Hern 7 Jan. 1830   Boon
Wisdom, Francis to Margaret G. Smith 21 Feb. 1839   Pk-B
Wisdom, Harison to Virginia Turner 21 Dec. 1837   Pk-B
Wisdom, James to Catherine Turner 16 June 1831   Boon
Wisdom, John to Dicey Crowder 22 Mar. 1832   Wash
Wisdom, Lewis to Mary Finley 6 Mar. 1829   Howa
Wisdom, Moses to Zilpha Dotson 13 July 1838   Boon
Wisdom, Taswell to Mary T. Dameron 14 Oct. 1837   Rand
Wisdom, Thomas to Charity Ballew 19 Jan. 1832   Cr-1
Wisdom, Thomas to Lucyani Gap 22 Mar. 1836   Howa
Wise, Henry to Nancy White 6 Dec. 1819   Howa
Wise, Nathaniel to Rhody Rustin 19 Aug. 1835   Cole
Wise, Philip to Sarah Hartle 25 Mar. 1828   CG-A
Wise, Philip to Catharine Fulbrite 18 May 1837   CG-A
Wise, Thomas to Nancy Goff 11 Dec. 1825   Howa

Wise, Thomas to Mariah Briggs 29 Oct. 1828	Rall
Wise, Thomas J. to Gabarella Poage 12 Aug. 1835	Mari
Wiseman, James to Katherine Tomes 13 Oct. 1839	CG-B
Wiseman, Lemuel to Mary Jenkins 2 Mar. 1837	Lewi
Wiseman, Lemuel to Ann A. Neil 14 Feb. 1839	Mari
Wiseman, Samuel C. to Nancy I. Gill 20 Feb. 1838	Mari
Wiswall, Noah to Mary M.A. Jones 20 Mar. 1831	Clay
Witcome, C.S. to Elizabeth Patton 13 June 1836	StCh
Withelin, John to Catherine Sutter 17 Nov. 1839	Perr
Withenton, John to Sarah Twitty 21 June 1833	Fran
Wither, John to Sarah Smarr 12 July 1835	Mari
Withers, Bushrod to Jane Reemes 1 June 1837	Pett
Withers, Jenkins to Margaret Steel 2 Apr. 1839	Coop
Withington, Francis to Polly Goodman 2 Apr. 1832	Linc
Withinton, Nelson Jr. to Rebeckah Decker 19 Sept. 1837	Fran
Withrow, Joseph H. to Ann Wright 20 June 1839	Linc
Withurington, Francis to Polly Parker 31 Oct. 1827	Call
Witt, Littleberry to Susannah Tooly 8 July 1823	Boon
Witt, Nelson to Catharine Conkle 12 Sept. 1822	Howa
Witten, James W. to Parallee M. Stephens 13 Sept. 1838	Mill
Witten, John G. to Isaphena McKinzie 12 July 1832	Cole
Wof, Absolim to Charloty Lakey 23 Aug. 1838	Howa
Wolf, Benj. to Mrs. Louisa Kinnison 12 Apr. 1832	CG-A
Wolf, John to Elizabeth Creeptree 1 May 1834	StCh
Wolf, John to Louise Durbin 18 July 1838	Lewi
Wolf, Michael to Nancy Furry 13 Nov. 1834	Cr-1
Wolf, Robt. to Rachel Watkins 18 Aug. 1836	CG-A
Wolf, Wm. to Annah Berger 12 Aug. 1829	Cole
Wolford, Henry to Rebecca Walker 12 Apr. 1827	CG-A
Wolfskill, Cyrus to Martha Herran 18 Aug. 1839	Howa
Wolfskill, Geo. to Elizabeth Lettral 3 Jan. 1837	Howa
Wolfskill, John to Polly Welch 28 Mar. 1819	Howa
Wolfskill, Joseph to Louisa Taylor 3 Feb. 1831	Howa
Wolsey, John B. to Martha Renfro 23 June 1838	Fran
Wommack, Hiram to Louisa Zimmerman 25 Sept. 1833	Linc
Wommack, Richard to Elizabeth Gilmore 16 Oct. 1833	Linc
Wood, Adam C. to Mary Wilson 9 Sept. 1830	Clay
Wood, Albert to Elizabeth Wood 19 Feb. 1836	Howa
Wood, Clifton to Eliza Snell 12 Dec. 1833	Boon
Wood, Davis to Rebecca Blevins 6 Aug. 1833	Lafa
Wood, Eli to Ann M. Jerman 18 Feb. 1830	Wash
Wood, Henry to Margaret Runkle 8 May 1836	Monr
Wood, James to Sarah Calvert 31 July 1834	Mari
Wood, James M. to Catherine Adair 20 July 1837	Morg
Wood, Jeriah to Ann Miller 21 Oct. 1824	Coop
Wood, Jessy to Ann Henderson 18 Dec. 1831	Md-A
Wood, John to Christiana McHany 15 Nov. 1823	Boon
Wood, John to Narcissa Breckenridge 5 Jan. 1837	Wash
Wood, John to Elizabeth Pryor 20 May 1838	Cass
Wood, John W. to Joanna Stokes 17 Nov. 1839	Buch
Wood, Lashly to Sarah McKenzie 9 Apr. 1828	Boon
Wood, Latney M. to Cordelia Owens 18 June 1839	Clar
Wood, Lewis to Mary Duncan 11 Sept. 1834	Clay
Wood, Melvin to Sereah White 27 Jan. 1833	Monr
Wood, Osburn to Fanny Smith 31 Oct. 1836	Cr-1
Wood, Rice to Matilda Gee 29 June 1837	Livi
Wood, Richard P. to Angeline Wallis 3 July 1838	Clay
Wood, Samuel to Nancy Crews 22 Mar. 1830	Boon
Wood, Spencer to Relief McConnell 10 May 1832	Pk-1
Wood, Vardy to Winey Forgason 25 Sept. 1837	Md-B
Wood, Watson to Lucinda A. Snell 24 Aug. 1833	Boon
Wood, Wiley to Emily Eaton 24 Sept. 1832	Wash
Wood, Wm. to Tabitha Roberts 12 Aug. 1832	Jack
Wood, Wm. to Laura Byington 2 Apr. 1835	StFr
Wood, Wm. L. to Eliza Hughs 20 Mar. 1832	Clay

Wood, Willson L. to Henretta Anderson 22 Nov. 1833   Mari
Woodcock, Henry to Minerva Wittington 3 Jan. 1837   Fran
Woodcock, Jesse to Rebecca Keen 12 Jan. 1837   Fran
Wooderson, Wm. M.K. to Elizabeth Woolard 13 Dec. 1838   Ray
Woodfin, Geo. to Maria Green 17 Nov. 1829   CG-A
Woodfin, Moses to Eliza Chenantt 27 June 1838   Morg
Woodfolk, Charles G. to Jane Allen 12 Apr. 1836   StCh
Woodford, Jesse to Polly Vance 25 Sept. 1828   Clay
Woodford, Julian to Martha T. Huff 9 May 1839   Morg
Woodland, James to Nancy Moody 8 Aug. 1833   StCh
Woods, Absalom to Elizabeth Williams 18 Mar. 1827   Coop
Woods, Andrew to Louise Chovine 6 Feb. 1806   StCh
Woods, Archibald to Elizabeth Kelly 12 Sept. 1822   Coop
Woods, Archibald to Dortha J. Hudson 3 Jan. 1828   Clay
Woods, Archibald C. to Elizabeth Houck 7 Apr. 1831   Lafa
Woods, Barna to Nelly Dail 9 Feb. 1832   Howa
Woods, Caleb to Margaret McBride 11 Jan. 1829   Howa
Woods, Christopher to Lusa Brian 13 Nov. 1828   Wash
Woods, David to Margaret Maupin 24 Sept. 1824   Howa
Woods, David to Sarah Reynolds 10 Oct. 1831   Call
Woods, Forrest to Mary Oldham 9 July 1837   Char
Woods, Garret W. to Frances Marshall 25 Nov. 1838   Rand
Woods, Green to Mary Estes 30 Nov. 1821   Coop
Woods, James to Jane Ogen 14 Nov. 1822   Boon
Woods, James to Martha J. Stone 1835   Boon
Woods, James to Amanda Devant 28 Jan. 1838   Livi
Woods, James H. to Sarah Hyatt 19 Apr. 1831   Cr-P
Woods, Jesse to Missouri Gilbert 5 Feb. 1835   Mari
Woods, John to Nancy McClure 6 Sept. 1821   Coop
Woods, John M. to Eliza J. Curry 4 Oct. 1838   Monr
Woods, Jonathan to Mary Cosney 1 Dec. 1836   Linc
Woods, Larkin to Mary Hawker 27 Jan. 1829   Howa
Woods, Levi to Rachel Shipley 22 Jan. 1826   Coop
Woods, Levi to Mariah Campbell 6 Oct. 1833   Coop
Woods, Nicholas L. to Leannatha Green 25 Sept. 1828   Howa
Woods, Peter to Nancy Collins 12 Dec. 1822   Howa
Woods, Sachel to Elizabeth Warren -- May 1823   Howa
Woods, Sidney S. to Martha Simpson 5 Apr. 1832   StCh
Woods, Solon H. to Martha A. Reid 5 Sept. 1839   Monr
Woods, Stephen to Polly Cummings 15 Mar. 1828   Howa
Woods, Stephen to Elizabeth Cowan 22 Oct. 1839   Howa
Woods, Thomas to Elizabeth Younger 22 June 1826   Clay
Woods, Wm. Jr. to Sarah Wilson 12 July 1827   Clay
Woods, Wm. to Sarah McGuire 10 Oct. 1828   Coop
Woods, Wm. D. to Elizabeth Jamison 10 Oct. 1839   Wash
Woodson, James to Mary A.E. Anderson 14 Nov. 1837   Char
Woodson, Richard to Mary A. Bennett 13 Dec. 1838   Howa
Woodson, Warress to Elizabeth McClelland 11 Apr. 1822   Boon
Woodson, Wm. to Elizabeth Lewis 25 Nov. 1834   Howa
Woodson, Wm. G. to Cynthia Thompson 9 Feb. 1837   Monr
Woodward, Albert G. to Rebecca A. Moore 3 June 1839   Clay
Woodward, John to Polly Douglas 21 Mar. 1833   Howa
Woodward, Willis to Elizabeth Reed 10 Aug. 1826   Md-A
Woodworth, Charles G. to Elizabeth Stone 24 Nov. 1829   Mari
Woody, Davis to Partheny Isbeel 23 July 1835   Gasc
Woody, Leonard to Permely Stark 20 Apr. 1837   Clin
Woolard, John to Nancy Liles 9 Apr. 1821   Ray
Woolery, Henry Jr. to Litvitia Beaty 31 Dec. 1829   Coop
Woolery, James E. to Elizabeth Wadley 11 Apr. 1839   Coop
Woolery, John to Priscilla Moore 16 Nov. 1837   Cole
Woolery, Joseph to Nancy Tittsworth 17 Aug. 1828   Coop
Woolery, Laurence to Betsy Beeman 2 May 1839   Morg
Woolery, Stephen to Polly Shirley 3 Oct. 1839   Coop
Woolery, Wm. to Margaret Thomas 1 Jan. 1835   Coop
Woolf, Fielding to Ruth Standford 10 Nov. 1835   Howa

248

Woolf, John to Sally Mullins 26 Nov. 1832   Coop
Woolf, Peter to Nancy Millsap 12 Feb. 1839   Char
Woolfolk, Norbern to Matilda Woolfolk 3 Oct. 1839   Warr
Woolfolk, Richard to Helen Wells 15 May 1828   StCh
Woolfolk, Robt. N. to Malrina Bowlware 22 June 1837   Mari
Woolfolk, Zachary to Ann A. Hindrick 9 Apr. 1837   StCh
Woolford, Frederick Jr. to Nancy Phelps 6 Oct. 1825   StGe
Woolford, Frederick to Eliza Logan 26 Nov. 1835   Wash
Wooliver, Alford to Sinai Compton 17 May 1835   John
Woolridge, Edmond to Elizabeth Ross 4 Dec. 1834   Coop
Woolridge, Starlin to Ann M. Roe 19 Dec. 1838   Coop
Woolsey, Geo. to Eliza Henderson 7 Nov. 1839   Mill
Woolsey, Noah to Sally Harvey 27 June 1835   Carr
Woolsey, Stephen to Abigail Woolsey 21 Jan. 1838   Carr
Woolsey, Stephen C. to Elizabeth A. Caton 5 Aug. 1838   Carr
Woolsy, Levi to Maranda Walls 29 Jan. 1832   Fran
Word, Thompson to Rachel Culp 4 Jan. 1838   Clin
Worden, John to Louisa Burris 1 Mar. 1839   Cass
Work, Henderson to Julia Hendrix 2 Oct. 1834   Carr
Work, Jacob to Sena Finny 12 Feb. 1837   Livi
Worker, Daniel to America King 29 Dec. 1831   Wash
Workman, David to Mary Hook 20 Oct. 1825   Howa
Worland, Stephen W. to Sarah E. Blacklock 22 Sept. 1839   Monr
Worldly, James to Nancy M. Prewett 1 May 1839   Ripl
Worsham, Archibald to Alsey Swift 4 July 1837   Pk-A
Worsham, Hines to Catharine Triplett 29 Dec. 1836   Pk-1
Worsham, John to Martha McQuary 6 Jan. 1831   Pk-1
Worsham, Richard to Elizabeth Triplett 30 Aug. 1827   Pk-1
Worsham, Wm. T. to Samenta A. Stokes 27 Mar. 1838   Call
Worthington, Joseph to Elizabeth Mitchell 27 Jan. 1836   Lewi
Wouldridge, David to Prudence Simpson 21 Feb. 1837   Monr
Wray, Blanton to Margaret A. Hultz 5 July 1837   Call
Wray, Robt. to Polly Gifferd 3 July 1833   CG-A
Wren, David to Delilah Grindstaff 23 Feb. 1836   Boon
Wright, Abraham to Mrs. Polly Rodney 19 Feb. 1828   CG-A
Wright, Benj. to Nancy Lewis 1 Sept. 1831   CG-A
Wright, Bryan to Nancy Belt 31 Oct. 1837   Lafa
Wright, Darlin to Nancy Riley 23 Jan. 1829   Rand
Wright, David to Lavina Smith 19 Oct. 1836   Rand
Wright, Drury to Elizabeth Shobe 8 Dec. 1830   Gasc
Wright, Evans Jr. to Milly Gideon 13 Nov. 1834   Rand
Wright, Foster P. to Nancy McLanahan 29 Aug. 1837   Morg
Wright, Geo. to Syntha Fowler 22 June 1837   Pk-A
Wright, Geo. B. to Caroline R. Merrell 15 Dec. 1836   Mari
Wright, Geo. D. to Elizabeth Cull 15 Aug. 1836   John
Wright, Geo. W. to Sarah William 30 Aug. 1838   Boon
Wright, Gideon to Nancy Culp 5 Sept. 1834   Rand
Wright, Grayson F. to Martha Anderson 14 June 1835   Mari
Wright, Harrison to Caroline Taylor 29 Nov. 1836   Cr-1
Wright, Jackson to Elizabeth Matlock 15 Jan. 1839   Cr-1
Wright, James to Louisianna Shaw 7 Dec. 1830   Boon
Wright, James to Burnetta Arthur 29 Dec. 1831   Cr-1
Wright, James K. to Myra Wright 5 Apr. 1836   Boon
Wright, James W. to Hannah Flynn 22 Oct. 1816   StGe
Wright, John to Eliza Wills 25 Dec. 1831   Rall
Wright, John to Eleanor Williams 2 Nov. 1833   Mari
Wright, John to Pelina West 2 June 1836   Monr
Wright, John A. to Susan E. Shannon 4 Oct. 1839   Pk-B
Wright, John C. to Mary E. Holding 23 Jan. 1837   Mari
Wright, John F. to Elizabeth Goodman 21 Jan. 1836   Pk-1
Wright, Joseph to Margaret Bennet 11 Apr. 1839   Linc
Wright, Leland to Martha W. Norman 10 Apr. 1837   Mari
Wright, Morgan to Sarah Lee 28 Mar. 1838   Warr
Wright, Oliver to Veany Pratt 28 Nov. 1839   Call
Wright, Robt. to Polly Ramsey 11 Sept. 1833   Ray

249

Wright, Sampson to Elizabeth Mullins 25 Oct. 1821   Howa
Wright, Scott to Susan Leadford 4 Nov. 1838   Pk-B
Wright, Scott B. to Mary Lewellen 16 May 1837   Rall
Wright, Thomas to Polly M. Cochran 11 Apr. 1825   Char
Wright, Thomas to Elizabeth Chambers 13 Nov. 1834   Linc
Wright, Thomas E. to Mary Bolt 24 Nov. 1839   Polk
Wright, Thomas J. to Caroline Gugar 20 Sept. 1831   Linc
Wright, Walter to Louisa Gibbons 18 Feb. 1834   Mari
Wright, Washington to Mariah Williams 23 Oct. 1834   Howa
Wright, Wesley to Polly Potts 12 Oct. 1826   Call
Wright, Wm. to Margaret Spraul 10 Jan. 1827   Boon
Wright, Wordden T. to Phebe Marrill 14 Nov. 1839   Mari
Wrightsman, Daniel to Jain Crockett 21 Oct. 1834   Clay
Wrightsman, Frances to Lucinda Officer 19 Jan. 1832   Clay
Wyate, Sander to Eliza Ralston 6 May 1838   Henr
Wyatt, Benj. to Nancy Simpson 16 Sept. 1830   Fran
Wyatt, Geo. to Harriett Compton 17 Oct. 1837   Mari
Wyatt, Gideon P. to Matilda Weir 18 Apr. 1839   Gasc
Wyatt, James to Mary Craig 10 Apr. 1831   Gasc
Wyatt, John to Jane Wilson 23 May 1830   Gasc
Wyatt, Samuel to Jane ---- 11 Mar. 1832   Gasc
Wyatt, Wm. to Elizabeth Burnsides 18 Sept. 1825   Fran
Wyatt, Wm. to Elizabeth McGoun 24 Nov. 1831   Gasc
Wyette, Francis to Arthusa Faulconer 25 Feb. 1837   Linc
Wygall, Wm. to Mariah Cooksey 29 Dec. 1836   Lewi

Yager, Aaron A. to Mary A. Ford 15 Dec. 1836   Monr
Yager, Henry to Elizabeth Hutson 12 Sept. 1839   Pk-B
Yager, Joseph to Emily Bennett 11 Oct. 1832   Boon
Yale, Richard to Liza Vale 13 Sept. 1827   Pk-1
Yancey, Wm. to Martha Ferguson 14 Mar. 1839   Call
Yancy, Albert G. to Elizabeth Rochester 4 Jan. 1838   Howa
Yancy, Thornton to Elizabeth Dean 29 Apr. 1834   Jack
Yantis, J. Alexander S. to Sarah Green 23 Nov. 1837   Lafa
Yarborough, Geo. to Elizabeth Steele 28 Apr. 1836   Cole
Yardley, Frederick to Missouri T. Loney 15 Oct. 1835   StCh
Yardley, Geo. to Sarah L. Wray 8 Mar. 1838   StCh
Yarnal, John to Delilah Yarnal 8 Dec. 1817   StCh
Yarnald, John to Jane Wilker 16 Feb. 1834   StCh
Yarnall, Amos to Elizabeth Tagart 1 Dec. 1836   StCh
Yarnall, Washington to Elizabeth W. Towers 22 Dec. 1838   StCh
Yartin, Richard to Ann E. Elliott 20 Aug. 1832   Coop
Yates, Abel to Phoeby Blanton 11 Apr. 1830   Jack
Yates, Benj. to Amelia Crider 9 Apr. 1829   Gasc
Yates, John to Ann Nichols 15 May 1828   Call
Yates, John to Elizabeth Dawson 26 Apr. 1833   Call
Yates, Jeptha to Jane Harrison 2 Apr. 1838   Call
Yates, Jonas to Martha Foster 6 Sept. 1827   Jeff
Yates, Nathaniel to Judith Moore 1 Oct. 1836   Clay
Yates, Pleasant to Harriett McCrary 6 May 1832   Clay
Yates, Thomas to Eliza Pierceall 14 Dec. 1835   Monr
Yates, Vincent to Nancy Estes 9 Sept. 1827   Call
Yates, Washington to Rachel Clarke 18 Jan. 1836   Ray
Yeargen, Bartlet W. to Loretta Westover 11 Dec. 1834   Wash
Yeaters, C.P. to Mary Millroy 25 Jan. 1838   Pk-B
Yeats, Joshua Jr. to Polly Milikam 18 Jan. 1827   Clay
Yeocham, Geo. to Elizabeth Hopper 17 Aug. 1837   Gree
Yielding, Richard to Mariah Wilds 17 Nov. 1829   Howa
Yoachaman, Soloman to Nancy House 12 Aug. 1834   Gree
Yoacomand, Levi to Polly Patterson 15 Oct. 1834   Gree
Yoalkam, Adam to Martha Ventioner 13 Jan. 1839   Barr
Yocham, Jesse to Mary Chance 17 Nov. 1831   Clay
Yocom, Jesse to Mary A. Adkins 31 Jan. 1830   Clay
Yong, James to Rosana Nichles 14 Feb. 1838   Perr

```
Yong, Wm. to Elizabeth Miller 27 July 1817                      CG-1
York, James to Jane Goff 21 Apr. 1820                           Howa
York, James to Tabitha Wilson 16 Apr. 1828                      Howa
York, John W. to Mary P. Collier 8 July 1828                    Md-A
York, Jonathan to Sarah Shore 12 Apr. 1838                      Lafa
Yosti, Francis to Emilie A. Morrison 7 Oct. 1839               StCh
Young, Alexander to Nancy Brown 14 Feb. 1833                    Cr-1
Young, Alexander A. to Ann Steel 16 Feb. 1837                  Gree
Young, Allen to Narcissa Kimbull 3 May 1832                     Md-A
Young, Awsten to Marget Critz 2 Oct. 1806                       CG-1
Young, Burd H. to Milly Carpenter 19 July 1838                 Lewi
Young, Charles to Nancy Greenawalt 4 Apr. 1836                 StFr
Young, Chesney to Rachel Lewis 13 July 1830                    Jack
Young, Clinton to Emily Miller 23 Oct. 1831                    Coop
Young, E.W. to Julia A. Parmorle 26 Feb. 1839                  Clar
Young, Elija to Polly Evans 19 Aug. 1832                        CG-A
Young, Geo. to Sarah McLaird 3 Sept. 1829                       Md-A
Young, Henderson to Theodosia Callaway 23 May 1839            Lafa
Young, Henry to Sary Lewis 17 Mar. 1835                        Rall
Young, Herd to Frances A. Gant 22 Dec. 1835                    Lafa
Young, Hiram H. to Edna Thornhill 10 Mar. 1831                StCh
Young, James to Emily Scofield 19 Mar. 1837                    Mari
Young, James B. to Martha Johnson 5 Aug. 1825                  Lafa
Young, John to Jane Wilburn 31 Jan. 1826                       Lafa
Young, Joseph to Sarah Byrd 22 Oct. 1805                       CGRA
Young, Joseph R. to Lucy Ellis 20 June 1833                    Howa
Young, Joshua to Nancy Hayes 12 June 1838                      Boon
Young, Lawson to Lydia Scofield 17 Jan. 1839                   Mari
Young, Meltonia to Angeline Carter 21 Nov. 1839               Lewi
Young, Oliver to Margaret Helderman 1 Dec. 1839               CG-B
Young, Pleasant to Margaret Gregg 13 Oct. 1836               John
Young, Richard M. to Matilda M. James 25 June 1820            StGe
Young, Rufus to Marinda Hailley 25 Feb. 1834                  Jack
Young, Samuel to Polly Bearden 11 Jan. 1829                    Rall
Young, Washington to Nancy Lake 18 Jan. 1824                  Rall
Young, Wm. to Elizabeth Catron 30 Nov. 1819                   Coop
Young, Wm. to Sally Linville 18 Apr. 1831                      Call
Young, Wm. to Amanda W. Sanford 9 Jan. 1839                    Rand
Young, Wm. to Mary A. Collins 11 Nov. 1839                    Lafa
Youngblood, James to Mary Mayberry 11 June 1835               Ray
Younger, Anderson to Harriet Calahan 25 Sept. 1838           Boon
Younger, Coleman to Eleanor Murry 30 Apr. 1829               Clay
Younger, James to Rachel Murphy 2 Feb. 1823                   StFr
Younger, John to Polly Johnson 17 Sept. 1839                  Plat
Younger, Littleton to Liza Sampson 30 Dec. 1833              Clay
Yount, Benj. to Ruth Sullivan 21 Mar. 1834                   StCh
Yount, David to Caty Waggoner 12 Dec. 1833                    Call
Yount, Frederick to Polly Mayfield 30 Dec. 1830             CG-A
Yount, Geo. to Eliza Wilds 18 Oct. 1818                       Howa
Yount, Geo. to Anna Cotner 4 Aug. 1836                        CG-A
Yount, Jacob to Katherine Mayfield 20 Nov. 1834             CG-B
Yount, Jesse to Libby Tinnen 4 Apr. 1822                      CG-1
Yount, Peter to Margaret Mowser 24 Dec. 1835                 CG-B
Yount, Smith to Polly M. Murray 8 Mar. 1835                   Cole
Youre, James to America Sharp 9 Apr. 1838                     Jack
Yourie, Anderson to Athaliah Wallace 24 Apr. 1835            Lafa


Zachary, Henry H. to Sarah J. Jones 15 Nov. 1838             Barr
Zeigler, Samuel to Mary Dotson 9 May 1839                    Perr
Zumall, Henry to Elizabeth Kesler 20 Sept. 1808             StCh
Zumalt, Abraham to Margaret Zumalt 17 Feb. 1829             Linc
Zumalt, Adam to Nancy Caton 6 May 1813                        StCh
Zumalt, Adam to Mahala --ills 12 Oct. 1834                   Fran
```

Zumalt, Adam to Laureta Birnside 25 Aug. 1837   Polk
Zumalt, Ephraim to Nancy Lankford 30 Mar. 1837   Linc
Zumalt, Levy to Delila Lankford 3 Aug. 1837   Warr
Zumwalt, Abraham to Juliet Hope 30 Sept. 1825   Call
Zumwalt, Eleanor to Mary Plank 17 Sept. 1835   Cole
Zumwalt, Geo. to Clementine Callison 5 Jan. 1837   StCh
Zumwalt, Isaac to Matilda Blythe 10 June 1826   Call
Zumwalt, Isaac to Sarah Crow 24 June 1837   StCh
Zumwalt, Jacob to Henrietta Cunningham 18 Aug. 1817   StCh
Zumwalt, Jacob to Sarah Zumwalt 18 Aug. 1836   Call
Zumwalt, Jesse to Nancy Grider 25 Aug. 1836   Fran
Zumwalt, John to Mary Crow 16 Nov. 1809   StCh
Zumwalt, John to Mary Petty 10 Apr. 1828   StCh
Zumwalt, John to Sarah M. Russell 2 May 1838   Polk
Zumwalt, John M. to Lucinda Zumwalt 19 Sept. 1837   Warr
Zumwalt, Jonathan to Mary M. Pearce 7 Feb. 1828   StCh
Zumwalt, Solomon to Nancy Grose 1 Nov. 1827   StCh
Zumwalt, Solomon to Lucinda Kent 20 July 1834   Warr
Zumwatt, Noah to Nancy Corhan 1 Apr. 1830   Linc

ADDENDA

Criswell, Wm. to Elizabeth Benedick 21 Sept. 1820   Howa
Ford, David to Mary Smith 6 Nov. 1828   Howa
Foster, Ezekial to Elizabeth Bowman 20 Mar. 1838   CG-A
Gladden, David to Nancy B. Stone 1 June 1838   Clay

257

Bass, Mary 207
  Nancy 197
  Nelly 41
  Paralee 67
  Polly 100
Bassa, Elizabeth 236
Bast, Sarah 208
Bastin, Mary A. 40
Bate, Ellen 155
Bates, Eliza A. 75
  Ellen 158
  Emily C. 234
  Louisa 198
  Patsy 31
  Polly 67, 207
  Rachel 101
  Sofiah 136
  Susan 74
Bath, Sarah J. 23
Batony, Mahala 109
Batterton, Malinda 4
Battle, Mary 30
Batty, Clency 180
Baty, Louisa 243
Baugh, Alcy 190
  Judith 43
  Lucinda 196
  Martha 112
  Martha A. 17
Baul, Cordely 146
  Nancy 95
Bauman, Lelah E. 244
Bauthel, Celeste 66
Baxter, Ann 34, 180
  Eliza M. 169
  Elizabeth 112, 236
  Luannah 181
  Mary 43
  Phebe 213
  Polly 218
  Rachel 83
  Sarah 34, 43, 240
Bay, Hetty 180
  Sally 172
Bayles, Amanda 133
Bayley, Elizabeth 24
Bayne, Mary A. 239
Baynham, Harriet A. 171
Beal, Winney 1
Beals, Mary 62
  Nancy 199
Beaman, Martha 71
Beard, Manerva 97
  Martha C. 64
Bearden, Polly 251
Beardsley, Viletta 225
Beasley, Amelia 243
  Martha A. 130
  Mary 119
  Sarah 199
Beason, Rhoda 5
Beatty, Elizabeth 105
  Mary A. 54
  Sally 6
Beaty, Elizabeth 121
  Jane 5
  Litvitia 248
  Martha J. 234
  Polly 38
  Rachel 27
Beauchamp, Cecile 190
  Elizabeth 185
  Marie 24
  Theodosia 163
Beauchemin, Marguerite 12
  Mary 119
  Victoire 132
Beaver, Perlina 43
  Susan 44

Beavois, Mary 200
Beck, Coly 26
  Lydia 110
  Nancy 110, 207
Becker, Sarah 46
Becket, Elizabeth 81
  Jane 192
  Malinda 100
  Mary 122
  Nancy 121, 132
  Sally 164
  Susan 227
Beckett, Abby 92
  Polly 183
Beden, Patsy 204
Bedford, Sally 18
Bedinger, Polly 39
Beeman, Betsy 248
Been, Nancy 49
Beesley, Nancy 7
Beherst, Adaline 79
Behurst, Elizabeth 223
Beil, Regina 124
Belcher, Harnah 166
  Jane 152
  Roady 189
  Sarah 95
Belew, Mary 191
Bell, Derinda 79
  Elenor 125
  Elizabeth 42, 63, 108, 119
  Emily 173
  Helen M. 67
  Lydia 164
  Margaret 48
  Martha M. 126
  Mary 54, 104
  Nancy 176
  Obedience 65
  Polly 65
  Rachel 9
  Rebecca 204
  Sallie 49
Bellamy, Ann 90
  Delinda 76
  Luand 192
Bellemay, Leah 110
Bellemy, Eliza 89
Bellow, Lucinda 107
Bells, Ann 225
Bellum, Mary E. 94
Belmare, Mary 16
Belmear, Mary A. 218
Belt, Elizabeth 104
  Nancy 249
Bemes, Pusena 96
Benedick, Elizabeth 252
Benge, Peggy 201
Benham, Dicy 134
Benn, Temperance 157
  Verlinda 200
Bennet, Margaret 213, 249
  Mary 125
  Nancy 114
Bennett, Adaline B. 160
  Eliza 79
  Ellis 13
  Emey 6
  Emily 250
  Jane 111
  Marget 150
  Mary A. 248
  Matilda 83
  Patcy 150
  Polly 98, 138
  Rebecca 225
  Rosina 190
  Sarah 28
  Susan 216

Benning, Alizar 173
  Huldah 144
  Mary S. 26
Bennings, Desdamona 182
Bennon, Keziah 164
  Polly 164
Benoise, Adeline 190
Benson, Ann 203
  Elizabeth 129
  Harriet 103
  Permela 245
  Sarah 4
Bentley, Emily 172
  Harriett 18
  Martha 216
  Rhoda 105
Benton, Martha 144
  Merry 217
  Nancy 241
Benus, Betsey 142
  Nancy 79
Beordin, Elizabeth 102
  Eulalie 24
Berd, Sabina 5
Berdon, Rhoda 146
Berger, Annah 247
  Nancy 99
Berk, Sarah A. 89
Berkett, Eva 31
Berkley, Martha 6
  Sarah 185
Berman, Polly 35
Bernard, Maria L. 66
  Mary 67
Berncer, Margaret 227
Bernier, Archangel 42
  Mary 61
Berribo, Angelique 145
Berry, Eleanor 136
  Eliza 237
  Elizabeth 110, 185
  Esther 15
  Lucy 187
  Margaret 19, 67
  Margaret A. 24
  Mary C. 148
  Mary E. 83
  Nancy 200
  Rebecca 126
Berryman, Nancy 28
Berthireaume, Polly 138
Berthold, Barbara 227
Bertin, Nancy 49
Bess, Adaline 206
  Catherine 204
  Eliza A. C. 116
  Elizabeth 200, 211
  Hanner 242
  Jain 241
  Katharine 199
  Margaret 240
  Mary 107
  Nancy 124
  Rilla 45
  Sarah 17
Best, Alcey 206
  Bary 99
  Polly 237
  Salle 17
Bevel, Elizabeth 51
  Matilda 196
Bevins, Eliza 200
  Elizabeth 123
  Malinda W. 113
  Martha A. 135
Bewley, Catherine 8
Bewly, Sylvia J. 201
Biddy, Polly 6
Bierden, Martha 49

Biggers, Dulcena 71
Biggs, Belinda 79
  Emily 27
  Larany A. 141
  Polley A. 227
  Susan 68
Bigham, Jane 68, 212
  Margaret 97
  Polly 20
Bigs, Fanny 139
Bilford, Delilah 127
Billings, Clementin 239
  Minerva 15
Billingsly, Tabitha 229
Billups, America A. 58
  Mary C. 75
Bilyeu, Sarah 146
Bilyew, Diannah 31
  Lydia 18
  Nancy 209
Bingham, Amanda 11
Bink, Eliza 111
Birch, Malinda 234
  Mary J. 234
Birchfield, Nancy 127
Bird, Catherine 65, 118
  Emily 241
  Jane 31
  Matilda 125
  Polly 238
Birditt, Susan 165
Birdsong, Betsy 231
  Jale 35
Birkhear, Julia N. 220
Birns, Eveline 25
Birnside, Laureta 252
Biscoe, Mary A. 211
Bishop, Ann 205
  Charlotte 182
  Elizabeth 11,, 177
  Francis 36
  Harriet 55
  Lucy J. 109
  Margaret 22
  Terrissa 84
Biswell, Elizabeth 43
  Polly 136
Biticks, Nancy 186
Bittle, Elizabeth 18
  Katherine 20
  Nelly 152
  Susanna 208
Biven, Matilda 141
Bivens, Ann 142
  Maryann 38
  Minerva H. 17
  Nancy 74
  Polly 127
Bives, Odille 131
Black, Dovey E. 97
  Isabella B. 135
  Nancy 186
  Narcissa 38
  Polly W. 163
  Purnacy 135
Blackaby, Mary J. 166
Blackburn, Elizabeth 3
  Evaline 119
Blacklock, Sarah E. 249
Blackstone, Elizabeth 107
Blackwell, Elvira 71
  Evaline 221
  Mariah 176
  Mary A. 37
  Nancy 216
  Polly 207
  Susannah 143
Blackwood, Margaret M. 21

Blackwood, Mary 21
Blag, Catherine 128
Blain, Elizabeth 239
Blair, Elizabeth 29
  Jane 103
  Nancy 183
Blais, Hetty 7
  Louise 138
Blake, Jane 208
Blakely, Elizabeth 109
  Emporia 63
  Nancy A. 50
  Polly 102
  Susannah 89
Blankenship, Diadana 50
  Mahala 38
  Malinda 19
Blann, Polly 73
Blanstel, Louisiana 154
Blanton, Mary 32
  Mary A. 236
  Phoeby 250
Blare, Margaret 42
Blasgame, Rode 162
Balssengame, Polly 159
Blattenburgh, Mary 103
Blauff, Margaret 107
Blecher, Milla 24
Bledsoe, Camantha 105
  Isabella 20
  Louisa 36
  Mary 2
  Nancy 195
  Ritta 111
  Sarah 2
  Tabithy 101
  Thesiah 93
Blent, Betsy 32
Blevin, Nancy 172
  Polly 204
Blevins, Amely 34
  Catharine 9
  Elizabeth 183, 199
  Eva 156
  Mary 41, 153
  Polly 92
  Rachel 179
  Rebecca 247
Blith, Susan 33
Blize, Elizabeth 161
Blizzard, Sarah A. 180
Block, Abby 124
  Delia 20
  Julia A. F. 140
  Louisa 125
  Rachel 1, 209
  Susan 21, 75
  Virginia 129
  Zephore 147
Blocker, Mary 153
  Sarah 91
Blockley, Mary 107
Blockmann, Marie 214
Blomenberg, Phillipine 74
Blount, Nancy 53
Blue, Affia A. 213
  Amanda 139
  Elvira 126
  Emuld 126
  Flora 82
Bly, Polly 110
Blythe, Margaret 169
  Matilda 252
  Sarah 167
Boalding, Laney 119
Boas, Mary 164
Bobenreid, Catherine 224
Bock, Helena J. P. 163

Bock, Minna 150
Boessheart, Ebrosina 230
Bogart, Eliza A. 31
  Elizabeth 133
Boger, Susana 233
Bogges, Naomi 88
  Orpha 29
Bogghess, Hester 171
Boggoss, Mary 54
Boggs, Jane 124
  Jinny 50
  Lidia A. 147
  Margaret 38, 82
  Rebecca 115
Boggus, Delila 88
Bogy, Felicita 119
Bohannen, America 56
Bohannon, Frances 135
Bohon, Jeremia 19
Boian, Disa 167
  Nancy 230
Bpice, Elizabeth 75
  Jane A. M. 195
  Malinda 154
Boid, Mariah J. 178
Boils, Margaret 118
Boilston, Elizabeth 7
Bold, Susan T. 189
Bolen, Elizabeth 217
Boli, Elizabeth 218
Bolin, Lydia 56
  Peggy 130
  Sealy 216
  Susana 1
Boling, Lucinda 204
Bollinger, Ana 100
  Barbery 208
  Catherine 7
  Eave 121
  Elizabeth 200, 205
  Katherine 154
  Margaret 104
  Mary 48
  Mary M. 21
  Polly 96, 113
  Polly C. 21
  Sarah 81, 225
  Sophia 240
  Susan 19
  Susannah 212
Bolt, Mary 250
Bolware, Emily 139
Boman, Edith 214
  Nancy 39
Bombaugh, Rebecca 221
Bomker, Sophia 170
Bond, Lydia 112
  Martha 159
Bonderant, Telitha 118
Bondurant, Martha 101
Bone, Celeste 232
  Mary 217
  Menerva 220
  Mira B. 128
  Nancy 201
Bones, Eliza 151
  Margaret 80
Bonham, Rebecka 136
Bonne, Mary 217
Boocher, Catherine 209
Booke, Sarah 230
Boolen, Elizabeth 144
Boon, Charlotte 166
  Delea 154
  Dicy 127
  Elizabeth 151
  Louisa 239
  Lucy 203

Brashears, Margery A. 79
  Mellisa A. 61
Brasher, Matilda 48
Brasier, Sarah 139
Brason, Polly 221
Brassfield, Cynthy 136
  Frances 211
  Polly A. 81
Bratten, Emily 173
  Severn 94
Bratton, Susan 170
Braucher, Christina 203
Braughman, Amanda 226
Brawley, H. 214
  Mary A. 88
Brawner, Kitteann 157
Bray, Elizabeth 145
  Jane 192
  Patsy 185
Brazel, Elizabeth 133
Breassie, Emily 35
Breckenridge, Elizabeth 26
  Letitia 196
  Milla A. 205
  Narcissa 247
Breese, Rachel 78
Brellen, Infinity 55
Brendenburgh, Nancy 165
Brenegan, Polly A. 213
Bressie, Elizabeth 241
Brewen, Elizabeth 59
Brewer, Bennety 238
  Charlott 143
  Elizabeth 125, 129
  Esther 48
  Hester A. 151
  Letty 48
  Lucinda 33
  Maria 183
  Mariah 129
  Mary D. 132
  Milley 26
  Nancy 61, 89
  Polly 210
Brian,, Lusa 248
  Mary 131
Briant, Temperance O. 173
Brice, Amanda M. 211
  Kitty 139
Bricken, Louisa 97
Brickey, Agnes 110
  Eliza A. 111
  Lydda 220
  Meriam 117
  Rhoda 134
Brickley, Lucinda 245
  Matilday 201
Bricky, Emily 237
  Louisa 92
Bricot. Mary M. 51
Bridges, Elizabeth 88, 93
  Jane 245
  Mary 124
  Mary A. 225
  Nancy 118
  Saleeta 50
  Susan 50
Bridgewater, Nancy 63
  Sarah 210
Bridwell, Mariah 35
Briges, Sarah 110
Briggs, Barbary 36
  Eleanor M. 66
  Eliza I. 36
  Jane 145
  Judith 94
  Margaret P. 39
  Mariah 247
  Mary A. 238

Briggs, Nancy 217
  Susan E. 238
Bright, Anna M. 48
  Elizabeth T. 151
  Nancy J. 162
Brigs, Elizabeth 146
Brinck, Zelia 179
Brinegar, Remey 90
Brink, Ketura A. 237
Brinker, Maria 123
Brinkle, Malinda 203
Brinkman, Sophie 237
Brisco, Sevilla 71
Briscoe, Artimissa 122
  Elizabeth 7
  Frances 27
  Frances W. 185
  Margaret 126
  Peggy 205
  Sarah 46
Brison, Catharine 29
Bristo, Elizabeth 217
Bristoe, Didima 62
  Mahaly 212
Brite, Hannah 167
Briton, Agnes 184
Britt, Amanda 179
  Ellen 179
Britton, Frances 184
Brizandine, Lucinda 11
Broadhurst, Elender 78
  Mary 219
  Sarah 27, 94
Broadhush, Ila 167
Brock, Elizabeth 184, 238
  Jincy 189
  Lucy 231
  Malinda 192
  Susan 14
  Susan C. 27
  Susannah 127
  Tabitha 78
  Tiny 186
  Wineford 128
Brockhaust, Mariah 31
Brockman, Burlinda 160
  Elizabeth E. 64
  Ellen 64
  Fanny 170
  Lucinda 41
  Mary A. 118
  Nancy 126
  Susan 241
Brocks, Melinda 70
Brokehoff, Elizabeth 127
Brook, Cynthia A. 84
Brookie, Sarah A. 163
Brookin, Sarah 112
Brookins, Elizabeth 137
Brooks, Eliza J. 179
  Fanny 45
  Genetta 88
  Margaret 96
  Mary 126
  Mary A. 72
  Matilda 68
  Missenier 72
  Nancy 115, 140, 152
  Narcissa 196
  Orpha J. 34
  Rachel 32
  Rhodey 245
  Sally 15
Broose, Margaret 92
Brooshire, Abigail 91
Brotten, Nancy 170
Broughton, Eliza 197
Brower, Sally A. 121
Brown, Adah W. 74

Brown, Ally 130
  Amanda Z. T. 136
  Ann 11, 99, 117, 234
  Anne 213
  Arthusia 236
  Betsy 30, 232
  Catharine 82, 142
  Catherine 2
  Clarinda 74
  Easter 119
  Eleanor 54
  Eleanor C. 95
  Eliza 203, 207
  Eliza E. 205
  Elizabeth 14, 50, 81, 133,
    149, 170, 174, 185, 195,
    202, 239
  Elizabeth A. J. 122
  Elizabeth Allen 175
  Elizabeth L. 197
  Emiline 61
  Eunice 171
  Euphema 188
  Frances 237
  Frances A. 169
  Frances E. 166
  Frances H. 28
  Hannah 175, 181
  Hannah A. 231
  Helen T. 93
  Hiley 20
  Isabella 103
  Jane 17, 123, 142
  Julia 242
  Kiseal 66
  Lucretia 61
  Lucy S. 25
  Mahala 193
  Malinda 17, 138, 206
  Malinda T. 133
  Malissa 230
  Mandana 30
  Margaret 15, 212
  Martha 67, 103, 186
  Martha H. 52
  Mary 39, 46, 68, 71, 73,
    91. 98, 203, 232
  Mary C. 150
  Mary S. 245
  Maryann 167
  Matilda 123
  Melinda 215
  Minerva 60, 116
  Miranda E. 105
  Nancy 50, 53, 78, 81, 93,
    104, 188, 235, 246, 251
  Nancy J. 56
  Patsey 205
  Patsy 216, 237
  Paulina A. 87
  Permelia 66
  Polly   20, 26, 36, 96,
    130, 226
  Priscilla 177
  Rachael 231
  Rebecca 142, 181
  Rebecka 114
  Rosanah 187
  Sally 102
  Sally R. 27
  Sarah 26, 47, 127, 185
  Senith 21
  Serena 73
  Susan 128
  Susanna 182
  Susannah 134
  Sylvina 154
  Syntha A. 218
  Tempy 170

261

Brown, Mrs. Terrance 170
  Verbina A. 117
  Viletty 194
Browning, Matilda 161
  Nancy 62
  Susan 11
Broyles, Ada 101
Bruce, Annthorett 134
  Marilda A. 130
  Rebecca 34
Bruer, Eloyser 119
Bruffee, Eliza 56
  Amily 243
  Mary 122
Bruffey, Margaret E. 5
Bruffic, Martha M. 215
Bruffie, Nancy 109
Brugiere, Judith 131
Bruin, Margaret 148
Bruk, Demerius 126
Brumley, Fanny 171
Brumly, Julyann 38
Brumman, Polly 133
Brummet, Polly 242
Brundage, America 244
Brunk, Tabitha 105
Brunt, Betsy 43
  Cinthy 176
  Peggy 100
Brunts, Nancy 244
  Rebecca 65
  Sally 105
Brurassas, Celeste 190
Brushear, Mary J. 46
Bruster, Mililda 88
Bruziere, Aneglique 38
Bryan, Widow 141
  Ann 106
  Betsy 24
  Cynthia 127
  Elizabeth 58, 109, 215
  Mary E. 7
  Melcena C. 139
  Nancy 180
  Parthena 31
  Polly 102
  Sarah 115, 192, 193, 236
  Susanna 159
  Susannah 201
Bryant, Catharine 181
  Eliza H. 75
  Eliza J. 159
  Elizabeth 75, 144
  Margaret 136
  Mary 66
  Mary A. S. 222
  Mary J. 177
  Nancy 146, 192
  Patience 85
  Polly 206
  Sarah R. 184
  Susan 21
  Susanna 50
Buatte, Eulalie 129
Buchanan, Elizabeth 113
  Nancy 143
  Sousan 226
Buchannon, Mary 136
  Nancy J. 1
Buchly, Mildred 201
Buckhanan, Margaret 106
Buckner, Elizabeth 216
  Frances 58
  Harriet 244
  Louisa A. M. 203
  Lucy 94
  Mary 62
  Mary H. 85
  Mary M. 23

Buckner, Mildred 36
  Nancy 8
  Sarah J. 227
  Sary D. 57
  Susan E. 119
Buckridge, Jane 75
Buckston, Claricy 10
Buddamen, Katherne 234
Buff, Elizabeth 153
  Rosannah 204
Buford, Adaline 169
  Amilia 186
  Frances 182
  Harriet 94
  Janetta 85
  Mary A. 225
Bugg, Ann W. J. 243
Buis, Artimissa 121
  Missouri Line 60
Bulinger, Barborah 7
  Catey 156
Bull, Kisiah 70
  Rebecca T. 161
Bullard, Elizabeth 18
Bullinger, Barbery 119
  Elizabeth 75
  Fanny 7
  Luffy 156
  Polly 197
Bullitt, Nancy 30
Bullock, Mary E. 162
  Sarah J. 24
Bumpiass, Sarah 25
Bun, Cynthia 155
Bunch, Action 130
  Cordelia 143
  Elvira C. 131
  Lucinda 53
  Orlina 206
  Patsey 177
  Sarah 113
Bundridge, Patsy 97
Bundrum, Dulanie 88
Bunds, Mary K. 148
Bunger, Agnes 234
Bunnell, Keziah 32
Burbanks, Laurinda 239
Burbridge, Anna 5
  Polly 6
Burch, Ann 75, 132
  Eliza 202
  Frances 86
  Jane 243
  Mary 143
  Nancy 86, 91
Burcham, Sarah 80
Burchfield, Jane 71
Burck, Julian A. 40
  Mary 72
Burckhart, Brunet A. 106
Burden, Frances 98
  Sarah 155
Burdet, Elisabeth 188
  Margaret 165
Burdett, Malindy 178
Burdette, Melvina 169
Burditt, Esther A. 199
Burdoin, Eliza A. 25
  Rachel C. 74
Burdyne, Jane 139
  Nancy 118
  Polly 174
Burford, Eleanor 96
  Frances 146
  Nancy J. 32
  Rebecca C. 66
Burgain, Mary 168
Burgan, Nancy 198
Burgen, Elizabeth 158

Burgen, Margaret 85
Burgur, Lavanna 210
  Mary 19
  Sarah 39
Burgess, Eliza 176
  Elizabeth 202
  Nancy 78
Burgher, Salina 209
Burk, Eliza 74
  Nancy 184
  Sally 204
Burke, Lucinda J. 33
Burkel, Nancy 220
Burket, Leeny 245
Burkhart, Elizabeth 179
  Mary J. 120
  Sally 240
Burkhead, Elizabeth A. 224
Burkheart, Elizabeth 12
Burkleo, Edna 32
  Elenor 116
  Mary A. 17
Burklow, Sulia 142
Burleson, Nancy 192
  Rachel 235
Burlison, Ann 166
  Sarah 50
Burman, Sophia 159
Burnam, Betsey 160
  Eliza J. 176
  Esther 119
Burnem, Marnen 87
Burnen, Elizabeth R. 57
Burnes, Nancy 81
Burnet, Constantine 156
  Susannah 32
Burnett, Ann 194
  Elizabeth 54
  Elizabeth A. 154
  Jane 143
  Judith 232
  Lilly G. 18
  Lucinda 55
  Mariah 33
  Mary 137
  Susannah 130
Burnham, Nancy 222
Burns, Elizabeth 33, 76, 133
  Elizabeth J. 198
  Enegline 33
  Lindy 45
  Lydia 183
  Marilla 141
  Mary 69, 202, 232
  Narcissa 213
  Pamelia 204
  Potisha A. 91
  Prisila 18
  Sally 10, 58
  Susan 74
  Susannah 152
Burnsides, Elizabeth 250
Burnsidy, Elisabeth 11
Burnum, Susanna 57
Burrass, Rachel 215
Burress, Margaret S. 71
  Rachel 53
Burris, Ann 84
  Elizabeth 114, 194
  Louisa 249
  Polly 168, 212
  Rebecca 160
  Sarah 136
Burriss, Lewhetty 34
  Lusinday 122
  Nancy 115
  Prudence 78
Burroughs, Martha A. 68
Burrows, Martha 46

263

265

Cole, Nancy D. 126
  Nancy G. 117
  Patty 219
  Polly 140, 242
  Rachel A. 101
  Rebecca 72, 136, 207
  Rosannah 13
  Suckey 50
  Susan M. F. 193
Coleman, Ann D. 210
  Catherine 110
  Jane 56
  Maria A. 64
  Sarah 46
Coley, Mariah 44
Colfer, Polly 174
Colier, Clarinda 138
Collans, Susannah 201
Collard, Isaphana 245
  Mary 193
  Nancy 126
Collector, Ebby 166
Collet, Elizabeth 15
  Mary 43
  Nancy 79
  Rabeka 241
  Rebecky 44
  Susannah 68
Collett, Minerva 220
  Nancy 150
  Sarah 206
Collier, Amalia 139
  Cordelia 73
  Elizabeth 63
  Frances R. 139
  Jane 172
  Lucinda 105
  Mahala 186
  Mary P. 251
  Matilda 245
  Susan O. 179
Collins, Adelina 169
  Ann 40
  Anny 43
  Catherine Gee 211
  Eliza 69
  Elizabeth 138, 161, 199
  Frances 212
  Jane 10, 191
  Jane W. 191
  Louisa 29
  Mahaly E. 39
  Malinda 184
  Mary 166, 230, 240
  Mary A. 25, 251
  Nancy 193, 234, 248
  Permelia 28
  Polly 94
  Sally A. 149
  Sarah 93, 137
  Susan 166, 173
  Susannah 137, 228
Colliver, Margaret 135
  Nancy 11
  Sally 17
Collman, Euprosine 24
  Hermoine 172
  Marie L. 222
Collmann, Celeste 16
  Judith 68
Colman, Sarah S. 109
Colovan, Fanney 78
Colvin, Betsy 173
  Catherine 51, 171
  Elizabeth 196
  Frances L. 38
  Jane 157
  Margaret 126

Colvin, Mary 208
  Nancy 192
  Rebecca 185
  Sarah 31, 75
Colwell, Betsy 227
Combs, Elizabeth 204
  Sophony 231
Comegys, Edney 6
Comley, Mary 227
Compton, Catherine 135
  Elizabeth 183
  Faraha 238
  Harriett 250
  Martha 37
  Matilda R. A. 16
  Polly 174
  Sinai 249
  Sindy 210
Comstock, Lavina 187
  Polly 207
Condry, Metelda 236
Conger, (?) 165
  Caroline 184
  Narcissus 127
Congo, Lucinda 140
Conkle, Catharine 247
Conley, Lydia 127
  Susan 76
Conn, Polly 104
Connelly, Sara A. 229
Conner, Abbigail 93
  America 57
  Ann 80
  Betsey 79
  Catherine F. 191
  Elizabeth 205
  Emily 127
  Jane 233
  Lydia 135
  Mary 80, 143
  Nancy 12
  Phebe 36
  Rebecca 227
  Sarah 88
Connor, Jane 192
Connoyer, Celeste 146
Conrad, Elizabeth 157
  Malinda 69
  Priscilla 134
Conrades, Analie 225
Constible, Elizabeth 149
Conway, Elizabeth 15, 233
  Margaret 86
  Margery 30
  Nancy 49
  Polly 104
Conyers, Sarah 6
Cook, Ann 177
  Eliza J. 49
  Elizabeth 34
  Frances E. 120
  Jane 73
  Mary 148, 158
  Permelia 187
  Sairna 89
  Sally 76
  Sarah 3
  Susan 200
Cooksey, Mariah 250
Cooley, Cassandra 97
  Eleanor 90
  Elizabeth 173
  Evalina G. 170
  Hannah 14, 20, 245
  Jane 230
  Jemima 239
  Malinda 229
  Mary 75

Cooley, Sarah 97
  Susan 196
  Tempey 57
Cooly, Ann 70
  Betsy 152
  Elizabeth 239
  Polly 205
Coons, Chalotte 93
  Louisiana 157
Coonts, Eliza 142
Coontz, Druzilla 168
Cooper, Abigail A. 108
  Amelia 30
  Ann 53
  Catherine 217
  Charlotte 189
  Eliza 5, 44
  Elizabeth 48, 77, 118
  Elvira 221
  Ester 56
  Eveline 163
  Fanny 42
  Frankey 37
  Hetta 113
  Lavenia 214
  Lucy 158
  Nancy 35, 85, 197
  Patsy 243
  Polly 20, 28, 36, 126
  Rodd 214
  Sarah A. 62, 127
  Susannah 231
Coots, Elizabeth 231
  Sally 86
  Tabithy 86
Cope, Elizabeth 156
  Susanna 142
Copel, Ann C. 221
Copeland, Ann 213
  Matilda 89
  Rebecca 202
Copher, Dosha 213
  E. 148
  Hetty B. 17
Copitt, Mary E. 101
Coplan, Nancy 193
Copland, Poly 217
Coplin, Caroline 36
Copling, Elizabeth 120
Coppedge, Cynthia 99
  Lucy L. 179
  Permela 6
  Zurbia 29
Coppege, Vicy 236
Coram, Nancy 72
Cordell, Ann C. 101
Cordil, Elizabeth 182
  Nancy 98
Cordry, Mary A. 236
Corhan, Nancy 252
Corlin, Parmelia 195
  Sarah 39
Corn, Juliet 31
  Polly 46
  Susannah 83
Cornelison, Sarah 243
Cornelius, Alzady 74
  Fanny 2
  Frances 226
  Mary 29
Cornett, Elizabeth 210
  Mary 5
Cornutt, Martha 40
Corum, Nancy 22, 242
  Susan W. 72
Cory, Barbary 202
Cosby, Sarah 205
Coshen, Phoebe A. 153

Cosner, Charlotte 215
  Maryan 101
Cosney, Mary 248
Costley, Mahala 112
  Sina 125
Costly, Lottie 125
  Margaret 27
Cote, Mary 221
  Rosalie 22
Cothman, Maurgerite 41
Cotner, Anna 251
  Fanny 100
  Katharine 45
  Mary 159
  Patsey 199
  Polly 72
Cotter, Ellen G. 61
Cottle, Esenau 7
  Harriet 51
  Sophrina 170
Cotton, Lucinda 151
  Mary 48
Couch, Elizabeth 235
  Lizzy 27
  Sally 181
Couiard, Dorcas 11
Coulter, Ann 228
  Evelina 20
  Julia D. 13
Counse, Rebecca 141
Counts, Rachel 95
Couples, Mary 220
Courcaute, Felicite 51
Courtner, Sally 182
Courtney, Lucind 204
  Nancy 77
Courtois, Marie 190
Coutis, Catharine 156
Covent, Betsy 27
Covert, Sarah 150
Covey, Elizabeth 40
  Marcha 115
  Sarah 245
Covington, Nancy 145
  Nancy C. 99
Cowan, Amanda 14
  Cynthia 213
  Elizabeth 35, 102, 248
Coward, Emaly 105
Cowen, Emily 175
  Stacy 232
Cowgill, Martha 70
Cowherd, Lucy C. 239
  Sarah A. 231
Cowick, Elenor 244
Cowie, Deborah 193
  Eliza 138
  Nancy 65
Cowin, Elisa 143
  Polly 151
Cowis, Patsy 230
Cowsert, Jane 80
Cox, Amy 57, 205
  Catharine L. 4
  Caty 172
  Cora 180
  Docia A. 30
  Eliza E. 70
  Elizabeth 91, 96
  Elizabeth A. 168
  Ellen 214
  Emily 238
  Fanny 98
  Franky 230
  Hannah 202
  Lidia 108
  Lucilla S. 209
  Lydia 34, 244

Cox, Mary 4, 11, 63, 135,
    165, 192
  Matilda 153, 181
  Neoma 38
  Patsa 77
  Rachel 128
  Rebecca 35
  Ruth 46
  Ruthie 42
  Ruthy 18
  Sarah 4, 27
Coy, Elizabeth 130
  Frances 90
Coyl, Iyden 31
  Patsy 188
Coyle, Dianah 15
  Elizabeth 191
Crabtree, Arenah 18
  Elizabeth 240
  Mary 179
  Nancy 174
  Parthena 89
  Rebecca 78
Cracraft, Nancy 187
Craddock, Emelia 101
  Juliet 91
  Margaret A. 121
  Mariah 211
Crader, Fanney 9
Crafford, Emily B. 211
  Nancy 204
Craft, Jetdida 237
  Martha 34
  Rebecca M. 142
Crafts, Elizabeth 59
Crag, America 87
Crage, Elizabeth 101
Craghead, Elizabeth 154
  June E. 36
  Nancy P. 125
  Sarah 53
Craig, A. 99
  Ann 148
  Catharine 133
  Catherine 208
  Charlotte 35
  Elizabeth 88
  Emily J. 77
  Jane 32, 229
  Lucinda 22
  Margaret 60
  Mary 216, 250
  Mary A. 146
  Sarah 223
  Susanna 155
Craighead, Mary 77
Crain, Frances W. 24
  Jane 23
  Martha 8
  Mary 148
Cramer, Agnes 51
  Caroline 57
  Harriet A. 86
  Lucinda 176
  Rebecca 105
Crane, Isabella 140
  Patsy 109
Crater, Catherine 224
  Melinda 170
Crates, Mary E. 46
Cravens, Martha A. 169
  Mary 200
  Nancy 18, 234
Crawford, Beveline R. 63
  Christine 63
  Cinthy J. 197
  Elender 111
  Eliza 144

Crawford, Jane 129
  Jemima 70
  Margaret 166
  Polly 61
  Sally 15
  Sarah 212
  Susanah 115
Crawley, Darcus 61
  Jane E. 60
  Patty 30
  Polly 164
Creasman, Rachail 127
Creason, Hannah 220
  Judy 46
  Martha 151
  Mary 179
  Milly 168
  Rachel 162
Creasy, Elizabeth 74
  Louisa A. 193
Creed, Louisa A. 185
Creek, Eliza 200
  Margaret 57
  Marthy 50
  Mary A. 20
Creel, Sarah A. 231
Creeptree, Catherine 2
  Elizabeth 247
Cresbongy, Polly 215
Crews, Jane 12
  Malvina 165
  Margaret 136
  Nancy 247
  Pauline 132
Crgel, Margaretta 241
Criddle, Letitia 210
Crider, Amelia 250
  Rachel 202
Crigler, Cynthia 35
Crimm, Lucinda 9
Crismon, Polly 116
Crisp, Elizabeth 117
  Hannah 47
Criswell, Leanner 114
Crites, Christina 244
  Elizabeth 45, 182
  Eve 139
  Hannah 62
Critesman, Ann 37
Critz, Charlotte 55
  Hannah 182
  Marget 251
Crizman, Juda 38
Crobarger, Harriet 152
Crocket, Elizabeth 164
  Julia A. 167
  Margaret 162
  Mary 28
Crockett, Ann 180
  Hannah 8
  Jain 250
  Jane 162
  Lovey 179
  Nancy 76
  Rebecca 99
  Sarah 71
Croff, Lavina 107
Crofford, Elizabeth 28
Croft, Hannah 211
Croley, Aba 165
Croly, Mary 109
Cromwell, Penelope 182
Cronester, Rebecca 214
Crooks, Adelina 119
  Amanda 91
  Malinda 239
  Sally C. J. 239
  Unicy I. 198

Crop, Elizabeth 44
  Esther 44
Cropper, Cynthia 203
  Mary 213
Cross, Anjilinah 7
  Annette 183
  Barbary 123
  Barthena 123
  Catherine A. 75
  Elizabeth 246
  Elizabeth A. 173
  Hannah M. 127
  Margaret 77
  Maria J. 122
  Mary A. 209
  Orpah P. 122
Crosset, Jane 238
Crossit, Eleanor C. 56
Crossman, Sarah A. 165
Crosthwaite, Franky 48
  Mary A. 101
Crouch, Eleanor 81
  Frances 177
  Polly 38
Crow, Ann 175
  Elizabeth 130, 142
  Eveline 55
  Harriett 137
  Lucinda 193
  Margarett 217
  Mary 252
  Nancy 203
  Rebecca 38
  Sarah 231, 252
  Susy 221
Crowden, Tabitha H. 191
Crowder, Dicey 246
  Judith 167
  Louisa 151
  Martha A. 129
  Mary E. 135
Crowley, Jane 109
  Louisa 82
  Matilda 205
  Mulah 4
  Nancy 211
  Polly 214
Crown, Eliza 67
Crowson, Rosa M. 241
Croxel, Mary 26
Crucher, Frances 227
Crul, Elizabeth 159
  Mary 153
Crum, Elizabeth 4
  Matilda 120
  Ruth 211
Crumet, Mary 199
Crump, Amanda 224
  Angeline 167
  Dinney 182
  Elender 57
  Elizabeth 88
  Frances 26
  Martha F. 204
  Mary 143, 207
  Parthenia 98
  Patsy 237
  R. 154
  Ruthey 113
  Sally 196
Cruse, Arminty 39
  Demonas 182
  Mary 8
  Vianna 219
Cukerdall, Almeda 163
Culberson, Ann E. 142
  Elizabeth 130
Culbertson, Eliza A. 70
  Harriet 138

Culbertson, Lear 199
  Mary 229
  Nancy 84
  Orra 208
  Pena 147
  Rebecca E. 240
  Uley 83
Cull, Eliza A. 240
  Elizabeth 249
Culp, Elizabeth 31
  Jane 37
  Mary 237
  Nancy 249
  Rachel 249
Culver, Mary A. 221
Cummings, Lucinda 238
  Polly 248
Cummins, Elizabeth 19
  Francis E. 203
  Laviny 204
  Lucinda 75
  Mary 55
Cumton, Elizabeth 129
Cundiff, Elizabeth 105
  Lucretia 164
Cunningham, Berebe 3
  Catherine 188
  Elizabeth A. 46
  Elizabeth C. 197
  Emily 147
  Francis 112
  Henrietta 252
  Margaret 64
  Martha 39
  Mary 110
  Mosila 41
  Nancy 111, 115, 244
  Ruth 167
  Sarah 110, 112, 141
  Theodotia H. 191
Curd, Mary C. 63
Curhat, Mary 91
Curl, Nancy 223
Curnutt, Lydia 18
Currin, Mary A. 3
Curry, Eliza J. 248
  Nancy 164
  Rosanna M. 230
  Sarah B. 63
Curtis, Bestey 202
  Ceily 160
  Esther 72
  Nancy 6
Cushing, Elizabeth 139
Cutbirth, Charlotte 107
  Elizabeth 107
Cutler, Sally 5
Cutter, Mary 177
Cylard, Margaret 47
Dagen, Marie A. 61
Dagley, Elizabeth 82
Dail, Nelly 248
Daile, Elizabeth 223
Dailey, Elizabeth 181
  Jane 118
  Sarah 49
Daily, Jane 20
  Melinda 62
  Polly 181
Dale, Barbary 80
  Dicy 197
  Eliza 91
  Emerine 115
  Emily H. 142
  Jane 3
  Levina 242
  Margaret 167
  Mary 209
  Mary A. 48

Dale, Melissa 108
  Minerva J. 86
  Nancy 152, 197
  Permelia 95
  Rachel 114
  Sarey 123
Daleney, Martha J. 238
Dall, Folly 107
Dalton, Mary 226
Daly, Alice W. 219
  Bridget 15
  Elizabeth 149
  Jane 61
  Louisa 199
  Lucy 22
Dameron, Frances L. 34
  Mary 68
  Mary T. 246
  Phebe J. 195
Damrell, Eliza A. 232
Dandy, Sally 106
Danford, Nancy 223
Daniel, Amanda 104
  Eliza 207
  Elizabeth 118, 126
  Julie 62
  Margaret 193, 194
  Nancy 37
  Vecinda 179
Danilson, Sally A. 17
Daniwood, Eliza 187
Danley, Martha 150
Danngilder, Mary 174
Danzal, Helene 66
Dapron, Mary A. 61
Darby, Elizabeth 37
  Susan 170
Darr, Perlina Y. 207
  Sarah 204
  Sarah A. 235
Darst, Mary 29
  Rosetta 96
  Zerilda 143
Darvies, Lucy A. 124
Daugherty, Anna 44
  Elizabeth 207
  Emily 83
  Mary N. 130
Daughtey, Nancy 77
Dauherty, Lucretia 36
Daulton, Louisa 203
  Salina 246
Daurst, Nancy 74
Davenport, Mary 88
  Polly 35
David, Elizabeth 98
  Hannah 57
  Sally 25
Davidson, Edith 163
  Elizabeth 23, 102
  Elizabeth M. 183
  Jane F. 100
  Lavina 114
  Lucinda 73
  Mahala 17
  Margaret 167
  Martha 97, 140
  Mary A. 121
  Paulina 15
  Polly 212
  Rachel 52
  Rebecca 30
  Sarah 163, 171
  Tilitha C. 62
Davies, Martha 13
Davis, Abigail 26
  Adeline 196
  Agnes 191
  Amanda 111, 168

269

270

Dunkin, Sally 188
  Spicy L. G. 117
  Veny 240
Dunklin, Mary M. 37
Dunlap, Betsy 189
  Elizabeth 53
  Elizabeth J. 89
  Elvira 196
  Mary 125
  Nancy 149
Dunn, Amanda 203
  Ann 35
  Araminda 156
  Catharine 220, 246
  Cynthian 51
  Margaret I. 174
  Maria 160
  Mary 39, 123
  Nancy 71
  Pheby 126
  Ruth 101
  Sarah 107
  Theresa 61
Dunnaway, Sarah 34
Dunnegan, Kisiah 3
Dunnica, M. 117
Dunnicah, Manima 126
Dunnicak, Sally M. 99
Duque, Mary 226
Duquet, Eloise 85
Durben, Perlina 71
Durbin, Ann D. 190
  Louise 247
  Malinda 192
  Sarah A. 198
Durham, Elizabeth 77, 165
  Jane 108
Durnang, Hillnry 3
Durning, Mary 82
Durrett, Eliza R. 29
  Marietta 83
Duson, Elizabeth 3
Dutch, Caroline M. 147
  Eliza J. 60
Dutton, Rhoda 137
Duvall, Leuisa 213
  Mahala 114
  Mary 132, 153
  Sarah 217
  Theressia 132
Dycke, Martha 219
Dye, Polly 88
Dyer, Elizabeth 47, 152
  Martha W. 236
Dykes, Catharine 181
Dyzard, Mary 102
Eades, Clarinda 155
  Nancy 106, 233
Eads, Mary 4
  Melve 3
  Polly A. 221
  Sally 163
Eagen, Lydia 241
Eaken, Polly 180
Eaker, Margaret 209
  Nancy 154
  Sally 157
  Susan 55
Eakins, Pethany 134
Ealam, Elizabeth 8
Eament, Melvina 93
Earheart, Elizabeth E. 38
Earickson, Eliza A. 19
  Nancy 183
Earls, Lucretia 10
Early, Elizabeth 105
  Mary E. 14, 219
  Polly 128

Early, Sarah 75
Earnest, Rachel 232
Earney, Rebecca 96
Easley, Sarah 137
East, Elizabeth 109
Eastbridge, Matilda 22
Easten, Jane 207
  Nancy 123
Easter, Elizabeth 50
  Nancy 144
Eastes, Ann 60
  Deliah 204
Eastin, Emily 82
  Susan 195
  Tillithi 114
Easton, Juliana 144
  Patsy 208
  Rhoda 67
  Rusella 6
Eastwood, Amanda 5
  Elizabeth 237
Eaton, Elizabeth 152
  Emily 247
  Jane 69
  Polly 54
Eavens, Rachel 91
Eavins, Gane 61
Ebenns, Elizabeth 227
Eckert, Marian 167
  Martha J. 169
Eddington, Lucretia 80
Eddleman, Susannah 244
Eddman, Mary 82
Edds, Elizabeth 71
Eddz, Mary 131
Edelin, Catherine O. 60
Edelman, Ann 75
Edes, Mary 207
  Rachel 214
Edgar, Ann 30
  Elizabeth 110
  Sidney 145
Edge, Mary 7
Edgman, Sinu 209
Edinger, Hannah 142
  Katherine 135
  Polly 121
Edminton, Loucinda 106
Edmonds, Susan 223
Edmondson, Leah 53
Edmonson, Elvira 242
Edmunds, Lucy L. 231
  Mary 236
Edmundson, Louisa 89
  Patsy 182
Edrington, Mary J. 95
Edward, Elizabeth 191
Edwards, (?) 208
  Adiline 135
  Amanda 77
  America 77
  Anna 73
  Cynthia 4
  Elender 86
  Elizabeth 133, 151, 212
  Elizabeth C. 139
  Emily C. 181
  Fanny 86
  Jane 142, 143
  Lotty 77
  Manerva 191
  Martha 8, 142
  Martha O. 139
  Mary 209
  Melinda N. 6
  Nancy 152
  Neely 202
  Sally 142

Edwards, Sarah 223
  Sarah A. 140
  Susanna 180
Egans, Nancy T. 213
Eggiman, Anna 17
Egleberger, Eliza T. 216
Egman, Everanna 193
Eichelberger, Betsy 139
Eidson, Ann 230
  Betsy 84
  Lucy A. 37
  Mary J. 134
Elam, Harriet 70
Elder, Eliza J. 136
Eldridge, Prudence 233
Elgert, Johanne Ch. 28
Elgin, Lucinda 135
  Rebecca 128
  Sarah 212
Eliot, Matilda 214
Elis, Ann M. 170
Elison, Ealenor 136
Elkins, Eliza A. 34
  Millia 100
  Polly 199
Ella, Mary 60
Eller, Martitia 119
  Rebecca 2
Ellice, Elizabeth 201
  Polley 155
Ellington, Mary 45
  Milly 99
  Nancy 99
  Patsy 12
Elliott, (?) 227
  Ann E. 250
  Cinthy 57
  Eliza 94
  Elizabeth 87, 238, 245
  Ellenor 132
  Hycinthia 182
  Jane 159
  John 227
  Julia A. 151
  Marie L. 62
  Martha A. 175
  Mary 7, 88
  Mary A. 108
  Mary E. 181
  Mary S. 5
  Polly 112
  Rebecca 183
  Rhody 220
  Rose A. 234
  Sarah A. 115
  Susan 60, 229
Ellis, (?) 224
  Belza 231
  Caroline 145
  Clementine S. 160
  Elizabeth 98, 138
  Emily 117, 197
  Hatty 129
  Isabella 79
  LaPlata T. B. 52
  Lucy 251
  Maria R. 236
  Marry 18
  Mary 87
  Mary W. W. 226
  Nancy 24, 241
  Rhoda L. 180
  Sally 227
  Sarah 228
Ellison, Eliza J. 161
  Nancy 152
  Polly 70, 235
  Sarah A. 214

Fort, Lucinda 191　　　　　　　　Freeman, Lurany 163　　　　　　Fulbrite, Catharine 246
　Martha 34　　　　　　　　　　　Martha E. 174　　　　　　　　Fulkerson, Basheba 34
Fortenberry, Sinthy 216　　　　　Mary 15, 74　　　　　　　　　　Catherine 194
Fortune, Lucy P. 177　　　　　　　Nancy 16, 22　　　　　　　　　Elizabeth 176
Foster, Amanda 211　　　　　　　　Pernina 230　　　　　　　　　　Elizabeth G. 107
　Caroline 17　　　　　　　　　　　Rachel 171　　　　　　　　　　Jane 42
　Delancy 80　　　　　　　　　　French, Celia A. 138　　　　　　Margaret 234
　Elizabeth 106, 173　　　　　　　Marian 28　　　　　　　　　　　Mary 135
　Emily 157　　　　　　　　　　Fretwell, Evaline 203　　　　　　Sarah 104
　Jane 100, 243　　　　　　　　　Hannah R. 93　　　　　　　　Fulks, Elizabeth 102
　Julia 98　　　　　　　　　　　　Lousindia 126　　　　　　　　Fullbright, Rodah 237
　Letita 75　　　　　　　　　　　Nancy C. 213　　　　　　　　Fuller, Elizabeth 186
　Martha 250　　　　　　　　　Freund, Katherine 15　　　　　　Selinda 184
　Mary 78, 164　　　　　　　　Frey, Frances 150　　　　　　　Fullerton, Mary 77
　Nancy 88　　　　　　　　　　　Mary 96　　　　　　　　　　Fullington, Patsy 198
　Narcissa 209　　　　　　　　Freymuth, Elizabeth 56　　　　Fulton, Charlotte M. 194
　Polly 9, 33, 226　　　　　　Frickey, Anna 6　　　　　　　　Funk, Delila 6
　Rebeca 113　　　　　　　　　Friend, Catharine 151　　　　　Mary 144
　Sally 190, 243　　　　　　　　Sarah 81　　　　　　　　　　Fuqua, Frances 173
　Susan 87　　　　　　　　　　Frier, Carline C. 135　　　　　Martha 39
Fountain, Elizabeth 57　　　　　Gabrela 167　　　　　　　　　Polly 4, 168
　Ivy 197　　　　　　　　　　　　Pauline 190　　　　　　　　　Sally 198
　Lucy 111　　　　　　　　　　　Rebecca 86　　　　　　　　Furgason, Malinda 185
　Polly 130　　　　　　　　　　Frieze, Matilda 37　　　　　Furgeson, Elizabeth 35
　Sarah 54　　　　　　　　　　Fristee, Eliza 72　　　　　　Furguson, Louisa 180
Fowler, Amelia 39　　　　　　　Fristoe, Frances 192　　　　　Lucy 140
　Catherine 97　　　　　　　　　Margaret C. 45　　　　　　　Martha A. 75
　Dorcus 43　　　　　　　　　　Mariah 124　　　　　　　　Furry, Nancy 247
　Elizabeth 138　　　　　　　　Mary A. 85　　　　　　　　Fute, Helen 190
　Jacintha 96　　　　　　　　　Mary J. 119　　　　　　　Fyffe, Elizabeth 203
　Jemima 239　　　　　　　　　Nancy 141　　　　　　　　Gabainal, Nelly 77
　Levicey 89　　　　　　　　Fristow, Mary A. 219　　　　　Gabel, Hilda 11
　Louisa 98　　　　　　　　　Sarah 207　　　　　　　　Gabriel, Nancy 237
　Lucinda 71　　　　　　　　Fritstoe, Laura 99　　　　　　Sarah 157
　Matilda 175　　　　　　　Fritzlen, Mary A. E. 82　　　Gaddy, Polly B. 28
　Minerva 136　　　　　　　Frizel, Elizabeth B. 237　　Gain, Ellen 129
　Oma 246　　　　　　　　　Frizell, Clara 122　　　　　Gainer, Fhebe 50
　Syntha 249　　　　　　　Frizell, Jemimah 40　　　　Gaines, Elizabeth 23, 190
Fox, Elizabeth 59, 215　　　Sarah 58　　　　　　　　　Felicia 191
　Malinda 69　　　　　　　Frizzell, Mary A. 144　　　　Margaret A. 186
　Malisa 222　　　　　　Frost, Ann 150　　　　　　　Mary J. 63
　Mary 204　　　　　　　　Hannah 168, 199　　　　　　Nancy 25
　Susan 227　　　　　　　Jane 154　　　　　　　　Nancy A. 93
　Susanna 206　　　　　　Unity 62　　　　　　　　Polly 112
Foxworthy, Clarissa A. 245　Frudelle, Eulalie 187　　Gains, Mary A. 89
　Isabella J. 246　　　　Fruend, Eliza K. 16　　　Gaithes, Matilda 180
Fraizer, Cleopatra 220　　Fruit, Susan J. 55　　　　Galbreath, Elizabeth 82
Fraker, Mary 92　　　　　Fruman, Ellen 48　　　　　Isabella 169
Frakes, Martha 44　　　　Fry, America 115　　　　　Margaret 17, 171
Frances, Rebecca 113　　　Catherine 29　　　　　　Mary 20
Francis, Amanda 171　　　Eliza 157　　　　　　　Parthena 21
　Elizabeth A. 185　　　Elvira 84　　　　　　　Peggy 98
　Jennie 59　　　　　　　Emeline E. 196　　　　　Sally A. 16
　Margarette 116　　　　Emily 81　　　　　　　Susan 187
　Martha 49　　　　　　Mary 12　　　　　　　Gale, Juliet 26
　Polly 12　　　　　　Mary A. 36　　　　　　Galebs, Olive 68
Francisco, Julia E. 157　Nancy 230　　　　　　Gall, Betsy 225
　Rachel C. 111　　　Pauline 214　　　　　Gallaher, Julia 117
Franklin, Polly 226　　Frye, Elizabeth 184　　Gallaway, Betsy 204
Fraser, Mary 63　　　　Margaret 170　　　　　Delilah 22
Frasier, Martha 208　　Fryer, Betsy 65　　　　Francis 22
Fray, Elizabeth L. 90　Fugate, Cathy 135　　　Leah 19
　Martha 201　　　　　Clarinda 8　　　　　Nancy 129
Frazer, Elizabeth 191　Esther 239　　　　　Sarah 19
　Lucretia 14　　　　Kitta 21　　　　　Susan 174
Frazier, Abigail 57　Lewisann 55　　　　Gallet, Jane 59
　Eliza A. 80　　　Maryann 170　　　　Gallingharst, Catharine 129
　Elizabeth 10, 115　Milly 224　　　　Gallitan, Ellen 154
　Mary A. 172　　　Nancy B. 125　　　Galliway, Margaret 193
　Nancy 172　　　Fuget, Emeline 176　　Mary 120
　Susan 210　　　Polly 3　　　　　Perlina 65
Frazuer, Polly 92　Theresa 68　　　　Gallop, Susan 93
Freeman, (?) 245　Fugit, Emelia 177　　Galloway, Polly 94
　Catharina B. 119　Fugitt, Perlina 226　Gamble, Louisa 145
　Elisabeth 109　　Fulbright, Elizabeth 237　Games, Margaret 196
　Elizabeth 45, 89, 121, 233　Margaret 107　Gan, Nancy 163
　Jane 8　　　　Polly 68　　　　Ganes, Catharine 167
　Jemima 24　　Rosa 68　　　　Gann, Matilda 233
　Lucinda 130　Sally 212　　　　Rosanna 83

Gilmore, Marth. J. 213
  Mary 57, 143, 202
  Mary J. 212
  Rebecca E. 98
  Roena 146
Gilstrap, Jane 218
Ginnings, Margaret J. 183
  Rachel 9
  Rhoda 211
  Sarah 35
Ginst, Mary 138
Gipson, Jane 180
  Mary 98
Gist, Cecelcernam 81
  Hannah 140
Given, Gorham 68
  Mary Thomas 230
Givens, Ann 118
  Charlotte 4
  Euphamia 68
  Hannah A. 186
  Hezeah 121
  Margaret 198
  Sarah Thompson 98
  Sinthy 14
  Surana 1
Gladden, Mary 140
Gladdin, Elizabeth 56
Gladney, Agnes 143
  Martha 77
Glasby, Ruth A. 142
Glascock, Dorothy 156
  Eliza 86
  Lucinda 175
  Nancy 174
Glass, Lucinda 199
  Margaret J. 38
Glasscock, Alletha 16
  Elizabeth 86
  Mary 93
Glaves, Elizabeth 238
Glaze, Sarah 149
Glazebrook, Sebtella 153
Gleaves, Eliza T. 159
  Mary F. 106
Glenn, Ellender 116
  Emaline 213
  Hester 56
  Malvina 170
  Mary J. 39
  Sally 66
Glove, Lavinia 129
Glover, Elizabeth 9
  Vashti 126
Gnash, Corden 160
Go, Ulie 169
Goatley, Elizabeth 242
Gobe, Jane 46
Goddard, Amanda 168
Godifrois, Mary 181
Godin, Jane 2
Godman, Ann E. 55
  Maria 123
  Tabitha A. 73
Godsey, Nancy 146
Goff, Eleanor 237
  Elizabeth 47, 84
  Jane 251
  Nancy 246
Goforth, Elizabeth 46
Goggin, Casandria 195
  Cintha 95
  Elizabeth 87
Goggins, Malinda 95
Goin, Jane 216
Goings, Elizabeth 70
Goins, Catharine 143
  Elizabeth 73

Golden, Matilda 65
Goldsberry, Lois 232
  Nancy 177
Golliher, Belranette 184
Gooch, Eliza J. 193
Goode, Cassandra 44
  Delilah 78
  Elizabeth 212
  Francis C. 168
  Mary 191
Gooden, Mahala 171
  Rebecca 71
Goodin, Mary 180
  Sarah 217
Gooding, Polly 9
Goodman, Elizabeth 249
  Jane 77
  Lucretia 26
  Polly 247
  Polly A. 82
Goodno, Harriet 222
  Vina 24
Goodrich, Sarah 152
  Sarah B. 214
Goodridge, Esther A. 67
Goodwin, Elizabeth 55
  Jane 176
  Mary 71
  Rodah 16
  Sarah 38
Gordan, Jane 8
  Polly 116
Gorden, Elizabeth 34
  Emily 54
  Nancy 111
Gordon, Elizabeth 241
  Levina 116
  Lucy J. 48
  Margaret 229
  Masinai 122
  Nancy H. 200
  Nancy J. 110
  Philena 71
  Polly 178
  Ruth 229
  Sally 88
  Sarah 155
Gordwin, Nancy 109
Gore, Mary M. 20
  Redulah 14
Gorham,, Jane 117
  Martha A. F. 107
  Nancy M. 139
Gorman, Margaret 218
Gosa, Malinda 106
Goslin, Angeline 226
  Charlotte 226
Gosney, Mary A. 10
Goss, Surilda 104
Gostings, Jane 189
Gotcher, Artemicia 101
Gotien, Angelique 62
Gott, Margart 128
Goudin, Francois 131
Gouge, Elizabeth 134
  Rebecca 41
  Sarah 41
  Susannah 146
Gough, Susan R. 196
Gould, Caroline M. 171
Gouldan, Sophia 40
Goveranau, Mary 164
Govero, Matilda 190
Govreau, Emma 49
Goza, Amanda 124
  Elizabeth 169
  Hiscey 188
Grabs, Helen M. 88

Grace, Elizabeth 198
Gradavene, Dorothy 13
Graffort, Margaret 214
Gragg, Elveary 106
  Mary 179
  Polly 29, 107
  Rachel 28, 96
  Rebecca 168
  Ruthy 105
  Salena M. 89
  Sally 148
Graham, Adeline 245
  Ann E. 120
  Ara 133
  Eliza 13
  Elizabeth 71
  Hesteran 33
  Jemima 72, 105
  Louisa A. 183
  Lucinda 180
  Margaret 160
  Mary E. 29, 75
  Nancy 185
  Polly 28
  Rachel E. 221
  Rhoda 140
  Rosanna 196
  Rutha 2
  Sally 54, 87
  Zerpha 130
Grahard, Margaret 232
Graidy, Frances 113
Graig, Fanny 40
Grainger, Martha 91
Granberry, Rebecca 75
Granbery, Rebecca A. 95
Grandby, Marguret 224
Granger, Katharine 1
  Raney 242
  Rhoda 235
Grant, Ann 14
  Catherine 172
  Catherine R. 215
  Eliza 171
  Elizabeth 141
  Miranda 91
  Nancy 13
  Polly 13, 82, 107
  Sally 77
  Sara 133
  Sarah 166, 167
Grass, Elizabeth 36
Graves, Agnes 15
  Ann 243
  Ann M. 196
  Eliza 243
  Elizabeth 203
  Elizabeth C. 110
  Frances 244
  Mary A. 131
  Milly 3
Gray, Betsy 212
  Cynthia 51
  Elizabeth 19, 95, 97, 155, 195
  Elizabeth V. 216
  Exceline 230
  Hany 18
  Lezertha 115
  Marietta 236
  Martha 51
  Mary 44
  Mary A. 139
  Minerva 83
  Nancy M. 235
  Peggy 97
  Rachel 95
  Sarah 70, 113

Gray, Teresa 180
Grayham, Nancy 35
  Polly 122, 163
  Sarah 133
Greath, Polly 108
Greathouse, Martha 139
  Nancy 162
Green, Ann 83
  Betsy 198
  Catherine 42
  Celia 213
  Cinthy 180
  Elizabeth 33, 64
  Emily 75, 184, 233
  Forlee 62
  Harriet 199
  Jane 15, 35
  Jemima 68
  Leannatha 248
  Louisianna 176
  Lucinda 120
  Maria 248
  Martha 90, 217
  Mary 68
  Mary W. 80
  Matilda 150
  Melissa 99
  Nancy 48
  Nelly 102
  Polly 96, 202, 211, 214,
    221
  Rebecca 203
  Ruth 147
  Sally 104
  Sarah 52, 58, 206, 250
  Sarah A. 32
  Sarah E. 60
  Silan 230
  Susannah 83
  Theresa C. 222
Greenawalt, Nancy 251
Greenee, Eliza 122
Greenhalgh, Eleanor 152
Greening, Bertha A. 11
  Elizabeth 61
  Nancy A. 228
Greenstreet, Anny 95
  Elcey 223
  Elender 26
  Jane 65
  Orba 217
  Orpha 131
  Sarah 219
Greenup, Elizabeth 200
Greenway, Rebecca 232
Greer, Christiana 135
  Emily 150
  Mary 185
  Mary S. 221
  Nancy 2
  Sarah 219
Greery, Catharine 201
Gregg, Elizabeth 236
  Margaret 251
  Mary 134
  Sally 243
Gregoire, Julia 183
  Mary 168
Gregory, Amanda 22
  Celia 187
  Elizabeth 228
  July 204
  Mary 114
  Nancy 41, 73
  Sarey 93
Gresham, Susan M. 86
Gress, Elizabeth 134
Greyum, Polly 155

Griden, Rebecca 195
Grider, Louisa 161
  Nancy 252
Gridley, Sarah A. 19
Griffan, Ann 63
Griffee, Nancy 67
Griffen, Maria 99
  Mary 188
  Nancy 240
Griffey, Mary A. 182
Griffin, Ann 91
  Catherine 209
  Rebecca 29
Griffith, Betsey 200
  Caroline 141, 148
  Clarissa 93
  Edith 52
  Evelina 64
  Harriet 180
  Jane 70, 163
  Mariah 114
  Martha 48
  Nancy 64
  Nancy S. 222
  Rachel 126
  Rebecca 245
  Sarah 148
  Sarah J. 146
  Winneford 81
Griffiths, Nancy 153
Griffy, Eleanor 235
Grifith, Frances 2
Griford, Magdalena 129
Griggs, Ann 162
  Catherine 241
Grigsby, Mary J. 41
Grimes, Gaberillen 141
  Hester 94
  Mary 164
Grimsley, Sophia 22
Grindstaff, Delilah 249
  Eliza 56
  Sarah 54
Grisham, Sarah 209
Groff, Elizabeth 86
Grogan, Nancy 8
Gromer, Mary 90
Groom, Elizabeth 162
  Sally 213
  Sarah 92, 147
  Saray 149
  Scinthia 95
Groomer, Eliza 34
Groomes, Polly 41
Grooms, Amely 141
  Elizabeth 65
  Lorinda 6
  Maria 9
  Mary 165, 171
  Nancy 104, 178
  Polly 46
  Sally 240
  Sarah 22, 171
Grose, Nancy 252
Groshong, Elizabeth 112
Gross, Elizabeth 127
  Fanny 21
  Mary 192
  Nancy 90
  Rachel 137
Ground, Elizabeth 143
Grounds, Catherine 165
  Polly 241
  Synthia S. 18
Grove, Edy 47
Grubb, Ann 8
  Louisa 161
Grundy, Minerva 163

Grunt, (?) 103
Gryam, Ann 67
Grymes, Lisa A. 137
Gueril, Emilie 133
Guess, Belinda 11
Guest, Nancy 166
Gugar, Caroline 250
Guignon, Margar(?) 181
Guilmaure, Jeannette 89
Guin, Rebecca 159
Guinn, Elizabeth 115, 195
  Isabella J. 46
  Paulina 128
Gumpstock, Olive 173
Gunn, Cynthia A. 12
  Dorshey 217
  Julia A. 5
  Kasander 226
  Mary A. 30
  Nancy 2
  Polly 104
Gunnell, Mary P. 174
Gunnels, Fanny 135
Gunnville, Mely 38
Gutherie, Fanny 154
Guthrie, Louisa 187
  Lucy A. 30
  Nancy 125
Gutter, Therese 78
Guy, Jane 142
  Sarah 40
Guyer, Elizabeth 180
Guyn, Alhay 211
Gwinn, Frankie 98
  Julianna 75
  Malinda 50
  Polly 9, 113
  Rachel 14
  Thatha 114
Gwynn, Eliza 168
H(?), Sarah 238
Hackley, Elender 107
  Fanny 142
  Margaret 137
  Martha 177
Hackney, Nancy 81
  Prudence 121
  Sally A. 84
  Sarah E. 31
Hackty, Elizabeth 241
Haddock, Nancy 69
  Penelope 177
  Sarah 60
Haden, Ann 50
  Elizabeth 10
  Jane D. 165
  Maxamilla 39
Hadin, Mary 170
Haelt, Sarah 241
Haff, Eleanor 3
  Ellen A. 168
  Mildred A. 168
Hafter, Elizabeth 127
Hagan, Christine 227
  Eulilia 210
  Louisa 64
  Mary 40, 68, 160
  Nancy 161, 190
  Sarah A. 43
  Sarrah 40
  Susann 160
Hagen, Adelia 36
Hager, Lussee 51
Hagewood, Jane 138
Haggons, Louisa A. 15
  Sodoiski 4
Haghn, Judith 121
  Pricilla 190

Haghn, Sarah 42
Hagood, Ann 109
  Mary 1
Hahn, Catherine 25
  Fanny 200
  Laney 94
  Matilda 199
  Sarah 199
Hahs, Elizabeth 126
Haigh, Maria 234
Haile, Catherine 107
  Nancy 105
Hailley, Marinda 251
Hainds, Elizabeth 67
Haines, Hily 10
  Polly 128
  Sally A. 75
Hains, Drewcilla 100
  Lucinda 26
  Mary 25
  Morning 192
  Susan 96
Haizlip, Julia A. 125
Halderman, Betsey 23
Hale, Elizabeth C. 95
  Joanna 173
Haley, Elizabeth 167
  Mary 165
  Nancy 207
Hall, Ann 205
  Ann M. 65
  Catherine 169
  Charlotte 93
  Cynthia 7
  Eleanor 135
  Elizabeth 31, 100, 128
  Elizabeth A. 81
  Elizabeth J. 191
  Elizabeth W. 33
  Giddida 208
  Grazilla 95
  Hariete M. A. 161
  Jane 168
  Juda 153
  Katharine 117
  Luiza A. 227
  Luvica 78
  Mahaly 178
  Mary 50, 56, 86, 184, 236
  Mary A. 81, 95, 218
  Mary I. 223
  Meekey 36
  Phebe 193
  Polly 185
  Rebecca 152
  Sarah 128, 171, 184, 228
  Sarah A. 97
  Sophronia 81
  Susanna G. 241
Halstead, Hester 32
Halter, Catherine 78
  Elizabeth 234
Halton, Elizabeth 71
Ham, Lucy 221
  Rachel 222
  Rhoda 180
Hamblin, Elizabeth 220
  Emily 219
  Mary 20
Hambright, Elizabeth 9
  Synthy 113
Hamby, Mahaly 233
Hamelton, Mary 30
Hamet, Catharine 173
Hamilton, Ann R. 22
  Catherine 118
  Clare F. 201
  Eliza J. 197

Hamilton, Elizabeth 52, 233
  Elizabeth J. 31
  Isabella 4
  Lucinda 127
  Malinda 20
  Nancy 119
Hamlet, Louisa 209
Hamm, Elizabeth 53
Hammer, Sarah 125
Hammers, Eliza 166
Hammett, Emeline 194
  Margaret 11
Hammon, Nancy 149
Hammond, Mary M. 238
  Polly 113
  Sarah 232
Hammonds, Elizabeth 27
Hammons, Catherine 121
  Sarah 231
Hamond, Elizabeth 92
Hampton, Hester C. D. D. A.
  157
  Sarah 192
Han, Prisilla 140
Hancock, Catherine 214
  Eliza 81
  Fanny 49
  Jane E. 21
  Leanora 17
  Martha 15
  Mary A. 233
  Polly 124, 193
Hand, Edy 118
Handcock, Catherine 192
  Crissy 118
  Louisa 45
  Nancy 62
Handley, Mary 118
  Sarah 158
Handon, Mary 9
Handsbrough, Lydia 85
Hane, Belinda 21
Hanes, Elizabeth 177
Haney, Elizabeth 213
Hanger, Minerva 24
Hanks, Heculen 8
  Susannah 10
Hanley, Patsy 31
Hanly, Catherine 243
  Dulcena 234
  Elinor M. 182
  Fanny 103
Hann, Melinda 223
Hanna, Anna 19
  Margaret 121
  Polly 159
  Rebecca A. 215
  Sarah 225
Hannah, Catherine 80
  Elizabeth A. 194
  Margaret 81
  Rhoda 127
Hannelly, Peggy 69
Hans, Maria 222
Hansborough, Adelia 196
  Mary E. 17
Hanshaw, Elizabeth J. 137
Hansly, Jane A. 215
Hansucker, Sary E. 50
Hardaman, Nancy 68
Harden, Polly 60
Hardester, Jane 171
  Rachel 55
Hardesty, Luvina 38
Hardick, Ann 47
Hardin, Elizabeth 113, 236
  Lucy A. 93
  Mary 134

Hardin, Mary B. 16
  Patsy 151
  Sally 165
  Susanna 218
Hardister, Ibba 218
  Mary 55
  Rebecca 246
Hardridge, Lucina 33
Hardwick, Betsy 57
  Darkess 64
  Maria 47
  Minerva 167
  Patsy 146
Hardwood, Mary A. 118
Hardy, Mary A. 79
  Susan 144
  Verlindie A. 132
Harget, Polly A. 189
Hargis, Celia 6
  Eliza 218
  Maria 44
Hargrove, Lucretia 66
  Nancy 149
  Susan 8
Hargus, Eliza 226
Hariford, Franky 173
Harison, Nancy 143
Harkman, Katharine 208
Harl, Jennitta 48
Harler, Nancy 99
Harlerod, Elizabeth 8
Harley, Rebecca 109
Harlis, Elizabeth 195
  Frances 195
Harlow, Elizabeth 186
Harman, Susan 219
Harmon, Nancy 14
  Rachael 219
  Sarah 42
Harold, Susan 76
Harp, Patsy 59
  Sarah 18
Harper, Abigail 33
  Almira M. 239
  Betsey 228
  Elizabeth 113, 238
  Evaline 237
  Jennetta 109
  Matilda 242
  Sarah 85
  Sarah A. 185
Harr, Emeline 190
Harrell, Mildred 36
Harriford, Polly 109
Harrilson, Temperson B. 142
Harriman, Susan 140
Harrington, Charlotte 8
  Elizabeth 178
  Elizabeth A. 52
  Mahala 46
  Margaret 17
  Polly 104
  Sarah 151
  Susan 17
  Susanna 17
Harris, Anna 103
  Attalanta 169
  Betsey 54
  Delila 225
  Eliza 8
  Elizabeth 2, 87, 225
  Elvina 228
  Hannah 104
  Joanna 45
  Lavena 131
  Louisa 152
  Lucy 2, 82, 209
  Lucy A. 68

Harris, Mahaly 97
  Malinda 7, 119, 220
  Margaret 22, 164
  Martha 116, 123, 153
  Mary A. 97
  Mary M. 61
  Maryann 72
  Matilda D. 80
  Morgan 168
  Nancy 143, 162, 209, 236
  Nancy J. 7
  Narcissa S. 110
  Patsy E. 78
  Perlena 75
  Polly 102, 156, 176
  Rebecca 243
  Rebecca D. 47
  Sarah 58, 155, 225
  Susan 53, 67, 119
Harrison, Cynthia 126
  Elizabeth 69, 92, 104,
    133, 162, 236
  Frances J. E. 89
  Jane 250
  Jane C. 68
  Judith 214
  Margaret 118, 145
  Mariah 133
  Mary 209
  Matilda C. 217
  Mildred E. 137
  Nancy 99
  Neoma 101
  Parthena 4
  Patsy 179
  Safrania 222
  Sarah 85
  Susan 225
  Virgane 8
Harriss, Elizabeth 52
Harryford, Jane 236
  Susan 198
Harryman, Kiziah 226
  Margaret 24
  Polly 24
Hart, Hannah 234
  Harriet S. 48
  Harriet W. 207
  Lucretia 172
  Mary 212
  Rebecca 160
  Sally 173
  Sarah 17
Harter, Eliza 71
Hartgrove, Milicia 117
Hartle, Malinda 11
  Mary 198
  Sarah 157, 199, 246
Harvey, Celia A. 225
  Drucilla 25
  Eleanor A. 224
  Elizabeth 22
  Louisa 22, 179
  Malvina 137
  Nancy 18, 133
  Polly 31
  Sally 249
  Sarah 164
Harwick, Eddy 2
Hase, Ann 78, 222
  Mary 44, 146
  Mary J. 76
Haskall, Maria S. 86
Haslip, Jane 163
Hastings, Ann 232
  Jane 60
Haston, Maria 235
Hasty, Betsey A. 24

Hasty, Clarissa 43
Hatcher, Margaret A. 35
  Tabitha 44
Hatfield, City Ann 78
  Polly 229
  Sarah 96
Hatley, Elizabeth 110
Hatten, Charlotte 91
  Mahala 188
  Sally 209
  Sarah 244
Hatton, Amanda M. 244
  Cynthia A. 12
  Lena 116
  Rebecca 65
  Sally 174
Haun, Anna 159
  Elizabeth 127
  Mary 154
Hause, Rebecca M. 169
Haustatter, Elizabeth 206
Havens, Juliann 150
  Rebecca 137
  Sinea 88
Hawk, Susanna 154
Hawker, Eliza 137
  Manervy 226
  Mary 248
  Nancy 138
Hawkes, Catherine A. 14
Hawkins, Ann 140
  Caroline 68
  Mahala 206
  Mary 78, 180, 231
  Mary J. 40
  Nicy A. 14
  Pheba 65
Hawthorn, Sarah 137
Hay, Elizabeth 155
  Frances 175
  Maria 66
  Nancy 31
  Susannah 79
Haycroft, Sarah J. 77
Hayden, Ann 125
  Caroline 161
  Catherine 29
  Eliza 166
  Elizabeth M. 93
  Emily 22, 216
  Leah M. 144
  Louisa 71
  Luvina 98
  Margaret 226
  Martha J. 201
  Mary 146
  Melinda 234
  Nancy 184
  Susan 23
Haydon, Amanda J. 101
  Harriet 186
  Keziah 211
  Susan E. 73
Hayes, Charlotte 170
  Delindy 119
  Malinda 218
  Mary B. 15
  Nancy 251
Haygood, Elizabeth 59
Haynes, Eleanor M. 225
  Elizabeth 189
  Hannah 198
  Lucinda 59
  Martha 59
  Matilda 130
  Polly 198
  Polly A. 127
Hays, Bethiah 203

Hays, Catharine 126
  Clarysa 91
  Elender 224
  Elinor 42
  Eliza 116
  Elizabeth 166
  Gracie J. 139
  Gunilda 112
  Hannah 152
  Hannah A. 51
  Louisa 56
  Lucinda 84
  Mary 105
  Minerva 167
  Minervy 68
  Nancy 32, 102, 113
  Paulina 113
  Polly 77
  Rebecca 211
  Sally 16
  Serelda 147
Haze, Sarah A. 82
Hazelton, Jane 70
Hazzard, Dorcas 95
Head, Agnes 132
  Ann 58
  Caty 7
  Cynthia 166
  Dicey 106
  Elizabeth 20
  Ibby 189
  Martha 181
  Mary 114
  Phoebe 149
  Rebecca 203
  Sally 104
  Sarah M. 182
  Susanna 206
Headen, Eliza 180
Headspeth, Melinda 106
Heafner, Therese 35
Heald, Mary S. 140
Heard, Polly 82
Hearn, Eliza 18
Hears, Ester 86
Heart, Elizabeth 182
Heartatch, Mary A. 172
Hearty, Patsy 52
Heasick, Elizabeth 95
Heaslip, Elizabeth 13
Heath, Eliza 201
Heather, Elizabeth 195
  Polly 100
Heatherly, Rebecca 153
Heathman, Nancy 197
Heberly, Adeline 227
Hebert, Julia 134
  Louise 17
Hector, Elizabeth 138
Hector, Amantha 58
Hed, Margaret 102
Heddleston, Nancy 232
Hedrick, Elizabeth 208
  Orpha 102
  Sarah 213
Heeny, Elizabeth 105
Hefner, Mary A. 98
Heiromrums, Catherine 23
Heland, Mary 187
Helde, Rosina 246
Helderman, Margaret 251
Helm, Lucille 105
  Peggy 52
Helms, Dicy 52
  Elizabeth 97
  Polly 52
Helton, Emaline 15
  Jane 11, 114

Hindi, Maria S. 137
Hindman, Susanah 111
Hindrick, Ann A. 249
Hinds, Nancy 7
Hines, Ale 201
  Ann 19
  Dicey 7
  Elizabeth 85
  Patsy 29
  Peggy 25, 26
  Polly 164, 204
  Susannah 242
Hink, Mary 49
Hinkle, Elizabeth 94, 110,
  166, 206
  Fanny 107
  Mary 45
  Permelia K. 162
Hinkson, Susan 145
Hinksons, Elizabeth 113
Hinley, Polly 218
Hinshaw, Celia 34
  Dianah 121
Hinson, Narcissa 35
  Sarah 122
Hinton, Betsy 35
  Margaret 106, 173
  Mary 71
  Polly 42
  Rachel 178
  Sally 5
  Sarah 64
  Winna 28
Hipkins, Elizabeth 125
Hire, Elizabeth 7
Hirsh, Nancy 174
  Sarah 195
Hitchcock, Liddy 90
Hitchock, Elizabeth 174
Hiter, Margaret 108
Hitt, Alsey 46
  Delany 134
  Racheal 10
Hiutt, Josephine 172
Hix, Auri J. 118
  Frances 144
  Jemima 44
  Sary 144
  Teletha 42
Hobbs, Mahala 133
  Margaret 12
  Mary A. 239
  Ruth 138
  Sarah 158
  Sarah A. 110
  Temperance 25
Hobeck, Dice 108
Hobs, Mary 174
Hobson, Nancy 89
  Ruth 147
Hocker, Verlinda 229
Hockersmith, Eliza 15
Hodg, Cintha A. 39
Hodge, Rebecca 202
  Sally A. 235
Hodges, Clerissa 192
  Margaret 119
  Mary V. 10
  Susannah 126
  Zeznlda 182
Hodgins, Ann C. 26
Hoff, Elizabeth 132
Hoffman, Johanne R. 104
Hofman, Sally 188
Hog, Elizabeth 223
Hogan, Sary 206
Hogard, Delilah E. 173
  Martha 45
  Mary 155

Hoge, Katherine 139
Hoges, Mary 221
Hogg, Jane 133
Hogue, Jane 193
Hoints, Polly 242
Hokell, Nancy 122
Holaday, Patsy 204
Holand, Mary J. 87
Holbert, Mahala 246
Holbut, Lucinda 164
Holcomb, Clarissa 181
  Elizabeth 133
Holcombe, Phebe 179
Holden, Honor 221
  Lavina 221
  Mary 30
Holding, Mary E. 249
  Rebecca 125
Holdman, Elizabeth 194
Holeman, Eliza A. 174
  Frances 25
  Sophia 96
Holida, Polly 17
Holiway, Margaret 19
Hollad, Martha 89
Holladay, Sally A. 16
  Susannah 101
Holland, Harriet 128
  Julian S. 82
  Mary 191
  Nancy 166
  Polly 208
Hollans, Melinda E. 61
Holleman, Nancy 184
Holley, Fanny 24
Holliday, Eleanor 160
  Eliza A. 56
  Margaret 62
  Mary 56
  Sary 101
Hollingsworth, Emily 177
Holliway, Mary 223
Holloway, Elena 58
  Jane 75
  Lucy A. 223
  Rachel 49
Hollway, Jane 98
Holman, Eleanor 193
  Elizabeth 113, 201
  Levan 98
  Lucy 72, 104
  Mary 157
  Nancy 234
  Sally 220
  Sarah 12
  Sophia 95
  Susan 73
  Vienna 239
Holmes, Casandra 189
  Elender 88
  Elizabeth 28
  Frances 191
  Jane 132
  Jane F. 85
  Margaret 242
  Mary 221
  Matildy 161
Holoway, Elizabeth 173
Holsclaw, Mary A. 125
Holsheiter, Agnes 17
Holst, Lisethe 233
Holster, Susanna 227
Holt, Ann 171
  Eliz. C. 89
  Jane 208
  Lydia 210
  Martha 64
  Mary 131
  Nancy J. 212

Holt, Susanna 16
Holtzclaw, Nancy 135
Holzcher, Ann M. 53
Homes, Eloise 216
Homesley, Nancy A. 18
Hones, Susan 105
Honey, Mary S. 242
Honsinger, Viney 10
Hood, Jane 190, 200
  Mary A. 209
  Rebecca 206
Hoof, Ann 201
  Barbary 45
Hook, Ann 99
  Mary 228, 249
Hooker, Rerran 141
Hooper, Alvira 243
Hoops, Martha 206
  Mary A. 206
Hooser, Sally 1, 210
Hoover, Amanda 60
  Elizabeth 175
  Malinda 187
  Nancy 130
  Rachel E. 119
Hoozer, Elenor 237
  Jane 213
  Martha 98
  Melinda 208
Hope, Jane 103
  Juliet 252
  Katharine 213
  Sarah 183
Hopkins, Eliza 37
  Harriet 126
  Julian 76
  Lucinda 166
  Mary 74
  Mary M. 101
  Minerva 127
  Purlina 8
  Susan 14
Hopper, Elizabeth 120, 166,
  250
  Elmira 120
  Hannah 141
  Jane 3
  Margaret 11
  Nancy 210
  Polly 108
  Rebecca 176, 217
Hopson, Ruth 242
Hopwood, Clementine 27
Hord, Louisa B. 77
Horine, Angelisy 136
  Ann 229
  Elizabeth 115
  Emily 231
  Mary S. 49
  Polly 232
  Susan 118
Horn, Nancy 240
  Polly 96
  Sally 195
Hornback, Christy A. 23
  Nancy 195
  Polly 77
Hornbuckle, Sarah J. 29
Horndon, Lucy 228
Horne, Elizabeth 72
  Mahala 235
Hornman, Elizabeth 151
Hornshell, Eliza 73
  Lucinda P. 98
Horrell, Barbery 55
Horton, Eleanor 118
  Elizabeth 113, 235
  Fanny 132
  Jane 207

282

Hunt, Isabella 221
  Lucretia 102
  Lydia A. 79
  Margaret 115, 235
  Martha B. 47
  Mary 100, 163, 185
  Nancy 5, 158
  Patsy 72
  Sarah D. 7
  Sarah J. 162
  Susan 59
Hunter, Agnes W. 122
  Dorothy 37
  Eliza C. 59
  Jane 64, 141
  Kathern 175
  Lucinda 129
  Margaret 186
  Mary 157
  Mary A. 147
  Melvina 243
  Nancy 40, 71
  Sally 153
  Susan 103, 193
Huntsucker, Charity 130
Hurd, Elizabeth 1
  Susannah 246
Hurley, Elizabeth 9
  Nancy 71
Hurt, Alsey A. 154
  Elender 173
  Eliza 8
  Jane 216
  Katharine 106
  Roxana 82
  Sarah 130
  Sydney A. 9
Hush, Lucinda 203
Husk, Lamah 89
Husley, Susan 122
Huss, Julia 69
Hust, Amanda 145
  Catherine 196
Huste, Elizabeth 2
Huston, Adeline 178
  Elizabeth E. 28
  Jane 218
  Nancy 136
  Sarah 147
Hutchason, Easter 99
Hutchens, Elizabeth 81
Hutcheon, Nancy 103
Hutchings, Caroline 137
  Dorothy 188
  Mary J. 182
Hutchins, Mariah 64
  Mary N. C. 190
Hutchinson, Elizabeth 18, 193
  Margaret 176
  Mary 174
  Mary A. 208
  Polly 171
  Sarah 109
  Thirza A. 166
Hutchison, Margarett 170
Hutson, Ceclia K. 67
  Elizabeth 229, 250
  Fany 191
  Luezsa 56
  Nancy 183
  Patsy 48
  Sarah 26
Hutton, Nancy 236
  Sarah 101
Hyatt, Elizabeth 2
  Lenna 108
  Luvey 162
  Rachel 97

Hyatt, Sarah 248
Hyden, Martha 114
Hyet, Lency 169
Hyle, Jane 43
Hynes, Phebe 135
Hyranymous, Sarah 98
Hyre, Catharine 33
Icenhower, Mary 171
Icenogle, Hannah 63
  Nancy 63
Igart, Elizabeth 153
Ikard, Sophia 131
Ikherd, Sarah 96
Indicut, Casander 171
Inge, Eliza 187
Inglebart, Elizabeth 52
Ingledow, Alpha 117
Inglish, Catherine 151
  Elizabeth 90
  Malinda 55
  Martha 133
  Mary 237
  Phoebe 4
  Polly 151
Ingraham, Elizabeth 132
Ingram, Barbary 172
  Barshaba 148
  Elizabeth A. 230
  Hannah 112
Inman, Amey 79
Innman, Susannah 186
Inskeep, Susan 150
  Tabitha V. 89
Ion, Mary 107
Ireland, Betsy 218
Irgim, Polly 136
Irons, Elizabeth 39
  Polly 83
Irvin, Charity 99
  Mary 237
  Rebeca 44
  Redonia 210
Irvine, Harriet 82
  Mary 109
  Minerva 98
Irwin, Anna 154
  Eleanor 43
  Elizabeth 17
  Louisa 201
  Martha 113
  Tabitha 14
Isaac, Emmaline 90
  Nancy 89
Isaak, Lisabeth 197
Isabell, Temperance 71
Isbee, Emely 30
Isbeel, Partheny 248
Isbel, Hardwitch 83
  Nancy M. 193
Isbell, Abigail E. 109
Isele, Elizabeth 77
Isenhaur, Mahala 120
Isgrig, Elizabeth 78
  Jane 218
Isgriggs, Eleanor 32
Isham, Margaret 204
Isom, Marcellite 61
  Odile 40
Israel, Letitia 235
Ivans, Christena 80
Ivers, Lydia 185
Jack, Evelina 171
  Livina 174
Jacks, Caty 6
  Elizabeth 6
  Fanny 175
  Malinda 118
  Polly 198
  Sophia 99

Jackson, Anny A. 118
  Amanda M. F. 102
  Catharine 67
  Caty A. 239
  Christian 99
  Elizabeth 174, 199
  Fanny 235
  Francis 223
  Jane 4, 168
  Lucinda 29, 59
  Malinda 129
  Margaret 18
  Maria 4
  Mary 113
  Mary A. 224
  Mary J. 22
  Matilda 111
  Minerva 162
  Nancy 105
  Nancy W. 127
  Parneaty 186
  Polly 170, 202
  Priscilla 24
  Rachel 42
  Sally 61
  Sarah 240
  Sarah A. 202
  Sarah J. 111
  Susan 36
  Susannah 245
  Synthis 122
  Zelphia 229
Jacobs, Celenary 32
  Elizabeth 246
  Elizabeth A. 128
  Katherine H. 215
  Lucindy 246
  Malvina 164
Jacoby, Eliza 179
  Leones 236
  Margaret 136
  Martha 111
  Susan 240
Jacson, Patsy 217
  Polly 38
Jahs, Jane 195
Jamerson, Nancy 104
James, Ann 89
  Anna 39, 134
  Anne 226
  Betsey 211
  Christena 211
  Elizabeth 68, 166, 214
  I. 193
  Ibby 34
  Katharine 156, 211
  Mahala 233
  Malvina 32
  Martha 2
  Martha O. 96
  Mary 92
  Mary A. D. 69
  Matilda M. 251
  Mildred M. 73
  Nancy 152, 188
  Nancy P. 75
  Polly 25, 62
  Rebecca 47
  Sally 201, 218
  Sarah 83
Jameson, Alemeda 66
  Amelia 9
  Durrika 34
  Eliza M. 147
  Emeline 118
  Louisa 112
  Lucretia 6
  Mary 119
  Nancy 13

283

Jameson, Polly 62
  Susan E. 95
Jamey, Eliza A. 10
Jamison, Delialah 134
  Eliza J. 46
  Elizabeth 174, 248
  Harriett 179
  Jane 77
  Latitia 115
  Louisa 197
  Lucinda 234
  Martha 108
  Polly 9
  Ruth B. 210
  Sally 156, 204
Janis, Emelie 132
  Etionetta 108
  Felicite 132
  Susan 51
January, Deborah 131
  Susan H. 34
Jarey, Mary 52
Jarvis, Polly 55
Jeans, Elizabeth 148
  Mary I. 231
Jeffers, Elizabeth 70
  Margaret 6
  Mary J. 65
Jefferson, Ann E. 70
  Catherine 152
  Margaret 196
Jeffres, Martha 109
Jeffries, Elizabeth 28
  Mary 150
  Mary J. 116
  Nancy 72, 159
  Sally 200
  Sarah J. 72
  Susan 30, 45
Jenkins, Amanda 73
  Elizabeth 156
  Esther 239
  Mary 247
  Peggy 70
  Rachael 167
  Rosy 192
  Sophia 234
Jennings, Elizabeth 66, 226
  Hannah F. 209
  Lockey T. 205
  Lucinda 119
  Lucy 85
  Mary 176
  Nancy 208
  Zilpha 149
Jentry, Sally 79
Jepson, Nancy 128
Jeringen, Keren 203
Jerman, Ann M. 247
Jesse, Atlanta 230
  Mary A. 171
Jewel, Elizabeth 172
Jewell, Angeline 245
  Hannah 31
  Sarah 36
Jimason, Sarah J. 22
Jimison, Polly 138
Jinings, Wineford 103
Job, Eleanor 80
  Malinda 47
  Melissa 30
  Pamela 151
  Sarah 44
Jobe, Lucretia 198
  Nancy 166
Joenes, Jane 220
Joffre, Catherine 150
Johns, Elizabeth 173

Johns, Elmira 150
  Frances 164
  Lydia 24
  Nancy 13
  Rosanna 235
Johnson, Widow 207
  Alice 163
  Ann 40, 93
  Anna 120
  Artemetia 27
  Avaline 69
  Betsy 218
  Caroline 63, 122
  Caroline P. 164
  Catharine 177
  Cynthia 121
  Effy 149
  Elenor 175
  Eliza 172
  Eliza J. 171
  Elizabeth 5, 9, 80, 93, 96,
    158, 165, 169, 189
  Elizabeth A. 102
  Elvina 173
  Emeline 113, 157
  Esther 81
  Eveline 72
  Frances 158
  Frances A. 116
  Hannah 162, 191
  Harriet A. 16
  Hortentia 186
  Huldah 180
  Isabel 5
  Jane E. 216
  Jane V. 133
  Jenisha B. 109
  Judah 121
  Katharine 109
  Lavina E. 230
  Lucinda 2, 23
  Mahala 231
  Mahaly J. 85
  Manerva 47, 95
  Margaret 41, 65, 139, 176,
    182
  Margit 55
  Maria 147
  Marin L. 163
  Martha 167, 172, 251
  Mary 2, 8, 9, 116, 121,
    123, 227
  Mary A. 25, 34, 120
  Mary J. 1
  Matilda 54, 107
  Matty 79
  Minerva 66
  Nancy 59, 61, 88, 93, 102,
    126, 148, 172, 178, 181,
    191, 241
  Phebe I. 185
  Polly 35, 251
  Purmelia A. 193
  Rachel 39, 183
  Reachel 185
  Rebecca 4, 218
  Sally 10, 33
  Sarah 125, 139, 165, 243
  Sarah A. 215
  Sarah B. 165
  Sarah W. 200
  Sophia 27
  Susan 27
  Susan R. 202
  Susannah R. 143
  Syntha 38
  Vatilla 191
Johnston, Catharon 220

Johnston, Cintha 239
  Clementine 79
  Dicn 65
  Dorcas 22
  Elizabeth 31, 227
  Emily 25
  Jane 33
  Kesire 8
  Lucinda 141, 216
  Mahala 26
  Margaret 13
  Rachel D. 61
  Sally 4
  Susan 237
Joiner, Nancy 108, 135
Jollin, Emilie V. 7
Jolly, Elizabeth 46
Jones, Agnes 27
  Ann E. 27
  Auza M. 145
  Betsy 244
  Borilla 164
  Catherine 85, 89, 142
  Catherine W. 19
  Charlotte 233
  Cynthia 238
  Delue 47
  Edy 190
  Eliz. L. 142
  Eliza 94
  Eliza J. 152
  Elizabeth 31, 76, 110,
    124, 146, 186, 219, 241
  Elizabeth E. 28
  Emiline 19
  Fanny 1
  Gracy 11
  Hannah 50
  Jane 122, 189
  Jemima 89
  Jenny k73
  Lennia 45
  Lisebeth 32
  Loucinda 154
  Louisa 6, 157
  Louizanna 110
  Luckey 107
  Lucretia M. 165
  Lucy 139
  Luizea 77
  Malinda 146, 234
  Malvina 75
  Margaret 97, 178, 206
  Maria 116
  Martha 42
  Martha H. 83
  Martha J. 234
  Mary 66, 89, 179, 242
  Mary A. 23, 212, 223
  Mary M. A. 247
  Mildred 149
  Minerva J. 188
  Myre 85
  Nancy 123, 164, 173, 213,
    215, 229
  Naomi 243
  Pamelia A. 95
  Parthena 39, 185
  Patsey 49
  Patsy 30, 221
  Penelope 154
  Polly 41, 144, 154, 211
  Rebecca 2, 29, 123, 172,
    222
  Sally 138, 150, 186, 242
  Sarah 62, 67, 84, 98, 107,
    113, 124
  Sarah A. 22, 124, 193, 224

285

289

Martin, Mary A. 145
  Mary C. 131
  Mary F. 168
  Mary R. 13
  Mary W. 167
  Maryann J. 74
  Matilda 148
  Morman 195
  Nancy 53, 125, 136, 206,
    210, 215
  Nancy S. 202
  Parthenia 203
  Phebe 50
  Polly 40
  Polly B. 187
  Polly M. 147
  Ruth 189
  Sally 115
  Sarah 72, 191, 218, 222
  Sarah G. 207
  Susan 21, 87, 234
  Tabitha 150
  Virginia 218
Martinall, Catherine 221
Martinau, Florance 131
Martindill, Nancy 42
Martineau, Louise 16, 155
Martinou, Julie 135
Marvin, Matilda 163
Maryotte, Elesie 197
Mase, Catharine 231
  Catherine 13
  Jemima 124
  Polly 113
Mason, Anna 40
  Eliza J. 57
  Elizabeth 178, 225
  Frances 59, 199
  Katharine G. 192
  Mary 177
  Mary H. 155
  Nancy 114
  Sarah 111
Massey, Catherine 228
  Elizabeth 103
  Lydia W. 110
  Maria 146
  N. M. S. 168
  Nancy 49
  Nancy D. 152
  Polly 49
  Susan M. 19, 20
  Vinecea 128
Massie, Cinthia A. 182
  Nancy 213
  Rebecca 240
  Susan A. 129
Massingill, Polly 54
Massy, Caroline 154
  Mary 150
  Peggy 111
  Susan R. 101
Masters, Basheba 34
  Caroline 191
  Elizabeth 178
  Fanny 11
  Isabella 50
  Mary 92
  Nancy 190
  Peggy 212
Masterson, Ann 147
  Eliza 87
  Hester 163
  Margaret 234
  Mary M. 120
  Polly 184
  Sarah 184
Mateer, Sarah 177

Mathens, Martha 91
Matheny, Sally 70
Matherly, Jane 95
Mathes, Elizabeth 244
  Katharine 152
  Sarah A. 4
Mathews, (?) 160
  Catherine 235
  Eleanor 87
  Elizabeth 88
  Jemima 39
  Margret 157
  Mary 220
  Patsy 236
  Rebecca 223
  Sarah A. 52
Mathis, Hannah J. 216
  Martha A. 235
  Nancy 50
Matier, Catherine 160
Matkin, Matilda 153
Matkins, Rebecca 194
Matlock, Elizabeth 249
  Juliann 196
  Keturah 217
  Teressa 42
Matson, Harriet 144
  Jemima C. 219
  Mary 142
Matthens, Elizabeth 162
  Polly 88
Matthew, Mary 12
Matthews, Ann 75
  Catharine 151
  Clarissa 12
  Elvira 28
  Louisa 45
  Mary 75
  Susan 199
Mattingly, Amanda 185
  Ann 68, 149
  Elisa 12
  Lucinda 166
  Maria 81
  Mary 23, 85
  Mary L. 207
  Mary M. 194
  Matilda 74
  Susanna 116
Mattock, Luiza 136
  Matilda 217
  Rachel 126
Mattocks, Susan 48
Mattson, Elizabeth 140
Mattuck, Sary 131
Maupin, Ann 229
  Charlotte 147
  Elender 138
  Elizabeth 42
  Frances 96
  Leah 104
  Lucinda 241
  Margaret 174, 248
  Martha 203, 223
  Mary A. 153
  Mary E. 163
  Nancy 239
  Rosey 8
  Sarah 18, 102
  Sarah J. 129
  Senia 9
  Zerilda 217
Maupon, Malinda 54
Maurice, Marie 131
Maury, Joanah 103
Maw, Narcissa 158
Maxey, Mary 242
  Mary M. 178

Maxwell, Catharine 129
  Jane 90, 198
  Lucinda 163
  Matilda 5
  Nancy 129
May, Deborah 144
  Frances 216, 243
  Lavinia 225
  Lucinda 17
  Mary 197
  Mileta A. 23
  Permelia 60
  Preciller 204
  Sarah 155
  Susan 56
Mayberry, Margaret 201
  Mary 136, 251
  Nancy 10
  Polly 69
Mayden, Alisabeth 216
Mayes, Frances 54
Mayfield, Katherine 251
  Polly 251
Mayhan, Catharine 230
  Marthay 146
Mayjors, Mary 107
Mays, Ambrosha 97
  Martha 155
  Polly 221
  Sally 173
McAdams, Jane 164
  Jemima 27
McAfee, Catherine 144
  Mary 153
  Mary M. 16
McAlister, Mahala 181
  Manerva 184
McAllister, Marget 3
McAlroy, Elizabeth 116
  Sarah 119
McAlvain, Avaline 31
McAnry, Dicy A. 225
McAtee, Lucy Eleanor 230
  Mary J. 220
McAttee, Mary M. 132
McAustin, Catherine B. 79
McBain, Eliza 141
  Harriet 115
  Sophia 47
McBride, Aranetta 232
  Isabella 105
  Janira 190
  Leviney 59
  Lucinda 36
  Margaret 248
  Tabitha 171
McCabe, Amanda 69
  Ann 206
McCafety, Katharine 71
McCafferty, Martha J. 78
McCain, Leuame 187
McCalester, Sarah 51
McCall, Rosanna 34
McCampbell, Moniza 48
McCampble, Sophia 243
McCann, Delilah 220
  Mary 220
  Matilda 49
  Polly 131
McCarman, Palen J. 174
McCarther, Elizabeth 188
McCarty, Ann T. 54
  Elizabeth 241
  Lucy 103
  Mary A. 215
  Matilda 69, 196
  Nancy 189
  Prudence M. 73

McCarty, Sarah 37
McCary, Nancy 48
McCauly, Mary J. 214
McCay, Jane 99
McChriston, May 96
McCinsey, Seery 180
McClain, Eliza 134
  Eliza J. 18
  Elizabeth 96
  Lottey 10
  Lynda A. 102
  Mary 78
  Matilda 20
  Minerva 134
  Racheal 140
  Sophia 218
McClanahan, Caroline 58
  Eliza 229
  Frances 192
  Jeanneat L. 61
  Mary 46
  Mary M. 166
  Rebecca 91
McClane, Julia 52
  Polly 109
McClard, Elizabeth 103
  Lenis 13
McClary, Emeline 158
McClay, Elizabeth 197
McClean, Ellen E. 220
  Lucretia A. 241
  Mary J. 170
McClellan, Barbara 63
  Barbary 180
McClelland, Elizabeth 162, 248
  Julian 227
  Mary 118
  Patsy 184
McClellande, Martha A. 129
McClellon, Adeline 109
McClenahan, Mary A. 16
McClendon, Louisa 233
  Mary 155
McClenehan, Nancy 40
McCleur, Jane E. 163
McClinny, Sarah 4
McClintock, Rebecca 148
McCloar, Amanda 218
McCloud, Daphne 192
McClure, Elizabeth 103
  Elizabeth M. 141
  Elmyria 138
  Isabel 210
  Kezeh 229
  Lucetta 50
  Mary 191
  Mery 101
  Nancy 110, 248
  Polly 67
  Sarah 29, 150
McCullough, Caroline 158
McCollum, Nancy 84
  Sally 9
McCombs, Jane 33
  Minerva A. 195
McConnel, Leny 231
McConnell. Elizabeth 108
  Mary 114
  Relief, 247
  Sally 211
  Sarah 54, 114
McCord, Jane 190
  Mildred T. 141
  Susan 34
McCorkle, Lidia 179
  Sarah 212
McCormack, Margaret 71
  Mary 64

McCormick, Ann 63
  Jane 188, 234
  Mary A. 23
  Nancy 162
McCorrle, Nancy 44
McCourtney, Elizabeth 57
  Nancy 78
  Sarah 36
McCown, Susanna 13
McCoy, Ann 163, 241
  Christiana 235
  Dincy 147
  Eliza 196
  Eliza A. 106
  Eliza J. 148
  Elizabeth 37
  Emily 12, 97
  Lucinda 65
  Lydia 192
  Mahala 35
  Margaret 220
  Mary A. 155
  Milda 95
  Nancy 131
  Peggy 221
  Polly 165
  Rebecca 43, 63
  Sally 128
  Sarah 86
  Susan 134
  Tempa 63
McCracken, Virginia 238
McCrary, Betsy 44
  Harriett 250
  Jane 4
  Marinthia 192
  Mary 123
  Sidney 2
  Susan 226
McCray, Mary 119
  Ruth 63
  Sally W. 74
  Sarah 212
  Sarah L. 12
McCreary, Lucy 93
  Nancy 25
  Polly 20
McCreery, Jane 108
McCroskey, Elizabeth 107
McCulah, Martha 237
McCullar, Ellendar 241
McCullock, Elizabeth 81
McCullom, (?) 80
McCullouch, Sarah 185
McCullough, Elizabeth 218, 227
  Jane 130
  Margaret 154, 230
  Sally 185
  Sarah 173
McCully, Elizabeth 9
  Jane 9
  Menervy 209
McCulter, Sally 8
McCulum, Eliza A. 172
McCune, Margaret 44
  Polly L. 69
  Polly S. 26
  Susan 156
McCurry, Mary 149
McCutchan, Zerilda 95
McCutchen, Elizabeth 31
  Harriett S. 76
McCutcheon, S. S. 52
McCutchin, Rebeccah 112
McDando, Sarah 128
McDanel, Delilah 67
McDaniel, Agnes 145

McDaniel, Betsy 98
  Cenith 181
  Eliza J. 49
  Emily 8
  Evaline 138
  Louisa 10
  Malinda 158
  Mariam 76
  Nancy 131, 231, 233
  Rebecca B. 95
  Sarah 143, 145
  Sarah A. 235
  Susannah 44
McDaniels, Elizabeth 43, 148
McDavitt, Mildred 115
McDelany, Sarah 196
McDermid, Charlotte 218
  Fanny 40
McDonald, Ann R, 65
  Anne 221
  Catharine 76
  Louisa 220
  Mary 82
  Nancy 182
  Rebecca 127
  Sally 76, 173
  Susan 76
McDonel, Mary 37
McDow, Jane 121
McDowel, Margate 169
  Margrate 120
  Polly 75
McDowell, Caty 28
  Eliza 53
  Eliza A. 158
  Hetty 102
  Lucinda 178
McElroy, Ann 69
  Eliza 163
McElwee, Margaret 112
  Sarah 152
McEntire, Emily 99
McFaden. See McFadden.
McFadden, Ginne 41
McFarland, Amanda 237
  Caroline 132
  Cassa A. 104
  Catherine 150
  Celina 68
  Cynthia 166
  Eleanor 69
  Eliza 61
  Elizabeth 148
  Elly 228
  Eveline 114
  Frances 74
  Helen 108
  Keron H. 21
  Lavina 89
  Louisa 52
  Lucinda 86
  Lucy 12, 244
  Mahala 60
  Mary 11
  Mary A. 140
  Nancy 215
  Polly 107
  Polly E. 144
  Rachel 11, 162
  Sally 9, 84
  Sary 11
  Sophua 61
McFarlin, Nancy B. 143
  Polly 144
  Sarah 84
McFawl, Sally 81
McFearson, Elizabeth M. 109
McFerron, Columbia 71

McFerron, Evina 71
  Tabitha B. 179
McGarey, Patsy 30
McGaugh, Charlotte 107
  Elvina 149
  Nancy 245
  Sally A. 100
McGaw, Elizabeth 222
  Susan 229
McGee, (?) 203
  Aley C. 44
  Amelia L. 73
  Cynthia A. 88
  Eliza 150
  Elizabeth 53, 162, 211
  Emaline 78
  Jane 216
  Katherine 121
  Mahaly 53
  Nancy 209, 224
  Polly 191
  Rachel 143
  Sarah 222
  Susan 47
McGill, Sally P. 18
McGinas, Elizabeth 56
McGinnes, Hester 165
McGinness, Alley 199
McGinnis, Martha A. 61
McGinniss, Virginia 106
McGirk, Mary J. 122
McGlandin, Frances 44
McGloflin, Sarah A. 65
McGough, Polly A. 37
McGoun, Elizabeth 250
McGowan, Nancy 172
McGruder, Ann M. 105
McGuire, Catharine 163
  Elenor 112
  Elizabeth 59
  Emely 30
  Jane 181
  Malinda 87
  Margaret 172
  Mary 219
  Nancy 169
  Sarah 155, 248
  Susan 26
McHaddan, Mary 214
McHaney, Nancy 203
McHany, Christiana 247
McHargue, Anna 66
McHeney, Elizabeth 215
  Martha A. 219
McHenry, Urissey 94
McHeny, Bertheny 211
  Nancy 211
McHill, Matilda 135
McHugh, Mary 5
  Sarah 181
McIlhenny, Casandria A. 186
McIllvain, Isabelle 145
  Lucy M. 145
McIlvain, Cythiann 62
  Susan H. 208
McIntire, Betsy 85
  Lucy 157
McIntyre, Elizabeth 187
McKamey, Elizabeth 195
  Louisinda 16
  Mary B 157
McKay, Edith 39
  Isabella 151
  Julyann 193
  Lenna 160
  Margaret 151
  Sarah A. 162
  Susanna 145

McKay, Thurzy 138
McKeammy, Rosey A. 207
McKean, Leficy 238
McKee, Elizabeth 158
  Jane 161
  Loudicey 106
  Nancy 60
  Polly 159
  Rachel 9
McKenney, Lucinday 112
  Mary J. 36
  Sarah A. 207
McKenzie, Sarah 247
McKey, Elizabeth 88
  Nancy 53
McKiney, Rachel 140
  Tabbitha 203
McKinney, Ailsey 222
  Amanda 28
  Elizabeth 123, 127
  Euphonia 8
  Levina B. 148
  Nancy 88
  Paulina 41
  Polly 178
  Sally 47
  Sarah 116, 178
McKinny, Keziah 86
  Lucinda 98
McKinsey, Sarah A. 142
McKinzie, Isaphena 247
  Katherine 60
  Mahala 164
  Malinda 151
McKipic, Polly C. 237
McKirk, Pimecia 139
McKissick, Catherine 41
McKissie, Rebecca 93
McKnight, Assentha 90
  Elizabeth 170
McKorkle, Millinda 91
McKoun, Elizabeth 146
McKpwn, Hannah 137
  Mary 11
McLain, Ann 149
  Charlotte 203
  Elizabeth 178
  Sary A. 93
McLaird, Sarah 251
McLanahan, Nancy 249
  Sophronia 152
McLane, Ruth 228
McLard, Jane 207, 233
McLary, Johannah 109
McLaughlin, Cena 45
  Jane 67
  Malinda J. 60
  Mary 33
  Priscilla 170
  Susan 178
McLean, Artenisia P. 146
  Matilda 20
  Tabitha C. 124
McLinn, Conthian 2
McMahan, Margaret 92
  Mary 12
  Oraminta 218
  Polly 147
  Sally 207
McMahon, Elizabeth 238
  Nancy Hasling 1
McMannus, Elizabeth 178
McMickle, Patsy 208
  Sophia 206
McMillan, Emma R. 123
McMillen, Eliza 87
  Hannah 15
  Henrietta 100

McMillen, Nancy M. 123
  Polly 188
  Rutha E. 11
McMillin, Jane 63
  Margaret 7
  Susannah 65
McMillon, Vicindarilla 187
McMurtrey, Clementine 147
  Elvinea 191
  Nancy 226
  Polly 147, 162
McMurtrie, Lydia 56
  Nancy 110
McMurtry, Susan 114
McMurty, Mary 22
McNair, Margaret 149
McNeal, Rebecca M. 166
McNee, Ann 213
McNeel, Elizabeth 15
McNeill, Sally A. 239
McNeille, Harriet 84
McNerwin, Mary 3
McNew, Sally C. 114
  Sarah 164
McNight, Elizabeth 131
  Margaret 104
  Nancy 174
  Permelia 103
  Polly 174
  Sarah 174
McNite, Delitha 189
McOnnel, Rebecca 64
McPerson, Sarah 145
McPheeters, Florence 133
McPherson, Elizabeth 147, 151,
    162
  Emily 147
  Nancy 38
  Nancy E. 135
  Rhoda 21
  Sally 207
  Sarah 69
  Susan 239
McQuarry, Mary A. 235
McQuary, Jane 218
  Martha 249
McQueen, Caroline 193
  Elizabeth J. 45
McQuester, Elizabeth 174
McQuiddy, Mary 65
McQuidy, Sally A. 67
McQuie, Amelia 236
  Elizabeth 236
McQuilly, Elizabeth 241
McQuitty, Isabella 53
  Mary 214
  Mary A. 50
  Percilla 50
  Sarah 94
McRae, Polly 49
McRay, Margueritte 188
McReynolds, Maria 83
McRoberts, Harriet 69
McSpadden, Elizabeth 84
  Nancy 214
McSy, Mary 125
McTabb, Fanny 216
McVickers, Mary 32
McWilliams, Elizabeth 82
  Elva 154
  Lucinda 245
  Magadorah 149
  Nancy 61
  Sarah A. 128
Mead, Henrietta 186
  Sally 232
Meadew, Margaret 147
Meals, Morthey 50

Means, Cynthia 13
  Elizabeth 51
  Jane 51
  Louisa 102
  Mary A. 142
  Scyotha J. 111
  Thursa 208
Meason, Elizabeth A. 109
Meazle, Martha 216
Medley, Cynthia 217
  Eliza 63
  Harriet E. 59
  Jane 43
  Sally 57
Medlin, Nancy 191
  Tabetha 214
Medlock, Susan 98
Meek, Alafair 113
  Charlotte 19£
  Janie 210
  Mary 184
Meelor, Louisa 108
Mefford, Cordelia 72
  Elizabeth 223
Mellone, Faney 97
Melton, Ann 232
  Lucy A. 174
  Mabel 20
  Rebecca 210
Melvin, Sally A. 15
Meng, Mary 170
Menifee, Jane 30
  Sarah A. 22£
Mercer, ElizaLeth 209
Merchant, Sarah 158
Mercil, Marie L. 179
Meredith, Elizabeth 222
  Mary 176
  Polly A. 166
  Sally 89
  Sarah 4
  Susan J. 76
Merfrey, Deanner 206
Merrell, Ann A. 18
  Caroline R. 249
Merrett, Sarah A. 49
Merril, Eliza 48, 202
  Larany 139
Merrin, Elizabeth 89
Merrit, Elmira 29
  Irenia 28
Merry, Louisa E. 47
Mescade, Josephine 81
Messersmith, Elizabeth 51,
  186
Meteer, Isabel 116
Metz, Sarah 169
Metzshingereen, Walburge 115
Meul, Sarah P. 243
Meur. Livisa 88
Meville, Sarah J. 204
Meyers, Margerate 127
  Scithe A. 228
Meyor, Angel C. D. 125
Mezings, Martha 82
Miars, Mary 161
Michael, Eliza 123
  Nancy 243
Micheau, (?) 16
Michel, Nancy 130
  Sarah 1
Michell, Dellia E. A. 160
Middleton, Irena 165
  Mary 42
Midlock, Artamus 16
Mier, Phebey 61
Miers, Lean 225
  Sally 239

Mifford, Elizabeth 30
  Jane S. 82
  Julian 118
  Mary A. 15
  Polly 111
Milburn, Susannah 36
Miler, Ann 79
Miles, Ann 66
  Catherine 232
  Catherine M. 97
  Cecilia 132
  Elizabeth 132, 134
  Helena 246
  Mary 68, 235, 240
  Mary M. 232
  Perneleanna 132
  Polly 47
  Rosanna 140
Milhomme, Marguarete 232
Milikam, Polly 250
Milington, Silvia I. 13
Millan, Ellaie 49
Miller, Adaline 162
  Amanda 124
  Angeline 182
  Ann 45, 247
  Ann L. 85
  Arilla 206
  Barnett 27
  Betsy 140
  Caroline 145, 210
  Catherine 51
  Clara 85
  Constantia D. 209
  Demshea 168
  Dolly 153
  Eliza 54, 199
  Eliza J. 6, 129
  Eliza M. 10
  Elizabeth 6, 10, 17, 52,
    56, 89, 180, 201, 203,
    209, 251
  Emily 251
  Fanny 41
  Hannah 88, 113, 12£
  Hannah M. 101
  Harriett 23, 68, 228
  Isabella 55
  Jane 45, 72, 106, 157
  Johanah H. 38
  Katherine 104
  Lavina 201
  Lucinda 90
  Lucrecy J. 20
  Lucy 157
  Luretta 14
  Lydia 219
  Mahala 140, 154
  Malinda 6
Maraine, 184
  Margaret 2, 44, 89
  Margaret G. 96
  Margarett 103
  Margaretta 195
  Margery 151, 238
  Maria 216
  Martha 147
  Marthy J. 194
  Mary 76, 93, 171, 209, 224
  Nancy 108, 126, 130, 149,
    233
  Polly 21, 52, 132
  Prudy 201
  Rachel 56
  Rhoda 109
  Sarah 51, 83, 179, 216
  Sarah A. 202
  Sevina A. 74

Miller, Sophia 90
  Susan 204, 223
  Thamer 27
  Unfsey A. 160
Millhallen, Elgerta 246
Millham, Dosha 175
Millheizer, Sally 234
Millhollan, Martha 245
Millhomme, Judith 227
Millin, Mary 173
Million, Mary F. 231
Millroy, Mary 250
Mills, Docia 235
  Eliza P. 171
  Elizabeth 42, 133
  Engeline P. 48
  Mary 144
  Mary S. 131
  Monica 232
  Sally 215
  Segia P. 38
Millsap, Barbary 20
  Nancy 87, 249
  Polly 96, 147, 245
  Zulica 43
Millson, Bathsheba 52
  Susanna 169
Milsap, Celila 87
  Nancy 159
Milsaps, Elizabeth 41
Milton, Fidella 108
  Mary 38
Mincher, Ruthy 217
Miner, Elisa J. 195
  Sarena 82
Minor, Cynthia A. 200
  L. 226
  Mariah 13
Minten, Elizabeth 108
Minter, Ann 243
  Ann M. 205
  Ruth 130
Minton, Francis 85
  Martha 79
  Nancy 146
Miot, Tarece 61
Misplay, Elmira 21
  Julia 24
  Theresa 232
Misse, Hortense A. 170
Missrt, Mary 62
Mitchel, Ann 55
  Catherine 231
  Mary 213
  Nancy 52
  Sally 18
  Sarah 208, 241
Mitchell, Agnes 76
  Agnes C. 157
  Agness 140
  Armerica P. 191
  Betsy 236
  Eliza 21
  Elizabeth 200, 246, 249
  Judith P. 79
  Louisian 229
  Martha 36, 96
  Mary 180
  Nancy 182, 219
  Patsy 148
  Sally 133
  Sophia 225
  Sophronia 182
  Susan 201
Mize, Hezziah 16
Mizee, Nancy 7
Moad, Elizabeth 173
  Nancy 4, 146

293

295

Nelson, Alcey J. 200
  Diadema 191
  Elizabeth 20
  Lucy S. 34
  Margaret E. 129
  Mariah 141
  Martha A. 173
  Mary 4, 80
  Mary J. 158, 167
  Nancy 164
Nesbit, Eliza 25
  Nancy 156
  Permelia 226
Neswonger, Polly 100
Netherton, Elizabeth 161
Nettle, Ede 241
Neuman, Henrietta 36
Nevil, Mahala P. 22
Nevill, Lydia 227
Neville, Mary A. 22
Nevins, Jane 65
  Sarah 103
Newberry, Elizabeth 221
  Mahala 129
  Polly 30, 65
Newbill, Amanda 53
Newby, Cynthia 158
  Eliza 182
  Nancy 153
Newel, Anna 35
  Elvira 121
  Myra 180
Newkern, Lydia 59
Newkirk, Rachel 59
  Sarah 148
  Susannah 194
Newland, Sally 241
Newman, Martha 33
  Mildred 71
News, Martha S. 181
Newsom, Nancy 242
  Rebecca 195
Newton, Experience 167
  Louisianna 229
  Martha 53
  Patsy 204
  Polly 51
  Ruth A. 130
  Susannah 51
Nicely, Nancy 8
Nichles, Rosana 250
Nicholas, Mary 74
Nichols, Amanda 245
  Ann 250
  Eliza J. 92
  Elizabeth 139
  Emily 10
  Hannah I. 235
  Judith 201
  Julia A. 132
  Mary C. 207
  Nancy 245
  Petitia 49
  Sarah 20
  Susan 6
Nicholson, Jane 61
Nickerson, Elizabeth 234
  Lucindy 130
  Mahala 9
Nickles, Ann 43
Nickoll, Emily 205
Nickols, (?) 186
  Rebecca 220
Nickolson, Elizabeth 117
Nicoles, Elizabeth 208
Nidevar, Susannah 72
Niece, Mary 146
Nifong, Elizabeth 131

Nifong, Mary 32
  Susannah 42
Nix, Rebecca 153
Nixon, Gustin Cath. 100
Noble, Mary 236
  Nancy 9
  Polina 200
  Rokyannah 108
Nobles, Emily 153
  Milla 153
Noblet, Eleanor 161
Noe, Lurinda 102
Noel, Eliza 40
  Pauline 60
Noell, Mary L. 75
  Sarah A. 30
Noland, Angeline L. 178
  Arrena 76
  Clarrissa 227
  Elizabeth 31
  Emerien 144
  Nelly 89
  Sarah 84
Noonan, Sarah A. 231
  Sarah M. 27
Noonon, Sarah 183
Norman, Martha W. 249
  Susan 193
Norrice, Matilda 185
Norris, Anna 115
  Cynthia 148
  Elizabeth 59
  Frances 208
  Harriet 63
  Nancy 181
  Parthenia E. 65
  Sally 120
  Sarah 64
  Vina 111
Norten, Eliza A. 3
  Maranda 88
North, Frances 233
  Marie L. 66
  Mary S. 99
Northcraft, Martha S. 116
Northcut, Malinda 52
  Mary 125
  Sarah 22
Northcutt, Elizabeth 125
Norton, Elizabeth 200
  Isabella 54
  Marinday 54
  Nancy 54
Norwine, Aluntdear 190
  Barbary 190
Norwood, Elizabeth 7
Nouel, Delila 242
Noval, Marguerite 64
  Mary 132
Nowlin, Amanda A. 140
  Elizabeth P. 6
  Lucy T. 204
  Martha 158
Null, Eliza 60
  Elizabeth 16
  Lavina 23
  Rebecca 133
  Sarah 61
Numan, Mary 196
Nunn, Elizabeth 3
  Malinda 214
  Nancy F. 32
Nurenhaus, Mary 112
Nyswonger, Catherine 9
Oakes, Elizabeth 139
Oakley, Susan 46
Oaks, Minerva 61
O'Banion, Malvina 88

O'Banion, Mary 236
  Nancy 68
O'Bannion, Nancy 223
  Rebecca 121
Obermaier, Mariana 169
Oberry, Elizabeth 210
O'Brien, Margaret 69
  Mary A. 126
O'Bryan, Emilee 152
Obuchon, Margaretha 22
  Mary 197
  Neville 176
O'Daniel, Ametes I. 205
Odell, Abigail 183
  Betsy 44
  Elizabeth A. 127
  Esther 181
  Jane 169, 194
  Mary 84, 169
  Matilda 116
  Nancy 172
  Peggy 169
  Thizziah 183
Oden, Harriet 127
  Hulday 117
Odenale, Jane 52
Odenel, Elizabeth 244
Oder, Crecy 137
Odey, Pauline 140
Odin, Margaret 40
Odle, Evira 168
  Ruth 219
Odom, Malinda 210
Oens, Alley 208
  Elizabeth 200
Officer, Lucinda 250
  Margaret 97
  Nancy 49
Ogden, Elizabeth 105
Oge, Cecile 52
Ogel, Martha J. 223
Ogen, Jane 248
Ogle, Harriet 232
Oglenice, Eliza 104
O'Gles, Keriak 19
Oglesby, Elizabeth 25
  Martha A. 76
  Mary A. 236
Oglisby, Mary 87
Ogresby, Julien 192
O'Haver, Elizabeth 103
  Hanah 79
  Sarah 211
Olba, Juliet 152
Old, Luise M. M. J. 213
Oldham, Eliza A. 81
  Mary 145, 248
  Mitalda 114
  Sarah 224
Olive, Angeline C. 198
Oliver, Agnes 171
  Elizabeth A. 25
  Judith P. 151
  Lucyann 157
  Margaret 34
  Martha 34
  Nancy 83
Olson, Ann 5
Omarrha, Mary 40
O'Neal, Elizabeth 244
  Nancy 228
Ones, Rebecca 193
Onsley, Elizabeth 100
Onstot, Mehala 19
Ordway, Elizabeth 192
  Rosanna 78
Orea, Melinda J. 209
Orear, Ann 199

Riggs, Hannah 43, 210
  Lucinda 144
  Luson 122
  Mary C. 133
  Nancy 189, 200
  Phebe 230
  Polly 169
  Rachel 51, 189
  Rebecca 76
  Rhodia 114
  Sarah 9
Riggsby, Susanna 173
Right, Sherlotte 92
Rigsby, Mary A. 196
Riley, Ann 202
  Betsy 239
  Huldy C. 18
  Katey 209
  Mary E. 246
  Nancy 245, 249
  Sarah J. 127
Rimell, Christena 175
Rimmell, Sarah 47
Rimon, Elen 12
Rindesbacher, Maria 210
Rine, Jane 208
Riney, Lucinda 132
  Lucretia 101
  Rosa 15
  Sarah A. 62
Ringo, Charlotte 141
  Emily 206
  Jane 10
  Nancy 164
Ripper, Elizabeth 29
Ripperton, Susan 55
Risher, Aggatha 192
  Charlotte 208
  Mary A. 37
Risley, Jane 186
Ritcher, Rachel 103
Ritchey, Ester 68
  Mary A. 192
Ritchie, Eliza 176
  Martha E. 110
  Mary 130
  Susan D. 141
Ritter, Betsey A. 153
Rivers, Margaret 23
Rives, Elizabeth 3
Roade, Susannah 78
Roades, Ann 123
  Rosy 77
Roads, Susan 12
Roan, Elizabeth 43
  Sarah A. A. 118
Roark, Lorenda 28
  Polly 28
  Sarah 112
Robans, Celia 176
Robb, Elizabeth 49
  Lucy A. 134
Robberson, Louisa 193
  Nancy 240
Robberts, Mary 222
Robbins, Abigail 146
  Azuriah 177
  Polly M. 6
Rober, Elleanor 129
Robers, Malinda 159
Roberson, Catherine 115
  Mary 111
  Mary A. 11
  Polly 212
  Sally 233
Robert, Briget 222
  Felicite 230
  Louise 64, 222
  Rachel 27

Roberts, Ana E. 233
  Caroline 133
  Catharine W. 214
  Dinah 190
  Eliza A. 67
  Elizabeth 107, 117, 138, 148
  Hannah 246
  Harriet 177
  Jenac 156
  Joy 96
  Kitty 44
  Lavina 69
  Luceta 225
  Lucinda 10
  Lucy 183
  Lydia 24
  Mahala 35
  Mahuldah 47
  Mary 99
  Mary E. 24
  Matilda 95
  Nancy 9, 37, 125, 180, 207, 218, 246
  Nancy J. 216
  Polly 12, 119, 164, 191
  Rachel 237
  Rosmary 112
  Sally 98
  Susanna 164
  Tabitha 247
  Vergain 116
  Vidilla 199
  Zerelda E. 15
Robertson, Catharine 72
  Catherine 116
  Caty 220
  Charlotte 84
  Courtney 47
  Dolly 88
  Elizabeth 127, 227, 242
  Elizabeth A. 121
  Ella 125
  Harriet 79
  Ivannah 154
  Jane 18
  Katherine 142
  Louisa 219
  Lucinda 235
  Margaret M. 198
  Mary 19, 123
  Mary J. 1
  Nancy 177
  Peridance 27
  Polly 222
  Rebecca 152
  Sarah 215
  Susan 187
Robeson, Judy A. 86
  Parthena 30
Robideau, Pelagie 24
Robidoux, Pelagie 210
Robinet, Sarah 141
Robinett, Leuisey 71
Robins, Elizabeth 183
  Lavina 141
Robinson, Ann J. 30
  Betsy 164
  Cassandra 181
  Eleanor S. J. 122
  Eliza 240
  Elizabeth R. 144
  Emily 37
  Harriet 168
  Jane 241
  Jeane 194
  Leona J. 115
  Lithe 109
  Margaret 134

Robinson, Margery 92
  Martha A. 154
  Mary 51, 99
  Mary A. 174, 182
  Nancy 189
  Polly 88, 112
  Rebecca 205
  Sally 62
Robirds, Martha 162
Robison, Elizabeth R. 3
  Martha J. 206
  Mary A. 150
  Nancy 34
  Peggy 86
  Sally 113
Robnett, Louisa 120
  Lucinda G. 143
  Mary A. 31
  Sally 137
Robut, Rebecca 133
Rochefort, Mary 30
Rochester, Elizabeth 222, 250
  Emila 60
  Margaret 206
Rock, Ann 115
Rockhold, Elizabeth 216
  Susannah 142
Roden, Malvina 31
Roderoque, Emily 187
Rodes, Elizabeth 201, 240
Rodgers, Mary J. 239
Rodney, Charlotte 152
  Luceal 220
  Maria L. 192
  Matilda 187
  Polly 249
Rods, Nancy 37
  Polly E. 22
Roe, Ann M. 249
  Elizabeth 22
  Polly 58
  Sarah 242
Rogers, Adeline 95
  Doshean 205
  Elizabeth 133, 157
  Frances 3
  Harriet 126
  Julie 194
  Mary 13
  Maryann 19
  Sarah 139
  Susannah 238
  Tempy 201
Roggers, Elizabeth 147
Roi, Julia 199
  Lewezy 186
  Mary L. 180
Roland, Elizabeth A. 148
  Levina 85
  Lockky 19
  Margaret 5
Rolin, Sinthy 187
Rollands, Lucinda 102
Roller, Barbara 191
Rollin, Enmical 36
Rollings, Ann 3
  Nancy 108
Rollins, Eliza 16
  Julian 26
  Nancy 164
Ron, Ann 46
Ronald, Eliza J. 211
Ronleau, Scholatique 52
Ronnalls, Fanny 233
Ronnolls, Martha W. 86
Rook, Sarah 19
Rookard, Percilla 195
Rookwood, Sarah 77
Root, Joanna 239

Rop, Elizabeth 108
Roper, Elizabeth 81
  Liza 73
Roques, Uln 177
Rorer, Ann 27
Rose, Elizabeth 130
  Louisa 72
  Mary 64
Rosebury, Matilda 239
Ross, Amyann 50
  Ann M. 194
  Betsy 203
  Cern 29
  Elizabeth 183, 249
  Jane 40
  Julian 1
  Lucy 76
  Lydia 11
  Malvina 19
  Margaret 101
  Mary L. 186
  Nancy 89
  Patsey 128
  Piety 118
  Prisey 57
  Rosannah 151
  Sarah 13, 167, 220
  Susan 144
Rossar, Ann 32
  Martha 192
Rossitter, Eliza 204
Rosson, Lucinas 31
Rothe, Christiane W. 212
Rouch, Polly 40
Roughton, Rhoda A. 44
Roulston, Margaret 45
Roundtree, America 215
  Catherine 159
  Louisa 234
Rountree, Louisa 205
Rous, Elizabeth E. 209
Rouse, Benuda 230
  Martha 176
  Urania L. 66
Roush, Mary C. 194
  Rebecca 174
Roussin, Mary 90
  Pelazie 197
Rout, Nancy 198
Routbout, Esther 70
Routen, Katherine 117
Routh, Margaret 120
Row, Elizabeth 169
  Rebecca 237
Rowarth, Luiza 152
Rowe, Anne 76
  Peggy 191
Rowland, Delany 184
  Diana 219
  Elizabeth 112, 194
  Elizabeth E. 148
  Emaline 66
  Harriet 147
  Mary 109
  Millender 99
  Patsy 72
  Polly 169
  Rachel 219
  Rebecca 62
  Rhoda 4
  Sally 126
  Sarah 66
  Susanna 198
  Susany 184
Rowley, Elizabeth 224
Rowlings, Elvina 175
Rownels, Sarah M. 192
Roy, Denicy 106
  Euphrosine 41

Roy, Francoise 134
  Margaret 177
  Marguerite 161
  Minerva 1
  Nancy A. 72
  Susan 80
  Tempy 15
Royers, Ann 34
Roynts, Martha 45
Rubey, Lucinda 73
  Malinda 103
Rubottom, Mary 137
  Servillity 137
Ruby, Sucothia M. 46
Rucker, Catharine A. 202
  Jane 167
  Julian 216
Ruden, Sarah F. 95
Ruder, Letitia 172
  Sarah C. 220
  Susan 89
Rudissel, Sarrie 151
Rudolph, Helen M. 162
Rue, Susan 48
Ruggles, Lucinda 168
  Mahalay 182
Ruhn, Ameline F. 164
Ruland, Ann 2
  Susan 103
Rule, Anny 243
  Elizabeth 96
  Euphema 69
  Franky 244
  Judith 146
  Leviney 237
  Nancy K. 44
  Olive 175
  Sarah A. 193
Ruley, Eliza J. 234
Rummons, Jane 133
Rundlett, Sarah A. 181
Runge, Freemelda 134
Runis, Rebecca 90
Runkle, Betsy 51
  Catharine 157
  Margaret 247
Runnels, Elizabeth D. 214
  Hannah 19
  Nancy 2
Runnuls, Cintha G. 206
Runyon, Sophia 235
Rupe, Delila 171
  Hannah 244
  Susan 148
Ruraifs, Alice 53
Rush, Miss 91
  Catherin 40
  Elizabeth 101
  Frances 87
  Margaret 92
  Sarah 224
  Susan 137
Rusher, Polly 13
Russ, Celeste 159
Russel, Elizabeth 23
  Nancy 20
Russell, Elizabeth 46, 122, 146
  Fanny 91
  Jane 134
  Martha 21, 66
  Paulina 102
  Rebecca 169
  Sally 228
  Sarah 29
  Sarah M. 252
Rust, Dukedella 70
Rustin, Rhody 246
  Senith 159

Rutenbiller, Eve 165
Ruth, Elizabeth 158
  Rebecca 184
Rutherford, Betsy A. 218
  Catherine 59
  Hannah 44
  Martha 115
  Marthy 27
  Mary A. 39, 128
  Rutha 215
Rutledge, Eliza 1
  Elizabeth 222
  Sarah 162
Rutter, Eliza 84
  Emeline 18
  Martha A. 18
Ryan, Cary 213
  Nahlcia 244
Rybolt, Christina 98
  Margaret 54
Ryland, Juliet V. 76
Rymal, Elenor 141
  Keciah 141
Saberfield, Malinda 187
Saddler, Ann 178
  Elizabeth 94
  Mary K. 80
  Sinthy 94
Sadler, Dizy 178
  Hetta W. 6
  Sally 124
Saffarans, Mary 74
Safferins, Catherine 142
Safford, Mary 200
Sage, Laemay 237
  Sarah E. 144
Sagelle, Aurora 64
Sagers, Desdaminia 52
Sailing, Mary 120
  Nancy 198
Sailor, Katherine 164
St. Arnoud, Catherine 161
St. Clair, Sally 21
St. Gemme, Marie T. 93
St. Leager, Elizabeth 218
St. Louis, Georgine 133
  Mary E. 41
Saintus, Regina 78
Saling, Elizabeth 116
  Mary 126
Sallee, Amilea 70
Sally, Nancy 120
  Susanna 16
Salter, Elizabeth J. 97
Salyers, Mary 153
Sampson, Jane 16
  Liza 251
  Mary 152
  Nancy 33, 110
Sams, Cyrenaann 221
Samuel, Martha 74
  Nancy 13
Samuels, Ann M. 144
Sanders, Aley 129
  Elender 40
  Elizabeth 19, 119
  Kiziah 192
  Mary J. 148
  Nancy 206
  Prudence 153
  Susanah 234
Sanderson, Jane 11
  Marian 104
Sandford, Huldah 120
Sandlan, Mary A. 158
Sandlin, Cyntha 196
Sandridge, Perenna 13
Sands, Martha 138
Saners, Lucat 22

303

306

Snider, Margaret 58
  Mary A. 110
  Sarah 21
Snoddy, Margaret 245
  Mary 19
  Mary A. 228
  Nancy 39, 83
Snodgrass, Elizabeth 48
  Matilda 211
  Nancy 69
  Polly 238
  Sarah 58
Snow, Eliza 117
  Matilda 196
  Nancy 196
Snowden, Eliza J. 235
  Jane 137
  Lucinda 26
  Martha 225
  Peggy 6
Sofframaus, Virginia 39
Solivan, Virginia 214
Sollars, Sally 129
Sollers, Mahala 86, 210
  Nancy 2
Solomon, Katharine 34
Son, Hetty 243
Sone, Elizabeth 88
Songbark, Jantha T. 234
Sooney, Nancy 47
Soper, Alemeda 72
  Martha 26
Sorell, Virginia 221
Sorrel, Eliza A. 12
Sorrell, Mary J. 223
  Nancy 111
Soule, Margaret A. 231
Soults, Mrs, 166
Souter, Catharine 93
South, Calista P. 201
  Elizabeth 109
  Margaret 118, 210
  Polly 27
  Spice 133
Southworth, Elizabeth A. 179
Spalden, Elizabeth 166
Spalding, Ann 162
  Catherine 194
  Hannah 83
  Lydia 170
  Mary 111
Span, Nancy 225
Spann, Agnes 100
Sparks, Eliza 178
  Elizabeth 147
  Martha 39
  Polly 233
  Sarah 62
Spears, Patience 5
  Sally 181
Speed, Edy 127
  Juliet 5
  Mary M. 144
Speer, Indiana 83
Speery, Elizabeth 94
Spellman, Ann E. 240
Spence, Elizabeth 176, 219
  Margaret 151, 180
  Mary A. 81
  Nancy 83
Spencer, Altezorah 108
  Ann 94, 153
  Elener, 41
  Elenora 138
  Elizabeth 212
  Jamima 152
  Mary 21, 48
  Mierria 21
  Nancy 97

Spencer, Sinthia 182
Spergin, Jane 35
Spicer, Lucy 235
Spires, Eliza 235
  Jane 73
  Mary 127
  Sarah 228
  Susana 152
Spiva, Elizabeth 226
  Jane 222
  Nancy 78
Splann, Jane 26
Splawn, Ellender 171
  Lucinda 142
  Patsy 211
  Rosa A. 68
Spoonamore, Sary 90
Spoors, Mary V. 80
Sportsman, Clancy 7
Spotswood, Elizabeth 157
  Emily 20
Spott, Catharine 219
  Eliza 186
Spotts, Margaret 108
  Sarah 17, 57
Spradling, Lucinda 171
  Polly A. 44
  Susan M. 48
Spraul, Margaret 250
Spraull, Elizabeth 159
Spreer, Elizabeth 181
Sprigg, Ann W. 105
  Mehala 158
Springer, Angeline 106
  Manervy J. 157
  Nancy 141
  Nancy C. 102
Sprowl, Martha 9
Spura, Elizabeth 28
Spurgeon, Rebecca 201
Spurnhoward, Mariah 115
Spurs, Hariet 1
Srum, Saly 204
Staats, Jane A. 237
Stacy, Elizabeth 234
Stadler, Elizabeth 197
Stadley, Mähala 13
  May 91
  Sarah A. 203
Stafford, Elizabeth 85
  Evaline 6
  Kitty 125
  Lovina 126
  Mary 52
  Nancy 110, 210
  Polly 188
Staford, Badelia A. 246
  Patsey 246
Staley, Grisellah W. 58
  Letitia R. 59
Stalkup, Katherine 149
Stall, Sarah 108
Stallard, Elizabeth 31
  Winna A. 176
Stallings, Lovey 72
Staly, Emily 29
Standage, Amy 56
Standeford, Jane 15
Standerford, Priscilla 168
  Ruth 10
Standford, Jemima 25
  Levicey 104
  Margaret A. 92
  Mary B. 237
  Patsy 127
  Ruth 248
  Sally 189
Standiford, Agnes 65
  Jemimah 25

Standiford, Mary 120
  Nancy 25
Standley, Alvira 7
  Lucy C. 75
  Marian 227
  Namoney 14
  Nancy 34, 201
Stanfield, Lydia 230
Stanley, Easther 231
  Jane 118
  Jemima 158
Stanly, Polly 231
Stansfer, Mary A. 135
Stanton, Ann 223
  Judith 195
  Margaret 157
  Polly 82
Staples, Ann E. 212
  Elizabeth J. 178
  Jane 99
  Lucinda 166
  Margaret F. 228
  Martha E. 208
  Sarah 22
Stapleton, Amanda 241
  Margaret A. 153
  Mary 17
Stapp, Celia A. 235
  Dinah 25
  Elizabeth 196
  Emeline E. 117
  Melissa 160
Stark, Betsy 232
  Elizabeth 200
  Emily 108
  Meriann 73
  Permely 248
  Polly 167
Starks, Huldah 57
  Margaret 102
Starnes, Polly 168
Stass, Nancy 54
States, Mary 87
Statler, Barbary 198
  Catey 135
  Margaret 21
  Polly 172
  Sally 126
Staton, Martha 180
Stayton, Catharine 236
  Ruth 13
Stealey, Hannah 186
Stear, Lucy 240
Stearman, Nancy 242
Stearns, Sarah 149
Steel, Ann 251
  Clementina 83
  Eleanor 122
  Eliza J. 50
  Margaret 111, 234, 247
  Mary 103
  Nancy M. 79
  Rachel 112, 236
  Sally 46
  Susan 47
Steele, Elizabeth 119, 250
  Margaret F. 63
  Polly 100
  Rebecca 145
  Sarah 190
Steeley, Clarissa 146
Steene, Mary A. 106
  Olla 226
Steerman, Belinda 169
Steers, Lucy 164
  Mary 193
Stegitmire, Feliciana 158
Stein, Ida 63
Steinbeck, Agnis 239

307

Steinbeck, Louisa 81
Step, Patience 221
Stephens, Agnes 241
  Ann 193
  Casander 197
  Elizabeth 189
  Fannie 95
  Francis 160
  Heziak 50
  Jane 165
  Letitia 235
  Louiza 35
  Macolia W. 61
  Malinda 90
  Martha A. 16
  Martha M. 43
  Mary 59, 197
  Mary A. 136
  Maryan K. 164
  May 161
  Nancy 175
  Olteny J. 156
  Parallee M. 247
  Polly 5
  Sally 20, 226
  Susan B. 18
  Susannah 96
  Zilphy 40
Stephenson, Curtis W. 5
  Dorothy 153
  Elizabeth 107
  Jane 108
  Margaret 124
  Maria 78
  Mary 15
  Mary E. 174
Stepp, Elizabeth 161
  Lucy 181
  Mary 48, 133
Sterguin, Barbary 113
Stetler, Catharine 59
Stevans, Creasy 176
Stevens, Amanda 59
  Eliza A. 6
  Elizabeth 23
  Josephine 113
  Lucinda 110
  Rachel 221
  Sally 232
Stevenson, Elizabeth A. 176
  Jain 78
  Margarett 81
  Martha A. 86
  Mary J. 236
  Polly 99
  Rachel 101
Steward, Jane 162, 187
  Leusindy 226
  Mary 228
  Sarah A. 227
  Sentha 145
Stewart, America 87
  Catherine 164
  Elizabeth 53, 87, 164
  Emily 66
  Jane 145
  Lascen 205
  Loutica 45
  Lucinda 112
  Malcina 203
  Mary 203
  Mary A. 47, 86
  Nancy 98, 214
  Sally 32, 206
  Sarah S. 159
Stice, Dicey 115
  Matilda 177
  Sarah 188
Stiegmier, Elizabeth 66

Still, Agness 150
  Rachel 14
Stillwell, Polly 183
Stinnett, Elizabeth 215
Stinson, Elizabeth 77
  Hannah 75
  Lorenly 192
  Marietta 49
  Polly 239
  Sarah 112
Stipe, Hannah M. 38
Stites, Mary A. 204
  Polly 173
  Susannah 173
Stivers, Emellina 121
Stockdale, Rachel 102
Stocknill, Mary 86
Stockston, Sally 122
Stockton, Huldah 23
  Mary 69
  Maryanna 236
  Polly A. 36
Stoe, Sarah 16
Stoga, June 221
Stoker, Polly 222
Stokes, Eliza 112
  Joanna 247
  Rebecca 189
  Sally 149
  Samenta A. 249
Stollings, Patsy 72
Stona, Letha 187
Stone, Charlotte 65
  Deboriah 63
  Dicy 134
  Dorinda 121
  Eliza 4, 47, 106, 166
  Elizabeth 243, 248
  Elizabeth M. 111
  Fanny 55, 118
  Harriet 209
  Jane 128
  Lizy 20
  Lucinda 29
  Martha 241
  Martha A. 136
  Martha J. 248
  Mary 163
  Mary A. 228
  Nancy 136
  Nancy B. 252
  Patsy 216
  Sally 4, 180
  Sarah 88
  Sarah A. 233
  Zerelda 142
Stonebreaker, Harriet 127
Stoneham, Elizabeth 142
Stones, Mary A. 37
Stooky, Nancy 204
Story, Ann 240
  Anna 19
  Catharine 96
  Lucitha 75
  Matilda 94
  Patsey 92
  Polly 85
  Prudence 122
  Rebecca 137
Stotts, Nancy 82
Stout, Ann 116
  Elizabeth 83
  Emerine 55
  Laviny 147
  Mahala 183
  Osa 213
  Rachel 216
  Serilda 184
Stover, Catherine 122

Stover, Emeline 28
  Mary 27
  Mary A. 49
Stovers, Poly 217
Stow, Martha 223
  Sally 187
Stowe, Polin 93
Stowers, Anna M. 216
Strader, Viney 205
Strain, Mary 96
  Nancy 137
Strange, Sarah 115
Strap, Elizabeth 44
Strawhorn, Marinda 101
Street, Fanny 230
  Laurania 33
  Nancy 229
  Sarah 246
Strel, Betsey 211
Stribling, Elizabeth 233
Stricklan, Rachel 35
Strickland, Abigail 69
  Elizabeth 218
  Mary 104
  Phoebe 49, 207
  Unity 48
Stricklen, Nancy 198
Strien, Luisa 176
Striklin, Lucretia 12
Stringer, Ann 181
  Nancy 55
Stringfellow, Nancy 199
Strode, Elizabeth 164, 229
  Mary A. 234
  Tetetha 240
Strong, Drussilla 135
  Mary A. 38
  Nancy 176
Strother, Cynthia 185
Stroud, Polly 31
Stroup, Polly 31
  Mahala 51
  Matilda 166
Stuart, Eliza 65
  Isabela 121
  Jane 36
  Sally H. 178
Stubblefield, Ann 198
Stufflebean, Ailcy 78
Stuttress, Mary A. 222
Sublet, Soffrony 49
  Zerelda 65
Subren, Catharine 3
Sucet, Nancy 40
Suddeth, Elizabeth 165
  Lean 207
  Margaret 183
  Susan J. 155
Suddith, Wilmina 85
Sudduth, Evalina 87
Suggett, Catherine 139
  Susan 139
Suhren, Catherine H. 232
Suiter, Miranda 104
Sulcher, Martha A. 70
Sulivan, Melvina 13
Sullens, Jane 123
  Rebecca 108
Sullers, Ann W. 49
Sullinger, America 143
  Elizabeth 86
  Maria 106
  Mary 104
  Sarah 21
Sullivan, (?) 158
  Cassor 53
  Eunicy 95
  Harriett 141
  Mary 31

Tong, Eleanor 167
  Harriet 137
  Jane 109
Tongue, Malinda 52
Tony, Elizabeth 179
Tooley, Elizabeth 158
  Jane 111
  Mary 239
Tooly, Polly 231
  Susannah 247
Toomey, Julian 63
  Mary 124
Toomis, Sally 8
Tooney, Susannah 10
Torrence, Margaret 110
Toun, Elizabeth 235
Tovel, Elizabeth 62
Towers, Elizabeth W. 250
Towler, Martha A. 239
Townsend, Charlotte 3
  Elizabeth 242
  Kitty 233
  Nancy 37
Townson, Martha A. L. 122
  Rhody 98
Tracy, Margaret 175
  Susan 36
Trail, Cintha A. 11
  Jane 110
Trale, Agnes 160
Trammel, Ann 63
  Rusheba 69
Trammell, Jemine 244
Tranuih, Sally 107
Trap, Nancy 136
  Sarah 103
Trapp, Decy 4
  Kiriah 120
  Mahalia 166
Travilion, Elizabeth 103
Travillier, Jean 157
Travis, Catherine 135
  Cynthia 226
  Elizabeth 121
  Nancy 103
  Sally 121
Treese, Margaret 63
Trent, Sarah A. 80
Tribble, Mary 187
  Permelia 161
  Susanna 225
Trible, Ellen 86
Tribue, Susanna 44
Trick, Eliza 231
Trigg, Dinah 4
  Judith 186
Trimble, Eliza 46
  Jane 136
  Mary J. 166
Triplet, Catey 87
  Rebeca 105
Triplett, America 42
  Ann 239
  Catharine 249
  Elizabeth 249
  Katharine 35
Tripp, Nancy 25
Trosper, Margaret 227
Troth, Mary 183
  Sarah 183
Trotter, Eliza 213
  Gabriella 239
  Margaret 154, 205, 210
  Mary 220
  Polly 147
  Rebecca 121
Trowley, Susan 125
True, Patsey 178
  Sarah 152

Trusedell, Nancy 145
Truitt, Mary 72
  Rebecca W. 105
Truman, Sarah C. 122
Trusdel, Thursa 176
Tucer, Jane 239
Tuckenay, Margaret 92
Tucker, Amanda M. 2
  Barbara 220
  Cecily 132
  Charlotte 140
  Clarissa 66
  Eliza 66, 87
  Elizabeth 42, 94, 107
  Frances 12
  Juliane 132
  Margaret 66
  Maria 102
  Mary 11, 94
  Mary A. 25, 61
  Matilda 74
  Nancy 94
  Perlina 118
  Sarah 61, 73
  Sarah E. 115
  Sophia 129
Tuckfield, Mary 38
Tudor, Elizabeth 16
Tuggle, Hester 2
  Nancy 87
  Susan 56
Tulbert, Maria 190
Tulette, Elizabeth 51
Tull, Polly A. 237
  Sarah 229
Tully, Eliza 68
Tuly, Nancy 119
Tunage, Margaret 200
Turbit, Drucilla 141
Turdy, Elizabeth 105
Turley, Ann 60
  Cisiah 231
  Eliza M. 145
  Elzira 147
  Helen 106
  Lavina 46
  Louisa J. 234
  Lydia 179
  Malinda 187
  Ruth 77
  Salinda 100
  Sophia 224
  Susan 71
Turman, Nancy A. 208
Turnbeau, Sary A. 58
Turnbow, Hannah 54
  Jane 228
Turner, (?) 7
  Abigail 88
  Ann 152, 199
  Catherine 43, 246
  Cinthy A. 203
  Elender 229
  Eliza 83, 237
  Eliza J. 178
  Elizabeth 103, 195, 204
  Ellender 43
  Emelia 154
  Jane 40, 135, 194
  Jean 149
  Jemima 29, 229
  Leathy 241
  Letitha 58
  Lovey 100
  Lucretia 180
  Lucy 118
  Mahala 51
  Mariann 48
  Martha 46

Turner, Mary 66, 205, 243
  Matilda 97
  Muluny 182
  Nancy 41, 85, 139, 230
  Polly 203
  Polly A. 85
  Rachel 168
  Rebecca 46
  Sally 51, 234
  Sarah 32
  Sarah A. 25
  Sophia 25
  Susannah 243
  Teressa 106
  Virginia 246
  Zelihe 79
  Zerilda 44
Turnham, Ann R. 7
  Eliza 32
  Mary 101
  Sarah C. 67
Turnidge, Elizabeth 215
  Jane 145
  MAry A. 140
Turpen, Anny 25
Turpin, Avarilla 233
  Elizabeth 211, 215
  Emily 138
  Jane 73
  Martha A. 149
  Mary 130
  Nancy 11
  Phebe 52
  Sarah 211
  Sarah A. 209
Tutor, Elizabeth M. 110
Tutt, Dollie M. 190
Tuttle, Elizabeth 243
  Martha A. 159
  Salina 147
Twimdeman, Elizabeth 20
Twisdell, Mary A. 105
Twittey, Nancy 6
Twitty, Ann 210
  Belindah 216
  Charlotte 51
  Ellen 99
  Fanny 160
  Sarah 247
Twyman, E. C. F. 5
Tygart, Sarah 88
Tyler, Bertha 23
  Borelly 23
  Charlotte 121
  Eve 144
  Jenita 133
  Lucretia 107
Tynnell, Jane 188
Tyre, Nancy 55
Ulelly, Mahalia 181
Umphries, Mary 11
Underwood, Dicey 112
  Elizabeth 124
  Elizabeth S. 21
  Julia A. 180
  Matilda 38
  Nancy 124
  Polley 91
  Zeriaha 183
Uno, Catherine 131
  Celest 190
  Marie L. 201
Unsel, Lucinda 29
  Tabitha 147
Updike, Sarah 242
Upgrove, Mahala 67
Upshaw, Polly 180
Uptegrove, Elizabeth 117
  Mary 148

311

Wells, Jermima 143
  Margaret 9, 147
  Patience 154, 197
  Patsy 56
  Ruth 227
  Sally 126
  Sarah 99
  Susan 171
  Virginia B. 222
Wels, Elizabeth 99
Welta, Rosanna 68
Welthy, Elizabeth 77
Welton, Elizabeth 69, 156
Weltsy, Alsey A. 107
Welty, Barbary 64
  Elizabeth 77, 203
  Kathryn, 112
  Mahala 240
  Polly 226
Wert, Margaret L. 190
Wescott, Louisa P. 77
Wesmeir, Catherine 232
West, Agnes 228
  Ann 199
  Betsey A. 141
  Cassandra 208
  Eliza 41
  Eliza A. 188
  Elizabeth 5
  Irine 111
  Jane A. 114
  Louise E. 76
  Lucy 65
  Lydia 35
  Margaret 89
  Martha 37
  Mary A. 159, 227
  Mary J. 56
  Matilda 106
  Nancy 188
  Pelina 249
  Sally 89
  Sarah 146
  Zerilda 137
Westbrook, Charlotte 222
  Elizabeth 100
  Lidy 182
  Mary 74
  Midist 99
Westerfield, Mildred 130
Westlake, Ann 95
  Nancy 174
Weston, Agness 159
Westover, Loretta 250
  Maria 228
Westy, Elizabeth 11
Whaley, America J. 216
  Barbary 130
  Elizabeth B. 4
  Narcissa 38
Wharton, Lucinda 130
  Lucy 188
Wheat, Nancy 145
Wheeler, Abigail 16
  Julia 75
  Mary 81
  Melinda 48
  Nancy 240
Wheeley, Mary 14
Wheeter, Catharine 240
Wheldon, Catherine 17
  Polly 238
Whelman, Phebe 43
Whetstone, Mary 17
White, Amelia 7
  Charlotte 75
  Christine 25
  Diannia 244
  Eliza 3, 231

White, Eliza J. 53
  Elizabeth 49, 86
  Elizabeth B. 240
  Emilene 4
  Fanny 76
  Hannah 196
  Jane 135
  Jurughe 50
  Leah 140
  Lidia 160
  Lucinda A. 83
  Lucy A. 118
  Margaret 132
  Margarett M. 156
  Margery 180
  Mary 19, 61, 166, 217
  Mary A. 75
  Mary J. 35, 71
  Matilda 21
  Melinda 83
  Nancy 22, 66, 78, 91, 246
  Polly 47, 88, 89, 123,
    157, 185
  Polly A. 118
  Rachel 55
  Rebecca 199
  Sarah 103, 195
  Sarah A. 59
  Sarah L. 92
  Sereah 247
  Susannah 229
  Theollis 137
Whitehead, Delila 225
Whitelock, Sarah E. 56
Whitelow, Eliza 6
  Julia A. 145
  Martha 5
  Mary A. 83
  Matilda 59
  Virginia 135
Whitely, Lavena 140
Whitenberg, Polly A. 161
Whitenburg, Malinda 149
  Rachel 91
Whitenburge, Margaret 99
Whitener, Catherine 90
Whitesides, Richanah 138
  Susan 148
Whitest, Lucindy 156
Whitinburg, Elviny 164
Whiting, Cynthia 184
  Lydia 71
Whitledge, Alcy C. 123
  Elizabeth 225
  Elvira A. 214
  Franckey 202
Whitley, Elizabeth 20
  Rebecca 187
Whitlock, Silvy 119
Whitlow, Pevina 177
  Lucy 229
Whitmire, Charity A. 46
  Sally 73
Whitner, Elizabeth 52
  Polly 89
Whitney, Elizabeth 234
  Mary 191
  Nicey J. 53
  Patsy 50
Whitsel, Margaret 243
Whitsell, Elizabeth 240
  Lucinda 119
  Margaret 184
  Nancy 18
Whitsett, Frances 43
  Polly 57
Whitson, Mary 214
Whitten, Elizabeth 68
  Emdiah 175

Whittenburg, Elenor C. 32
  Liza 58
Whittenburgh, Rachel 164
Whittey, Iby J. 140
Whitton, Catharine 53
Whitty, Mary 240
Whitworth, Elizabeth 48
Whoopaugh, Nancy 180
Whorton, Elizabeth 188
Wiatt, Louiza 213
Wicks, Susan 142
Wideman, Jemima 9
  Mary 180
  Patsey 229
Wieligman, Catherine M. 197
Wiggans, Elizabeth 49
Wiggin, Alice 84
Wigginson, Saphira 189
Wigham, Elizabeth 12
  Phebe 159
Wilbourn, Tempy 7
Wilburn, Caroline 231
  Jane 251
  Rebecca W. 18
  Rosanna 140
Wilcocks, Salley 238
Wilcockson, Irena 205
Wilcox, Delvina 45
  Elizabeth 7
  Eunice 128
  Leannah 36
  Polly 190
  Sabry 205
Wilcoxen, Nancy P. 5
  Rebecca 197
  Sarah 217
Wilcoxson, Elizabeth 34
  Sarah 177
  Sarah S. 203
Wild, Polly 242
Wilds, Eliza 251
  Elizabeth 187
  Maria 28
  Mariah 250
  Melissa 219
  Polly A. 114
  Rachel 185
Wiles, Amanda 218
  Narcisses 140
Wiley, Ann 189
  Delitha 67
  Eliza J. 157
  Lydia 63
  Mary 46, 65
  Peggy 176
  Polly B. 221
Wilfley, Elizabeth 60
  Nancy 14
  Phoebe 11
Wilfong, Elizabeth 21
Wilhite, Eliza 97
  Elizabeth 48, 245
  Elvira K. 165
  Nancy 152
  Sally A. 158
Wilhoit, Elizabeth 232
Wilker, Jane 250
Wilkerson, Amy 172
  Emily T. 177
  Leviney 33
  Martha 219, 223
  Nancy 70, 206
  Sally 219
Wilkey, Hanner 84
Wilkins, Letty 138
Wilkinson, Elizabeth 103, 121
  Martha 34
  Mary 58
  Nicy 62

314

315